All rights of distribution, including via film, radio, and television, photo-mechanical reproduction, audio storage media, electronic data storage media, and the reprinting of portions of text, are reserved.

The author is responsible for the content and correction.

© 2018 united p. c. publisher

Printed in the European Union on environmentally friendly, chlorine- and acid-free paper.

www.united-pc.eu

Julian Harrison

A Year in Melancholia
Living with Mental Illness

The Situation

I live with my wife Lesley and thirteen-year-old son Elliot in Wigston, a suburb of the city of Leicester in the English East Midlands. I have three other children – technically my step-children though I have never considered them as anything other than my own. Rachel, the eldest, is approaching her thirtieth birthday and is currently in Sri Lanka with her partner on an extended stay in Asia that will also involve them doing some relief work in Nepal. Luke, the next down so to speak, is an architect in London, working long but productive hours and forging for himself a successful career. Joel still lives with us but not for long as he too is about to face his biggest adventure to date, travelling with a friend to Thailand, Vietnam and Cambodia. Elliot, my not so little boy any more – he's nearly my height and has size ten feet! – is doing really well at school and though beginning to show the inevitable signs of adolescent dissension, is wonderful and loving as a friend as well as a son. I'm so lucky to have him.

My Lesley – I could talk for hours about her virtues and of my love for her. I guess this will become apparent to you as the days pass. She works in the NHS but the value of her being is not confined to what she does throughout a working day. She is my soulmate as well as my wife. She is my carer and deals will all the practical aspects of life that I find so difficult to face and address. She provides a shoulder to cry on and a solace and sounding board for my turmoil.

As for me, well I'm currently starting a new career – for what it's worth – as a self-employed 'consultant'. I took voluntary redundancy in September this year after spending ten years working – latterly in the areas of equality, cohesion and human rights – at a local authority in the East Midlands. My twitter page (@leicsparta) describes me as a 'Father of four, fighter of discrimination, admirer of Beethoven, lover of rugby league...and supporter of Millwall and Sparta Prague!', every individual component of which deserves – and will be given – some degree of explanation.

I was diagnosed with clinical depression soon after Elliot's birth in 2002. Subsequent psychotherapy treatment revealed that depression has been within me since childhood. I have been on increasing amounts and varieties of medication ever since that diagnosis and have also received Cognitive Behavioural Therapy (CBT) and other forms of talking therapies. I am well known locally as a mental health advocate and activist as well as for my work with communities and in relation to the Holocaust.

Julian Harrison
31st December 2015

Introduction

I've never written a diary before. To be honest, I've never contemplated doing one either. So I guess the first of many questions to answer is 'why now'? Well, the initial and still primary stimulus is my mental health. For those of you who don't know me so well, I have clinical depression and Obsessive Compulsive Disorder (OCD). Over the course of many years – since I 'came out' about my depression – I have tried to be open and honest about this disability that has been a part of me since childhood. I have given talks and I have been there to listen to others struggling to come to terms with mental ill health. Knowing of my transparency and 'open book' status, people have turned to me to ask questions, to receive feedback and advice, to gauge their own situation and so on and so forth. I have always tried to be reassuring but truthful, supportive and sincere. To tell people how it is for me. I have talked about low mood of course, but I have also told of the physical manifestations of my depression. I guess this has been surprising to some, people with a simple yet understandable appreciation that equates depression solely to mood and emotion. And yet if I'm honest, it is often the physical consequences of a depressed mind that have caused me the most concern. They are plain for all to see. They cannot be disguised. They address full on the questionable assumption that mental illness is a hidden affliction. From this, therefore, has come the desire to put down on paper on a daily basis how depression fully impacts upon my life. A 'warts and all' documentary that talks about anger and shyness, worry and fears, physical idiosyncrasies as well as a fevered mind, quirks and habits and coping – or not – with emotional depths. To this end, I hope my account will help others who also have a relationship with mental illness. I sincerely wish to do my part to increase understanding and awareness, to put to bed some common misconceptions. To tackle the stigma and discrimination that still accompanies depression and other mental disabilities.

2016 also promises to be a watershed year as far as my health – and therefore my life – is concerned. I see my mental health consultant in mid-January. At my last appointment he asked me to consider the possibility of changes to my anti-depressive and anti-psychotic medication. Realistically, my options are limited. I have reached the 'ceiling' with regard to my current drug regime. Yes, they have kept me on a stable footing and have certainly kept the dark clouds at bay over the course of the last twelve months, but in terms of making my life more liveable, giving me some fulfilment, some positivism, even – heaven forbid – some enjoyment, I may have to relent and give some other pills their chance. What is always hard to face for a depressive, is change – any change, however miniscule, trivial, routine, fleeting or otherwise – and I know that I don't do this very well. That is why I have been given some time to contemplate what this may mean. I say 'may' because, as anyone suffering from depression will tell you, there is no certainty as to how one's body will cope with new medication. I may become worse, more fearful, more anxious, more morose, more lethargic, even more suicidal. But I may not, and I guess I owe it to myself and my family to take that chance. However, it's not just my mental state that is giving me cause for concern. Physically, I'm a wreck. My blood pressure is rocketing, my liver condition is weak, I'm overweight and have little appetite for exercise. All these things stem from either my mental illness or the medication I have to take to combat it and its symptoms. For years I have had to juggle with the fact that in order to keep my depression in check, I have had to sacrifice elements of my physical health. Depression can drain the life out of a body. It can add weight not just to a troubled mind, but to the rest of ones anatomy as well. I mean this quite literally. At times, I feel like I'm carrying the heaviest of rucksacks on my back, that my legs are walking through the densest possible mud. That an invisible force is pushing down on me preventing even the raising of my arms or the turning of my head. These are factors that will impact on even the most robust of athletes, let alone someone approaching his half century in age. Something will have to give in the New Year though. I'm hoping that the change in medication will play its part, but if I want to abate – let alone eradicate – the perils of physical ill health, somehow I need to raise my efforts to do what I can in terms of exercising more and eating more sensibly. Again, I have little choice if I want to stay alive.

I'm conscious that I'm not painting the most optimistic of pictures as 2016 nears its opening. But this is my reality. A book on depression is never going to be a bundle of laughs, but I hope in the days and months to come that some element of comedy, of light-hearted thoughts and amusing anecdote will rise to the surface, at least occasionally. It's not a coincidence, I suggest, that some of the world's great depressives also happen to be some of the world's divine comic talents. I hope Stephen Fry would recognise – and perhaps even welcome – that description, because he is the first person that comes immediately to mind when I think of the juxtaposition of two apparently diametrically conflictful states of being. I have just finished reading his marvellous autobiography 'The Fry Chronicles' – which probably accounts for him being foremost in my thinking! In this and his later – and more recent – set of memoirs[1], Stephen begins by reminding his readers of how he has got to where he is. His résumé of his formative years is beautifully crafted and of course superbly articulated. He not only covers all bases, he brings his past to life, giving one a sense of fulfilled accompaniment. It is as if the reader is his best friend, his closest companion. I cannot hope to replicate his style and craft, but neither can I really use his method as some sort of guide. The reason is quite simple. I wouldn't know where to start. How does one relay in a very short period of time, all that has transpired over the course of forty-seven years? What have been the highlights? And the lowlights? I can't even distinguish between them in some respects.

My life has been a series of contradictions and complications in many ways. It seems to me that I've always been an outsider – at school, at university, in working environments – and yet my deepest wish to belong has not always manifested itself in my actions. I've faced discrimination and bullying without always knowing how to recognise acceptance. I've wanted the company of people, whilst also embracing the solace of loneliness. I've longed for the release of tension and worry but cannot contextualise this cathartic state unless it is somehow complete and free from all possible and potential forms of turbulence. It is quite literally one hundred percent or nothing! I talk but crave for silence. I laugh but at the same time cry. I guess I'm one mixed up, complex, lump of flesh and bone. Everything seems to come back to the same thing though. The depression that has been my lot since childhood. It has consumed my mind and body to the extent that anything I do either emanates from it, or has ramifications and repercussions for how it reacts. It is a living being within my living body. It is my own close companion, my twin state, my alter ego. As I don't know a life without it, I can't seem to contemplate a life free from its presence. It has become my confidante as well as my affliction. That is probably the greatest apparent contradiction of all. The daily account of my life that you are about to begin, I trust will elucidate in everyday situations what I mean by this. Of how I can't live without depression whilst trying to fashion a life that keeps its most acutely damaging manifestations at arm's length.

Before we do start, however, there is one practical caveat that I need to disclose. In the last years of his life, my father wrote a diary. By this time, he was crippled with coronary heart disease and, although it was never diagnosed, depression. In it, I recall that he referred to his daily description of what remained of his life as 'the diary of a dying man'. It is a heartrending read. An account of immense bravery and integrity. However, at times it is difficult to stomach. I keep it upstairs in my library and every now and again, I will delve into its pages, looking for something, some inspiration perhaps, some welcome advice and guidance. I guess though I return to his words when I'm feeling acutely depressed. And what I find in some passages makes me worse. The passages to which I refer are not those that deal directly with his struggles with life and impending death, they are those that involve some criticism of his family – myself in particular. My Dad left nothing out. His honesty at times is brutal and harsh.

Whilst I understand that he was simply reflecting his innermost thoughts and feelings, to be judged by someone I looked up to and admired as well as loved is not conducive to dealing with one's own depression. I turn to his words because he died in January 1988 – when I was nineteen years old – and they are all I have of him now alongside the odd photograph and of course my memories. In writing a diary of my own, I am determined not to leave such an aftertaste with my own family. I will try to be every bit as sincere and thorough as my father, but I will not criticise or be judgmental of my own nearest and dearest. They don't deserve it and I will not enforce it upon them. Truth be told, they are my rocks and they form my appetite for life. But of course, in daily considerations there will always be times – remote though they may be in my case – when one is annoyed or even angry with one's closest companions. When this is the case, those feelings will remain inside me. I trust you, the reader, will forgive my discretion.

Here we go then. Whatever else this will be, it'll be a journey. See you at the end…fingers crossed!

Julian Harrison
31st December 2015

January

Friday 1st January 2016
Predictably, given my naturally pessimistic inclinations, 2016 hasn't started well. Something has happened in Rachel's relationship with her partner – something obviously serious as he has flown home from Sri Lanka. We won't know the full story until she rings tomorrow, but already the impact on Lesley is apparent. The poor love, she has had a rotten time recently. She was attacked whilst taking our English Springer Spaniel, Millie, for a walk in a Leicester park at the beginning of December. It was a cowardly as well as vicious assault which has left her with some depressed fractures to her face as well as damage to her retina. All being well, the physical scars will soon heal and disappear. The mental ones, as always, are more severe and enduring. She is more fragile and emotional than at any time I can remember and deserves the type of sensitive, dependable and unwavering support that I want with all my heart to give. The self-doubt that is my nature is playing havoc though with my determination to be strong. I just wish she didn't have to depend on such a frail and troubled mind as my own. However, I can be

physical without being necessarily mentally resolute so plenty of hugs and cuddles are the order of the day. God help us if she too succumbs to mental ill health.

The New Year is of course supposed to be the time to look forward. To make new resolutions and plans, to focus on positive change and adjust to new horizons. I've never really been able to do this. Yes, I can say that I'm going to do things and practically I probably have a better track record than many in succeeding in whatever it is I set my stall out to do. I finished my book on the Holocaust in 2015, for example. What has always been apparent though is my inability to change my mind and temperament. I can do practical things, but they don't seem to impact on my mood and on my overall demeanour. Accordingly, the changes that do occur in my life are so miniscule in scope, so trivial even, that they soon become meaningless. Has the completion of a major study on the Holocaust made me feel better? Yes, it gave me some satisfaction, but the reality is that instead of giving me the confidence and surety, the optimism and hope that I have contributed something to the genre, I have agonised about how it will be received once it has been published? The potential reaction has overcome the sense of achievement. I have also worried myself silly over the intricate details of things such as copyright and acknowledgement of sources. At times, I have even wished I'd never done it at all!

Looking forward as well is the antithesis of my depression. I have been asked on a number of occasions by various consultants, what I actually look forward to? My honest answer, every time, is nothing. I cannot even recall occasions – and there must have been at least some –when I looked forward to something in my past life. I do have to say, though, that December is my most favourite month of the year. Nevertheless, when it comes, the reality never matches my anticipation. I expect to be unfulfilled and disappointed. Now that it has gone, yet again I realise that it's passed me by. It is perhaps the best illustration of a general tendency. I have this persistent and yes, depressing, habit of looking back at times and situations that I now wished I had made more of. The tragedy is that I recognise that this will transpire at the time in question but still I am incapable of maximising periodic potential and truly living the moment. I guess what I really need is the impossible – the ability to know for sure at the time that my worries, concerns and fears are groundless, that things will turn out well, that they will be as I wish them to be, not as I fear them to happen.

I hope that makes some sort of sense?! If it doesn't, perhaps it will on reflection, once you have seen what else I am to write in this journal!

Day One is over. Three hundred and sixty five – as it is a leap year and there is an extra twenty-fours to endure – to go!

Saturday 2nd January 2016

I'm sure there will be some repetitive topics and themes as the days and months go by. Change is one and has already received some attention. Logic, reason, rationality – whatever derivation you choose to adopt – I suspect will be another. In probably its broadest and most populist analogy, these words are deemed to be the very opposite of whatever terminological manifestation of mental illness you choose to cite. 'Madness' can't be logical, can it? Otherwise it wouldn't be madness! However, therapeutic treatment is geared towards helping the 'patient' see things more logically. To see the wood for the trees, or whatever similar idiom one can think of on the spur of the moment. Therapy has helped me immensely not necessarily to understand mental illness – although it has contributed to that – but to enable me to take actions that can bring me out of its darkest corner and tightest grip. Cognitive Behavioural Therapy (CBT) of course is about practical measures that emanate from the relationship between thought, feeling and behaviour. If you can use CBT in your daily routines, I do believe there is respite from torment because it stimulates and encourages you to take the bull by the horns (sorry, another idiom) and quite literally, help yourself.

What doesn't work – for me anyway – is an explanation of how, when and why depression hits in the first place, and under what conditions it reoccurs. Yes, there are sometimes direct causal links. I know that my last serious bout, which began around September 2014 and lasted until the following Spring, was immediately attributable to my working environment. However, that is – again for me – a rare example of an immediate cause and stimulant. Most of the time, the serious depression that I experience in episodes descends for no apparent, accountable – and therefore logical – reason. I also can't determine how deep I will go and how long it will last, irrespective of how much I use CBT and other treatments as a daily dose of therapeutic medicine. Depression like this is unpredictable and devastating. It acts against your will and takes over your life like nothing else.

I mention all this, not just because it's an important scene setter, but also to warn you not to always expect consistency and – those words again – logic, reason and rationality. What I think you'll find more of is random unpredictability. Things that may make sense to me may be totally off the wall to anyone else. Also, things that I find entirely reasonable one day I may not be able to define, describe or even register the next! Such is the nature of a depressed mind. I would suggest, if I'm honest, that everyone's brains work like this to greater or lesser extents. It's just that the brain of a depressive has more peaks and troughs. It's both erratic and dramatic at the same time!

Reasoned appraisal and consideration is what our Rachel and her partner need right now. They've decided to take a break in their relationship to assess where they are and where they want to be – either together or separately. I guess, though it's distressing, it may actually be good for them as they near that time of life when decisions about more long-term things usually need to be faced. I do hope that they can resurrect what has always been to us a wonderful togetherness. They are both sensible and will work things out for the best – whatever that may turn out to be. Lesley spoke to her at some length this morning and I know they both feel better for hearing each other's voice.

Rachel, of course, is a seasoned traveller, which is the least that can be said of Joel! His impending trip to Asia is growing increasingly near – this time next week he will have gone – and he is fully immersed in all the final preparations whilst working virtually to the last minute to earn as much as he can. I'm really proud of him as he's turned himself into a capable as well as loveable young man. I know his Mum will worry constantly whilst he's away – all Mums would do! – but he's going out into the big wide world with a sense of security, determination and boldness, attributes that he has only recently – and probably unconsciously – added to his character and DNA. He's also going with someone who's been before, so that helps!

Sunday 3rd January 2016

One thing I do get some enjoyment out of is reading. I guess I could be described as an avid reader. I have turned what was initially Rachel's room when we first moved into this house in 1998 into a library, a veritable treasure trove of books particularly on certain subjects. I'm speculating, but you can probably determine a great deal about someone from the books he or she reads. I don't just mean their interests – that would be too obvious – but their character, their values, their approach to life etc. I am a bit of a specialist and up until fairly recently I only read non-fiction. Accordingly, I have most of the leading works on the likes of the Holocaust and Nazi Germany, but also on Jack the Ripper, the Titanic, Mallory and Irvine, the Kennedy Assassination, the Russian Revolution and the Cold War. What you may deduce from this combination – add depression, trench life in the First World War, Millwall and Leeds United into the equation as well – I would be fascinated to gleam! Your hypothesis may not be pleasant on my ears or kind on my mind, however!

The thing about reading for me is that it has to be an intellectual exercise. I have to learn from books. There is no point in reading them for me if that was not the case, even those that may be considered 'trashy' or popular. I need to see how an author has crafted a story or related facts. I need to witness the skill of, and creativity behind, writing. I need to know things I didn't know before. There is also a mental health dimension, as you probably might expect. There are two essential elements. Firstly, I have to read books in a certain order. This may change upon the purchase of something new, but essentially it has to be pre-established. I can't just pick one up off the shelf and effectively 'go with the flow'. Since I've started reading historical fiction as well, that pre-arranged ordering now needs to alternate fiction and non-fiction. If I, by accident, go out of synchronisation – and it does happen occasionally – I feel I'm somehow 'cheating' and betraying the work of the author I have pushed further on down the queue. It's as if I'm inflicting some mortal wound on the poor person! Not just hurting their feelings but their whole personae! The second thing is that I have to read with a degree of intensity that is sometimes hard to describe and definitely hard to accomplish. If I don't understand something, I cannot simply gloss over the point in question, confining it to irrelevance, I have to struggle to grasp the full complexity and sometimes enormity of what is being stated. Skim-reading is a complete no-no! I'm not as bad as I used to be. At one point, I thought that I hadn't properly read a book unless every single word had registered. That would include the acknowledgements section and even the reviews and biographical notes. I would have made one hell of a proof-reader! At work, colleagues would often ask me to go over papers, proposals and reports with punctuation and spelling as well as delivery of meaning in mind. What I'm essentially talking about here, what lies behind my method of reading, can be encompassed in one word – perfectionism. It's something that is, and always has been, part of my being, my approach, my way of dealing with practicalities. At some future point in this journal I will turn to it in much greater length and detail.

The reason I'm talking about books however is that a changeover has just occurred. I've finished reading another excellent Bernie Gunther novel by Philip Kerr and have started 'The Diary of Dawid Sierakowiak'. This is very topical as Dawid was a victim of the Nazi genocide, and specifically of the Łódź ghetto, a place I visited only last month. Indeed I discovered Dawid's grave in the extensive Jewish cemetery that dominates what was the eastern edge of the ghetto area. I did wrestle with the question of whether to read it before I went to Poland or afterwards. Doing this did not involve the simple 'flip of the coin' type of decision-making that reflects much of what people actually do. No, for me it became a massive dilemma. How could I best serve and make the most of what Dawid had to say? By reading in advance or upon reflection? I'm still not totally convinced I made the right decision but the moment has now passed, which at least has made any further deliberation superfluous on that score.

To be honest, that is a tactic I often use if I can't come to some resolution. Wait until circumstances – fate or otherwise – lessen the odds, determine the situation, pave the only remaining path to take. If only all of life could be like that? But, of course, it can't!

Monday 4th January 2016

Today marks the beginning of the new me. Or at least the beginning of changes I am in a position to make to my life. A new diet, a new exercise regime, a new schedule for working, a new work-life balance. This feels like quite an overhaul, but I'm determined not to fall into the trap I've often experienced of asking too much of myself, being too optimistic and too goal-driven, effectively setting myself up for failure. I recognise that this is probably the case for the vast majority of people who make New Year's resolutions. But I think the stakes I'm playing for are that bit higher than average, as I explained in my Introduction.

I began work at 9.00 this morning. When I get some paid work – and hopefully that is a 'when' rather than an 'if' – I can adjust that to mirror my working pattern when I was employed by the Council. That meant starting at just after 7.00. With a short break for lunch, time to write this journal and then a reasonable – but not excessive – amount for exercise, that should leave me with enough 'me-time' to make life bearable. Yes, I know, exercising and writing should do this as well, but 'should' is a dangerous word for a depressive. I put inordinate amounts of pressure on myself at times because I slavishly follow that word 'should', considering it a stipulation rather than a choice, a rule as opposed to an option. There are occasions when I can't seem to eradicate it from my thinking. "I 'should' be able to do this." "I 'should' be capable of withstanding that." And so on and so forth. Even now, having thought and decided upon a time framework, I am still uncertain as to how I will react when the moment for 'leisure' arrives. Will I feel that I haven't done enough 'work'? Will I consider that I haven't achieved what I set out to achieve during the course of the day? You can see just how this could play out!

A little bit of self-discipline is needed of course. But it needs to be combined not just with a degree of flexibility, but an equal amount of self-kindness. I mustn't – yes, I realise that this is another 'should' type word – yield to the burdens of self-penance, overdo things and succumb to self-pity. What if I do fail to achieve my targets? Who suffers? Does it actually matter?

Strangely, I have more confidence in my ability to diet than anything else. I know in recent weeks I've let myself go, but I've done so with the understanding and 'comfort' that I'm going to be different come January. And it has been Christmas! This has involved me saying things to myself that I know are dangerous, that I know can lead to mental trauma if left unchecked. I've had these mental intrusions before and have sometimes wondered if I do suffer a little bit from anorexia. Anyone who saw me and who didn't understanding this devastating condition would probably laugh at this, but I can't help but think it's true. I need to watch myself then. The last thing I need is yet another variety of mental illness! How much can someone realistically cope with?

Tuesday 5th January 2016

Sadly, the twelfth day of Christmas (unless you belong to the eastern Orthodox churches of course where it's not Day One until Thursday). All over again for another eleven plus months. Is there a more depressing day in the year? Lesley was up early to take down all the decorations so I was greeted with a very ordinary and somewhat barer front room on my arrival downstairs. Christmas may never really meet one's hopes and expectations, but even an underwhelming festive period surely beats normality and the drudgery of week-by-week routine.

Anyway, I did it! Not only did I survive Christmas but also my first bit of genuine exercise since trudging through the streets of Łódź in early December. Admittedly, it wasn't very strenuous – or even long for that matter. Ten minutes on the bike, twenty on the Flabelos machine – which if nothing else does wonderful things to your digestive system (I swear that a mere ten minutes of severe 'wobbling' can cure the most obstructive constipation!) – and then some upper body weights to finish. Not only that, but I stuck to my planned food intake as well. What a success! I just need to keep that up for another twelve months and…I'll probably look and feel exactly the same! Please ignore that last comment. That's depression talking, as they say.

Talking of depression talking, I heard – though only fleetingly – what appeared to be a fascinating and insightful interview with Ruby Wax on Radio Five Live yesterday afternoon. Ruby is another example of a comic depressive, as you probably know. She is also someone who has used her experiences and her condition to 'wax lyrical' (sorry, I had to get that pun in somehow) about what can be done in very practical ways to deal with one's worries, anxieties and inner agitation. Though she always strikes me as a very positive person, she is obviously very much aware of the fact that talking 'positively' and enthusiastically doesn't necessarily equate to a transformation in mood on behalf of the listener, or indeed the speaker. One of the things I heard her mention yesterday which really stood out for me was her consideration of the benefits of mindfulness. What she said was simple but true. Mindfulness can help many people in many different ways. However, for people with a severe and/or long-term mental illness, it offers a way of coping and a way of alleviating the harshness of symptoms. It can take the edge off the bitterness of despair, the sourness of illness. It can't, however, cure. It's not that easy, straightforward, or indeed that powerful an antidote. I don't feel pessimistic or defeatist when I say to myself and others that I will never be free of depression. To me, that's just a statement of fact. Of logic rather than mood, if you like. That doesn't mean that I don't try things that I feel may help, whether that be medication, talking therapies, exercise, diet, meditation or even listening to music. You have to believe that they will make a difference though. Not necessarily absolute remedies. But things that can – either singly or more often, collectively – have some soothing, mitigating impact.

Ruby also dealt perfectly with the old chestnut of telling someone simply to 'perk up'. "I would never have thought of that" she said. And I completely concur! I've had that so many times in numerous word combinations. 'Cheer up, it may never happen'. 'It can't be that bad'. 'You need a kick up the backside'. 'When's the funeral?' 'It doesn't hurt to smile'. Do people really think that works? That you can literally click your fingers, give yourself a metaphorical kick up the arse, put a forced smile on your face, and, hey presto, that's the answer? Some obviously do. These, I guess, are people who don't understand the difference between being sad or upset and being truly depressed. Others, I put it to you, just don't think!

Wednesday 6th January 2016
I visited my friend John this morning to discuss our working plans for the year ahead. John is the most dynamic person I think I

know. He always has new ideas, new connections, new opportunities. And more importantly, he acts on them. With John, things happen. That's why I'm so fortunate that he has taken my involvement in Holocaust related work and wants to build an entire working programme around it and its relationship to conflict. Between us, we make a good resource, one that can be taken out into communities to raise issues, to discuss challenges and to come up with solutions. I suspect he would say that I keep his feet on the ground, that I give him some perspective. He gives me prospects, possibilities, latitude and confidence.

I returned home at lunchtime to an empty house. Lesley has taken Joel to an interview for a position with Eurocamp which he would take up, fingers crossed, once he has returned from his travels in Asia. This could mean that he will be away for virtually an entire year. Once, I would have gulped and secretly welcomed that prospect, but not now. He is such a character. I miss him so much when he's not around. I need to tell him that before he goes. Not to make him think twice about going, of course. But to make him realise how much he is loved and valued. A measure of Joel's allure can be gleamed from what he told us about the interview when he came in from work on Monday evening. "It's in Hertford, in Norwich, in Cheshire", he proclaimed. While I tried to get my head around the prospect of him being in the Home Counties, East Anglia and the suburbs of Manchester all at once, he then corrected himself. "Sorry, 'Northwich', not 'Norwich'". With 'Hertford' becoming 'Hartford', it then made sense!

Of course, it wasn't a completely empty house. Millie was here, waiting patiently at the front window for my return. I would love to be a dog. For them, it seems to be all about routine, about pretty strict patterns of behaviour and recognising clearly-defined prompts. Clearly, us humans train our dogs – whether they be working or otherwise – to be so. But they take it to a level that is beyond even the most meticulous of trainers. Millie sits in different places depending on the circumstance, for example.

Before we go to bed, I even go through the charade of asking her if she wants to go for a wee outside. She jumps up, follows me through the back door, looks around for ten seconds and then promptly goes back inside, sits on her mat, and awaits her treat! The passing of urine is now pretty much a side-show! To show me that it's not just her, I see a man walking his dog pretty much every day through the upstairs window when I'm 'wobbling' on the Flabelos. On every occasion, they stop at the same spot on the pavement, he makes her sit down and then they cross the road. She may not quite have mastered the automatic repose of sitting yet, but she's certainly got one thing absolutely exact. She moves to the same position on the pavement – the very same – every time, irrespective of where her master is. I wonder if he notices himself? He must do. For dogs, routine must equate to comfort and reassurance. Such predictability also sends a message to those around them. "I'm OK, I'm happy and content. You've no need to worry about me." It also earns them approval and praise, acclaim for their loyalty and dependability. If only that could be me. I can do the routine stuff. Ordinarily, my OCD as well as my depression makes me a supreme embodiment of everything foreseeable. Indeed, most of the time I crave routine. I want things to be the same as they were the last time I did whatever it is it was. I relish patterns, systems, procedures. I want to work like a clockwork toy. But not all the time. Sometimes I want to be alive. I want exposure and excitement. I want things to be sporadic and random. I want to feel fresh and invigorated, capable of bursting out of my self-imposed straitjacket, to realise and embrace freedom. Sadly, for me, this is normally a sign that I'm becoming ill. Instead of feeling rejuvenated, I start to worry. Depression hits home and not only do all those new cravings evaporate, but everything that I see as normally comforting, suddenly becomes overbearing and frightening. I very rarely even get to glimpse let alone internalise those feelings that have so tantalisingly been within reach. Having had years of depression, my brain has automatically adjusted itself to see instead fear and danger. What a life!

Thursday 7th January 2016

London! I had an interview today for an Associate Caseworker position at the Parliamentary and Health Service Ombudsman. If I get it – and the interview went reasonably well, I think – it will suit my new working arrangements down to the ground. The work of the Ombudsman revolves around providing a final decision on any complaint in relation to Central Government Departments or the NHS that has exhausted all previous attempts at resolution. Caseworkers are paid per completed case and can work at home. Ideal.

Interviews are naturally tense situations but the forty-five minutes I spent being grilled about my competency for the post were nothing compared with the really challenging part of the day – getting on the train itself! This is one of my pet hates. Let me explain. Whenever I book a train to London – for football or on other occasions – I reserve a place in the Quiet coach. I just find noise in a confined space intrusive and at times, frightening, and even though not everyone obeys East Midlands Trains restrictions on the use of mobile phones, sitting in a relatively quiet area tends to calm and relax me. Now, the Quiet coach on the service to St Pancras always seems to be Coach A and is either at the very front of the train or the last compartment. In addition, I try if I can to book a seat at one end of the carriage, so that I am next to the toilets, and, more importantly the entrance/exit. The reason for this is quite simple. It avoids as far as possible having to get up in front of people and walk through a compartment. The problem is that at my station, the southbound platform is short. It can only accommodate five to six coaches. If Coach A is at the back of the train, it means getting on two or three compartments further up and having to walk through carriages that are usually full to the brim of people, all of whom I think are looking at me, scrutinising my passage through their train space. I never know how I'm going to react and am so focussed on not looking anyone in the face and even more importantly, keeping my feet so that I don't brush against any one person or, heaven forbid, lose my balance if the train starts to move, that I am forced to adopt exclusive tunnel vision.

Now, I'm nearly six foot and weigh eighteen stone. I'm a big man. I'm hard to miss and there is never enough space to walk seamlessly and effortlessly from point A to point B. I crave invisibility – in actual fact, that is my one wish if I was to have some superhuman power – or even some form of teleportation that can work instantaneously, thereby eradicating all obstacles, tangible, physical and of course, in my mind. The period immediately before the arrival of the train is the worst part of the day. I am fraught with nervous tension. I just wish the moment could be over. I pray incessantly and feverishly that Coach A is at the front so that I can literally take ten steps at most to getting on the train and finding my seat. Even that doesn't alleviate every cause for concern, though. What if someone is sitting in my reserved seat? What do I do then? I have to either alter my plan and look somewhere else, thus completely throwing me. Or I am forced into interaction with someone that I haven't planned. It's a positive nightmare.

I have thought about asking for assistance from the station personnel. But think about it. I suspect their entire focus in relation to disability is on providing a ramp for a wheelchair-user. How they would react to an apparently fit and able man like me trying to tell them that I'm terrified of walking onto a train and through a compartment, is not quite so clear cut! I don't want to see confused looks on their faces, or some evidence of any doubts in their mind. I could be doing them a complete disservice. Rail companies may well train their staff to deal with people with mental disabilities as well as physical. But I don't want to take that chance. I don't want to be looked on in some pitying or disparaging fashion – by staff or fellow passengers. Again, I don't want to draw attention to myself and almost elicit probing scrutiny. So I keep things to myself and hope beyond hope that things will turn out well.

Yesterday, thank God, they did. Coach A was at the front and my seat was empty upon arrival!

All that, simply to get on a train! What an effort it is. How uncomfortable it becomes. How traumatic if may turn out to be. It doesn't always end once I'm sitting where I'm supposed to be and the train moves off. You would be forgiven for thinking that I'd automatically be relieved. And nine times out of ten, that is the case. However, very occasionally, I allow myself to reflect in a severely punitive way and scold myself incessantly for being pathetic and melodramatic. I know I'm wrong to do so. I know I would react angrily if I saw this reaction in others. But I can't help doing it to myself. I become my own worst enemy!

Friday 8th January 2016

Rachel skyped us this morning. It was great to see her and, as she is now in Barcelona with her friend Susie, the wireless connection – or whatever it is that makes Skype work – was that bit clearer and smoother. She had a long conversation with Lesley – with the occasional intermission from me offering 'wise' counsel (!!) – and though there were tears, I think both will have felt a lot better from having such close and prolonged contact. They'll be even closer very soon when Lesley flies out to Sri Lanka at the end of the month.

Whilst Lesley is off to see her Manager about a return to work – she's been off since the attack last month – I'm going out into the wilds of rural Leicestershire to meet a bloke about a school. Curious? This isn't some pending venture, some potential educational initiative, rather it's to address elements of my past – and his, I would suspect. The impact on my life of my experiences at a Scottish boarding school have been considerable and far-reaching. They will inevitably be the subject of close scrutiny at some future point in this journal. But not now. Suffice to say that the person I'm meeting is a fellow alumnus. Though he is significantly older than me, we have both been quite forthright – with each other and on Facebook – about negative experiences of that school. He in particular has been instrumental in drawing the school's attention to some totally deplorable things that have happened to pupils in the past and how the school itself has a duty to address these and not solely focus on the welfare – educational and otherwise – of its present incumbents. It will be interesting to meet him.

Today is also Joel's last day at home before he commences his big adventure. There will be tears again tomorrow. He seems very relaxed, as if he's going to the pictures in town, rather than thousands of miles away to foreign shores! That's him in a nutshell though!

Saturday 9th January 2016
Last night I got really frightened. The catalyst was my decision to forego the ready meal Lesley had left for me and to have chicken nuggets and chips instead. At the time it was virtually an automatic process. I just couldn't stomach the mushroom focussed mess that was potentially my tea and the first things that I found in the freezer were…yes, a slightly less rapidly cooked fat-orientated substitute of fried chicken and potato! However, as I was eating it, I began to believe that what I was devouring was poison. It didn't stop me clearing my plate but as I sat there afterwards and contemplated what had passed into my stomach, the belief intensified and became more and more real. For a moment I was honestly expecting death. I started to imagine pains in my chest and arms. I felt faint and defenceless. For an hour or so, my mind kept churning over and over the same thoughts and fears. They wouldn't go away. I tried so hard to logically address what was happening. To use my CBT experience to push away the anxieties. Eventually a combination of reason and distraction succeeded in calming the turbulent ocean that my mind had become. I told myself that it can't have been poison as my heart is still ticking and I'm fully conscious and that I can rid myself of some of the fat by exercising in the morning. Anyone reading this who has no experience of mental illness will wonder how and why this seemingly self-evident conclusion could not be reached straight away, or even used as some form of protective shell to keep the immediate panic and consternation at arm's length. The answer

is that that is not how a depressed mind works. Logic doesn't enter its parameters. It feeds on fear, not reason. It races away at its own speed, following its own direction, shoving aside everything in its path, leaving a trail of damaged threads and infected matter. The only way to stop it is intervention. This can involve medicine and therapy at its most severe. (I occasionally use Diazepam as a calming sedative, for example). CBT, once learned and practised, also helps me, as it eventually did last night.

Trying to make sense of things this morning, I couldn't help dwelling on coincidence. Two people I know of have recently died quite suddenly. The first was a lecturer at De Montfort University and a tutor on Lesley's law course.[2] The second was the ex-Newcastle goalkeeper, Pavel Srníček. The former Czech international collapsed whilst running prior to Christmas and sadly never recovered. Two tragic but apparently random events. The connection for me was their age. Both were forty-seven, as am I. I've now got it into my head that this is no coincidence, that it's some form of pressing portent, a horrible premonition of the fate that is to befall me. Lesley, during her most vulnerable moments recently has said that she fears something bad is going to happen. I seem to have connected all these evidently indiscriminate happenings (including last night's fears), made two and two equal five, and concluded that I am to be the direct victim of circumstance.

It's a good thing I'm seeing my consultant on Thursday. I'll be able to mention this to him and see what he says. In the meantime, I have my learned experience of CBT to fall back on. It is so useful, but it's exhausting. It becomes a real physical as well as mental challenge and it doesn't always work. But it's what I have.

Sunday 10th January 2016
We took Millie for a long walk this morning. She's been very unsettled these last few days. Lesley thinks it's because we

haven't exercised her as much as she is used to. I also think it's because – with Joel leaving – she's detected some kind of upheaval in our domestic situation. Dogs seem to have a sixth sense, some powerful internal antennae that connects with what is about to happen irrespective of any other form of tangible communication. If she settles down over the course of the next day or two, I think I'll be proved right. I wasn't entirely enthusiastic at the prospects of a walk, if I'm completely honest. It's certainly not that I don't enjoy walking. Rather, it's the fear I have of the ramifications of exercise, particularly away from the confines – and the shelter – of my own home. Some time ago now, I took Millie for a long lunchtime walk, had a dizzy spell half way through and barely made it home in one piece. I almost fell through the front door and if Joel and Elliot hadn't been there to take care of her and put me to bed, I'd have been in a real state. That episode I think has stayed with my subconscious being. It seems to stimulate my brain to project within me some kind of forceful radar that says 'be wary, danger ahead'. It's a significant example of mind over matter, but of course in a negative sense. I think I'll struggle, I detect the onset of fear and worry, I ruminate over the prospects of becoming faint, and so that of course, without question, is what is going to happen. And it often does. The very instant I start to sweat, my muscles begin to strain and my heart to thump, I trigger that process of panic that leads, inevitably it seems, to the dire physical consequences of fear within my mind. The trick for me is to use CBT in either a preventative or alleviating fashion. This morning, yesterday's fears were still very much with me. However, so too was Lesley, and that provided that necessary degree of comfort and reassurance to enable me to function rather than malfunction!

Well, he's gone. We put Joel and his mate Dave on the Megabus to London yesterday afternoon, and this evening they will fly from Heathrow to Thailand. Joel was so excited yesterday. Admittedly he was still under the influence of alcohol following his leaving 'do' the night before, but it was clear he was just itching to get off. It was great to see him looking so exhilarated, so full of anticipatory yearning. When I think back over the years of being his Stepdad, I would like to think that some of what I've tried to do for him and with him has been of benefit, that he thinks I've been of at least some help and support. My depressed mind can't stop ruminating over the bad times though. Those many occasions when we argued, those angry moments, the period when I had virtually no relationship with him whatsoever. It was always his Mum that was the calming factor. It was Lesley who pulled him through, who stayed with him, who always seemed to believe in him. It is her that he owes his gratitude, rather than me. I've tried. God I've tried. I just wish I'd been more understanding. That what I've learned as a parent could have helped him more through his formative years. I'm probably being quite harsh on myself. At least I hope I am! There's always been a bit of me though that his seen him continuously as my little boy, that vulnerable lad, the youngest of our three before Elliot. I still have a tendency to revert to the language that I used then to him, to behave as if he's eight rather than twenty-four. This trip is the turning point for him in many ways. It's the last element of his youth but also the first of his adulthood. It will make him a man in so many new ways. I have to make sure that it is equally as climacteric for me so that we can move what I now think is a productive relationship forward in the right way.

Looking back over what I've written so far in this diary, I think I'm going to have to try and write more concisely perhaps and with a greater sense of perspective. I have a whole year – minus ten days now – in which to write about the things that happen to me but also, more importantly, within me. I don't need to explain all in the first month! Otherwise, this journal is going to be one akin to 'War and Peace'!

Let's see what happens anyway.

Monday 11th January 2016
This is going to be a challenging week. On Thursday, as I've already mentioned, I see my consultant. But it's not just my health that's on the line this week. On Friday I'm meeting people

in relation to some health-related community engagement work. I put together a proposal to do this as well as broader equality proofing prior to Christmas and it seems they like what I've had to say. This could be quite significant. As far as the work itself is concerned, it focuses on applied research and specifically on how specific NHS projects can utilise more fundamentally and successfully, links with communities and in particular those that are marginalised, socially excluded and with key health issues. For me, it would allow me to continue what I've done, I think with some degree of competency, over the course of the last ten years or so.

One of the most difficult things I had to address in my proposal was what to stipulate as a payment! I suspect – in fact I know – I've undercharged. Certainly in comparison to what may be considered the 'going rate' for consultants in the NHS, and indeed the wider public sector. But not only am I not accustomed to putting a monetary value on my work, I just don't like doing so. I guess that again depression plays its part here. Such financial undervaluing simply reflects my overall state of mind, my natural tendency to think badly of myself, to detrimentally consider what I do to be of limited worth. Even though in the proposal document I simply laid out what I could do, the process of transforming those words from an exercise in promotion and in writing into practical delivery is another matter. It's not that I've falsified or over-exaggerated anything. I was strict on myself in only stipulating what I was able to do given my experience and knowledge. It comes down to inner belief and overcoming serious internal unsureness. It's always been the same whenever I've had a break from work in the past – mostly as a result of a breakdown in my mental health, of course. Every occasion has involved wrestling with my self-respect and self-conviction. Increasingly, I seem to forget things I've always known. It's as if an attack on my brain has left tangible physical scars that include a deficient memory and massive self-doubt. If there is overconfidence, then there must also be, quite logically, under-confidence. I've never had the former, but am blighted continually by the latter. What I must tell myself now is that I've always regained what I feared I'd lost in the past – at least to enable me to function in a working capacity – and that there is no reason why that can't also be the case this time. Telling myself is one thing, it goes without saying, believing it is another. 'I can work. I can do what I said I could do. I can achieve. I can be successful. I can meet the expectations of others'. They may not satisfy my own perfectionist inclinations, but they are good enough.

I should also know today whether my interview last week at the Ombudsman's office was successful or not. I'm hopeful, though not expectant. Whatever will be, will be.

David Bowie died today. An immense talent, cultural icon and global superstar, he was also, by all accounts, a thoroughly nice bloke. The world is sadder for his loss.

Tuesday 12th January 2016
Continuing yesterday's theme – as it still dominates my thoughts – I can't help but wondering if my relatively good mental health of recent months is down to my no longer being in a workplace? Or perhaps even of having no paid work to do? I think the former is definitely the case. There is no doubt that for the latter part of my time working for the Council, the working environment was a contributory factor in keeping me depressed. It didn't lead to depression itself. That was already there. It just didn't help in any recovery. I also know for certain that my last depressive episode of consequence was triggered directly by things that had happened in the office. Though there was a distinct inevitability to it all, it still took my consultant to point out at the time that if I wanted to keep myself safe and remotely sane, I shouldn't be at work. His intervention was crucial. I'd have carried on regardless – as I had done on many previous occasions. Medical intervention brought me to my senses. It also took the decision out of my hands. Here was somebody – someone with knowledge and expertise – telling me what to do. I was no longer capable of deciding for myself. When I'm severely depressed the

ability to decipher between one thing or another becomes not just difficult but frustratingly intolerable. I can't decide whether I want tea or coffee sometimes! I become the master of indecision. Perennially 'on the fence'. Whether trivial or substantial, it's all the same. I need to be told, to be instructed, to have my mind made up for me.

The latter supposition – whether work itself is harmful to me – is less clear-cut. I sincerely hope not of course. The last thing I would ever want is to be permanently redundant, not earning my keep, not contributing to the family income. It would be such a massive blow to my self-esteem. I'm not sure I would recover. In the past, whenever the length of absence from work has triggered a reduction in sick-pay, I've felt awful. Helpless, futile, disempowered – these are all words that come to mind when I recall the aftermath. I've always therefore felt that the ability to work and to earn is paramount to my ability to stay relatively well. But what if that is no longer the case? What if work itself – or rather my capacity to do it – is making me worse? I guess time will tell. It's a fearful conundrum though. And it will weigh on my mind. Of that there is no doubt.

Wednesday 13th January 2016

The first major disappointment of the week (my automatic use of the word 'first' is obviously in expectation that there will be more!) came with the news that my application for the Ombudsman's post had been unsuccessful. I can handle their decision – the outcome, if you like. What I always find more challenging to come to terms with is the process by which that decision was made, involving as it must, some form of judgement. Somewhere along the line, something I have done, or said, or written, has been perceived to be lacking in some way. It hasn't met the required standard. It hasn't pass the relevant test. It has been deemed 'deficient'. More often than not, anything other than the proverbial and metaphorical 'perfect ten' causes me intense self-analysis and savage self-scrutiny. Thinking trap after thinking trap then follow, the most damaging being the 'all or nothing' variety. I'm either brilliant or I'm crap. There's nothing in between. At the moment, in relation to that job, that specific set of circumstances, I feel the latter. Proper perspective is what I need, but that is often hard to come by.

I had a meeting with two old friends in a pub in the West End of Leicester last night. It was great to see them and chat over plans to carry on working with Gypsies and Travellers even though only one of us now has a formal role to do so – in terms of a job description that is. I hadn't been to this particular pub before and so a process of planning, almost of 'prior acclimatisation' immediately kicked in. Whenever I have to go to somewhere new, I can't just turn up, I have to plan in as meticulous a way as possible beforehand. I need to somehow overcome fears of ignorance and uncertainty. I don't want to be a stranger or be seen as one. Accordingly, I not only looked at where the pub was on Google maps, I went down to the 'street level' function, so that I could physically see on my PC what the pub looked like, where it's entrance was, what the streets were like around it for parking, what my route would be, what physical obstacles there may have been and so on and so forth. I then had to plan a timescale. What time to get ready, when to have something to eat, how long to allow for the journey and to find a parking space, when to go the toilet so that I wouldn't have to use the facilities in the pub. All this I did, but of course one can't always prepare for every eventuality. When I arrived outside the pub five minutes before we were scheduled to meet, I found that virtually every street had a 'residents permit only' parking status. What do I do now? I began to panic. I even thought for a moment of going home and then offering some plausible – but false – excuse as to my absence. Luckily I found somewhere that allowed you to pay to park. I was saved! I didn't even have to pay as it turned out, as it was after 6.00 pm. My worries were not over, though. I got to the pub, looked through the windows and couldn't see my friends. The thought of going into the building and waiting provoked too much anxious insecurity. Those of you that have seen the film 'An American Werewolf in London' will remember the very first scene when the two intrepid young explorers from the States enter a rural Yorkshire inn. Immediately, the conversation stops and all eyes turn to the front door. That was, and always is, my fear! I am the perennial stranger, the outsider, the exclusive one. I don't want to be, but I am – at least in my own mind. So what did I do then? I stood outside the pub, pretending to have a conversation on my phone so that it looked a little less conspicuous, until my friends arrived as they duly did within a few minutes. All that for a drink and a chat! It's no wonder I'm exhausted after going out. It's not the physical exertion that expends energy, it's the mental challenge that drains and uses up virtually all my battery capacity.

Thursday 14th January 2016
D-Day! As my new consultant's name begins with the letter D, it seems appropriate to use these words to describe the challenge of another appointment. But, of course, this promised to be no ordinary or routine consultation. I was here not just to discuss how I'd been since I last saw him, but to consider a change of medication. As it turned out, though, he recommended not to go ahead – at least for the moment. He said that he detected signs of improvement since my last appointment in October and that, as a consequence, he saw no reason to do anything other than continue with my current regime. It does make sense. In fact, I had been thinking the same, if I'm truly honest with myself. If there had been a decline or even if things had remained the same, the option to revert to new drugs would have been a more conceivable and sensible one. But as it is, I will carry on with my faithful companions, Duloxetine and Quetiapine. He doesn't want to see me for four months, but mentioned the proviso that I can always get in touch in the meantime should things deteriorate. He asked me if this relative improvement could be attributed to anything specific. My immediate reaction was to say 'not working'. However, I fall back on my thoughts from Tuesday. Is it not having to face that particular working environment that has led to this current period of sustained stability? Or is it the fact that I'm not doing any paid work at all? I don't know. I can't know and I won't know until there is a change in my working

circumstances. Everything is supposition. Nothing can be determined to the level of satisfaction and ease I really yearn for. I can't manufacture future certainty.

I am glad though not to be facing the trials and tribulations of changing medication. It is a daunting process and in the past it has caused me no end of discomfort, physical as well as mental. One particular drug – and I can't remember which – caused pronounced withdrawal symptoms. I was all over the place for a couple of days. There was little respite from a fervent dizziness and nausea. One usually has to gradually reduce one's dosage of the current medication to nothing before starting, and gradually increasing, its substitute. It is demanding on your body and your mind cannot be reassured that things are going to get better straight away. If anything, one needs to prepare for the worse, that you will initially be vulnerable, more depressed and potentially suicidal, before the new medication kicks in. It can be worth it. Of course it can. Every change of drugs that I've had in relation to depression has been a positive revision. The problem is that you can't guarantee it. Like depression itself, being on particular drugs is a very individualistic experience. What works for one person, may not work for someone else. It can even be more subtle than that. What elicits stability in some cases, can prove to be a potential cure in others. It all depends on the uniqueness of the individual. The other thing that can blur proceedings is the issue of side-effects. They can be exactly the same as the symptoms of the illness itself. Depression can cause weight gain or loss, sleepiness or insomnia, dizziness, muscle tremors, nausea and any number of other physical or mental ailments. If you look at the potential side-effects of anti-depressive medication, all or the majority of these things are stipulated in depressive clarity and force! It can be difficult to determine, therefore, whether what you're going through is the illness or a consequence of its treatment! Of course, drug companies have to state every conceivable possibility when it comes to repercussions. They need to cover themselves for every potential eventuality, after all. This apparent interrelation as well as the uncertainty of outcome can lead people though to wonder what they are letting themselves in for. To question whether the process of change is worthwhile. I suppose, when it comes down to it, it's a gamble. You simply don't know, but you want to give things a try. Who knows, the new drug may be the breakthrough one in your case. I'm still searching, I have to say. Stability has been the best result I have achieved so far. It may be that's the best result I'm ever going to get. As I've said before, I've resigned myself to that being the case, without being unduly pessimistic. I've never been resistant to change, though. I'll give most things a go, including any medication that may help.

There was a lighter side to my visit to the Centre. Firstly, my new consultant is a spitting image of the actor Christian Bale. In the last film I saw of his, he was playing Moses. For a brief second and no more, I thought I was caught up in some form of biblical providence, some divine assessment, some heavenly conference. I had to shake my head and blink my eyes to return to reality! The other thing occurred in the waiting room. When I'm particularly anxious or stressed, I have the habit of tapping my feet. It's just a nervous twitch, but it's remarkably durable. I'm like an incessant morse-code telegraph in human form. I even swear on one occasion that my foot was signalling 'SOS'! I'm not always aware that I'm doing it either. It seems to happen not only when I'm awaiting something in trepidation, but when I'm watching Millwall (no comments please!). Well this morning, there were three of us in the waiting room and every one of us was tapping our right foot! Not only was this mildly amusing, there was a strange feeling of community, of commonality, of togetherness. Depressives of the world, unite. We have nothing to lose but our minds!

Friday 15th January 2016

Another disappointment. This morning, I had my meeting with NHS personnel at Leicester General Hospital. If you remember, this was in relation to some potential community engagement and equalities work. How did it go? Well, whilst it wasn't what I'd hoped for, I suppose it wasn't a disaster either. I'd thought that it would simply be about agreeing (or not) the details I had included in my proposal. What transpired however was a little more circumspect. They weren't as far forward in terms of making decisions as I'd thought they'd be, and they asked for a little more time. This is fair enough and I suspect if I was in their shoes I'd ask for the same. I think what will materialise is pockets of work (initially on a trial basis) rather than the full proposal that I had formulated and costed. The challenge is, of course, my ability to see this as a result, a positive step, and not a reflection on my full capabilities. Easier said than done. What I should glean from the meeting is their confidence in my approach, my sincerity, my skills and my adeptness. Why oh why can I not feel even the tiniest morsel of confidence in myself?

The inability to make music my profession has been one of the deepest regrets of my life. I was trained as a youngster to be a classical musician. It was why I went to boarding school, gaining a music scholarship that not only paid a substantial part of the school fees, but which also enabled me to have access to the very best 'cello teachers in the land. I would have lessons with leading figures at the Royal Academy and Royal College of Music in London and at the Royal Scottish Academy of Music and Drama in Glasgow. My teachers all thought I had promise. I had talent. I know I did. I could move audiences with my playing. I managed to master some significant works in the repertoire. But what I didn't have was what I required most of all, the dedication and perseverance to succeed. I only realised this when it was too late. Instead of practising with the necessary intensity and focus, I would largely go through the motions. Putting in the hours (though not always) was one thing, but it was quality, not quantity that was required. Focus on technique and study is a prerequisite for all successful musicians (it's no different to talent in sport, for example), whereas I just wanted to play pieces, to make a wonderful sound, to revel in the joys that my playing seemed to bring others. I would also take any short cut that I thought could lead to performance, not recognising that I was side-tracking fundamental aspects that only a true and professional music-maker would assimilate. I only recognised this in my last year at Durham University when I applied to music colleges for postgraduate study. I know my teacher then knew that I was over-reaching myself, but he didn't say anything. Presumably he didn't want to hurt my feelings. When I auditioned, it was obvious I was wasting my time. Even now, I think the people I played for were embarrassed at my proficiency – or lack of it to be more accurate. They recommended arts administration, saying quite truthfully I think that an adequate performer would have a greater appreciation of the demands of staging professional music. I didn't want this. I didn't want to be 'adequate'.

All this haunted me as I drove away from the hospital. Life would have been so much simpler, and possibly more enjoyable, had I managed to make a living out of musical performance. All you have to do is practice, turn up and play. What you're involved in though is high art, invoking passion and beauty, enabling escape and reflection, achieving and exemplifying all that humanity has to offer in its most noblest and passionate splendour. That could have been me. No dissent, no turmoil, no argument, no opposition. Just music. I know I'm painting an over-generalised, over-simplistic and rather utopian ideal. But indulge me for one wonderful moment before depression takes over. Would depression have enabled me to successfully deal with the challenges of performance? Probably not. But would I have been able to use my job as an artist to keep depression in check? Possibly. Unfortunately, but pertinently, I will now never know.

Saturday 16th January 2016
Well, that was the week that was. It promised much, but ultimately delivered little. It's quite astonishing to think that the most positive thing that happened was probably the appointment I had with my consultant. Oh irony of ironies! What is usually an occasion beset with despondency was this time even a little up-lifting. It wasn't a breakthrough by any means. But it at least evidenced some improvement in my mental state compared to

last October. It gave me a boost, even if that was probably more due to the decision not to change my drugs and to maintain the status quo. We're back to that fear of change again, aren't we?

I just hope that the lack of progress on the working front doesn't immediately temper the little headway that came my way on Thursday. I can feel the struggle rising within me though. It's like a potential tidal wave of fear and doubt and it promises to wash over everything unless somehow I can keep it in check. All I desperately need is a break. Some respite in my mind and some movement in getting some work. Things could change significantly if only… I can't even finish the sentence. 'If only' has become a metaphor for my life in so many ways.

It's been a quiet sort of day. It's Lesley's university weekend. Two full days of lectures. She's been working hard this week in preparation. How she manages to do this when she's at work as well I just don't know. At the moment, she's not of course. The doctor has advised a further period of sickness absence and I think she's recognised that she needs this. It's not in her nature to ease back, if that's the right phrase. However, it's her mind that needs to recover and until that degree of mental strength returns I think it's sensible that she stills the urge that I know is within her to return to her desk. Her manager agrees with this is well, so there's no pressure there which is a godsend.

Sunday 17th January 2016

Every Sunday morning I do the ironing. It's one of many routines that comprise my living week. It's not as time-specific as some. Ever since I can remember, Saturday (except in the Summer) tends to focus around kick off at 3.00 pm and Sports Report at 5.00 pm. It's not that everything stops at those times, it's just that my mind tends to go elsewhere, to wherever my teams are playing (and often losing!). I can be in town shopping, at home working, on a short break relaxing. It doesn't matter. Something in my DNA ensures an automatic, subconscious adjustment to the world of football. There are other routines, so many others.

When I was working at the Council for example, I would get up at 5.45 am so that I could be at my desk at seven, thereby avoiding those anxious moments that always accompany walking into an office of people. More often than not, I was the first to arrive. I could work silently, I could be silent and all around me, there was silence. No need for interaction with others. No interruptions. No distractions. Just me in my tiny space in the corner of the huge open-plan workplace. Getting in so early also ensured that I had no problems parking. I had my choice of thousands of spaces! It was unproblematic. It was easy. It was comfortable. There was no anxiety.

I guess routines are an expression of control. They provide order and stability. They make sense even if they may appear unusual or bizarre to others. Living with a mental illness has always meant wrestling with this issue of control. It's what I fear losing most of all. Doing so would feed the common suppositions that are associated with that word 'madness' – irrationality, wildness, irresponsibility, unreliability, even danger and violence. Routines provide, for me, some means of thwarting the destructive path that uncontrollable madness can take. And yet at the same time, keeping and developing routines can also constrict your mind, making you a slave to habit. You lose spontaneity. You become robotic. Moreover, if you don't, for whatever reason, meet the expectation that has become your way of living, you may begin to experience feelings of self-doubt and failure. You end up criticising and judging your very being using the criteria that you, yourself, have instigated! As with everything, it comes down to balance, finding it and doing your best to maintain it with a certain level of flexibility – controllable flexibility of course!

Deep thoughts for a Sunday morning! Back to the ironing. You won't be surprised to learn that ironing is one of those pastimes that is ripe – and hazardous – for a depressive who is also a perfectionist. My aim for every item of clothing is complete smoothness. Like a millpond in the dead of night, free from waves, free from ripples, free from any external influence. I have to deal with every crease, I have to provide symmetry and beauty. And this is ironing, not architecture or some meticulous example of classical art! It means it takes me ages. It's not helped, of course, by having a teenage son who puts absolutely everything in the washing! Every week I iron five white shirts, three pairs of black trousers, two black pullovers, a PE kit and occasionally even a tie and a blazer! And that's just what our Elliot needs for school. I don't begrudge him though. I was a thirteen-year old once. More years ago than I would care to mention, of course. I can remember the obsession with bodily cleanliness, with looking good, even stylish. I tell myself that Elliot is a beautiful person and if I can play some small part in that personae by ironing his clothes well, then I would do it all week to my heart's content!

The first snow of the winter fell overnight. I love the snow. I love its purity and its freshness. I love the transformation it brings to mundane surroundings. What I don't like though is driving in it! When I woke up this morning I was initially comforted not just by the beauty outside but by the thought that I didn't need to go out. However, when I got downstairs, I found Lesley had left a note asking me to do some shopping for dinner! Immediately worrisome thoughts began to infiltrate a mind that until then had been an idyll of serenity. 'Driving was bound to involve an accident.' 'No matter how careful I am, I can't control the behaviour, the obviously reckless behaviour moreover, of my fellow drivers.' 'I would be a tortoise surrounded by budding Lewis Hamilton's!' The only way to still my rising anxiety was to go and get on with it. You'll be glad to hear that I was fine. No cause for concern. Aside from our estate, the roads were clear. No-one appeared in a rush to go anywhere. I survived!

Monday 18th January 2016

My Dad died twenty-eight years ago today. My memories of that time are still very vivid. I remember well the overnight train journey I had to take to get me home from the north of Scotland where I was working. How lonely it was in the carriage. How much I wanted to sleep, to escape just for a short period the trauma that I knew was to come. I remember his reaction when I appeared on that Sunday on the ward where he'd been taken. How emotional he was, but how determined he seemed not to cause concern. Still focusing on practicalities. Still trying to stay optimistic. I remember leaving him as he wanted to speak to Mayla, his sister. How I knew at that moment that I would never talk to him again. I remember the vigil around his bed in the early hours as he gently slipped away. As if it were yesterday.

My Dad was my hero. He still is. We were close, so close. We did so many things together. Music, football, politics. The list could go on. We laughed and we joked. We shared and we reflected. We cried and we comforted. We debated and we learned from each other. I do know though that my relationship with him after he passed away contributed to my evolving mental illness. Putting him high on such a pedestal meant that I could never criticise, or even think of criticism. He placed demands on me as the oldest son to look after the rest of the family after he'd gone. How could I not rise to the challenge? And yet the challenge was an impossible one for someone already afflicted with depression. Anything that went wrong from then on, I felt culpable. I was letting him down if I didn't resolve matters. The perfectionism within me was preserved and solidified by the faith my Dad seemed to have in my capabilities and my responsibilities. I didn't realise it at the time but I was setting myself up to fail. Only the psychotherapy treatment I received years afterwards made me come to my senses. Made me appreciate that Dad was human, not superhuman. And that I was too. Those weeks of therapy were devastatingly painful. For the very first time in my life I was encouraged to think of my Dad as anything but perfect. I saw for the first time not only his frailty and failings, but also his misgivings and the unfairness that lay central to what he expected me to do. I even felt resentment, and that hurt so much. I scolded myself as a consequence. I tortured myself incessantly. Those feelings have stayed with me to the same degree as the sadness of bereavement. They have become less harsh, less piercing, throughout time. I have learned to cope with them.

I know that I developed OCD as a direct result of the immediate aftermath of his passing. Whilst I was a student at Durham, only a matter of months after he died, I began at night to go through an elaborate, but insistent ritual. I would say to myself that I couldn't go to sleep until I had a perfectly developed, beautiful and unimpaired image of my father. At the start this came to me easily and effortlessly. But as time went on, as the days turned into weeks, the weeks into months, disturbing and invasive thoughts penetrated this panacea of love. The more I concentrated and tried to force my mind to think in a wholly positive manner, the more it failed me. The images became distorted, the thoughts more conflictful. I wrestled with myself every night, trying desperately to convey my perfect appreciation of my Dad through a mind that was not working as I wanted it to do, a mind that I thought was becoming diseased. My 'solution' was to invent new rituals. I started to check things. I started to count. Only if I did things in a certain way and a certain number of times (my number was, and still is, seven), would I be able to demonstrate and feel within me my abiding and unequivocal love for my father. I was damaging myself without any conscious understanding of what I was doing and where it would lead. It became permanent without my recognition.

Things are a lot better now. My Dad has become human again. I have learned to see him in a more rational, more normal, way. I'm still afflicted though. Bereavement at such an early age leaves a mark. For me, it didn't cause depression. That was already there. It did though provide a helping hand in its penetration of my entire being. It assisted a path that was already being tread. It consolidated an already existent disability. It allowed an affliction to germinate, to cultivate soil already ripe for illness.

I miss my Dad so much. The single most disturbing thing I've realised this morning is that I can no longer remember his voice.

Tuesday 19th January 2016

Apparently yesterday, being the third Monday of the first month, was the most depressing day in the calendar. I use the word 'apparently' advisedly because not only am I not sure who exactly is making this claim and which criteria have been used, I am even less clear as to who has been consulted in relation to this supposed 'fact'. I would suggest that the last people to be involved would be people like me – long term depressives. For us, depression is a part of every day. There is not always a logical external stimuli that leads to our depressed state. For most of the time in my case, depression just happens. Why and how is not always easy to decipher and pinpoint. Of course, for others experiencing different forms of depression this is not necessarily the case. The most obvious example I suppose, given how I started talking about today, is those that have Seasonal Affective Disorder (SAD).

Given the circumstances, yesterday was never going to be one of my best. In fact, it turned out to be not too bad. I had some productive conversations with two good friends, both of whom were encouraging and supportive to me not just in terms of work but in relation to my health. I was able, I hope, to be equally so to Lesley. Given what has happened to her lately and the fact that she has time on her hands she can feel quite low, absorbed in circumstances and worried as to what next is going to go wrong. It is one of the most curious things about my mental state that I am sufficiently lucid and practically-minded to give the kind of advice and guidance that I find difficult to apply to myself. Logic would dictate that I should be able to transfer the recipient of my supposedly 'wise words'. In other words to self-advise. This is of course a key component of Cognitive Behavioural Therapy (CBT) and there are occasions when it works. I find the way to a conclusion, to a decision, to a way forward. But not all the time. I can say things to myself, I can instruct myself, I can give myself the proverbial 'kick up the backside'. But sometimes words are simply words. I hear them, but cannot translate them into practical action. They echo inside my mind, persistent noises, imploring attention, but the more they sound, the less clear they become. They fail to register and I learn simply to switch myself off. I suppose it's often easier to give advice then to receive it, but this inability to change, to heed my own warnings, is one of my many pitfalls. The solution for me is to continually work at developing your own CBT-inspired acumen. The more you practice and use what you have learnt, the greater the number of hits rather than misses. It's hard work but it's one of the better weapons I have in my perennial fight to stay sane.

Wednesday 20th January 2016

What a mixed morning. On the plus side, I heard from the NHS. After deliberation and the necessary approval from the powers that be, they are keen to proceed with the engagement work initially on a trial basis. This is a huge relief as I was beginning to fear that nothing would come of it. They want to see me again on Friday morning which is excellent. It means that I have some form of target and will have a more defined and purposeful structure to my working week.

Less positive was my attempt to produce my own website. In characteristic fashion, I was worrying about it for most of yesterday. I even had a dream in which I was trying to follow instructions that became increasingly hazy and unintelligible to the extent where I was simply making it up, using random words and images, pressing 'enter' and 'OK' to bizarre questions, producing absolute nonsense. There were also occasions when I would press the keyboard time and time again, trying desperately to make it work. It wouldn't type anything. It simply moved up and down making a louder and more disturbing noise. What emanated was the sound of my own frustration, nothing produced other than agitation, desperation and anger.

The fact that I dreamt about the task I had conditioned myself to doing reflects of course the extent of my rumination yesterday. I knew it was going to happen, but I couldn't do anything to stop it. Why was this the case? The simple answer is that I was entering the unknown. I'd never done anything like this before.

I'd never needed my own website. I didn't know what I was going to face, what questions I was going to get asked, what choices I would have to deliberate over. Though I'd got an end product in mind, how to get to it was vague. What I had in mind as a result was, of course, the most superlative website imaginable. Beautifully presented, engaging, stimulating. The right combination of words and images. No spelling errors. Perfect punctuation. But I didn't know how to achieve it. I was lost. I was clueless. When I sat down in front of my PC earlier on today, racked with nerves but committed to action, what transpired was a carbon copy of my initial fears and subsequent dream. 'Déjà vu'. I knew that I was defeated, that the challenge was too much, that the struggle would only result in cross words, a loss of temper and an uneasy sense of failure. I did the most logical thing. I called John and asked if I could take him up on the offer he'd already made to help me put the thing together. Why I didn't do this in the first place, I don't know really. I guess I wanted to prove that I had the skills and more importantly the confidence to do it on my own. I didn't want to bother anyone else. I wanted to rise to the challenge. I wanted to master a new venture. It all came crashing down around me. But it didn't completely destroy me. I made new arrangements. I had the insight and the sense to do so. That is a little comfort.

On a different note, last night was a crazy one in the east end of Glasgow. One of my football teams, the one (the only one) that is successful, managed to score eight times. Celtic eight, poor shell-shocked Hamilton Academical one. I followed the game on the laptop. At one point, when they were already five goals to the good, if they'd have carried on at the same rate, the game would have ended up 15-0! I was actually gutted that they only scored eight and absolutely mortified when they had the temerity to let one in at the other end. Nevertheless, I had a smug smile on my face come 9.30 pm. I only wish I could have dreamt about Celtic rather than bloody websites!

Thursday 21st January 2016

What a strange day yesterday turned out to be. After completing my diary entry, we took Millie for a walk in the Country Park. I was perfectly OK for the first circuit but about half way around the second, I began to feel increasingly dizzy and lightheaded. Immediately, my step was less sure, my confidence went and my breathing seemed to become shallower. I have these 'attacks' quite often and sometimes I seem to bring them on myself through worrying, thinking and believing that they are about to strike. A self-fulfilling prophecy, in other words. I'm not sure if they are panic attacks in the strictest sense of the term, but panic is certainly at the heart of whatever it is they are. Resting and eating in combination seem to be the best remedy and although this wasn't the case yesterday, I usually begin to recover quite quickly. Whenever I raise the matter with doctor or consultant, neither seem entirely sure as to whether the root of the problem is physical or psychological. It could be a side-effect of the medication. It could be a consequence of high blood pressure. It could be something to do with sugar levels. It could be a mixture of all of these things.

As it turned out, I still wasn't feeling particularly refreshed even after shoving some food down my neck and sitting down, so when we got home I went to bed and slept for a couple of hours. That did the trick. Nevertheless, my mind was still restless and so I decided it was high time that I underwent another physical health MOT. I have to have these fairly regularly to test how my medication is impacting on a variety of things – cholesterol, liver function, thyroid etc. Sometimes, an ECG is recommended. Thankfully, I've always passed this particular test, whereas some of the other checks have revealed problems. My blood pressure in particular is causing me and my GP some concern. Even though I've been prescribed additional medication to address the spiralling readings, I know it's not under control. It could be that that causes the physical distress I mentioned earlier? My health is now so complex that I suspect it's virtually impossible to determine exactly what is causing what. Anyway, I shall ring the doctors' surgery later today to make an appointment.

That, however, was not the end of the saga. In the early evening I started to feel increasingly worried at the prospect of my impending return to working life. All the little sources of concern that constitute real stress began to rise within me like a powerful juggernaut incapable of stopping or turning. I knew that my mind was again under attack from within. I started to deliberate, to speculate, to reach abstract conclusions. Nothing seemed to offer the definitive outcome which would lead to the respite and solace I was seeking. I sought reassurance in Lesley. But ultimately I felt I needed something more. I'd slept in the afternoon. All I saw in front of me was a long, protracted evening of distress and nervous tension, without the saving grace of fatigue giving it a natural ending. I told myself that what I needed was sedation. I therefore took Diazepam. Even though recourse to this drug always elicits concern – it's powerful stuff, not to be taken lightly[3] and it can only be a provisional measure – on this occasion I just couldn't see any other way out. It succeeded in shutting the door to the mishmash of confused thinking that had threatened to overcome me. Calmness and torpidity became welcome substitutes. But only temporarily. And at what cost?

The morning after brought the inevitable recrimination. Why couldn't I stop or control what was going on inside me? Why didn't the therapeutic lessons I have learned over many years work? Why did I have to resort to Diazepam? Was self-sedation absolutely necessary? If I hadn't slept during the day, could I have used the natural force of tiredness instead? Even if that was the case, would dreams have continued the agitation as they had done twenty-four hours earlier?

Is this what working again is going to involve? Is this the life I can expect? Oh God, if only there was a better, less destructive, way out.

Friday 22nd January 2016

I had my first meeting as a paid consultant this morning. I was so nervous. I kept waking up at half-hourly intervals from the early hours onwards, so when I eventually got out of bed it was with a trembling frame and a pair of leaden feet. I had to follow the procedures and customs that have become the norm to enable me to get to the hospital complex at the right time, find a parking place and then the correct meeting room in the building. This initial planning may meet your expectations given what you know already about my mental illness. What I'm now about to say, you may, by contrast, find somewhat strange and even a little outlandish. To ease my nervous state, I try not only to enter where I'm supposed to be before anyone else, but also position myself in such a way that I can see everyone when they enter, as well as also leaving me a clear pathway to an exit. I don't want to feel psychologically trapped, so I have to ensure that physically I am not equally constrained. The latter I hope will impact on the former, thus calming any existent nerves. It works, at least for me, and is no different, I guess, from reserving a place in a train compartment in the first or last row of seats.

Everything worked well this morning. My plans came to fruition and I found myself sitting at the table, work book out and pen at the ready a full ten minutes before the meeting started. The problem I now had to face was how long I would be on my own. I could not, of course, control when others would enter the room and as it happened, it wasn't until bang on nine 'o'clock when the flow of people began. This was too long a gap for me. I found myself fidgeting with an anxious ear to the door, uncertain of what to do, worrying about first impressions, concerning myself with how I looked and even how I smelt! What would they be like? What would they think of me? Would they understand me? What could I say as an ice-breaker? Could I weigh everything up sufficiently and competently to ensure that I didn't say the wrong thing or do something extraordinary and out of context? Please, please, let them like me. Let them respect me. Let them value me.

This is an extraordinary amount of pressure to inflict on an already anxious mind. But I can't in any way circumvent my rituals. They are there for a reason, as protection, as a method of control. I wish at times that I could simply turn up and get on with things without a care in the world. But that isn't me. I don't think it's ever been me.

Reflecting afterwards on my morning, I measured it a success. I felt at home, comfortable and welcomed. I contributed things which seemed to go down well. I left, I hope, as positive an impression on them as they made on me. Thank God the inauguration is over though!

It's a big day for Elliot today. He's spending the weekend in London with Luke and his partner, Megan, which means his first solo train journey. We've eliminated all the risks. We'll put him on the train at our local station as there is public access to the platform. The service doesn't stop anywhere else before St Pancras, where Luke will meet him once he's gone through the barriers. I know they have some great things planned for him, including a trip to the theatre and to an Italian restaurant, so he'll have a whale of a time. His trip south coincides with Luke's Christmas present to us, a weekend retreat in rural Staffordshire, something which we could both do with, time away from home and respite from all the minutiae that make life challenging, even for a non-depressive.

Elliot has also 'graduated' this week to the teenager pad we have outside. I ought to explain. The initial garage at the property was converted to a stand-alone facility before we bought the place in 1998. We did it up to accommodate each of the children in turn when they 'came of age'. It doesn't have a toilet or washing facilities, something that didn't really bother Joel as the most recent resident. I won't tell you how he got round that problem, but with a garden surrounding his enclosure, I'm sure you can guess. Only for number threes I hasten to add! And not every time! Boys! Elliot is so proud of his new accommodation. He's managed to entice Millie to share the space and even his bed, though I don't think he was totally expecting her to take up as much of his duvet as she obviously does! It will be good for him. It shows our confidence in him and gives him a little more independence. Ironically, at around the same age as Elliot is now – thirteen – my Mum and Dad renovated our existing garage into something similar for me! The only difference was that the garage then was attached to the house, rather than being totally separate. How similar the wheels of time can be.

Saturday 23rd January 2016
A really lovely day. Not one without its element of depression, but one of my best for a long while. After dropping Millie off with Lesley's sister, we made our way to our hotel in the depths of the Staffordshire countryside. After dropping our bag off, we then proceeded to Lichfield station to take one of its regular commutes into Birmingham. After a spot of lunch, we had a look round, did a bit of shopping, took in Leonardo DiCaprio's latest film 'The Revenant' and had just enough time to have a pleasant meal at a French restaurant before catching the return train.

Lesley remarked during our meal that 'it was nice to have me back'. I pressed her on what she meant and she replied that my mood seemed up-beat, that I was talking in a more positive fashion, in other words that my outward appearance was more relaxed, more settled and that I looked – dare I say the word – happy. She's not wrong. I often think that too, and that has certainly been the case today. Things are not quite so encouraging and assured, however, when you take other physical and psychological manifestations into consideration. These are the characteristics of depression that I have been relaying and describing since the start of the New Year. Even yesterday, a virtual panacea of hope and cheer – relatively speaking – there were still signs of restlessness and unease. Part of my planning for the day, for example, involved researching train journeys from Tamworth into Birmingham. I needed to know where our outbound station was, how long the journey would take, how frequent the service as well as all the relevant timings and prices. I had also got it into my head that the best thing to do would be to take a taxi from and to our accommodation. All that went out the window when at the hotel we were advised to travel not from Tamworth, but from Lichfield. Parking at the station was also advisable, our affable host continued. It shouldn't have been a problem, but all of a sudden I started to panic inside and was only calmed when we were on the train itself with Birmingham New Street looming ever closer on the horizon. To re-orientate my mind from a confirmed plan to new circumstances doesn't come quickly and it certainly doesn't come smoothly. Lesley of course knows all this. She can detect the very instance my mind starts to deviate and I start becoming unsettled and distressed. It's not just the big indications she notices, it's the minute, apparently random and even fleeting characteristics of depression that she recognises. She intervenes at the right time though. She gives me the space to work through it, but knows that if that isn't possible, a reassuring word, a sensitive and calm look, a close hug can often work miracles. Sometimes all it takes is for her to hold my hand.

I couldn't get over the change in Birmingham. From the post-war period onwards, and certainly during my formative years, Britain's second city was the subject of many a cutting remark and endless self-deprecating jokes. My Mum, being a native, was at the sharp end of my Dad's savage sarcasm and pointed wit – he would continually make fun of Birmingham the place and the people – and yet she herself didn't entirely disagree with the sentiments expressed! According to her, you needed a sense of humour to come from Birmingham! But what a difference a generation makes. The city is now vibrant and exciting. It's increasingly prosperous and appealing to those with no axe to grind and no inherent bias, one way or the other. To be blunt, it looks good and it feels good. Mum is now proud of her Brummie origins. She may not always admit it, but you can tell. She even wants to spend a day in the Bullring and the cultural centre.

More significantly, my Dad, if he was here, would I suspect feel likewise!

Sunday 24th January 2016

I knew it wouldn't be long before football became a topic for discussion. Yesterday all the teams with which I have some affinity and affection won their respective matches. Leeds struggled to beat Bristol City, but beat them they did. Millwall won at Chesterfield, coming from a goal down to win 2-1. Celtic and Wrexham both went one better, winning more comfortably I suspect than their respective scorelines suggest. Tottenham – for whom I've always had a soft spot – continued to impress and are threatening to break the monopoly of the Premier League's top four; and in Scotland, my two minnows, Stranraer and Elgin City, beat Cowdenbeath and Berwick Rangers respectively. I can't recall a day ever when this unusual combination of results transpired to make me a happy football supporter! It seemed to reflect the lovely day that we had away as well. Usually, at least one of my close teams will let the side down and provide a blot – however temporary – on the proverbial psychological landscape. But not yesterday! Oh no.

I know you'll be trying to work out how I come to follow so many different – and of course, unconnected – teams. For the majority, they reflect first experiences of the game. The first match my father ever took me to was Stranraer versus Albion Rovers in 1978. We were on holiday nearby and so it seemed the most natural thing in the world to see what the locals did and go where they went on a Saturday afternoon. The same is true of Wrexham, my local side when I was growing up in North Shropshire, and Elgin, the club closest to our holiday static caravan in Speyside. I've only ever seen one game there – and that was before they joined the major league in Scotland – a fervent and tempestuous fixture with local rivals, the beautifully named, Forres Mechanics. Both Celtic and Spurs have remained on the periphery of my supporting career. I've taken Elliot to matches at Celtic Park and even though he doesn't really enjoy the sport, he does like weekends away over the border and will watch the game, but only if he can have his iPhone going at the same time. If Spurs lose I'm not terribly bothered, but I like to track their fortunes and as they – and Celtic – have been relatively successful, winning more matches than they lose, they provide a much-needed and welcome contrast to my two more focused obsessions, Leeds and Millwall.

Those of you that know your football will be aware that supporters of Yorkshire's finest and the pride of South London do not get on. So why, you must be asking, can I follow them both? The answer revolves around depression. Leeds United have always been my club. My father came from Leeds and was a massive fan, as were other relatives, some of whom worked behind the bars and in the tea-rooms at Elland Road. My aunt's ashes were even scattered in the goalmouth! Ever since I can remember, the Leeds result was the first I looked for on a Saturday if I couldn't actually be there to witness it. I went to matches with my Dad and then graduated – after a period of watching Everton as it was much closer to where we lived – to going on my own and taking my younger brother. It was a great time to watch Leeds as they motored through the then Second Division to become Champions of England in a matter of years. Even though the bubble quickly burst and the team spiralled downwards, being relegated amidst financial uncertainty into League One for the first time, I would go to games regularly. What began to happen though was a curious and alarming affliction. I would become so obsessed with the team, feeling so intrinsically linked to its fortunes that my whole mental state rose and fell with them. I became convinced that Leeds United were controlling my inner state and vice versa, but only in a negative way. If Leeds were successful that was down to their playing strength, their physical attributes and their ability to dominate other sides. However, if they couldn't do this, if they conceded goals, if they lost, it was down to me. It was my fault. I was to blame. Our fortunes were intertwined. The relationship had become so fixed, so determinant, that I convinced myself that other forces were at play. God – or some other being, fate or otherwise – was punishing me through an external force. This situation elevated ninety minutes of a game of football to something out of all proportion to what it was. In my warped mind, I could not only influence, but actually dictate how things happened on the grass in front of me. It was like some virtual game on a PlayStation. Only I was hampered. I was disabled. The players wouldn't do what I willed them to do. They wouldn't listen to me. They would do the opposite in fact. They were taunting me. They were laughing at me. They were the reflection of my innermost anxieties. In this damaging relationship, a defeat would reinforce the depression that was already there. Indeed, it would do more than that. It would twist the knife that I held myself, in my own two hands. It would batter my head with my own fists.

All this is very difficult to explain and even now, looking back at what I've written, I'm not sure I've got it right. But it will have to do. Suffice to say that this couldn't continue. It was leading me to places I knew could be cataclysmic. After a dispiriting 2-0 home defeat to Watford in which I came close to having a fight with a fellow supporter, I decided I couldn't watch them anymore. It had to end. My love for Leeds United was too much. It had led to something I couldn't control, something that could destroy. I've never gone back.

I couldn't though leave the sport. Being a football fan is one of my strongest identities. I love the game. I love the positive things associated with being a fan. The pride, the feelings of camaraderie, the singing, the gesticulating, the passion. I decided, therefore, to go and watch someone else. To go somewhere where things were less determined and fatalistic. To go somewhere safer. But where? The obvious port of call, as I live here, would have been Leicester. But somehow fate led me to Millwall. Truth be told, I'd always liked them. Nobody else did. But that was the point. It's not for nothing that Millwall fans sing the refrain 'No One Likes Us, We don't Care' with such fervour and spite. It really is them against the world. It had always seemed like some kind of self-reflection, some established self-realisation. I didn't like myself. To what other team could I therefore belong? I'd followed their fortunes because they were reviled, because they were a small club fighting to survive irrespective of how others saw them. It didn't matter to them that they were despised by other football people. It was irrelevant how much they were hated, how vehement others felt in their opposition. 'Please God, Don't let Millwall get promoted' screamed one tabloid as Millwall threatened for once to be successful. It had to be Millwall. Millwall made me feel at home. They have done ever since. There are times when my love for the club, my identity as a fan, threatens to spiral in the same way as it had previously with Leeds. But for now it has remained in perspective. I can treat defeat in the same manner as victory. It doesn't condemn me to eternal misery or damnation. It feels right. 'We are Millwall, from The Den'. And I am too.

Monday 25th January 2016

I think it may be worth exploring in a little more detail a theme from Saturday. I talked about my mood being not only stable but assuredly cheerful. I also stated that some elements of depression were also continually present irrespective of my overall demeanour. Some may not understand this or even see it as a contradiction. Such people almost definitely see depression as being entirely associated with one thing – whether someone feels low. Following on from this, the measurement for depression – how severe it is – relates to how low one gets. And that's it. There's nothing else. But how wrong can you be? Depression is a combination of physical as well as psychological symptoms, of which mood may well be a pivotal one. But it is not the be all and end all. As I have found so far this year, depression can be every bit as debilitating irrespective of low mood. Part of the confusion I guess stems from the general definition of depression. The Oxford Dictionaries defines depression (the general term not the illness) as "feelings of severe despondency and dejection"[4]. Accordingly, using this criterion alone, one can see how common usage of the term becomes almost the accepted, unequivocal, unambiguous practice that one finds all the time in day-to-day parlance. 'It's depressing watching Millwall', for instance. 'That's a depressing image'. 'That meeting was enough to make anyone depressed' etc. These are not descriptions of a devastating illness. They relate solely to mood. They also imply a state that is not only temporary, but essentially fleeting. No-one watches Millwall all the time. It only takes a second to avert one's eyes. A meeting is finite. And so on and so forth. The choice we have as a result of all this may actually be quite simple. Either we change the English language and eradicate use of 'depression' completely, unless it refers to the mental illness. Or we educate people to see depression in a new, broader and more complete sense, to refer to a condition every bit as severe as any other serious medical affliction. To provide a context that is not only more accurate, but is more supportive to those who have it. People who are misunderstood, their illness trivialised, their daily struggles dismissed as 'quirky' or 'strange'. Depression is not just a state of mind, it's a state of being. It's all-consuming. In theory, it can attack all parts of the body. It affects not only how you see yourself and the world around you, but how you behave and take your place in it. To see it as anything else, is not only inaccurate. It is unfair.

Tuesday 26th January 2016

If the British public is to become better educated with respect to depression, and indeed mental illness more generally, then its portrayal on television needs to become more consistent as well as more impacting. Thankfully, there are signs that this is beginning to happen. There is a superbly created and delivered story-line on EastEnders at the moment. Stacey, whom we know has a history of bipolar disorder, has now developed a condition called Postpartum Psychosis, a condition so severe that her grasp on reality has virtually disappeared in a matter of episodes. We have seen her struggles and watched intensely the dramatic impact that such a deterioration has had on those around her, in particular her partner and close family. The actress who plays her, Lacey Turner, should not only be congratulated but acknowledged and even rewarded not just for her talent, but for her homework and her obvious attention to detail. It's awful to watch, but compelling at the same time. One of the best combinations for drama. What I hope she realises is the gratitude of those of us who have a real-life relationship with mental illness. To have someone go to the lengths she has and to put in a performance that should serve to educate as well as 'entertain', is really awe-inspiring and gives us hope that a more compassionate as well as empathetic future is on the horizon.

Television – particular prime-time television – has the capacity to make a real difference in contemporary society, making mental health equality more reachable. And yet in the past there have been some truly awful depictions of mental illness, some of them even reserved for the comedy domain. As if a scene set in a psychiatrist's office could somehow be funny? How is this even appropriate, I ask myself? To some, and I have seen the arguments expressed quite succinctly, any situation is potentially funny, any theme acceptable territory. I just don't agree. For those of us who have to experience such a situation in real-life, for those of us in particular who have had to relay suicidal inclinations or seen as a consequence, hospitalisation, to see that context delivered on television with the aim of making people laugh, is hard to take. By contrast, I well remember the first time I ever saw OCD represented on television. It was, as far as I can remember, part of an episode of 'Casualty'. It's many years ago now and I can't remember the actor concerned, but what I do recall is the problems he experienced simply getting through a door in the Emergency Department. It made an immediate impression on me as I was having a really hard time dealing with the onset of the condition. I had no idea, come to think of it, that there was anything called OCD, that there was some form of label, some defined illness that matched exactly my thoughts and my behaviour. OCD is alarming to experience and to watch. It looks agonising, strange, desperate, unbalanced, all at the same time. And it feels like this as well. For years I tried to keep it hidden, worrying continually that my secret would reveal itself, thinking that what I was doing was 'madness' personified. It used to take me 45 minutes to leave my office or my flat, and even then I would agonise as I left, constantly going through imaginary scenarios, trying desperately to keep calm and to stay sane. Often, I would go back and the whole process would start again. I was on the brink. I know that now. And then there, on national television, was someone who behaved like me. It gave me the confidence to go to a doctor and broach the subject with him. This is the positive impact of well-researched television. It has the capacity to change lives.

I do hope Stacey's story has that impact. I'm sure it does and will continue to.

Wednesday 27th January 2016

Today is Holocaust Memorial Day. A day of reflection, of remembrance, of tears, but a day to reaffirm action against the seeds of genocide – antisemitism, racism and other forms of discrimination. This year's theme is 'Don't Stand By', particularly apt in this day and age when to observe but not to react seems so prevalent. Along with Lesley and Elliot, I attended the annual memorial event at Oadby and Wigston Council yesterday evening. It was probably the best I have been to here in my home borough. The involvement of local schoolchildren is always something the organisers pride themselves on and this year we heard some powerful testimonies from young people who had taken the time and the care to register and show interest and a depth of understanding that I am sure will serve them – and others – well. I'm always very proud of Elliot on these occasions. He has attended the last four or five events and is obviously moved and committed to demonstrating the compassion and empathy needed if we are to make sure the horrors of the past don't repeat themselves. On our way home, he said to me that he goes because it is important to go. There's no better reason.

Holocaust Memorial Day is particularly poignant for me. It has been my life in so many respects over the course of recent years. I have written a book that is due out shortly. I have been to so many sites – camps, ghettos, factories, former homes, synagogues, museums, cemeteries, hospitals, the list could go on. I have talked and listened to people in various places in Germany, the Czech Republic and Poland. I have taken hundreds of photographs. I have assimilated knowledge, listened and read about events, taken note of messages and diary entries, thought about issues of significant depth, and presented to others the results of my time and endeavours. Despite this, I still feel ill-informed. I need to know more, to digest further reading, to see more places, to have more conversations. To do justice to the lives that were so savagely taken away. To honour my dead brothers and sisters.

It was good to see so many at the event and to catch up on one or two old acquaintances from my time in full-time employment[5]. One remarked that I looked more at ease with myself, more engaged, less haunted and stressed in comparison to my tenure as an employed local government worker. Of course such a change is going to be more evident to someone I don't see regularly. And yet the observation gave me mixed feelings. On the one hand, it is comforting to hear that my personae is as it apparently is, or at least how it seems to be. However, I can't help feeling aggrieved at what I obviously lost and went through before, the devastation that environment wreaked on a mind already beset with depression. I don't think it's an exaggeration to say that the experience I went through for so many years nearly killed me. I was proud of the work I did and the impact I think it had, but I can't help feeling let down and even bitter at the cost. In many ways, it was unavoidable. These are challenging times and the job I was doing was demanding and often fraught with tension and conflict. Equality and cohesion work, if done properly, is like that. That I committed myself to it unreservedly didn't necessarily help my mental health, but I couldn't do it any other way. People respected me for precisely that approach. They knew what they got with me. I sacrificed a lot, but I'm pleased I did.

Thursday 28th January 2016

Lesley leaves tomorrow afternoon to spend ten days with Rachel in Sri Lanka. I know they are both looking forward to it and that, given the rather traumatic things that have happened to both of them recently, they need to be together. When Lesley asked me months ago if I didn't mind her going, what could I say other than 'yes'? There was no hesitation on my part and certainly no inclination whatsoever to disagree. Not only does she deserve a break in and of itself – particularly as she does so much more here at home than we sometimes appreciate – I think she equally needs a break from those carer responsibilities that she carries, not just for Elliot, but for me as well. And yet, I have to admit this morning to feeling terrified at the prospect of her not being around. This is a totally and utterly selfish position on my part. But I have to be honest to myself, if not to her. I can't let her see my fears and uncertainties over the course of the next twenty-four hours or so. I want her to feel confident in my abilities to cope. I want her to 'know' that we'll be fine without her, that she can spend the time she needs with her daughter content in the knowledge that we are missing her, yes, but dependent on her, no. And yet, of course, this is one big charade. Elliot will depend on me, as will Millie. They, I hope, will feel I am up to the task. But do I feel this myself? Do I have the confidence that I want to evoke? No, I don't.

My OCD, for one thing, will return with a vengeance. I can't delegate the checking procedures that become the norm to anyone else. Lesley won't be here, and Elliot himself is beginning to exhibit those characteristics of obsession and compulsion that I know so well. I feel such overwhelming guilt when I rely on him or even when I seem to expect him to fill his mother's mantle. I have to overcome it, but it's not easy. I have to reassure him when I feel bereft of self-assurance. I have to calm him when inside all my organs are wrestling with themselves. I have to guide him, when I know not what to do myself.

I just pray that nothing goes wrong whilst Lesley's away. In the past when she's had a mini-holiday with friends, I've been able to manage because I've had the safety net of her voice on the other end of the telephone. However, this time, because of the distance and the costs involved, that option isn't going to be available to me. She's going to be virtually incommunicado. So I am alone. It's true that my Mum is coming for a few days next week. That will certainly help me, but I have to rise to the challenge of being totally responsible for our small family unit and its home in the meantime and despite the belief that I know others have in me, I can never seem to translate that into sufficient quantities of self-confidence, or indeed in any.

There is a selfish streak within my depression. It's a trait I utterly detest, but cannot prevent. When I'm not well, it rises to the surface. It's all about me, about my position, my comfort, my welfare, my survival. I hate it. Already I'm beginning to recognise the feelings, the onset of mental attack. Please God, let things go smoothly. Let me cope with any challenges. Let me prove myself. Keep the wolves at bay. Don't let them destroy me.

Friday 29th January 2016

I'm now the proud developer of my own website. I can't claim the status of creator as I needed John's input to start me off and get me going. As is so often the case, I've found it to be not half as complex as it seemed when I sat, motionless, staring forlornly and cluelessly at my computer screen last Wednesday. Such is life. I've managed to overcome virtually all the hurdles I've faced to date. There are some things that I can't get my head around, but John, bless him, has offered his services whenever such obstacles arise. I'm quite proud of what I've done, even though it's been quite limited.

It's another achievement though. That's what I'm saying to myself. Another feather in my cap. Another thing to cross off the list. Another metaphor etc.

John was also instrumental in helping me to publicise my book this lunchtime. He invited me to come to his Social Media Café (which I do most weeks) and do an informal presentation using the theme of Holocaust Memorial Day and the same photographs I used in November at his Reportage Club event. It amazes me how I'm able to talk on occasions like this with sufficient degree of competence, authority and clarity. Of course, I know my subject to the extent that I don't appear to need a script or even cue cards. But even still, I don't seem to get phased when confronted with an audience in such a context. I don't even get nervous at the prospect. It was interesting to register my immediate panic and uncertainty when he asked me to go around the room in an attempt to drum up interest. That I just couldn't do. There is a clear distinction in task which obviously has an impact on my confidence. Speaking in a more controlled setting, with my own agenda is one thing. I know what I'm going to say, more or less. However, in the other situation, I feel more circumspect. Trying to persuade people may involve a conversation. How do I know what will be asked? Even if I can predict, I can't say for certain. What if they don't want to listen? Can I handle that sense of rejection?

I remember sharing the platform with a senior police officer at an Interfaith event some time ago. The subject was mental health and I had offered to speak – and just speak, no supporting equipment, no prompts, no distractions – on that old subject of me and my mental illness. My companion, on the other hand, had a slick PowerPoint presentation. When I confessed at the end that there was no way that I could have performed with the added pressure of conforming to script, somehow juggling my words with a click on the right button, enabling instantaneous fusion of diction and image, he responded with the comment that he likewise could not have done what I had just done. He was genuinely in awe of my ability to talk lucidly about myself, about issues such as self-harm and suicidal ideation. To me, that was the most straightforward thing in the world. No pretence, no fabrication, just the truth. I guess it just shows how human beings are wired differently, and that maybe those of us with a mental illness are more naturally attuned to think and act in certain ways that others may find difficult or even incomprehensible.

There are times, for example, when I think I can speak to Parliament! But talk to a bus driver or to a shop assistant? Have a discussion on the telephone? No chance.

Saturday 30th January 2016

What a difference a week makes. This time last Saturday I was about to set off with Lesley for a wonderful weekend retreat. Seven days on and she is thousands of miles away. Her plane landed in Colombo about an hour ago and she will soon be re-united with Rachel to begin what I'm sure will be a memorable week together. Whilst I'm thrilled at this – and I know how much Lesley has looked forward to it – for me a totally different period of time awaits. The moment she left yesterday afternoon, I felt an immediate change within my body. Insecurity, anxiety, loneliness and terror now became my watchwords. It was that sudden a transformation. As if someone or something had switched me from one state of being to another. Every noise in the house, every time I used an appliance, every change in the weather outside, every new situation – no matter how miniscule – suddenly evoked danger. The whole edifice in which I live – both structural and theoretical – had in an instant become menacing, threatening to cut me off from the life I normally lead, glowering over me like the darkest of clouds, banging on every door and window, intent on sweeping me away like the most powerful of floods.

I don't know how I got through yesterday evening. The minutes dragged. Seconds slowed down like a fading heart-beat. Every tick of the clock resonated like thunder through my mind. Painful. Foreboding. I tried my hardest to put on a show of defiance and, for Elliot, of calmness personified. Reassuring smiles and words. 'You've nothing to worry about son. I'm here. I'll look after you. I'm in control.' But inside me every gesture only succeeded in condemning my insincerity, reinforcing the total contrast that was my true frame of mind.

I try not to believe in fate. To reject its power. To ignore its presence. The future can't be pre-determined. It can't be controlled. It can be influenced, of course, but that's all. Whilst wishing with every ounce of my being that the days until Lesley's return will be peaceful, without incident, without worry, without fear. That nothing will break down. That nothing will go wrong. I know that this is beyond my ability to regulate. It's that word 'control' again. Thinking the worst doesn't mean the worst will happen. But the same is true if you flip the coin over onto its other side. I tried desperately last night to calm my fears, to rationalise my situation. But it didn't work. What alleviated my worries about things going wrong within the house or with the car was not the careful, deliberate and thoughtful use of methods I've learned over the years of therapy treatment, but rather their replacement with even more catastrophic potentialities. I kept seeing Lesley's face as she waved her goodbyes. I wrestled with the horrific thought that something was going to happen to her. Some element of calmness did eventually come, the more reasoned me did begin to emerge. It has perpetuated itself this morning, for which I'm profoundly grateful. It hasn't swept all the doubts and fears away though. If only it could be next Sunday morning. I can't resort to Diazepam from this time until then.

Sunday 31st January 2016

Well, I survived Day One without Lesley. It was difficult at times, but I had Elliot as a companion and support – and Millie, of course! What Lesley's absence does do, naturally, is bring Elliot and me much closer together. We become a much more cohesive unit, doing the practical things as well as being aware of each other and enjoying our mutual friendship. I remember my Dad telling me that his father advised him to make his sons his friends. That's stayed with me and has always resonated as good, solid advice. Of course, there must always be an added component, parenthood, and at times when you're being punished for some misdemeanour, it can seem as if your father is your worst adversary. But perspective has always reinforced the good in the relationship with my Dad, and I hope that has continued in the way I have tried to be the same with and to all our children.

Elliot has had a lot to cope with recently. By this I mean not just what has happened to his Mum and my ongoing disability, but the onset of adolescence and his emerging sexuality and sexual orientation. I think he is now firm in the knowledge that he is gay. It has taken a little while, as is natural, for this to become a more fixed identity among the many identities that comprise every human being. That he felt no inhibition, worry or fear in telling me and his mother is very humbling. In my experience as an equality officer and specialist, I am well aware of how demanding a challenge the process of 'coming out' can be. And not just with respect to sexual orientation either. Mental health can be every bit as stressful and formidable an identity to come to terms with and to divulge. With us, his parents, Elliot can be himself and he is himself. The wider and broader context he is yet to face. He is aware of what it can involve – he's been experiencing homophobic bullying at school which has resulted in close contact between us and the school's pastoral care team – but equally he knows how rewarding and uplifting both the decision to be out and open, and the processes involved in doing so, can be. His next step, I suspect, is to have some conversations with his sister and brothers – when he can, of course, because none of them are easily available at the moment!

He has also had to deal with the emotional turbulence and practical difficulties associated with his own mental health. He has had OCD for a while and is currently receiving treatment which, through his hard work, perseverance and bravery, is beginning to make a difference. Some of the rituals he had only a month ago are now gone. Others persist, but he now has a way to address them that he knows works. He has confidence in those helping him, including us, but what he still lacks is sufficient confidence in himself. He doesn't have depression, but low self-esteem (one of depression's most predatory symptoms) seems to be particularly acute at times. I took him to his counselling session on Friday and it was a remarkably moving experience. His mentor focused almost entirely on the issue of self-esteem and Elliot reacted in a manner that made me so proud. He worked really hard, putting himself under intense scrutiny, addressing those obstinate traits and reactions that he is well aware can become the norm unless he himself confronts them. This was penetrating self-analysis. But he delivered. He felt so much better as a consequence. Of course, as with all talking therapies, it's what you do in between appointments that will make the decisive difference, the breakthrough even. It's also what measures your determination and sheer guts. And he's only thirteen! What an inspiration he is to me. I'm so proud of him.

I started this entry with the issue of survival. Of course, I've also made it through the first month of the year! I wonder what February will bring?

February

Monday 1st February 2016
Two hours into the new month, I lay awake, unable to sleep, tormented by the most horrible of images, shaken beyond belief by what kept going through my mind. All I saw was a fire in the back room with Elliot, in bed, trapped by the walls, unable to move, helpless as the flames raged closer and closer. I wanted to force my way through them but couldn't move. I was as ensnared by my demons as he was by the inferno, constrained by some external force intent on punishing me for my negligence or for some other reason. I lay there fighting the vision, desperately seeking reason and rebuttal. I knew it wasn't happening there and then, but was it a premonition? Should I act now, before it was too late? Should I give in to my fears, wake him up and get him upstairs with me? With every minute of agony, I seemed to grow wider awake. I sought salvation. I sought peace of mind. Eventually, sleep came and with it the flames of the nightmare disappeared. Even then, my night was not to stay in slumber. An hour later and my mental torment had been replaced with the most painful of stomach cramps. I knew

they were a consequence of the vagaries of my mind. I could deal with them quite easily though. I popped a pill. If only that was equally true of what was going on inside my head.

Needless to say, it wasn't the sharpest of awakenings when my alarm went just after seven. I got up relatively early to ensure that Elliot was also awake and getting himself dressed and prepared for the beginning of the school week. For some reason, his alarm hadn't gone off, so it was a good job I was the backup plan. To put things in perspective though, at least he wasn't burned or dead! It's interesting, but disturbing, that with Lesley away, some of Elliot's initial OCD insecurities have resurfaced. I guess it shouldn't be surprising. If mine can return, why shouldn't his? He's been seeking reassurance from me for things that have virtually disappeared from his radar over the course of the last month or so. It's so difficult to be hard with him and not relent to his requests, but if I give him what he wants, it won't do him any good in the long term. With OCD you need to have the strength and the skills to work things out for yourself. Getting someone else to do it, thereby delegating responsibility, may provide immediate relief, but it will only be temporary. It adds to your dependence, it consolidates and intensifies the inaccuracies in your thinking, it perpetuates the disorder, literally and synonymously. It won't resolve matters. If anything it can make things worse. What a hypocrite I feel though, given my reliance on Lesley. I too seek the short cut at times. I also feel the need to seek reassurance, to beg for encouragement, to be given the answer – and the order – I crave.

I decided to take Millie to the country park before lunch. She loves the freedom to explore, and, being a Springer, she indulges the right to roam to the maximum. As I was walking around, trying desperately to keep her in sight through the trees and undergrowth, I was aware that I was far from sure of myself. Every possible worst-case scenario began to pepper my mind, one after another. I knew only too well what the problem was. I couldn't exert the control I needed to calm my own fears. The only way to do that would have been to keep her on a lead, in close proximity and not allow her the leisure to do what Springers do naturally. That would have been not only unreasonable, but positively draconian. I couldn't do it. When I'm with Lesley in the park and elsewhere, places where we can let Millie off the lead, there is no problem. I have her with me, to deal with anything going wrong, to provide the calmness and yes, the reassurance. I convinced myself this morning that if I let Millie out of sight for just one instant, she would run away, she would get into trouble, she would get run over, she would impale herself on some fence, she would be attacked. It's this way of thinking, this catastrophizing, that lies behind the reluctance I often have to take her out. It's not laziness. It's fear. It's not that I don't want to do it, it's that I find it so challenging. Everyday pastimes such as this become, not a pleasure, but a trial. Every second is nerve-wracking, exhausting and debilitating. I knew this morning that there would be an immediate consequence. My body would again be punished. It was incapable of reacting positively. It couldn't restore a sense of equilibrium. It would not be able to withstand the onslaught. It would inevitably follow the lead given by my mental illness. I realised as I tramped around the paths that I was getting dizzy and feeling short of breath. Mind over matter, and a diseased one at that. The more I ruminated, the greater the propensity to worry, the less well I felt, the more remote the chance of self-recovery. I am my own worst enemy. At times, the fight is with myself.

Tuesday 2nd February 2016

A much better night's sleep, although having got up at seven to supervise Elliot I was so tired – barely keeping my eyes open as I watched morning telly – I had to go back to bed and get another hour under my belt!

There's sleep and then there's quality sleep, sleep that is restful and soothing, sleep that succeeds in recharging batteries. I get plenty of the former, but very little of the latter. The dreams that I have tend to be very vivid and extremely challenging. They nearly always have a foot in the past, to times at school and at university for example, but with a current twist. I'm as I am now but trapped – in time and in situations not of my making. I am forced to experience events and to face trying, testing examinations of my character and temperament and I never win. I am always the outsider, struggling to break out, desperately attempting to make my true feelings heard and to be able to make decisions that ease the tension and address the predicament in which I find myself.

As a result, sleep is exhausting. It's a psychological struggle. I'm aware that my brain is working overtime but I can't stop it. Other than medication, there is no remedy. Most websites on depression that I am familiar with will state that two of the symptoms can be insomnia and oversleeping. Two extremes. It's the same with eating and not eating. However, for me, there's a third – with respect to sleep that is – the state of restless sleep. There are times, for example, when what I have gone through during my sleeping hours is more vivid and more real than anything experienced during the day. It's as if I come alive – psychologically – when I close my eyes and lay my head on the pillow. I even seem to feel physical sensations of touch. As a result, it's no surprise that I'm knackered when I finally get up. I can hardly lift my head and my body seems to have the weight of the world pressing it down into the mattress. The temptation to sleep on is so acute. Sometimes I have to give in. Physically I can't do anything else. However, when I wake up a second time there are often intense feelings of guilt and self-recrimination. 'What a waste of time that was. What a waste of space I am. Look at what other people are doing? Full-time jobs, busy lifestyles, lots of responsibilities. And look at me? Sleeping my life away'. I'm reminded of that immortal line in 'The Full Monty' – "it's surprising how tiring it is doing nowt", or words to that effect. It's a line that says a lot but still masks the true reality. Physically there may be inaction, but mentally, one's brain is behaving like an Olympic athlete. Or in my case, a man hauling a heavy load through deep, sapping, mud.

Wednesday 3rd February 2016

My Mum arrived yesterday afternoon to spend a few days with us. It was lovely to see her even though she looked quite frail as we met her at Leicester Station. Just having her around, especially given Lesley's absence, is not only nice but comforting. I've already had some positive conversations with her this morning about Elliot's OCD and my own new working situation. These are not easy things for her to comprehend, given the changes in both our circumstances, but I was really proud of her for the way she grappled with the enormity of what I was trying to convey. I often feel that I don't involve her in my life as much as I should do. This isn't because I don't want to, it's simply because I don't want to upset her. The desire to protect, instilled in me by my Dad, is still strong and this is an exact manifestation of that promise I made to him all those years ago. I tried to tell her this morning of my difficulty in coping with change, even a fleeting one such as her visit. Of the challenges I face readjusting to different dynamics, different conversations, different relationships. Of how I need to continue the core elements of my life, to maintain the fabric of my existence – sitting in the same chair, watching the same TV programmes, following the same routines – and how any potential interference can register as threat and can lead to uncertainty and even indifference. I feel this when one of the kids comes home too, so it affects all the people that are close to me. It's so difficult to explain. You don't want to come across as casual, uncaring, rude and unfeeling, particularly to one's loved ones, but at the same time you wish you could explain exactly and thoroughly how human interaction, any human interaction, can provoke anxiety and indecision. How I would relish true telepathy!

Of course, I will always be her child to my Mum. Having her here has made me examine what being a child was and is like, because there is no doubt that I feel positively childlike at times as a result of my mental illness. There are occasions when I would like nothing better than to cry like a baby, to sulk like a child, to be a truculent adolescent. I often wish to return to infantile ways, to experience again the reality of growing up. I'm sure those of you who know me well, and Lesley in particular, would argue that I sometimes succeed in all these things! It's not that I necessarily want to go through my life again, to have a second chance. What I'm seeking is the inherent innocence and simplicity that characterise life in our formative years. I want to be free, if only temporarily, of responsibility, of the complexities of adult life, of my current predicament. This is why whenever a child visits our home with their parents – whoever it may be – I feel an immediate affinity with the young rather than the old. I want to play with them. I want to talk in childish ways, to reflect on childish life. Because the alternative is too difficult, too emotional, too challenging. It's escapism. I know it is. But when I'm ill, it's natural to want to escape, to avoid the thinking and the behaviour that I see as contributing to my illness. If I'm honest, though, the element of choice is often taken away from me. It's not just that I want to be child, I can't help being one. I need someone else to tell me what to eat and when, who to talk to and how, what to do and why. I need someone else to make arrangements, to deal with all the many decisions that comprise living. If I can't decide if I want coffee or tea, how can I address more complex and demanding situations?

Thursday 4th February 2016

My day started with an appointment with my GP. At times, engaging with our Doctors surgery is an exercise in patience, self-restraint and humour of some magnitude! Getting and keeping an appointment, making an administrative change in medication, ensuring that my consultant's latest notes have been received and uploaded on to their system, establishing that the prescription that goes to my pharmacy is accurate and up-to-date…the list detailing the potential calamities that can and have happened could go on. This morning, though, it was a model of exemplary service. I was greeted at the desk not only with an engaging smile but with an apology for the ever so slight delay. My appointment was at 9.05. I got seen at 9.05. When I returned to reception afterwards to make a further appointment for some blood tests, I was offered a choice of day and time! I even got called 'Sir'! I was really impressed. Seeing a doctor can be a daunting experience and for those of us with a mental illness that have difficulties when things go awry, it can be really challenging to deal with administrative frustrations in a public place. Pent up nerves can easily translate into loss of control and temper. The last thing you want is to make a spectacle of yourself, but it's not easy to have sufficient amounts of self-possession and staying power when your reaction to the slightest thing going wrong is to catastrophize. Many is the time I've found my voice raising, my demeanour fragmenting, my whole being shaking. I know what's happening but there's little I can do. Without having the self-assurance necessary to deal with the situation, my only alternative is to take myself away.

The appointment itself went really well. I'd gone because sometimes it's impossible to decipher whether physical symptoms such as extreme tiredness and occasional dizziness are a result of your mental illness, the medication you take to address your mental illness, or something entirely separate. One of my perpetual fears is that I attribute everything to my mental state and miss the signs of potential cardiovascular disease, diabetes or anything similarly severe. As my Dad had both of these illnesses and died as a result of the former, I can't afford to take any chances. This morning though, I got as much reassurance as I could hope for. My GP went through my last blood test results, taken in September. Aside from the normal problems with my liver function (due to medication), things were relatively stable. She took my blood pressure and was able to tell me that it had come down from the alarming levels of only a short while ago. The extra medication is obviously working. She did suggest some lower level tests – blood count, iron and Vitamin D levels – but explained the reasoning and context with real understanding of dealing with someone who has a tendency to equate two and two with eight!

It seems therefore that what I'm experiencing physically is a direct consequence of either my depression or its associated medication. Though it won't alleviate the symptoms, it does contextualise, rationalise and explain them. It's what I wanted to hear.

Altogether it was positive and I hope it translates into increased confidence. The initial signs weren't great. I'm sure that visiting a doctor itself is a psychosomatic experience. No sooner had I arrived home than I was crawling into bed, suddenly overcome with fatigue. And when I took Millie out later on, the little muscle niggle that I sometimes get in my left arm, I convinced myself was the onset of cardiac arrest! Good news doesn't always automatically metamorphose into a refreshed and more vibrant being. In my case, I'd just settle for it doing so every now and then!!

Friday 5th February 2016

I'm not embarrassed or ashamed to say that I shed a tear or two this morning after dropping Mum off at the station to catch her train home. Irrespective of the challenges I face adjusting to a new person in my daily life – even for a short period – it was so good to see her and to be with her. I hope it's just depression talk when I say that I can't help feeling that something worrying is on the horizon with respect to her health. It's not good. It's becoming more and more obvious and I can also see it in what she says and how she says it. She's obviously and understandably preoccupied to a large extent with looming health concerns – appointments, diagnoses, medication etc. – and it seems to me that she's finding it hard to overcome ailments that normally would have passed relatively quickly and without much consequence. I hate to admit it, but she's getting old and increasingly frail and I guess that has to slow one down, even though that's hard to reconcile when it's your Mum.

I think she had a good few days with us. We introduced her to cinnamon and raisin bagels and Dominos pizzas. Elliot gave her some sound instruction on how to get more out of her smartphone. He also amazed her by following recipes for chocolate brownies and cupcakes from the Internet! Millie made a fuss of her, as is her wont, and astounded her with her energy, vitality and downright cheek. I was able to have some good conversations with her, addressing some serious and complex issues, though I did try to avoid the subject of politics (Mum's political views are somewhat different to my own leftist leanings!). Mum in turn was very generous in Waterstone's, buying us new books even though neither Elliot nor I are short of things to read at the moment. It was just lovely to have her around, just to see her fall asleep in front of the television and to hear her booming voice first thing in the morning.

Now that she's gone, the house feels unnaturally empty. I wish I could have confidence that things are going to be fine. I know my depressive nature and instincts work against me in this respect, particularly as one of the thinking traps I regularly fall into is a tendency towards black or white thinking. I live so much of my life at opposite ends of a spectrum (well, mostly at the bottom end if I'm honest) but I can accept this to a certain extent when things revolve solely around me. It's when I let others, particularly my family, into the equation that I feel the desperation more avidly. This is of course unavoidable. I'm not a hermit. I don't live on a deserted island. I'm not alone in some prison cell. Other people are part of my life. I'm an interdependent human being. What I'm trying to say is that I would be able to cope for most of the time if I knew for certain that my depression was not impacting on anyone else, or that I felt no responsibility for other people. But it does and I do. As a result, I want more than anything to protect others, particularly my loved ones. The protection that I mean though is not a natural one, it's an all-consuming, one hundred percent totality. There's a strong bit of me that wants to achieve the impossible, namely to ensure – or actually guarantee – the ongoing safety and welfare of my family. I know this is unrealistic. I can't be totally responsible. I can't oversee their every movement. I can't be with them twenty-four hours a day, seven days a week. I can't be a protective wall that wholly shields and shelters, keeping out all dangers, all threats, all illnesses, all diseases. But I desperately want to be this and, more ominously – as far as my mental health is concerned – if I can't do it to the levels I seek, to the extremity of absolute success, I consider it a failure. Rather, I consider myself a failure.

All that can be said this afternoon in conclusion as I finish this entry is that I feel very lonely and extremely powerless.

Saturday 6th February 2016

Thursday was 'Time to Talk' Day, an initiative of the Time to Change mental health programme. It provides a stimulus to encourage people to be open and to have conversations about their own circumstances and about mental health in general. It coincided with the release of more distressing figures on suicide, this time courtesy of the Office for National Statistics[6]. It is so obviously superfluous to say that suicide is a serious issue and yet it remains, perhaps understandably but certainly not helpfully, largely a taboo subject. I am well aware of commonly voiced – if not necessarily held – views that see suicide as an inherently selfish act. There are others, equally habitual, that view it as cowardly or as some form of 'easy way out'. I can only talk from my experience and my own perspective, and it is this. That suicide is selfish only in the sense that it is an action focused primarily on one's self. There is an important caveat, that the broader context of family and friends is not necessarily absent in someone's mind. It's just that the overwhelming urge to take one's life has superseded all other thoughts and considerations. To this end, the notion that suicide is easy, facile and/or weak and spineless, I have to contest. Given what I know and have gone through myself, nothing could be further from the truth.

I am part of a group of people that are more susceptible than others to the tragedy of suicide. For one thing – and to state the obvious – I'm a depressive. I experience episodes that involve my mood plummeting to the depths of human feeling and emotion, and moreover, staying there for some time. But I am also other things. I'm a man and I'm middle aged. Statistics have suggested for some time that this is a combination to raise concern when it comes to taking one's own life. I also have a legacy, a relationship with suicide that is not just confined to the past. It's something that can and does reoccur. It hits when I'm at my lowest ebb. It lures me into somewhere dark and empty but at the same time dangerously seductive, a place where my life is literally on the edge. I recall with some trepidation, disquiet and fear just what that has meant. Words though are insufficient to describe the agony of suicidal ideation. It is torturous, it appears endless, it removes logic, it elevates all the destructiveness of mental illness to a level which one's body and mind can barely tolerate. During this time, I wrestle within myself with an intensity that is impossible to convey. All the issues, the considerations, the implications of the removal of one's own life strike me with incessant menace and with a level of purpose that my mind struggles to control. With me, I have to seek clarity of thought. I have to struggle with overwhelming surges of emotion. I have to reason it out, to ensure that I'm certain that the path over which I'm deliberating is the only one available for me to take. I never have been so far. That's why I'm still here. For others who confront suicide or have it literally in the back of their minds, what I've described may be totally unfamiliar or different in fundamental or more subtle ways. Everyone is unique and as I said previously, I can only speak for myself.

My last confrontation with suicide occurred on 23rd August 2014. It was slightly different from before in that things appeared much clearer and even calmer in my mind and my only fight was with the issue of inevitability. I'd gone to London, ostensibly to see Millwall at home to Rotherham United. Even before I'd got to the ground, when I was sitting in Waterstone's near Piccadilly Circus, I felt an elevated sense of futility and disconnect. It was as if it wasn't me, as if I was some interested and involved bystander, looking in on myself, incapable of independent action. I made my way via the Jubilee Line and the Overground to The Den, taking my place in my usual area of the ground. The match was a blur. I know the result – Millwall lost 1-0 – but again I felt ghostly, invisible, detached, almost resigned to whatever was going to happen next. After the game finished, the result unimportant, the experience vague and irrelevant, I began to make my way back to Kings Cross St Pancras. I eventually found myself at London Bridge station, on the northern bound Northern Line platform. I was just behind the yellow safety line, but in front of me was clear concrete. The desire to walk just a few yards to oblivion began to sweep over me. It was such a simple act. The only thing to think about was timing. To move my legs to coincide with the arrival of a train. To this day I don't know how I didn't do it. I saw the train coming. It was on time. The moment had come. But something stopped me and when that second, that window of opportunity, came and went, it didn't return. Whatever it was had shaken me back to reality, back to normality, back to reason, back to life. Lesley was waiting for me at the end of my journey. As I walked towards her she could tell something serious was wrong. I told her what had happened and in doing so, I began to appreciate the full enormity of what I'd just gone through. It was the nearest I'd come.

Since then I've realised more than ever the importance of talking, of being brave enough to let someone know what's going through your mind. It doesn't have to be someone close to you. Anyone prepared to listen is a potential life-saver. The foremost thing, the imperative if you like, is to talk and to share. People are responsive. People are caring. People matter and people can make all the difference in the world. For anyone contemplating taking the ultimate step, please think again and make human contact. I'm always here for one.

Sunday 7th February 2016
Though it's been an intense week, today has been a breeze and a delight. At last, some light relief – for me and, I suspect, for you the reader too! Lesley is now home – alive, well and very brown. Elliot and I picked her and her friend Sue up from Birmingham Airport earlier on this morning, a moment that I'd continually rehearsed in my mind ever since we saw them off last Friday. It was every bit as good as I'd hoped and envisaged!

She's had a glorious time, by all accounts. Being with Rachel was obviously the main attraction and purpose behind her trip, but to combine that togetherness with the cultural headiness of new experience can only serve to magnify every sensation that makes being a human being worthwhile and consequential. I'm sure it could be described as a holiday of a lifetime, though that supposes that such an experience can only happen once. Can you actually have more than one? It may well be a contradiction in terms, but I'm now waffling! I only hope being back here with me this week isn't the massive comedown that I would expect if I was coming home to be with myself!

I love an airport. It's an environment in which you tend to see the better side of the human race. Occasionally not, I must admit, but generally speaking it's a delight to see people excited at the prospect of holidays or even of simply being in a plane and to be there to witness moments of reunion is a privilege. This morning, I couldn't help but smile when a little girl waiting patiently outside Arrivals at last saw her father. She ran up to him with such pleasure and giddy excitement, flinging her arms around his neck and hugging him tightly. I wanted to do the same when I saw Lesley, but adult discretion and conformity somehow tempered the moment! I had to wait until I got home!

I used the word 'intense' at the start of this entry. I'm aware that this may imply a week without cheer, humour and indeed enjoyment. This would be wrong. It did have some lovely and memorable moments. Seeing and being with my Mum in particular. It also included what I consider to be some good news about my physical health. So, all told, I can't complain. I've survived being without Lesley. Nothing calamitous happened. The adjustments in routine worked, even if they caused some insecurity and anxiety. Everything was actually pretty mundane, but it did feel within my orbit of control. Without Lesley by my side though there is no doubt that I am as vulnerable as I am lovesick.

Monday 8th February 2016

It wasn't a surprise to see Lesley struggling to keep her eyes open as she sat on our settee early yesterday evening. She hadn't had much sleep on either of the two plane journeys that brought her home, but was obviously conscious of jet lag and the need to keep awake for as long as she could. By 6.30 pm, however, she had to admit defeat and it wasn't long before the familiar snores began to emanate from our bedroom upstairs! I didn't mind at all. It was just so good to have her home.

As the reader, you will have noticed that a greater proportion of what I've written so far has dwelt on what has been going on in my mind, rather than what I've actually done tangibly or materially. Of course, the two cannot be separated entirely – physiologically, one needs the former to do the latter – but it is symptomatic of the fact that much of my life revolves around the mental rather than the physical. What is also telling is how much of that mental activity relates not to the stimulus of the here and now, but to the potential. In other words, what the future 'may' bring either as direct consequence, or as a result of random and abstract connections and deductions. From this, one can only conclude that the life of someone experiencing severe and/or long-standing depression relates as much to issues of fear and worry about unreality, as it does to manifestly happening situations. A percentage of that 'unreality' may, it needs to be said, be based on fact or potential fact, but if my case is anything to go by, a significant amount relates to fantasy. This is not the fantasy that equates to wonder, sparkle and fairy tale, à la Disney. It's the fantasy that deals mostly in distorted disquiet and nightmare. It is creative imagination, I guess – that much is fundamentally connected – but it's the imagination of a brain accustomed to thinking the worst rather than its converse, to dealing in pessimism rather than optimism.

I suspect that if you look at the history of mental illness and of the terms used to describe it, you may begin to see how what was once more commonly termed 'madness' begins more and more, through time, to relate to present diagnosed conditions. I hate the term 'mad'. It stigmatises. It demonises. But sometimes, to convey meaning, one has almost to accept the deficiencies of the English language and state that OCD in its physical manifestation, for example, looks 'mad'. When I am rattling a door again and again to ensure that it's locked, or when I am counting out loud seven times to ensure a switch is off, it looks disturbing. When I am hitting myself around the head (my self-harm characteristic) in a fit of desperation, it appears frightening. When I lose my thread of conversation or my temper, it is visually unnerving. One can see it. It is apparent, visible and potentially threatening. However, these situations don't happen to me regularly. For most of the time, the equally menacing trains of thought that can culminate in such behaviour lie within me, unable to escape, unable to be seen by others. One of the conclusions that needs to be drawn from this if mental health is to be understood and treated in ways akin to its physical counterpart, is that if you can't see something, it doesn't mean it doesn't exist. You can't see air or the wind. But we know it's there. It's no different. One needs to probe in order to help. To take more of an active interest. To persevere and to show empathy and support. Helping people is not difficult. It just requires a greater degree of humanity and the perception to know that what goes on within one's head can be treated and addressed. It just needs to have an outlet.

Tuesday 9th February 2016

I met up with my ex-colleague Sean this morning. It was good to see him. He's been a loyal friend, one of only two from my last days at the Council who have kept in touch with me. Sean embarked on the same path that I have trodden, only four years previously. With him, similarly to me, it was mental health that contributed directly to his decision not to put himself through the rigours of a selection process and to take Voluntary Redundancy instead. I wonder how many people working in the public sector alone have made the same choice and for the same reason? Thousands I would surmise. People with talent, skills, knowledge and experience who simply could not face the prospect of an internal interview and potential rejection. There will also be some who did not have the belief or faith that they would be treated fairly. People convinced that, irrespective of equality law, their mental health would count against them. This is the current reality of life as an employee with a mental illness. Evidence even points to the fact that a high percentage of employers wouldn't knowingly employ someone with my sort of background. They can't use mental illness as a reason, of course. That is illegal. It just means some other criterion needs to be applied and stated.

I met Sean at a coffee shop in the city centre. It's a place I know well. Indeed, it's been my preferred and regular haunt for meeting people for work purposes for years. I know the procedures. I know the lay-out. I know the people. It should pose no problem for me. Pretty routine, you may think. But no, not a bit of it. To begin with, I have to assess when I should arrive. Ideally just before the appointed time. But how do I know when my companion will arrive? And does it matter? The answers are 'I don't' and 'yes'. To explain. When I'm in a café or a restaurant it is imperative that I place myself so that I look out at my surroundings. (I may have mentioned this previously, but I can't remember at the moment.) I guess this stems from a fear of being trapped, being hemmed in, being restricted in my movement and in the choices available to me. I need an exit route and I need it to be clear and visible. Accordingly, if the person I'm meeting arrives before me and chooses the seat I need, what do I do? Do I ask him or her to swap? That virtually necessitates explaining why. Or do I keep 'schtum' and try to cope with the anxiety that I know is the inevitable consequence? Assessing my arrival time therefore is important. And from that, I have to work backwards, allowing myself enough time to drive into Leicester, park the car and so on and so forth. It's a lesson in guesstimates! It becomes a virtual military exercise!

As it happened, Sean was waiting for me outside the café! And though we moved seats once we had got our drinks, I was able to position myself appropriately without compromising him. I know he would have understood, but to have that conversation would have meant sharing it with others seated around us, and I would have been reluctant to have bared my soul this morning.

On other occasions, I wouldn't have thought twice, but not today. Don't ask me why. That's just how it was.

Wednesday 10th February 2016

A while ago now, a Scottish comedian (I can see her face, but for the life of me can't remember her name), appearing on the BBC programme 'Would I Lie To You', read a statement on which the other team would customarily deliberate and conclude either 'Truth' or 'Lie'. The words she used were, of course, deliberately crafted for full comic effect, but the general gist was as follows: 'A day before I go to somewhere I've never been before, I do a dummy run to ensure that I know where I'm going'. Her statement produced immediate laughter in the studio. Her teammates – with an eye to winning the game – maintained a straight face, but the three panellists facing her had no such restraint to consider. Their bewildered expressions fed a series of questions intended not only to elicit the truth behind the story, but to create the necessary atmosphere of entertained incredulity. Our heroine faced probing that questioned not only her sincerity but her state of mind. It couldn't be true. No-one would do something so daft. As soon as she said the words, though, I turned to Lesley and said 'that's me. I do that'. As I watched, a growing sense of discomfort and helplessness began to overwhelm me. 'If it's true', I said to myself, 'then that lady has some nerve and guts'. 'If it's a lie', I countered, 'it's in poor taste'. It turned out to be the truth.

Today, I face the task of going somewhere I've never been before. I've been asked by an old friend to do a talk on the Holocaust in Greenwich. It means not only facing the old hurdle of getting onto a train to London, but then taking a tube journey to the end of the line at Woolwich Arsenal. I have to change at Bank, leaving the Northern Line to take the DLR (Docklands

Light Railway) to its final destination south of the river. From there, I head north on foot towards the town centre, and take a number of right turns to my destination. Yes, as you can see, I've done my homework. I couldn't afford to undertake a full rehearsal and actually go to London, so I did the next best thing. Via Google maps, Underground plans, real life street images and other means, I was able to take a virtual journey instead. I've allowed myself enough time and have found out my friend's new mobile number just in case of an emergency. I've therefore done all that I realistically can. So it has to be sufficient. There is no doubt though that, if money was no object, I would have journeyed twice in two days. Here in Leicester, without the necessary financial straitjacket, I do do that. It must sound odd, and look bizarre, particularly as sometimes it necessitates knowing where reception (my initial port of call) is and even deciphering how to get through the security behind a front door. Do I have to press a button and request entry? Anyone seeing me – twice – would be forgiven for thinking that they have some innate sense of déjà vu'!

It's amazing to think that the prospect of travel compounded by finding my own way, is itself weighing on my mind far more than delivering a speech and showing photographs to an audience of fifty!

Thursday 11th February 2016

I did something entirely out of character yesterday. Instead of wishing to be, and to remain, invisible and anonymous, I wore something that had the potential to draw attention to myself. As I was giving a Holocaust address, I decided that I would wear my Kippah, not only at the event at which I was talking, but throughout my entire journey there and back as well. It wasn't an easy decision. Not only was I demonstrating my identity as a Jewish man, I was opening myself up to the possibility of antisemitic abuse. It is a sad fact of life in twenty-first century Britain that people from some communities in particular feel the need to hide or even deny an aspect of their identity, even if that is its primary manifestation. I know many local people from our Gypsy and Traveller communities, for example, that do this in order to safeguard jobs and to circumvent discrimination in one or more of its many forms. Jews are no different. Youtube clips of visibly identifiable Jews simply walking through the streets in some areas demonstrate an appalling level of provocation and direct abuse. I wanted to test the water myself. Would I be subject to verbal threats or pointed remarks? Would I be challenged in other ways? The answer, thankfully, was no. I did get a few stares and there were times when I felt incredibly self-conscious, nervous and rather more open than felt comfortable, but the vast majority of people didn't react at all. Maybe my physique – at nearly six foot and eighteen stone, I'm a big man – had something to do with it? I prefer, for once, to lean towards the positive and say that for people that came across me yesterday, albeit fleetingly, my Jewish identity didn't matter at all.

The event itself went really well. I think I came across as both knowledgeable and engaging. Certainly what I had to say and show elicited numerous questions and prompted considerable discussion. I do feel at home when I present on the Holocaust, its lessons and its current legacy. I am able to inform, introduce history and geography, show the value of insight and direct experience of visiting places and of meeting and talking to people. It also enables me to showcase and use what I have learnt over many years working in the equality, diversity and community cohesion domains. It brings it all together and more than anything else, I feel confident and valued. It's such a refreshing change from my normal existence. It doesn't mean that all symptoms of my disability simply disappear, however. My concern with appearance and how I come across is still intensely acute and domineering. My fear that I may lose my memory or thread and consequently stall is also quite deep. It relates, of course, to control. Probably the most pertinent issue though is that of perfectionism. In my delivery, I can't be adequate or satisfactory. I have to be exemplary. I need people – and that means every single member of an audience – to feel moved, to follow every word, to show interest and to be involved in the intensity of the moment. If I see someone yawning, I can't accept that it's because they're tired – which given an evening meeting is the most logical explanation. To me, it's because they're bored. And if they're bored, it's because I'm not engaging enough. It's my fault. I haven't done my job properly. I can't hold an audience. I'm no good. I should give up. That's the chain of thought that goes through my mind and, unless challenged, becomes cemented as the truth.

Though all the indications are that I succeeded last night, I still can't seem to reward myself, to give myself the proverbial pat on the back. On the other hand, I'm not ruminating over my performance either. I'm not seeking or brooding over perceived faults and weaknesses. I'm not judging myself. For me, that is a result!

Friday 12th February 2016

Today is a massive day for me, and therefore for this diary. On 12th February 1996, my lovely brother Danny passed away. Throughout my life, even following his death, Danny has proved to be my greatest inspiration. He was gentle and kind. He was unassuming and natural. He was talented and energetic, eager to learn and to share his knowledge and wisdom. He had genuine beliefs in the goodness around him without always recognising that the light that shone most brightly emanated from within him. Anyone who met him could never forget his presence, his impact, his wonderful hugs and kisses and his purity. He was a true gift from God. Undoubtedly, the greatest, most positive example of the goodness in humanity that I have ever known.

Danny also had Down's Syndrome. Because of this, he was condemned. Condemned by people around my family at his birth, people who warned my father that he should build a wall around our house – 'to keep them out, rather than Danny in', my parents always insisted. Condemned by those working with the 'mentally handicapped', to use the terminology of the time, who resolutely stated that he would never read or write. He did both, taught diligently and lovingly by my mother. And condemned by medical practitioners who didn't even have the decency to inform us until Danny was ten that he had a hole in his heart, and who refused to countenance the possibility of a heart-lung transplant, the only thing that could save him and prolong his life. 'You will be hard pressed to find any surgeon in the land who would even consider operating on a person of this kind', was the savage rebuttal of one consultant. Accordingly, Danny was condemned to die, despite our efforts, our support and our refusal never to give up hope.

He was only twenty-five when he breathed his last. Even though it's been twenty years, I have never forgotten that morning. He had been moved from Shrewsbury to Whitchurch, to our local cottage hospital where he had a lovely room to himself, spacious and quiet. For over a month we knew he wasn't going to survive. We'd been told that medication would ease his discomfort and pain, that as a consequence, it would look as if he was rallying and making progress but that we should not be deceived. It was inevitable. Only a matter of time. There were occasions when we allowed ourselves the luxury of the tiniest sliver of optimism. We wanted to reassure, to keep up appearances for him, to maintain some semblance of normality despite the tragic predicament that enslaved us. At the last though, he was struggling so hard simply to breathe. Mum and I were with him when he eventually succumbed. He looked peaceful. I remember taking the oxygen mask off his face when I realised he'd gone. I just wanted to look at his features one more time without any impediment or interference, without the signs of illness. At the very moment he passed away, a furious thunderstorm broke outside. Lightning flashed, hailstones beat at the window, the sky darkened. Then as if by command, the sun broke through and a glorious rainbow shone above the building. It was positively Biblical. The world crying in agony, but soothed by the love and compassion of the Almighty. God had taken him to be with his Dad.

Danny and I were more than close. I preceded him into this world, but when he arrived some eighteen months later in March 1970, my life was changed forever. I wasn't just his brother. I was his friend, his protector, his helper, his confidante. In later years, I was his carer too. Following my Dad's death in 1988, I became his surrogate father. I relished the role. I thought it was what I had been born to do. Nothing was more important or more enriching. For me, Danny was my better half, my alter ego. He brought out the best in me. He made me feel wanted and valuable. I didn't realise though that what I had become in relation to him had some elements that I should have recognised were not healthy. It wasn't anything that Danny had done, or my parents could prevent. The combination of being the eldest son with a disabled brother and an increasingly poorly father proved destructive. It was in this context that the roots of my mental illness lay. Ironically, when Danny was born my parents were told that one of two things would happen to them as a result of the associated stress and worry. Either they would separate or one of them would become seriously ill. As it happened, the former was never going to happen. Danny brought us closer together as a family unit. He was the glue and the magic that made our collective life both strong and vibrant. Illness though did strike my father. He developed coronary heart disease when I was very young, an affliction that grew steadily worse until it eventually claimed him when I was just nineteen. What nobody foresaw though was the impact on me. The pressures of having to cope, of becoming independent at an early age, of having to accept that Danny would require more attention and care than was perhaps normal, of taking over responsibility for his life and having to make decisions that I was ill-experienced to face, let alone address. Of becoming a Dad to one's brother. It all took its toll. I didn't realise it at the time. How could I? This was life. I didn't know anything different. I just had to get on with it. I was supposedly strong and dependable. I could be trusted to do what was right. I could deal with the consequences. I was knowledgeable. I was insightful. But was I? In the midst of all this, I was becoming ill. I put on a brave face. I had to look tough and unyielding. I had to assume and demonstrate command. I had to give the appearance of being emotionally stable and reliable. I had to persevere and to always be focussed, consistent and strong-willed. Nothing could be allowed to phase me. I had my family to look after. I didn't realise that the situation was sowing the seeds of my downfall. Mental illness had subsumed me. It had overwhelmed me. It would now never leave me.

Looking back now it appears obvious. But hindsight is a wonderful thing. I can't blame anyone, particularly my family. They weren't to know. We were a unit that was facing unimaginable pressures. They did what they thought was best, for me and for all of us. I've forgotten to mention our Sammy, my younger brother. I took over that responsibility, that protective shield, that motivating force for him too, but I also relied on him to step up to the mark. To become an adult before his years. I don't know if that was right. I torture myself at times, thinking of what I should have done differently. Even now, I sometimes feel that I let Danny down because he died. I also ruminate over whether I should have told him that he was dying. I didn't, because I wanted to protect him. But was I right to do so? Should I have allowed him to prepare? What could I have done to ease that pressure though? There are times when I resent my Dad for making me promise that I would take over his mantle, but then I punish myself for thinking that I didn't do precisely that. That I wasn't capable, that I was weak and puerile.

One thing though remains abundantly clear, unwavering and without deviation. Danny was a gift to me. Being with him, being his brother and much more, was never a trial or a burden. It was life-enriching and I would never have been without it. God bless you my brother. I love you so much.

Saturday 13th February 2016

After the emotional challenges of yesterday, today has been mild in comparison. I always feel a little guilty when this happens, as if I've betrayed the intensity of feeling by not continuing to experience it. I can rationalise this though. I tell myself that no-one can live their lives at those levels. That attempting to do so can only damage oneself, increasing pressure and expectation to a state that can't be met ad infinitum. Danny wouldn't want me to grieve in such a manner. Remember yes, but grieve no. It's not always easy to distinguish between these two situations however.

After I'd written yesterday's entry, what stayed in my mind for a long time was the question of whether what I'd put truly reflected my recollections and feelings. Were there other things that I should have said? Though I recognised this as a thinking trap, as part of my illness, it was still difficult to persuade myself that this was so and that I had no need for self-recrimination. To accurately convey what this feels like is virtually impossible to do. I do beat myself up (literally sometimes). I agonise over minutiae such as wording and interpretation. I see connections all the time that I feel I have to explore and explain. I want to achieve absolute perfection, but scold myself when I can't fulfil my own expectations. Eventually my internal brooding gave way to a calmer state, but not without a mammoth struggle. Solace began to seep into my mind, enabling me to gradually come down and relinquish the battle with my own self.

So what happened today? Well, not much really. We took Millie for a walk in the Country Park and then went into Oadby for a coffee and to buy one or two things for tea. Elliot spent much of the day on his laptop. Lesley watched a film in the afternoon. I read my book for a while and exercised on the flabelos. Oh, and Millwall, who all of a sudden seem to be in danger of becoming successful, beat Rochdale away 1-0!

Sunday 14th February 2016

Valentine's Day. Lesley and I decided to forego the customary buying of presents and exchange of cards. We concluded that we love each other enough to do without them! It's not only the annual day of love and romance, however, it's Lesley's sister's birthday. And that means a family get together and meal out. Alarm bells were already primed for ringing yesterday when I contemplated that fact, but today they are audible and vociferous in their action. The fact of the matter is that if I was really ill, in the grip of a depressive episode, there would be no dilemma. I wouldn't go. I couldn't go. It would be too much. But I'm relatively OK at the moment. I can face it. There's a bit of me that thinks I would enjoy it. The greater part though is still hesitant and unsure. If only I knew how long it would last. How much I'd have to endure. That would be OK. I could pace myself in the same way that a long-distance runner judges how to run a race, using just the right amount of body fuel at each stage. There's no difference. For me it means assessing when to talk, how much to say, how long I can remain silent, when I can begin to countenance closure and withdrawal. I don't want to appear rude and indifferent. Yet I can't hide what is growing within. The stress and tension must have some form of visible outlet.

What I'm really talking about, I guess, is tactics. Tactics to maintain a level of meaningful contact with others whilst addressing the growing agitation within me. I often look around me on similar occasions and think how nice it would be just to experience it for what it is to others, a treat, a time for enjoyment and revelry. To just go with the flow without the need for tactical awareness and application, to avoid any semblance of pre-planning, to not have to use subterfuge and duplicity as a potential last resort. For what can I say to people if I've reached the end of my tether? Do I tell the truth? Do I say that I find social occasions and people – even my own relatives – daunting and frightening? Do I explain why? Do I lay myself open to reaction to mental illness? Or do I simply tell a fib? Do I say I have a headache or that I feel sick? Do I make up some other pretext to go?

The reality is that I have done both in the past. Sometimes I feel so desperate to be somewhere else that I simply don't care what I say. I need to leave. That is the only thing that matters.

Monday 15th February 2016

A strange thing happened to me over the course of the weekend. I developed a really bad sore throat and as a result, felt genuinely off colour. I'm hardly ever ill in the conventional sense of the term, by which I mean falling victim to everyday infections, colds and flus. I sometimes think that God, fate or some other immovable force of nature has decreed that I should be excused common ailments, as if I have to cope with enough with my mental illness. Most of the time, what I seem to have all relate to varying degrees either with depression or to the medication I have to take to address it. I know, for example, I'm susceptible to Irritable Bowel Syndrome, that I have numerous headaches and that my muscles can ache in very strange places. I accept these in the same way that footballers view hernias and groin strains as occupational hazards. I don't react to them as illnesses in themselves, in other words. They are just part of life, part of everyday life at that. I sometimes pop pills to treat them, but I would never consider going to see a doctor. What's the point? He or she would take one look at my file on their computer screen and acknowledge what I already know, that they come with the territory of the mentally afflicted.

When I worked at the Council I would never consider taking a day off work for anything other than my mental state. The only exceptions I can recall were a particularly nasty stomach bug and a prolonged nose bleed that necessitated a trip to Leicester Royal Infirmary! Anything else, I would just persevere, sit back and think of Yorkshire, or whatever similar metaphor you choose to cite! On too many occasions though, my thinking became illogical and focused almost exclusively on the need to 'compensate'. Let me explain what I mean. I have had to take a lot of time off work over the years as a result of depression. This was officially recorded, as it should always be, as disability-related absence. No matter what I try to do to address my disability, this is something I can't help. Once it hits, it stays hit. Recovery time can never be predicted. It's not the same as many physical ailments in this respect. For me, despite this sense of inevitability and helplessness, I have often felt guilty as a result.

I know that people are having to cover for me in the office. I am well aware of what my illness means in terms of my dependency on Lesley and my family at home. As 'compensation' for all this, I feel compelled to ignore common bugs and conditions and work through them as best I can. I even do this ahead of any future depressive episodes. I say to myself 'I'm going to be severely depressed again at some point, so I have to 'store up' some work time in advance as some form of temporal reimbursement.' I know I don't have to do this, that it is inherently unfair on me more than anything else, but the forces of habit and compulsion seem to be so strong and so hard to ignore. I also know many other people with a variety of mental illnesses that do exactly the same. They seem to feel the need – as I do – to justify their employment and their worth as an employee. They are well aware of negative attitudes towards mental health, attitudes that punish and blame, that accuse and denigrate, that belittle what is happening and what is 'acceptable' in terms of severity. It's hard enough dealing with mental illness without having to prove oneself as a result of other people's perceptions. But invariably, that's what lots of people feel they have to do.

Tuesday 16th February 2016

The BBC's new season of programmes on mental health opened last night with Stephen Fry returning, ten years on, to examine changing attitudes towards bipolar disorder. The original series, 'The Secret Life of a Manic Depressive', I remember well. Probably for the first time on national prime-time television, we saw the devastation wreaked by a mental condition on so many people from wildly different backgrounds. It was undoubtedly pioneering and now, a decade later, it was fascinating to see not only Stephen's own journey through the myriad of issues and consequences, but also to glimpse how others too had fared and were coping with living under the dark clouds. What we saw was destruction, the consequences of illness, but, just as tellingly, of people's attitudes towards it. A young man on a commuter train, his manic episode caught on camera and downloaded onto YouTube, the savagery of human response, the vindictiveness and sheer hatred of some who obviously couldn't resist the urge to chastise and lambast. But why? It's difficult to find a reason. He wasn't hurting anyone. He was in a world of his own, caught up in the mania of his illness. On the other side of the coin, though, we witnessed what can only be described as a revolution in empathy and understanding. Of people being able to describe what was happening to them and to receive, not rebuke, but compassion and genuine warmth of feeling. For me, the overwhelming lesson to learn is that treatment is important. Of course it is. But an underlying supportive environment is equally necessary. A society that understands, is aware, is vigilant and is sensitive and benevolent. That is what will truly make a difference. For every new medication, for every developing therapy there needs to be a concomitant bedrock of true consciousness. We still have a lot to learn. Stigma and discrimination, still rife in many respects, is every bit as debilitating and harmful as the illness to which it relates.

It may be coincidence, but on the very day that this new season, entitled 'In the Mind', was launched, the Government announced that an extra £1bn per year would be allocated to help boost mental health services.[7] This is obviously welcome, but I do hope that it is spent wisely. Ensuring treatment is available, timely and thorough is, of course, key. But just as important is investment in grassroots projects that provide support and things such as advocacy and training. I've seen some fantastic local work here in Leicester, but not all of it has survived the tests of time and resource. Realistically, new monies won't do anything other than scratch the surface unless there is an accompanying movement towards greater awareness and empathy. And local projects do a wonderful job educating and providing that warmth, strength and encouragement that can make all the difference.

I am well aware how much my treatment costs the NHS and, indirectly, the tax-payer. The investment in time is one thing, appointment and treatment time with my consultant and GP, but

I also take five drugs as medication on a daily basis. Duloxetine as an anti-depressant; Quetiapine as an anti-psychotic; Ramipril, Simvastatin and Indapamide for the physical consequences of the former. It all adds up. Indeed, I take Quetiapine in its modified or prolonged-release form, which is significantly more costly than its more routine substitute. I do pay for my medication and, thank God, there is an option to pay annually for a set amount rather than per prescription. Otherwise, my medication would cost me an extra £580 a year! It's difficult to get your head around all this and to assess how much it costs just to keep one person – me – alive. Considering the depth of the mental health crisis that we in Britain are facing, of countless undiagnosed cases, of substantial unmet needs, of restrictions in service and treatment, it seems to me that what is being proposed by the Government is no way near enough. Mental health still appears to be playing catch-up. This is, I guess, the legacy of years of underinvestment, the consequences of a devastating lack of recognition and intent.

Wednesday 17th February 2016

After four days of discomfort and four restless nights of pain, I finally admitted defeat this morning and rang the Doctors surgery to make an appointment to see someone about my throat. I've been taking Ibuprofen and yesterday bought an anaesthetic throat spray but it doesn't appear to have done the trick. If anything I have felt progressively worse. Much to my surprise, I got through without having to go to the end of an automatic queue and it was an even greater shock to the system to be told I could see someone in little over an hour's time! In the event, though, I was told nothing I didn't already know and the advice was to do things I was already doing. Still, at least it reassured me that I hadn't contracted glandular fever or, more seriously, throat cancer. I'd looked both of these conditions up yesterday and as a result had to spend some time bringing myself down from the self-inflicted worried frenzy that I knew would be the consequence. Why I did this, I'm not sure. I knew what would happen. I guess my best-case scenario was to read symptoms that were wholly unlike what had developed so that I could immediately banish all possible contemplative deductions. What I read though was simply a regurgitation of everything I was experiencing, only to a greater level of severity. I even managed somehow to imagine new features and convince myself that every conceivable trait or symptom of cancer was evident within my increasingly painful, red-raw throat. I am the ultimate self-fulfilling prophecy when I'm like this.

What induced me to further think the worst was the dream I had. The relationship between dreaming and mortal fact, between subconscious and conscious, has a particular resonance for those of us who are mentally ill. Last night I dreamt that I was an invalid, hospitalised and condemned. My bodily functions seemed to have deteriorated to such an extent that I was one plethora of disease, deformity and defect. I couldn't walk, I couldn't sit. All I could do was lie there, totally dependent on others. And yet I wasn't being treated for physical symptoms. All anyone could focus on was my mental state. The rest of me didn't matter. It was taken for granted. In fact, if anything it had been written off. 'What do you expect?' seemed to be the recurring leitmotif, an incessant indictment of my health per se. 'You are mentally ill. That's all we're bothering about. That's your treatment allocation, your casefile, your raison d'être'. It was as if no-one had considered the possibility that someone as mentally vulnerable as me could possibly have a bad leg, a sore throat, a strained back, a broken neck, cancer or Multiple Sclerosis. The common denominator everywhere was mental illness. My mental illness.

How to interpret dreams has become a regular part of my reflective self. In this case, all I could think of was that people only expect me to be ill in the mind. That my whole personae relates to my brain and its deficiencies. And consequently, they find it difficult to imagine that I could be sick in any other way. That has been my experience at medical appointments in the past. When I've told people of feeling tired and dizzy, or of aches and pains, all that comes back is concern about my mental state, that my body reflects my mind. It's as if I can't be physically ill in itself or for any other reason. I know I talked recently about the reassurance I felt when a doctor told me that my physical complaints were entirely the result of mental illness and its treatment, but I suspect I am always going to need that same diagnosis, that same encouragement and contextualisation. Otherwise, so my deficient logic dictates, I could be cancerous and nobody, let alone me, would be any the wiser.

Thursday 18th February 2016

I appear to have turned the corner as far as my sore throat is concerned, although my sleep was once again disturbed last night. This time, in the early hours, I brought up some bile, and that horrible sourness in the mouth induced a fierce and bitter coughing fit. I remember sitting on the toilet lid in the bathroom trying to sooth the combination of pain and alkaline 'taste'. When I eventually took myself back to bed, my breathing seemed more noticeably audible, but it wasn't the sound of breath itself, but rather a gurgling reverberation in the mouth, akin to water bubbling under intense heat. It obviously went away in my sleep, but at one point it seemed to perfectly accompany Lesley's light snores as if deliberately imitating some Stockhausen masterpiece! Anyway, when I eventually woke up, it was without the sharpness of pain of previous mornings. I think I've got a slight fever, but I don't mind that.

Lesley and Elliot are going to Oxford later on today to spend a few days together, it being half-term. It will do them both good, of course, but I know that once again those same feelings of trepidation will enter my consciousness virtually as they disappear down the road. I have Millie for company and will enjoy the peace and quiet, but I just wish I could really savour and make the most of that experience. I've always been someone who likes solitude. But only if it truly brings tranquillity, and if I'm honest, I can't really remember what that feels like anymore. I must have done at some time, because the feeling does register as a recollection in my brain. It just doesn't materialise at any point now. Being alone sets in motion a series of thoughts that fundamentally clash, my contentment at not having to speak and make an effort, for example, juxtaposed with the worry and helplessness of my isolation. I can't be great company anyway when my anxieties threaten to get the better of me. It's Millie I feel sorry for this week. I wouldn't want to be stuck with me for three days!

I would hazard a guess that if I looked back at this diary so far, there will be numerous contradictions and inconsistencies. What I say one day at variance totally with an entry from another time. I have resisted the temptation to reflect back with this in mind and instead concentrate solely on the present. That way, I'm being true to myself and to my disability. If there are the sort of clashes to which I refer, that's just me. If you wanted regularity and conformity, then I'm sorry. This isn't a scientific paper, it's a journal about mental illness. Of course, this isn't an easy path to follow because of that word 'perfection'. I have had to dispel already any thoughts and inclinations that seem to steer me towards attempting to write the authentic and quintessential manuscript. At times, my desire to record is superseded by an overwhelming urge to write in a style that tries to emulate literary greats such as Oscar Wilde and role models like Stephen Fry. As if anything less than intellectual mastery and artistic creativity is a waste of time. Please just accept me for what I am, not what I think I ought to be.

Friday 19th February 2016

There was a time last night when I honestly thought I was going to die. What made it more terrifying was that it literally came out of nowhere. I'd just taken two Paracetamol tablets as per the medical instruction I got on Wednesday and almost immediately I began to feel sick. My stomach bloated, I started to panic a little. As a result of this sore throat, I'd taken a lot of tablets in a twenty-four hour period and even though this regime was only repeating what I'd already been through one day earlier, the fact that Lesley wasn't around to reassure or pick up the pieces seemed to be the catalyst for sheer hysteria. I worked out what I'd taken. In addition to my daily medication of seven tablets, I'd had the maximum amount permissible of both Paracetamol and Ibuprofen plus an IBS relief pill to settle my stomach. Some twenty-four tablets in total! I kept telling myself that I'd done nothing to exceed the recommendation or supersede the advice I'd been given, that I'd checked on Wednesday whether there was any incompatibility with my routine medication, that I felt sick precisely because my body wasn't used to dealing with so much, that I didn't feel like I was about to pass out, that if I did I could seek emergency medical attention. The whole issue was compounded though because I just couldn't make a decision. I felt totally incapable of deciding on a course of action even though I knew what options I had available to me. I just wanted nature to take its course, for fate to intercede. Luckily I could speak to Lesley on the phone and in the course of her reporting in on their journey and on their short break so far, I was able to raise the subject in a manner that I hoped didn't give any cause for worry.

Even so I spent much of the evening transfixed in my chair in the living room. I still felt a bit queasy and I know that was genuine. However, I soon began to experience other pains and aches – a tightness in the chest, some discomfort in my left arm, a little dizziness – or at least I thought I did. Were all these things in my mind? Or were they real? I so often force myself to believe in my own fears that it's so difficult to distinguish fact from fiction. I had to concentrate hard to enable me to decipher one from the other. In the end I calmed myself by acknowledging that my troubled mind was working overtime again, making two and two make five once more. I did go to bed briefly wondering whether I'd wake up, but by that time tiredness overcame me and I gave in to what I hoped would be the serenity of sleep.

This past week has been awful health-wise. Because of the sore throat and the draining nature of its related symptoms, I've not been able to exercise. Because I've not been able to exercise, I've lost some of the physical fitness I've gained since the start of the year. Because of this, I've become fatter and more unhealthy. Because of this, I've put myself at greater risk of severe illness. Because of this, I'm going to have a heart attack or a stroke. Because of this, I'm going to die very soon. And there you have it! Catastrophizing, depressive 'logic'. From a sore throat to death in a series of related steps. This is a classic thinking trap. I know that. I recognise that. But internalising this, contextualising this, putting things in their proper perspective, all this I find difficult, though not impossible. I guess, when it comes down to it, the more you practice addressing these traps, the more you use therapeutic techniques that you have experienced and learnt, the less challenging it becomes. There is a way out. It's just bloody difficult and it takes it out of you.

Saturday 20th February 2016

Was it my imagination? Or did I just experience the same twenty-four hours twice? It certainly feels that way. I ended up last night sitting in my usual seat, spending hour after hour trying to read or watch television when all that really seemed to matter, all that was foremost in my mind, was my current obsessive fear, my health status. Yet again I was as certain as I could be given the circumstances that I was on the threshold of impending catastrophe. The catalyst this time was the food I'd bought to give myself a treat. How ironic! I'd been to Marks and Spencer's and bought a cheesecake during the day (which must prove, without doubt, that the day was different and that it wasn't déjà vu!) and after a pretty nondescript salad I decided to indulge myself. With every mouthful, however, rather than relishing the taste of a pudding I love, it appeared to be condemning me to an early grave. Again, I couldn't rid the thought in my mind that I was poisoning myself. I don't think I am being melodramatic, because afterwards it was as if I'd self-harmed. The feelings of guilt and self-recrimination combined with sheer disgust were that intense.

I think I need to mention this to my consultant at my next appointment because it's becoming too common, a recurring trend I could do without. I find myself scolding my lack of discipline, berating my weakness in giving in to dietary indulgences. I also keep saying to myself that 'food is the enemy'. These exact words. At times, I only feel comfortable when I think I can starve myself. That I can live on water alone. This is not good. Healthy eating is one thing, but I can't let the obsession with trying to achieve this control me the way it is currently threatening to do. I know I'm on the slippery slope to another potential calamity if it does.

One of my problems – one of my many problems, I should say – is that I think too much. I know this is true because a past consultant has said as much. The distinction that he made to contextualise the matter was between quality and destructive thinking, that using experience and knowledge is productive only if you focus on it being so and use it accordingly. My trouble is that in order to try and achieve this, I resort to more thinking. Indeed, I think and think and think and am not always selective. I don't filter thoughts that are harmful. I simply accept them all like an avalanche of all-consuming cogitation that includes bits that are useful but much that is the opposite. When I'm on my own, thinking is all I seem to do. I constantly ruminate. I ask myself question after question. I'm analysing, I'm deciphering, I'm probing, trying to find solutions to things that sometimes I barely understand, answers to the imponderable. It also seems that this deluge of mental activity exists in inverse proportions to my physicality. The more sedentary I am, the more my mind races, thoughts entering and leaving at a furious pace, uncontrollable and unrelenting. I would say, if I could, that sleep provides the natural remedy of rest, but quite often it doesn't. My dreams can be so vivid, so inherently demanding and exhausting, that there is little respite. I don't really know what the ultimate answer is. Well no, that's not quite true. Medication helps. Confiding in your loved ones is also a good step, but these can't be the definitive solutions. You need to take responsibility yourself. I guess it comes down to practice. To learning how to take charge of your thoughts. To use them to your advantage. Therapy can point the way, but you need to be master or mistress of your own mind. I try to do this and I suppose, if I'm honest, given the fact that I am mentally ill, I am reasonably successful. But I'm not as successful as I want to be. I know that when I fail, there are consequences. At the moment it just seems that I'm failing more often than is good for me.

Sunday 21st February 2016

It's a good job that I was poorly last week as this week promises to be a really busy one for me. I still don't feel myself. I took Millie for a longish walk yesterday and I'm still feeling the after effects some twenty-four hours later. In fact I fell asleep in front of the television this morning which is most unlike me. Back to this coming week though and at the moment, I have to admit to feeling a little daunted at its prospect. I'm interviewing tomorrow. On Wednesday I have two back-to-back meetings, both concerning mental health projects. On Thursday I travel to a hotel at East Midlands Airport to attend a Health and Social Care event and I end the working week with a morning meeting at Leicester General Hospital followed by a trip to London where I'm conducting a tour of Jack the Ripper murder sites! I'll leave you to mull over that last one for the time being and let you have the details, and an explanation on another occasion!!

For those of you accustomed to busy weeks as a natural tour de force, this may not sound like much. But for me, bound by the parameters set by mental illness, this is immense! The reason why is, of course, the fact that each of my commitments requires mental preparation of a kind that is more regimented and exhaustive than is 'normal' (whatever 'normal' actually means!). Also, I have to pace myself mentally as well as physically to ensure that I last for the full requirements of the job and am able to contribute as much as possible and in the manner I have established as necessary and meaningful. Then, finally, there is the aftermath. The weighing up, the self-monitoring of my performance, the inquisition even. This happens whether it's a trip to the post office, a shopping exhibition, picking Elliot up from school or a full-scale exam, interview, talk or business meeting.

For me, there isn't any decipherable difference. I can't forego or dismiss the need for self-analysis. I just can't.

Lesley and Elliot are due back any time now from their short break in Oxford. I've spoken to them on the phone each night they've been away and it sounds like they've had a busy and enjoyable time. I think Elliot's main motive for choosing Oxford was the prospect of visiting University colleges. He's slightly ahead of his time in this respect (he's only thirteen!) but it's no bad thing to set your stall out now and have long-term ambition. Whilst there is bound to be a bit of me that hopes he eventually chooses Durham, I think he is well capable of Oxbridge entry. He just needs to keep doing what he does best – work hard, listen, absorb, challenge and revel in the process of learning. I know I have to keep his feet on the ground, but that applies to me too. I don't want to push him or even live my life through his achievements with all the concomitant pressure that that involves. It sounds the easiest thing in the world to say that all he needs is the right support, an encouraging environment. But it's true. I just know when it comes to it that he'll be fine. He'll just get on with things. It's me and my reaction – to success as well as failure – that worries me much more.

Monday 22nd February 2016

Lesley begins her third week of a phased return to work today. I think she's doing really well. Whether she does too is another matter though. As I suspected would be the case, the real challenge to overcome is within her mind and in particular managing her own expectations. She has successfully negotiated the initial return and conversations both with her colleagues and with Victim First who just happened to ring her on one occasion when she was in the office. It wasn't ideal, as it was bound to impact on her emotions, but looking back now it was no bad thing that she felt able to cry in the workplace. It's been interesting and, I have to say, rewarding for me to be able to advise and support her for once through mental ill health. I was able to give her perspectives that only someone accustomed to that experience could really comprehend and offer. That vulnerability may hit at any time. That keeping things controllable, not setting yourself up to fail, is the key to work and life progression. That mental frailty is physically demanding and exhausting. That being able to be open and honest with yourself as well as with others is a definite advantage. That simply being in the office, dealing with basic minutiae such as emails, is still necessary work. That dealing with these things is an achievement. And so on and so forth. I hope it's helped. She certainly seems more confident and self-assured.

Addressing mental illness may be one of the most relevant and expedient examples of the idiom 'do as I say, not as I do'. Over the years I have been approached by many people aware of my disability and my openness, seeking advice, support and guidance with regard to their mental health or that of one of their loved ones. And every time I've said what I've said, I've reflected afterwards on whether I actually practice what I preach. Nine times out of ten, I don't. I guess one of the problems is that some of the basic tenets of support (whether self-support or otherwise) are relatively easy things to say and to convey. Seek help, speak to someone you trust etc. They're not necessarily so easy to do though. What does one say? How does one approach someone? What do you actually want them to do as a response? What are you seeking in terms of support? Do you actually know yourself? Dealing with the aftermath of contact can also be extremely challenging. You are bound to end up wondering if people's feelings towards you may change, that their actions, their words, every aspect of their relationship with you may become different. Not necessarily fundamentally, but subtly. I'm often asked, for example, if I would always advise people to be honest about what's going on inside their head and about any potential or actual diagnosis. My answer is never definite, one way or the other. You want to say that 'yes, being open, being transparent' is always the best policy. But whilst you can manage your own approach to mental illness, you can't determine other peoples. Stigma and discrimination are powerful enemies to the depressed and to anyone experiencing mental ill health. They are prevalent and they can be soul-destroying. You end up giving a very unequivocal answer. 'It depends', I will say. 'If you are certain about the person to whom you are opening up, then it shouldn't be a problem. If you aren't, then it can be.' You need to be prepared for the possibility of a changed relationship, of people behaving differently, more distantly, more selectively, less certainly, less confidently. I suppose my approach is based on the identity I have worked hard to feel and portray. That mental illness can be an asset. It's debilitating, but not embarrassing. It's demanding but can be rewarding. It's something of which I'm proud. I don't want to hide. I don't need to hide. It's your problem if you can't deal with it. But I'm here to help you do so if you want me to. It's taken me many years to come to this. The journey has been agonising at times. Plenty of tears, much self-doubt, intense anger, considerable frustration. But I'd definitely say it's been worth it.

Tuesday 23rd February 2016

As you are aware from previous entries, I have a tendency to have dreams that are both vivid and true to life. The other night though I had one that was relatively new. It's true I've had it before, but I'd dismissed that almost as a one-off. However, it returned on Sunday and I suppose I now have to accept that it may be repetitive. It's not that in itself that bothers me (i.e. its potential recurring nature), it's what it was about. Actually, more accurately, it's who it was about. My Dad has been off-limits as far as dreams go. I don't know how, but in some way my conscious desire not to think ill of my father for so many years impacted on my propensity to dream about him, or not as the case may be. I'd obviously built up a fairly impregnable barrier that prevented my subconscious overruling its diametrically opposite. Dad just didn't appear in any of my dreams. At times his personae filled my waking hours. I would talk to him as if he was physically present. I would conjure up his image, try to recreate his voice and his words. I would consult with him, confide in him, cry on his ghostly shoulder. But I couldn't dream of him.

On Sunday though, I did, and it wasn't pleasant. What I dreamt was horrifying and troubling. I can't remember the full nuts and bolts, the specifics of words or contexts. I know school was involved in some way. I suspect I was leaving the place, whether temporarily or permanently I can't recollect, as I seemed to be packing all my life's features into the trunk I used whilst I was at school. I use the word 'features' advisedly, because what I was storing were not just physical objects, but memories, failures and achievements. All that was me seemed to be on the floor in front of me, all destined to be hidden away in a dark place. What I do remember quite succinctly was packing bundle after bundle of banknotes. My Dad was questioning what I'd done to come into such a vast fortune. I told him I'd won it as winnings after a bet and some kind of game. He wouldn't accept it. He didn't believe me. He kept trying to remove the money from the trunk. He was accusatory, scathing in his comments. As we exchanged angry words, the temperature of the argument increased, as did its scope. More and more he admonished me, calling into question my character, my integrity, my decency. He gathered support from those around me, people at the school. Everyone began to berate me, to continue the tirade, to join in the bandwagon until it became an incessant barrage of verbal and physical rebuke. I could withstand this no longer. I snapped. I fought with my Dad. I tried to constrain him, to shut his mouth, to push him away, even to punch him. I could see his discomfort. I knew I was pushing him towards cardiac arrest. My Mum tried to stop me, but she couldn't. I was brutal and unrelenting. Before calamity could strike, however, I woke up and I did so on every subsequent occasion as when I returned to the world of sleep the same dream kept resurfacing, gnawing away at my battered mind.

What did it mean? My fear is that somehow this is all linked with the worries my Dad had for my future in his last years. I had failed at school, twice making a hash of my 'A' Levels. I was devoid of ideas, lacking in spark and interest, fully submerged I know now in depression. For Dad, increasingly weak physically and tired mentally, this situation was beyond his capabilities. I know he worried but he didn't realise how mentally ill I had become. He was too locked into his own vulnerabilities, too self-absorbed (and this is no criticism) to appreciate my anguish. Was my dream my attempt to get him to register? To acknowledge my situation? Was it telling him to go away, that I'd found a path for myself, even if it was one paved – in banknotes – with the seeds of self-destruction? I just don't know. At the end of the day, fathers worry about the future of their children. That's what parents do. It's what I'm good at! My consolation is that before he passed away, he knew that I'd gained a place at University to read Music. My immediate prospects were assured.

Wednesday 24th February 2016

This afternoon I face one of my most nerve-wracking of challenges – overlapping engagements. I have a meeting at 4.00 pm and then an event that begins at 5.15 pm. It means managing a situation that will inevitably cause anxiety, however meticulous my preparation and successful its operation. Do I leave the meeting early and get to the event on time? Or do I stay longer at the former (not knowing when exactly it may finish) and risk being late for the latter? It really is a 'no-win' situation. My gut feeling is to take the first option. I find it much more challenging to enter into an environment in which everyone is already present. In the past, when I've been in precisely this predicament, I have often given in to my fears. Even though I've thought I could do it, enter a room and risk everyone looking at me, I've not been able to follow it through. Quite literally, I've fallen at the final hurdle, sometimes stalling at the door, not being able to open it. Engulfed by embarrassment, shame and fear, I've just walked away. Option one though is not without its own hurdles. It means having to interrupt the normal procedures of the meeting, having to excuse myself, risking irritation, inducing possible bad feeling, gathering up my possessions amidst scrutiny and possible silence and then leaving with the feeling (if not the actuality) that all eyes are following me through the exit.

I don't want to let anyone down. That's the bottom line. If I take the second option, I run the greater risk, I suppose, of not having sufficient mental strength and stamina to go to the event at all. That would be worse in the long term, even if it would initially keep the trauma wolves at bay. Does it matter if I go to the second engagement? Well yes, it does. I've said I'm going. There are people on a waiting list that could have taken my place if I don't turn up. It would be good for me to go, to show my face, to contribute. People, heaven forbid, may even be looking forward to seeing me.

Both engagements, moreover, focus on mental health. Part of me argues that as a consequence, there is likely to be a much greater level of awareness of the pitfalls of attending events, of going through precisely what I've already explained. There may even be an expectation that people leaving early or arriving late will need an empathetic response, or a sympathetic appreciation of people not arriving at all despite their best intentions and their underlying wishes. We've all been there, so the argument goes. The greater part of me however recognises that these are important things for me to be at. People know me for being open and forthright in relation to my own mental health and to the issues that govern and impact on people like me. It's not therefore a question of wanting to go. It's the fact that I need to go.

If both engagements were being held in the same building, it wouldn't be so bad, but unfortunately they're not. At the Council, I was accustomed to back-to-back meetings ending and starting at exactly the same time. Although I would do my best not to put myself in such a situation, I could resign myself to the fact that all that would be required is to walk from one room to another. There would be nothing else involved, nothing to think of, no obstacles to negotiate other than exit and entry through a door. Today, I have to drive into the city, park my car twice and deal with rush hour traffic getting from meeting one to event two. The venues are not too far apart, but too distant to allow me to park in one place and walk to both. How long do I leave it? Where should I park? What if there are no spaces available? My nightmare would be to leave the first, have difficulties getting to the second and be late for that as well!!

It's complex. Too complex. As you can also see, a great deal of nervous energy will be used up. It has already started in actual fact. I can feel the tension beginning to rise, fully three and a half hours before I have to leave. If only I could be assured that I will feel OK and look presentable. If only teleportation was possible. If only I had the gift of invisibility. If only I didn't feel like this in the first place. If only....

Thursday 25th February 2016

I've spent today at an event on Applied Health Research at a hotel on the East Midlands Airport complex. It was a full day, the first I've had work-wise for a long time, and my head is spinning a little as I write this in the sanctuary of my own home. Even though much of the specifics were beyond me – it's a constant amazement to me how jargonised people's vocabulary can be and how peculiar it is to individual sectors – I think I got the general gist. Coming into something new, like I am to this terrain, is never easy and I was reminded of this during one of the presentations. The subject being discussed was 'comfort' – a complex and, yes, uncomfortable, one for anyone with a mental illness – specifically, the challenge of moving from a position within one's comfort zone to one without. The context was health to academia and vice versa, the position in which most in the audience would find themselves working, and indeed, moving. For me though, what was acutely relevant was the difference between the meetings I went to yesterday evening and today's event. Yesterday, I was in my natural element. Both meetings focused on mental health and involved people with a variety of mental illnesses. I was at home, at ease, confident, without fear or embarrassment. I was able to speak with authority, contribute with meaning and intent, listen with understanding and follow the discussion in its entirety, every nuance, every context, every situation, every viewpoint and every issue. Moreover, I felt that every person present was a brother or sister, people with whom I share something that can be highly toxic and destructive at times, but something deeply resonant to us all. Today, by contrast, I struggled. I didn't even know how to introduce myself. Within the context of the event, I felt that every word I uttered was irrelevant and without foundation. I felt a sense of scrutiny that was quite overbearing. When isolated in discussion, I was like a rabbit caught in a headlight, unable to move, incapable of speech, uncertain as to how to react and deeply conscious of my inadequacies. Luckily I was saved by some of the people I did know, people with whom I will be working on specific projects and who have been, in a very short space of time, both friendly and supportive.

I know what I've described will come across as unnecessarily negative and self-critical. Anyone faced with the novelty of circumstance and context would probably feel the same. But I'm a depressive. And I'm a depressive with an obsession with perfectionism. That dreaded word 'should' hovers menacingly over every situation in which I find myself. I should be able to cope. I should know these initiatives. I should have done some research. I should be capable of understanding complex matters. And so on and so forth. How I should have done these things doesn't enter into the equation! The point is, I should!!! Cognitive Behavioural Therapy (CBT) does help me to regain perspective and logic and I shall turn to it with determination as well as familiarity tonight. In a day full of strange acronyms, CBT is one I know only too well!

Friday 26th February 2016

It seems rather apt to expand on the issue of 'comfort' raised yesterday for the simple reason that the event I attended highlighted not only the discomfort of ignorance and unfamiliarity, but also the anxiety induced by its very nature. I've been to hundreds of similar events over the years, and every single one involves negotiating a significant obstacle. If you are similarly experienced, you will know that in addition to the formal parts – the speeches, the workshops, panel questions and answers etc. – there are also the 'comfort breaks' (going to the toilet to you and me!), the 'networking' sessions (translated as 'talking to others'), refreshment and lunch arrangements. In other words, sections of the day that are informal, social and supposedly more relaxed. I use the word 'supposedly' advisedly because for me, they are anything but so. Instead, they are fraught with tension. They are ominously anticipated. They are, in actual fact, dreaded. They can even induce panic attacks. Whereas others revel in the freedom, diversion and distraction, the ability to laugh and joke, tell anecdotes as well as enjoy the excitement of meeting new people, I simply wish to crawl into a corner or into my own shell. I just want anonymity. The prospect of going out into a room full of people, some of whom you will know, the greater percentage of whom you may not, and precipitate or engage in discussion without the barriers imposed by formality and expectation, is quite simply terrifying. I hate it. I'm no good at it. I can't cope with it. I start to shake. I stumble over words. I fear I may come across as odd or weird, that the social niceties observed by everyone else will not come to me at the right time or in the right manner. I want to be understood, but that may mean divulging information that is not appropriate to the setting. Who wants to be met by someone trying to explain depression, shyness or fear when you are supposed to be winding down, enjoying a well-earned tea or coffee? I just wish it could all go away, that the minutes go quickly, that there are refuge points to which I can go, that there are opportunities to escape or to look engaged. Anything that doesn't serve to highlight me as incapable, deficient, stressed or different.

I have some coping mechanisms, some of which may strike you as utterly bizarre. I lock myself in a toilet, for example, or retreat to my car. I stay in the meeting room looking through any information I can find. I even pretend to have imaginary conversations on my mobile! My logic here is that it's perfectly understandable and acceptable for people to catch up on messages during breaks. Even though I rarely get them, if I give the impression that I have and that I'm following them up, then no-one will think twice about looking at me. I have, of course, to ensure that my phone is switched off first! I can't risk someone actually calling me when I'm supposed to be talking to someone else! The conversations I have are simply made up. I tend to pretend that I'm the recipient of news, the reactor to a situation. That way it appears that I'm listening and don't have to talk as much. I have to gauge not only what would be considered as mundane, so that I don't draw attention to the conversation, but also when to stop and even where to do so.

Yesterday, I was supported considerably by a new colleague whom I approached at the first interval to ask for her help. I explained my predicament and asked her if she wouldn't mind looking at the various information stalls for me and gather up anything she thought might be of use. She actually responded that she would go a step further and be with me throughout the period in question and at lunch. Having someone that understands, that you can depend and rely upon, that is willing to be so supportive can take away much of the anguish and worry that is building up to boiling point. It's the same as having a support worker for physical needs. There's no difference. You just need the reassurance that such a trusted companion naturally brings. So many people I know don't feel they can ask for that type of support. I'm lucky, I guess, in that I can do so, even though there are still occasions when I can't bring myself to raise the question and others in which there simply isn't anyone that you immediately feel comfortable approaching. Of course, being open about your disability is almost a pre-requisite. How can you seek help such as this if you can't explain why you need it? And, believe me, there is often the need to explain in detail. Unlike visible disabilities when the need may be self-explanatory, all too apparent. Unlike other hidden disabilities where there may be almost automatic recognition and appreciation. Mental illness and its impact, its symptoms, its manifestations, more often than not doesn't elicit the same sense of immediate understanding. Would someone quite naturally think of anxiety, shyness and panic, or of physical traits such as lethargy or shakiness if they were told someone had depression? More often than not, I suspect the answer would be 'no'. As a result, I often feel I have not just to explain, but to justify my reasons for seeking help. It seems, when I do so, that I'm forced into something much more fundamental. I have to justify my disability.

Saturday 27th February 2016

I am so tired today. I got back from London around midnight, but even then, after an evening of physical exercise tramping around Whitechapel and the City of London whilst delivering what I hope was a stimulating tour, I couldn't sleep and watched telly well into the early hours. Why my interest in Jack the Ripper, you will probably be asking? Well, it stems, I suspect, from a broader fascination in historical mysteries. Ever since I can recall, I have been engrossed in trying to find conclusive evidence or at least a persuasive argument in relation to a wide range of bygone conundrums. History was always my favourite subject at school, and this provided me with the knowledge and the appreciation of trying to decipher and explain how things came to be, so that I could then apply it to specific contexts and enduring mysteries. Amongst my pet hobbies in this regard are the fate of Mallory and Irvine on Mount Everest, the Kennedy Assassination and notorious 'whodunnits' of which the perpetrator of the murders in Whitechapel all those years ago is probably the most widely known and perhaps the biggest challenge. I have all the books. I've studied document after document. I've scrutinised all the theories. And I've spent many hours walking the streets, exploring not just the murder sites themselves, but relevant buildings and thoroughfares, seeing for myself the changing nature of the environment and sadly, the gradual erosion of old East London. There must be some degree of romance within me (though Lesley will verify that it's barely perceptible!) because I was deeply affected by the implications of some of the developments we saw last night. Old streets, ancient buildings, even things such as period street lights, all being sacrificed in the name of 'progress'. Lots of things do remain of course. There is still the evidence of old Jewish shops, for example, as well as those wonderful homes built originally for French Huguenot families that dominate some of the side-streets around Brick Lane.

The 'lucky' recipients of my expertise not just in Victorian crime, but in all the associated issues of social exclusion, poverty, discrimination and community cohesion, were a party of sixth formers from my old school and their two geography teachers. They were on a two-day visit to the capital as part of the 'World Cities' programme of study and I'd responded to an appeal for anyone who could offer some related activity to complement their formal schedule. Meeting people connected with the school is not always an easy thing for me to do, given that my experiences when I was a pupil there were not always that positive and have had a lasting legacy. I will go into this more at some future point, but for now it's probably sufficient to say that hearing the sounds of 'refined' accents combined with the parlance specific to that school and its setting, were a little unnerving at times. They were really nice young people and their teachers were more than welcoming and enthusiastic, it's just that I felt a reluctance within me to probe into their school experiences or even to recognise that I shared something quite fundamental with them. At the start of the tour, when one of the teachers mentioned that I was a former pupil and asked me to expand on that, I have to admit that I felt almost embarrassed to do so and reveal my past. I didn't want to dwell on it and although I responded to the inevitable questions, it wasn't something that I would have naturally felt open and comfortable to discuss. Besides, it wasn't relevant to the evening. I was there as a tour guide, not an old student.

Given the fact that school is a frequent setting for some of the most disturbing of my dreams, I know that sometime within the next ten months or so, I will need to confront my demons and deal with their impact and their consequences. Not to do so would not only belie the openness I want to show and convey in this diary, but it would also perhaps perpetuate some of the rawness behind this part of my depressive state. Even though I know that the roots of my depression do not lie in my schooling – they were already there, ripe and fertile beforehand and would still have been even if I had not won a Scholarship to go north – what I went through in those formative years didn't necessarily help my embryonic mental afflictions. In some cases I would go as far as to say that they succeeded in keeping open wounds that were already laid bare, open and beckoning to infection and something more permanent.

Sunday 28th February 2016

After last week's exertions culminating in Friday's guided walk around Whitechapel, this weekend has been one of rest and recuperation. I hadn't planned anything, which is a good job really as I've been so tired, in both mind and body. I've had lengthy lie-ins on both days and even then have struggled to summon up enough energy to get out of bed. It just shows how much nervous and physical energy I consume even when it seems to me – and I'm sure most definitely to others – that I'm not actually doing a great deal. It being Sunday, I did the ironing this morning and then ventured to Aldi with Lesley to do our weekly shop. After returning, I sorted out my invoice and expenses details so that I'm up-to-date with what I've earned and what I'm owed. For most of the time though, I've been watching sport on the telly. Nothing's really grabbed my attention, if I'm honest. I couldn't face the prospect of West Brom versus Crystal Palace yesterday evening so turned instead to the delights of international Rugby Union. The wrong choice as it turned out. I just don't understand the other form of rugby. Too many times the whistle goes, something's happened in a ruck or a maul (and I don't know which is which) to grab the attention of the referee, the players then position themselves for one set piece or another, it takes an inordinate amount of time to satisfy the official, and it's all so disjointed, stationary and broken up. I'm sure people who know the game will contest my description, but all I can say is that I'm proud to be a Rugby League man. Our game is simpler, faster, more skilful and infinitely more entertaining, but then again I'm biased! As it happened the round ball contest at The Hawthorns appeared to be an absolute classic. Five goals, a bit of controversy and a game played at a genuinely high-level tempo and with a touch of style as well. Typical!

Monday 29th February 2016

I am reading a wonderful book at the moment. 'To Reach the Clouds' is Philippe Petit's written account of that momentous period of his life in which he planned, organised and carried out what he termed 'le coup', a tightrope walk between the two towers of the World Trade Center. I know the story well. I was mesmerised by the documentary 'Man on Wire' and totally captivated by the more recent film 'The Walk' which I have to say is probably the most gripping piece of cinema I think I have ever experienced. To me, to walk in the clouds as he did on that beautiful August morning in 1974 is probably the single greatest achievement in the history of humankind. Amidst all human achievements, it still stands out simply because it still retains that core element of impossibility that has perhaps been relinquished in other spheres. Our minds have become accustomed to witnessing other notable feats created and experienced by our fellow humans, feats that at one time did appear to be beyond human comprehension and fulfilment. I'm thinking here of things such as space exploration or momentous inventions, scientific endeavours perhaps, or human creativity in the spheres of music or the arts. We have succeeded in pushing the boundaries back so much that when we witness a new world record in athletics or experience something novel in terms of sound or as an aspect of our fascination with new technology, it appears simply as an extension of what we already have and know. It doesn't mean it's not remarkable, just that it's contextual, easy to consider and envisage, predictable even. Philippe's wirewalk, however, is so much more than this. It still astounds. It takes your breath away because no matter what we know, no matter how much we are familiar with his expertise, it still appears absolutely impossible. It defies not only logic, but utter belief. I simply can't comprehend to this day how someone could not only walk over such a void on something so slim and apparently fragile, but then kneel, lie down and salute one's audience. It became not simply an exploit of skill, a demonstration of intense concentration, but a performance of such majesty. It was beautiful, pure and serene. It had everything. It was the supreme act of a unique individual.

I know what attracts me to Philippe Petit. It's not that as someone who has never had a head for heights, what he did and still does encroaches on all my fears and elements of phobia. It's because he is what I could never be – flamboyant, impulsive, extrovert, unpredictable, single-minded, a crowd-pleaser, a risk-taker. He doesn't seem to care about how others feel about him. He isn't fazed by expectation, normality or routine. I look at him and the only things I can see that we share in common are our pre-occupation with detail, our perfectionism, our irritation when things go wrong and our obsessional behaviour. In other words, all elements of my mental illness. It is as if I have to be ill to be synonymous in any way and even then it's with what others (thought hopefully not he) consider to be the less positive aspects of his character. What attracts people is the 'joie de vivre' that epitomise all the things I initially stated, not those by-products of a genius that are there simply to prove he is mortal. Who remembers Beethoven for his depressive illness rather than his artistic creativity?

The other thing that is worthy of note is that Philippe recognised the supremacy of his act. He knew that on that wonderful day he had surpassed himself, that this was the ultimate sensation of a sensational talent. He had gone beyond any confine or challenge, any ritual or passion. He had excelled beyond human imagination. How wonderful that must have been to realise and to feel. But how then does one deal with the rest of one's days? How do you reconcile life afterwards with that brief period of utter sublimity? That must be a challenge and a half. For me though I deal with that reality all the time and I have never had my wirewalk moment. Or if I have, I didn't realise it.

March

Tuesday 1st March 2016
It's been noticeable recently that I've felt the need to schedule and itemise parts of my day in more detail. Today, for example, I've allocated a couple of hours to one piece of work but then followed it with mundane activities (taking work receipts to the General hospital, cleaning, exercising) before a doctor's appointment at ten to four brings the curtain down on my more structured, more timetabled, routine. The point is not that I'm doing different things – that always tends to be the case – but that I'm stipulating, pre-planning and recording what I'm doing, at what time and for how long. It feels at the moment that unless I do this, I won't have the self-discipline or even the normal ability to decipher what needs to be done and when. It's as if I simply don't trust myself. Some may call this good planning, of course. The need for structure in relation to a project or with regard to exam revision, is always a good thing. But I seem to need to itemise things that normally I would take for granted. I know that when depression is at its most severe, I do need to follow patterns and procedures that are similarly outlined, so that I do

small things for short periods of time and have some sense of shape to my life and hopefully some achievement as a result. But I'm not severely depressed at the moment! I'm relatively OK. So what is behind this need for detail, this desire to plan?

I suspect that one explanation may lie in the fact that I'm beginning to attract little pockets of work and in the same way that a student prepares for exams in different subjects, there is a concomitant need for order in my planning. I do find it difficult to adjust to things when I have a lot on. I much prefer to attend to one matter to its entirety, before starting anew. My brain can cope with this. It makes sense. It achieves continuum. It avoids distraction. At times, even though I can register a myriad of thoughts – random as well as connected – flowing through my mind at any one time, as a whole my brain feels the need for parameters and for regulation. It's like a river flowing in one direction, but interrupted in its flow by rocks, bridges, foliage or whatever else one usually finds floating or swimming in our waterways. There are also times when I feel this desperate need to complete a task all in one go, or even immediately. I can't wait. I can't deviate. Otherwise my train of thought or my desire to fulfil will be lost, perhaps irretrievably. When I panic, this is definitely the case. It's simply impossible for me to contextualise what's happening. There is an immense urge within me to resolve, to finalise, to put to bed, to make it go away – whatever it is. If I'm honest in my reflections, I think this tendency has become more acute as time has passed. Perhaps that is why I'm trying desperately to gain some foothold on things temporally, to create structure by dissecting tasks into component parts. This would mean going against the inclinations that have become more rigid within me. To battle against the tide. To try and dam the river.

I know I'm probably reading too much into this. I'm almost certainly catastrophizing again, but what bothers me in terms of trying to make sense of things is that as my life clock continues to tick, I'm only able to process an increasingly limited number of 'tasks' or items at any one time. I'm slowing down, in other words. I'm becoming less adaptable, less able to cope with complexity as well as change, more rigid, more regulated, more robotic and one-dimensional. Can my brain manage? Can I expect it to react positively to things unforeseen or unexpected, or will these things just not register at all? It's one thing not to gain pleasure from life's quirks, facets, qualities, unpredictability's and similar manifestations, but not to realise that they are happening, that's more worrying.

Wednesday 2nd March 2016

For once, my visit to the doctor was not of a routine nature as far as my mental health is concerned. Blood tests taken after my last visit have revealed that I am Vitamin D deficient. I didn't really know what that meant until I looked it up on Google, and found that in addition to one of the main causes being a lack of exposure to the sun, one of the potential symptoms or by-products is depression. I have to confess to being a little unsettled and indeed shocked by this revelation. Surely, after all this time, it can't be the case that all I had to do to 'cure' myself of mental illness was simply to get a sun-tan! It can't be that simple, can it? Have I been kidding myself all these years? Perhaps I didn't need psychiatric treatment after all? Just a prescription to revel in sunlight!

My simple causal explanation, as I suspected, didn't add up. My doctor reassured me that things were more complex in my case. That my depression was a more fundamental disability, that it is an underlying condition not triggered by one factor or even necessarily a combination of factors. In other words, that I'm depressed as a result of mental illness, not a deficiency in sunlight or Vitamin D. I guess he could have gone further and added exercise and maybe other things as well. It seems therefore that my awareness and understanding of my own situation has not been shattered. It remains the case that depression came first and that physical aspects connected to it are subordinate and supplemental. Basically, I'm mentally ill because I'm mentally ill. No other reason. No direct physical cause. No attribution. No simple connection.

Not only did I guess as much, if it was as simple as that, then Vitamin D deficiency or any other single manifestation would constitute the basic test for depression. Everyone would be screened accordingly. My doctor also revealed that I had been tested for this before, some three years ago, and though low, it hadn't registered then as something for concern and remedial action. So, depression came first, as it always seems to have done. You may detect – particularly if you are semantically inclined – that I was more than comfortable with my doctor's explanation. I was, in actual fact, relieved. What this amounts to is effectively this: that I want to have the reassurance and the knowledge that my mental illness is, to all intents and purposes, pure as well as long-standing, independent and distinct as well as severe. This may strike you as bewildering and perhaps even a little disturbing. It certainly is a position that requires explanation.

I'll now do my best to provide that.

When depression is at its most potent, its most severe state, there is nothing I want more than to be relieved of its aggression, its pain, its terror and its potential for disaster. Even when it's just there, as it is most of the time, as a permanent state of being, less dramatic but still evident and disturbing, I want to be able to control it, to temper it, to alleviate its rawness and its debilitating impact. But do I want to lose it completely? Or permanently? No, I don't. I know that I don't. I'm very firm in my conviction here. I certainly do not want to relinquish my identity as a depressive. Over the course of so many years, I have managed through sheer tenacity and determination, to transform it from one of illness to one of strength, from one of frailty to one of pride. Let me reiterate. This is not about the symptoms of depression per se. They remain horrible, parlous, at times overbearing. This is, instead, about how it feels to be labelled or perceived. It's about what you feel in relation to yourself. How the impact of illness is internalised and consciously recognised. Depression is a part of me, every bit as much as my limbs or organs. It is a companion, an uneasy companion yes, but still a companion. And a companion that is fundamental to my whole world ethos, my entire orientation as a person. If I wasn't depressed, what would I be? I don't know and I don't really want to find out, because, pure and simple, it wouldn't be me. This is a difficult concept to explain and probably even harder to visualise, understand or accept. I want to get better. Of course I do. And having Vitamin D supplements may indeed make me feel better – it's a no-lose situation – but I know that I'm never going to be rid of depression completely. Not only am I comfortable with that, I'm also positive with its implications. This isn't depression talking. It's me.

Thursday 3rd March 2016

I had a meeting with my friend John this morning. I don't seem to have seen him much lately, mainly due to the fact that I've been busy on Fridays when he organises his Social Media Café at the West End Centre. As always, it was great to see him and chat about positive work, current and planned. We're working towards putting together a package entitled 'Active Citizenship', which aims at encouraging and assisting people to become more engaged and influential within their local communities. It just combines what we currently do and specialise in, and together I think it has real mileage. The great thing about our conversations is that we both appear to come away suitably inspired and invigorated, with tangible things to do, real actions based on both substance and vision.

John is organising Military History Live in June, an event at which my forthcoming book on the Holocaust, 'Suspended Disbelief', will be officially launched. Providing it is ready, of course! It should be, as my publisher has now received the manuscript back from the editor and consequently all that really remains prior to printing is for me to insert relevant photographs and then for the final checks, what hopefully will amount to no more than crossing i's and dotting t's. It's funny, but as the whole enterprise nears its conclusion, I'm becoming more and more impatient and increasingly nervous as well. All the hard work is done, but it's what happens from now on in that will ultimately present something concrete and conclusive. It feels like the final four hundred metres of an Olympic marathon, the once around the stadium conclusion to an epic race. Here now, everything is laid on the table. One can see it unravelling in front of one's eyes, with myself cast as the lone runner, fatigued, leg-weary, caught up in the moment and the achievement, the end goal tantalisingly close, desperate for it all to be over but conscious that all camera lens' and the eyes of the world are focused on those final few yards and the finishing tape. That one brief, historically momentous finale and then respite.

What has been troubling my mind ever since I handed over my final draft, is what then transpires once someone else scrutinises it with critical aforethought and mindset. Inevitably there will be changes. For me, beset with perfectionism, what I produced was my definitive perfection. Yet, that won't be the case once publisher and editor do their jobs. What does that say about what I initially wrote? That it wasn't good enough. That it was deficient. That it was lacking in substance and style. This translates, in my warped logic and constantly sensitive brain, to recognising imperfection. There is a stunning scene in Milos Forman's film adaptation of Peter Shaffer's 'Amadeus', when our hero, Mozart, appears on stage at the end of the premiere of his opera 'Die Entführung aus dem Serail'[8], to be greeted by the Emperor who, unsure of how to critique musically what was beyond his capabilities as an enthusiastic amateur to recognise, simply states that 'it had too many notes' and that all that needs to be done is to 'cut a few and it will be perfect'. Mozart, never one for decorum or deference, replies by asking him which notes he had in mind! I'm certainly no genius when it comes to writing or indeed anything else. Far from it. However, what Mozart knew was perfection, I perceive and internalise as perfection. It's that old chestnut again. I'm either great, or I'm crap. If I can't be the former, I must be the latter. It's not notes that bother me, obviously, its words. I've written a lot. I know that. But to my mind they were necessary. I wouldn't have written them otherwise. If, in the process that's happening as I write, there is a decision to significantly reduce what is there either for financial expediency or literary necessity, I will take that badly. I know I will. The more I worry about it, the more I'm convinced that that is what is going to happen. My mind is racing ahead of myself again, contemplating the worst, fearing its impact, visualising my reaction. Why can't I just live in the present? Or at least view the future with some degree of optimism? I don't want much. I'm not greedy. Just a little would be adequate. It would give me some semblance of comfort, something to clutch at with at least a degree of positivism and confidence.

Friday 4th March 2016

I had to do something this morning that's been worrying me for quite a while. I haven't been back to the Council building since the start of October and that was only two working days after I'd left their employment. This morning I had to attend a meeting as a mental health representative on a body of people from various communities relevant to the Equality Act 'protected characteristics'.[9] I was therefore there for the first time not as a local government worker but as an ordinary member of the public, someone volunteering to scrutinise the equality work of the Council. A classic case of 'gamekeeper turned poacher' (and yes, I've worded that deliberately in reverse) you might say, although, to be honest, I was never much good at the former and certainly never saw myself in that protective, guarded role or fashion. Indeed some would say that I was always the poacher, the only difference now being the transformation from working to open the door from within to banging on it incessantly from the outside. I have to add that anyone characterising me as such would see their hand being shaken heartily, gratefully and with much relief!

The scars I bore from the working environment I had to endure whilst working there are still quite fresh and certainly very raw. Despite receiving much needed and valued support from my

Line Managers and some colleagues, my overall experience over more than ten years of work was not favourable. It was certainly not conducive to positive mental health, at least as far as I was concerned. Too many times I felt that my disability wasn't recognised, that it certainly wasn't understood and that it counted against me in my efforts to remain in work and to maintain the level of service that I considered my position demanded. Every time I came back to work after a severe bout of depression, for example, some people would simply ignore me. Others obviously considered it difficult to approach me, and when they did, couldn't find the words to ask how I felt. It seems the most simple and most obvious thing to do when someone returns after illness, whether that be two days off with a cold, or seven months off with depression. You ask 'how are you?' 'Are you feeling better?' I know it can be challenging sometimes to find the right words, but this isn't rocket science. Besides, I was always open about my mental illness. It wasn't embarrassing to me. It wasn't a taboo subject, one to be avoided at all cost. One of the difficulties that people with mental illness often face when returning to any environment, whether work or otherwise, is the perception people have that if they can see you at work, you must be well. You must have recovered. You can't be ill anymore. Of course, this isn't usually the case. Moreover, in the most fundamental sense, I'm never not ill (and sorry for the double negative, but I thought it a more accurate use of words!). Depression never leaves me completely. I just learn how to handle it and can do so with more efficiency when I'm relatively well ('relatively' being the operative word). People do expect you to be something that you're not and are never going to be. You wouldn't expect a footballer recovering from a broken leg, to suddenly sprint one hundred metres as soon as he or she has the cast removed, would you? You also wouldn't consider someone getting over a severe bout of tonsillitis to immediately sing a Wagner aria, or for a cancer patient undergoing chemotherapy to be able to work at their post, without rest, for a full working day. Expectations need to be managed. That's why people experience rehabilitation. That's why employers use phased returns to work. That's why an atmosphere of support and understanding needs to be cultivated and continually worked on. So that people don't feel, as I did, that they are being treated differently, that they aren't being included, that their value isn't recognised, that they are being compared to others less favourably and more critically.

Of course, it is people that need to change, as it's people that comprise organisations. The Council at which I worked had all the required policies and strategies. They had the right procedures. They focused on maintaining standards that had received external verification and recognition. They provided internal mechanisms for support and external means of challenge. I should know, I worked directly in these areas. Moreover, I knew some wonderful people there that took great pride not just in their jobs but in the manner in which they helped others to do theirs. My Line Manager for most of my time there was one. She excelled herself in her desire as well as her ability to know me, to help me, to support me. But, as with all organisations, no matter how big or how small, it is people that remain key and if some decide or know no other way than to treat difference with indifference, to exclude rather than be inclusive, to discriminate whether consciously or otherwise, then it's a reflection on them first and foremost. You just hope that the organisation has the knowledge and the confidence to react and to address in the appropriate fashion. And if it doesn't, there is a need to challenge.

To return to this morning. I felt decidedly ill as I uneasily sat in my front room pondering what was to come. The meeting itself wasn't really the problem, of course. It was its context. Though I felt the need to restrain myself when discussions took place on areas of work that until October last year I was engaged with. The insider knowledge that I had didn't rest easily with what I heard at times – something about theory and practice, what was one but not the other, and all that – but I felt I had to keep my distance, this being my first engagement as an 'outsider', so to speak. All the ingredients of the morning outside the formalities posed problems and placed demands on my mental strength and resilience. The journey itself, the same roads and roadworks, the first sight of the concrete labyrinth that is Council HQ, parking and greeting at reception, getting through the doors, seeing familiar faces and so on and so forth. I felt physically sick at one point and throughout, my tummy was in knots and spasms. I was expecting the onset of dizziness and sure enough, it didn't disappoint in its appearance and sensation. As the meeting drew to a close, it was palpable how much these physical symptoms of stress and anxiety began to subside, to be replaced by calmness and a feeling of immense relief. What did that place do to me over so many years?

Saturday 5th March 2016
We journeyed down to London yesterday evening to spend the best part of the weekend with Luke and Megan at their new home in Highbury. Luke, quite rightly, was very house proud. It was the first time we'd been there and within minutes, Luke was giving us the guided tour. Very kindly, they'd relinquished their room so that Lesley and I could have their bed with Elliot on a mattress that, with a small degree of manoeuvring and improvisation, they managed to squash into the corner beside us. It was snug but very comfortable. Luke is such a lovely person. He's very amiable, always attentive, kind and considerate, generous in his approach and amusing in his verbal repertoire. He always has things to say, can contribute to virtually every conversation and his personality is so welcoming and warm, it's so wonderful to witness as a parent. He's done incredibly well for himself, given the problems he has had with dyslexia and the rather slow start he made to his education at primary school. As soon as he entered secondary school, he seemed transformed into someone bursting with enthusiasm and determination, recognising his limitations, but maximising those assets to learning that meant that he was always destined to succeed, given hard work.

Luke is also blessed with character attributes that I can only look on with envy and a modicum of nervousness. This is, I hasten to add, all about me as a depressive and not him as he is, because the traits to which I refer are so alien to my condition, so fundamentally diametric to anyone who experiences mental illness in the same way that I do, that they are bound to clash when in situ. Luke is essentially spontaneous and laid back. Though he doesn't avoid the need to make arrangements, they are always subject to flexibility and circumstance, never definitive, never complete even, but forever adaptable. There are also other times when he just makes things up as he goes along, content and able to be quick on his feet, to make a decision irrespective of whether it may prove illogical or problematic in the long term. Other than major catastrophes (I recall that he rang home from Australia once when his bank card was swallowed up by a machine leaving him penniless!), he's seldom flustered and appears very comfortable in his easy-going manner, never letting the minutiae of daily living get to him. As you will know well by now, I need the opposite. I have to have certainty, well-constructed and thought-through plans, definitive and conclusive arrangements. I also ruminate, of course. When confronted by the type of approach in which Luke thrives, I immediately begin to worry. I can't help it and though at the time I wish fervently for others to be and think as I do, including my own family, when I look at things in hindsight, I certainly do not wish for this to be the case. Why should I expect anyone else to be as intricately focused, so concentrated on detail, so caught up in planning and so potentially distressed as I am wont to be?

I know Luke knows this, bless him. Apparently he was so concerned about the impact on me of the changing parking arrangements that he had made for us that he asked Lesley not to tell me what was going on. For this, I felt a sense of pride and guilt at the same time. Pride at the perception of my son, of his solicitude and thoughtfulness, but also guilty at the pressure he obviously experienced, pressure created by me and my mental health condition. Luke is also aware of the fact that social situations are never easy for me. I can do things in small doses. I can also cope if I know when something is going to come to a natural end. But if there isn't that sense of aforethought and planning, I can get easily fazed. When it comes to it, what I'm really talking about is conversation. I just find it taxing and tiring. I just can't deal with those seemingly interminable occasions when people just sit down to chew the fat about anything and everything, those long gatherings of family or friends when the sole activity, the sole purpose of coming together, is to talk. I try to concentrate and to contribute, but as time goes on, it feels more and more awkward and incongruous, contrived and bewildering. I never used to feel like this, but in the last ten years or so my estrangement in such situations has become increasingly marked to the extent that I experience real pain and anxiety after a certain point in proceedings. That point will vary depending on how well I am at the time, but it's always there. When I begin to feel that I'm approaching that defining moment, I try as hard as I can to determine a way out for me. Otherwise, nervousness can transmute into impatience, impatience into tension and tension into tangible suffering and torment, a state of affairs that inevitably will need outing and resolving. I know I'm becoming less controlled and it worries me that I will say or do something unacceptable and embarrassing. That I'll appear rude and uncaring. That I will apportion blame or verbally attack someone or something. I can't control it. The tension is too much. The experience too overwhelming. The only effective release at times like this is to walk away, to be on my own, to suffer in silence and in isolation.

Sunday 6th March 2016

There was once a time, many years ago, when football clubs reflected the geographical location of their surroundings. Every football club, that is. In this modern era, when money predominates, that is no longer necessarily the case, particularly at the elite level. Not only is there an increasing tendency to build new multi-purpose, modern but soulless grounds in out-of-town spaces, but the social circumstances, especially the finances, of players is at such variance with those of the average fan as to be essentially other-worldly. Luckily that is not the case at my beloved Millwall. Yes, the new Den is nothing like its original incarnation on old Cold Blow Lane, but the essential footballing experience down South Bermondsey way is still as it always has been, hard, tough and very raw. There is something genuinely 'democratic' about watching Millwall. Not only are the fans very much a part of what the club is all about, playing an active role behind the scenes, but they wield a significant amount of influence during the ninety minutes of a match. I know what you'll be thinking, especially those who equate Millwall with one thing and one thing only – violence – and I can't and won't pretend that there are supporters who behave not only inappropriately but offensively and unacceptably at times. But all Millwall supporters really want from their players is determination, guts and commitment. And anyone who doesn't give it, is quickly made aware of their deficiencies! In addition, Millwall supporters tend to come from the immediate area around the territory of The Den, or else they originate from these same districts of South-East London but have moved away to pastures new. Bermondsey, New Cross, Peckham and the like are ostensibly working-class in build and nature. They are tough, unyielding neighbourhoods. What you see is what you get, whether on the streets, in the markets, in the pubs, across the housing estates and, fittingly and entirely consistently, at The Den. At a recent home match against Peterborough, either the stewards or the police, I forget which, tried to restrain an elderly man. The response from the fans was to prevent this and, to all intents and purposes, to chase the police out of the stadium. Yes, this was over the top, and yes, it cannot be condoned, but the response that led to the overreaction was a genuine sense of grievance. So many times, I've seen wonderful examples of sportsmanship, concern and humanity from Millwall supporters, a sense of respect and solidarity towards local examples of social deprivation and social exclusion. Millwall's community scheme – award-winning I may add – has long focused on attempts not only to include local people within the club and its activities, but to address real social problems, alleviating genuine hardships and inequality. A few seasons ago, Millwall forewent the usual clamour to find a financially-rewarding sponsorship deal and instead formed a relationship with Prostate Cancer UK, using the charity's logo on the club shirts to draw attention to a damaging health condition. And, let it be said, Millwall are not a club that can do without financial investment, particularly in this competitive day and age. Millwall's reputation is not without substance, but it is still decidedly one-dimensional. It's far easier to attack the club for the violent or racist behaviour of a small minority than it is to recognise the tremendous goodwill and commitment towards its local communities.

I was thinking about all of this as I made my way via London Overground to The Den yesterday for the match against Blackpool. Time has stood still in the streets around the ground. The same high-rise flats, the same tenement buildings, the businesses built into the railway arches, closed-down shops and low-price supermarkets, traditional pubs and cheap car lots, the perception of poverty and disadvantage everywhere, this despite the looming presence of The Shard in the distance, a tantalising glimpse of affluence and privilege one may say, but there again, these are not attributes that would sit easily with your average resident in the tough streets around The Den. Happy with their lot. No, that would be patronising. Pride in their attributes and their club. Most definitely.

As to the match itself. Millwall, for once, were well worthy winners. Blackpool didn't help themselves with some charitable defending, a decidedly lacklustre and inept performance, epitomised by the antics of their right back who got himself sent off with fifteen minutes to go. By then Millwall were already two up and they went on to get a third with a Steve Morison penalty towards the end. Even I, pessimist as I am, the ultimate natural worrier, could afford to relax a little as they saw out the final minutes with some ease and composure. A good day at the office.

Monday 7th March 2016

I forgot to mention that last week I got offered a job. This wasn't commissioned work related to my consultancy, but an opportunity for me to be employed by a national charity. You would think, I'm assuming, that this would automatically be envisaged as 'good news'. However, in the world of a depressive, things are never straight forward or clear cut. Yes, ultimately and upon reflection I did think positive things. I was grateful. I felt humble and appreciated. I was honoured even. Nevertheless, my initial reaction was 'shit, what do I do now? I have to make a decision. I can't do that!' I realised afterwards that I actually resented being put in this position. Imagine that. You are contacted, out of the blue, by someone who wants you to work with them, someone who values what you can do, someone who considers you ideal for the task, someone who is willing to give you an opportunity to excel, someone who will pay you a salary. And your first impression is to curse them! How ungrateful. How bizarre. How plain stupid! However, you need to realise that being forced into a corner whereby you can't avoid having to decide some course of action is something a depressive like me will try and dodge wherever possible. The dilemma, the indecision, the trepidation is tangibly painful. I can't delegate here. I can ask for someone else's opinion, of course, but only I can make the choice. I can't tell you how much of a challenge this tends to be. I deliberate and deliberate. I ruminate constantly. I mull over different options, I tell myself different things, conflicting things even. I try to work out implications that are impossible to decipher. I do anything but come to a conclusion, to delay the climactic moment. Even then, I know that whatever decision I come to will leave me having to deal with the anxiety of contemplation. It never stops. Did I make the right decision? Could I have done something else? Is there another way, an option I didn't consider? What will people think of me? Will the person in question think twice before asking me again? Have I blown all my chances, now and into the future?

Perhaps what I need to tell myself is that one's gut reaction tends to be significant. That it will tend to lean towards a particular line of thinking. Maybe this is enough to go on? I really don't know. Aaarrrggghh! In this case, my initial thought was that it was wrong for me. It would have meant working directly with the

Council, with people I knew in my old section. Not people who I ever had a problem with, but still people that I associate with a context from which I had the need to flee last year. Moreover, it was equality-related work. It would have meant addressing, scrutinising, challenging work which had a personal connection. It would, I know, have meant re-examining in some detail things that I had deliberately left behind, things that I can comment on and help guide from afar, but not from within the immediate vicinity. I decided, in the end, therefore, to say 'thank you but no'.

Was I right to do so? Please, brain, stop!!

Tuesday 8th March 2016

It's gone four o'clock and my head is positively aching with a combination of pain, stress and sheer fatigue. I've spent literally all day staring at the words of my Holocaust manuscript on the computer screen, trying to decipher what's been changed and, annoyingly, correcting typos that I'm positive were not in my original draft. To say it's been a bit of a slog is a gross understatement! As I became increasingly accustomed to finding little errors – words that have been joined together, unobserved paragraph breaks, footnotes without breaks in the script – the more I focused on trying to find more. My mind refuses to be satisfied, my craving for perfection remains unfulfilled. I can't let it go! It's become a saga of epic proportions. The irritating thing is that all I was asked to do was to insert relevant photos into the text. That's all. It should have been straightforward. But as soon as I saw the first mistake, my task metamorphosed into something distinctly different, something genuinely exasperating and tiresome. I've cursed, I've shouted, I've grunted…why can't anything be simple? I've finally decided on a course of action. I'm going to have one more run through with footnote typos in mind and then that's it. I'm sending it back, as complete and as resplendent as I can make it. It's not perfect, but I've convinced myself that I'm trying to achieve the impossible. That I could still be looking at this in ten days' time and still not be satisfied. For once, I'm allowing myself to aim for 90% rather than the full house.

In all honesty, that's not a bad policy to follow. We are conditioned from our early years and particularly through the education process, to always strive for excellence. That translates, in effect, to 100%, to A*, to a level of distinction. We doggedly persevere, from one exam to another, with the ultimate score and assessment in mind. We're told to aim high. We're pestered and we're cajoled. We're encouraged and we're supported. We're shouted at, we're comforted. We're admonished, we're praised. All for something that is not just difficult or in some cases nigh on impossible, but, if you think about it a little, perhaps essentially self-destructive! If that focus on perfection carries on and permeates our life outside formal education – which it is highly likely that it will if you are that way inclined – we will effectively spend our lives failing. What quantifies a perfect cake? Or a perfect drive in a car? What equates to a perfect discussion? Or a perfect wash? How do you gauge a perfect piece of DIY? That it looks nice? That it's sturdy? That it's cost-efficient? That it lasts? What about a perfect relationship? The list could go on and on.

Yes, sometimes, more times than we currently allow, we should set ourselves up to succeed, but also to fail (if failure means non-perfection, that is!). I do do this occasionally, but I know I should do it more. Perhaps I should allow the odd crease in the ironing? Overlook a punctuation error in a report? Settle for 75% rather than anything more? After all, if everything that you do could equate to University marking, 75% is as much a first class degree as the proverbial one hundred! It's worth thinking about.

Wednesday 9th March 2016

Looking back at yesterday's entry, I realise I've missed an obvious point. Last Thursday I wrote about my fears regarding my book being returned with wholesale changes and of the impact that may have on my confidence and self-esteem. Well, it's come back, with little appreciable amendment. Whilst I wouldn't go so far as to say this is a triumph, what can this really mean other than a tangible result! Certainly, it's a massive sigh of relief. It must have been OK. It's passed the first test. Now for the general public! Oh my word, what if people are critical? What if no-one buys it? I need to physically stop myself there. I know that it's sold, because people have told me they've pre-ordered a copy. They wouldn't have done so if they weren't genuinely interested in what I have to say. The whole purpose of the book was to ask questions, to get people to think more deeply about the issues. If that happens, irrespective of whether people agree with any conclusions I've made, then again I will have succeeded. I need to set my parameters appropriately, without recourse to ill-serving judgment. To take on board constructive comments, to internalise new advice and guidance. In a nutshell, I must also learn not to beat myself up!

Our Danny would have been forty-six years old today. I think of him so often and can't help wondering what he would be like now, into middle-age. I would hope that the things that count would have remained pure and unchanged. Those wonderful sloppy kisses, those loving cuddles, his love of music and television, his passion for reading and for writing. He would have been a magnificent uncle to my children. He would have played with them as kids. He would have listened to them and cuddled them in times of need. He would have been the closest and most giving of inspirations. What I wouldn't have wanted, of course, is a continuance of the pain and discomfort he felt towards the end of his life. That was agonising to see. It destroyed me at the time and still does when I think back. I can still see his face. I can hear his laugh. I can feel his embrace. I torture myself still at his passing. I've never stopped grieving, if truth be told. I know it's often expressed, but I disagree with the notion that time heals. It enables you to cope more effectively. That much is true. But it doesn't take away the anguish and the hurt, the devastation of loss. One day, I will be able to write his story. It will be a brother's perspective of what he was, what he brought to my life, how he changed it in so many fundamental ways. I will tell of his humanity, his grace and compassion. I will talk of his achievements, his pride and his motivations. I will do my best to capture the essence of his being, the impact he had, the enduring legacy he left. I need to do this. For years, I've been frightened of the challenge, of the effect it would have on me. I couldn't face addressing what I no longer have. I guess I've associated writing about him in terms of loss rather than in positive celebration of his example of life. It means a re-orientation of thought, but I think I'm now able to meet that test, that process of reflection and conveyance, and thereby give to all at least something of what he gave to me.

Once I've finished this diary, I will turn my attention once more to Danny, my brother, my friend, my champion of the world.

Thursday 10th March 2016

I could hardly raise myself from my bed this morning. Just to move to sitting position seemed to require enormous effort and for some moments I had to resist the temptation simply to lie back down from whence I had come. Much of the morning has passed in that same lethargic state. I've worked, but it's been slow progress. I've written things and read reports, but at frequent intervals I've lapsed into reflection and rumination, occasionally interspersed by playing mournful songs on YouTube. I don't know for sure what's going on. My initial thoughts were that this was some kind of depressive hangover from yesterday, some still unfulfilled grief from the loss of my brother. This may well be what's nagging away at the back of my mind, but at its front, I've barely been able to focus on any one thing in particular. Long silences, staring into the distance or even at the plain wall in front of me. On a few occasions, I've even felt a little tearful, as if it would take only a slight prod or stimulus for me to break down completely. Nothing seems important today. I'm in perpetual 'no man's land', unable to go forward, but equally averse to drifting back into past recollections. Aimless and without purpose or motivation, I appear condemned to suffer not just in silence but in solitude. I hate to say it, but this is how I am at the onset of a depressive episode. I don't want to do anything, but I can't contemplate doing nothing. I want to escape, but can't move. It's as if the tiny flutter of my heart beating or the most miniscule of head movements is enough to grate ferociously in my head. My body has become immersed in mud or encased in concrete, it's every movement laborious, protracted and irritatingly defined. Noise emanates everywhere, despite my almost inaudible state of being. I can't do anything without alarm bells ringing incessantly and piercingly within me, advertising to no-one but myself that I'm in trouble. The mountain has taken over from the proverbial mole hill without my knowledge or permission. Is this the beginning of another period of deep depression? Of course I hope not, but only time will tell. It may be fleeting. It may be otherwise. All I know at the moment is that I'm in a vulnerable place. How, when and in what direction I move will depend not on my conscious efforts, but on the nature and course of my disability. I can move with things under my own steam, but I can't set that process, or its direction, in motion.

Friday 11th March 2016

The only thing I can say with any degree of certainty is that this is not a one-day depressive hangover from Wednesday. I awoke this morning in much the same way as yesterday. I couldn't afford the luxury of going back to sleep as I had meetings to attend and perhaps that was a good thing. It meant a focus of the mind, maybe, or a distraction, however temporary. The fact that I not only went but could contribute to the agendas should have given me some degree of confidence I guess, but that hasn't really translated as such in terms of my perceived reality. I was half-tempted when I got home to email Carol, one of my work contacts, to check that I had come across reasonably coherently and that I hadn't said or done anything out of the ordinary. I do worry about how others see me and what they think, but when I'm ill I become so pre-occupied with image and behaviour – my own of course – that I fret about every single mannerism. The nature and extent of my self-analysis is positively cruel. It's slavishly dogmatic and punishing in its condemnation. So far I have resisted the temptation to check. I've convinced myself that I will put my own depressive twist on any feedback anyway, so what's the point? I also know from past experience that what I think is being conveyed to others is often the product of my depressed inner self. In other words, it's not visibly apparent. It's not seen reality. My deductions and fears are baseless. I know too – and this may be a contradiction in the light of what I've just said – that I can mask things to a certain extent. This comes from experience. Years and years of having to pretend that I'm in control and capable, when the reality is that I feel anything but. It's not just me. Think of celebrities – comedians, musicians, artists, TV panellists, actors, sportspeople – and consider how often what they produce in terms of their 'thing', their specialism and that personae that goes with it, is different from their innermost state of being when it's running wild and subject to depression or any similar mental condition. I remember Gary Speed, the ex-Leeds footballer and manager of the Welsh national team appearing on lunchtime television the day before he took his own life. Was his anguish apparent at the time? No. It was only afterwards and with a trained eye, that one could perhaps detect that things were not right. People do perform when they are ill. And people do manage to cope by hiding, by putting up a façade intended to deceive, but of course also to reassure. To say everything's fine when it's not. I can do this and I do do this, but only to a certain extent. When I go over a certain pivotal state, I'm no longer able to carry on the deception. I succumb to my illness and to my true self at that time. I therefore become visibly ill. The irony is that when this actually happens, when I recognise how ill I really am, I also experience some sense of relief. I don't need to pretend any more. I can just be me. I shouldn't be fooled, particularly within my own family. Lesley knows when I'm getting worse. The signs are there, even if I don't always recognise them. No matter how hard I try to convince others – rather than myself – that I'm OK, I can't carry on the pretence. The masquerade must stop.

Saturday 12th March 2016

The one thing I've noticed from my last two entries is how different in nature they were to write. I'm assuming as well that they must come across as similarly at variance with my usual style and content. Having resisted the temptation to alter them, to at least make them less rambling, more coherent and yes, more logical, I think they may serve as a useful illustration to me and to you, the reader, of how things change when low mood strikes. One thing that always seems to accompany this is increased confusion and memory loss. It's difficult to explain how frightening it is to lose one's thread. I know I must be challenging to deal with. I tend to get exasperated very quickly – mostly with myself – and somehow it seems much more onerous a task to make myself clear and understood. Whether this is because words simply come out without much pre-thought, or whether my delivery changes, I don't know. Lesley does say that I mumble and I am aware that I'm much quieter. It must be this – coupled with the exhaustion of conversation – that makes me reluctant to engage with other people. I resort to one word answers. I don't seek discussion or even the barest essentials of dialogue. I shy away from opening my mouth at all. I've nothing I want to say and I can't bear the thought of entering into something which I find tiresome but also agonisingly prolonged.

I woke late this morning. A combination of fatigue and a late night at the opera in Nottingham meant that I felt justified in staying in bed a little longer than usual. Though I'm not sure that I've turned the corner, or even that I've interrupted the descent into a depressive trough, I do feel better for the immersion in Mozart that we experienced at the Theatre Royal. I can't remember a time when Mozart wasn't part of my life. From my furtive attempts at playing simple tunes on the piano when I was a kid, to my A Level thesis (on the da Ponte operas) and the hours I used to devote to wallowing in the luxury of his harmonies and melodies whilst at school, to playing in the orchestra in a production of 'The Marriage of Figaro', to reading of his life and trying to understand his genius, to countless car journeys accompanied by opera, symphony and choral masterpiece, to endless re-runs of 'Amadeus', it's been a lifetime of learning and pleasure. A devotion, I would go so far as to say. 'Così fan tutte' is one of my favourite Mozart experiences, a comic opera for sure, but one that combines the thread of comedy with a dark exposé of infidelity and betrayal. I know I'm a purist and I dare say even a bit of a 'musical snob', but I can't help feeling that Mozart's genius was rather lost on many of my companions in the theatre last night. Of course there is the potential to laugh, chuckle and smile, but some around us in the audience seemed to think they were experiencing an episode of 'Gavin and Stacey'! Hearty laughs, prolonged reactive conversations, even pre-emptive chuckles and anticipatory one-liners accompanied not just the recitative but the musical ensembles as well. I wanted to shout – to no-one in particular – 'this is Mozart, you philistines, not Rodgers and Hammerstein! 'Don't you realise the genius here? Don't you appreciate the supremacy of structure and form? Can't you treasure the musical characterisation? Don't you see the irony of the story? Of the blatant exploration of social class relations?' It didn't spoil my enjoyment, though. Art such as this has the potential to elevate one into a different stratosphere, but only if you engage in the challenge of understanding. I dare say that for many people, it's simply the melodies and the plot that entertain, but I would argue that to enrich, one needs to go much further as a listener. If you can do that, if you can rise to the challenge, the rewards are infinite and immeasurable.

It wouldn't be an exaggeration to say that music, particularly that of Mozart and Beethoven, has saved my life on many an occasion. Indeed, one of my coping mechanisms when I'm struggling is to turn to the latter. Knowing of his own battles with depression, what Beethoven produces seems to emerge from the fog of mental illness like a shining beacon, penetrating and offering clarity and direction.

It's no coincidence either, that Mozart's music is often recommended as a calming influence on babies and young children. Why? Because there is obviously something inherent in its creation that stimulates but also calms. Sheer beauty implores attention. Sheer magic captivates.

As for me on this day, I can only hope that what I went through last night works to relieve and to galvanise.

Sunday 13th March 2016

As I've mentioned a few times, there are always physical indicators of mental ill health. One of these – for me at least – is muscle pain. It's been noticeable over the course of the last few days that not only have my muscles been tired, they've ached more than usual as well. My lower back in particular has been causing me some grief. Regardless of how long I've been sitting in one position – which of course would be a natural cause of possible pain – it just seems to be more evident, more wearisome and more deflating. In other words, it's not just the pain itself that's bothering me, it's the fact that it's having an overbearing and adverse impact on my mind. The same could be said of the aches I keep experiencing in my lower right leg, over the top of my shoulders, in my left ear and jaw area and in the right side of my tummy. I'm becoming a physical as well as a mental wreck and the two are inherently intertwined. There must be some clinical explanation for this. It happens all the time. It's no coincidence. It's a manifest illustration of somebody's declining mental condition. I personally see a connection between the lethargy that overwhelms my body when I feel low, the fact that I become statuesque, incapable of moving with the same level of freedom as is my norm, and the correlation therefore that my muscles become attuned to a more sedentary nature. If they're not used to moving, if they become more 'sensitive' to movement, then it follows that they are less adaptable to the demands of everyday life. When 'forced' into action as a consequence, they ache more and become increasingly perceptible, more distinctive as a source of pain and discomfort. All I can realistically do is massage myself, rub copious amounts of ibuprofen gel into the affected areas, take one or two more pills and hope for the best. I know full well that the only real remedy is to deal with what's going on within my head, but I have no real indication of how long that affliction is going to take to run its course, irrespective of what I can do to help it to do so.

Lesley's been at the University on one of her study weekends, so Elliot and I have been largely left to our own devices. I've done some things that needed doing – washing, ironing, taking Millie out, cleaning up – and have watched some sport, but all told, it's been a distinctly unrewarding and unremarkable weekend. Leeds and Celtic both won 2-1 away from home yesterday and Millwall were within seconds of doing the same, only to concede an equaliser with virtually the last play of the match. I tried to engage with Saturday night television, only to feel frustrated and despondent watching people enjoy their recreational time with such evident gusto and carefree abandon. I'll no doubt have the football on again this afternoon, but there's little if any anticipatory excitement within my aching torso and depressed mind. I just want today to end, really. I've wanted to ever since I got up this morning.

Monday 14th March 2016

When I started writing this diary, I did wonder how I'd be able to continue when low mood eventually came. I was in no doubt that it would come – sometime, sooner or later. That wasn't the issue. Rather, it's whether I would be able to write about its reality and impact with any sense of true description, characterisation or possible explanation. Well, it's been with me now for a number of days, and I have been able to persevere and write things. That much is true. I don't know if I've managed to truly encapsulate what's been going on, however. Is that even possible, I guess I must add as a supplementary question? I do owe it to myself, and to you, to try, so here goes.

The pain and sense of loss and desolation is truly agonising. It numbs your whole being, but at the same time pierces your flesh and hammers at your soul. Every waking moment drags with a sense of protracted struggle, one that is both desperate and soul-destroying. I just want the next moment to come quickly and then the next, and so it goes on. Hour after interminable hour. Day after endless day. Everything slowing down, everything burdensome and complicated, beyond my capability and comprehension. Within a short space of time, I've become different. Less responsive. Less alert. Less motivated. Less stimulated. More taciturn. More lethargic. More muddled. More inarticulate. Increasingly disengaged. Flatter. Monotonous. Vacant. Robotic. Morose. Isolated. Uninterested. Futile. Fatalistic. A veritable shutdown. I'm treading water, but that water is not clear and easy to negotiate. It's muddy and thick. There's something inherent within it that wants to overcome. I want to relent, but there's that small element that wishes to fight, that essence of human spirt that remains intact and resistant to destruction. It's increasingly desperate, my attempts to remain on the surface. There's something inside me that is sucking the life out of my whole being. A constant drain, sapping what energy is left, taking away the vestiges of mental cognition, imploring unconsciousness and seductively persuading me to succumb to sleep, to stillness, to nothing. When I awake it may be gone? There's hope, but there's also experience. I know what to expect. I'm prepared for it. I'll come through. I'll survive. It won't defeat me. I just don't know when that 'normal' me will return. How long do I have to endure? How much will it take out of me? And what will be left for me to salvage?

Tuesday 15th March 2016

I put a message on Facebook yesterday saying that I was having another low period. I'm never quite sure whether this is a good thing to do or not. Actually, I should add that there is another more fundamental question to do with whether it really matters or whether I should be bothered about this, but that's me for you. Always having to think of all the imponderables, never satisfied unless I am one hundred per cent – or as near as damn it – certain one way or the other. When I do resort to telling everyone and anyone via social media, I earnestly hope that people don't see it as eliciting sympathy. It's most definitely not that. However, what I gain from people's good-natured responses makes such a positive difference that my premeditated thoughts are focused on what my initial message will precipitate. To some of you this may seem a very thin dividing line or even splitting hairs, but I assure you that there is an important distinction for me. I know I react positively to seeing what people have kindly and thoughtfully written. It gives me a boost. It makes me feel valued and loved. It does reenergise me and gives me a much-needed foothold for me to cling to and use as a catalyst to help myself. I can't tell you how much I appreciate people taking the time to leave me their thoughts, their goodwill, their offers of support. I don't necessarily want people to feel sorry for me, but if they do, I welcome that as an honest response to my predicament. It's a very natural thing, I know, and it's people's innate inclinations and reactions that I really need and am very fortunate to receive. It's interesting that nobody tells me to 'pull my socks up' or 'look on the bright side'. I have had those comments in the past and there are occasions when I still get the sensation of intention behind those phrases rather than the actual words themselves. I'm very fortunate to have around me people who understand what mental illness is and what it isn't. People who are sufficiently knowledgeable to realise that if I could pull my proverbial socks up and that that is all that is required to recover, then it would be the first thing I'd do! Phrases such as this are really hurtful. They belittle the experience of mental illness. They trivialise its impact. They stigmatise the sufferer. They simplify and undermine the complexities involved. On a much wider level, it's probably telling that there is now a much greater awareness of these issues, particularly the damage that unthoughtful but much-used wordage can do and, of course, convey. We're maturing as a society when it comes to mental ill health. Having said that, we still have a long way to go. Examples of stigma and discrimination are still far too prevalent. Understanding and awareness is still in its relative infancy. Words are an important part of this equation. They are a powerful antidote to suffering, a calming and reassuring mechanism for good. They can also be punitive and destructive, stigmatising and belittling. Like in every context of life, we need to learn how to use them appropriately, positively and helpfully.

Wednesday 16th March 2016

Another strong motivation for my writing on Facebook is my desire to be open and transparent. I have nothing to hide. I'm not embarrassed about my condition and feelings and find talking about them to be quite natural and logical. Challenging, yes. Difficult, most certainly at times. But demeaning or in any sense degrading, definitely not. Why should this be so for me? Because depression is such an engrained part of my whole self and has been for so long, that it's as accustomed a topic of conversation for me as holidays, weekend pursuits and the antics of friends and relatives are to others. Please don't misunderstand me. I'm well aware of the stigma and discrimination that still tends to accompany mental ill health. How can I be not? I know too that my routine conversations about depression and OCD and how they impact on me can lead to difficulties in the sense that other people may treat me differently, even with discriminatory intent. I know that some people may find such transparency odd, unsettling or disturbing. But that is for them to come to terms with. Not me. Why should I alter my approach to myself simply because others cannot or will not relate to it? Being candid, plain-speaking and unashamedly detailed, though exacting and tough at times, can only help others who are more reserved and circumspect, to be the same if it means that they can fully confront what is happening inside their minds and talk to others of their issues. Our society requires a more mature and productive context for mental illness to go alongside the need for greater understanding and compassion in relation to those who suffer.

I would like to hope that this open approach has paid off with regard to Elliot. If this afternoon is anything to go by, it has. I had to take him to his initial CAMHS[10] assessment. He was very nervous beforehand, as is understandable, but once he overcame those natural hesitations he was superb, answering the questions with thoroughness and a lucidity that really belies his age. He talked of his troubles. He explained his trains of thought. He outlined in some detail the manifestations of his OCD. He was not shy, neither did he hold anything back. Most impressively, for me, he was assured and comfortable when faced with someone probing him about his life and his feelings. I'm not sure I could have been as such at his age. The outcome was that he now goes on a waiting list for Cognitive Behavioural Therapy, but also for some group activity related to anxiety management. Both, I believe, will do him no amount of good. As he left the building, I could see his pride at what he had just done. It wasn't just that he was relieved that it was over. He knew within himself that he had just achieved something quite considerable. He had conquered his fears, but he had done so in a manner that was obviously both liberating and enriching. I can't express how proud I am to be his Dad.

Thursday 17th March 2016

Whoever designed the Government website by which one can register as self-employed quite obviously did not have mental illness in mind when doing so! Actually, to be fair to the individual(s) in question, it is probably the process itself that is the problem, not its superficial camouflage, its dressing up, so to speak! Irrespective of whether you insert nice friendly, relaxing images or try to reassure constantly through various methods of terminology, it is never going to be an exercise devoid of stress or anxiety. I know I'm probably quite typical in this respect, but as soon as officialdom looms, I begin to panic. Legal requirements (and money for that matter!) seem to induce in me an overwhelming rush of adrenalin and sheer terror! I quite literally go to pieces. I can't focus. I can't concentrate. My powers of understanding and logic go out the window. I read and re-read every sentence without it really penetrating or even disturbing my consciousness. I can't get out of my mind the horrifying thought that whatever it is I put on the form, it's bound not just to be wrong, but to lead to some punitive consequence. I'm going to be fined, or worse! The catastrophizing thread that leads from one simple question to a spell in prison is laid out before me in overt and accentuated detail. To be honest, it's not the consequence that is the fundamental issue. It's the fact that question follows question and therefore decision follows decision. I can manage my name and address, even my National Insurance number. But it's when I'm given choices, or asked a succession of related questions designed to decipher what kind of service I want or what position I am (or whatever), that's the time for me to become a quivering wreck, incapable of commitment or resolution.

I set out the other day to become officially self-employed. It took less than a minute for me to give in, to recognise that I was out of my depth. What I was trying to follow just became a mess, a conflagration of words and even letters that seemed indecipherable and beyond my capability to digest and comprehend. It wasn't helped by the fact that the site was so complex, so concentrated, it became impossible for me to focus on one thing at a time. Instead of one question per page, which would have been easier, there seemed to be a constant barrage of interconnected requirements, a mass of options and associated links. I was like a toddler trying to read the most undiluted, compressed version of 'War and Peace'! I craved simplicity, clarity…and the odd image! I had to call for Lesley. Immediately, she took control. Her organised and uncorrupted mind made the process appear so straightforward and coherent I could have laughed and cried at the same time.

There is, though, a big lesson for Government departments and indeed any organisations here. What if I didn't have Lesley to hand? It's alright saying that you can call a helpline if you're stuck, but what if you can't use the phone? What if your communication skills and confidence are so negligible that you can't make that connection? The likelihood is that, like me, all you really desire is immediate gratification, an end to the task in question. Resorting to email is fine, but what if there isn't a prompt reply? You end up begging for a resolution. So what is the easiest thing to do? You put the most appropriate answer down just to finish things. It may not be the right answer though. It may be that you're not maximising use of the service you require. It may be that you just don't understand what's being asked and you therefore stipulate something or give an answer that is simply quick rather than accurate. Your desire to escape supersedes everything else. And what could you be left with? Potentially, consequences that are far-reaching, frightening, maybe even damaging, simply because you can't cope with a process that is far too intense and fraught with worry.

Even now, I'm not sure what I put on the various pages. Lesley knows though and therein lies my salvation and my coping mechanism. What would I do without her?

Friday 18th March 2016

I've spent all day at a training workshop on improving healthcare for multi-ethnic populations. When I'm unwell, I face a huge dilemma when it comes to things such as this, aside from whether I actually go to them at all that is. On the proviso that I do attend, how do I participate? Do I keep things to a minimum and effectively play it safe? Or do I try to engage as normal? There isn't an easy answer to this conundrum. The former rather isolates me. It marks me out as different. The latter runs the risk of failing to meet expectation. I do have a reputation for positive contribution and engagement – I know I do, and I'm proud of that. However, with it comes a presumption that not only will you participate as normal, but that you will do so in a fashion that is constructive, enthusiastic, knowledgeable and articulate. What if, as a result of my mental state, I can't deliver? Am I setting myself up to fail? But can I avoid this? So, back to basics. I have to somehow decide beforehand whether my involvement will serve to increase my confidence (and possibly aid my recovery) or, by contrast, solidify the fears that I won't meet expectations or, worse, that I will appear incapable or unable to do my job. So much to think about, and I'm not even through the front door yet!

I did decide – or rather it was half decided for me through a little bit of peer pressure – that I would go for it. As it happened, I was able to contribute, but it felt contrived, awkward, forced even. I wasn't sure whether what I was saying was pertinent, let alone logical. I couldn't gauge from people's reactions. I didn't get that reassurance from seeing nodding heads or approving smiles. Or at least I don't think I did because, if I'm honest, I wasn't sufficiently aware of what was going on around me. It was as if there was a distinct atmosphere haze, that people were blurred, out of focus and consequently out of recognition. I felt very lonely and isolated as I spoke, a voice quite literally 'crying out in the wilderness', craving attention and gratification but consumed by doubt and ambivalence. When I wasn't speaking, I was conscious of feeling physically uncomfortable. I shuffled around on my seat, trying to eradicate the aches and pains that seemed to consume my body. I felt lethargic, sleepy and slow. Turning my head was an effort. Keeping in tune and time with the surroundings, with the conversation and level of debate was difficult. It became an immense intellectual challenge. Lacking the powers of concentration, I wrestled more and more with the simple task of staying with it, invoking increased demands from within to focus amidst the confusion of interrupted cognition. The more I tried, the greater the challenge. I couldn't keep up with the pace and with the pressure I was putting on myself just to understand. It's no wonder that I now feel completely shattered.

I was grateful for the fact that I had good people around me. A supportive environment shouldn't be too much to ask, but in my experience it doesn't always come with the territory. I have that now and I treasure it. I truly do.

Saturday 19th March 2016

We're having some new chairs for the front room delivered this morning. Instead of looking forward to revelling in newly-acquired luxury, I'm actually dreading it. It's not just that I'm attached to my old chair, it's the fact that something new and perfect is about to enter my domain and all that can happen – in my mind at least – is that the perfection is going to be spoilt. Gradually, over time, things will happen to the chairs – drinks spilled, Millie's hair and mud from her walks, dust and scrapes – to erode the immaculate condition of what we've just bought. For me, I would be content at this moment in time just to look at the chairs and never actually sit in them! I've always felt like this about new things. I had a new camera as a Christmas present a number of years ago and, unlike my kids who immediately open and discard the box, tear at the packaging and simply can't wait to switch on whatever it is, I just put it on a shelf for months. I just couldn't face the prospect of trying to adjust my mind to a new object. I was scared that I'd do something to spoil it, to break or damage it. I didn't want dust or anything to settle on it and scar it with the evidence of everyday living. It took one heck of a leap of faith to eventually devote some time to what had been given to me, and even then I had to do it in stages. I spent ages, for example, looking at the instruction manual, trying to devour every single step of the process of making it work, before even turning to the object itself. I'm the same when it comes to new clothes. Straight away I put whatever it is on a hangar and there it stays for a week or more. Like an evocative painting, I marvel at its texture, its colours, its shape. The prospect of blemishing it by exposing it to my body, my sweat in particular, is just too much to bear. I protect it intensely, doing everything I can to ensure that it doesn't get dirty. Even when it does, there is a further obstacle to face, particularly for white clothing, in that I don't want to wash it and make it lose its purity, the novelty of its brightness. My reluctance to buy anything new, therefore, doesn't just stem from the natural frugality of a Yorkshireman, it's a reflection of my relationship with perfection. It's not just my perfection that obsesses me, it's that of things around me.

The other thing this morning that is weighing heavy on my mind is my tiredness. The thought of moving furniture around, even though it shouldn't take long, is daunting in the extreme. When just moving out of a seat is difficult, anything up and above that appears virtually impossible. It's hard to describe the nature and extent of the fatigue that attaches itself to mental illness. It's both mental and physical, but it's difficult to distinguish one from the other. I sometimes find myself panting even when I'm sitting down, contemplating my next move. I guess it's the feeling of weight that is the common factor. If you can imagine the heaviest object attaching itself like a leech to your body – and everywhere on your body at that – then you may begin to appreciate what it's like. The sensation of heaviness, of every movement being cumbersome and sapping, of the prospect of having to move eating away at you, telling you that you can't do it, that you have to stay still, it all plays on your mind, convincing you that if you need to move, you need to do so with caution and to pace yourself. The urge simply to do nothing is overwhelming.

And despite all this, I've told Lesley that tomorrow morning I'm going to clean the house! My friend and former colleague, Chantelle, is coming with her family for Sunday dinner and, as Lesley has a painful back at the moment, I have to step up to the challenge of making things presentable. Oh God, how am I going to do that?

Sunday 20th March 2016

What a day! Somehow I can't quite believe that I came through it relatively unscathed. Apart from one heck of a tired body and mind, that is. My morning was mostly spent cleaning and ironing, not jobs that I relish – hardly surprisingly – and today, of all days, I couldn't fall back on the coping mechanism of doing things in short time spells with breaks. I had to compromise on perfectionism. Not an easy thing to do and at times I had to resist the almost unbearable temptation to ensure that every stain, every blemish, every piece of dirt was accounted for. Time, you see, was not on my side. Or it was if you wanted an excuse not to do things as thoroughly as usual! (if you catch my drift) I persevered, under Lesley's watchful gaze, covering the essentials, the observables, making sure that nothing stood out for our guests. Every time I clean, I want to preserve my efforts as much as I can and for as long as I can. That means exercising the impossible. Yearning for people – and dog – not to spoil what

I've done by using equipment and surfaces that I've cleaned, even having the temerity to walk on my sparkling, unsullied floor! Just look at this, I say to myself. How can you ruin what I've laboured so hard to produce by carrying on the process of everyday living? It's not fair. You're provoking me. You want me to do it again and again. To cover up after you. To erase every fault, every smear. To perfect every imperfection.

Following a haircut, beard trim and shower, I made my way to a community centre in the city where I was due to deliver a talk to a group about my mental illness, its origins, development, manifestations and impact. The group has only recently come together, inspired by the vision of a good friend of mine, and works at promoting positive messages in relation to mental health, helping those in need, offering support and guidance and trying to dispel some of the many myths and misconceptions that sadly still surround the domain. I was the last of three guest speakers and I had a real tough task on my hands to follow my predecessors, both of whom spoke openly, bravely and with tremendous dignity. I wasn't sure how long I would have and to be honest, I was only expecting to speak for ten minutes or so. However, when I got to the venue, I was greeted by the organiser with the words 'thirty minutes OK for you?' In almost every other field – the Holocaust probably being the only exception – I would have struggled with the immensity of the time requirement, but this didn't faze me at all. I was comfortable and actually grateful, that I had some room for manoeuvre, that I could dwell on some issues that ordinarily I would have to skirt over. I hadn't prepared anything as such, but I'm accustomed to doing this now so it wasn't difficult to have a broad agenda in my mind and simply talk. I began by describing my near brush with suicide at London Bridge station in 2014, proceeded to talking about my life, my growing awareness of mental instability, the diagnosis, my symptoms and their ramifications and concluded by offering some thoughts on whether depression really is a 'hidden disability' (I don't believe it is) and on how I believe that my condition – despite its ravages, its challenges and its agonies – has helped me in a positive way. It seemed to go well and I was quietly pleased that, despite my current low mood, I'd still been able to deliver something that people appreciated.

Very soon after I got home, Chantelle and her family arrived and we had a very pleasant couple of hours eating, drinking, catching up and getting to know her husband, and their lovely daughter. Even though I really had to force myself to raise my game and contribute when, truth be told, I simply wanted to sit and doze, they were such good company that it wasn't as hard as I'd anticipated to join in the conversations and enjoy their friendship. Chantelle is virtually the only regret I have about leaving the Council. I miss her everyday presence, her compassion and her ease at making me feel valued. She was so welcoming when I joined the Authority all those years ago, and despite us working in different fields, I've always relished her insight as well as her encouragement and solidarity. I hope she feels the same. Those few hours – which sped very quickly – took it out of me though and for much of the remainder of the evening, I remained locked to a chair trying to keep awake, unable to exert myself into doing much more than watching a screen. It felt acceptable though to wallow and 'chill'. The self-critical pressure that I exert on myself, that self-accusatory scrutiny that persists in forcing me to justify my use of time and even my existence, still nagged at my consciousness, but, for once, I managed to keep it from biting.

Monday 21st March 2016

One thing I forgot to mention yesterday evening that did threaten to disturb the calm that I had worked hard to maintain was something so simple, so inconsequential, that in the cold light of day it seems difficult to contextualise or reason. I made the mistake of looking at my emails at one point and found that one mass email that I'd sent on Friday obviously hadn't been delivered to at least one of its intended recipients. Instead of looking to see whether it was just one individual or all ten, I purposely deleted it to prevent myself knowing and thereby possibly acting. This was a massive mistake as I spent fully an hour speculating and ruminating. I found it impossible to reach a conclusion that would quell the growing anxiety within me and instead catastrophized, reasoning that it must have been all ten and that the problem was something to do with my email system itself, not just with one individual message. Then began the one plus one equals five train of illogical thinking, spiralling me into such doubt and helplessness that I thought I would have to resort to diazepam. I tried the Lesley route, asking her to help me to look at the issue logically and dispassionately, but she was unable to provide me with the categorical certainty that I was seeking. It never strikes me whenever this happens that what I'm asking for is the impossible, that there isn't the unambiguous sureness that I crave. I'm not capable of reasoning this out and coming to that same conclusion. I effectively want the miraculous. I ended up determining on a course of action, to reduce each of my email group lists to five rather than ten, just in case it is the number of recipients that is the issue. However, for an hour or so, and just before bedtime as well, I realised that this whole problem was threatening to be the straw that broke the camel's back. The fact that I didn't decide to take sedative medication was a good thing in hindsight, I suppose. I managed to keep myself above water through my own cognitive efforts, even if I was treading wildly and intensely at times.

This morning it seems like the proverbial mountain and molehill. Ridiculous, incredulous, trivial and simply plain stupid.

In reflection, I often wonder at how I get myself so hot under the collar, but I've determined that this isn't any use to me because all I succeed in doing in ruminating over what has already happened is to scold myself incessantly and harshly. And for what? I can't change the past. It doesn't stop me looking back though, even this realisation and understanding.

If only I could just live in the moment and look forward. But I can't. The past seems to be both my refuge and my punishment.

Tuesday 22nd March 2016

I am unpleasantly irritable when I'm in the midst of a depressive episode. It seems to go with the territory. I recognise it. I know I'm doing it. But I can't seem to do anything about it. The problem stems from the fact that I don't see it coming. I can be fine one second – low yes, but also calm and placid – and then all of sudden I'm something totally different. It doesn't take much. There aren't even any particular stimuli. It can be something somebody's said or not said, something somebody's done or not done. Something tangible and obvious, something hidden and imperceptible. I'm aware of what I'm doing when I'm doing it. I am conscious of the fact that my fire has been lit. I know that I'm being unreasonable and overdramatic. But my mind refuses to adjust my behaviour. It's as if there is total disconnect. The irrationality, the nonsense, the 'madness' if you like, consumes me. It directs my body and my mouth. It's like a sudden onset of a fearsome fever, one-directional and unrelenting. Only when the balance between brain and action changes in favour of the former do I begin to calm myself and to recognise what's happened. I'm full of remorse afterwards. I beg forgiveness. I hope for understanding, for empathy, for consideration. I pray that any damage I've done – not physical but emotional – is brief, minimal and soon forgotten. I'm embarrassed. I'm appalled. I hate myself. I don't recognise what I've become but I know it's still me.

If left unquenched, the fire can lead to something far more terrifying. I'm talking here of self-harm. I am not immune from its vicious but compelling clutches. It's such a hard thing to describe because in my experience, there's no denying the fact that, despite its awful severity, it can also be attractive and seductive. It's only afterwards, when I'm more together and conscious of my surroundings, that I realise what has happened and reflect, mercilessly, on what I've done. I'm full of self-recrimination and sorrow. I'm ashamed, particularly if there's been a witness. I pray for deliverance, for reprieve, for non-judgmental reflection. I hope I'm not tarred emotionally and with respect to others' confidence. I hope I'm not castigated or vilified. I just want to break down and submit, to fall into Lesley's arms and stay there, protected and comforted. I'm aware that this is all me. That what I've done impacts on others, particularly my loved ones. I don't know how to make it right. How to be what I believe I should be, the protector, the strong one, the rock. How to regain my dignity, my respect and the strength of my desired identity. How to recover the trust, the confidence, of those close to me.

Fortunately, in my case, episodes of self-harm are rare. I don't cut or scratch. I hit my head, sometimes very hard and more than once. My reasoning, if you can call it that, is quite simple. I believe that the inside of my brain harbours my problem, my disability, my disease. I want to target it at source. I want to punch it out. To physically dispel it. My head is the cause of my struggles, my agony, so to rid myself of its fierce and piercing manifestations, all I need to do is hit it and hit it hard. It's logical isn't it? Or so I convince myself. My other deduction connects to the first. That the consequence of this physical battering is often a headache or maybe even concussion. My mental torment has transferred into a physical pain, and moreover, a physical pain that can be alleviated by medication or sleep.

I haven't self-harmed for quite a while now. But I'm very much aware that during this current low period, when irritation and frustration tend to be more evident, I'm also more susceptible to harming myself. I need to be vigilant and I guess I need the help and understanding of others to keep an eye on me and to react when whatever warning signs there may be begin to materialise and threaten to overwhelm what has become a vulnerable interior and exterior.

I must be a horrible person to live with or be around at times.

Wednesday 23rd March 2016
There seems to be a lot going on around me at the moment. I use these words advisedly because there's probably no more than usual. It just appears to be the case. When it's difficult to

see beyond the next day or even the next task, anything over and above that is largely out of reach, beyond my capacity to digest, contextualise and address. With myself, I have work and I also have quite varied work. Each day brings its own challenge and its own uniqueness. Take today for example. I began by addressing some email correspondence in relation to a couple of health-related initiatives with which I'm involved. As I scanned through what I'd received on Outlook, I saw a number of other opportunities for me to link up with people interested in working on very broad programmes to do with community empowerment and the active citizenship stuff that I'm working with John to develop. I then decided I needed to rework my email community groups into smaller numbers which necessitated some mind-numbing admin readjustments. Then, following a break for exercise and to see the end of the England – Afghanistan Twenty20 international (which England came perilously close to losing!), I made my way to the Friends Meeting House to a meeting of a mental health group which I'm currently helping by providing them with an evaluation report. Spending a couple of hours with some lovely, but obviously quite vulnerable, people certainly gives you a sense of perspective and a reality check, and yet I felt so at home there amidst not just the sad reality, but also the creative freedom of mental illness. To see people energised and captivated by a marvellous project was truly humbling.

I know I'm living life a little bit more on the edge at the moment, given my low mood. I'm able to cope with the demands of what work I have. I can keep my head above the surface, recognising that my obligations are sufficiently flexible to accommodate times like this. It's when I try to keep up with the vagaries of family life that I began to lose that sense of reality that requires thought and action. It seems that everyone, bar Luke possibly, is experiencing testing times. Rachel and Joel are still overseas. Their return to home shores is now imminent, though still dependent on extraneous factors, complicated by relationships on the one hand and the start of a new job in Europe on the other. Elliot is finding school a bit of a handful and I know will be glad of the pending Easter break. Yet again, he's being bullied and once more I find myself facing a visit to the school's pastoral care team. Different people seem to be involved but the issues don't seem to go away. He's also adjusting himself to the demands of exams and assessments, knowing that there are huge expectations on his very young shoulders. I've tried to take the heat off him, by getting him to realise that his happiness is our primary concern, that we just want him to do his best, irrespective of the result, but being a high achiever brings its own internal pressures, and I think the real challenge is within his own mind. Lesley is coping wonderfully with the trials and tribulations of getting back into work but it's all the other things that seem to be lying in wait on the 'things to do' list that keep focusing and refocusing her attention. She seems to attract dependency, bless her. People turn to her for help and practical assistance, and, such is her kind and giving nature, she doesn't turn people down or even put them on hold. How she deals with all that goes through her mind, I just don't know. I'm bewildered at the very concept.

Life, its complexities and its variance, goes on therefore. Whilst I am forced once more into survival mode, around me nothing stops. I become a reluctant witness at times, frustrated but incapable, bound by my disability yet desperately fighting to remain lucid and involved. I try to concentrate on small steps, little challenges, intermittent connection. If I can do this, I'm still useful and I'm still relevant. It's not much to cling on to, but it's something.

Thursday 24th March 2016

What a night! It's not surprising that I have difficulties getting up at the minute when my sleeping hours are so vivid and lifelike. It's difficult to conceptualise what I go through as rest because most of the time my sleep is anything but restful and otherworldly. If anything, I seem to come alive. I experience all the physical sensations of living whilst conscious, whether that be pain, fright, anger, worry, exhilaration, anxiety or whatever else. I am also very much aware of how tiring it all seems to be. It's as if I'm undergoing real physical exertion. I'm walking, running, jumping sometimes. I'm pulling at things. I'm pushing stuff away. I'm kicking and lashing out. I'm holding my head. I'm grappling. I'm stretching. But all the time, I'm asleep. Of course, only rarely do I remember what I dream about. I should write it all down as soon as I waken, as various therapists have told me to do over the years. I do remember part of last night's dream related to being on top of a very tall edifice, having to negotiate the challenge of moving from a precarious position to one of relative safety. I couldn't make my mind up whether to move or not. I was really wrestling with the notion of whether I cared sufficiently what happened to me to make a decision on my next step. If I wasn't bothered, it didn't matter what I did, whether I lived or died in the effort of moving, or whether I remained, hanging by a thread, awaiting whatever fate had in store.

All this is, as you will no doubt appreciate, entirely relevant to my current depressive episode. Trying to learn from my dreams is one of the reasons why I would be reluctant to take anything that prevented me from having such evocative analogies of my troubles, or even a tempering of their clarity, irrespective of how disturbing or how challenging and anxiety-inducing they are. I need them sometimes to contextualise where I am, to propound choice, to illustrate danger or to point to what I can do to help myself. As such, it is easy to see how I often live my life through sleep. Not to escape from reality, but to help me make sense of it. On the other side of the coin, though, I'm very conscious and quite scared at the impact this has on my sleeping behaviour, particularly when I'm ferociously lashing out. Lesley needs danger money at times. Last night I found myself trying to grab her in my sleep and I've often kicked out and made contact with her leg as I furiously try to escape from whatever situation is trying to confine me in my dreams. It's probably one of the reasons, thinking aloud now, why I tend to sleep with my legs stretching out the other side of the bed. That way, any physicality is directed at the wall rather than her. I'd much rather have bruised toes or worse making contact with concrete than hurt anyone else. Please don't misunderstand me. I hope I'm not coming across as some form of violator or bully. I'm most definitely not, and am appalled at the possibility that you may think me so. Lesley understands, bless her, and she helps me when I'm most upset by waking me up. I can be screaming, quite literally.

I guess it's a very thin line between what we mostly understand by the terms 'dream' and 'nightmare'. I can't really distinguish between the two. Perhaps for me, it's more accurate to say that my dreams are nightmarish in essence in the sense that they are often vivid, disturbing and scary, but wholly attune to living reality. Whereas my nightmares – if by that we mean things and situations that are out of this world – are infrequent and, precisely because of their outlandish nature, actually less distressing.

The consequences of all this are many and varied. One thing, though, always remains the same. During times of despair and crisis, when all that I've described elevate to maximum levels, I find little respite, during the day or at night. I don't rest properly. I can't rest properly. Tiredness needs an outlet, but when I sleep I only use up very small proportions of the rest I need. I never meet the required amount. I certainly never exhaust the supply. I'm destined to struggle until my mind begins to readjust and I come through the other side of the dark tunnel.

Friday 25th March 2016

Good Friday. Though, to be honest, I can't see what's so good about this one. I'm sorry if that appears sacrilegious or disrespectful to those of you of the Christian faith, but I'm speaking from a purely secular point of view with respect to one more day in the calendar and one more day in my current depressive episode. As a Jewish man, though, I'm tempted to make reference to the fact that this day has been, over the ages, a particularly sensitive one for the Jewish people. Traditionally, it's been an occasion for many Jews to retreat behind their front doors, aware of the heightened threat of antisemitism emanating from the age-old accusation that Jews killed Jesus Christ. It should be hoped that that phenomenon be confined to the historical scrapheap, but sadly, I suspect in many places throughout the world, it hasn't been and sadly, never will be.

To Christians, wherever they may be, I most sincerely send warm wishes and greetings at this special time of the year for them. My Mum, being one, will most certainly be experiencing an elevated spirituality and a closeness to Jesus and to God over the course of the next few days, and I'm thinking of her and her co-religionists with a fervent wish for global peace and religious reconciliation.

Lesley and Elliot will be out for much of the day. This morning they've gone to a cookery class (!) and this evening they're going to the circus in Newark. I couldn't face the prospect of either, so Elliot's invited his friend Maddy to use my ticket for the latter. Truth be told, I'm no fan of circuses at the best of times. It's probably a legacy of the fact that when I was a kid, they seemed always to be on the telly – often on different channels at the same time – and such being the restricted choices available (effectively BBC's One and Two and ITV), it felt like saturation, and an irritating one at that. Elliot's always liked them though. It just shows that not everything is handed down from one generation to the next!

What will I be doing today then? Honestly. If I had to say the first thing to come to mind it would be 'seeing the day through to its conclusion'. I can't summon up the energy to do more than go through the motions. I'll probably do a bit of work, watch the television, read a bit, exercise a bit more. Nothing exciting and nothing exceptional, certainly nothing out of the ordinary. I will have a shower. That I must do. When times are rough, taking care of yourself becomes a massive challenge. It's not laziness, it's a sense of futility that's at play here. I just can't see the reason why cleaning oneself, usually a routine part of everyday living, is that important. I have to force myself to do it. Yesterday,

I just couldn't be bothered. I wasn't going out. Nobody other than Lesley and Elliot would see me. I didn't smell. I wasn't dirty. So why bother? When I think of when I'm relatively well, when the slightest trace of sweat precipitates an immediate wash, the contrast is both amazing and alarming.

Saturday 26th March 2016

There are times when I just can't find the words to describe depression and its consequences. I think today is one of those. Words just seem completely inadequate. Looking back at what I've written previously and specifically those adjectives that obviously came to mind at the time, none of them do justice to the way I feel just now. Desolate. Futile. Agonising. Dispiriting. Purposeless. None of them. If depression at its most severe is hard to describe, it is most definitely harder to live with. If only I could wish away the time in oblivion. Sleep isn't enough, because of my propensity to dream and to dream vividly. It has to be oblivion, a state of being where one simply doesn't register what is happening, when nothing disturbs the darkness, the paralysis of the mind, where nothing lives aside from a pumping heart. It's so close, so tantalisingly near, to what I suspect is the reality of death. Except that I hope death leads to something more pure and spiritual, a reunion with loved ones without the pain of living, the heartache of loss or the futility of an aimless existence. I know this is dangerous. That a couple of steps further into the darkness may bring the immensity of suicide nearer to contemplation. I think I have to let Lesley know, so that she can keep a watch over me.

It's the contrasts that I find really challenging. I want to sleep, but I don't want to dream. I want to be busy, but there's nothing that can keep me focused. I want to be active, but I crave rest. I want to be at home, but its walls seem confining. I want to be alone, but I yearn for company. Wherever I am at any one time, I want to be somewhere else. Whatever I'm doing, I want to move on. I'm not able to live in the moment. It's too hard, too painful.

For a brief period this morning, there was an element of respite. Having got up and made my breakfast, I flicked through the film channels, only to find 'Amadeus' mid-movie. I can't begin to relay the effect this film had on me when it was first released. It was positively inspirational. It impacted on me musically as one would expect. I think my 'cello playing moved on to a different level, one more crafted, more spiritual, more enlightened even. Certainly more mature. But my musical appreciation and understanding grew much more succinctly and fundamentally. I became consumed by music, particularly that of Mozart. I appreciated its form and structure, its simplicity in melody amidst the complexities of harmonic usage. Its boldness and radical overtones. Its power to captivate and to move emotionally. Moreover, not only did it make me a better musician, it made me more appreciative of beauty in life. It empowered me. It lifted me. It enriched my whole being. I used to go to sleep with the sounds of Mozart in my ears.

The film is now thirty-two years old. I find that too hard to believe. Maybe if I can reconnect with its message and its impact, I will be able to find a way out of my current predicament. Herr Mozart may once more come to my rescue.

Sunday 27th March 2016

Today is our wedding anniversary. Eighteen years ago this lunchtime, Lesley and I were formally married at the Registry Office in Leicester. I can honestly say that was one time when I was truly happy. I remember well loving every moment, wanting each one to last forever. I was eager, impatient even, to begin married life. I looked forward to things. I revelled in the new responsibilities, particularly with three young children, and couldn't wait to share what I had and what I'd been through with my new extended family. Despite what has happened to me health-wise since, our marriage is stronger than ever, as is my love and devotion to my family unit. Amidst the indecision that hampers my daily reality, irrespective of my inability at times to make the most elementary commitment to things, to decipher one path, one course of action, one object from another, the most important decision I ever had to make, I got right. That was to ask Lesley to marry me, to entwine our lives for all time.

I just wish I was able to give her a more encouraging outlook at the moment. The last thing I want today of all days is for her to worry about me. I'm doing my best to at least look more positive and engaging, but it's hard to take on depression at any time and almost impossible when you're at your lowest ebb. I'm trying. We took Millie to the Country Park this morning and went for a coffee in Oadby afterwards. I didn't really want to go, but then again, I wasn't too enamoured at staying at home either. It was an effort, but I made it. I told her last night of what I'd written in my diary yesterday. She's concerned, obviously, but we've been there before and I guess that experience will always stand us both in good stead for the ongoing battle with my demons. She suggested that I contact my consultant and I think she's right. My next scheduled appointment isn't until 19th May and that seems an awfully long way away as I write. I suspect that the issue of changing medication will arise again and this time it's hard to make a case for the status quo. I'll ring on Tuesday and see if I can be seen earlier.

Lesley also made me aware that my desire to seek isolation may not always be the best one as far as Elliot is concerned. It's true that when I'm really low I withdraw into my shell. It's a coping mechanism for me but I also tend to think, without questioning the logic, that it has to be better for everyone else. That way those concerned don't have to put up with any tension or anxiety engendered by my mood. They can be themselves without feeling any pressure to compromise. They can smile, laugh and be jolly without compromising on guilt or awkwardness. However, Lesley made me think about whether this is always necessarily the best course of action. On reflection I think she's right (again!). Elliot is no fool. He knows when things aren't good. He's had his own lifetime to realise this and to make his own adjustments. He is aware of the challenges of depression and of mental illness. He has a condition himself now of course. I shouldn't treat him like an infant. My desire to protect may well project an unintended impression to alienate, or at least to push him away. That is certainly not my intention but I now see how what I tend to do may result in him feeling this way. We have good and occasionally very deep discussions about vulnerability and illness. I have never tried to be anything but honest with him, but I guess that standpoint is threatened when I become very ill. I don't lie to him. I never do. But I'm not as open as I am when my mind is more intact. The bottom line is that I need to learn the lessons from my relationship with my own father. He too tried to protect, to cushion and to shelter and in doing so, he often erected a shield around himself, his condition and his innermost feelings, a shield on which was stated 'I'm OK, don't worry, but don't ask'. Love too was his motivation. Nothing else. But of course I wasn't duped. I was too astute, but didn't want to impose on his upset, his grief and his own depression. I would hate to think that there were any barriers between Elliot and myself, no matter how unintentional their construction and ongoing fabrication. So I need to make some changes. My way, my methods, my approach is now much clearer. Thanks once more to my rock, my wife.

Monday 28th March 2016

I woke up this morning with really aching shoulders. Actually, come to think of it, I went to bed with them as well, but they were ten times worse when I eventually got up. This always happens when my mood is low. Irrespective of how much exercise or simple movement I do, I seem to attract aches and pains. In actual fact, it's probably in inverse proportions to bodily motion. The less I move, the more I suffer. I'm sure there are proper, credible physiological explanations for this. Probably something to do with restricted movement, with rigidity and the impact on muscles, tendons and all the mechanics that contrive to enable someone not just to move from position one to position two, but to move any and every part of one's anatomy. Yesterday, I spent an inordinate amount of time in one chair. From roughly two o'clock to gone ten, my only movements were to the toilet and to the kitchen, and even then, these were hardly frequent. Lesley and Elliot had gone around to her sisters for a family Easter meal. I just couldn't face the prospect of loads of people and non-stop conversation, noise and bustle, so I stayed at home to fend for myself. One meal to prepare isn't much of a radical departure from my sedentary existence. I only had to ensure synchronicity between microwave and oven and their respective cooking times. That's all. It was pre-prepared, package-orientated and simple. In just over twenty minutes, that was it. All done. Thinking back now, with the benefit of hindsight, I should have spent more time moving around the house at least. I must have sat there for fully seven hours in total! And, added to that, I couldn't get myself comfortable. Whether it's because the chairs are new and I'm still adjusting to them, or whether the problem emanated solely from within me and I'm just using the chairs as a convenient excuse, I don't really know. For some reason, my new chair seems to be less flexible, less soft and a bit more restrictive. In my old one, I could flail my legs over the sides, I could virtually lie down with my feet resting on the fireplace, everything (almost) was possible. What I mustn't do is let my predisposition for the used, the familiar, for routine and ritual, cloud my ability to adapt to something new and something that should be inherently uplifting. It's not every day one gets new furniture after all!

Today, I've at least gone out. I went with Lesley into Market Harborough. Just for a coffee and a quick look around the shops. As an Anniversary present, Lesley bought me a book on the Titanic (another one of my specialist interests!) and I would have reciprocated with some clothing except Lesley just couldn't find anything she liked that wasn't an extortionate price. So I owe her one. We did a bit of food shopping as well and on our return, I took Millie out onto the green so she could have a bit of a run around. She's so fast on her feet. One minute she's there, the next she's galloping away into the distance and she never, ever seems to tire. Oh, to be young! She must be an awful tease to other dogs. One of her mannerisms (one that I find particularly endearing) is to go up to dogs twice her size, try to cajole them with a lick or a sniff and then, if they rise to the bait and get a bit agitated, she simply runs off or around in a circle, knowing full well that, unless it's a greyhound, she won't be caught. It reminds me of the immortal Muhammad Ali or Sugar Ray Leonard at their majestic best! A quick jab, a swift uppercut, a powerful blow to body or head and then a dance, a jiggle, a swaying upper body. 'Come and get me!' It's tantalising and its effective and it's beautiful to watch. It puts a smile on my face and for that, especially at the minute, I'm particularly grateful!

Tuesday 29th March 2016

Unquestionably, there is a real need to talk about mental health. For some, despite the issues of stigma and discrimination, this is a relatively straightforward process. Not easy. Never easy. But systematic, perhaps even inexorable. I've met a few natural speakers recently, but no-one better than my new friend Annie. Completely new to the concept of speaking in public she may have been, but the authority and emotion she managed to convey on the two occasions I've had the pleasure of listening have been nothing short of incredible. Nothing contrived, nothing forced, nothing hidden, nothing embellished. Just plain, honest, talking. It's people like Annie – and Sarah, another new acquaintance – that inspire you to want to do likewise, to reach audiences through the power of truth and honesty. However, whilst this is all well and good, and undoubtedly it is to maximum efficacy, there has to be a further dimension, an added responsibility, if you like. And that is to try and help others to do the same. People who may not think they have anything useful to say. People who are reluctant or naturally shy. People who are scared of the effects of stigma and discrimination. People who believe they have much to lose but very little to gain. People who have been almost coerced into silence through fear and trepidation, but who offer so much to those that they let in to their immediate vicinity. Please don't misunderstand. This is not about compelling people to be open and to talk about their own condition or mental illness in general if that is the last thing they want to do. This is not a mandatory act or some form of insincere peer-group pressure. It is about releasing something that wants to come out but doesn't know how, when or maybe even why. There has to be a pre-existing will and a determination, however dormant. There has to be a motive and a desire to help, both oneself and others. From my experience, it has not been my own capacity to speak openly that has fuelled my desire to be involved in mental health activism, it is the propensity to develop that skill and fire in others. People are interesting. No, more than that. People are fascinating. Every single one of us has a story to tell, experiences to relate, a message to give. In this world where restraint and fear often rule, there is nothing more liberating as a proponent and as a recipient to be free to talk as one would wish, knowing that the impact of one's words can make the difference between living and simply existing.

Wednesday 30th March 2016

Everything seemed to come together last night. I had vivid dreams – this time about Danny and school. I woke up in the early hours with terrible aches around my knee and when I awoke more permanently – around 8.30 – I could hardly raise my head from the pillow. There are times when these things are the most tangible, the most penetrating, evidence of a depressive episode, even more than low mood. To be honest, in times of acute depression, I think I take low mood almost 'as read'. I'm aware of it. How can I not be? But its persistence, its durability, makes it almost imperceptible. I'm more conscious of any brief light-hearted relief, such as something funny on the telly, or a Millwall win (as happened on Monday night!), than the agonised state that has overwhelmed and condemned me. This may strike you as odd and it probably requires spelling out. If you are constantly low in mood. If that is your lot, so to speak, then its characteristics become your accustomed position, your everyday existence. You take it for granted. You live and breathe it. Only a diversion from its destructive course, only a manifest change, fleeting though that may be, breaches the camouflage of depression that has become so all-consuming. It attracts your consciousness. It penetrates the fog. For the rest of the time, the agony of mental illness simply exists. The pain, the discomfort, the heaviness, the futility, all those things and more become simply the norm. They are by no means inconsequential or indeed indiscernible. They are monumental in their own way. But they have become routine, 'mainstream' if you like.

As for my day, I've already been shopping at Aldi, I have no scheduled meetings but do have some work I need to do. I'm also taking Elliot to the cinema this afternoon, and at some point amidst all that I'll do some exercise on the bike and the 'wobble machine' aka Flabelos. Nothing strenuous, nothing arduous, nothing challenging and – with the exception of our film outing – nothing memorable. One day merges into the other at the moment. I'm barely conscious of what day it is, if truth be told. Enduring each one. Surviving each one has become my raison d'être.

Thursday 31st March 2016

The last day of March heralds the return of Joel from his travels!

As I write, he's already landed at Heathrow, from where he'll make his way to St Pancras to catch a train home to Leicester. It certainly doesn't seem three months since we were dropping him off at the coach stop. I suspect that this time away will have changed him to a certain extent, but only to sharpen and develop those alluring parts of his character that make him what he is, a wholly nice guy. I'm thinking in particular here of things such as confidence and self-regard, but also of matters to do with motivation and independence. The very fact that he's only here for two weeks before he sets sail again, this time a little closer to home, to France to take a job with Eurocamp, is illustrative of these new dimensions to his already strong disposition. I can't wait to see him.

One thing I've been conscious of these last couple of days is that my mood seems to be a lot worse in the mornings. I guess this isn't surprising. The prospect of another day to get through, of hours of potential nothingness at best and pain at worst, it's enough to make one consider the merits of at least trying to live a normal life. I am literally forcing myself to go through the motions. I have to physically tell myself to do things, to drag my weary body from one situation to the next, to readjust a heavy mind from one task to another. I'm looking at the time in the bottom right-hand corner of my computer screen. It currently reads 10.26. Translated into the language of depression, that's nigh on twelve hours to endure before I face the next hurdle of sleep and dreams. Twelve hours equates to 720 minutes and to 43,200 seconds. That seems a lot. It is a lot. The temptation is strong to begin counting, but, as everyone knows, time drags when you're constantly looking at a clock. That's the last thing I need. I want time to pass as swiftly as possible. Realistically, when it comes to around 7.00 pm, I begin to see the finishing line in sight, and consequently, my mood seems to improve slightly. I seem to get a bit more chatty, a little more cheery and optimistic. Whether that's because I've survived another day or am anticipating the darkness of sleep, I'm not sure. Probably a combination of both. If I had to analyse this – and in writing these words, I've rather compelled myself to do so – it is clear that one thing I am definitely doing is wishing my time, and therefore my life, away. This isn't healthy. It's positively destructive. It may be depression talking, but it's still my life, my time and my use of it. Or misuse as the case may be.

It reminds me that I need to ring my consultant and see if I can bring my appointment forward.

April

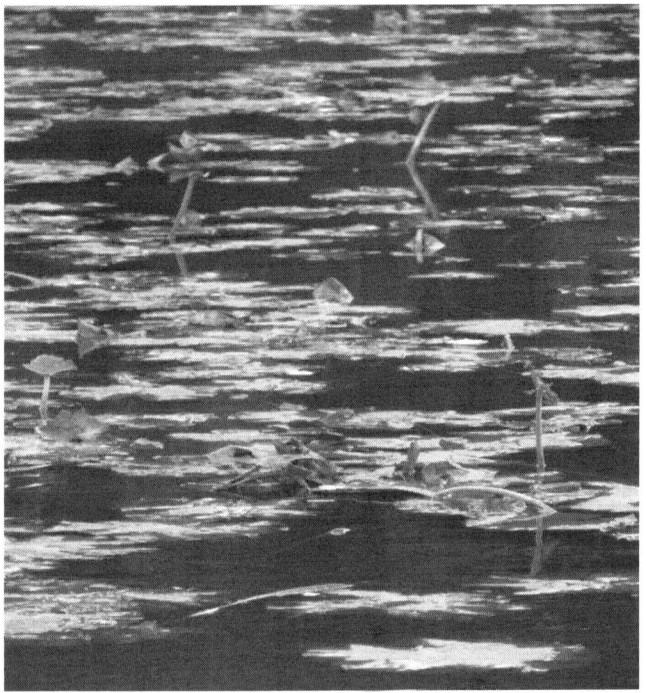

Friday 1st April 2016
How I managed to get up this morning I will never know! I had to be up earlier than usual as I had a nine o'clock meeting at the Leicester General site. Subconsciously anticipating this, I awoke at just after seven, but could I raise my weary head from the pillow? I lay there, knowing full well that the longer I did so, the heavier my body was becoming, the more resistant to movement I would be. I realise that I've described this feeling in previous entries, but its persistence and its importance as far as mental health is concerned merits repetition. An overwhelming sense of weight and gravity consumes my whole. I'm not just pinned to my bed, I'm strapped in with a colossal all-pervading 'essence', a virtual body cushion or smothering blanket pushing downwards, creating an unequivocal impression in the mattress,

a silhouette that becomes more and more defined as the seconds tick by. Somehow, I managed to raise myself to a sitting position and sat there for what seemed an eternity before eventually summoning up enough motivation and strength to force myself upwards. It was intense and it was unbearable. Even as I sat downstairs watching early morning telly and eating my cereal, I could feel my eyelids becoming increasingly heavy. The temptation to submit to their evident need to close was tantalisingly strong, but in the end I did resist. Life had to carry on!

As you are probably expecting me to clarify, the reason for such marked tiredness lay not in what I had done physically, but what had saturated my mental stamina during the course of the night. Dreams, dreams and more dreams. Dreams of such stark reality. Dreams that inundated my every sense with a vividness and a graphic encapsulation of issues that have focused my mind over the years, many of which have refused to leave my subconscious. In one, I found myself leading a charge into a mass of people, determined to fight, my fists flying, my body tensing at the prospect of hard physical contact. In another, I was observing a school performance of an opera having been denied the opportunity to take part myself. I had been kept in the dark, deliberately overlooked. The frustration, the insult, the embarrassment. These were acute sensations, as was the anger that overtook them all, threatening to engulf me and to culminate in even more overt vilification. The message last night was strong. I had been left behind, ignored and forgotten, but I wanted to be seen, felt and heard. Whatever obstacle you, life, may put in my way, I will fight it irrespective of outcome.

Luckily, I was wanted and respected at my meeting, and I was able to contribute despite my fatigue and my current low mood. It's been such a positive move for me, working in this new domain and with people who are genuine, warm and simply nice. I hope they feel I have earned the trust they evidently have in me. I got home around lunchtime and since then have done a few jobs, sent some emails and updated my work schedules and administration.

After the big build up yesterday, Joel got in touch to say that he was now staying with Luke in London for a couple of days! I do envy them both, because Joel is like his brother in the sense that he can change his mind, completely alter his plans, and not be fazed at all. They do make a habit of it, but when you're young I guess you have greater freedom to go where your heart is, to make adjustments whenever you wish, to literally go with the flow and make it up as you go along. You must take advantage of it because life can not only be restrictive, it can become dictatorial in its fashion, in its requirements and in its routines. For those of us with a mental illness, there is probably a much greater likelihood that this will be so. Anyway, Joel is now due at a quarter past midnight tomorrow morning! Lesley is going to meet him off the bus, probably cursing him at the lateness of the hour whilst enjoying his return at the same time!

Saturday 2nd April 2016

I forgot to mention that I rang the other day to see if I could bring forward my next consultant appointment. As I half suspected would be the case, I can't. 'These appointments are like gold dust', I was told. Unless there are any cancellations – and given what I've just said, there aren't likely to be many, if any – I'm going to have to wait until 19th May. I have to admit that my initial response was actually positive. The prospect of an earlier date with destiny, especially given my current low mood, wasn't that appealing, if I'm honest. I can safely predict a change of medication and, as I've mentioned before, that brings with it so many challenges, new fears, new worries, new uncertainties. Can I afford to wait for another six weeks or so? Yes, I think so, but there again, I'm not entirely sure. The champion of indecision and doubt at play!

Even though the UK Government keeps telling its people that the budget for mental health is increasing, that there is a real drive to creating parity of finance and of esteem with physical illness, the proof of the pudding is very much in the eating. I haven't noticed any change in service delivery or capacity, and I don't know anyone within the system who has. The waiting lists are still inordinately long. There is still a real dearth of qualified psychiatrists, psychotherapists and other practitioners given the prevalence of mental illness in our society. Hospital places are still insufficient with respect to supply and demand. Campaigns that encourage us all to look after our mental health and to ask for support are very much in evidence, but if the system can't cope with a heightened awareness of illness and vulnerability, it's almost setting itself up to fail, or at least be questioned. Anticipation of treatment is one thing, it's availability in the short or even medium term is another. If people can't get what they need in time, the consequences can be serious, if not disastrous.

It's a good job I'm not more severely ill than I am, though of course, I would have the option of Crisis support if things got worse. I guess it is frustrating though that the system as it is can't respond to a dip in mood that doesn't warrant hospitalisation. On numerous occasions my consultant (whoever that has been) has reassured me that I can call him or her before my next scheduled appointment if things change and if I need specific help. To be fair to them, they really mean it. They don't say these things for nothing. I see every time an honesty and a commitment to help. But the current state of play doesn't allow for this more flexible approach. It doesn't give the consultant what he/she needs, and of course, this is even more the case when it comes to the patient. I have been lucky in the past, and quite recently actually. My previous consultant, for example, managed to fit me in once on the very day I rang. Though conscious of time, he didn't throw me out after ten minutes, but listened thoughtfully and carefully, made sure he understood the consequences of what I was telling him, and gave me the service that I desperately needed. I was so grateful. But it really is pot luck. This week I haven't been so fortunate and so I now have to play the waiting game. I'm good at that though!

Sunday 3rd April 2016

What a weekend I'm having! I seem to have spent virtually all of it in front of this screen. The reason? Well, shortly after completing yesterday's entry, I received an email from my publisher containing the first mock-up of my completed book on the Holocaust. With it came the request to look through it, correct any typos and make any final adjustments or amendments. A straightforward task, but one that I've been awaiting with some trepidation and, I have to admit, a certain degree of anxiety. This, effectively, is it. My last chance to effect any changes, my last opportunity to be in command of the process before printing and publication. I felt a massive weight of responsibility, because, as usual, my overwhelming wish is for perfection. The other challenge, miniscule in comparison, is the extent of my manuscript. I knew what I'd written was lengthy, but to see it result in over four hundred pages of text was a surprise and a bit of a thunderbolt. By end of play last night – at eight o'clock I needed respite! – I'd only been through four chapters out of eighteen, around a quarter of the book page-wise. It was also a surreal experience re-reading things that I'd written two years ago. I hadn't realised how detailed and how complex some of what I'd had to say had transformed into logical and readable script. I was quietly impressed because it read like a real book. That may sound absurdly obvious, but when you're short on confidence, seeing something tangible that you have produced, an achievement realised, is a bit of a shock to the system. But a nice shock, I have to admit. My challenge now is to do what I need to do whilst trying to keep things in perspective. I've been comprehensive so far – the mistakes I've found have been few and far between, small fry really, perhaps even indiscernible to the average reader – yet I know the comparison between the need to properly review and the compulsive and obsessive urge to reflect and ruminate, amounts to very fine margins, particularly in someone with OCD and depression.

The other noticeable thing over the course of the last twenty-four hours or so has been a lifting of my mood. Whether the book has played its part in this, or maybe even the return of Joel, I'm not too sure but, to be honest, I don't really care at the moment. All I know is that when I look back at what I wrote last weekend, when I remember the dire straits I felt I was in, what I feel now is appreciably, perhaps even acutely, different. I'm not over the woods yet. I'm experienced enough to know that. But the signs are there that I may be over the worst. I've become more communicative. I've felt able to join in with conversations without feeling the unbearable sensation of estrangement. I've been able to adjust to things, to concentrate more, to look forward a little. What hasn't left me is the lethargy, the aches and pains, the physical realisation of deep depression. But of course, most of these things never really go away whatever my current state of mood. They simply become more bearable and less impactful. Have I turned the corner then? I think maybe I have. I just need again to achieve and retain perspective (that seems to be the word of the day!). Not to get ahead of myself. Not to fall victim to the temptation to set unrealistic recovery targets. Not to run before I've learned to walk again.

Monday 4th April 2016

I've had quite an interesting morning as it happens. I was interviewed on television by a friend of mine as part of a wonderful project she herself has launched and developed, all to do with inspiration. She herself is one of the most inspirational people I have the good fortune to know, but her stimulus has been rooting out and bringing to attention those whose natural intentions have been to help others in a wide variety of ways. It wasn't a surprise to find my good friend John had preceded me in the studio because he too exhibits all those same qualities. Surrounded by such positivity and enthusiasm I hope 'inspired' me to talk about relevant areas of my life that somehow met the appropriate criteria of the project and the interview. Mental health was central to that discussion. Though I tried to convey its intensity, enormity and the challenges that naturally come with it, I was keen to get the message across that having a mental illness shouldn't form an immovable barrier if one is sufficiently motivated and determined to do something, no matter how big or small. It shouldn't shatter dreams and ambitions, neither should it dictate one's horizons. I do believe this, though of course I'm under no illusion as to the inherent difficulties and the extra burden that we have to carry as a community of people.

You might think that being interviewed would be an automatic guarantor of stress and anxiety. It's strange but I've never really experienced that. Even going back twenty years or so when I was regularly featured on BBC Radio Leicester and indeed on national television and in the newspapers as part of my work in rugby league. I always looked forward to the opportunity to talk and to be heard. It wasn't in any way, shape or form, a 'buzz'. It wasn't that form of 'looking forward'. It's probably more accurate to say that it never proved a hurdle or an obstacle. It never threatened to overcome me. It wasn't something that I dreaded or would do anything to avoid. I simply went with it. That's remained with me, irrespective of the depth or otherwise of my mood and the extent and nature of my mental illness at any one time. I could probably say with some degree of confidence that talking in the media about mental ill health during the course of a depressive episode has maybe heightened the energy and potency of the experience, for me and for any listeners. Though I can't really speak for the latter, of course!

Job interviews are somewhat different! I get really nervous beforehand and though I work hard to ensure that I try to keep calm and attentive, it's not easy when mental illness is pulling at you and wanting to take you in randomly diverging directions. Somehow, though I know that it's an extra hurdle to overcome, that it increases the demands you place on yourself, it's difficult to say 'please take my mental illness into consideration'. Part of you thinks – given the prevalence of stigma and discrimination – that such an admission will backfire. You don't want to give the impression that you are making some sort of excuse. Neither do you want people to feel sorry for you. It's virtually an impossible balance to control. Unless you know the people who are interviewing you or you are aware that they know about your disability, you can't gauge exactly how to deal with the issue. You know it's impacting on you at the time, but can you be confident that those facing you in the room or over the table will be sufficiently knowledgeable or aware to ensure fairness as well as encompassing reasonable adjustments for your condition? How can you? You don't know them.

The last question I was asked during the interview related to from where I derive my own inspiration. Without hesitation, I answered 'Danny'. For his achievements, his tenacity, his drive, ambition and enthusiasm for life. But for so many other things as well. Without him, I'd be nothing. His impact on the way I try to live my life has been monumental. He was the glue that ensured solidarity and cohesion within our family, but his presence and his humanity reached people in the most fundamental of ways. He always showed love and compassion. Short in stature he may have been, but physically and mentally he was immense. How I miss him.

Tuesday 5th April 2016

It's funny what an immersion in one piece of writing can do to one's mind, and particularly when you try to write something else! Since Saturday I've been trailing through the final draft copy of my Holocaust book, chapter after chapter, paragraph after paragraph, line by line. I'm now on page 315 out of 429, so I'm very nearly there. What a revelation it's been. As I alluded to on Sunday, it's been hard at times to reconcile what I've been reading with the fact that the words originated within my own head. On many occasions, I just cannot remember the physical act as well as the mental focus of writing. Did I really construct that argument? How did I come by that story? Did those connections really take place within my mind? I seem incapable of coming to any firm conclusion as to the merits – or otherwise – of the book. At times, I can't believe that this is my product. It's as if I'm reading the very best contribution to the field of leading historians and social commentators. I think it's that persuasive. The self-doubt within me then takes over. Was I simply the physical means (the writing part) of portraying someone else's ideas? Was I just processing what someone else had deduced or discovered in their research. In other words, I seem to force into my head an actual disconnect between the mechanics of writing and the creative impulse that leads to it. It's so hard to explain. It really is. The bottom line, I suppose, is that my lack of confidence in my own ability has superseded every other consideration. It can't be my work. I'm not capable of that level of understanding. Somehow, I'm just the messenger of somebody else's inspiration and talent. These ideas, false though I know they are, just won't go away.

The other thing to note, as I said initially, has been the effect of reviewing one book on my capability of writing another. For the first time in a while, I found writing yesterday's entry a real burden. Not because I had challenging things to say necessarily, but because I couldn't trigger that switch in my mind to move from one context to another. My brain simply couldn't adjust that quickly. It couldn't translate what was being asked of it. It remained in some form of time lock! It's not just the fact that I'm writing about different things. The style and manner of writing is different too. It's more personal, obviously, for one. But it's also geared towards a different purpose. As cricket has been very much in the headlines recently, with England reaching – though ultimately losing – the World Twenty20 Final, it's perhaps apt to use a cricketing metaphor to illustrate my point. It would be like tasking a batsman who has spent the day surviving an onslaught at the crease in a five-day test match, to go straight into a twenty overs-a-side fixture and to launch himself immediately onto the attack, with quick runs the charge. One needs time to adjust. To steady oneself. To re-orientate. To re-focus.

Maybe this is a reflection on my increasing inability to multi-task. I seem to find this a much more challenging exercise than I used to. Indeed, sometimes, the prospect of just such a scenario can lead to real panic and anxiety. It's as if too much is being asked of a machine – in this case, my brain – so almost inevitably, it has to shut down and one has to start all over again. If I could only control what I'm doing and what I have to do so that this multi-layered approach to life is marginalised or even eradicated, then I would be able to cope. I'm sure of it. But life simply isn't like that. I even get confused and frustrated when Lesley tells me of the numerous things that she is doing or having to deal with. Just listening to that intensity and synchronicity of action, is enough to start me off on a path towards bewilderment and ultimate closure. I'm sure I'll return to this at a later date.

Wednesday 6th April 2016

A mixed morning. Two productive and interesting meetings but an awful lot of waiting around and twiddling of thumbs. Indeed, I calculated when I got back home that I'd spent longer waiting for the meetings to happen than their actual duration! To be fair, it wasn't the fault of the two people concerned. Sometimes circumstances simply dictate that it's going to be one of those days. Firstly, traffic and secondly, a police matter resulted in both of them starting late, but I can't complain, as they were both putting themselves out to see me in the first place. As you might expect, I hadn't really planned for either of them being delayed, let alone both. As a result, it meant having to readjust timings and thinking a little on my feet so that I used my time productively. It didn't work. I couldn't really decide what to do after the first meeting and ended up wandering aimlessly around the city centre, not sure of where I wanted to go or indeed how long to devote to anything I did settle on doing. I ended up frequenting Waterstones and Tesco Express without spending a single penny, hopping into and out of shop fronts and alleyways to escape the rain, looking out for anything to catch my attention. Nothing did. I should just have gone to Caffe Nero for a drink, as was my initial intention!

It made me think of how precious time really is. Both my dates this morning lead tremendously busy lives. Indeed the second of the two had only flown in from Turkey late last night after a short, unexpected trip. Most of the people I know in the world of work are the same (not taking trips to Turkey, I mean!) and I guess I was as well when I worked at the Council and even in my working life prior to that. How much of what I did though was productive, and how much time did I really waste? How could I have done things differently and how do I ensure, now, that I maximise the potential of each moment? I think back to my father, a Secondary School teacher, a man committed to the process as well as the ideals of education, someone inspired to play a role in guiding and developing talent and potential. He spent thirty odd years doing a job that he initially loved but which eventually played its part in damaging his health to such an extent that he tragically left us at the age of only 55 years. There were other factors at play, that much must be said, but teaching – at one time a calling, an inspiration and an art – became for him an empty hollow, devoid of substance, eating away at his strength and motivation. I look back at my ten years at the Council. What did I actually achieve that matters? I'm told I did a lot. Those words were even spoken to me this morning. But I'm struggling to conceive of anything substantial, anything that really impacted on people and their lives. Ten years of struggle and perspiration. Ten years of reports and publications. Ten years of policies and strategies. I tried. I most certainly did. I spent more time than I'm sure my bosses would have wanted meeting people in communities, listening to them, trying to understand and then support them. I made a conscious and unilateral decision that that was the best way of serving the public, not being chained to a desk and to a telephone that my fragile mental health meant I could rarely use anyway! Did I ultimately make a difference? Who knows? If I could safely say that I'd made a contribution, I would be satisfied with that. I can say those words very easily, but do I believe them? I'm not so sure.

What I am certain about, what I know did happen as a result of ten years in that environment was that my mental health deteriorated to an alarming extent. I wasn't well to start with, of course, but I ended up struggling to maintain any sort of working operation, any semblance of a productive working life. I was ruined. I'd become a shell of my former self. I couldn't continue. I know that now. Ironically, voluntary redundancy was probably the best decision I ever made as a local government worker! Like father, like son? There's similarities.

I'm ruminating. I know I am. I just hope that I don't spend the rest of my life in this state. Thinking time away without there being any end product, or any noticeable outcome that I can be proud of when I eventually follow my Dad to the next world. I hope I still have the opportunity and the chance to make an impact.

Thursday 7th April 2016

I'm feeling rather fragile today. In fact, I'd probably say I was a bit shocked. The catalyst is two-fold. Firstly, I finished the review of my book late yesterday afternoon. Though the focus in what I've been doing has been on finding and drawing attention to grammatical errors and typos, this doesn't mean that I've not been reading and trying to digest what I wrote. I just can't seem to make my mind up as to whether what I've put together and argued is coherent and logical, or whether it's actually far too complex and condensed. In depression speak, is it good or crap? Sadly, I'm tending more towards the latter. I stated in the Introduction to 'Suspended Disbelief'[11] that the book was a series of separate essays. Linked of course by the subject matter and often by the same examples and issues. In other words, that it wasn't a chronological account, or even a homogeneous whole. However, I can't get it out of my mind that all I've succeeded in doing is making the same point over and over again. My Dad used to say that Vivaldi wrote one melody and then six hundred or more variations on it. That that was his entire repertoire! Well, I feel like his written-word equivalent! There's a strong part of me as I write that wants to scrap the entire exercise, pull out of the process and start again. Only I can't. It's too late. I have to go with what I've got. I pray that not only is this my depressed mind taking over, masking fact and reality, but also that people reading it will be kind to me and find what I've done both interesting and stimulating. I'm not sure how

I'd cope if reviews were unkind, even though they may be honest and actually correct. What have I done? Have I wrecked my budding writing career during its very first lap?

The second issue has, irony of ironies, been in relation to feedback on the work I'm currently doing with a mental health project. Recently, I've felt under a bit of scrutiny, receiving questioning comments in relation to my approach, suggesting that I should be modifying things that I thought were already agreed, done and dusted. I'm almost certainly blowing things out of proportion, but it's beginning to hurt. It's not that I don't mind constructive criticism – though my ability to cope with it does largely depend on mood – it's that in this case it's made me feel completely inadequate and disconnected. Do I know what I'm doing? And what I'm doing it for? I'm starting to doubt myself again. The irony doesn't really need spelling out, but I'll do so. The fact that it's a mental health project, it includes people like me, it addresses issues and challenges that I face, seems to be significant. Do I not even register with what should be my natural domain? Am I too aloof, too particular, too disengaged from my own community? Am I an outsider even here?

I'm probably undermining myself. I'm possibly ruminating in self-pity and self-criticism. But I feel in pain. I feel inadequate and useless. I'm also very much on edge. In times like these, how I react to things can be so randomly uncontrollable and illogical. It's worrying and it's dangerous. I don't want to blow a fuse. I don't want to verbally lash out. I don't want to overreact. I don't want to give in to the temptation to self-harm. But I can't seem to stop it. If I had a choice this very moment, I'd want to lock myself up and tell everything and everyone to go away.

Friday 8th April 2016

Doubt. What a monumental word that is! An integral aspect of daily life yet one that poses what appear at times to be insurmountable challenges. Just think of all its manifestations. Doubt over what to do. Doubt over where to be. Doubt over what you are. Doubt over what other people think of you. Doubt over your own credibility. Doubt over your own capabilities. Doubt over your own purpose. I can't think of a single word that has such immense magnitude. And one that encompasses all the traits of mental illness as forcefully. At times, I am consumed with doubt. I am almost powerless in its wake. Like a cancer, it attaches itself to my brain and spreads in all directions, effecting every part of my conscious and subconscious, permeating every sense, every thought. It is, of course, the very antithesis of what I crave and what I need. Certainty is that comfort for the mentally ill. It takes away deliberation. It prevents rumination. It is, rather than what it might or could be. Wherever possible in my life, I search for the ultimate truth, the unambiguous reality. In absolutely everything. From the minutiae of what I want to drink, to the more demanding aspects of life such as employment, health or even relationships. However, my feeling is that doubt is a far more pervasive aspect of life than its diametrically opposite. The ability to make decisions is part of the make-up of being a human being, after all. If it wasn't we would simply be robots, pawns in an absorbing game of chess. Or perhaps that should be bullets in Russian roulette? Subsumed into the will of someone or something else.

If only I could handle doubt more effectively? At the moment, it has engulfed me. Everything I do, think or say has suddenly become a matter of such close scrutiny that all I seem to do in response is doubt. If I could get immediate clarity or reassurance, then I would. My recourse of turning to Lesley is there. It's always there. But if I over use it. If I rely on it too much, it can become destructive. I don't help myself. I'm reliant on her, and indeed others, to do it for me. It's not conducive to good mental health. It provides immediate relief and gratification. But in the long term, unless checked, it can turn one into that proverbial robot, unable to function unless switched on and operated under someone else's steam.

Ultimately, there is a very thin dividing line between living in such a fashion and being taken into care, hospitalised and removed from the realities of ordinary living. And I don't really want that.

Or do I?

<u>Saturday 9th April 2016</u>

I've started this morning something that I've been putting off for at least a couple of weeks. A while ago now, I made it my intention to send an update on my work situation to all the people I used to be in contact with during my tenure at the Council. Whilst I was working there, I used to send regular emails out to hundreds of contacts in the community and in organisations that included government updates, funding news, the latest reports and information on events, courses, initiatives, jobs and other things. It also used to feature news stories and any interesting articles relating to equality, diversity and community cohesion. I was told by some that if they didn't receive this information from me, they wouldn't get to hear of it at all, so it did meet a real need. Indeed, it was the mainstay, the bedrock, from which other community cohesion related work would emanate. Information is power, so they say. So providing it was a key aspect of empowerment. Such a simple concept really, and an easy thing to operate once you'd done the hard work in engaging with people as well as putting together the mechanics of creating and developing relevant Outlook lists and regular sources of information. I became quite famous locally, principally because of an email address!

Using the rationale that I still have something to offer communities in my new role as an independent consultant, I determined to send an email to those same people and others outlining what I can do and in effect, promoting myself as a new business.

On the surface, you're probably thinking, where's the problem?

Well, it boils down to this. Firstly, my new operating power as far as emails are concerned is pretty restricted, certainly in comparison to what I was able to use at the Council. I've tried before to send emails out to groups of ten or so, and I've never been sure whether they've actually succeeded in reaching the relevant people or are still floating around somewhere in cyberspace! I used to get emails back saying that there was a problem with one or more of the recipients, but that was it! Was it one or all ten? I used to panic and, almost inevitably, think the worst. That I was trying to speak to people, desperate to make contact, but in vain. Undoubtedly, there were ways of ascertaining the real situation, but the more I ruminated, the more I didn't want to know! What a paradox. It was as if the prospect of knowing the truth (thereby eradicating the doubt) was too challenging, too shattering, too demanding of my fragile nervous system. I just couldn't go through with it.

The other think gnawing away at my confidence was the issue of whether people really wanted to hear from me at all, particularly as I'm now, in effect, trying to sell myself as a product that equates to tangible pounds and pence. Very occasionally in my previous guise as a local government worker I would get short and sometimes even nasty emails back from people telling me not to bother them. They could be quite hurtful and I could never understand why there was a need to respond in such a manner when all I was trying to do was to help them by providing what potentially was useful information. What if people now tell me to do one? What if my good intentions as well as yes, my need to obtain work, results in people being offended? The prospect of being thought of as interfering, as capitalising on past connections, of acting in some kind of mercenary fashion, is really troubling. I'm not sure at the minute, of how I'd react if I was accused of being so or if people rejected out of hand my offer of support. Such is the fragility of my position, and the nature of my nervous tension. I'll only know if I go ahead and send the emails. It's a leap – or perhaps that should be a plunge – of faith!

Sunday 10th April 2016

Sure enough, it had to come, didn't it? Someone, for some incomprehensible reason, couldn't resist adding a critical and indeed almost spiteful comment to their request for me to delete their email address. Why? I just don't know. What is it in the DNA of some people that they feel almost compelled to inflict upset on someone for something of nothing? All I was trying to do was to promote what I can do to help others! The impact on me was as I feared. Initially angry, that quickly turned into despair and then uncertainty. I felt demoralised for much of the evening, unsure of myself, fearful of further contact. I couldn't let it go despite Lesley's assurances and support. It even affected my sleep. I didn't resort to Diazepam, so I guess that is a sign that, despite my turmoil, I had some semblance of control. Though it stretched my capacity, my limitations, to the full.

I often wonder if people realise the impact of a careless or insensitive comment. If they did, would they still feel the compulsion to offend? It's a hypothetical question, of course. However, living with a mental illness makes me, I know, more attuned to how easy it can be to upset people. The maxim, 'treat others as you would wish to be treated yourself', is, of course, assuredly the point here. If the boot was on the other foot, and certainly if I didn't know someone well, my initial reaction would be to assume that my contact, my protagonist, was equally sensitive for whatever reason, mental illness or otherwise. This would be my outlook, my framework for dialogue. Not the other side of the coin. I don't need to know that someone is fragile. I just go under the pretext that they might be. My contention is that this is a far better, more humane, way to deal with a fellow human being. This doesn't mean, by the way, that you don't make your point, that you aren't strong or unequivocal in your meaning and intention. It just means that you're more respectful and even, in the world of work, more professional. I remember once at work being lambasted by a Councillor for something that I'd done. When, in my response, I told him that my mental state was not good at that moment, when I showed him the emotion that was welling up inside me, he immediately relented, asked for forgiveness and then offered his support. That was quite a reaction. One of compassion and understanding. I thanked him most profusely for showing me respect, kindness and a degree of consideration that I really needed at that time. I like to think that it made him pause for reflection as well. His reaction and attitude stood out for me, for the simple reason that with others, things had been markedly different. No inclination towards the impact on the other person. What mattered to them was not so much to make their point, but to put me 'in my place'. To reinforce hierarchy, power and position, irrespective of the impact and consequences. To me, that comes down to one thing, and one thing only – bullying.

Monday 11th April 2016
The trouble with days that you want to avoid is that they come too quickly. I've got a pretty daunting week, at least that's how it appears at its onset. When I made arrangements for various commitments, it seemed an age away. Even at the back end of last week, its imminence didn't register. I was, for once, caught up in the moment, neither looking forwards or backwards. But now it's upon me and I'm worried. I have twenty-four hours to go before I'm into its actuality. I'm anticipating being not only nervous but positively worked up. What is it that I'm doing, you'll be asking? And when I tell you, please reflect for a minute before responding! This week, starting tomorrow morning, I am leading focus groups and interviews with staff, volunteers and members of the mental health project I've mentioned a few times in past entries. I shall have to not only obtain and retain people's interest in the questions I need to ask, but commit their answers and the nature of the discussion to paper at the same time. It's multi-tasking, but it also amounts to effective engagement. What I'm currently petrified about is the possibility of people not wishing to get involved, of there being active dissent and criticism, of being under pressure and intense scrutiny. Of course, it's part of the task to ensure that people are switched on and that the conversation flows in a positive manner. I'm just not sure I'm up to it. But I have to go ahead. Cancelling is not an option.

Postponing likewise. It would simply be delaying the inevitable. There are some things I can't avoid and it looks like this is one of them. Ironically, the first people that I meet in the morning are members of the Confidence Building group. How I could do with a bit of that!

Tuesday 12th April 2016

'Panorama'[12] made particularly compelling and disturbing viewing last night. Its focus was on the deficiencies within the current mental health system, and particularly with respect to CAMHS. As if things weren't bad enough, what came across during the course of only thirty minutes was frightening and quite disgraceful. Of course, I have a vested interest not only as a result of my own mental illnesses but because of Elliot's recent referral. What I witnessed, though, was enough to question whether all the waiting for treatment was actually worthwhile. Even though the programme concentrated on one tragic story, I have to say from my own experience and knowledge that this is far from being a unique set of circumstances. The poor girl in question had spent the latter part of her life being shunted from one hospital to another, none of them particularly close to her home town, experiencing what amounted to serious neglect and dereliction of care. She'd been effectively institutionalised, shut off from her own family and from a culture of understanding and empathy. What she needed she didn't get. What she wanted seemed immaterial. Her family were effectively powerless, unable to get close enough for long enough to intervene without the full machinations of the sectioning process being triggered. Recourse to the girl's diary would have revealed the full enormity of her predicament. She talked of 'absolutely hating' the environment in which she was trapped. She continually pleaded for positive interventions and for someone, anyone even, to take the necessary time to just give her some attention, some care, some educated perception and relevant cognisance. It didn't happen and it proved to be fatal. She ended up taking her own life.

It is easy at times to blame the immediate medical support structure. Most of the time, this is unfair because the problems are more systemic than particular. However, in this case, there were occasions when I simply couldn't believe what I was hearing. Of a patient with a history of self-harm and obviously severely ill, being able to access the metal binding of notebooks with a cursory remark ('You're not going to do anything with this, are you?') that actually drew attention to the danger! Of her being allowed to look forward to a home visit or transfer and then having that entitlement withdrawn at the last minute. Of a building up of hope and expectation to be quickly and suddenly thwarted. It seemed that she had no effective outlet, no trusted contact, no valued relationship that she could draw upon when she needed to. It was thoroughly upsetting, but – and this is the sad bit – not entirely surprising. One has to wonder at the quality of treatment as well as its availability. But if the system is not geared towards implementing thorough safeguarding measures simply because of the paucity of resources, it's hard not to look any further than at government level when one is trying to assess responsibility and apportion blame. Even when one takes into consideration the inevitability of human error, one is left with a whole edifice that is beyond the capabilities of its staff to rescue. People who work within the mental health system are doing their level best, I am sure. Every single worker I know is not only focused and hard-working, but is dedicated to their patients, and desperate to make things work. But it's like swimming with one arm behind your back. Despite best efforts, all you can do is go around in circles. It was mentioned in the programme that the entire national CAMHS financial allocation is only 0.7% of the entire NHS budget. 0.7%!!!!! If we were going out of our way to create an underclass of severely troubled young people, we couldn't be doing any better with resources such as this!

I've said it before, and no doubt I will say it again, but not only does there need to be a massive increase in financial investment per se, there has to be a focus on where that is best spent. Money, in this respect, needs to be given to grassroots projects such as the one I'm working with this week. It needs to go towards supporting a community infrastructure where people are encouraged, and supported, not only to help themselves, but to help others who share an illness and an outlook. It requires bravery, because this would in some ways be a novel act. But if you look around at the community in which I am a part, the community of the mentally ill, I can positively say, without fear of contradiction, that where there are avenues and paths of support that involve us and enable us to help ourselves and our friends in need, there is a far better chance of inculcating a culture of self-sufficiency and care which is absolutely vital. We are part of the process of recovery, not just an NHS number or an object for medical scrutiny. We are also part of the process of prevention, of maintaining a level of positive mental health in ourselves that thereby avoids, potentially, the need for more serious intervention. Please don't get me wrong, I'm not advocating this as an alternative to clinical and medical investment, but as a necessary addition. More hospital beds are undoubtedly needed. More psychiatrists and psychotherapists need to be trained. More mental health nurses need to be available. More training on mental health and its complexities needs to be a part of every GP's personal and professional development. But all this won't be enough if we can't help ourselves and our fellow men, women and children to feel valued and supported through well-constructed and delivered local projects. We just want to help, that's all! Just give us a bit of trust.

Wednesday 13th April 2016

Continuing yesterday's theme and discussion, it struck me as I was listening to the girl's sister read from her diary that I could have done something to help her. This isn't some idle boast or an illustration of an inflated ego – you should know by now that overconfidence is most certainly not one of my mannerisms! – but more a recognition that what I suspect she needed most of all was someone to put time and other matters aside and simply be there to listen and to talk to her. However, the crux of the matter is that that someone has not only to empathise but to have personal experience of mental illness. So often it's such a relief when you're trying to explain how you feel and what's going on in your head to be with someone with immediate and close knowledge and appreciation of what it is you're trying to communicate. You don't need to use words. Just a knowing look or gesture can be enough. There's a very real sense of telepathy at work. Yesterday, for example, when I was having a conversation with someone about the symptoms of OCD, I mentioned the fact that one thing I do have trouble with is the telephone. However, this was something that exceeded simply using the thing to communicate. This was about my fear that somehow if I didn't put the receiver down properly, I would be continuing the phone call and accumulating a substantial bill. My remedy to this is often to continually pick the receiver up, put it down again and so on and so forth. Or to repeatedly press the 'end call' button. His reaction said it all – 'Oh, thank God, there's someone else!'

Returning to the Panorama programme, I felt very much a kindred spirit. I knew that if only I'd been able to be by her side, I could have done something. I knew what I would have said. I kept imagining the conversation we could have had. It wouldn't have been a big thing for me. It actually would have been second nature. This would not have been a substitute for therapy, of course. Despite my first-hand experience and a lifetime's knowledge of depression, I'm not trained or qualified to be an adequate substitute in this regard. But that's not the point. What she needed in addition to medical support was the closeness of someone from her own community of the mentally afflicted. Someone like her. Someone like me.

Thursday 14th April 2016

At around one o'clock this morning, I was conscious enough to realise that Lesley was shaking me and urging me to wake up. She told me that I had been screaming in my sleep. In the cold light of day, I can remember what it was that triggered that reaction. I dreamt that I was in a room or small apartment. It was dark and I was lying spread out on the floor, as if hurt or constrained. There were two doors, one in front of me, one behind. They were fragile and they were shaking. Someone was trying to get in. I could see their silhouette through the glass panels. I was helpless. I wanted to remain hidden, to blend into the darkness if I could. I tried to remain silent as well as invisible, but it didn't work. Somehow, I could be seen, my fright and anxiety as evident to whoever it was outside as it was to me trembling on the floor. I decided to try and scare him away. The glass was soaking in condensation and I spread my hands as widely as I could and pushed at it, trying to invoke a feeling of danger despite my own desperation. I wanted the person to see only my handprint. That, and nothing else. I then realised that I was shouting. It seemed at the time as if I was imploring my unwelcome guest to go away and leave me alone. However, Lesley told me later that what I was actually bawling at the top of my voice was 'I'll f…..g kill you!' I'd somehow become the threat rather than the refuge, the perpetrator rather than the potential victim. That was scary. My dream – or rather my nightmare – had been turned on its head.

I've wrestled with the subject of its meaning all day. What is it in my subconscious that leads to such palpable, such striking and horrifying outbursts? What is burrowing its way inside my head like a cancerous growth that culminates in such a confrontation? Why am I torturing myself in such a fashion? How and why do such shocking manifestations of my existence come so readily and yet so unexpectedly? I hadn't had a bad day yesterday. I had no discernible anxieties as I went to bed. I wasn't conscious of any outstanding issues I needed to resolve. And yet that didn't stop the demons in the night from trying to take over my mind.

I was in a daze for much of the morning.

I'd woken up with a banging headache. Probably not surprisingly! I tried to deal with it through tablets and then enforced relaxation. It sort of worked, at least taking the edge off my discomfort. I was able to function. I had commitments which

I met. And yet, the fear has stayed with me throughout the day. Who was I trying to kill? And why? Was it actually my own shadow on the other side of that door? I think that's the most frightening aspect of all this. That what I was intent on doing was to eradicate myself.

Friday 15th April 2016
The end of the working week, and what a week it's been. I'm truly glad it's all over. On reflection, I guess it's gone well. I did all that was asked and required of me. I managed to negotiate the potential hurdle of the focus groups and interviews. They were demanding. I have to say that. I found I had constantly to be alert and at times, to think on my feet. There was never any chance that they were going to run entirely as I'd expected and perhaps even hoped. Therein, of course, lay the possibility of self-destruction. I could only do so much as preparation. I couldn't even safely anticipate what was going to happen, such was the diversity of people and opinion that I had to try and capture and encapsulate. For someone who forever searches for certainty and predictability, it was a lesson in self-management and self-control as much as it was in the techniques of the task in hand. It did help to have an empathy with those with whom I was in conversation. Time after time there was an innate intuition between us. We could finish each other's sentences. We communicated with a knowing nod, smile or grimace. Because what was being relayed quite often was my own experience. I still have more sessions to do, and they will be stretched out over the course of the next month or so. But the worst is over. And at least I now have a degree of confidence, even if I suspect I'm still lacking in other areas – competence being one!

My book too is on its last lap prior to fruition! I've scrutinised the manuscript. I've drawn attention to things that require adjustment. I've even inspected the correlating corrections! It looks complete. Actually it looks great. If only a book's appearance could always mirror its contents. I'd be laughing! All that is needed now is the process of printing and the finished product, after three years of meticulous planning, focused research and simple hard labour, will be in my own hands. I can't wait for that moment.

It wouldn't be a week in my life without its downside and upsets. After a fortnight's presence, the whirlwind that is Joel has once again left us for pastures new. He left for France in the middle of the night, this time as a working man for he is spending the summer period as an assistant at Eurocamp. As is his wont, he didn't entirely do all that his Mum asked him during his brief sojourn at home, but his presence was immense and tremendously uplifting actually. He seems now to be able to take whatever life throws at him, and even his own ambitious plans, in his own sure strides. He looks forward with confidence and a degree of adventure that, as a parent, can be a little frightening, but is also wonderfully invigorating at the same time. He knows what he wants to do, where he wants to go, and how to live the life he wants. What could be better than that? All I can say on the day of his departure is that I'm very proud of him and I'll miss him very much.

Saturday 16th April 2016

Another turbulent night. I'd gone to bed slightly troubled by worries over my physical health. They'd been accumulating during the course of the evening. I hadn't exercised and I'd eaten some things that I knew weren't good for me. Wracked by guilt and concerned at the prospect of impending illness, I'd tried desperately to dispel thoughts that, no matter how much I used reason to negotiate, had become intrusive and disturbing. I thought I'd succeeded. By the time Lesley came to bed – she'd been out at the theatre with Elliot – my mind was elsewhere and other matters had taken over. I was tired, I was relaxed and I was ready for sleep. Around one in the morning, however, I was awake again. This time, it wasn't what I'd dreamt that had frightened me, it was the prospect of going back to sleep. I felt a tightness, as if something was crushing or squeezing the life out of me. It was a horrible sensation and I honestly thought that if I went back to sleep, I would die. I was so convinced. Distraught and helpless, I lay there trying desperately to keep awake. Every time I shut my eyes the prospect of everlasting darkness seemed to consume me, like a tormenting demon, omnipresent and omnipotent. Eventually, I could resist no longer. Sleep overcame me, but it wasn't welcome. It seemed to bring infinity and to be honest, I was both surprised and relieved when I next woke to find I was still here and no longer subsumed by my own vivid and distressing imagination.

Though not everyone is the same, I am one depressive who is constantly tired. As a consequence, I could break records for sleeping. Irrespective of what I do during the day, I have no trouble shutting my eyes and drifting off into another world. If only that process was cathartic in some fashion, or helped me to relax and recover from whatever things I have to address in my waking hours, I wouldn't complain. It's not nice to be constantly knackered, but if there was an alleviation, a direct remedy for my fatigue, I would happily accept the situation and simply go with the flow. But there isn't. There isn't even a recharging of batteries. If anything, sleep leads to a pervasive tiredness that is never satisfied nor expunged. Constantly demanding, perennially debilitating, it never goes away. No matter what I do. I never recuperate. I'm never refreshed. I can accept that, to a certain degree. But when I also have to deal with vivid nightmares, horrendous obstacles, tormenting spectres, constant dilemmas that only serve to confine and punish me whilst I'm supposed to be resting, I wonder if life really is worth living. Fate, circumstances, God, whatever or whoever it is, please just give me a break.

Sunday 17th April 2016

It just goes to show that you should never take things for granted. I thought I was OK again. But this afternoon proved that I'm not perhaps as well as I had imagined. A simple tea at Lesley's sister's house in honour of their mother's birthday was not something that I particularly feared or felt nervous about as the morning passed into afternoon. But I'd only been there a matter of minutes when I knew something wasn't right. The same old anxieties, fears about people and conversations, hit me with a force that I hadn't expected. Ordinarily I never find these things particularly easy. That much is true. But it had never occurred to me not to go and I was expecting to have 'enough in the tank', a degree of confidence and assuredness that not only would stand me in good stead, but would actually allow me the luxury of enjoying the occasion. Not a bit of it. I felt conspicuous by my presence, lost and isolated, withdrawn and unsure. I needed Lesley by my side, to feel her hand, to be my shield. But then, I couldn't surface from behind that protection. It was just too much. I survived the opening of presents and the eating of food, but that was all. I had to make my apologies and leave.

Life can be so cruel. I can't enjoy what others deem natural and habitual. Where others relax and revel in each other's company, I freeze and feel compelled to simply endure. My existence is wholly dependent on this companion that I have, this alter ego called depression. I can never go anywhere without it. It feeds on my fears and exacerbates my worries. It distorts my reality and diminishes my personality. It simply exists, wherever I am, whenever I am, and however I am.

Monday 18th April 2016

Something strange happened to me this morning as I was walking into Wigston. I suddenly became pre-occupied by the ground I was walking on, particularly it's cleanliness. For some reason, it seemed to me that everywhere there was dog poo, even where there was no visible trace. I even found myself trying to dodge any suggestion of a 'blemish' in the natural colour and texture of the concrete. It must have looked bizarre to anyone around me. I was momentarily obsessed by shit! It's not even that I'm unaccustomed to having to deal with the issue. Taking Millie out inevitably leads to clearing up after her. Never a nice job, but it's not one that I do everything to resist, or even feel unable to endure, given the association between hygiene and

OCD. But today it became the most important thing in the world. Funny!

I was meeting a friend of mine for coffee. I haven't seen her for a while, so there was plenty to catch up on. However, I have to admit I found it difficult. Not because of her. She's naturally chatty and I've always found her enjoyable company. No, it was entirely me. It all seemed so much of an effort, as if I was having to continually force words out of my mouth. I get like this at times. It's not even necessarily that I have nothing to say, it's simply the process, the mechanics if you like, of keeping within a conversation. If I thought about it or even pre-empted what we'd discuss, we could have been there for hours. As it was, I seemed constantly searching for what I call 'verbal stamina'. If I could get away with a 'yes' or a 'no', or even a nod or shake of the head, I felt the urge to acquiesce. But that doesn't do much to promote a collective contribution to dialogue, so inside I was caught up in the effort of cajoling more words out of my reluctant mouth, anything to seem connected and focussed. Speaking is no different from moving in this important respect. When depression hits, both are affected, and for the same reason. Lack of motivation. There have, however, been occasions when I've become quite adroit at hiding behind the façade of conversation, when I've talked enough and in a manner that obviously is sufficiently engaging to convince whoever it is that I'm with that I'm OK. This morning was one of those times. Whether I'll suffer for it later, whether I'll have used up my daily quota of words, remains to be seen!

Tuesday 19th April 2016

Dealing with new things has emerged again as an issue over the course of the last couple of days. At the weekend, Lesley bought some new bed linen and pillows. The former looks nice and the latter is suitably soft and yielding to the touch. All is well, you would think. Not a bit of it. To begin with, I found the new duvet cover in particular to be itchy. It seemed excessively dry, if that makes sense. A bit rough too. As for the pillows, my last combination was a perfect match for my sensitive head. Their replacements have left me with a dilemma. One is too low, two is too high! My perfection pilgrimage, you see, doesn't stop with my own behaviour and attitude. It permeates everything with which I come into contact, including now, my new bedding! I've tried so far to resist the temptation to insist on the return of the old. Not only would this, quite understandably, annoy Lesley, it would once more encapsulate my mental blockage concerning anything new. I would be giving in! As a result, I'm trying to make it work. I'm telling myself that there's nothing wrong with the texture of the duvet cover, and that I can quite easily adapt myself to the new heights and contours of the pillows. It will take a bit of time, but I think it will be worth it.

I've found it a little harder though to address a problem with some new Adidas jogging pants I bought a week or so ago. I wore them for the first time yesterday and almost immediately, I spilt some drops of bleach from the newly cleaned washing up cloth. Sure enough, rather than drop harmlessly to the floor, they found their way onto the bottom of my brand new pants. They just had to, didn't they?! As a consequence, amidst the deep blue of the clothing, there are now specks of pink! I tried washing, I even tried colouring the blemishes with a biro. Nothing worked. Never mind, I said to myself, I only brought them to wear casually around the house. I'm not going out in them. Only to take Millie for a walk. It doesn't matter. But of course, it does, doesn't it? At least for me! Having wrestled with the predicament of what to do, I decided that I'd chance my luck and take them back to the shop I bought them from and seek an exchange. The only problem then was that I couldn't find the receipt. No matter, I've got the labels. That will suffice. As we were going to bed, Lesley asked me what had happened as she could clearly see vestiges of pink on what should have been a complete blue. After I'd explained and then told her of my determination to replace them, her immediate and unequivocal response was that the shop wouldn't accept them without a receipt! So now, I'm back to square one. Do I chance it at the shop, or do I find a more durable and workable blue felt-tip pen?

I still don't know. I'm now so tired and fed up of thinking – particularly as all I seem to do is to invent new problems or scenarios – my mind has gone numb. It's over-exercised itself. It's strained and exhausted. Perhaps I'll just resort to Plan C. Simply go and buy a new pair! It's more money – perhaps a needless spend – but at least I'll have peace of mind!

Wednesday 20<u>th</u> April 2016
Yet another interrupted night. I'd only been asleep for ninety minutes before I was awakened by a savage coughing fit and a horrible burning sensation in my throat. I'd managed to bring up some bile and it had then, literally, 'gone down the wrong way', into my lungs rather than my stomach. For fully half an hour I was in extreme discomfort. I ended up sitting on the floor in the bathroom spitting into the toilet in a desperate attempt to ease the situation. All my efforts succeeded in doing, however, was to make me vomit. I then couldn't get rid of that toxic cocktail of sick, bile and saliva, its taste and substance vile and acidic in equal measures. Every time I spat out, all that seemed to happen was that it would all come back from within in greater measures. I really did feel that I was drowning in my own bodily juices. I realised that I was panicking and debated whether or not I should wake Lesley up. I decided not to, to persevere in my sojourn by the toilet seat, to pray for some absolution. Eventually I made my weary way back to bed and lay there listening nervously to the terrific gurgling sound that emanated from deep inside my body. Every time I breathed in, it seemed to invoke further curious sounds. Still feeling swamped by bodily liquid, it was so hard to try to wrestle back control, not just of what was going on inside my digestive system, but of a mind that had been invaded by an uninvited intruder. Tiredness must have overwhelmed me at some point – I don't know when exactly – and the rest of the night was uneventful.

It seems that I've been talking much more about my sleeping hours lately. It's no coincidence. At times I think I live my life in reverse. Robotic, routinized and predictable during the day, yet impulsive, flexible and more engaged when asleep. I do crave sleep sometimes for that very reason. I feel more alive. Life is more exciting. It's unpredictable, that's for sure, but it's just that sense of spontaneity that attracts. It can be such a massive contrast to the search for order and control that characterises having to live with depression. My mind becomes free, if you like. Free to create, free to reflect, free to summon. But also free to disturb and free to frighten. It's like a game of Russian roulette, and I suppose sometimes it appears to be that deadly. You never know what you're going to get. You're incapable of conscious interference, so you simply have to go with it until interruption comes – whether forced or natural. This scenario explains succinctly and clearly why I'm more tired when I awaken in the morning. I've often spent eight to ten hours locked into contexts from which I can't escape, situations that are real and vivid, reincarnations of past experiences combined with current twists, depictions of me that I only recognise in the moment. It relates to all that people try to do with their lives, in effect, to make them interesting and worthwhile. To give them a purpose. That's my night, not my day, though. And because of this, that essential component of human existence, the ability to connect concretely with other human beings, to influence and be influenced, to learn and to teach, to revel in the company of others when you yourself feel properly alive, alert and liberated enough to engage and contribute. All that is missing. I can only dream of the 'quality' of these interdependencies, rather than experience them in some tangible, actual sense. If only I could transfer some of that freedom, that reality, that focus to at least a part of my waking hours?

Thursday 21st April 2016

A much more relaxing day. I certainly needed it after the exploits of yesterday. I spent the majority of it at an event at the Leicester Tigers Rugby Union ground geared around supporting disabled people, older people and carers. It promoted services and products, but also showcased the wonderful array of innovative projects that are currently underway in the Leicester area.

Superbly organised by John, Laura and their team from the Centre for Integrated Living, it was a really uplifting experience. Imaginative, creative, visionary but also well-delivered and with a conscious and pre-emptive recognition of the need to accommodate the diversity of people and their needs. It was very well supported as well, though that fact coupled with the sheer size of the endeavour caused me a few problems, health wise. I'm never good when it comes to attending events. Mostly, this revolves around issues of unpredictability and the number of people in attendance. I can do a little to prepare myself for the former. I can read all prior information. I can find out things such as parking arrangements and the lay-out of rooms. I can judge interest and even plan a schedule for myself. What I can't do, though, is say for certain how busy it is going to be. I can predict. But I can't stipulate. As it happened, my arrival coincided with a packed entrance lobby. It was a veritable hive of activity. I felt immediately a little unsure of myself. I was conscious, for example, that I couldn't dwell in conversation with the people I knew from the host organisation. They were simply too preoccupied with the need to ensure that people were aware of what was happening and where they needed to go. I therefore made my way, steadily if a little warily, up the stairs and into the main exhibition hall. There, I was greeted by row after row of stalls, people making their way from one to another, organisers and exhibitors checking their equipment and supply of information, guides looking for business, caterers serving queues of hungry and thirsty guests and loads of information screens. Everywhere you looked, there were people. Thankfully, right in front of me, in the middle of the room was an area where you could sit down and ponder. I would spend much of the rest of the day just there.

It worked out well, actually. Rather than find people, they could find me. I had no shortage of interesting companions. I was included in the programme as an expert in equality, diversity and human rights and to be honest, even if I wasn't specifically identified, there were plenty of people who already knew me and were keen to have a chat. That made my predicament a lot easier to handle. I just couldn't face the prospect of moving around the room, from stall to stall, from organisation to organisation. The prospect of being approached, of being caught dwelling for a second too long in front of an information stand, is positively scary at the best of times. I just don't like it. I feel I'm being scrutinised, judged and sometimes even pitied. It increases my already considerable levels of nervous tension. Put quite simply, I'm just no good at doing that sort of thing. It's the same in shops. Too much of an interest in one item seems to bring upon me the attention of a shop assistant eager to capture a potential sale. If I wanted someone's help, I would ask. I don't need someone breathing down my neck. There have been occasions when, as a result of this, I've either bought something I didn't actually want or I've fled at a great rate of knots! I respect the fact that people are only doing their jobs or, in the case of an event such as yesterday, doing what they need to do to secure interest and to be in a position to offer advice and guidance, but that doesn't actually help me. It doesn't take away the reality of contact and the potential for dialogue for which I may not be prepared. The only veritable solution to this is for me to become invisible. That way I can drift around as I please, without pressure, without discernible appearance. If only it was possible!

Yesterday, though, I made my own space. I created my own comfort zone. And luckily, I didn't feel conspicuous by my own presence. I was helped not only by some wonderful friends who happened also to be there, by John the ever-supportive and me-conscious host, but also by some new acquaintances from the mental health project for which I'm doing the evaluation work. They had a stall close by. Never manned by less than four people, staff and member alike, many of them came across to talk to me and to compare notes, not just of the event, but of our respective mental conditions. It's so good to find people who share mannerisms that one thinks are peculiar only to oneself. There is a sense of telepathy, of intuitive understanding and empathy when this happens that is genuinely comforting. A problem shared etc.

I stayed for virtually the entire duration of the event. From ten to just after five. I never thought I would when I first arrived, my psyche full of nerves and hesitant anticipation. But I'm so glad I did. I was exhausted at the end. Nervous tension can take more out of you at times than the most strenuous of physical exertion. More importantly, I was pleased for my good friend John. What a job he did. And how inspirational he is. I just hope he gets a well-deserved rest as well as the accolades he deserves.

Friday 22nd April 2016

One of the highlights of Wednesday's event was meeting a young man by the name of Robert. It turned out we had a lot in common. Not just the generality of a mental illness, but also some of its specific nuances. He too, for example, had a thing about entering a crowded room. However, it was what he showed me that immediately caught my attention. Robert, you see, is an artist of considerable pedigree. Now, I'm certainly no connoisseur when it comes to painting. Music yes, but other forms of art, most decidedly no. I do like to think, nevertheless, that I can appreciate talent as well as sincerity and beauty, and in Robert's case, all these positive elements seemed to combine effortlessly with a vision and an attention to detail that was simply stunning.

Of course, the fact that someone obviously hampered by a mental illness should produce work of such quality and depth is no surprise. We – and I'm referring here to the community of people who experience mental ill health – are as capable of achievement and are as likely to achieve as any other group within society. There is nothing that is beyond us. And I mean that most sincerely. If a depressive can lead whole states at times of crisis, as was the case with Winston Churchill and Abraham Lincoln, for example, that surely illustrates the point I am making in a manner that defies dispute. However, if you look within the arts domain, the list of famous devotees of various artistic enterprises who combined that talent with a mental illness is extensive. From Beethoven and Donizetti to Tolstoy and Dickens. Michelangelo, Paul Gauguin, Francesco de Goya and Vincent van Gogh. Hemingway and Dostoyevsky. Edgar Allan Poe and Tennessee Williams. From Cole Porter to Billy Joel and Robbie Williams. I could go on and on. What I saw the other day was another perfect illustration of the marriage of talent and artistic endeavour on the one hand, and the insight and perception gleaned directly as a result of mental illness on the other. I've known countless people who have found art to be a cathartic release for their built-up frustrations and ongoing suffering. People who use art to express what is within in a manner that encapsulates most clearly that reality. People who have found that added dimension, that extra quality, that intrinsic meaning to their competence and expressive flair, that reason to do what they do so well. I know I had that once with music. I still do when I listen. It's no coincidence that I turn to Beethoven in my darkest hours as the perfect embodiment of all that I am with all that I would have liked to be and all that is humanly possible.

I hope Robert gets the break he deserves. His work and his humanity requires a bigger stage, one that he can harness and make his own. All he really needs is that confidence and the necessary support to get him on to that platform in the first place. Getting over that obstacle will be the difficult part for him. Difficult, but certainly not impossible. I wish him all the luck and success in the world.

Saturday 23rd April 2016

The dreaded subject of money came up in conversation with Lesley yesterday. Though she was quick to reassure me that we were still financially solvent, the very mention of the issue was enough to quicken my heart beat and send my mind racing. I can't think of another topic that leads to such sudden, even automatic, catastrophizing. It's always been the same. Every time I have ever ventured into examining finances, I've done so with the sure knowledge that there is going to be some mental illness payback (if you'll excuse the pun!). It's one of the reasons why Lesley takes charge of our collective balance sheet. All that she said yesterday was that she wanted to review our monthly outgoings. Straight away, I convinced myself firstly that we were somehow not in a position to pay the mortgage and all the necessary bills; secondly that we would have to curtail even more our spending to 'starvation' levels; and thirdly, that it is all my fault. I couldn't get it out of my head that my new working arrangements, my self-employment status, my success – or otherwise – in obtaining new work, were all leading to financial meltdown. That I was reliant so much on Lesley to do absolutely everything, to be the breadwinner, the home organiser, our income analyst, our decision-maker, our rock, and that I contributed next to nothing. Nothing seems to bring me down more than my conviction that I am useless and pointless.

One thing that we have been doing for the past month is monitoring our daily outgoings. Everything we spend goes on a list that is then analysed at the end of each week. This works well for me because implicit in its existence is the need not just to account for what we spend, but to actually spend as little as possible. This comes quite naturally to me (yes, I know, all the Yorkshireman jokes!) and I have now made it my mission to spend as near to nothing as I possibly can. Obviously, there are things one cannot avoid – food and petrol come immediately to mind – but it's astonishing how much little things cumulatively metamorphose into significant elements on a spreadsheet. I'm thinking here of trips to coffee shops in particular. One doesn't always consider something like this as having a real impact on a weekly budget – though for some of course these are things that simply are unaffordable – but if you get into the habit of frequenting your Costas, your Starbucks, your Caffe Nero's and their local variations, what you once considered automatically as just an element in your day, a way of passing an hour, suddenly becomes something much more. Accounting for everything, however, can lead to a very real mental health issue. And it is this. If you are scrutinising in such a way and in such detail, and if that transforms into issues of guilt, every single item, no matter how necessary, routine or mundane, can become a potential nail in a coffin. The pressure not to spend simply leads to self-reproach and remorse when one does so. It's a question of balance and I'm never sure or confident enough to recognise when I have achieved this state of affairs. And so I go on feeling guilty, feeling ineffective and unproductive. St Paul, of course, said that 'the pursuit of money is the root of all evil'. Even though this discussion isn't about greed and the love of material things, I can't help wishing to alter a word or so to reflect my circumstances. Perhaps, to a depressive, it should instead read 'the spending of money is a root of all uncertainty'? A thought to ponder.

Sunday 24th April 2016

I was absolutely distraught this morning. In the early hours, once more a horrid, vivid dream led to my lashing out in my sleep. The details of my fantasy are less relevant than what it led to, but nevertheless it is important, I guess, to set things in context. I was being forcibly driven from a bedsit. Why I was there I wasn't sure as my alternative was to return to Lesley and my family and this is actually what I was desperate to do. However, my departure was being 'assisted' by people who also lived in the house and indeed in the street. They wanted me gone and were doing everything in their power to get me out as quickly as possible. Physical ejection combined with my possessions being literally thrown into a massive suitcase that was perched precariously on the top of my car. At one stage, however, one person in particular was adamant that he could use the circumstances to throw way lots of his unwanted items. My suitcase had become a skip. The more he put in, the less room there was for my stuff and the more the car sagged and groaned with the increased weight. I recognised him as well. He was an old schoolmate. It was then that my 'dream' turned into a living nightmare. In trying to stop his antics, I decided to punch him. You can probably guess what happened. My somnolent action became a real physical gesture. Still asleep, disturbed and pressurised, feeling trapped and targeted, I ended up whacking Lesley. I immediately woke up, my subconscious exertion translating into conscious recognition. I felt so awful. All I could do was to profusely apologise. Desperate for understanding, Lesley, bless her, immediately knew what had happened. I guess she's become accustomed to it. Irrespective of the fact that all this had occurred whilst asleep, I couldn't get over the fact that I had physically hurt her. She was OK, thank God. I hadn't connected with real force, but that wasn't the point. For a while I lay there on my back, my mind continually turning over the same horrific thoughts. Desperate for absolution, I tried to reason with myself. This wasn't a premeditated attack. It wasn't even a conscious reaction. I wasn't a wife batterer. I wasn't guilty of domestic violence. I couldn't knowingly inflict such pain. My mental cogitation soon affected the rest of me. I felt physically sick, my stomach turning, in spasm and in real discomfort. I had to resort to medication to get me to calm down. Eventually sleep embraced me but it was with real trepidation that I awoke some hours later. Lesley virtually laughed it off. She was unhurt. She wasn't marked. She had the perspective that I was struggling to generate. I've probably said this before, but I really do need to mention this to my consultant when I next see him. It's become too traumatic to ignore, too impactful to dismiss. I don't know what the answer is. Separate beds, separate rooms. Physical separation? Please God, don't let it come to that.

Monday 25th April 2016

After yesterday's drama, I'm pleased to say that I – and more importantly Lesley – both survived the night! Joking aside, I thought it may be interesting just to dwell on what my dreams have led me to believe, because this is a significant consequence with regard to my general mental health. In short, I have convinced myself that certain things that I have dreamt – and dreamt repetitively – have within them an element of truth. In some cases, I even firmly believe them to be indisputably and wholly true, without hesitation, consideration or variation. I seem to be beyond the capacity to rationalise them, for the simple reason that I can't recall or summon up from within me anything sane or realistic to refute what they state and reinforce. They have, in a nutshell, become internalised as fact.

What sort of things am I talking about? As examples, I can immediately think of the following:

1. That I had a more traumatic time at school than I probably did. That it was a source of perpetual conflict. That all it did was undermine my confidence and self-esteem.
2. That someone who I was really close to at school actually disliked me. That she simply endured my presence. That she was doing everything she could to discard me.
3. That, somewhere in the metropolis of Leicester, I have a secret bolt-hole. That I return to it at times when I want to avoid scrutiny, when I want to hide. I can even picture it, a bedsit, a single room, but one that has been grandiosely decorated, chandeliers on the ceiling, elaborate mirrors and precious art on the wall. My meagre possessions, my limited furniture – a table, a chair, a single bed – all seem out of place and context.
4. That I owe the landlord of that room thousands of pounds in unpaid rent. That she – and it most definitely is a she – lives elsewhere in the building and wants me out. She is tired of my excuses, of my forgetfulness. She is intent on damaging me.
5. That I went to more universities than I actually did, and did more courses, more subjects, than I could possibly manage. That I'm forever behind in my studies. That I'm succinctly out of my depth. That I'm continually threatened with expulsion.
6. That I lived at various times of my life in abject poverty. That I could never escape from its strictures. That I was forced to sell things, treasured things, to survive. That I was reduced to begging, unable to help myself, incapable of making money.
7. That my Dad and I had become adversaries. That our relationship had turned sour. That he didn't believe in me. That he judged me. That he always thought the worst of me.

> That he wanted to punish me. That I resisted and resorted to physical violence. That I knew that in doing so, his physical condition would deteriorate.

This is all scary stuff, particularly the last one. Thankfully, that one in particular is less prevalent, less dominant in my mind and more susceptible to dissecting and dispelling. The mitigating factor is, though, that it has only surfaced recently. The others have been with me for years. Psychologists would, I am sure, be able to explain and unravel all this. I think their essence, their permanence, their transference into reality, is a reflection of the fact that they have been with me for so long. If you continually tell yourself something, even if it's subconsciously within your sleep, you begin to rationalise it as the truth. As fact.

Is it also paranoia? Is it hallucination? Is it distorted reality? Yes, I think it is. Sadly, I wish it were only these things. That way there would be a bit of me that would dispute the evidence of their existence. I seem to have gone beyond that. I seem at times to be living in my own disfigured and twisted world.

Tuesday 26th April 2016

It's turning out to be a very quiet day. I did have a meeting this afternoon, an interview for a project actually. But as my contact has not got back to me to confirm the arrangement, I'm presuming it's off. I'm quite relieved, as it happens, because it's enabled me to spend some time working at home without fear of distraction or interruption. How I used to cope in an office environment, I will never know. That's probably a rhetorical question for the simple reason that I didn't – cope that is! The sanctuary of my own workplace in the kitchen, the quietness, the stillness and the solitude all contribute to a much more productive working arrangement – for me at least. I used to have to consciously focus on eradicating the busy atmosphere around me, to have, in effect, 'tunnel vision, when I was sitting at my work station at the Council, and that was before I actually got round to doing anything! Everything I did there I did on the backdrop of firstly having to shut myself off from the hustle and bustle, and that was often an immense if not impossible task in itself.

I'm told that hot desking is about to be implemented right across the workplace in my old section. I would never have been able to deal with that. Such a policy, to my reckoning, also flies in the face of disability equality. It seems to me to be inconsistent with the legal requirement to offer and implement reasonable adjustments. Even if such considerations are in mind – and I sincerely hope they are – it presupposes the fact that disabled workers are entirely comfortable for their disability and associated symptoms to be out in the public domain. At least amongst their fellow workers, that is. For how else is the issue of people not being able to meet the requirements of the hot desking arrangement and therefore being 'permitted' not to do so going to be dealt with when everyone is of the opinion that it is a blanket policy? It almost coerces those people who wish their disability to remain a matter for them and perhaps their manager alone, to 'come out'. Or at the very least, it puts added pressure on them to do so. Unless managed properly, it's not a situation conducive to a healthy atmosphere.

To change tack. I had another dizzy spell at lunchtime. The usual thing. It hits me very quickly, and without warning. I can be fine one minute and then this feeling of light-headedness, breathlessness and haziness overcomes me. It's like a sudden adrenalin surge, but without the trigger. What causes it, I don't know. Every time I mention it to a doctor, they seem to think it's related to my mental condition. They do the tests – bloods, blood pressure, ECG etc. I pass them, or at least those that I expect to pass (I've given up on liver function!) and so it goes on. They feel like a panic attack but without an apparent stimulant. Again, no trigger! Food helps to take the feeling away. Rest as well. If I didn't know better, I would bet time and time again that they relate to my blood sugar levels. I am prone to diabetes. I've done the self-assessment tests. I have the family history. My medication increases its likelihood. But every time my doctor checks for the illness, there is no sign. I'll mention it to my consultant at my next appointment. Gosh, I'll have a lot to say to him!!

I can't let today go by without commenting on the result of the inquest into the Hillsborough Disaster. At last, at long last, it seems that justice is eventually a reality. I remember that day very vividly. I wasn't there, but as I'd spent time as a teenager on the Kop watching Liverpool[13], it always struck me that I would have been standing there alongside people who would eventually die in such appalling circumstances. I also remember being in the city that very night – at a concert at the Philharmonic Hall. It was like intruding on private grief. There was a palpable feeling of shock and devastation everywhere. The streets were deserted and where there was people, there was also silence. I'll never forget it. For it to take twenty-seven years for the truth that was always there to be 'officially' and 'institutionally' recognised is nothing short of a national scandal. I just hope that for the families and friends of the '96' there is now proper peace.

Wednesday 27th April 2016
Though I have to go out later to conduct two more interviews for the Mental Health project, today promises once more to be relatively quiet. I have Lesley at home with me. She's got the next three days off work, primarily to devote some time to her law studies. Knowing her, she'll try to cram in a variety of odd jobs as well! I know she's taking a friend of her parents to an eye appointment tomorrow, for example. Her ability to switch from one thing to another, to multitask effectively, always astounds me. As for me, I have a lot to be getting on with. I'm going to try and finish writing up the results of the focus groups/interviews I've already done for that project. I'm on the last legs now with regard to doing any more. I then face the complex task of turning a wealth of information into something meaningful and productive, a report that can be used to move things forward a little.

I spent a lot of time yesterday thinking about Hillsborough. As someone who spent so much time in the 1980s on the old football terraces, what happened on that fateful day has always been within my imagination and experience to visualise and even internalise. I know what feeling uncomfortable standing on overcrowded lumps of concrete was like. At the time – and before the tragedy – one just put up with it. It was part of the footballing experience. I can remember one game at Elland Road for example, where my brother and I arrived to find a more than expected mass of people trying to gain entrance. We were still queuing outside as three o'clock approached, every one of us frantic to pass through the turnstiles before someone decided it was full to capacity. When we eventually got in, about ten minutes after kick-off, we were met by a wall of backs. It seemed impenetrable. I couldn't see how any more could be crammed in, and yet behind us were still hundreds of people expecting to see a game. We couldn't move in either direction. At that moment Leeds scored, and the crowd to a man – and it was an all-male affair – started to move. People jumped up, pushed forward, leapt on each other. It was chaos. The ecstasy of a goal. It was our opportunity not just to join in the celebrations but to access the enclosure. For fully a minute or more, we were caught up in this melee of moving bodies, every one of which was momentarily released from pent-up tension, like an athlete at the start of the hundred metres. When it began to calm down, we were twenty yards to our left and half-way down the terrace, and yet I couldn't recall my feet ever touching the ground.

At the time – pre-Hillsborough – this was what you watched football for. The ecstasy of a goal, the cathartic loosening of every internal inhibition, the crazy yet permissible need to jump on the person next to you, knowing full well that someone was going to do the same to you. We never thought we were in any real danger, even when you weren't fully in control of your movements. Crowd dynamics were the equivalent of a ride on a rollercoaster. Thrilling, unconventional, scary, yet fleeting and infrequent (particularly if you were a Leeds supporter!). You did feel breathless at times. After it settled down, I often found myself blowing heavily, trying to catch my breath and regain my composure. It must have been from the pressure. There was no other explanation. After Hillsborough though, you realised that this was potentially something else. This really was dangerous. It could take your life. Of course, everywhere you went there were the cages. With the metal pointing inwards at the top, you could climb them, but it was the devil of a job to get over them, particularly if you were a little overweight. The pins at the top were like numerous blunt daggers thrust into your torso. But that was the point. You weren't designed to get over them. They were there to keep us in, to restrict our movement, to entrap us like animals. When I go to football these days, the experience is so different. It's hard to imagine and certainly to describe to youngsters what it was like then in comparison to now. But to those of us of a certain age, fanatical fans of our teams and our generation, we could imagine the Hillsborough experience. We didn't have to have been to that one ground. Everywhere was potentially the same. I have to admit that it scared the living daylights out of me. How many times had I, unknowingly, been in a situation that could have been life-threatening? What would I have done had the pressure got too much? I knew the signs of pressure, just not to that extent obviously. Would I have been able to help myself? Was I innocently taking my younger brother into a death-trap? How could I live with myself afterwards had I survived and he not?

That's why Hillsborough is important to so many people, I guess. Not just those immediately concerned, the wonderful families and friends of the ninety-six people who were unlawfully killed, but to every last one of us who experienced the terraces of old and lived, thank God, to tell the tale. That's why the campaign for justice touched so many people. They were our brothers and sisters who perished because of a state of mind that equated fans with worthless commodities. Who died because the powers-that-be, whoever they were, decided that the deaths of those innocent people, mattered less than the perpetuation of the status quo.

Thursday 28th April 2016

One of the interviews I did yesterday was with a woman who has only just been discharged from a period on a psychiatric ward. Still understandably shaky and very cautious, we had a long conversation that went far beyond the requirements of the work I've been tasked with doing. I've never been sectioned or spent time voluntarily as a patient, but I've been with so many people who have that it's a situation that seems very familiar, though disturbing at the same time. Yet again, I found someone talking about what appeared to me to be basic inadequacies of a system that appears incapable of doing 'what it says on the tin', to paraphrase a popular TV commercial of yesteryear. Simple things in many respects, such as being afforded the time and the space to get to know your surroundings, of being treated as a person rather than a number, of being given the opportunity to become accustomed to routine and more importantly, the people around you. All things that are absolutely vital in the treatment of mental illness. Indeed, things that I would say are more pivotal when dealing with mental conditions than with any other form of illness. I know I've been close to being detained under the Mental Health Act. The last major depressive episode of my time at the Council comes immediately to mind. The questions I was asked by my consultant at the time to determine my pending course of action I knew afterwards were really focused on whether that choice was going to be allowed to me or not. If I had stated, for example, an intention to soldier on at work despite having just talked about finding my route to the top of the building in order to throw myself off it, I'm convinced he would have started the process leading to my detention. Whether hospitalisation would have helped me then I don't know. Whether it would ever help me is, of course, a question I can't really answer. All I can say from my experience of listening to people who have been there is that I would have my doubts. Yesterday I heard a clear message that rather than aiding her recovery, her time had simply exacerbated her condition, leading to further uncertainties and fears. It hadn't helped. It had kept her safe maybe, but that's all. Maybe that was actually enough? Maybe that is really the primary purpose? What I'm not saying – or suggesting – is that hospitalisation never works. That would be plain idiocy and a wild overgeneralisation. People obviously do recover on wards. But maybe not all? What it does reveal, I think anyway, is that there are obviously severe shortages in terms of staff, in terms of time and in terms of options. These are things that are often beyond the capabilities of current staff to address. It's the system, and the lack of investment in it, that is really the issue. It needs attention. It needs overhauling. It needs prioritising. The other thing that was clearly apparent from my conversation is a disconnect between letting a patient go from a ward and what happens afterwards – in terms of continuity of treatment that is. Yes, there is the Crisis team, but it was abundantly clear that what would help my newly-acquired friend was not anything available in the clinical system, but her familiarity and her participation in a community mental health project, in this case the one I'm doing some work for. It was her involvement in that that would aid recovery, maintain some sense of normality, keep her focused and slowly but surely reactivate her energy and reassert a sense of self-esteem and self-worth. But are projects such as this one even known to all that work inside the system? And even if they are, are they actively promoted? The further issue, of course, revolves around funding and the priorities for our fragile mental health infrastructure. It comes down to the age-old matter at hand. There is a serious need not only for greater connections between clinical treatment and practical, community-based activity, but also for greater investment in the latter that does not come at the expense of the former. It's an addition, not a replacement, a complement not an alternative. And it's a vital one.

Friday 29th April 2016

Mild panic set in this morning! I left home at my usual time to get to my fortnightly nine o'clock meeting at Leicester General. It's only a short drive so I didn't think I'd have anything to worry about. However, for some unaccountable reason, everyone in Leicester appeared to be going my way. I kept getting stuck behind stationary traffic. When one queue lifted, another began. I started to feel the tension rising within me. I can't ever be late for meetings. It's one of those situations that I find really difficult to handle. The thought of walking in to a crowded room, the agenda already begun, faces turning to the door, searching for a seat, scrambling to get out a pen and notebook, apologising at every opportunity, looking and feeling flustered, taking time to regain some composure. The dreaded legacy of unpunctuality goes on! As I drove, I was virtually begging people to move. I then began to shout and scream. Why hadn't I left earlier? Was I simply complacent? Why hadn't I foreseen traffic problems? You see, my aim is never to arrive on time. It is to arrive at least ten minutes early. All my coping mechanisms are geared towards this. I can choose my seat in the room. I can hang up my coat at leisure. I can get a drink without having to think of anyone else. I can prepare my papers. I can check that my pen works. I can get the extras ready if not. I can see the door and greet people as they come in. I can focus on that alone. By ten minutes to nine, I was still at least two traffic lights away. They seemed stuck for an eternity on red. Would I get through them before they turned once more? Finally I arrived at the car park. Only five minutes later than usual and five minutes before the meeting was due to start. My problems, however, weren't over. I paid my money at the machine and got a ticket. I put it on my dashboard but as I went to close the door, it kept blowing away onto the floor of the car. Leicester General's tickets don't have a sticky bit to attach to your windscreen and as it was really windy, I couldn't get out of the car without risking my ticket disappearing from view! Can you believe it? I tried one last time, only to find that the ticket simply wasn't there. I desperately searched under the seats. The clock was ticking. One minute to nine. I'd have to get another ticket. Spend another three pounds. Finally, a little bit of luck. I found my displaced, precious item in the door compartment. Now, back to the task in hand! I'd have to somehow wedge it onto the dashboard. Luckily Lesley's specs were at hand. I placed my ticket under them and positioned them accordingly. At last, I was saved, momentarily at least. But at what cost? I rushed across the road, through the doors, up the lift to reception. I got my visitor's badge. I signed in and nearly sprinted to the meeting room. Envisaging my nightmare scenario, I prepared for the worst, only to find people still missing and those present casually getting drinks, passing the time of day innocently and without a care in the world! The meeting eventually got going at around ten past nine, those present seemingly, yet understandably, oblivious to the traumatic start to the day that my mental illness had inflicted on me. I know in two weeks' time that I'll be ready and waiting to go even earlier than usual. My body clock will need to be adjusted once more. Anything to avoid the consequences of time and its potentially calamitous impact on my psyche and composure.

Saturday 30th April 2016

I don't mean this to be flippant or disrespectful given the subject of my entry of a few days ago, but watching football, I am convinced, can be seriously bad for your health! Today, I made my way to The Den to see Millwall take on Oldham Athletic. I haven't been for a while, but that didn't stop me having to go through the usual and familiar pre-match rituals. I take the same train at the same time. On arrival in London I frequent Waterstones near Piccadilly Circus, before leaving at one o'clock to take the Jubilee Line and the Overground to Surrey Quays. From there I walk to the ground, taking the same route, entering at the same turnstile, eating the customary pie whilst watching whatever game is being shown on the telly. I then go up into the stands, earlier than most, so that I can sit in my usual seat. It's all done deliberately. Any deviation would potentially be disastrous. You see, following my habitual pattern, is an absolute must, if I'm going to feel comfortable and – and it's taken over here as it did before at Leeds – if I'm going to do my bit to contribute to a Millwall win.

Today, given the fact that Oldham have been flirting with relegation for much of the season, there was a tangible sense of inevitability that my team would gain the three available points. We scored at the start of each half and at the end of the first.

Perfect timing. Oldham had a lot of possession but lacked a cutting edge, their plight summed up by possibly the worst miss I've ever seen at a game. Their substitute forward, from literally a yard out with an open goal, succeeded in hitting the top of the stand! The irony, for me, was that he used to play for Leeds! Despite the luxury of a comfortable lead throughout, the quality of the opposition and Millwall's run of good form, all the usual manifestations of anxiety and tension prevailed. We go to football for those ecstatic moments when someone puts the ball in the opposition net. The sheer thrill and exhilaration is hard to beat. You feel momentarily on cloud nine. You share your adulation and your cathartic release with others around you, irrespective of whether you know them or not. You jump, you punch the air, you clench your fists, you shout, you scream. It's absolutely wonderful. It's intoxicating. It's the best feeling in the world. But, given that goal and celebration take up only a few minutes, it's fleeting. For the rest of the time, I – and I'm sure I'm not alone – find myself consumed by nerves, frustration and apprehension. Every time the opposition come close to our goal, I'm fearful. My right leg starts to jitter, my nervous cough becomes incessant. I can't speak. It's like a massive inhalation of breath. It stays there for what seems like an eternity, awaiting a release. When we attack and contrive to miss an opportunity, I can feel the exasperation, the sense of unfulfilled expectation. I am let down. I've been allowed to feel eager. I've been coerced to wait on tenterhooks, to anticipate what could be that defining moment once more. It's not come. All those anticipatory feelings of joy have been thwarted. Will they come again? I don't know.

For someone with a mental illness, football – if you are passionate enough – can give you something that you don't necessarily encounter in everyday life. That sense of achievement. That moment of joy and ecstasy. But it can also contrive to exacerbate all the characteristics that trap you in your condition. If you suffer from anxiety, if you're prone to panic, if you find it difficult to escape from routines, if you simply can't enjoy life, then for most of the time, football can act like a powerful, but unrequited stimulant. It promises much. But ultimately fails to deliver. As I left the ground today, I was thoroughly exhausted. Those moments that I crave had come and gone. I'd left them behind. Ordinary existence had taken over once more and I again felt as I am day to day. I looked around me. Happy faces, cheerful gestures, engaging conversations. People fleet of foot, eager it seemed to celebrate a 3-0 victory.

As for me, I made my way back to St Pancras, alone and thoughtful, ruminating once more, content but no longer jubilant. The reversal to normality, you see, had begun at the final whistle.

May

Sunday 1st May 2016
Carrying on the football theme, today could be the finest moment in the history of Leicester City FC. Whether football fan or not, it could also be one of those defining occasions for everybody living in or in close proximity to the city. An opportunity for people to say 'I was there', 'I remember it well'. Because today, little Leicester City could become Champions of England! I won't go into how this has come about, firstly because it's not essentially relevant to this diary and secondly because it would be hard to encapsulate what has been in essence a sporting miracle. All the superlatives have been used. The story will be one of legend. It strikes me though that for one community of people, this may be 'bitter sweet' at best, difficult to handle as certain, and potentially debilitating at worst. For us depressives, situations in which it is 'expected' that people will be joyous and exuberant can become occasions for immense inner turmoil. Why can't I feel like that? Should I try and pretend? What's best for me? What tactics should I employ? Shall I just endure and wait until it is over? Christmas, I guess, is probably the most evident

example of what I mean. Seeing and being overwhelmed by festive good cheer can serve to aggravate and inflame feelings of loss and anxiety. If you don't feel as others do, their behaviour, their excitement, their joy only magnifies your own sense of alienation and despondency. The gulf between you and them only increases. If you are a Leicester City supporter and a depressive, emotions could be at such odds that it may be confusing. Depression cannot be wished away in one momentous gesture. It can't be beaten by something incidental and other worldly. If it could, it wouldn't be depression. You may feel a disconnect that is hard to stomach. You want more than anything to be part of the celebrations, part of that communal feeling of togetherness, of shared rejoicing and triumph. But you can't give yourself entirely to those sensations. Your mental illness, your depression, is too powerful. It keeps you in check. It still permeates your feelings, your sensations, your ability to react and to sustain. You're caught in a trap. The expectation can't be fulfilled, no matter how hard you try and how much you wish it to be otherwise. Even for those of us who aren't City fans, but who live here and wish the team well for the sake of your geographical community, for the goodwill of the area, for the impact you know it will have on so many facets of life, it is a time for longing and a time for reflection. You're part of it, but not in the same way. You're caught up in it, but not in the same manner. You feel the emotions of others, but you can't internalise them. You see the exhilaration, but you can't empathise. You remain an outsider. You are still a depressive. Your condition still dictates, still engulfs, still determines your way of coping.

Monday 2nd May 2016

As it happened, City only drew with Man United, a result that still leaves them two points off the title. It will happen though as not only do I think it impossible for them not to gain those elusive points, but I can't envisage Tottenham winning all their remaining games either. It's just now a matter of time.

We had a busy day yesterday, which probably accounts for my more than usual lethargy this morning. Not only did I clean the house and do my usual stint of ironing, but we had to take the car to a garage as the exhaust was only hanging on by what seemed like a thread! A friend of mine, Pete, was also coming around for Sunday lunch/tea. It was good to see him. He's been a faithful friend and a caring one. He'd been to the pub to watch the Leicester match, very much a first experience for him as he's not a football fan at all. It just shows how much people have been swept away by the current success of the team. By the time he left, it was going on nine o'clock and I was yearning for my bed.

Today promises to be more leisurely, which is only right as it's a Bank Holiday. Mum arrives at Leicester Station at ten to five this afternoon. She's staying for a couple of days which will be nice. Though I have to work, it will still be good to have her around and at least now, working from home, I don't have that necessity to be somewhere else all the time. I still have things to go to this week, but only now and then. I seem to have settled into a fairly regular work pattern. There's always something to do. I have tasks, projects and targets. I have commitments, routine and exceptional meetings to attend, a steady – though sill limited – income. Things appear to be progressing. There is potential work on the horizon via a number of old sources. I will have the opportunity of extending my involvement in ongoing initiatives should I wish to take them. People seem interested in what I have to offer. So I can't complain really. I think developing a website of my own has been a sound move. Putting it together wasn't easy though. I had the information to hand. I knew what to include. But I'd perhaps not anticipated the inherent need to 'sell myself'. Suddenly, I had entered the realms of business. I had a product – me – that required a certain approach, a means of promotion and advertising that I was unaccustomed to achieving and one that I found immensely stomach churning. I had to use words that made me cringe. Words that embarrassed me. Words that I was afraid people would deem to be overconfident, self-centred and boastful. All I was doing was what seemed to be required, but it just wasn't me. My mental illness was inherently at play here. How could I elucidate self-confidence when it's one of the things I ordinarily lack? How could I give reassurance, when that is one of my most pertinent needs? How could I instil reliability and portray competence, composure and expertise, when these are all qualities that I don't often feel in myself, or at least, have to search for within my psyche? To me, it seemed an exercise in hypothetical assurance. Not a falsity as such – I didn't tell any fibs – but something that was decisively what I could be, rather than what I naturally am. I've talked to other people who have done what I've just done and who feel as I feel, and they all recognised that sense almost of embarrassment. It's obviously not only me. I said to one person that in order to do what was necessary, I felt I had to become someone else, someone akin to David Brent[14] at his most cringe-worthy self-inflated best. He knew what I meant. 'We all have to do it', he said in encouragement. I just pray that those qualities that I hope I have within me and to which I aspire – relating to empathy, lived experience, sincerity, honesty, clarity and so on and so forth – and those passions that people who know me would hopefully recognise, will still shine through amidst the muddied waters of business promotion. I'm still me. I'm not anyone else. And I'm honestly still the person you think I am. Fingers crossed!

Tuesday 3rd May 2016

Well, there wasn't long to wait! A Chelsea goal eight minutes from time led to the biggest party ever seen in Leicester's long history![15] We could hear the fireworks going off within minutes of the final whistle and seeing the television coverage this morning, I'm convinced that half of Leicester never made it to their beds last night! I'm genuinely thrilled, especially for those friends who are die-hard City fans who could never have believed in a million years that this could happen. I remember when Leeds won the title in 1992. The feeling was absolutely immense. For a short period of time, my mental illness was relegated to subsidiary status – though it never entirely went away. I do recall consciously experiencing a massive sense of regret, however, when things did begin to sink in. That regret was based on the fact that, irrespective of my wishes and desires, depression would determine the nature and the duration of my celebrations, such as they were. It wouldn't let me go. I couldn't join in the revelry to the same extent and in the same manner. I remember thinking that any time now I would revert back to normality, that monotony and endurance would once more engulf me. It was just a question of when. I couldn't even consider living in the moment because I knew that if I did, if I even attempted an emotional release, letting my wishes oversee my condition (even if that was possible), the crash – when it inevitably came – would be too much to handle. The fall from delirium to depression would be too big. The difference in emotional states too extreme. The situation potentially dangerous. So, I had to keep things in check. I tried so hard to enjoy the experience and I did to a degree. But that shadow, that dark shadow of depression, never left me. It was just waiting for the moment when I relented, unable to sustain the pretence, incapable of carrying on the façade. And then it hit me. And it hit me hard. The awful thing is that I always knew it would, and that's the perennial problem with any form of celebration for a depressive. Momentary release often leads to devastating reverberations. It's akin to the worst kind of hangover, only on a permanent basis.

Wednesday 4th May 2016

Well the party in Leicester shows few signs of abating. I ventured into the city yesterday for a meeting and everywhere you looked there were visible signs of celebration. I wanted to go down past the stadium to have a look for myself but every approach, from whatever direction, was congested with traffic, everyone apparently with the same intention! It's difficult not to be caught up in it, but as the day went on, that sense of alienation within me began to grow. I'm not a City supporter, of course, so that will have had something to do with it. But I've lived here for nearly twenty-five years so I think I could claim at least some attachment to the place and at least a morsel of credibility as an involved citizen. However, it's not manifested itself in terms of identity and emotion. I'm pleased. Of course I am. But I can't seem to feel and to experience that same sense of belonging. I still feel an outsider. That's the truth of the matter.

And there's something more. This will be hard to describe accurately and unequivocally. In a nutshell, seeing the euphoria on the streets and on my television screen has actually been a painful process. I'm jealous. I'm envious. Not of the success of someone else's team but at the capacity of so many people to be so consumed with unadulterated joy and pleasure. It actually hurts and that then compounds the guilt I have that I can react in such a self-centred way. I know that I cannot begin to envisage and internalise, let alone express, what so many others are feeling. What they're going through is just alien to me. To that extent anyway. And so that feeds a sense of bitterness, of anguish, of disappointment, of loss. I don't know whether I'll ever feel as they do. I certainly can't remember ever experiencing sensations of that enormity and quality. Did I? Once? And is it just that I've forgotten? I just don't know. I'm often asked by consultant and doctor when the last time was that I was really happy. My answer is always that I can't remember. If it ever was there, it has been suppressed by long years of depression. It's not part of my emotional vocabulary any more. If it ever had been.

Thursday 5th May 2016

My brain is positively whirring as I write this. It's tired. It's confused. It's overworked and it aches. My brain, that is, not my head. I'm trying to make a deliberate distinction here. I've spent the vast majority of the day at an event focusing on mental health and in particular mental health commissioning. I can't pretend that I got much out of it, because I didn't. This was partly due to the fact that its target audience was actually the mental health voluntary sector as opposed to individual service-users, although many were one and the same. What didn't help was the language, the complexity of the terminology. Let me give you some examples. Social Impact Bonds. Preventative interventions. Social investors. Innovative service delivery. Outcome focused culture. Better contract management. Evidence base. Potential for replication and scaling. Baselines assessment. Intervention model. Outcomes metrics. Transformation opportunity. Outcomes-based contracting. Co-production model. I could go on. Now, I like to consider myself to be reasonably intelligent and certainly conversant with the jargon that accompanies institutions. I worked for a local authority for nearly eleven years, for goodness sake! But even I was struggling at times. I hate to think how an ordinary member of the public manages to keep abreast of what's going on when faced with this intellectual convolution and challenge. I do know actually, because they used to tell me as part of my job! I've been away from 'public sector talk' for six months and I was stumped! It was hard going, taxing to the extreme, and to be honest, I'd given up at lunchtime. I tried to maintain focus, to keep wrestling with the exercises, but I simply couldn't keep up the pace. I'll need at some point to sit down and try to dissect and then digest what I've been told today because it is important. It may serve to determine how services for the mentally ill in Leicester are commissioned, supported and developed for the immediate future, no less.

I know I wasn't helped by the emotional upset of seeing my Mum leave this morning. The time she spends with us goes so quickly and I always wish I'd made more of it. Depression can be so cruel at times. It serves, for example, to stifle my speech, my ability to converse, my motivation to connect. I want so much for things to be easy, for the conversation to flow, to be able to chat away, to find out more, to reveal more, to revel in the process of human contact. But I just can't. It's too difficult. It's frustrating and it becomes too large a hurdle to negotiate. I do enjoy just being with her and I hope that that's reciprocated. I feel comforted by her presence, but at the same time I find it hard because I know the barriers created and enforced by my mental condition are set and unyielding. I love her so much. I also want to be her little boy again. I want her to take away my pain as she did so many times in my formative years. I want to play games with her. I want to laugh and cry with her. I want to joke with her. But depression has made those things not impossible, but so much more demanding. As we left each other at the station, I knew how upset she was. I wanted to let myself go. To cry and to shake. To hug her. To not let go. I've been the strong person in her life for so long though that the mantle refuses to transform, to adapt to new circumstances. I maintained – or tried to – that element of solidity and dependability that I hoped carried her through those awful times when we were coming to terms with the loss of Dad and Danny. It's still there. It was only as I was driving away, seeing her looking for me, that I gave in and the tears came.

Friday 6th May 2016

Simon and Garfunkel's 'The Sound of Silence' is one of my favourite songs. Even though the song is a much more complex matter in meaning than the nature of silence, it focuses for me on the value of that essence, on its beauty, its tranquillity and its serenity. This afternoon, I absolutely craved a world without noise. A world of peace and of simplicity. A world without interruption, without interference, without confusion. It's been a busy week, full of meetings, full of human contact. I seem to have stumbled from one situation to another and in every one, I have met the expectation of contribution. It's been taxing. I can't remember a time when I've been truly alone, content within my own sphere of existence, satisfied just to do nothing and to let the world go on in its indomitable way, endless in its duration, seamless in its process. The other day, I felt that need to such an extent that I seemed on the verge of screaming. Within me, a growing sense of frustration and entrapment coincided with a tension and anxiety that I was finding increasingly difficult to suppress. It all stemmed from the fact that I couldn't find respite. Everywhere I went, I was compelled to talk and to engage. On a number of occasions, I felt the temptation to resort to Diazepam. I was uptight and frustrated, but, more ominously, I also sensed a growing anger, a violent outburst in the offering. I wanted to shout away everyone and everything. I wanted to physically dispel the hustle and bustle of life. I wanted no part of it. 'Please go away. Leave me alone', I wanted to scream. It wasn't people as such that I wished to disengage from. But life itself. People I could deal with as long as I could resort to peace and quiet whenever I felt the need, whenever my mind demanded it. Even today, in the meetings I've had, I've found the conversation difficult, the need to come up with words and sentences, challenging and arduous. They just wouldn't flow. I had to consciously contrive the mechanisms by which I could communicate, and communicate effectively and meaningfully. It was like a complex and tiring physical exercise, one without an end, one devoid of relaxation, one absorbed with effort, an everlasting struggle. The people I was seeing were lovely. It wasn't my company that was the problem. It was entirely within me. Talking had become too demanding, too strenuous. If only I could convey to you, the reader, in its entirety, just how much. But that too, necessitates words and, to be frank, I've had enough of them for one day. I want to be in a field, surrounded by trees. No roads, no buildings, no people. I want to look into the sky, to revel in the cloud formations, to experience the breeze and the sounds of nature. I want to feel my heart beating. I want to listen without discomfort, without resorting to reaction, without being compelled to play my part. I want peace without effort, tranquillity without boundaries. And I want it whenever I need it. Whenever everything else becomes simply too much to bear. 'No one dare disturb the sound of silence', wrote Paul Simon. He also talked of 'echoes' and of 'whispering'. A world where silence is precious, where noise plays its part, but only in moderation and in tandem with that wonderful, that evocative, 'sound of silence'.

Saturday 7th May 2016

Looking back, yesterday's entry seems almost surreal. I don't think I was in a good place, though it didn't necessarily feel that way. I guess it was a build-up of intense anxiety that needed some kind of release, even if that only materialised in a vision of utopia, a sensation of yearning and contemplation. My field wasn't real. It was only a dream. But it represented hope.

Today actually promises to be a quiet one. Lesley and Elliot are going over to her sister's later as they are holding a surprise party for their step-Grandad. I just couldn't face the prospect of a family gathering, particularly one that will involve revelry and, of course, endless conversation, so I've cried off. I do feel guilty, as I always do, but, thinking of me and my sanity, it is the best solution. Lesley will be able to have a good time without worrying about how I am, as I know she does whenever I take part in something like this.

As for me, well I intend to do some reading, but also, it being Saturday, I will watch some sport on the telly. It's that time of year when the football season merges into that of rugby league and cricket, when hopes are high whether you are at the end or the beginning of your respective fixture list. Millwall will be in the play-offs. That's brilliant on the one hand – the prospect of a date at Wembley is so tantalisingly close – but not so great if you are a depressive. It means constant anxiety, the potential for unfulfilled delirium. It's effectively a kill or cure. Unless you win, it's devastating. And this is Millwall, not Real Madrid! As for the rugby, well it's still relatively early in the campaign, though for Leeds – the current Champions it must be remembered – the season is effectively over already. Struggling at the wrong end of the table, dumped out of the Challenge Cup last night by Huddersfield, the only battle on the horizon is one of staying in Super League. Who would have thought it? It's every bit as shocking as Leicester's success in the round-ball game, but for all the wrong reasons!

Depression in sport is a massive subject, but one still relatively unexamined and undiagnosed. Focus has tended to be restricted to the elite level, to high-profile individuals struggling to cope with fame, money and glory. Yet, even analyses based on these presumptions do not tell the whole story. They tend to suggest that it is something inherent in the context, the sport itself, that is the problem. Of course, this may partly be the case, but what also must be remembered is that depression – or indeed other mental health conditions – is in itself the dominant and determining factor. Depression is indiscriminate. It can hit anybody at any time, whatever their circumstances. This alone should put to bed one of the most damaging but still remarkably enduring misconceptions – that money can always buy you happiness, that fame and fortune combined should, necessarily, culminate in a life free from anxiety, paranoia and any other vestige of mental illness. It's simply not the case.

I'm not surprised to see a number of prominent examples from the world of cricket – I'm thinking of Marcus Trescothick and Jonathan Trott here. The demands on anyone who has, as part of his or her job, to spend months away from home on tour, sometimes across the other side of the world, are not only immense, but obviously, for some, impossible to address. I could never have coped with this – and in another entry on another day, I'll tell you of my own experiences. The novelty, the unfamiliarity, the change of circumstance, the constant vigilance, the pressures, the everyday concerns (diet, washing of clothes, socialising, being with people you may not necessarily get on with, and so on and so forth), are not only harsh with respect to having to cope, they can be devastating. They place demands on anyone, but for someone already vulnerable, already afflicted by depression, they can be dangerous and even, potentially, life-threatening.

The sporting context, however, is not confined to individuals or even to sportsmen and women, the actual players, the contestants, the athletes themselves. The sporting figuration (to use a sociological term) includes administrators, doctors, medics, physios, managers, coaches, sponsors, spectators and supporters, to name just the obvious participants. Depression can apply to any and to all of them. I've already mentioned my devotion to one football club and how that culminated in a relationship so intense, so intrinsic to my health, so directly intertwined in fortune and despair, that I had to walk away. On another occasion, I'll talk about my experiences working within a sport, within my sport of rugby league, and how depression managed to curtail my involvement, govern my perspective and ultimately damage my passion and interfere with my health and sanity.

I'll leave today though by referring to a story that I first came across probably ten years ago. It relates to a footballer who played for a non-league club who was diagnosed with depression whilst at his prime. He felt so isolated within the dressing room, unable to share his news with his team-mates and colleagues, fearing – probably with some justification – that what he would say would be disbelieved, misrepresented and misunderstood. The stigma and discrimination that accompanied depression then – and still does – determined his course of action. He had tried to live his life almost in reverse, spending much of the day alone and asleep, only to surface when darkness fell to enable him to avoid, as much as possible, human contact. He talked of crawling across the floor at times, so despairing and so painful his emotional state. It was every bit as debilitating and as restrictive as any physical condition. Ultimately, he couldn't keep his 'secret' to himself. His fitness deteriorated. His appearance began to give cause for concern. His ability to communicate and to engage in conversation diminished to such an extent that he simply couldn't function. He was found, one day, in the dressing room that he thought had been vacated, by one of his team-mates. He was crying his eyes out. Unable to share what he was going through, to 'confess', to 'admit' as it were, he said that he'd been diagnosed with cancer. The words came tumbling out before he had any element of control. It was the first thing he could think of that wasn't the truth. Moreover, it was 'uncontroversial'. It was an 'acceptable' illness. It was understandable. It didn't come with added baggage. It didn't question his status as an athlete or as a man. Before he could undo what had begun, word reached the club hierarchy. They arranged a benefit match for him. They began fundraising to enable him to go to the United States for some pioneering treatment. Everyone in the club was involved as well as much of the local community. It focused and unified all concerned with one notable exception. He was now living a lie. How could he get out of it? How could he now 'come clean'? He ended up going to America, living for weeks on end in a hotel room, ruminating constantly on what he should do. It nearly killed him. He attempted to take his own life. Consumed by guilt, destroyed by an illness of the mind rather than body, trapped by his own admissions, constricted by his circumstances, cruelly constrained by the stigma of depression and now on the verge of self-inflicted death, he decided to come home and tell the truth. He hoped, beyond hope, that there would be some understanding, some appreciation, some compassion. He expected disappointment, even an element of anger, but what he got instead was incomprehension and hostility. He was sacked by the club, his career now at an end, his identity – one that he had held dear – changed forever. It's a sad tale, but not an uncommon one. It illustrates the devastation not only of illness itself, but of people's reaction to it. It draws attention to the need for greater awareness, for empathy, for involvement of the right sort. For the kind of society that doesn't discriminate. For a society, therefore, that is more like depression itself in this most fundamental of aspects.

Sunday 8th May 2016

My own days as a sportsman are long since over. I think the last time I pulled on a shirt in anger must have been fully twenty years ago, when, short of players as we often were, I filled in as a makeshift hooker for Leicester rugby league against Bulwell. At least I went out with a bang, scoring a try in a comfortable win. Nowadays, such is the lethargy that has now consumed my entire being, I struggle to get out of bed! This morning I woke late, roused myself from the sanctuary of my bed and made my way, slowly, downstairs. After breakfasting and my weekly dose of ironing, Lesley suggested that we go out and do something. My mind was willing, but my body was weak, so I hoped that what she had in mind wasn't too arduous. Luckily, it wasn't. Recognising the temperature outside – it's been in the early twenties today – and the potential impact on a Millie who would run around all day if she had the chance, she proposed a brief trip to Wistow to let her out for a run around the fields (Millie that is, not Lesley!), followed by Market Harborough for a coffee and some shopping. It sounded nice, but even as I got dressed, the old fears about whether I'd find it too demanding began to surface. These days they tend to be accompanied by worries about dizziness and feeling faint, so my first task is always to try and control my ruminating mind. If only I could conceive of this as a thinking trap, pure and simple. I'd be able to deal with that. But there is now some substance to my fears. I can't pretend that I'm not knackered and my dizzy episodes are becoming more frequent. There is the possibility, I guess, that in worrying about feeling faint, I'm not only anticipating being so, but also that I'm bringing it on. That again, it's all in my mind. But I'm not convinced of this. I'm really not sure though. I don't want to tempt fate by telling myself I'm fine, it's depression talk, I'll be OK and then drop dead from a cardiac arrest! What I do need to do though is become much more focused and disciplined with regard to exercising at home and eating more healthily. I started the year with every good intention and I kept it going for a long time. However, I know I've let it slip. If I can begin to feel good about my physical health again, regain some of that lost confidence, then maybe these recurring fears will ease off and perhaps even go away entirely. I have to have some faith. If only that faith wasn't directly connected to my own being. If it was faith in someone else, or faith in something else, that wouldn't be bad. This time, however, it's all down to me. To ask a depressive to believe in him or herself is a mammoth undertaking. Not an impossible one. But I can't help thinking that the odds are stacked against me, nevertheless.

Monday 9th May 2016

I woke up feeling decidedly queasy this morning. So much so that I had to cry off a meeting I had with a good friend of mine whom I haven't seen for quite some time. Phil has bipolar disorder, but that hasn't prevented him carving a real niche for himself, combining his passion for music with his desire to help others with a mental illness. He is the lead singer of a band whose creative impulse and inspiration lies in the road to recovery and in addressing stigma and forms of discrimination. I can't think of any other set of musicians who use as their direct stimulus a health condition and its ramifications. He's taken his band onto a local mental health hospital unit, not only to perform, but to teach people how to play, to make music collectively, to share in its joys and innovation. He's also been the principal instigator of a recovery manual that mixes good tips and sound therapeutic lessons with photography, poetry and other art forms – all geared around mental health – sent in from across the country as part of a nationwide competition.[16] I've spoken at his events on a number of occasions and it has been a real privilege to do so. I'm disappointed at not seeing him, but we'll rearrange.

Of course, I can't just accept that I feel sick. I need to know why, because otherwise my mind will start racing, making connections that don't actually exist, ones totally random and abstract, illogical but still persuasive – at least to me. I've already started. I've got into the habit again of taking a Boots IBS[17] Relief or Colofac before I go to sleep. I have had an irritable bowel in the past. For me, it's been one more manifestation of anxiety and mental distress. Nervous tension does hit me in the stomach and taking this medication has always helped. I did recognise at one point though that perhaps I was taking far too many tablets. They're not designed for daily use on a recurrent basis. So, with enormous willpower, I succeeded in breaking the routine. However, I'm back to square one again. I'm sure it's a question of mind over matter. The slightest degree of discomfort quickly transforms – before I even realise it – into something much bigger, but I'm not sure that it's physically credible, if that's the correct term. I think I'm imagining pain and therefore I'm feeling pain. I can't seem to relax or find any other way out than to, again, pop a pill. It can't be good for me, especially when combined with the full cocktail of medication I have to take only a few hours earlier. The situation is exacerbated if I feel a headache coming on as well. Perhaps – and this must be plausible – the headaches are a result of the tension I'm feeling in my digestive system? Perhaps again my mind has become so agitated, so unsettled, so exercised (or should that be 'exorcised'?), that it becomes overworked and needs something to help ease the anguish? Sometimes I feel that nervous apprehension in other places as well. My back or my shoulders. My thigh or my arm. I end up trying to negotiate the temptation, the massive temptation, to take pill after pill to try and quell the turbulence that is affecting my whole being. That mental undertaking in itself is anxiety-ridden and so the cycle goes on! I've become so accustomed to taking one tablet after another that I don't have the foresight or the insight to realise that although some are necessary, others aren't. Some of you may consider all medicine superfluous and I certainly respect that opinion. But it's not mine. What I need is the mental strength to negotiate everyday hurdles, common afflictions, without feeling that I have only one way out. I've got to start again then. I've cracked it once. I can do it once more.

Tuesday 10th May 2016

Well, I resisted the temptation last night! One out of one then. A hundred per cent record of achievement! How often do I record that?! It certainly wasn't easy. As usual, the cramping sensations began to increase nearer my bed time, and as I was lying there watching the telly, they were still tearing at my stomach, pulling it in one direction and then another. I tried rolling onto my side and that seemed to ease the discomfort. It made it difficult to see the screen though, my neck at a very unnatural angle. I began to think that all I was trading was a pain in the stomach for one in the neck, and so I, once more, turned to lay on my back, urging myself to continue the resistance. Whilst manoeuvring my body to negotiate physical dimensions, I tried continuously to relax, to urge my unwilling mind to be still and calm. I thought of suitable and appropriate sensations – of drifting, of looking at the sky, of floating – but, try as I might, I couldn't win the battle. The worries, the hesitance, the reluctance to change, they were all still there. When weariness came, I was able to allow my body to move without distraction. I turned on my side again, the gurgling from within still an unwelcome accompaniment. Luckily, sleep came quickly and with it the relaxation, physically, that I'd been craving all evening. What I have to do now is make this my new habit, to allow it to become routine, to secure it as an automatic reaction. This way, I'm reasoning, my mind won't be as troubled. It will recognise the pattern. It won't fight it.

I forgot to mention at the weekend that Lesley had talked to Rachel and my wonderful daughter is coming home this Saturday! It will be so good to see her, especially as she's been through so much since she last set foot on home territory. A relationship break-up is never easy, but this one has been difficult because of the circumstances in which it happened. She'd been with Toby for so long, for one thing, but that coupled with the fact that it happened thousands of miles from home and from her mother, must only have served to compound the trauma. I'm no good at expressing myself on the phone – I can hardly speak and never welcome the interaction as it makes me panic. I much prefer to use the written word via Facebook or email, but this time actions will speak much louder than any word can. I just can't wait to give her a hug and a kiss. It will be great for Lesley too. She will have someone around that isn't restricted by depression, someone to talk to, someone with whom to pass the time of day, someone that is able, willing and free to interact with without inhibition or limitation. The same goes for Elliot. He loves his big sister and misses her dreadfully when she's not around. He'll come out of his shell a bit more, simply because there's an additional person around, someone who loves doing the myriad of simple pleasures that make home life just that, a pleasure. It will be good for me too. Rachel is such good company. She's also, by nature, a busy person. She gets things done, things that I often – because of my lethargic state – can't seem either to start or at least to finish. She does take that pressure off me. What I can't envisage, she just does. I guess what I need to do though is not become as dependent on her, as I am on Lesley. I write those words slightly tongue in cheek. As if I actually have a choice in the matter! I don't choose to be dependent on anyone. It just comes with the territory. What I can control or influence, I do. What I can't, I have to take on the chin. I don't like it, even though it eases my anxiety. I don't wish it, even though it enables me to cope. It's the ultimate in double-edged swords.

Wednesday 11<u>th</u> May 2016

I've just come back from doing the weekly shopping at Aldi. I'd volunteered to go last night, thinking that I would be helping Lesley with one less job. I knew, though, as soon as I'd uttered the words, that I was inviting trouble. You see, shopping is one of those things that I find intensely challenging. I suspect it's the case for lots of people with mental illnesses, whatever the nature of their condition. It's not necessarily the surveying of the aisles, the actual accumulation of goods, that is the problem – though if the stall is particularly busy it may become so. No, it's the time at the tills. As soon as I park my trolley and a queue begins behind me, I suddenly feel in the spotlight. Like a rabbit caught in headlights, I sense pairs of eyes surveying me, scrutinising my every moment, waiting for something to go wrong, almost imploring the moment when my carton of milk falls to the floor or my box of eggs gets smashed by a heavy item. I also feel their breath, their frustration at the fact that I've beaten them in the payment process. They want me to be swift, without hesitation or deviation. They wish me to sail through in breakneck speed, every item accounted for and packed away so that they too can be on their way. Of course, if I do drop something or the package tears through some unintended act of clumsiness, that will hold them up even more. I can't win. They want something to laugh at, someone to be the focus of their light relief, but if I provide them with the entertainment they crave, I make them wait even longer. So their amusement turns to anger! A similar sensation takes place in the car park afterwards, particularly if there is a shortage of available parking spaces. I'm putting my shopping in bags to put in the boot of the car. I sense the presence of another vehicle, waiting behind me. Like a predatory wolf, it's waiting for the moment to pounce. Its owner is well aware that spaces are at a premium. He or she needs to react quicker than any other person looking on for the same purpose. A fleeting delay, a momentary hesitation, and the opportunity may well be taken away. But – I yearn for them to appreciate – I have to take my trolley back. I have to reclaim my one pound. I'll be as quick as I can, but I can't run. That would make me even more conspicuous. I try to look as cool and as unaffected as I possibly can, but inside my heart is thumping, almost breaking through my rib cage. My mind is full of permutations, none of them comforting or reassuring. Please God, let me escape. Make it all go away. Place me somewhere else. Anywhere else but here.

It's over relatively quickly of course, but those moments of tension are every bit as intense and uncomfortable as waiting for my train, boarding it and then walking through two or three packed carriages to find my seat. The sensations are the same, as are the ramifications. If something happens, I know that it's going to weigh on my mind throughout the day. I won't be able to dispel it, to laugh it off, to dismiss it as irrelevant. I guess what also troubles me is the fact that I feel so helpless. I concentrate so hard to ensure that I place my items on the conveyor belt both quickly and methodically. It becomes a real mental exercise, an examination of my competence. But despite this, I feel that I'm really vulnerable to some external force that I can't prepare for or prevent from descending. It's that force that is going to mess with me. It's that force that is going to interfere. It's that force that is really in control. Call it what you will – and fate or destiny seem the only words that immediately come to mind – I can only do so much to keep it at bay. I'm doing my best, but that may not be good enough.

Two further things come to mind as I bring this entry to a close. Firstly, for some, shopping is just a routine exercise, a necessity of life of course, but something automatic, a process that is carried out without much effort and with the minimum of fuss. For me, it's a whole different ball game. My reluctance to volunteer therefore is not down to laziness – even though some people, unaware of the mental health implications and unaccustomed to its variability, may see it as such. It's because I'm wary. I'm full of doubt. I'm consumed by anxiety. I'm actually scared. Secondly, if I had a choice – and I do – I would always try to visit the supermarket at a time when I can reasonably expect it to be less busy. Such times can't always be predicted, but sometimes they can. In this world of twenty-four hour service, I bet you your bottom dollar that in addition to the shift workers whose visit is time-constrained and others who prefer nocturnal shopping for whatever mundane reason, a fairly high percentage of those who do their shopping during the course of the night will be people experiencing mental ill health. It's just easier to handle, to exert your own control. People around you aren't so rushed. Queues will be shorter or non-existent. You can even choose your moment accordingly so that others aren't around when you wish to pay for your goods. It's an altogether more comfortable experience. And that's worth something amidst the hectic pace and nature of modern-day living. So, if you ever find yourself having to frequent a shop during the early hours, have a look around you and if you detect nerves or distress in a fellow consumer, just offer a smile. It can make the world of difference.

Thursday 12th May 2016

At the moment, I seem to move from one stressful situation to another! After yesterday's escapades and trial of endurance in Aldi, today, I'm faced with one more test of character and mental capability. Having workmen scheduled to come to your house to do a job is a scenario that I know lots of people with mental health conditions find difficult to contemplate and undergo. I am no exception. But what is that is stressful? Or, more accurately, what is that elevates that stress to an intensity that threatens to harm your mental health? I can only answer for myself, even though I'm probably saying things with which others would concur.

Firstly, it's the anticipation that necessarily prevails. I ruminate over what may happen. Irrespective of how routine I expect the work to be, I can only think worst case scenario. There is always bound to be something more complex, something over which I will be expected to make a decision or at least to have some knowledge or input. And I just don't know what that may be. I worry therefore over the issue of conversation. I don't want to appear ignorant or confused. I want instead to seem in control and unflappable. But it's all pretence. The longer I'm forced to wait, the more anxious these things become, which leads me onto the second issue. That of not knowing when exactly to expect their arrival. Today hasn't been too bad. The job in question was a new windscreen for Lesley's car, a necessary prerequisite if it's going to pass its forthcoming MOT. Lesley told me initially that they would be with me anytime between nine and five. Not a great help to me. Not much help to anyone really. However, at just after nine o'clock, I got a phone call telling me that they'd be here between eleven and one, and sure enough, as good as their word, they arrived just before midday. Lesley had already left me some instructions. I had the relevant Insurance document. I knew I'd have to pay an excess fee and that I could do so by card. This should, therefore, be as straightforward as it is possible to get. Even though when they came to the door and reiterated all that, I still felt restless and slightly panicky. They insisted the job wouldn't take too long. Famous last words! The third issue is job duration. If I'm expecting a certain length and what transpires is a much longer job, I begin increasingly to worry. Of course, that had to happen today, didn't it? I sat there watching through the window, unable to cope with doing anything else other than to occasionally glance at another mundane sports show on the television. I was urging them to finish. I tried to read their faces to ascertain if things were going wrong. At one point, one of them drove away in their van, leaving the other to remove the damaged screen. (That one of his techniques was to use his head didn't exactly reassure me!) Then...nothing. For fully thirty minutes I wasn't sure what was going on. The driver hadn't returned. Surely they knew they'd need a particular windscreen?! The minutes dragged. I tried to relax. To think of other things. To give myself something else to do as a distraction. But I couldn't! I was so fearful of knowing the facts, of confirming my suspicions, I simply could not venture outside to ask. Eventually, the van returned and the job recommenced. When, at last, I heard the knock at the door, the signal that they'd finished, I was told that the delay was something to do with the glass and its fittings being glued on. (Isn't that always the case?!) I paid the money, signed the forms, texted Lesley and then, and only then, could I finally breathe out. It had taken two hours. Two hours during which I could do little but fret.

As a relevant aside, last November I attended a workshop in London co-organised by Mind and British Gas. The latter wanted to know about the quality of service delivered to people with mental illnesses and whether they needed to take special measures, specific actions, to cater for just the sort of eventuality I've experienced today, plus others as well. It was quite insightful of them really, and I applauded their foresight as well as their apparent determination to ensure that we too as a community received the best possible service. It became clear during the discussions that, in actual fact, there is loads that companies such as this need to consider. We tried to instil in them the continual need for engagement, for consultation, for flexibility in design and approach. I remember making the point – and it came back to me this morning – that it would be really helpful if vulnerable people such as those with a known mental illness, could be informed as soon as possible at the start of the working day when exactly they could expect to see whoever it is that is coming to address a problem or to hear from the appropriate person if they required advice and guidance on the telephone. Obviously, it would help to resolve or address the issue sooner rather than later, but even if that were not possible, if we knew that it would be at a certain time slot later in the day, we could at least get on with our lives during the course of the morning. It would also mean that we could prepare for whatever it is – visit or otherwise – at our own pace, in our own way, with time not a factor as a constraint. Just a small thing. But an important one, at that.

Friday 13th May 2016

Though long and tiring, today has passed without a prolonged attack on my mental capability. I've had a succession of meetings, all of them productive and thought-provoking. I've managed to contribute to the discussions and to listen and take on board the thoughts of others. I think I've been engaging and positive. I hope I've been incisive and proven valuable. Sometimes it is difficult to know for certain. You find yourself constantly looking for signs, for indications that somebody appreciates what you're saying and what you're trying to do. I often get it completely wrong. I actually 'over look', if that is really a credible term! I'm so concerned about how I come across that my mind begins to play tricks, producing connections and leading to deductions that either aren't there or are simply false. Sometimes it works both ways. Not only does depression lead me to fear the worse, to see the bad in everything, to internalise feelings that are self-destructive, on other occasions my yearning to succeed, my desperate need to be valued leads to me effectively 'clutch at straws'. Any semblance of a smile or a positive word in response to what I say or do leads me clinging on to the last vestige of hope left inside me. It elevates a simple gesture to something monumental in significance. This may seem like an entirely positive thing. But it isn't if, as is virtually always the case, something erodes that 'utopia' and I come crashing down like a heavyweight stunned by an uppercut! Once on the floor, it is difficult to get up. Either way, I'm at the bottom. It's just the manner in which I got there that is different.

Lesley, poor love, was due to have a well-deserved evening out with her friends tonight. However, during the course of the morning, she got a phone call to say that John, her step-Grandad had been taken to A&E. After spending most of the afternoon trying to ascertain what had happened – to be met mostly by silence as the Department wasn't answering their phones – she decided around five to go down there herself. He's obviously not well. Lesley has said on a number of occasions recently that she's concerned about his breathing. However, the medics haven't been able to accurately diagnose the cause of the problem. One minute it's the asbestos he used to work with, the next it's a possible heart attack. You would think it wouldn't be that difficult in this day and age, but I'm probably being a bit unfair. Anyway, it was gone ten o'clock by the time she returned. Unbelievably, they were going to release him at that time but Lesley managed to convince them that it wasn't a good idea to let a ninety-two year old man go home to an empty house that late. This time, it should have been obvious. Surely our NHS isn't that heartless or thoughtless to allow such a thing to happen? I wouldn't have thought so, but... I guess it comes down, once more, to resources and the availability of care, including that of beds. It's a sad indictment of where we are that someone that vulnerable, in obvious distress, isn't worth, automatically, time in which to recover from the immediate symptoms at least.

Saturday 14th May 2016

Last Saturday, I said that I'd go into more detail about how depression played its part in my own involvement in rugby league, a sport in which I was fortunate to have had a paid role and an opportunity to make a real difference to its landscape and vision. On the surface it might appear the height of good fortune to have landed a job in a terrain that was very much my passion. I certainly thought so at the time. However, within a very short period, my dreams began to turn in a very different direction, eventually to become living nightmares. Whilst it is certainly the case that professional sport can be a merciless environment and even I, on its periphery, felt that to be true, on reflection it was depression that was the determining factor in how things turned out for me.

It started to have an impact during my first job working within Student Rugby League. I found it increasingly difficult to communicate with those around me. There was a nervousness and a tension, a feeling of being an outsider that I couldn't reconcile with the identity I thought I had. I began to get paranoid thoughts. That I was being examined, scrutinised, judged. That I had to achieve and continue to achieve a level of expertise and attainment that was simply impossible to sustain. When it came to showcase events like the annual Varsity Match between Oxford and Cambridge Universities – an event that I had to organise and for which I had to arrange and sell corporate hospitality – my need for perfection, to be faultless, reached unprecedented levels. Everything over which I had influence became exclusively a test of my ability to actually deliver. Any blemish – no matter how slight – in the catering I ordered became my responsibility, and mine alone. If the programme looked anything but flawless, it was down to me. If my volunteer helpers didn't perform to elite standards of care, the buck stopped at my door. If the game itself wasn't a classic, and a model of excellence, somehow that too was my fault. And so on and so forth. I couldn't distinguish between areas that I could control and ones that I couldn't.

That continued when I was successfully appointed to the position of Administrator of a competition called the Rugby League Conference. I had history here. I was one of a number of individuals who had helped to instigate it in the first place. We had recognised that the amateur game outside of the heartlands in the north needed a national structure, one worthy of a new era for the sport, most visibly demonstrated by the creation of a Super League and a move to playing during the summer period. These were halcyon days. Rugby league was set for a breakthrough. It was a time of optimism, but also one of realistic aspiration, of tangible goals, of moving in a monumental direction. The competition first ran as a pilot in 1997. By the time the sport's governing body, the Rugby Football League, was in a position to appoint a full-time administrator, it had two successful seasons under its belt. When I got the job, it was like coming home. I was welcomed. I felt appreciated. I wanted so much to do well. However, it wasn't quite what it seemed. There were underlying tensions within its infrastructure. There were inherent difficulties in trying to push through a more professional undertaking whilst remaining amateur in name and in pounds and pence. I began to feel a responsibility that not only wasn't commensurate with what I was being paid but in what I could realistically achieve. Simply getting games on was still, quite often, a struggle. Whereas I was expected to be influencing long-term direction, not only for the competition itself but for its place in the bigger picture that was the new national structure for the sport, I found the routine organisation of fixtures to be taking up most of my time and energy.[18] It became obsessive. I became paranoid. It was fertile territory for the full enormity of depression to feed on. Despite consistently developing and relaying up-to-date information on things such as registration of players, insurance, the appointment of match officials, safeguarding and other areas of protection, I began to internalise not just their communication to clubs but also their application at every level. I started to consider every single element of club administration to be my responsibility. If one player was not formally and properly registered at any club, it was again my fault. If insurance wasn't paid and in place at every club prior to training, let alone the playing of fixtures, I was to blame. If a bona fide referee wasn't available, I looked no further than my own front door in terms of culpability and accountability. I ruminated constantly. I continually checked the accuracy of my every word with the sport's national administration. If something was out of place, if there was even a hint of confusion in what I relayed, if the most miniscule of misinterpretations could be deduced, if I'd included too much or too little, I expected catastrophe. It became too much to bear. I was checking absolutely everything. Everyday. Sometimes all day. Those to whom I turned for reassurance I felt must have considered me strange and a continual pain in the backside. The bottom line was that in absolutely everything that the competition embraced, on and off the pitch, in season and out, I felt solely accountable. The process of catastrophizing was recurrent. If a player, for example, sustained an injury during training and if, despite my appeals and the information I'd forwarded, he (or she) hadn't been properly registered or included within insurance policies, then it was my fault. I then quickly turned that situation within my mind into one in which the player then can't work. He (for argument's sake, he's a bloke) finds he can't pay his mortgage. He loses his house. His marriage breaks down. He's denied access to his kids. His life falls apart, a life that he eventually takes. He's dead. In a series of connections, every one the worst possible scenario, what culminates in his passing was caused by his failure – my failure – to be comprehensively covered when he first threw a ball in anger on the training park. This was my everyday existence for month after month. Looking back, I now know that I had a succession of mini-breakdowns, each one eating away at what remained of my mental capacity and strength to cope. It couldn't go on. There came a time when I could no longer watch the sport I loved, even on the television. It just started the process of depressive rumination immediately and without exception. I'd became a living exemplar not only of what could go wrong, but of rugby league's every manifestation. It was every bit as close and as direct as my relationship with Leeds United. It was, in effect, killing me. I decided to quit. I had no choice if I wanted to stay alive. I worked out my notice and left, leaving behind all my hopes, my cherished dreams, my ambitions. Looking back now, I'm not even sure of what I ever actually achieved. And that's sad.

Sunday 15th May 2016

It's been quite a night. Elliot's first sleepover here resulted in six young ladies from his year at school spending the evening in a front room redesigned for the occasion with mattresses, cushions and duvets whilst revelling in the fantasy that is Eurovision. God knows what they did after it had finished because I was aware throughout the night that they were awake and still full of the excitement, the exhilaration of youth. I suspect endless films, a continuous supply of soft drinks, crisps and popcorn, and the comparing of notes about their schoolmates and any and every thing that matters to a group of thirteen-year-olds. He'll be grumpy today. Kids always seem to be when they're tired!

We were banished to our room at eight when coverage began from Stockholm. It was actually quite nice and relaxing. Millie joined us, bless her. I think she was a bit overawed and uncertain as to what was going on downstairs. She nearly put a dampener on things (quite literally!) when, nervous and unsure, she urinated on the temporary bedding in the front room! At just after ten, Lesley left to pick Rachel up from Leicester Station. It was so good to see her when they returned. It's been a long time and it was wonderful just to hug her again. Already, I can see a difference in Lesley and in the days to come I know that will provide the tonic that we all need at times to help us get through the predictability of everyday life. They are a good team. They've taken Millie out together this morning and I know the conversation will be flowing, ebullient and cathartic at the same time. They've a lot to catch up on.

As for me, depression will inevitably constrain what I do. I'd love to be able to feel free and uninhibited whilst chatting away. To dispel the fears, the restraints that are imposed on me when I enter the realm of conversation. But I can't. I try, but all I can realistically hope for is the occasional contribution, not the painless assurance and exuberance that others without illness can expect and do enjoy. When was the last time I was able to be as others are? I can't remember. Of course, interaction with Lesley is comfortable and comforting. It doesn't have boundaries. It isn't constrained. But I guess what I'm really referring to is the ability to participate in conversations that involve people who I'm not with – or haven't been with – on a daily basis. Including my own children, my Mum and my brother.

I simply can't recall a time when I truly looked forward to the process of engaging with others, of exchange being inherently liberating, rewarding and enjoyable.

Was there ever such a time?

I think there was. Immediately, I remember the circle of friends I had at University, even at school. My first workplace. My family when I was a child. When we were all together here before Rachel began the exodus to University, to be followed by Luke and Joel. It's different to other manifestations of depression, such as when I was last genuinely excited about something, or when I last felt truly and unequivocally positive about what others may term an 'achievement'. Maybe this is something to draw upon? To use as a weapon to tackle the adverse symptoms of my illness? To focus on to show that depression hasn't always been as it mostly seems? As ever, I'll try.

Monday 16th May 2016

It was Lesley's birthday yesterday, and I think she had a day she'll remember for quite a while. In addition to Rachel, Luke and Megan hired a car and drove up from London for a surprise visit, which I suspect was the icing on the cake. Only Joel was missing – but as he's currently living in a tent and holding fort at reception at Eurocamp in Southern France, he has a viable excuse for his non-presence! Elliot didn't indulge much in the festivities, which was probably not surprising considering he'd just gone twenty-four hours without sleep. He did his best before tiredness descended, bless him. As for me, well I tried to keep a low profile. I would have given anything to have had Lesley to myself, to celebrate with her and only with her. But that would have been selfish and self-indulgent. I can't compete with everyone together and as we were all going over to her sister's for Sunday lunch, I knew that I would be facing the usual challenges and having to utilise my customary coping strategies. It was very obvious yesterday when I'd reached my limit. Sometimes, things change very slowly. I'm allowed the luxury of some time without having to address my fears, a time during which I gradually experience the warning signals that herald an end to my ability to cope. I have time to prepare, to readjust, to forewarn. Yesterday, it came so suddenly, it was immediately debilitating. Within an instance, I'd turned from eating my meal and being able to contribute to the discussion, to a situation where I was simply glued to my seat, unable to speak. I began rubbing my forehead, much out of desperation I think now. It was an automatic reaction. Perhaps I was trying to keep panic at bay? Or was it a sign of my distress? Maybe I was actually trying to communicate to others that all was not well? I tried to catch

Lesley's eyes, to let her know. All the time, feelings of anxiety began to consume me from within. I no longer felt in control. I was no longer able to discern what was going on. I couldn't communicate. But I daren't move. I was trapped. Every second seemed to solidify my body, to terrorise my mind. How do I get out of this without appearing strange and melodramatic, without giving people a glimpse of the turmoil inside? Eventually, I forced myself into action. With a quick word to Luke sitting next to me, I rose from my seat. The first thing that came into my mind was to say that I needed to make sure Elliot, sleeping at home, was OK. It seemed a valid reason, an acceptable deception. I had to stop myself from running out of the house. As I trudged home, I could feel the tension dissipate. It was a tangible sensation of relief and respite. I'd done what I could.

Tuesday 17th May 2016

I fervently wished that this morning would never come. I don't know what happened yesterday. As the day progressed I seemed to sink further and further into a state of uncertainty and disquietude. My ability to cope diminished to the extent that I was left facing problems that were of my own making, or at least had been made within my fragile mind. It was as if something or someone had turned a tap marked 'confidence' and left it dripping, gradually eroding my sense of inner belief and self-assurance. This succeeded in making me hyper-sensitive to new thoughts and situations. I just wanted everything to freeze. I was at the limit of my capability, my capacity to deal with everyday matters.

I knew as I went to bed that today would be an examination. All the things that I've described recently have resurfaced. We're having workmen in to re-do our ensuite bathroom, for example. I have a list of questions that Lesley has asked me to put to them. I just feel so wary of my ability to deal with this that I'd do anything to get out of it. All I have to do is ask. To communicate. But I'm so scared. I can't account for the level and intensity of this feeling. It must seem bizarre and probably a bit pathetic to those of you unaccustomed to the vagaries of mental illness, but it's such a tangible feeling. It's biting. It's fierce. It's self-inflicted punishment of the most acute type.

I then have to go shopping. I volunteered once more. Why? Because I want to be of some practical use. I want to contribute something to the functioning of our house. If I can't deal with officialdom and organisation, what am I left with? Cleaning. Washing. Ironing. And shopping. The first three aren't so bad because they're solitary endeavours. The fourth? That's a different matter. To make things even worse, I asked Lesley to give me a list. Why on earth did I do that? What I've got now is another task. Not only to go shopping, but to buy specific items. What if I can't find them? I'll have to ask someone. I'll have to enter into dialogue. What if the shop doesn't have them? Do I go somewhere else? If I fail to buy one item, just one, I know that will have an impact on my sense of self-worth. In my mind, I'll have failed. The pressure is already building as I write this. Shopping today has become not just a mission, but a test of my whole purpose and of my competence as a person.

Finally, I have to finish a job application. It's for some part time work in relation to Holocaust Memorial Day. Its work I can do as a freelancer. It's work that I'm experienced in and in which I feel comfortable. I've completed all the required administrative elements of the form (past employment, references, contact details etc.). What I'm left with is the part in which I have to sell myself, the part in which I have to show that I've met the job description and have the associated necessary attributes. I have to write in such a way that I'm deliberately and purposefully conceiving myself as a product worth having. I have to promote my skills, to show off my qualities, to demonstrate my experience. I just feel so ill-equipped to do this. Depression has made this necessary task so hard to fulfil. How can you try to convince someone else when you are so lacking in self-confidence yourself? Every word I write seems false. Every sentence so unreal. It's all very well saying that you need to put yourself into a different mode of thinking. If that mode is not within your scope, if it's not part of your psychological DNA, it becomes a task that is easier said than done. Think of it this way. Would you expect someone recently bereaved to stand up in front of a room full of people and talk assuredly and confidently about their achievements and talents without any sign of mental distress or discomfort? No you wouldn't. It would be asking too much. Only the most hard-hearted of person would disagree. But that is what this feels like to me. This is the enormity of my task today. I just hope I survive to meet sleep tonight with some semblance of self-belief still intact.

Wednesday 18th May 2016
I'm having a bad day. Physically, I feel rotten. I think I've caught Rachel's cold as my throat feels decidedly like rough sandpaper. However, as usual, it's my mental state that I'm really concerned about. I feel very low, disillusioned and a little fatalistic. I was shattered this morning to learn that there has been a further delay to the availability of my book. I was counting on it being ready and accessible this week, but now, I'm told, it will be another month. I can't help but feel let down. I've met every single deadline I've been given, only to be met with one issue, one problem, one obstacle after another. I know I'm impatient, but I think after preparing myself for a launch this January, I have a right to be by now. If this new and additional set back was of my own making, I would readily hold up my hands and take the flak. However, it is not. My catastrophizing mind has led me to the conviction that everyone who pre-ordered a copy on Amazon will now cancel their order. I can't get that thought out of my head. I've tried to deflect people away from this by posting on Facebook, on LinkedIn and on my website, but I can't realistically do any more. And yet, I feel assuredly helpless – if that isn't a contradiction in terms. Misfortune and upset such as this can have a devastating impact on a person who is ill in the mind. We're not as able to rationalise matters as those free from such affliction. We can't summon up inner resources, resources of recovery and confidence, to the same extent. We fear the worst. We expect the worst.

As I write this, I really do wish I'd never put pen to paper, or whatever the equivalent phrase is in this modern technological age. I wouldn't be letting people down. I wouldn't have to face such disappointment and anxiety. I wouldn't be setting myself up to fail.

I'm not bothered about money. I just want people to read what I've laboured so hard to produce. I'm so scared that it will now be lost. That my efforts will have been in vain. That people will give up on me. Obviously, at least from the correspondence I've had today from my publisher, I care too much. I'm full of unrealistic expectations. I don't understand the process. I'm naïve. I shouldn't let it worry me. This last phrase is crucial to an understanding of mental illness. It's such an easy thing to say. It's commonly heard. But its implications are significant and damaging. If my psyche was so easy to control, so malleable, so predictive, so responsive, everything would be alright. One could simply dismiss the feelings, the sensations, as readily and as straightforwardly as turning off a running tap. But it's not like that. Worry is one thing that I am good at. I have it in abundance. It controls me. Not the other way round.

And all this after I survived the ordeals of yesterday! And survived well, I thought. It just goes to show that life has a persistent habit of kicking you in the teeth, irrespective of the protection one tries to put in place. Depressives feel those kicks a lot harder than others, I suggest. Not only do they also recover more slowly, they constantly anticipate the next wave of attack. It's not a question of if, it's one of when. You only have a certain number of teeth, after all is said and done.

Thursday 19th May 2016
I had my latest consultant's appointment this morning.

It's come at the right time I think. Yesterday I suspect will prove to be more than just a temporary blot on the landscape. I know the all-too-familiar signs. I never look forward to seeing my consultant. I don't mean that in a derisory or critical way, of course. Indeed, I really do like mine. I've only met him on a couple of occasions and we've already established a rapport and a sense of trust and confidence. That's really all that you can hope for. No, it's just that what we talk about is almost exclusively dark and painful and I can never be totally sure whether what comes out of our discussions by way of outcomes will work or not. It's the same for everybody. I'm hoping for something that can't be given. Something that is simply impossible. A one hundred per cent guarantee of success in terms of making me feel better. No such assurances can be made. There are too many influential or mitigating factors, depending on how you look at it. I believe in my consultant though. He remembers what I talked about on previous occasions. He offers sound advice. He works through my fears. He recognises my anxieties. He doesn't make connections that aren't there. He guides my thinking, my responses. He explores options. He asks my opinion. He's flexible and reliable.

I'm very lucky really, especially given what I've heard from so many other people in my position about their equivalents.

This morning we investigated further the issue of whether my current mood is likely to be fleeting or not. We thought not. There are too many indications that what I'm going through is the beginning of another depressive episode. We dwelt on all the manifestations, mental and physical. He probed and he reflected. And, most importantly, he acted. Recognising that panic and anxiety appear to be common factors of my depression. Realising that because of this, things – unless checked – are liable to move quite quickly out of my control, that mountains will develop from the proverbial mole-hills, he has prescribed some additional Quetiapine, this time immediate release, for me to take whenever such a situation threatens my mental stability. I have been taking Diazepam for this, but he thinks these will work more effectively, essentially because they work to counter depression as well and will kick in more promptly. They are liable to sedate me more thoroughly and conclusively, but I don't mind that. He had already asked me what I'd like to do when I sense such a threat. All I could say is that I'd like something to knock me out for a couple of weeks! If only humans could hibernate?! Or whatever the equivalent is in the summer!

I also talked to him about my sleeping patterns. As you will recall, these have been giving me some concerns, particularly my habit of lashing out in bed. I told him that I was fearful about what I could do, with Lesley in mind, given the vivid and horrific nature of my dreams. He was quite concerned. He asked me if I snored, which I do. He asked me if I feel rested, which I don't. He asked me if sleeping during the day was an option, which it is. He then asked me if I thought I ever stopped breathing. I wasn't expecting this one, to say the least! How would I even know? He then said that it was possible, given my mental state but also my physique, that I suffered from sleep apnoea. Thinking about it afterwards, it makes sense of the constant thread of my dreams, that of being constrained, imprisoned, forcibly punished, of my resultant desperation in trying to escape and to fight back, to inflict damage on my persecutors.

Anyway, the upshot is that he's referred me to a sleep clinic, which I guess I knew existed but only because of television programmes. As is customary for the NHS, particularly in relation to mental health, there's a long waiting list. So there you are, potentially another addition to my already extensive health curriculum vitae.

One other thing struck me about this morning. I looked at people's faces as I sat in the waiting area. Was mental illness so evidently marked in facial expressions? Could you really see mental pain and discomfort? Of course you could. What I saw was a wide variety of emotional representations, but all of them consistent with the reason why we were there. I saw discomfort, agitation, resignation, bewilderment, confusion, uncertainty, fear and many others beside. The thought then struck me that if I could see these things in other people, they could also see them in me. How did I look? Given the fact that a mental health clinic is one of the few places where I don't have to try and put a brave face on things, where everything is open, transparent, true and real, I must look like what I am, a long-term depressive. And people tell me that mental illness is a hidden disability! Not one slight bit of it.

Friday 20th May 2016

Millwall are playing the second leg of their play-off semi-final against Bradford City tonight. Whilst this should be an occasion to enjoy and in which to revel, all I can feel is deep anxiety. This is more than the natural concerns of a supporter, the combination of nerves, expectation and passion that most feel and actually savour. I, in contrast, am genuinely scared. Not at the result as such. But at its ramifications. I really do wish that it was all over. That I am protected from the fate of my club, that I could wake up in a fortnight's time without having to endure the process of participation. I don't want to be involved. I really don't. But I am, whether I like it or not. Why am I like this? I guess I've already talked of these matters in a previous entry. Millwall have now replaced Leeds in the way I feel connected and therefore, responsible. If we lose tonight – and we're two goals ahead from the first leg and therefore in a really good position – I know I will blame myself. Somehow, my fragility will have permeated the psyche of every player in blue and white, affecting their capabilities, destroying their confidence, hindering their movement. My logic dictates that I am somehow controlling their every pass and tackle. Or rather that I am impairing them. My consultant asked me yesterday if I would feel the same level and nature of responsibility should they win? Of course not, I replied, without really thinking. That's different. Logically it's not, surely? But this isn't about logic. This is pure madness. Sheer irrationality. I'm too close. It matters too much. I've become Millwall.

I can't face the prospect of disappointment at the moment. I know it will eat away at me in a way that is far more damaging, much more thoroughly and destructively than can really be imagined bearing in mind that it is, after all, just a game of football. I've pinned too much hopes on my team. I've enshrined in them all my immediate aspirations. It's too much of a kill, without the possibility of a cure. My mental capacity to cope is at risk. I can't regain the perspective I have when I'm relatively OK. In fact, it's gone completely. I've tried desperately hard to retrieve it, to sit myself down, to talk it through within my mind. But it hasn't worked. And now it's too late. In five and half hours time the game will have kicked off.

I've deliberately avoided the most obvious implication of all this. That I can no longer be a football supporter. That somehow, I will have to walk away for good from the game that has been my companion, my treasured friend, all my life. For the sake of my sanity, this may have to happen. I will lose so much, but at least I won't be putting my health, perhaps even my life, at risk anymore. And all for the sake of a ball.

Saturday 21st May 2016

Well, we drew, which meant we won! Please forgive the deliberate ambiguity. With our first leg victory, a 1-1 draw at The Den was enough to see us through to Wembley. At around ten o'clock last night I could finally draw a line under the evening's events and for the first time in a couple of horrible hours, I drew breath. I'd managed up until around 7.30 pm to keep things in check. I'd tried to keep myself busy and to distract myself as much as possible. It worked to some extent but try as I might, as kick-off approached, I couldn't stop all the familiar signs of footballing distress from hitting home. My stomach started tying itself in knots. My nervous cough emerged once more. I started to sweat profusely. I began counting down the seconds until full-time as soon as the ball was first kicked! I had to follow it somehow. For the first half, I relied on Twitter, continually clicking for updates, knowing that short of watching the game itself, this would be the quickest and most reliable form of commentary. It was all going so well. We'd gone 1-0 up. All the comments were reassuring and celebratory. No problem. Then, just before half-time, Bradford equalised. Suddenly, all change. Hesitancy. Uncertainty. Tension. Panic! I couldn't go through the second-half in the same manner. I began to, but could no longer take it, so I switched channels on the telly. Just as I did so Jimmy Abdou, Millwall's Comoros international (there's not many teams that can say they have one of those!), blasted a chance over the bar. From then on, the game was absolutely terrible...but at least Bradford never really looked like scoring. From twenty-nine minutes left, I started the countdown, minute by minute. Lesley kept reassuring me. 'They'll never score two goals in ten minutes' she said at one point. 'Hold on, love, this is Millwall', I responded. 'Anything's possible'. With twenty seconds left, I finally relaxed and enjoyed the moments of victory. Sadly, they didn't last long. Within half an hour, my normal state had returned once more. Depression couldn't even leave me long enough to revel and wallow. It had to have the last say.

Sunday 22nd May 2016

It's a beautiful morning. The sun is shining. All I can hear outside is birdsong. Even the occasional sound of aircraft doesn't interrupt the peace and tranquillity. It's a day for relaxing, for doing nothing, for enjoying the serenity of a life without unnecessary intrusion, without cause for concern or worry, without rumination. Oh, if only this could be so! Whilst all around our little house, I can picture just that environment, that context, that vision. Inside my four walls, I can't comply. I just can't join in. I'm not allowed to. I'm prevented from doing so. By what? By the force of my mental incapacity. By my depression. I can't be free of it. I know that to be the case. It permeates. It resonates. It indoctrinates.

It's very apt therefore that this afternoon I am speaking at an event about that very subject of mental capacity. It's part of some important work that I'm doing with two colleagues to draw attention to the impact and the intricacies of the Mental Capacity Act. Of what that means in a practical sense and of how you can prepare for the possibility that someone, somewhere and at some time – someone with legal authority and medical expertise that is – can decide that you cannot make decisions for yourself because mentally, you are too ill. The erosion of rights and responsibilities, the withdrawal of the most fundamental right of them all, to freedom, is an area intrinsically related to the issue of mental illness. For the simple fact is that if your mental condition deteriorates to such an extent that you are deemed a danger to yourself or others, you can be 'detained under the Mental Health Act'. In other words, 'sectioned'. This scenario is, relatively speaking, recognised and reasonably well understood. But that other legal edifice, the Mental Capacity Act, most certainly isn't. I knew that such powers existed, but, until recently, I didn't know they were invested in a single act of Parliament. And yet it can be nearly as constricting, as potent, as authoritative and as devastating as its more well-known counterpart.

You can, however, prepare for any such eventuality, by simply making it known what you would like to happen if, at some time, your 'capacity' is questioned and as a result, those freedoms that so many of us take for granted, are legally taken away. You can state, for example, what you wish to happen in respect of treatment. You can also appoint someone, anyone you wish, to make decisions for you in relation to things such as your property or your financial affairs. That person, chosen and trusted by you, is thereby entrusted to act in your best interests. You also have the right to make what is called a 'Statement of Wishes and Feelings', which can be about anything and everything. Though the latter can be over-ridden if it is deemed that what you have said is not in your best interest, it can't be ignored. These are really important factors. They mean that you still have powers, but 'in advance', if you like. But who knows about these things? There must be countless thousands, possibly millions of people in this country that may be aware of the fact that there are limitations imposed on someone when they are considered to be mentally unwell, but who don't realise that that person still has an opportunity – and a legal right – to influence and in some cases determine, what happens to them. There is a danger that we become too compliant, too resigned to our fate, too unconcerned about the consequences of illness, too trustful even. Think about it. If 'the state' (for want of a better term) can remove you from your home, put you into a hospital, determine the length of your stay and impose conditions with respect to your treatment, all because medical authority has deemed you to be too ill, it can certainly take away other aspects relating to your liberty and your right to act yourself in your best interests. Please don't get me wrong, I'm certainly not saying that 'the state' is necessarily wrong to do so. It is there to establish procedures for protection and to make sure they are applied fairly and humanely. What I am saying though is that the powers-that-be need to do much more to ensure that people – particularly people who already have a mental illness – are aware of what can happen should they become 'sufficiently' unwell. They also need to enshrine protection and care over detention, to make it clear that the erosion of an individual's liberty and ability, is not something that is taken lightly and that all concerned in the process have (or at least 'should have') your best interests at heart and in mind. To show the caring face of the mental health system (and to make sure that it does have one – which is another sensitive issue!). To reassure people. To offer hope and take away fear. Doing so not only helps those to cope with the possibility, and practicalities, of institutionalised care. It may well act in a preventative sense as well.

Just a thought! Or two!

Monday 23rd May 2016

There was an excellent programme last night on England's World Cup triumph in 1966. I found it incredibly moving, surprisingly so really. I think what probably made me more emotional than I had anticipated were my closing remarks on Friday. Though I wasn't around on that iconic day fifty years ago, my early football memories were of an era not too different from that illustrated. I can even remember watching some of the players – Bobby Moore, Alan Ball and Martin Peters in particular come to mind. It reminded me of what initially drew me to the game but also of what I – and football itself perhaps – have lost. I thought I'd reflect today on those twin issues, in the hope that somehow I can cling on to something that has been important to me for so long, something that I don't want to give up, but which I fear may play too dominant and intrinsic a role in my ability to keep some sort of perspective on life.

I can think of so many things. Of the excitement of going to matches at Wrexham[19] and eventually at Leeds with my Dad. Of the anticipation on Saturday mornings. Of wearing wrap-around scarves. Of buying a rosette at Elland Road. Of collecting programmes. Of buying my first copy of Roy of the Rovers whilst on holiday in Scotland. Of the smell of Bovril, cheap burgers and onions. Of supporters wearing caps and beanie hats. Of getting my first Leeds kit for Christmas. Of standing at the Racecourse Ground[20] next to my Dad. Of my Dad going to games in a suit. Of eagerly, but nervously, awaiting the announcement of half-time scores. Of Sports Report on Radio Two with its famous jingle, still played today. Of players long hair and the odd perm! Of Panini football albums and my first season collecting what were then cards that you had to stick yourself into their respective places. Of obtaining Allan Clarke, my favourite player, to complete the full set of Leeds pictures. Of Dad buying me packets of cards from WH Smiths. Of the old-fashioned kits. Of Spurs and of Ardiles and Villa wearing what still is my favourite all-time shirt. Of black, and only black, boots. Of Shoot magazine and annuals at Christmas. Of Dad paying £3.20 (yes, that's right, £3.20) for the best seats at Elland Road. Of Leeds contriving to lose my inaugural match having been 1-0 up against Manchester City. Of the hurt and disappointment as a result. Of listening to the 1975 European Cup Final in a caravan whilst on a family holiday. Of watching my first Cup Final in colour, also in 1975. Of zealously pinching the Sunday Express newspaper to find out which games were featured on that afternoon's 'Star Soccer'. Of nervously finding the courage each Saturday night to ask my Dad if I could stay up and watch 'Match of the Day'. Of muddy pitches and heavy footballs. Of the special atmosphere at evening games under the lights. Of seeing stadia for the first time. Of the tiny souvenir shop at Elland Road where you literally had to fight to get to the front and be served. Of silk scarves, tied around your wrist. Of seeing George Best playing in a testimonial match at Wrexham. Of Dixie McNeil knocking holders West Ham out of the FA Cup in 1981. Of Kenny Dalglish at Elland Road, still the greatest player I've ever seen live. Of dreading Monday mornings at school if Leeds lost. Of World Cups without England. Of the novelty of international football. Of seeing teams representing countries that seemed so far away. Of the Peruvian, Cubillas, destroying Scotland in 1978. Of club teams behind the old Iron Curtain. Of pennants advertised in magazines. Of Leeds United jigsaws. Of playing in the snow with orange balls. Of half-times being only ten minutes. Of Jimmy Hill and the resonant sound of his voice. Of giving Cloughie stick whenever he came back to Leeds. Of half-and-half woollen hats featuring your team with Celtic or Rangers. Of players having other jobs. Of upcoming youngsters such as Trevor Francis and Ian Rush. Of crying when Tony Currie left to join QPR. Of fences around the pitch. Of packed terraces and crowd surges. Of old-fashioned floodlights. Of World Cup theme tunes. Of running fights between rival fans. Of policemen giving 'deserving hoodlums' a kick up the backside. Of the electronic scoreboard at Elland Road. Of badges you had to get your Mum to sew onto jackets.

So many memories. I wish I could have them all again.

Tuesday 24th May 2016

The problem with reflection – particularly if you devote too much time to it – is that there is an inherent danger that you begin to live your life in the past. I think I probably do this already. In many ways, it seems easier. The element of choice, of having to make decisions, is taken away. You can't undo what's done. In addition, the issue of control is irrelevant. You are not engaged in the perennial struggle to retain involvement and influence as you want them to be, as is the case with the present and, potentially, the future. However, this is essentially over simplistic. For one thing, it presuppose that you are able to select what you recall from what has been. That only good memories resurface through your own will and capacity to choose. For a depressive, the reverse is more likely to be the case. For every positive recollection, there are numerous negative ones. I can't seem to exert the control (yes, that word again!) to relegate one to the dustbin of time and retain the other to indulge and inspire me. I get more of the bad ones, and the more I devote to their remembrance, the more they become confused and entangled with my present situation. In essence, the fears and anxieties I once had, complement the ones that I have to address now. Secondly – and this applies to everyone - to separate totally the past from the present and future is, in fact, impossible. You draw upon what you have been through, what hopefully you have learnt, to guide your approach to living today. For someone with a mental illness, though, it is more problematic. Random things tend to hit me in totally unconnected contexts, for example. I struggle to provide myself with a platform that is logical and coordinated, and one that gives me some sense of assurance as to how to act. It's really difficult to explain, but I'll try by way of an example. Seeing Elliot come home after a bad day at school (which everybody has from time to time), his face sad, his posture resigned, his words despairing, can lead me to recall my own educational experiences – in a totally different setting – and instead of being able to offer advice with a sincerity and conviction that I wish to portray and install in him, it leads me instead to worry about whether he too will succumb to depression, whether his life will, in fact, mirror mine. I say to myself that this is inevitable. Just as my life, I convince myself at times, is determined by the fate of my father, so will his with respect to me. This doesn't impact on what I tell him, of course. I give him advice that will, hopefully, help him. I am positive. I am reassuring. I am supportive. I am all the things a responsible and parent should be. But do I feel it inside? Do these things blot out my depressive rumination? No, they don't.

To try and remedy matters, I have to work really hard. I have to tell myself and force myself to believe that Elliot is different to me. That to devote all your thinking to some determined twist of fate – that one person's life will be exactly the same as that of someone else – isn't reality. It isn't logical. It's not rational. It's a thinking trap. One that I can overcome. Elliot is much more fortunate in so many ways. Though his OCD is an issue – and one that we are dealing with – he hasn't got depression. He may be sad at times. He may be anxious at others. But he doesn't have what I know I had at that age. And even if, in the future, he does experience depression as a mental illness, he is much better equipped to dealing with it now than I was then. I didn't even know it existed, let alone recognise it as part and parcel of the way I viewed and experienced life. That, I guess, is some indication of how we have developed as a society with respect to mental health awareness and knowledge.

Wednesday 25th May 2016
I'm heading into a busy couple of days. This afternoon I'm going along to the AGM of the mental health group that I'm evaluating to give a report on where I'm up to. All the focus groups and interviews are done now – I had to rely on Rachel to do the last one as it coincided with my consultant's appointment – so all I have to do is collate everything, finalise my conclusions and submit my completed report. I'm well on track to deliver what I promised, so in my book, I have to see that as a result! The fact that they want me to continue working with them, this time on business planning, is a positive sign, of course. I've obviously made some kind of impression and I'm really pleased, because it would have been difficult, I think, to have walked away from the project at this time, irrespective of a job well done. Tomorrow I have a succession of meetings, culminating in an event at The Race Equality Centre in the city. They have organised an EU Referendum Campaign question and answer session geared towards people from Black and Minority Ethnic communities, but obviously relevant to all. I'm curious as to what will come out of that simply because my strong suspicion is that people will vote on 23rd June on their gut feeling rather than on any underlying

or accumulated knowledge of the issues at hand. People just don't know enough. They don't understand the full complexities and implications of whatever decision they make. And it's not their fault. I've seen a number of campaign broadcasts and every one of them simply tries to address the claims of the rival camp. When you are faced with such apparent contradictions, and when the politicians continue to use language that is too convoluted, you do wonder how anyone can come to some form of conclusion and then use that as a basis to tick one of the boxes on a ballot paper. The conspiracy theorist in me tends to suspect that complex language is deliberately used to complicate and to hide, to cast a veil over the key matters at hand. I worked in local government too long, methinks!

It's great to have Rachel home. Aside from her simple presence, she has always been someone who gets things done, who doesn't put off until tomorrow what could be done today. As a result, jobs that Lesley and I have been talking about for ages are now underway, some of them completed. Elliot's old bed/desk/cupboard thing (!!) has been dismantled, for example, and we now have a clear space to begin the task of turning his former abode into a guest bedroom. Rachel thinks ahead, sees issues before they materialise, plans accordingly and thereby elicits confidence. Maybe it's the teacher in her? She's always been like that though. It's so good to have someone around who can help Lesley to organise and to carry through all the things that have needed to be done for some time.

I've been useless. I can't pretend otherwise.

I find it so difficult to contemplate big jobs, let alone start them. It's not laziness. It's the motivation factor (as I've mentioned on a number of occasions). Sometimes my technique, my means of action, in doing bits of a task at a time – one job a day – doesn't work. The jobs are too big to dissect into pieces small enough for me to manage. I can't even begin to see the end product. And as a result, the enormity of what I'm contemplating starting is too much. When you find it challenging enough to wash or even to get dressed, taking on the removal of years of accumulated junk is too daunting and overwhelming. It would be like climbing the Eiger on the basis of moving two metres – and only two metres – each day. And doing so without sustenance and the necessary equipment!

Thursday 26<u>th</u> May 2016

For once, I awoke this morning with a smile on my face. I heard the merry sound of a package being delivered downstairs. No ordinary package this. It contained my ticket for the Play-Off Final at Wembley on Sunday. Irrespective of the speed of our post service and the efficiency of the production and distribution company, I couldn't help beginning to worry yesterday at the prospect of having paid out for something that would somehow get lost or mislaid in the post. In the event, I had nothing to fear. I've a ticket now in my possession. Others, judging from Facebook, haven't yet been so lucky. I guess from the law of averages that some will be making all sorts of enquiries and having to undergo last-minute journeys in order to finally have that golden ticket in their hands. It's sod's law. Wembley being Wembley – or perhaps it's the Football Association that are responsible? – there are no tickets on sale at the ground on the day. I can't help thinking that other arrangements may have been possible had Millwall not made it to the Final. We seem to attract specific measures, laws unto ourselves!

I've found it difficult to motivate myself today. Having woken early, I was sorely tempted to go back to bed after breakfast. Not because I was tired necessarily, but because it would pass a few hours. I resisted, but I'm not sure that was the wisest thing. I feel tired now but it's too late to relent. I'm caught in a trap of indecision. What should I do? What's the best thing for me? What would I like to do? I can't answer these questions. I just don't know. And trying to find out would, basically, be a waste of time and, more importantly, of nervous energy. I find myself in similar predicaments quite regularly. Indeed, it's become a bit of a habit. To explain. I'm rarely content with the moment, with what

I'm doing or where I am now, at this minute. I want to be somewhere else, doing something different. However, when I get there or when I do this, the same thing happens again. I'm constantly trying to catch up with what I'm looking forward to, but when I reach it, it doesn't satisfy my hopes. It doesn't meet my expectations. Unrequited fulfilment. False premises. Dissatisfaction. Disappointment. I don't even know the words I need to use! It's like forever trying to catch a bus. You see your opportunity when it stops, but just as you reach its doors, the driver pulls off again. And so it goes on. And when, just suppose, you finally haul yourself on board, you find it's the end of the line. The last stop!

This sense of never being happy, of never being able to find exactly what we're looking for in terms of joy, contentment, peace and relaxation, is prevalent amongst depressives. That doesn't mean that we, robotically, react in the same manner or even that some among us don't find catharsis, that moment in which we think we have succeeded, or that place that tells us we've arrived. We're all different. But the sense that we find lacking a situation which we thought would be almost utopian, that we applied ourselves to achieving, that we've journeyed long and hard to seek, is very common. I think even Del Boy in the wonderful 'Only Fools and Horses', said something about being a millionaire not being as great as he thought it would be! That there was still something missing. That your dreams do not necessarily match your goals or achievements.

As I think I've said before, I've often been asked by consultant and doctor alike, 'when were you last happy?' I respond that I don't know. I can't recall what genuine happiness is. If I was asked 'when would you be happy?' the same thing would apply. I can't foresee a situation that isn't temporary. Millwall winning on Sunday would make me happy of course. But it wouldn't cure or even halt my depression. I would soon revert back to type. And, what's worse, I'd probably regret not making the most of the occasion or the situation. There'd be recriminations.

But that's depression for you!

Friday 27th May 2016

Most certainly a day of contrasts. The morning and the early part of the afternoon was devoted to health-related work. I attended the fortnightly meeting at the General before crossing the city to take up John's kind offer of a stand at his Social Media Café. We were again presenting on the issue of mental capacity and the advance planning project on which we have been tasked to engage with communities. It was different from Sunday because this time it was one-to-one interaction, which, whilst it gave us time to go into detail and discuss pertinent issues, meant that we didn't reach anywhere near the numbers that we had done previously. That's the name of the game though. The nature of the event determines our approach and the results. I suspect that, although we only talked to six people, what we got back from them will be potentially more insightful and comprehensive. We'll see anyway. Just as I was about to leave after five hours of almost solid talking, I was collared by a friend who wanted to ask me about antisemitism in the Labour Party! A very different topic! I suspect that my forthcoming book had prompted him to think about this issue and the far bigger context of anti-Jewish behaviour, and so it was a pleasure to offer my thoughts and to deliberate over the matter at hand. This is undoubtedly one of the things I was hoping would be a consequence of writing about the Holocaust and its legacy. That people will look at topical issues, about current circumstances and make some informed connections, perhaps examining their own pre-conceptions and questioning their own understanding. I don't want people to necessarily agree with me. What is much more important is that people think for themselves with a greater appreciation of fact and context.

I was thoroughly shattered by the time I got home and after a quick, but late, lunch I went upstairs to read. My eyelids soon began to feel heavy and it wasn't long before I was asleep. The rest of the day was spent idly. Deliberately so. I was still tired as

I made my way upstairs once more just before ten. It's revealing just how much a morning such as today actually takes out of me. It's equally disturbing when I think that for people in work, what I went through was simple routine, an everyday occurrence. I've tried not to dwell on this though because I know it will trigger the rumination that only seems to hinder me and lead me to analyse what I do and what I am through depression-tinted spectacles.

Saturday 28th May 2016

Only one more day to go before Wembley.

I should be excited. And, to be fair, there's a bit of me that is. Nevertheless, the greater part of me is nervous and a little percentage could only be described as sheer fright! I can't help thinking that tomorrow will be a test of my future relationship with football. I'm not sure, given my current health status, that I can afford to be so caught up with something that is essentially out of my control. If you think about it, it's bizarre and ridiculous. The thought that my outcome on life, and the quality of my life, is dependent on no more than fourteen[21] people that I don't know performing to a standard necessary to beat another group of fourteen in a game that involves a ball, is scary. I'm sure they are aware of their responsibility to the fans, but this is much more than making me happy. This is about my entire mental framework. It's Russian roulette again!

I think I'm already preparing for the worst. And that doesn't just mean a Millwall defeat. It means rejecting the future as far as football is concerned. Already I've started thinking about the halcyon days when I was younger, about football as it was. You saw that on Monday. There are a plethora of books that have suddenly appeared that focus on that bygone age when football was something to which an ordinary person could relate without having to factor in money and greed. I've added them to my 'Wish List' on Amazon. I want to revel in them, to live my footballing life through them.

To coin that immortal football-related song, 'Que sera, sera'.

Sunday 29th May 2016

I'm actually writing this on the morning of Monday 30th. It's been rare for me not to keep things up-to-date by doing my entry for the day on the day itself, but this had to be an exception. I didn't get home until nearly eight o'clock and, such was the devastation I felt, I simply couldn't face the prospect of doing anything other than stare into space when I eventually felt the weary embrace of my living room chair! Yes, Millwall lost, but it was the manner of defeat that was the true shattering consequence. Even in the morning, in the lead-up to the game, I couldn't stop saying to myself that we were going to lose. I'd tried to keep things low-key, in perspective, so to speak. I took an early train. I mooched about St Pancras station upon my arrival, spending some time in a book shop, buying myself a drink and watching people go about their business, those queuing for the Eurostar in eager anticipation of a holiday, it being the school half-term. Even after I'd made the journey up to Wembley Park on the Metropolitan Line, I'd sought to retain some sense of normality. I walked slowly up Wembley Way, trying to savour the atmosphere, taking in the sights and sounds of a distinctive pre-match atmosphere. Into the ground early, I revelled in the true majesty of my surroundings. It is one heck of a stadium now. It gleamed in the sunshine. It looked sparklingly new. Nothing was out of place. The pitch looked like a snooker table. It was truly beautiful. History and nostalgia alongside modern facilities, cleanliness, symmetry and sheer size. I've been to Wembley, old and new, around ten times – more for rugby league than football – but each experience is both unique and a privilege. Everyone around me as they made their way to their seats shared a sense of thrill and excitement that was intoxicating.

And then the match started and it all went wrong.

We were in the game for precisely 88 seconds. That's how long it took Barnsley to breach our defences for the first time. One shot. One goal. Within twenty minutes, we were two down. Their danger man, Adam Hammill, ran across our back four before planting a wonderful curving shot into the top corner of our net. As soon as he hit it, I knew, even from the other end of the stadium, that it was in. We looked shell-shocked. We just hadn't started. Though our usually dependable centre-half, Mark Beevers, pulled a goal back before half-time after a corner had resulted in confusion in the Barnsley defence, we never looked like we could push on and grab the equaliser in the second-half. With a quarter of an hour to go, the smallest player on the pitch – he had the stature of Ronnie Corbett, believe me – somehow contrived to plant a free header in our six-yard box into the back of the net, despite our apparently Premiership-bound keeper (height six foot one) coming out to challenge. It was utterly ridiculous. Preposterous even. But there it was. That proved to be the signal for crowd trouble to begin both high in the stand to my left but also around me. In the latter case, it set Millwall fan against Millwall fan. It was highly unedifying. What had we become? And again!

In the immediate aftermath, the sense of disappointment was hard to describe and to quantify. On the pitch, we just hadn't done ourselves justice. I don't think we ever really recovered from the shock of the first couple of minutes. Our passing game was virtually non-existent. We kept reverting to long balls up to our front two, but they were delivered more in hope and anxiety than with any real accomplishment or pre-set tactical delivery. We were over-run in the middle of the park and couldn't cope with Barnsley's flair and pace down the flanks. Moreover, we failed to 'give it a go'. That seemed to be the common assessment on the tube afterwards. Losing is one thing, but losing with a whimper, without utmost effort, determination and perseverance is something else. It didn't look like the usual Millwall out there. I guess that's the obvious conclusion. I know we're short on quality. Every Millwall fan accepts that. But what we lack in technique, calibre, skill and technical mastery, we usually more than make up with those attributes that have determined our teams throughout the years. Attributes based around sheer guts. Unfortunately, some of our fans, a tiny proportion yes but a meaningful minority nevertheless, decided that they instead would add some fight to the occasion. I fear that their actions may prove the more lasting legacy of what had turned out to be a day to forget.

Monday 30th May 2016

I was virtually in tears as I took in the damage in front and around me yesterday afternoon. When I finally persuaded my reluctant and suddenly languid body to leave my place and walk out of the ground, I was struggling to control what any minute I feared would become the floodgates of despair. I somehow managed to do so, but every bit of my being was defeated, immersed by emotion of a far greater magnitude than anything I've previously felt at a football ground. I knew then that this was more than one bad result. I knew it the other day, of course, as my diary will testify. I seemed to be walking away not just from one place on one occasion, but from a lifetime of involvement, many years of memories, and from an identity that was once a badge of honour and pride, and which now lies shattered and, like ashes in a heavy wind, prone to fly away into the skies of yesteryear.

Is it really that catastrophic, that terminal, in the cold light of day? To be honest, I don't know. I've had a long chat with Lesley this morning. She can definitely see the agony that I'm in even if the context is not one that she fully understands. She's never been a football watcher, let alone a fanatical supporter. I think she does appreciate the hold that a lifetime's immersion has. She also recognises that football has the propensity to give somebody some of the highest of highs. But it's difficult to describe the cost to one's mental stability if those dynamics – sport and mental illness – combine in the way they have with me. I tried to equate my predicament with that of medication. That what both anti-depressive and anti-psychotic drugs achieve is a flattening of the breadth of highs and depths. The highs don't go so high, but conversely, the lows don't go so low. It can mean that your entire emotional frame of reference, its magnitude, is shrunk to manageable proportions. Football acts in a very similar way. If I somehow decide and then are able to diminish its significance in my life, I risk being more able to withstand the lows, even eradicating completely those directly connected with football, at the expense of limiting the number and scale of highs available to me. It won't cure my depression. Football is still, largely, a peripheral element to that – albeit a significant one. It may mean my life is more boring. It may make it less pleasurable. But it may also help me to rationalise by taking away one element of complete irrationality. In the end, I can't win. What I may gain is offset by what I could lose.

I think all I really know at this moment in time is that there has to be a change. I might not know what that change may be, what it actually looks like and in what direction it takes me. But I can't go on as I have been. Millwall has become like Leeds before, something that matters too much, something in which I pin too many hopes and aspirations, something that is largely unsustainable when it comes to the one thing that I always try to seek when it comes to achieving some semblance of mental stability – that of control. I can't even do what I did before, and start going to watch somebody else. I just know now that the same thing will happen again. The issue is to recognise what I've always been – a fervent, overly passionate football person – that that identity is too firmly entrenched, too resistant to temporary modification or even to change of allegiance and that it's that broad distinctive character that is the matter at hand. To be (a football fan) or not to be? That truly is the question.

Tuesday 31st May 2016

Starting another working week always seems to be harder following a much-anticipated weekend. Today – despite the extra day that comes with a Bank Holiday – is no exception. It didn't help that I woke just before six o'clock with a blinding headache either! I'm a physical wreck at the minute. I keep bringing up phlegm – the legacy of a heavy cold a week or so ago – and on Saturday part of my back tooth came away when I was chewing Lesley's fish risotto. (It wasn't as a result of the meal, I should hasten to add) I haven't properly exercised either for at least a fortnight and I felt very leg-weary on Sunday evening despite my activity being confined to one trip up Wembley Way and another back down it again. All this may be a reason for the uncertainty I feel generally. Leaving my footballing experience and dilemma aside, I have to say that I really don't feel at all sure of myself. At my recent consultant's appointment, we both felt that I was heading for another depressive episode, and yet last week there were signs that this may not be so. As I write this, reviewing how I was yesterday, there was again a curious and unsettling mixture of low mood and easy conversation. These are essentially opposites when it comes to an assessment of my mental state. The latter simply doesn't exist when I'm in the grips of a severe bout of depression. I felt very sombre in the morning and at times during the course of the afternoon, but I didn't hesitate when asked by Lesley if I wanted to go to Costa Coffee at lunchtime and the evening was largely relaxed and anxiety-free. So where am I exactly?

It's funny but if I'm honest, I'd rather be one thing or the other, not stuck in some temporary and unpredictable mental health 'no man's land'. I know where I am then. In a trench – either my own or the enemy's! There is little though that I can do. Irrespective of my deploying the tactics and techniques that I've accumulated over the years to help me to live with depression, the illness itself is too immense to determine and control – at least for me that is. It will lay the path for me. It will put its own obstacles in my way. It will decide and dictate how far I fall and for how long. I just wish that it would make its own mind up! And it would be nice if it would let me know at some point!

June

Wednesday 1st June 2016

May certainly ended on a high note. Lesley and I went to see 'Don Giovanni' at The Curve last night and it most definitely lived up to all my hopes and expectations. It is, of course, a work of supreme genius. A masterpiece. The subtlety and irony of such a dark story being told within the genre of comic opera has always mesmerised me. Mozart achieves something that, on the surface, is hard to believe. Working with a libretto is one thing – the conveyance of a story – but achieving through music the characterisations that he does is art at the highest possible level. One has to listen carefully and work hard to see this, but if you can master that delicate skill, the riches you gain are monumental. Whether it be the depiction of social class or the portrayal of infidelity, obsession, confidence and a whole gamut of other human mannerisms, Mozart's attention to detail – the use of key changes, of melodic line, of harmonic context – is staggering to behold. And yet at times it sounds so easy, so straightforward, so effortless, so logical. It's beyond music with a heart. It's controlled and it's beautifully contrived. Mind has triumphed alongside emotion. They co-exist in majestic synthesis.

It's a pity that performances such as this nearly always occur in the evening. I could have sat and dwelt on what I'd heard for hours afterwards. I didn't want anything – especially sleep – to disturb my concentration and the spell under which I had let myself be submerged. In actual fact, if I'd had my way, I would not have moved from my seat in the theatre. Having to face, straight afterwards, the routines of everyday life, the mechanics of existence if you like – driving home, making a drink, taking medication – brings you back from spiritual elevation in a most abrupt manner. Mortality takes over once more. The immortality that you have just experienced fades from memory far too quickly, simply because life has to go on. For three wonderful hours you are in a bubble, a protective environment in which you experience the beauty of creation, the supremacy of musical intellect, an intensity of emotion hard to describe and to recapture, and then within ten minutes you are back to normality, negotiating roads, fuelling your bodily needs and so on and so forth.

If I could, I would immerse myself in music all the time. If any single thing could address my depression to such an extent that it would make life bearable and worthwhile – other than the love of my family that is – it would be exposure to music. But it would have to be total exposure, an all-consuming, all-pervading, experience that shuts out everything else. And sadly, that is impossible. Only in a coma, if you had the ability to hear, can I envisage such a scenario and still be alive. You can't dispel the monotony of life. You can't escape from having to deal not just with life's challenges, but with its commonplace characteristics. You have to come down from cloud nine. Maybe it's just those routine moments that make the contrast with high art so impactful? Maybe you need the contrast to appreciate fully what you see as uplifting and life-enriching? I guess there's something in that. However, it is revealing that in other spheres of life considered exciting – football comes immediately to mind

– all I ultimately envisage is let-down, a fleeting exhilaration quickly subsumed by anxiety and despair. In music, however, I have a conviction that I will be allowed to take myself away into a different stratosphere, not because I am being pushed into it as some sort of therapeutic remedy, but because my own will and destiny seem to point the way there. I have confidence that I will be able to maintain a level of detachment from reality, that music will keep me there by its own will and through its own power, a power that has a hold over me in a similar way to depression, but which is positively and wonderfully different in its nature and in its impact. I have to thank my Dad for this. Only now, after so many years, am I truly appreciating what he tried so hard to let me see for myself.

Thursday 2nd June 2016

I had a personal disaster last night. One that threatened to put me into a state of intense panic. My mobile phone suddenly told me that I had an 'Unregistered SIM'. I couldn't understand this, especially as I'd sent texts yesterday and received a phone call from Lesley no less than an hour earlier. Whatever we did – turning it on and off, taking out the SIM card and cleaning it – didn't solve the problem. Immediately, my catastrophizing mind went to work. I envisaged losing potential clients, missing out on opportunities, being overlooked and disregarded. I thought of who may be desperately trying to get hold of me. Of loved ones in trouble. I began to convince myself that I would soon be financially broken, that as a result I would lose the house, my surety, my stability, my bedrock. My family would desert me. I'd become a recluse, a lonely, bitter and despairing figure. That suicide would come as a relief. All these things overwhelmed me in a very short period of time. Indeed, they came automatically with a sense of inevitability and logic that defied any attempt to intervene and to address. To be honest, I didn't even have the time to react. I couldn't do anything to prevent it. I'd gone from position A to position Z in an instant. All I was left with was the need to challenge the damage that had been done. To try and install some reason. To attempt to think my way out of the trap that had already captured me. In the cold light of day, this is quite significant. The fact that I could go so quickly and so assuredly into a state of anxiety, without conscious interference, is something, I guess, to which I'm accustomed. But I rarely dwell on this apparent fact. I deal with the consequences, yes. I have to. But I don't always analyse or try to learn from what has happened. I just accept them. Now that I look back, it is another sure-fire indication that depression has a mind of its own, a level of control and impact that defies my ability – or perhaps at times, it's even my inclination – to do anything to stop it. The simple fact is that it's too immense a proposition. It's too strong an adversary. It's far too powerful to combat. It dictates rather than suggests. It states rather than implies. It determines rather than offers. It's a heavyweight punch landed on a blinded opponent. You don't see it coming. You don't even sense its existence and its threat.

Once I'd calmed down, we came to the only possible conclusion. It's knackered. Not a technical term I admit. But that's about the gist of it. I've had it for over ten years. It's ancient, really. It only does the basics in the sense that it acts like a phone rather than the complex, diverse, all-singing-all-dancing technological wonders that are the custom today. Lesley, bless her, said she'd come with me to a phone shop to assess what can be done, if anything. As soon as she'd offered I began to regain some composure. Some control, some decisive intent, had been resurrected. The prospect of having to deal with this on my own was probably an element in my initial reversion to panic. I knew I was out of my depth. I wouldn't be able to process whatever it would have been that I was told. My mind would still be in turmoil. I'd be asked to make a decision. To make a judgement. And I just would not have been capable. This is my reality. And it's the same for millions of others who have a mental illness. How those who are on their own cope with things like this I just don't know. It's hard to imagine the sense of trepidation. The terror, even. If it was me, I'd just hide myself in a corner of a room, put myself to sleep and hope and pray the predicament goes away. I'd be looking for a miracle, a divine intervention. I was on my own once, of course. Before I met Lesley. And looking back now, I realise that that is what I did a lot of the time. Eventually, when forced into action, I always looked for the easiest option, whatever that may have been and irrespective of the consequence. The easiest option was also the easiest to influence and to control. I was probably exploited. Almost inevitably I would have made countless errors, chosen the wrong course, gone along with the most simplistic of resolutions. It would have cost me money. But hardship I could cope with. Mental turbulence, I couldn't.

Friday 3rd June 2016

The return of the wanderer. Our Joel arrives home today, a little bit earlier than we had expected when he set off for the summer season at Eurocamp in southern France in mid-April. Bless him, he doesn't have much luck when it comes to injuries and ailments. This time, he's damaged his ligaments playing football! As the camp authorities can't effectively deal with his restricted state they've told him to go home until he's better. So now we have Joel and Rachel back. All we need is Luke to fall out with Megan and his housemates and lose his job and we'll have a clean sweep! Though it's not the ideal situation, I am, of course, looking forward to seeing him especially as the timing coincides with the beginning of the European Football Championships which will mean I have a viewing companion.

As I've mentioned before, a new person, a new dynamic, a new set of circumstances – they all combine to leave me feeling a little unsteady and uncertain of my place and of my ability to cope. I know there'll be challenges, not because of anything obviously contentious or inherently conflictful, but because it's a change. And I'm not good with that. I don't know anyone with a mental illness who is, as a matter of fact. It's difficult to explain, especially as there's a tendency for people to conceive this as a problem with the person or situation that is defining or involved with that change. It's almost an automatic reaction and though it's understandable for people to think this, it really isn't that at all. The problem is with change itself. It forces new conversations. It necessitates new arrangements. It compels you to alter your position, your way of doing things. It may require the most minimal of adjustments, but that's enough to make you wary, to elicit anxiety, to foresee problems, to dread practicalities. It makes me feel so guilty as well. That here I am thinking of myself, my disability, the impact on me of the arrival home of someone I love very much. There'll be times that I'll begrudge him his 'right' to 'spoil my stability'. That's how I'll see it. There'll be moments when I'll wish he wasn't here. I will resent his presence. I will doubt his sincerity (irrespective of the evidence of injury staring me in the face). I will judge him and I'll be jealous of him, of his easy-going ways, of his natural charm, of his flowing conversation, of his innate ability to love and be loved. That's how it will make me feel. And this will be nothing to do with anything he's done. It won't be attributable to any element of his character or persona. It's all within me. It could be Joel or Myleene Klass, Luke or Stephen Fry, my mum or Beethoven's ghost. The person, my feelings towards them, are irrelevant. It's my tendency to treat change as an imposter, as a bully. That is the issue.

Saturday 4th June 2016

"Oh my God, he's won the title back at 32". Boxing commentator Harry Carpenter's immortal words at the culmination of the iconic 'Rumble in the Jungle' in 1974 when the full enormity of Muhammad Ali's achievement in beating George Foreman first hit home. Today, forty-two years on, the world is in mourning. The Champion of Champions passed away earlier this morning, succumbing to a fight that even he could not win. There's not many people to whom the epithet 'global legend' can genuinely be fixed and widely acclaimed, but Muhammad Ali is one of them. To my mind, the most emblematic of all. There was and never has been anyone else who could seriously compete. The Reverend Jesse Jackson said on television this morning that he was the 'voice of our time'. Yes, and what a voice it was! That distinct, totally unique, way he had not just of expressing his confidence but in entertaining his public and encapsulating a lifestyle, providing a commentary on social affairs, a voice for the downtrodden, for the marginalised and brutalised. If he hadn't been a boxer, he would have made one heck of a poet. But that was Ali. He was always more than just a sportsman. He was never content to be simply the most supreme of boxers. When he said he was the greatest, it had more far-reaching application. Not just in sport, but as a civil activist, as an anti-draft campaigner, as a voice against the Vietnam War, as a humanitarian. He was the greatest of and at them all.

His fight with Parkinson's Disease was, of course, well known. But I hope as we reflect on his life, and as time and destiny provide their own accolades, that his impact within the sphere of disability is also recognised, because for me and I'm sure countless others with long-term, life-spanning conditions, he was always an inspiration. He never shied away from showing the impact of what had consumed his mind and body. He projected a determination not just to address and combat his disability, but to showcase it to demonstrate that it did not determine who or what he was. He was still the greatest. He was still the Ali we had always known. In that public face, his disability was simply another dimension to his persona. It didn't consume him. It didn't stigmatise him. It didn't let him down. If anything, it seemed to give him added strength. I'm talking here of identity, of status, not of the devastating physical and mental impact of the disease. There is an important distinction. In this way, Muhammad Ali would never be beaten. Nothing could destroy him. Nothing could diminish what he was, what he stood for and what he will always be remembered as.

He 'floated like a butterfly' and he 'stung like a bee'. Today he's floating just that little bit more. He's looking down on humanity with brotherly love, interest and with understanding. His embrace is all-consuming. His life is an example. He knew it as well. He has met his Maker as a friend, as a human exemplar of all that was required of him. He's done his job. He's fought his fight. His legacy, though, will endure. It is to float but also to settle. To offer a precedence and to pave a way to a better future, a more equal society, a more compassionate society, a more responsible society. The sting, though, is with us, those he has left behind as mortals. In the First Epistle to the Corinthians, it is stated, "O death, where is thy sting? O grave, where is your victory". Ali almost certainly didn't have this in mind when he uttered his own immortal words, but it's fitting that there is a continuity, a consistency, a completion between the lines. The world is feeling the effect of that sting this morning. The impact of the blows he unleashed in the ring have transferred to us all today, physically, mentally, spiritually, metaphorically but overwhelmingly. We are reeling. We are bitten. We are in pain. We are crying.

Muhammad Ali. Rest In Peace.

Sunday 5th June 2016
I need to have a chat with Elliot later on today because his OCD has threatened to become uncontrollable again. It's our fault, not his. We've neglected things and allowed a laxity to set in that could undo all the good work that he has managed to achieve by himself over the course of many months. Once you let things slip, things can rapidly become out of control. You put off trying to challenge its onset. You convince yourself that any leeway is temporary. You maintain that you have a hold over things. And soon enough, you are dealing with evasion and falsity. For one so young, he's done brilliantly. It's certainly not as bad as it once was. But in some cases, the more difficult ones, the situations that are the most severe, he never went on to tackle their existence and their impact with any degree of authority and confidence. I don't blame him at all. OCD can be absolutely devastating. You want to hide away from it. You want to believe with an intensity and sincerity that is absolute that it will simply disappear. You wish beyond all wishes that it will leave you alone. But it just doesn't work like that. You have to continually work at things. It's challenging and it's difficult, but there is no

other way. When you're as young as he his, that's a harsh lesson.

It's now up to me to help him rediscover the impetus to tackle it that I know he has within him but which has lain dormant for some time. For me, it's my duty as a parent. But it's more than that. For any father or mother with a mental illness, one of the most worrying and troublesome of issues is the prospect that what you have will pass on to your kids. I've thought about this so much. With the three older ones, it's not been anywhere near as bad. In fact, if I'm honest, I haven't given it much thought in their case. That's not because genetically, biologically, they are not mine. It's simply because they were already long in years when my depression began to become a real problem for me. Even though I've been depressed since childhood, they only began to see it when they were teenagers. I'd managed to keep it hidden from them. I don't know how, but I did. Or at least I thought I did. I'm starting to doubt myself, now that I've written those words! I think Lesley probably acted as a buffer whenever things threatened to reveal themselves, whenever I was down or anxious, panicky or angry. I could tear myself away and try to deal with things on my own. With Elliot, though, it's been different. I can see myself in him. I know there are aspects of his character and his mannerisms that are pure me. In the same way that I have always felt that fate has handed me down from my own father his own insecurities, uncertainties and doubts, so that tendency towards continuity I feel is evident and perhaps even a little predetermined with Elliot and myself. He has asked me if he too will become depressed, if mental illness will pass from father to son. I've tried to calm him without lying. I've said that there is evidence – though I can't quote source as I speak – that people are more prone to become mentally ill if one or more parent also has such a disability, but that there is no inevitability about it. He's not bound to 'catch it'. It's not contagious in that sense. Of course it isn't. But it may be more likely. What I've always thought – and I've told him this – is that if he does receive a diagnosis of depression or indeed any other mental illness, he will be more able to cope with it simply because he will be more informed and because he comes from a culture within his own family which is open and transparent. He'll be able to ask questions without fear of revelation. He will be able to seek reassurance from a position of strength. He can see with his own eyes what can happen. He knows how it impacts on me. But he's also aware of how I try to tackle it and not let it defeat me. I may say the reverse – and have done in this diary – but my actions when I'm relatively well should convince him that living a normal life is not just possible, but highly probable. And when I'm ill, I'm still here. I may be restricted in lots of ways, but I'm still capable of doing some things, not least showing love and support to others.

Elliot has lived with mental illness all his life, because of me. It's not something that he should necessarily dread or fear with an intensity that is inherently debilitating or even catastrophic. He is an intelligent person and a determined one. I know he has that in him, even if I sometimes see the same lack of self-confidence and self-worth that used to hinder my own personal development. When I was young, without diagnosis, without surety, without treatment, without knowledge, I was largely on my own. I didn't know what was happening to me. I knew something was wrong, but I wasn't able to give sense or credence to what that was. In the grand scheme of things with a desperately ill father and with a brother with Down's Syndrome, it seemed relatively unimportant. Elliot has a more positive and sure environment in which to handle whatever it is that life throws at him, even if that is mental illness.

I just have to live up to my responsibilities and to the confidence that he has in me. I mustn't let him down.

Monday 6th June 2016

I lost it this morning and for the first time in quite a while, I self-harmed.

Now that the incident is over and peace has been restored to my mind, I feel numb and pathetic, shocked and embarrassed. It's as if I can't register what happened, or at least contextualise it. But what's done is done.

The catalyst was something that I inadvertently did on my PC. Somehow, whilst trying to speed up the operation of the galleries I have on my own website, I must have pressed the wrong button. All of a sudden my screen – and everything on it – was stretched. All the icons, all the images, all the documents. Everything. If I knew what I'd done to make this happen, I could perhaps have logically reversed matters. But I didn't. I had no clue whatsoever. I tried every conceivable process. I opened all the likely apps, but nothing seemed to work. I didn't even really know what to say when turning to Google for help. Joel came down. He seemed to recognise what I'd done, but he couldn't decipher how to rectify things. Rachel, bless her, tried her best as well. All to no avail. It was when she said, to try to ease matters, that I could still access everything, that I finally admitted to her what was really wrong. It was the fact that something had changed, something fundamental to me, and that irrespective of accessibility, that meant distortion and it meant disruption. It was too significant for me to ignore. I couldn't work through it. I would no longer be able to use the computer. How I managed to contain my frustration and despair in front of the two of them, I really don't know. I could feel things rumbling away inside me. I began to well up. I could feel the tension, the bitterness, the self-loathing consuming me from within. There wasn't an outlet. I wanted to punch the screen. I kept my composure whilst Rachel was still fiddling, but I was tottering on the brink of madness and when she left the room, at my urging, I could no longer help myself.

I punched myself with both hands on the side of my head.

It helped, but only momentarily. Though it stunned and hurt me, it was a pain that I wanted. A physical pain, a tangible dimension to my suffering. A discomfort that could distract me from the turmoil inside. As soon as the moment passed, however, I returned once more to what I'd been beforehand. I was sorely tempted to keep battering away, to hit hard and straight, to try and dispel the disease within my mind. To use physical force – rather than mental persuasion – to clear my head and to eject the demons. Before I could do so again though, something happened. I've no idea what. It must have been a spark inside my brain that was desperately trying to make me understand, to calm my agitation. Some semblance of rationality and normality was trying to make its way through the fog of insanity. I really don't know whether it was this, or something else entirely, but whatever it was, it made me stop.

Within minutes, my PC had returned to normal. How, why and as result of what, I can't say. I'd already tried restarting it a number of times, but on this occasion, my prayers – though I can't say I was conscious about saying any – were answered. Things returned to normal with a degree of simplicity and inevitability that defied belief. I didn't know whether to laugh or cry! It was over. It was as if the bloody thing had a mind of its own. That after having had its mischief at my expense, it decided to put me out of my misery. It had teased. It had provoked. It had succeeded in derailing me completely. But now it just wanted to continue as if nothing had happened.

It's been a few hours now. My head is still spinning slightly. Things do feel a little hazy. I haven't been able to put it behind me. It's still there, only now the dominant feelings are of regret and of failure. I feel unworthy and dirty inside. I'm broken at the minute. There's a strong compulsion to add to my pain. To deliberately do so. To inflict my own sense of punishment on myself. But I must resist. It's so difficult though. It's taking up all my energy, every ounce of positive determination and motivation. It will exhaust me. There will be a cost. Out there, life continues. It is a warm day, it's a lazy day. The world carries on, seemingly oblivious to my heartache. Birds are still singing. I can hear distant traffic and the sounds of lawnmowers. Somewhere, a radio is playing. What I've gone through today is hidden to all intents and purposes. No-one else knows. Only me.

Tuesday 7th June 2016

Yesterday was nothing short of a nightmare, from start to finish. I simply couldn't recover from what had happened in the morning. It was just too much. As the day progressed – time passing with a heavy, reverberant but always slow tick of the clock – I descended inexorably into a mire, my whole entity increasingly restricted and trapped like a victim of the most deadly of quicksand. I gave up, if truth be told. I knew that whatever I did was destined to end in failure, so I resolved not to attempt to resist but to relent to the strength of my foe. There are times when you have to pick your fight. You have to believe that you have at least some remote chance of winning, or at least of forestalling your adversary. As the hours passed yesterday, I knew I was lost. I withdrew to the sanctuary of my own company and eventually to the confines of our bedroom. I wasn't capable of doing anything else. I tried to read but I couldn't concentrate. Television didn't really engage me. I resorted to looking out of the window at the slowly descending sun, wondering about what was happening out there in the outside world, but also imagining peace, solace, tranquillity, the serenity of what I hope is life after death.

Though it was a retreat, it wasn't without tactical aforethought.

If I could at least conserve some energy, to retain a modicum of optimism, I may be able to wake up and draw some inspiration to go again. I think that has happened today. I've been able to do some more preparatory work in advance of an important interview I have tomorrow in London at the offices of the Holocaust Memorial Day Trust. Concentration has proved challenging, however, and I have had to resort to short bursts of mental activity. I'm easily distracted and I'm not convinced that much is going in. To anyone with a long-term mental illness, to someone who experiences mental instability, uncertainty and pain each day, interviews are inherently unfair. If you think about it, the one active part of your body that you need to be functioning at optimum level during the course of an interview is your brain. If it can't do that – not because of anything that you've done, irrespective of your sense of commitment and the intensity of your will, but because it is essentially diseased, perpetually malfunctioning – then you are at a natural disadvantage. It would be akin to a penalty shoot-out competition to decide positions in a team or to secure a new contract in which one of the competitors has a broken leg. No reasonable adjustment is allowed. No prevailing circumstances will be taken under consideration. That person is expected, on one leg, to beat the goalkeeper. Or at least to compete with others with both limbs intact. It simply isn't possible. I guess by some fluke and a high degree of good fortune, the 'invalid' may somehow succeed, but it's highly unlikely. Let's put it at that.

What am I to do tomorrow then? I'm unwell. I'm prone to panic. Every part of the day will be strange and a little daunting. I will have consumed significant amounts of nervous energy negotiating trains and tube lines before I even get to the location. I need to know now where I'm going to sit, where the toilets are, the size of the room, the length of my ordeal. I've already done all that I can. I've used Google maps and images to plot my route to the door. I've assessed time considerations. I know the names of those that are interviewing me. What they look like even. But what if there's a change? I can't dismiss that possibility, but if it happens, it will throw me. And then I will be expected to perform to such a standard that I outshine my competitors and give sufficient reassurance to the interviewers that I am capable of doing the job. I could, of course, tell them about my mental illness. I could explain the circumstances of the last few days. But how do I know that they will respond in the right manner? How convinced am I that they will see what I say not as some form of excuse prior to the event, but as a reasonable assessment of my mental state prior to their adjudication? I don't know them. I can't tell. I can only say that at the moment of writing, I've dismissed that possibility because I can't help but think that any declaration will count against me.

I must do my best and I will do. That's all I can do. That's all I can ever do. It's just so disheartening to think – and to believe – that that in itself will never be good enough.

Wednesday 8th June 2016

I've decided that I hate interviews! This probably isn't an earth-shattering revelation. I mean, who does, in all honesty? For me though – as I think I explained in January when I last went to London for this purpose – it's far more than just the period of time when you are sat in front of a panel, trying for the life of you to think of something relevant and incisive to say. It's the whole experience, the nervous anticipation, the travel arrangements, negotiating when to eat and drink (if to eat and drink), ensuring that you arrive on time, making an impression, not saying anything daft outside the confines of the interview, keeping your composure, your self-discipline. In short, everything! Today, I also had to address the fact that it was boiling hot, with a closeness that made me even more sticky and uncomfortable than is normally the case in June. And it was London! Remembering what happened last time, when I totally underestimated the length of time it would take me to get to Westminster from St Pancras, I deliberately arrived half an hour early. I wanted to arrive without looking dishevelled, without a bead of sweat on my brow. So I took it steadily. I decided against a coffee or something to eat. I didn't want to upset my stomach. I do get really anxious about going to the toilet when I'm out and about. There's nothing tangible to account for this. I can't think of a time when I've not been able to negotiate being 'caught short', for example. But it really gets to me. The prospect of embarrassment, of discomfort, of having to suddenly disappear, somehow always seems to reverberate within my head. I can imagine it. Even though it's never actually happened, I always believe it's going to happen. That's the point. Sometime. Some day. Some place. It's one of the reasons, for example, why I always book a train seat next to the toilet. The thought of getting up in the middle of a carriage as the train hurtles onwards, of trying to stay on my feet as I anxiously make my way to one end or the other, of people looking at me, guessing where I'm going, secretly laughing like pre-pubescent kids, suddenly alert to my insecurity. It absolutely terrifies me. I guess the fact that I very rarely eat or drink when I'm out is related to this paranoia. There are occasions when I deliberately forfeit any opportunity to take refreshment. I put up with a rumbling stomach and a heavy thirst. I tolerate headaches caused by de-hydration. I damage myself. That's the bottom line. It's probably another form of self-harm, if you think about it in that context. When I go to Millwall, I always eat the same things at the same places before the match. It forms a ritual and it is part of my elaborate but self-defeating cognition that equates routine with fate. If I don't follow the same pattern, I'm causing my team to lose. That sort of thing. But what I do also relates to the availability of toilets. I eat and drink when I know that I'm in close proximity. Otherwise, I don't.

Anyway, I'm digressing slightly. Back to today and the interview itself. A depressive is never likely to think optimistically about performance. It comes with the territory. Sure enough, I've convinced myself that even though I answered each question quite thoroughly – in terms of time, that is – what I actually said was pure waffle. That I just let my mouth go with the flow, making connections that weren't logical, consistently going down blind alleys, contriving arguments that weren't consistent, using facts that didn't relate. And so on and so forth. I hate to think what I sounded like. And then there is the issue of promoting yourself, of putting forward your best side. This is all very well if you have one – or at least if you believe you do – but if you haven't and you don't, it just feels like empty words, false promises, rhetoric without substance or meaning. One of the questions I had to answer today actually hit the nail on the head. I was asked to rate my skills in communication on a scale from one to ten, where the former is hopeless and the latter is complete mastery. What could I say? I actually told them that I had a mental illness and that being asked to assess myself given this overriding fact was an exercise in total futility. I tend to believe I'm shit, especially when I've had a difficult couple of days, as I have done this week. I could be given a gold medal for some astonishing feat, and I'd still think of myself detrimentally and critically. I can never persuade myself that I'm actually good at anything. So, in the end, I lied. I couldn't say 'one' or 'two'. That would have been the truth according to my distorted and diseased mind. But it wasn't sensible. It would hardly endear me to an organisation wondering whether or not to make use of my supposed talents. So I said 'eight'. I tried to quantify it by saying that this was based on other people's assessments of my capabilities, rather than my own. I was also asked to talk about what I considered to be my major life achievements. What achievements, I said to myself? I haven't done anything! I gave some answer that mentioned fathering step-children and writing books, but if I didn't convince myself, how can I expect to convince anyone else?

Anyway, it'll be next week before I know the outcome. I'm not counting my proverbial chickens. That's my way anyway. It's not a bad philosophy to take when it comes to things such as interviews. If you expect the worst, anything other than that will be a bonus!

Thursday 9th June 2016

Looking back at what I wrote yesterday, there is – at least to me – an obvious connection between substance (the words) and the manner in which I put them to paper. I remember writing without being conscious of the need for structure, to construct sentences that flowed from one connection to another, to apply logic to argument, to effectively instigate a beginning, middle and end. In short, I was rambling. Before I knew it, I'd already written my paragraph but I wasn't sure what I'd actually put down. I knew that I was digressing. The fact that I recognised that at the time bears that out. Thinking carefully, that was probably the only time when I was aware of what I was doing. Everything else just happened. That moment aside, and upon reflection, it is logical to summarise that I should gain some confidence from the fact that I didn't have to change much, if anything, after reading things through afterwards. That discipline in writing came almost naturally. That shape, reason and consistency flowed through my proverbial pen just as much as individual words. But the truth is the opposite. I was scared at the prospect that freedom to write actually equated to what was going through my mind rather than the end result on a PC screen. In other words, that I was veering towards madness. That I couldn't influence, consciously, what was going on. That I wasn't able to exert any sense of check or balance whilst I was writing.

I achieved it. But I didn't feel it. That's the point.

As always, what I'm really talking about is control and the perennial battle to achieve it. At times it seems that what I'm really striving to attain is something absolute, something actually impossible. If control was fixed and total, we would be no different to the most well-constructed, best-serviced robot. Everything would be predictable, pre-determined even. The medication that I am on, I fully realise, attempts to achieve a level of stability and security that is not much different to the realisation of control in its most reachable and consummate state. But whilst I don't want to be wild, sporadic, loose, disorderly, maniacal or any other word that resonates when one thinks of the absence of control, I also don't want to be conditioned to the extent that there is no latitude to what I do or think. In short, I don't want to be a robot, but at times I want to have the control associated with such a thing. When it comes down to it, it's all about balance. But balance is a thing that tends to be associated with mental ill-health and mental illness. At times I don't have any notion of what that actually means and what it constitutes. When I'm conscious of the dangers involved, I try to exert a level of control that relates to every single aspect of my being. That's why I need to think about when I eat and drink. That's why I need to be near to a toilet. That's why I deliberately place myself at the end of a railway carriage. That's why I plan things meticulously. That's why I use Google maps to see a building I've never set foot in. That's also why I take routine medication at the merest hint of a headache or stomach upset. As soon as I begin to realise the sensation of discomfort, I can't simply wait and see how it will develop, I have to act. I have to immediately wrestle back the control that threatens to take the situation away from my conscious influence. In virtually everything I do, I'm never far away from this continual battle. Balance as well as control becomes my fixation.

For any person with depression, or indeed virtually every mental illness that I can think of, the consequences of not winning that battle is thought of as being dire and catastrophic. It may not actually be so, but that does not form part of the thinking process, a process in which extremity rather than continuum is the prevailing state. Everything is either black or it is white. One end or another. I'm either in control or I'm mad. I'm either totally balanced, or completely unbalanced. There's nothing in between. As a result, my warped sense of logic dictates that unless I achieve the ultimate state at one end of a continuum, I am destined, inevitably to fall under its diametric opposite. And I'm scared beyond measure of that prospect. If there, there is no sense of logic or rationality. There is no ability to help oneself. There is only confusion, uncertainty, loss and fear. Vulnerability rules the day. Insanity is pervasive. It's got you where it wants you.

Friday 10th June 2016

I spent yesterday afternoon over at the Glenfield Hospital site as part of a Mental Health Expert Panel convened to answer questions and enter into discussion with University of Leicester medical students. I've done a few of these now and generally find them really interesting. This latest one was no exception. I am always the token service user, the patient, the potential 'guinea pig' on the panel, and that provides quite a unique dynamic when it comes to how these things pan out. I'm considered an expert, but of a different kind. An expert through experience (through a life span in my case), through affliction and suffering, through continual involvement, but also an expert of a kind when it comes to trialling new ideas, potential diagnoses and of course, developing treatments. Sitting alongside me yesterday were two clinicians, one a psychiatrist the other a specialist in learning disabilities. The former I'd met before, as part of a previous panel. As a threesome, we seemed to click. We complemented each other's contributions, providing additional insight from our different perspectives and trying our best to instigate in those listening not just an inquisitive mind but also perhaps a specific interest and immersion in our respective fields. I was told that only 4% of medical students go on to specialise in psychiatry, which seems to me to be disturbingly low. So from this fact alone, there is a real need for young, enthusiastic as well as informed and trained, new blood. Of course you can tell those that are more focused and more interested. They ask more insightful questions. They are more receptive to answers and to subsequent discussions. They are constantly scribbling on paper or banging fingers on an IPad. And they have a tendency to remain alert or, at the very least, to stay awake. One or two people in the second of the two groups we had to perform to were certainly struggling with the latter! I couldn't necessarily blame them as it was the end of the day, the room was unbearably hot (even with fans!) and if you aren't positively enthused by the specificity of the subject (and not everyone is, of course!) it can be heavy stuff.

We touched on so many areas. On the importance of communication, on person-centred treatment, on patient attitudes, on diagnosis, on funding, on the need to involve carers, on the role of the voluntary sector, on GP competence, on stigma and discrimination, on comparisons with physical illnesses and disabilities, on involving the patient, on the value of social skills. And much more. It was hard work, but rewarding I hope. One example I trust is suffice. One of the students talked about carer input and the need to ensure that carers too are properly supported. The case that she has been given to analyse involved a young person with Down's Syndrome. I was able to suggest (from my own personal experience of course), that there can be a tendency to think only of primary carers when it comes to things like offering carer assessments, and that the needs of other carers, particularly siblings, are often overlooked or at best, marginalised. She mentioned, in response, that the young person in question had a twin and was genuinely grateful for that fresh insight, the consideration of an additional dimension, that I was able to give. I hope therefore that at least one sibling of someone with a learning disability may be spared some of the potentially traumatic trials and tribulations that can result from the assumption that they are not as involved as their parent(s) and that therefore there is no requirement to look carefully into their own needs, now and into the future. I suspect that the number of young carers (of their brothers and sisters as well as parents) who go on to develop mental illnesses that relate fundamentally to their time as a supportive mechanism to others is considerable. I'm also guessing that this phenomenon is not as well understood as it should be, and that the numbers involved may actually come down to guesswork. People in these situations often feel guilty about thinking of themselves. Their focus is on the supposedly greater need. They are entrusted (and I would imagine also in many cases, coerced), into relegating their own issues, their own requirements, their own mental stability, their own future, their own lives, to a far distant second. Or at least to having to take care of those things themselves. To be strong, when you feel only weakness. To cope when you are struggling yourself. To be independent, when it is dependence that you actually crave. Lives may be as determined from experiences as a child in these contexts as in many others. I'm only one example, after all.

Saturday 11th June 2016

I am so tired this morning. I had trouble rousing myself from my bed. I was dizzy when I stood up from my chair to make a coffee and had to steady myself for a moment. I even felt weary when I made my breakfast. In everything I've done, lethargy has ruled the roost. Why? It can only be my mental condition. I've done nothing especially onerous, nothing physically that could explain my fatigue. I haven't overexerted myself. I'm not going down with anything. I'm just mentally shattered and more than a little depressed. If I could only bottle what I'm going through, create something tangible and evidential that could demonstrate succinctly and unambiguously to those people unaccustomed to addressing the challenge of mental illness and who may not be aware of the connections between mental and physical health, I would even say I would be momentarily 'happy'. People need to believe the fact that your mental state can and does shape your physical capacity and capability, your outlook, your pedigree, your shape, your acumen, as much as it does the other way around. But the balance between the two is strongly in favour of the latter. Most people accept without question the relationship between physical illness and the way one's mind reacts to it. But somehow the concept that being mentally frail has a similar direct correlation to physical fitness, is beyond some people's conscious affirmation. People don't accept it as readily. In fact, some people reject it out of hand. I guess it's another manifestation of the state of mental health awareness and also the prevalence of stigma.

What hurts even more this morning, paradoxically, is that I've had some good news. Not only has my book finally been printed and awaits its public bow next week with its launch at John's Military History Live event, but I managed to get the position that I'd interviewed for on Wednesday. I had the phone call last night. I wasn't expecting a positive outcome, as you know, but for once my achievement has outshone my fatalistic position, inclinations and approach. I obviously wasn't as bad as I thought I'd been. Despite these lifts, I still remain irreparably consumed by the darkness that comes with long-term depression. Indeed, it's a pretty firm soundbite of the extent of my disability that supposedly positive things do not do anything other than fleetingly suggest that the fog is lifting. It doesn't give me clarity. I'm still not able to see through it. All it does is convey to me the possibility that I may be able to at some time. Almost as soon as this registers within a brain that is perennially heavy and slow to adjust, than my normal state reasserts its dominance and pervasiveness. The fog descends, becomes close and menacing once more. And I don't know when I'll see fresh air again.

Sunday 12th June 2016
I have a strong sense of déjà vu this morning. I could – if I was lazy and unconcerned with literary pedigree and consistency – just use the same words that I did twenty-four hours ago. Because nothing has really changed. My energy levels have sapped to such an extent that if I was a car, my driver would be frantically looking for a garage to fill up with fuel. The one thing that is perhaps different to yesterday is that there may be an additional component to my fatigue – an extra explanation if you like – that still relates directly to mental health, but not in the same manner. And it is this. It was Joel's birthday yesterday – he's now twenty-five – and in the evening members of Lesley's family came round for a meal to celebrate the occasion. Family gatherings, as you know by now, are not situations that I particularly relish. I find them hard to cope with. Even though this time there was the distraction of the European Football Championships – and England's first match – on the telly, the expectation of having to take part in new conversations, of needing to accommodate new dynamics, still had to be met. I tried, but as usual it was too much.

The aftermath always leads to self-recrimination, but this time I think I had consumed so much nervous energy in the hours leading up to people's arrival and then during the course of the evening itself, that it was almost inevitable that it would take its toll the next day. I found it hard to go to sleep – I guess I was still on edge – and it wasn't until the early hours when I finally felt sufficiently tired to no longer dwell on what I'd been through, to finally 'put to bed' (quite literally) my own evaluation of my performance. It's a reflection of my mental state that in a situation that most people find inherently enjoyable, one free from everyday worries and concerns, I still find myself in a context that merits self-analysis. It's no different from how I feel following a meeting, or an event at which I've presented. The pressure inside me necessitates dwelling on what I did, or didn't do. What I said, or left unsaid. It's a pressure that links succinctly to the issue of perfectionism. Did I pass the test? Was there anything I could have done differently? What on earth did other people think of me? What impression had I left on everyone else? And this, let me remind you again, is a consequence of a few hours of family togetherness over a meal, drinks and football. It wasn't a job interview. Nor a pitch for a product. It wasn't the delivery of a piece of work. Nor a medical assessment of the state of my health. It was supposed to be fun in a relaxed atmosphere!

One of the things that served to haunt me soon after my decision to go down its path was the fact that I slipped quietly away once I'd felt too over-burdened with my own anxiety. Rather than make a big 'song and dance' about saying goodbye to everyone, I just left. It was certainly the easier thing to do. But was it the right thing? I told Lesley that I was going to go out in this way and she understood and was fine with it. But would everyone have that same level of understanding and empathy? Would some find it rude, disrespectful or perhaps even offensive? I've done it before and there's been no problem. But that didn't serve to quell my fears as I lay in bed upstairs listening to everything going on below me. By the time I wondered whether I could in fact remedy matters, people had already started to leave. It was classic fait accompli! The legacy of my decision was the disquiet that I felt in the hours afterwards. Was it also my punishment? If it was, it was certainly severe and impacting.

Monday 13th June 2016

I've probably said this before, but in terms of treatment, self-help really, there is one heck of a contradiction that relates fundamentally to the correlation between mental and physical health. It's one that virtually every person I know with a mental illness recognises and has to face. Pure and simply, we are told that exercising is good for you and that we should try to extend what we currently do. As if we hadn't thought of that! But the problem, the inherent difficulty in stating what might appear to be the obvious, is that for most of the time when we're ill, we're also bloody knackered! Not because of the fact that we've been overexerting our bodies, not because we're on some strenuous exercise regime, not because we're training to become Olympic athletes, not because we want to relive the glory days of our sporting youth. No, because we have a mental illness and that, in itself, is energy sapping, positively debilitating and exhausts every part of us, not just our brain. Whenever I'm in a GP surgery and one of the many doctors I get to see says something to the effect that it would be good for me to increase the amount of physical activity I get through in a week, I look at him or her with that tired but resigned expression and say that actually I would love to do that, but when it's hard enough to raise your head from a pillow or to make it down the stairs (let alone up!), it's almost impossible to suddenly raise your game and do much more than you're currently able to withstand. It's the equivalent of being told to go for a short walk having just completed a marathon, of being asked to mow the lawn after spending a couple of hours in the gym, of being required to clean the house following a gruelling swim. It's not impossible, but it's downright hard. Actually, it's more than that. What I've just talked about are physical responses. The mental equivalent is probably more exacting. What I mean here is that in all the examples I've cited, you have already shown your commitment to exercise. You have already demonstrated that you can perform and that you recognise what is good for you. What you're being told now is that that is not enough. That you've still to prove yourself. That there are still expectations. That you need to do so much more just to keep your head above the water, just to satisfy what someone else has determined is your capacity and your capability. Such a scenario, I would put to anyone, is intrinsically shattering. It serves not to enthuse or to stimulate, but, in total contrast, to demotivate and to stigmatise. Every time I commit to exercise, I am battling with my body and with my mind. I'm having to try and energise a being that, as a result of mental illness, is already heavy, slow, cumbersome and weary. I'm attempting to resurrect something that has been infused with lethargy. And I haven't yet mentioned the potential side-effects of strong medication! Think of it this way. You are in a 100m race. You are lining up alongside your fellow competitors. The finishing post is within sight. In actual fact, it's tantalisingly close. Your goal, your sense of achievement is within consciousness in the same fashion. Suddenly, though, you are asked to step out of your lane. You are taken to one side and told that for you, and only you, a separate route from start to finish has been determined. Instead of track, you have to plough your way through heavy mud. You're not given an advantage, a head start. You're expected to race with those around you as an equal. Suddenly, all the ambition, the motivation, all the built-up energy reserves, all the advance planning and preparation. It's all dissipated. In its place, reservation and doubt wrestle for control. You can't contemplate what you're being asked to do. You're bound to lose. There's no guarantee that you'll even finish. Your body, conditioned for one task, is suddenly incapable of adjustment. You realise that the impact on your heart has multiplied considerably. If you lose, you're useless. Your perfectionism has reaffirmed that on many an occasion. But how can you win? How can you even compete? What's the point of even trying? You may actually harm yourself. You're putting yourself under too much pressure. What you have before you is now something else. It's ceased to be a contest. It's no longer a goal, an attainable goal, a realistic goal, a purposeful goal. It's now simply self-harm. Self-destruction. You stand to lose whatever you do. You can't gain anything at all. It's time to cut your losses. It's time to pull out. It's time to admit defeat and try to move on. Perhaps in the future there will be more realistic challenges? Perhaps there won't? But that's all that you can now genuinely apprehend. It's all there is. Possibility is the best you can hope for.

Tuesday 14th June 2016
I've got up this morning, but the fact is that I remain alarmingly unmotivated. All I see ahead of me are obstacles to be

overcome. There's nothing that I would say as I write this that I'm looking forward to, but to a certain extent I can accept that. There's nothing new in that position. What is particularly worrying is the fact that every single thing that I know is going to have to be experienced seems especially daunting, even writing this diary entry. It's all just a succession of challenges, every one of which has the potential to bring me right down. If I was to try and analyse what I'm about to face with some sense of rationality, I'm sure that I would be able to dissect each single situation and see it for what it is. I'm also pretty certain that what I would conclude is that there is nothing especially difficult in any of them. As such critical analysis is beyond me today, all I can really deduce is that what I'm struggling with is life itself. And that's depressing.

Take food as an example. I have to eat if I am to remain well. I know that. It's a basic fact of life. You need fuel to make your body work. But surely eating is more than simply a biological necessity? Can I not hope to think that it may be enjoyable as well? Of course, what translates subsistence into pleasure is the type of food you eat and the way it is prepared and cooked. Potatoes without seasoning remain just potatoes. Potatoes can also be roasted, boiled and fried and are usually seen as an accompaniment to something else. What makes them special is their elevation into something that people experience almost as a treat. I still see chips from a chip shop in this way. But of course what you are eating when you consume chipped potatoes is something inherently unhealthy. If you can reconcile that fact, or even if you have the ability to put that negative component completely to one side, you can still enjoy the experience of eating. And loads of people do and can. Unfortunately, I'm not one of them. I automatically recognise the bad side. Indeed, that is the natural side for me to realise. I see fat before I see indulgence. There are times when I have to eat things such as chips as fast as I can so that I can keep the demons at bay until afterwards. So that I don't have to face in a prolonged sense the dilemma of whether to eat them or not. Once I've done so, I no longer have to circumnavigate the element of choice. I no longer need to make that decision. The damage may be done, but it's a thing of the past, not a current quandary. Eating in such a way is, I'm sure, decidedly unhealthy as well. It can't help your digestive system to treat eating as if you're in sprint finish. However, it also means that any revelry, any pleasure you may gain from eating something you see as a treat, is quickly over. You may not even register the fact that this is supposed to be gratifying at all. It's over in a flash, and one of your own making. The manner in which you eat – designed to curtail the depressive essence of the experience – also succeeds in diminishing any sense of delight and satisfaction. If you can't win, the best you can hope for is a draw. In actual fact, that's what you are aiming for, if you think about it. The negative to negate the positive. And vice versa. But who, in the grand scheme of things, goes out of their way to continually seek stalemate? Every day, every part of a day. Isn't there supposed to be more to life than that?

I remember once during a psychotherapy session, I was asked by my therapist what food and drink I would buy if I wanted to reward or treat myself. I remember answering cheesecake and Dandelion and Burdock. She then instructed me to go immediately afterwards to a shop, buy them and luxuriate in their taste, savouring every mouthful. She talked about using the experience in a positive sense, to realise that life is about giving yourself indulgences, allowing yourself pleasure, saying within your own mind that you have deserved what you're experiencing, that it's a reward, a comfort, a salvation even. I did exactly as she said and I tried so hard to adjust my thinking, to focus solely on flavour and texture, to allow myself to salivate and to dwell on every single morsel of food and drop of fluid. It worked momentarily, but the consequences were more devastating than I could have imagined. I couldn't sustain that fleeting sensation. It was like trying to keep a heavy weight above your own head. Eventually, your muscles give way. It's natural and it's inevitable. And when they do, because of the exertion you've put in to the effort, you are left with even greater aches. You may even have damaged yourself. My world soon reverted back to what I was accustomed to experiencing. My mind resorted to what it knew, to what came 'naturally'. Depression had restored itself once more. That moment of indulgence was too minute to recollect. I'd already forgotten what it felt like.

Wednesday 15th June 2016
Joel had some shattering news yesterday. One of his friends from University, someone to whom he was really close, took his own life. Along with the devastation, Joel immediately began to reflect on what he could have done. Alongside the tears came the self-recrimination. Whilst both are understandable, only the former has any real credence as a logical and convincing reaction. I tried to make him understand that people who have passed through that stage of pain and are determined to end their life have made a conscious choice to go. It's what they want. I know from personal experience that there is sense and even comfort in that decision. I have never been so far along that path, of course. There was always something that made me hesitate and think again. But I do know what it feels like to embark on that journey. That everyday concerns, routine worries, all the anxieties and distress that comes from living under pressure (whether self-imposed or not) are relegated, perhaps for the first time, to subsidiary status. They may even evaporate completely. I don't know. As I said, I've never been that far.

I'm certainly not trying to convince people that suicide is the only way. It's not. I'm just telling it as it is, in an attempt to make people understand that it is an act that is based on experience of pain. That it is something that has logic, even if it is based in tragedy. I'm just trying to give people an added awareness of what it involves. To make sense of something that most people conceive of as being incredulous as well as selfish. It's not the former and to the person involved, it's not the latter. People at this stage of their lives, the ultimate stage if you like, are convinced that their loved ones, their friends, their associates, will be better off without them. There might be immediate anguish, heartbreak and desolation, but in the long term these things go. Life eventually goes on, and without the person involved, it is a freer life, one less focused on living pain. I'm not saying that this is true, by the way, I'm trying to portray the thinking of someone who has determined to end things but who knows that there are loved ones he or she has to leave behind, people who have to deal with the consequences but who can recover and live the lives they want.

Of course, it's never that simple, as Joel, bless him, is finding out to his cost at the moment. People are desperate to intervene. The good side of humanity comes to the fore. People want to help, to resolve, to reassure, to ease the pain. People do care. People are always part of the solution. Suicide can be prevented. It's not always last-minute intercession. For every high-profile case of someone stopping somebody on a bridge from throwing themselves over the edge, there are countless more examples of people spending more time with those that they realise are distressed and perhaps even resigned. However, the signs are not always obvious. Indeed, sometimes they may appear contradictory. The person concerned may even seem happier, living with a newly-acquired freedom of heart and mind. This is entirely logical, if you think about it. Life and all its tribulations have been addressed. The individual has moved beyond that. He or she is looking towards a future in another sphere. In a practical sense, therefore, there is a need to look for changes surrounding the person in question. Changes in attitude, in temperament, in ethos, in outlook. But also changes in a practical sense. People leaving instructions with regard to financial affairs or with respect to other tangible arrangements. Saying goodbyes in subtle ways. Resolving long-standing disputes. A sole focus, a preoccupation even, on immediate issues. There are some insightful websites that deal with these matters and I would urge anyone and everyone to have a look. It could be that you do so just in time to prevent someone from taking that journey from which there is no return.

Joel was saying lots of sensible and commonplace things as he reflected, painfully, on the decision that his friend had made. 'If only I'd talked to him earlier. If only I'd gone and seen him. If only I'd been there'. Understandable though they are, these are reflections that only make sense if you have the gift of foresight and the legacy of hindsight. His friend apparently did have depression. Joel knew that from their time together as students. Nobody, particularly with the geographical distance between them and taking account of the separation that comes following the intensity of campus relationships, could somehow accurately know that in a set time-framework, their friend or loved one would eventually take their own life. Not even God has that power if the person concerned is consciously intent on keeping it within. I tried to get through to Joel that if his friend had wanted help, if he had wished to involve Joel – or indeed anyone else – he would have done so and said so.

If there is a lesson from tragic circumstances such as this, it is that we all need to be more aware of how people around us act as well as feel. Mental illness can be seen. Mental distress is apparent. It may evidence itself in diverse ways, but it is not hidden totally. If you believe in God, there is a relationship to be had there that I believe can not only be beneficial but may be life-changing or life-preserving. If someone is absolutely intent on taking their own life, God can provide that comfort, that reassurance, that peace. Those are my beliefs. But if you don't think that way, there are still things that us mere mortals can do. We do have significant powers, powers that can provide avenues for the distressed, powers that can influence people's decisions, powers that do provide compassion and solace, powers that can persuade, powers that can affect change. A more thorough awareness of mental illness and specifically of suicidal ideation would certainly help. But deep down, I think it's more fundamental than that. We need to take care of each other, not when we wish to, but when the circumstances allow us and the conditions dictate. We may not always be successful, but the type of society I mean may actually play a part in making people contemplating taking their own life, think again. They may realise that life is worth living, that life has substance and meaning. That life is the preferable option.

Thursday 16th June 2016

It seems that the whole of the country (well, England and Wales at least) are gearing themselves up for the crunch match at the European Championships, which kicks off at two o'clock this afternoon. I suppose it's one of the luxuries of self-employment, of being your own boss, that you can simply allow yourself to work when you want to and take time off for things such as this. When I was working for various organisations, I seem to remember making it a priority to book annual leave whenever key football matches just happened to be scheduled during the working day. However, in this day and age, particularly with social media and live coverage via PC's, the clever – or sly, depending on which way you look at it – employee doesn't necessarily have to sacrifice holiday entitlement to follow what's going on. If you work in an office, it's all there for you anyway!

It begs the question of how much actual work people realistically do each day in such a working environment. Obviously, football tournaments are not everyday occurrences, but I know of lots of people who would follow the cricket or the Olympics from their desks and many more who would be permanently switched on to news updates and now even social media outlets. Then consider toilet breaks, making coffees and teas, routine socialising at desks, chatting to people in passing, visits to staff canteens and other commonplace occurrences, not forgetting the smokers amongst us who require regular inhalation of tobacco! It all adds up, doesn't it?

Why am I mentioning this? What's the relevance to mental health? Well, I guess there are lots of connections, things that could be mentioned, the most fundamental of which is addressing the stigma that often comes with flexible working. Equality law requires employers to consider reasonable adjustments for disabled employees and indeed others. For those with physical and sensory ailments, this tends to equate to specialised equipment, whether they be chairs, visual aids at people's desks, hearing loops and such like. For those of us with a mental illness, one of the most common aspects of adjustment relates to the ability to work more flexibly, whether that be different working times, longer lunch hours and, quite commonly, working more from home. The problem comes when people have preconceived notions as to what that means. Put more bluntly, some people seem to think that if you're not at your desk, visibly working, you must be skiving! I've had to face attitudes such as this throughout my working career. There was a time when my boss asked me to tell him of any occasion when people mentioned something that related in some way to my working hours. Quite often, it was their impression that I only worked part-time. Sometimes, I just thought that that was a clever way of hiding their real conviction, that I wasn't actually 'pulling my weight'. Nothing is more offensive in the workplace than people's false assumptions about dedication, motivation, deceit and laziness.

The consequence for me was that I overworked, for the simple reason that I felt I had to prove myself. When at home, at my own PC, addressing work issues and concerns just as I would have done in the office, I meticulously kept a record of what I was doing and for how long I was doing it. If I stopped to go to the loo or to make a cup of tea, my 'stopwatch' at my side was put on pause. I didn't count this as work. I wouldn't have made such a distinction in the office, of course, and nobody does, but at home, it seemed to matter. I also worked longer hours. I was constantly in surplus. Never, in my whole time working at the Council, was I ever behind in terms of my weekly or indeed monthly work balance. Why did I do this? Firstly, because I suspected I would have to account for myself far more stringently, and secondly, because I knew that at some point in the future I would be forced to take disability sick leave as a result of my depression. Therefore, I felt I needed to 'get ahead of myself', to work the hours that I would miss because of the effects of my disability in advance, so to speak. The same would happen once I returned to work as well. The thing is, I know lots of disabled workers, many of them with a mental health condition, who both feel and do the same. Who, as a consequence of stigma, cruel attitude and unproven assumption, think that the only way to counter that is to change their own behaviour, to work harder and longer, to close every loophole, to be ever vigilant, to think ahead and to cover themselves. To prove not only that they can do the job, but that they are without question the most responsible and efficient of workers. Some – and I've done this myself – actually volunteer to, and take on board, other people's workloads, for the same reasons. It would be like Wayne Rooney deciding that he alone can take to the field for England. Not because he wants to, but because he feels he has to, to dispel any criticisms over his work ethic, efficiency, reliability, diligence or backbone.

This is one of the reasons why I am particularly interested in the issue of mental health in the workplace. People are discriminated against because of their mental disability, but fear of discrimination is just as pertinent and perhaps even more commonplace. It all adds up. If people feel pressurised, they are prone to become ill. That simple relationship is, of course, much more dramatic and hard-hitting when it comes to someone who has an existing mental illness, someone who perhaps cannot handle stress and anxiety as well as those without. The need to prove oneself is, I suppose, part of every competitive working environment, but this is something entirely different. This is brutal and it's unacceptable. People who are mentally ill, who have to deal with all that that involves on a daily basis, don't need the extra demands imposed on them as a result of other people's ignorant, prejudiced, false and distinctly unfair attitudes. I remember on one occasion in the office, I made a note of how many times particular colleagues went out for fag breaks, how many hot drinks they made and how long they took making them, how often they would stop for a chat about sport, food, weekends, holidays and so on and so forth. As that proverbial watch stopped on every occasion, the amount of actual working time lost was quite staggering. But of course, these things don't actually matter. People don't record them on their work cards for the simple reason that they are not expected to. How that reconciled with some people thinking as they did about my battle with mental illness and how that impacted on my need and my ability to work, was difficult to stomach. Their socialising at work was one thing. My working at home was another. One rule for them. Another for me.

Friday 17th June 2016

I had to go to my former workplace this morning for a meeting of the Equalities Group of which I'm now a member. I wish I could describe accurately how I felt as I drove onto the complex and then entered the premises. It was a combination of nervousness, dread, regret and terror with more than a touch of anger mixed in. My whole working tenure at the Council flashed before my eyes and for a moment, when I was caught up in the emotion of remembrance, it seemed like I was back again as a committed but disillusioned officer. It was significant that for those fleeting seconds, a mirage of time, I also felt positively sick. It wasn't a pleasant experience. I do hope that with time, those feelings will dissipate and I'll be allowed to get on in my present state, as a service-user and member of the public. I suspect this will be later rather than sooner though.

On my way home afterwards, I took a slight detour. I had to go to the dentists with Elliot but that wasn't until much later in the afternoon. As I'd never been to this particular surgery before, I felt that I had to do what amounted to a 'dummy run'! This involved not just finding the address, but assessing what roads to take, where to park and the time duration of my journey. It wasn't enough just to look on Google maps. I couldn't rely on what I could glean within the confines of my own home. I had to physically go there. It added miles and minutes to my journey but it was time and money well spent. Instead of sweat and nerves, I could pace myself, breathe more easily, knowing that I'd done all that I could in terms of preparation. If I had the time, I would do this more often. I certainly never fail to have the inclination. It's a necessary part of adjusting my mind to new challenges. It's a coping mechanism. And it's an important copying mechanism. If you think it sounds bizarre, I have to tell you that I'm certainly not alone. You will recall in February that I relayed the story of the Scottish comedienne on Rob Brydon's excellent 'Would I Lie To You?'[22] As soon as she told her story, not only did I insist that she was telling the truth – I knew she wasn't fibbing – I also suspected that she had a mental health condition, though that wasn't revealed on national television, as you can probably appreciate. What was interesting in my reaction was that whilst I was so relieved to hear that someone else thought and acted as I do, I was also quite upset that everyone else, panel combined with willing audience, thought it was inherently funny in that almost unbelievably whacky and incredulous sense of the term. It made me want to shout at the screen – 'I don't want to do this. I don't want to draw attention to myself. I have to do it. It's the only way I'm truly able to deal with the situation'. I was virtually imploring those consumed with hilarity, 'please don't laugh. Please try to understand'. Perhaps using the situation as an example on prime-time television may make some people think a little more deeply and appreciatively about what makes someone feel that they have to put themselves through this enforced sense of déjà vu? I certainly hope so, because it's not nice to see people's instant reaction when it's something you feel is unavoidable and that reaction is simply to laugh.

Saturday 18th June 2016
What a day! At long last, I held a copy of my new book in my hands and was able to reflect on what I'd done. The book was being launched at John's Military History Live event and it was with nervous trepidation that Elliot and I made our way into town to take our places at the stand John had kindly created to advertise 'Suspended Disbelief'. Though nerves threatened to get the better of me at one point, I was able to function, to talk to people and to discuss relevant issues, even to the extent of making a public speech to officially and formally announce the

arrival of my new contribution to Holocaust writing. I was really pleased with what the publishers had done. It looked elegant. It had, to my mind anyway, that necessary combination of gravitas and accessibility on the front cover that promised much. That's really all you can expect from outside appearances. People were clearly impressed, though I did feel I had to point out to them that they hadn't read it yet! Clearly, proof of the pudding is in the eating! John, as ever, was wonderfully supportive. He couldn't do enough to make me feel at ease. He kept returning to ask if everything was OK and if I needed anything. To put on something as superlative and as comprehensive as an event geared towards military history in anything approaching the depth and substance that was achieved is something essentially monumental and yet he does things like this so well. Nothing seems to faze him. He oozes confidence and reliability. He has an innate charm that seems to draw inspiration and devotion from those around him. And yet he is so humble, so grounded, so down to earth. He makes you feel special and valuable, and that's no mean achievement with respect to a depressive!

I could also say all those things and more about my Elliot. I was so proud of him today. I'd asked him to come down with me early to help me set up, knowing that Lesley was bringing her parents at a later time. I expected him to then leave with them, but instead he insisted on staying with me. I was so touched. He gave me the courage, the necessary stimulus I needed to be proud of my achievement. He kept me entertained and did lots of little things that when collated and added together resulted in my having for one day at least that sense of acquired belief in myself that I know I lack most of the time. For him to hug me and say he was proud of me, meant absolutely everything. The feeling is most definitely mutual. I'm a very lucky man to have a boy like him.

Sunday 19th June 2016

I'm planning on having a very easy day today. Not just because it's Father's Day, but more because I have such a busy week ahead, one that is not just full of different engagements, but one that is potentially fraught with challenges and possible pitfalls. I can't say I'm looking forward to it. It should be exciting, particularly as the first two days are an induction for the Holocaust Memorial Day (HMD) Trust position I've just managed to secure, and I guess that when I'm actually in the room with my new colleagues, it will be. It's just that I have to negotiate so much around the actual working sessions and, for once, I am not in a position to influence let alone control what I do and how I go about things. The thing is, the HMD Trust have literally organised everything, from travel to hotel accommodation, even to booking a venue for an evening meal. They mean to be helpful, of course, to take away any of the hassles that might accrue especially given the fact that things have had to be arranged fairly quickly. But, for me, it's become an even more daunting prospect than would usually be the case. (I hasten to add that no fault whatsoever can be attached to the organisers – thorough, professional, anxious to please and support that they have been. How were they to know?) Let me give you some examples. The seat they've booked for me on both trains (to and from the capital) is in the middle of an ordinary compartment, which, as you know well by now, is not something I would have booked for myself for all the logistical nightmares that revolve around it. They've given me a relatively tight schedule to transfer from East Midlands Trains to the Jubilee Lane on the Underground. That means I will almost certainly be focused more than is usual on the time. Should there be delays, how will I react? The check-in time for the hotel is in the middle of the afternoon's working session which either means I will have to carry my luggage around with me or ask at Hotel Reception if they can store it until later. The latter, which is obviously the more preferable arrangement, involves dialogue with people I don't know about practicalities. I may be forced into having to make a decision. We're obviously going en masse for something to eat in the evening. That means socialising, small talk, getting to know people. It also means having to cope with a public venue. I'm not sure I've mentioned this before, but when in a café or restaurant, I always try to seat myself in a position where I'm looking out. I get quite paranoid at the prospect of people I can't see behind me. I get it into my head that they're scrutinising my every movement, my every word, and that somehow, for some inexplicable reason, I'm the focus of their laughter and merriment. I don't think this is quite as unusual or as strange as it sounds. After all, dogs and indeed other animals, also prefer this perspective. Their concern is the danger of physical attack. My concern is the same, only from a verbal or attitudinal perspective. But whilst when I'm with Lesley, this is understood and accepted, how do I broach this issue with people who don't know me? I have already sent an email to the organiser in which I mentioned that my mental health condition may necessitate some additional support. I was in two minds before I sent it. After all, I've only met her once. I just have to hope that she's taken it in the right way and that I haven't somehow alarmed her. She might think I'm strange. Impressions are just everything when I'm in this position of doubt and heightened concern. In the end, it comes down to this. Whilst for others, the challenge of a focused and intense induction process relates to what happens within the working room and during the course of the arranged sessions. For me what happens outside that environment is the more taxing and 'dangerous' prospect. That doesn't mean, by the way, that I'll find the work any easier than anyone else. Far from it. I'll be no different to the others in that respect. For me, when other people are relaxing and winding down, I'll be doing the exact opposite. I'll be under severe pressure from the very moment I leave home tomorrow morning, until the time when Rachel picks me up from the station on Tuesday afternoon. Perhaps they'll be someone like me doing the induction as well? A kindred spirit. A source of confidence and reassurance. That's something positive to finish on at least.

It had to happen at some point. Actually, it's probably a surprise that it's taken this long, almost six months into the year and this diary. But for the first time, I'm having to write these entries days after the events and experiences that are their focus.

The reason for this is quite simple. I just haven't had the time. Every single day this week has seen me busy virtually from start to finish, with little respite and little opportunity for thought and reflection. My energy levels have been severely challenged, but even these have been miniscule in comparison to the demands placed on my mental health and stability. It's literally been overwhelming, and as I attempt to do justice to the week that's just been, I am conscious of the need to be selective and to prioritise the most powerful of emotions, the most exacting of circumstances and the most insightful and representative of legacies.

There are lessons to be learnt from what I've just been through, and despite being forced to rely on memory and therefore dwelling on choice rather than all, I do hope you'll bear with me.

It's not the easiest of tasks, when all is said and done!

Monday 20th June 2016

I made a decision today at 5.15 pm that in many ways epitomised my perennial struggle for control and comfort in the midst of mental illness. We'd finished the first day of training at the HMD Trust and, as people were leaving to head back to the hotel to freshen up in advance of an evening out at a restaurant, I was taken to one side by the principal organiser. I'd emailed her yesterday as I thought I needed to mention the fact that I may need some additional help during the course of the two day induction because of my disability. Bless her, she'd obviously thought carefully about what I'd said and reiterated the promise and availability of support from the organisation. Without necessarily thinking the whole thing through, I said that I would find the next few hours particularly demanding and would very much appreciate the opportunity not to go but to rest up, recuperate and relax in my own time instead. She was brilliant about it, but despite her reassurances, I immediately became convinced that I was letting her and my new colleagues down. I walked back to the hotel and as I lay on the bed, gazing out of the window at the busy thoroughfare that was the nexus of the Vauxhall transport hub, I found myself ruminating over and over again about my decision, particularly as I'd been keen for her to tell the others the truth. How would they take it? Was I being, in some way, too open? Especially giving the fact that I'd only known these people the matter of a few hours. There was no way of telling.

I recognised though that I was at the end of my tolerance level. I couldn't push myself any further. If I had, I felt I really did run the risk of my not being able to control the toxic cocktail of emotions and pressures that were regurgitating within my mind. I was, in actual fact, feeling the need to shout and scream, to break down and cry, to fall apart and let everything take me to a place and moment in which I could be as I wanted to be. Without preamble. Without boundary. Without restriction. The parameters of what could be described as 'normal' behaviour had already been breached. What happened now needed to be personal and to take place in private.

Tuesday 21st June 2016
It was probably me, but I did feel that people did look at me and treat me a little bit differently this morning. The interaction felt a little more forced and I remember distinctly feeling that what I said and did was being scrutinised, as if my 'madness' was being assessed for its visibility and impact. Nobody said anything. Certainly nobody treated me badly or disrespectfully. It was just that I felt largely on the periphery of things. This was particularly the case during the lunch period where support workers such as myself joined with staff in a communal meal. With one exception, it seemed that no-one wanted to talk to me. I felt so alone, isolated, insecure and vulnerable. In the firing line and yet invisible at the same time. What I couldn't decipher was whether all this was really the case or whether it was just the haziness and distortion of a confused mind. Was it me? Or them? I didn't know and I still didn't when I tried to reflect on things afterwards.

During the course of the day, I needed to address two matters that had really bothered me the previous night. The first revolved over the issue of 'conflict of interest', whether what I do in relation to my book and in any future planned educational work that involved the Holocaust could in some way lead me to be at loggerheads with the HMD Trust. Luckily, this was quickly put to bed by a member of staff. The second was more worrying for me as it was a more immediate concern. I wasn't sure that I had enough time to journey across London to catch the train they'd booked for me, without subjecting myself to unnecessary anxiety. The last thing I wanted was to arrive at St Pancras out of breath, sweating profusely, agitated in demeanour and thereby drawing attention to myself. Again, I shouldn't have worried (how symbolic are those words?). I was allowed to leave early. To pace myself. To take my time. To do as I wanted to do and when. The support and understanding was there, automatic and freely-given. I was tired at the end of it all. But at least I wasn't flustered and overwrought! And, perhaps more importantly, my confidence in the organisation I'd just joined and the colleagues with whom I'd be working, was as near as possible to high and comforting as I am ever wont to feel.

Wednesday 22nd June 2016

Today was the first of a three-day conference on Mental Health and Cultural Diversity, organised by De Montfort University. It was certainly an interesting topic. The interplay between mental health, ethnicity, cultural norms and competence and the prevalence of discrimination, particularly of racism, is a powerful subject and an increasingly relevant one. Its focus on persistent inequalities felt very real, a permanent presence across a complex landscape. However, for me, it generally disappointed. The most hard-hitting component of an agenda that was far too packed, was a session in which a number of service-users talked about their experiences, offering their own insights and summations. All of them were young and middle-aged men and every one of them had a different thing to say and to draw upon. I felt very much at home in their language and in the representations they gave of their lives. However, what was interesting – and probably telling – was the fact that these very people, people who had spoken so eloquently and powerfully, were absent in all the subsequent sessions. Of course, it could have been that they didn't have the time to stay. But somehow, I doubted that. Their absence and that of any contribution, was as disquieting as the stories they'd had to tell. It was as if there was a fundamental disconnect between establishing the issues (how things are) and deciphering and debating what to do about them, between identifying the problems and proposing solutions. To be blunt, it seemed to me that what appeared in practice was not just the boundaries to which I've just alluded, but a significant one between patient and clinician. The former says what the matter is. The latter says 'leave it to me'. It seemed to set the tone for the whole conference. As a service-user I felt intellectually ill-equipped and organisationally bereft of the opportunity to state my case, to make my contribution, to be part of the solution and not just the establishment of fact. It was as if my involvement wasn't deemed either necessary or appropriate!

I was always going to have problems keeping up with the pace. Too many presentations, sessions that were inordinately long, little time for recuperation, no or very few opportunities for genuine discussion. It was a test of concentration, durability and focus, but also of tolerance and patience, and it shouldn't have been.

Thursday 23rd June 2016

If anything, Day Two was worse! The practice of speakers prolonging their stay at the lectern had already been established the previous day. How supposedly intelligent men and women thought that they could get through thirty, forty, even fifty slides during the course of a twenty-five minute presentation defied belief! Only a few of them seemed to have tailored their speech for the occasion. The rest were intent on planting themselves in front of a microphone and staying there beyond their permitted time not only to say what they wanted, but to take up all the minutes they obviously thought their words deserved and warranted. I found it not only arrogant, but also increasingly disturbing and annoying. If that wasn't enough, the language some of them used was unbelievably complex, far too convoluted, incomprehensible and unnecessarily intellectualised. Not everyone in the audience was a high-flying academic, after all. I made a note of some of the terminology: ethnic density, collectivist societies, cultural congruity, co-production models, interdigitate, equipotentiality, protoculture, co-creation, gene-culture co-evolution, home-grown algorithms, social entrepreneurship...and my two favourites... 'Neo-Cartesian duellism' and 'phenotypic plasticity'!

Now, I like to think that I'm reasonably intelligent and, of course, I have a lifetime's experience of mental illness and mental ill-health, but at times I really struggled to follow proceedings. I recognise that any conference should be challenging as well as stimulating, but there has to be a balance with respect to accessibility and an inherent position on involvement, particularly if you want service-users/patients to engage actively, effectively and meaningfully in what is going on. The most engaging speaker of the day, for me, was a British academic now working in Toronto, Canada, who spoke very clearly and unambiguously about the need to 'talk our language'. The context wasn't directly similar, but the point remained absolutely valid! I suspect the irony was lost on some of his co-academics!

Friday 24th June 2016
One thing I didn't mention in yesterday's entry was the showing of a film about a young Ghanaian man being sectioned and his consequent battle for identity and dignity. It was a little dated, but the points raised remained of total relevance, extremely powerful and upsetting in their impact. The reaction amongst many of those present, the academic contingent mainly, was to decry and belittle the attitude and actions of the professional workers shown in the film. Whilst I totally agreed with this, I unfortunately found their own behaviour equally divisive. It

actually had a similar effect on me – not to the same devastating extent, of course – as the relationship depicted on screen. I tried to make the point in the subsequent discussion that in my experience, societal attitudes (and those of people I have encountered in the workplace as a specific example), had proved to be much more inhibiting and destructive in their impact than anything I'd encountered within the mental health system – whether they related to consultants, doctors, therapists, nurses and so on and so forth. Yes, I've experienced what could be called 'restrictive outlooks', particularly amongst GPs, but those professionals whom I have relied upon to treat me thoroughly, compassionately and with dignity, have, on the whole, lived up to my expectations. However, I was actually talked down by one of the so-called 'experts' who carried on with his agenda totally disregarding what I was saying and seemingly oblivious to the point I was trying to make. That he was encouraged to do so – he being the professional, me purely a service-user – only served to reinforce the marginalisation I already felt. I spent the rest of the session looking at my shoes. I didn't want to raise my head and make eye-contact with anyone. But inside, I was simmering with anger and frustration.

Of course, I am well aware that I am fortunate that my status as a reasonably educated, white, middle-class male protects me to a large extent from the additional discrimination experienced within the mental health system by African and Caribbean men, for instance. Nevertheless, to be subjected to this type of treatment in a context in which my voice should be as reasonable, well-founded and significant as any other was thoroughly dispiriting. I felt totally isolated and dejected as I left the room.

I can't let today go by without reference to the result of the Referendum on UK membership of the European Union. Inexplicably – to my mind at least – the electorate has decided to turn its back and to go it alone. I was shocked when I turned on my telly to hear the news and throughout the day, my feelings fluctuated between anger, desolation and incomprehension!

God knows what my Dad must be feeling in his heavenly home. He was a true European, a pioneer of town-twinning, an educator and a practical exemplar of the need to communicate across languages. I'm too ashamed to call myself British at the moment. Or maybe that's actually English? The Scots had the conviction as well as the good sense to want to remain part of a broader network of nations. Maybe we should move north of the border? If they'll have us, that is!

Saturday 25th June

Yesterday, I couldn't rid my mind of the thought that I smelled. Whether I actually did so or not wasn't the issue. What was, was my perception. I began to be aware of this during the course of the Conference's first session, and as time went on, the feeling became more and more entrenched. I felt so embarrassed. I didn't want anyone to be near me, so convinced was I that I was repugnant and potent in equal measures. Where this all came from, I'm not completely sure. I often feel that people avoid me in public settings. When I go to Millwall, for example, no-one seems to want to sit in the seats either side of me. The same thing has happened at the Conference. Unless they were people I already knew, those strangers who entered the various rooms in which I was already sat, seemed to gravitate well away from me. I kept asking myself whether the smell was tangibly real or some kind of metaphorical expression of my mental illness? Perhaps I don't just act, look or feel 'sad and mad'? Perhaps depression actually smells as well? Is that possible? It can't be surely? Looking at the issue logically and hopefully with a degree of dispassion, I must give off, without necessarily knowing it, signs that I am aloof and remote, even if I don't want to be. Perhaps I look scared or even agitated without conscious effort. Maybe my inner turmoil really is visible and apparent? I would probably go with that one, especially as it is consistent with the notion that I've already mentioned and, I think, evidenced, that mental illness is not necessarily a 'hidden' disability. Strange are the thoughts that dominate the mind.

Sunday 26th June 2016

One of the words frequently used at the Conference as an alternative to 'patient' or 'service-user' was 'survivor'. I've come across this so many times before. I know of mental health organisations, for example, that use it in their title. Though I've never really considered it as a way of describing my identity or indeed my experiences, some people are the total opposite. I suspect the truth is that it is a reaction against the notion of being a 'sufferer' and in that sense, it does strike some sort of chord. Even though using the word 'suffer' is so common with respect to everyday illnesses, it shouldn't define what you are day by day. We all suffer in so many respects, and not just with regard to medical conditions, but when it becomes a means of asserting an identity or even casually referring to someone else's, it is far more problematic and contentious.

Going back to the word 'survivor' and my thoughts on its application, there are a number of things that come to mind that prevent me wishing really to associate myself with this term. For a start, how can I be called a 'survivor' when the experiences to which that word relates are ongoing ones? I guess you can be called a continual 'survivor' – people sometimes think of themselves as 'born survivors' in this sense after all – but what is it that I've actually survived? Mental illness itself? Societal attitudes towards it? Stigma or discrimination? The process of treatment or recovery? All of these things carry on in perpetuity, at least for me. They are continual in their nature. They never really end. They are part of a process that is not absolute in its boundaries and its manifestations.

I've experienced lots of different things, some of which have had a definitive ending. As an example, whilst it may well be pertinent and appropriate to refer to myself as a survivor of the British public school system (though its legacy has been remarkably and depressingly impactful), it would be very strange to apply that to something like childhood. Both have a distinctive and recognised end, after all. You could also apply the term to life itself. That's a continual process with an end that, irrespective of religious thinking and internal conviction, I will not survive. To consider myself as a survivor of life, to me, seems awkward and a bit weird. Of course, life and mental illness are closely related in my case. They entwine. They interlink. They are interdependent. I can't completely divorce one from the other. Accordingly, if I apply the term to one, I should apply it to the other. It's all or nothing.

To that end, I'll stick to identities that I feel more comfortable using. At the end of the day, that's the most important criterion, after all!

Monday 27th June 2016

The start of the working week, but a false dawn for me. After the exertions of the last ten days or so, I decided to give myself today off to recharge my mental as well as physical batteries. So much seems to have happened and I think, all things being equal, that I haven't done too badly. It's entirely symptomatic of the way my mind works, of course, that my initial thoughts are to evaluate! I can't seem to help that process of self-reflection and of judgement. I have to have some recourse to assess myself. It's always been important to me, irrespective of the fact that it isn't necessarily conducive to positive mental health. It's always so difficult to let go, to say that what's been has been. I seem predestined always to put pressure on myself, to adjudicate, to examine, to de-brief not just in terms of what I've done and how I've done it, but also the thinking and the feelings that went alongside the actions as well. Where does this all come from? I just don't know. Perhaps it's simply my DNA? My father was the same, after all. It seems that my only recourse is to purposefully try to opt out of something that comes automatically. I have little control over the process in terms of where it comes from and how it starts. My only intervention can be how it pans itself out and if it threatens to derail me. Then, and only then, can the damage I am doing to myself be addressed, and this only becomes obvious when my behaviour – as opposed to my thinking – begins to change. When I start to panic. When anxiety hits home. When I get agitated. When I start to feel aggressive. When I lose any sense of conscious thread. When I begin, in a nutshell, to lose control. It's not always me that notices these changes, of course. Quite often it's Lesley who has to intervene in some way, shape or form. To make me realise that I'm not OK.

So what have I done today by way of relaxation? I've watched some telly. I've read some more of my book on Mozart. I've caught up with some of my emails, and I've done some gentle exercise. Unfortunately the latter seemed to precipitate the uncomfortable light-headedness and dizziness that I often experience. I ate some food and sat down at my computer to try to see it out naturally, but respite wasn't forthcoming and I had to resort to going back to bed. Sometimes, there just isn't any other option. It's worrying though. Despite everything I went through last week, I was absolutely fine, despite my concerns that it would hit right in the middle of something involving other people. I would say that I controlled it, but that would be misleading. It's not something that I'm conscious of until it actually strikes, so I have no way of knowing what or how I take preventative action. If these things happen for a reason, I can point to the fact that four hours after it began, I got a phone call from my Doctor to say that my next blood tests are due! Uncanny? Spooky? Telepathy? Who can tell?

Tuesday 28th June 2016
As I suspected would be the case, sleeping during the day resulted in a restless night.

I had no problems falling asleep, it was the quality of what happened afterwards that was impaired and the impact on me today has been significant. Waking up feeling that you haven't properly rested has an effect on anybody, but when that merges into the usual mental health traits and consequences – lethargy, disturbing dreams, vivid recollections, anxiety and the like – it rather sets the tone for the rest of the day. I wonder if what I had planned for today also played a part? I'd earmarked today to be my first adventure into the working realms of the Holocaust Memorial Day Trust (HMDT). Following my induction last week, which outlined suggested next steps, their preparation and commencement needed to be addressed sooner rather than later for the simple reason that if I allowed myself to dwell or procrastinate, what should have been routine would elevate into a new, potentially formidable, challenge. This is new stuff. Not the Holocaust itself, of course, but the demands and machinations of the job. As this involved getting started on new software – Office 365 – my natural tendency to worry about things I'm not familiar with, would, I knew, quickly become a sizeable obstacle to have to begin to address, unless I was brave and effectively 'took the plunge'. It's difficult to accurately describe this phenomenon, which seems to impact on absolutely everything that is new.

Again, it's that element of control that is the pertinent issue. If I'm a beginner – at anything – I have to try to establish some sort of procedure, some logical process, some initial success, some quickly acquired expertise. Otherwise, I can just as rapidly evaporate into frustration, anxiety and distress. I have to have a quick answer to my initial tap at the door, for the longer I stay outside, the louder and more volatile my attempted entry becomes. And, of course, the more firm and unyielding the door. I panic very quickly. And I have little patience. What is, on the surface, and possibly to you the reader, a minor inconvenience to be addressed with a little help and support afterwards, becomes to me a major barrier that I have to resolve here and now if I want to retain some element of self-respect and inner confidence. You wouldn't believe the number of times I've had to resort to mood stabilising medication. (Well yes, you probably would actually!) I probably need to clarify that this is especially the case with new technology. Something I have to do rather than something simply to read. New information I can deal with. It's the process that matters. Reading is fine. Acting upon something I've read is something entirely different!

I've been OK today. I went straight into the software as soon as I sat at my desk. Though there is novelty, there is also much that is familiar. It's an extension of Outlook, really. I've familiarised myself with the basics – my mail, my calendar, my groupings – and personalised things like my profile, my email signature and my 'out of office' acknowledgement. I've answered and sent emails and updated my Calendar until the end of the year. It's a start, but I don't want to hedge my bets and do anything more on it today. There are other things I need to do as a result of last week, things that come much more naturally to me, things that are not so anxiety-ridden and potentially catastrophic! A bit at a time. That's the trick.

On average, I shall be working on HMDT matters one day a week, so I can look forward now to next Monday morning with a little bit more confidence! I hope!

Wednesday 29th June 2016

Ordinarily, I am extremely sensitive to the use of words such as 'crazy' or 'mad'. This stems, of course, from their inaccurate, casual, offensive and remarkably persistent use specifically in relation to mental illness and in the mental health domain, for such usage only serves to stigmatise and to legitimise discrimination. However, today, I'm struggling to think of alternatives when considering the absolute mess inflicted on this country as a result of the majority decision to leave the European Union. That the England football team seemed to have got in on the act and joined the bandwagon only serves to epitomise this sense of abject misery and shock. Their inept exit from another European superstructure at the hands of the football colossus that is Iceland left most of us wondering whether to laugh or to cry! Incredulity and bewilderment just don't seem to do justice – terminologically – to the seismic shock the English nation has had to endure, football fan or concerned citizen alike.

I feel, therefore, a sense of approval and perhaps even legitimacy as I consider using those common but brutal words to describe UK – and particularly English – society at the moment. Scotland and the North of Ireland voted to 'stay in' of course – not that it's actually done them any good or made any difference in the cold light of day – and at the time of writing the Welsh footballers are left to carry the flag for the Home Nations at Euro 2016. But for England? Is Armageddon too strong a word to use?

Whilst only the hardiest of England supporters will find it difficult to get over the latest competition debacle – we're used to it after all – the ramifications of Brexit[23] as far as mental health is concerned is much more difficult to decipher or to predict. We're left with speculation, and for our community of the mentally ill at ease this is a position inherently fraught with concern and danger. We always look for certainties, but there's very few of those at this moment in time. Speculation can – and I guess always should – have some roots in grounded opinion and even in fact. So let's perhaps see what we actually can glean? For a start, any insecurity or financial volatility in the economic markets will have an impact on things such as national budgets and spending powers and almost inevitably in these circumstances, future support of the NHS ranks high in people's minds and in budgetary priorities. We all know that mental health has lagged behind its physical counterpart in these regards for far too long. The case for increased investment has been made over and over again. Nevertheless, even when we're told by our powers that be that new money has been found, I'm yet to meet anyone anywhere that has seen any discernible change or impact when it comes to accessing services on the ground. And that's in reaction to a supposed increase! The possibility that yet again, the poor relation that is mental health will have to take a hit because of the current economic climate surely cannot be ruled out, despite the protestations of politicians and government ministers.

Then there is the issue of human rights. The roots of our current system – legislation, procedures, initiatives and the like – lie in the aftermath of the Second World War, and specifically the

Holocaust and the refugee crisis that came with it. Fundamentally, this was an international response to an international failing of mammoth proportions and all that we now take for granted has become so because of the genuine international goodwill that ensured that this was something that we all had to play a part in and to protect, whatever country we emanated from. That the UK Government has long considered opting out of international jurisdiction in this regard, proposing plans to form our own Bill of Rights as an alternative, is a longstanding fact and admission. But of what, exactly? Of the refusal to accept that others may know better than us? Of the unwelcome intervention of external (i.e. foreign) power? The Human Rights Act and all its surroundings 'does what is says on the tin', to paraphrase a popular TV commercial. Why on earth do we feel the need to do something different? And, significantly for our theme, what are the possible ramifications for minority rights, including those of people experiencing mental illness and ill health?

Sadly, the days following last Thursday's monumental decision have seen an outbreak of increased hate crime. It would appear that some people, somehow, have translated European exit as acceptance and approval to attack anyone not considered to be essentially British. For some unaccountable reason, they see a sense of legitimacy in their actions. Whilst of course this is not the case, it is the fact that this tendency can be tangibly evidenced that is the real issue of concern. Tragically, I can see a rise in racism and other forms of discrimination as being virtually inevitable, no matter what we do as a society to try and stop it. Will this new discriminatory fervour find its way into other domains, including disability? Will the targeting of other minorities, the most vulnerable of communities, be more commonplace? I sincerely hope not, but it can't be ruled out. As a Jewish as well as disabled man, I am genuinely worried. Almost in a moment of time, a flash if you like, Britain has become – potentially – a country polarised not just by the decision of whether to stay or to remain, but in other ways as well. The operative word here is 'potentially'. Now is the time for everyone not just to pull together but to deplore and to take action against any manifestation of hate. If we don't, we all know where the slippery slope can lead us – the Jews and the disabled amongst us in particular.

Thursday 30th June 2016
One hundred years ago today, my Grandad would have been in a state of mind that I cannot really imagine. Almost certainly, he was in preparation for the most brutal and calamitous day in the entire history of warfare, the first day of the Battle of the Somme. My use of words is deliberate. You see Grandad rarely talked of his experiences during the Great War and as he died when I was only a small child I never had the opportunity to hear of his memories and reflections first hand. What I do know though is significant. To begin with, he was a non-combatant stretcher bearer in the Royal Army Medical Corps, which meant that he would have billeted in Field Hospitals when not in the front line. There was a hospital of this kind in a little village called Mailly-Maillet. Equidistant from the larger towns of Amiens and Arras, on a straight path between the two, it wasn't its geographical location that was of consequence for my Grandad. It was its name itself. In one of those remarkable quirks of fate, he went on to marry a woman called Mahalah (shortened to Mayla) Mallet. The uncanny similarity of names was one of the few things my Dad handed down to me whenever he talked about his own father and his recollections of those tragic years. I remember many years ago now, when Elliot was a toddler and we still took Luke and Joel on holiday with us, I made a sole pilgrimage to the Somme and visited this tiny outpost. It's nothing remarkable. Just an ordinary, picturesque, quiet French village, with a long main street and a church. One thing does set it aside, but not from its near neighbours, and that is the presence of a War Cemetery. One amongst hundreds, of course, but for me, the most poignant. How many of Grandad's immediate comrades were buried here? How many fell on that tragic first day? Did he lose close friends? How did he grieve? Was he even allowed or given time to do so?

Words are completely inadequate when contemplating how he must have felt on this date all those years ago. Scared. Frightened. Tense. Nervous. Fatalistic maybe. Surely they can't even come close? I'm sure he would have wanted it to be over. He would have prayed for mercy and for the salvation of life. Even though he was only a teenager himself, he may have thought about the circumstances by which he had arrived at that point in his life. He may well have reflected on the fatuity, the irrationality and yes, the 'insanity' of his situation and those of all around him. Undoubtedly, he would have viewed those charged with responsibility for the context of war – the statesmen, the politicians, the military leaders – in a very unfavourable light. Of course, they were not with him on that day.

It was my Grandad's decision not to bear arms that inspired the pacifism of my father and, in turn, of myself. He wanted to do his duty, but not to kill or maim. Somehow, he survived the horrors of no-mans-land, but came back to Leeds a different person. Not for him were the military parades, uniforms and salutes that became the most evident illustrations of remembrance. To him they epitomised the vibrant and rampant militarism that had led to war in the first place. He kept his thoughts and his memories largely to himself, though I remember as a young boy his soft voice singing to me the songs that he had shared with his comrades at the Somme and elsewhere. He was a gentle man, a kind man, an inspirational man. These were qualities that may in some way link to what he went through when he was only a few years older than our Elliot is now. They were traits he learned to live his life by, not only as an act of remembrance but as a statement of integrity and as a living epitome of peace and togetherness. God bless all those who lost their lives at the Somme, from all countries. 'Keep the home fires burning' Grandad. George William Harrison (1898 – 1973). Rest In Peace.

July

Friday 1st July 2016
During a meeting yesterday, I had another nose bleed. It's becoming a bit of a habit again. Some years ago now, I had one just after getting into the office. As I'd got quite used to them, I didn't think much of it until it dawned on me after ten minutes or so that there was no sign of it stopping. I sat there with my head down, one hand correctly pinching my nose, the other gathering sheet after sheet of tissue paper, until I finally exhausted my stock. Toilet paper was then produced, but still no halt. Eventually, I began to feel a little faint, dizzy and weary. A first aider duly arrived and, after quickly evaluating the situation, advised me go to Accident and Emergency. By this time, my shirt was claret, my neck was claret and my nose looked like it had gone ten rounds with Mike Tyson. I was a mess. To cut a long story short, the inside of my left nostril was cauterized, Lesley was sent for and I made my way home. I – naively, no doubt – thought that that would be the end of it. Not a bit of it. Around six months ago, the bleeds started again. Always in the same nostril. Never a deviation. I have obviously got a weakness

there, but I can't help wondering if one or more of my medication may somehow be at least partly to blame. After all, if you look at the potential side effects of virtually all the drugs I take, it seems that every ailment from sweats and shivers to cardiac arrest and even death is mentioned. A relatively minor thing such as a nose bleed must surely be included in every conceivable bracket? All things said and done, it may be that I just have to put up with them.

It made me think though of how far I've come in relation to my experience of Obsessive Compulsive Disorder (OCD). There was a time, some fifteen years or more ago, when a bleed of any kind would have been a catastrophic occurrence. The sight of blood would almost inevitably lead me to mild or even severe panic. It wasn't the fact that I was bleeding per se that was the issue, it was the possibility that blood may transfer from my body onto that of someone else. At that time, I was utterly convinced that I was HIV positive. There was nothing to firmly suggest that this was the case. I didn't inject myself with anything. I wasn't an addict of any kind. My days of sexual excess as a young man were definitely over – I'm not sure they ever really existed, to be honest with you! I was happily married with three beautiful step-children. I didn't stray. I wasn't interested. I'd found my soul mate and was eagerly embracing a life of enjoyable, yet challenging, domesticity. And yet, within my head, I couldn't rid myself of that conviction that I was infected, diseased, tainted and unclean.[24] As a consequence, the most minor of scratches would scare me half to death. I would immediately think it inevitable that I would pass my 'contamination'[25] on to others, including, of course, my own family. Before I did anything else, I would search for a plaster to cover the blemish on my skin, no matter how small it was. Most of the time the wound wouldn't even warrant a lick, never mind a covering, but I could never afford to take that chance. At least that was what I thought. I got through so many boxes of plasters. One after another. At one point, I even started buying them in batch! Things came to a head at a rugby league event I was at in London. I'd cut my hand. I can't remember how, but I do remember there being running blood. I'd stemmed it to a certain extent and it was now drying on my skin. Before I realised it, I was being introduced to someone and I automatically stretched out my arm and hand to greet him. It was a reflex action, but before I could think and react, it was too late. I recall apologising profusely and within my mind I was imploring him to immediately go and wash his hands. But what could I say? 'Sorry mate. I think I've got HIV and I've probably passed it on to you'. That would have been ludicrous. What would he have thought of me then? What would he have done? I was effectively compromised. All I could do was draw attention to the fact that my hand was bloody and let him take responsibility for whatever he did as a result – if he did anything at all of course. For the rest of the evening, I was in a world of my own. The self-recrimination. The guilt. It was eating me up. I couldn't stand it any longer, but there was no-one to whom I could turn. I was trapped in my own insanity, suffering through my torments, my mind going to places I never wanted it to go. I was powerless and I was so alone.

It was my worst OCD moment.

Perhaps I reached my nemesis that day? At least as far as my obsessions were concerned.

I've experienced worse moments since then, but they have all revolved around depression rather than OCD. From that time on, particularly as I received some effective therapy treatment, my OCD has remained confined to routines around numbers and persistent thoughts of fires, burglaries, and domestic disasters. But with regard to blood and HIV, they barely enter my consciousness any more. As I walked away from the meeting yesterday, I remembered that I hadn't washed my hands afterwards. I looked at them and saw remnants of the short deluge that had come from my nose. It was dry and relatively thin, but it was still, obviously, blood. I casually walked to the nearest public toilets, even opening doors as I went, and I then cleaned myself up. My heartrate didn't fluctuate. No sweat ensued. My demeanour remained calm. The situation was under control.

And so was I.

Saturday 2nd July 2016

It's Mum's birthday today. She's seventy-five years young. We're journeying over to Shropshire tomorrow to help her celebrate the occasion. As Sammy and his family are doing the same, I just hope she has a relaxing and certainly more peaceful day today! My Mum is a most remarkable lady who has achieved so much in her life despite some tragic setbacks. She's had to face her own illness – a heart defect since childhood – but moreover she's coped with the heartache of being widowed in her forties and, probably more devastatingly still, the loss of our Danny, her second child, in 1996. What she did for him was monumental. When all around us said he would never be literate, she made it her mission to ensure that he could read and write. She also helped him to be an independent, decision-making person in his own right, someone who still needed help but who had an opinion and a perspective that was unique and special. She involved him and encouraged him. She supported him and guided him. She nurtured him and she nursed him. He was able to stand on his own two feet sure in the knowledge that the security he still required was no more than a heartbeat and a step away.

As for me, I owe her so much.

She never had any doubts about my capabilities. She sacrificed much to ensure that I too was able to be what I could be. If there was one thing though that I don't think she's ever really come to terms with, that would be my mental illness. Of course, it wasn't until the turn of this millennium that she – like I – had the verification of a diagnosis. But I think, deep down, she's always known that there was something wrong. She's tried hard to understand. She's read widely on the subject. She's listened.

She's sought the advice and guidance of others. But there's always been within her, perhaps, an obstacle that has always prevented her recognising what has happened to me. And that is, I suspect, the guilt that I know she feels quite intensely. To her, I'll always be her boy and in that respect, someone she feels she has to shield, protect and embrace. But no-one could withstand the onslaught that depression has been and still remains. Not even her. The circumstances of my childhood, Dad and Danny and their respective disabilities, these are factors that simply were, facts of life, a horrible and determining aspect of my growing up. How we dealt with them as a family was one thing, their impact and ramifications were something else. She's often said 'we did the best we could', and she's right of course. But within that context, somewhere, somehow, were the roots of my mental illness. She couldn't have known that. I couldn't have known that. And more importantly still, if we didn't know, how could we address it? How could it have been prevented? Mental illness wasn't the recognised, familiar and open disability then that it is now. It had all sorts of connotations, the sort that still serve to stigmatise and discriminate. I sought help, but what I received was transitory, restricted to time and space, couched within the terms of bereavement and loss, never something that was even considered to be enduring and long-term. What we know now is telling. That I was depressed as well as grieving. That I was mentally ill as well as mentally unhealthy.

I've tried hard over the years to reassure and soothe my Mum's worries and regrets. To tell her it's nobody's fault and certainly not hers. To lay the blame squarely, clearly and unhesitatingly at the door of depression, its manifestations and its ability as a disability to consume all involved wherever it rears its head, including carers, families and friends.

When all is said and done, human beings are not perfect entities. Neither are we robots. We react as we see fit, conditioned by things such as education, awareness, interdependent relationships and context. Sociologists may use the term 'configurations'. We do what we can. We try. We persevere. We react and where possible, we try to prevent. Try is the operative word here. As long as we do this, that's all that can reasonably be expected.

And my Mum has always been a trier.

Sunday 3rd July 2016
I always find a visit to my childhood home a slightly daunting prospect. Mum and Pat, her new husband, have made many changes to suit their lives together, but still the echoes of the past remain. I see ghosts everywhere. Of Dad and Danny. Of Joey our family Golden Labrador. But also of me. A very different me. One innocent in the ways of the world. Childlike and untainted. Free and without care. Ambitious and full of energy. Hopeful. Optimistic. Talkative and engaging. All the things that have abandoned me or I have lost myself over the years. I am, quite literally, a shadow of my former self. I kept thinking yesterday how hard it must be for Mum and Sammy to see me as I am and to still try to embrace me and include me. I actually feel like a ghost when I'm there. I struggle to participate in conversation and activity. I'm like a perennial bystander, reluctant and sometimes unable to converse, oblivious to everything tangible around me, but haunted by the spectral presence of my lost father and brother. I can't always have been like this, but in the same way I can no longer remember the sound of their voices, I too am restrained by the departed, the departed me. I can't recall ever being anything other than what I am now. I love my Mum and my brother, but I fear that I've made myself peripheral to their lives. I don't want to be. But I can't engineer the change that would enable me to return to what I once was. I don't even know what that is any more.

Monday 4th July 2016
I think I'm probably working a bit too much at the moment. Whilst I welcome the opportunity to work and am more than a touch

grateful for the fact that I have some work to do, I've got to get a better work/life balance. I know that.

Work can be a powerful antidote to the perils of depression, but it can also serve to spiral you towards that state if its meaning changes within you. The former can serve to increase self-esteem and build confidence but the latter has within it the seeds of potential destruction if you cannot see things for how they are, if work becomes a slave, a mechanism to beat yourself and a terminal dead-end for hopes and ambitions. I don't want to be a robot, tirelessly and mechanically driven to achieve outcomes and outputs. I don't wish to be identified and labelled solely by my working life. I can't let work become an outlet for failure. I mustn't give in to the temptation for blinkered vision. It doesn't take a lot for something in which you invest considerable time and effort, some component of life that you put on a pedestal, to come crashing down around you, to lose its impact and its thrust, to transform from positive to negative. As much as work can liberate and consolidate, it can also restrict and fragment. It can disintegrate into a myriad of tiny pieces, each one a sharp edifice that hurts and wounds. Your composure and dignity as well as your actual plans can shatter so easily and so decisively. You become quite simply a distinct element in the process of your own downfall. You sow the seeds of your own destruction.

I have to retain some confidence. I have to trust that I am able to recognise the signs, the time to take a step back, to have a rest and to recuperate. Ever since I left the Council, I've been able to work. I haven't stopped. And, more importantly, I've battled through spells of depression without having to give up that important part of my identity. I've persevered. I've made adjustments. I've planned ahead and acted accordingly. I can therefore succeed in keeping my working life clear and active, despite everything else, irrespective of the danger that always looms on the horizon. Had I still been working there, I honestly don't think I'd have been able to continue. Well, I know I wouldn't. I'd have been on disability sick-leave again, victim of my own determination and drive, attributes that sometimes cloud the reality of mental illness, that mask its mannerisms and its manifestations, that hide its true impact. Like a sprinter trying to change into a marathon runner without altering speed, you will burn yourself out without realising, you will ultimately collapse with the strain of effort. Your body can't cope with the tunnel vision of your mind.

Tuesday 5th July 2016

What a mixed day today has been. Having focused so much on my working life yesterday, today has been one of those days when everything work-wise seems to have clicked. I'd allocated a whole day to producing a plain English Executive Summary of an Evaluation Report. In actual fact, I finished it just after lunch. I don't know how or why, but the words seemed to flow, the issues I'd worried about simply melted away, and the formatting that is always important in documents of this kind just fell into place. I was even able to include some fancy speech bubbles, without spending an inordinate amount of time working out how! I'm also up-to-date with regards to Invoices and money coming in. A number of outstanding payments have been settled this week and my bank balance looks refreshingly stable and perhaps even positively healthy.

It's a good job though, because all of a sudden we're having to spend some money on basic things, including the installation of a new boiler. That is actually ongoing as I write. How we survived for so long with our previous antiquated relic defies belief. We think it's as old as the house itself – and that's some thirty years now! For the past ten years, British Gas have told us during the course of our annual check-up that even though there's been no noticeable problem, if things did go wrong, they wouldn't be able to get the parts. We were living on borrowed-time! This has meant, particularly when I've been alone in the house during the winter months, a persistent dread, an ongoing state of nervous anticipation, perennial thoughts of doom and gloom. I've waited for something to happen. I've sometimes jumped when the thing cranks noisily into gear. I've often checked the state of our radiators, trying to measure performance and reliability. I've ruminated over the possibility of leaked carbon monoxide. I've sat there waiting for the moment, THE moment when our risk of delaying action ultimately backfires. It never has and now it never will. By the time Lesley comes home this evening, we'll have a brand new, all-singing and dancing system! But the cost – and I don't mean the financial expenditure – has been significant today.

As I sit here downstairs at my desk, I daren't go and see what's happening. The last time I ventured upstairs, the carpets were rolled back, the floor boards were up, our cupboards have had to be moved, there is a thin layer of dust all over our bed, and still the sounds of drilling intersperse with loud bangs, fierce rumblings and ominous silences! The problem has been that for some unaccountable reason, the builders of the house installed the boiler in a bedroom! The disruption that would have ensued had we wanted our new one relocated downstairs would have been too severe, so it's moving only a matter of centimetres instead.

The fact of the matter is, that I just can't cope with the situation.

I can't get myself to calm down. I'm expecting bad things to happen. I'm anticipating problems. Insurmountable problems.

Interaction with the two lads who are doing the job has been a struggle. I just want them to go. But I also know that if I'm not meticulous in insisting that things are put back in their place, I'm liable to let them off, to leave things undone, just because I want them out of the door. If only Lesley was here. But she isn't. I can't expect her to be. I have to deal with this. I have to answer their questions. I have to provide them with all that they need, but I don't have much idea as to what that may be. What if I don't know? What happens then? My blood pressure must be rocketing. My only remedial measure is to take a tablet, but I'm reluctant to do so because Elliot is here, having a day off because of a teachers strike. I sense his nervousness as well.

How long will they be? When can I, at last, switch off? And I know, I just know, that I won't be content with how they put everything back into place. It won't be the same. My perfectionism, my OCD will gnaw away at my powers of recovery and my ability to cope.

I just want it to be over!

Wednesday 6th July 2016

I sometimes think I've reached a new level of insanity. Take yesterday for example. I was exercising on the Flabelos in what I suppose you could now call Lesley's dressing room[26]. The room overlooks our stone-covered front drive. (It also provides a view up the adjoining street, but that's neither here nor there). As I focused more closely, I kept seeing facial patterns in the gravel. It seemed to me that everywhere I looked, a sea of faces was scrutinising my every movement. But each one wasn't human. They were all made by the way the stones lay on the ground. They seemed uncannily real and, moreover, they were uniquely and unequivocally demonic in their shape and in their apparent demeanour. I couldn't escape the glares, the grimaces and the accusations. I was being judged. It really felt like that. I tried hard to look away and to tell myself forcefully that they were all simply figures of my imagination. But to no avail. This has happened to me so many times before. I remember our old dining table used to have a pattern that also played tricks with your eyes. Or maybe it was just my eyes? It wouldn't happen all the time, I should stress, only when I seem to be a little rattled or uneasy, or during a period of acute depression. With the workers being here yesterday, I guess that explains it!

You will probably have noticed that I haven't used the word 'hallucination'. Even though that is precisely what I'm describing, I'm very loathe to use that word because I know what that use may mean or even result in. It's a question I've often been asked by doctors, consultants, occupational health people and therapists. Do I see things that aren't there? Do I hear voices inside my head? Do I think I'm somewhere other than where I am? Has my imagination become reality? I have to say that at various times, the answer to all these questions has been 'yes'. However, on saying that, it's not always so easy to differentiate between what could be described as 'normal'[27] states of being, and something that is entirely abnormal and potentially 'maddening'. To illustrate what I mean here, I often talk to myself. We all do. I don't know a single human being who doesn't. I find myself having conversations. I ask myself a question. I answer it. I deliberate on something. I ruminate out load. I test out some wording. I give it approval – or not, as the case may be. It's not always done in my head either. But this is entirely commonplace. As I said, everybody does it. Nevertheless, I sometimes don't recognise the voice that I'm hearing as mine. And I'm not sure whether it's a real voice, or something confined within. Is this different? Is this where the distinction occurs? Am I really hallucinating here? There are also occasions when what I 'hear' alarms me. I want to rid my head of its presence and of its impact. Disturbing thoughts can penetrate through the mist of confusion. They won't let me go. They tell me something I dread to hear. Something appalling. Something catastrophic. I have to work really hard to recover my composure.

Dreams, of course, work in this way too. I've already mentioned in previous entries that I have a propensity to experience nightmares of a particularly savage and realistic nature. Though the circumstances and contexts may change, the themes are always the same. Disapproval. Loss. Rejection. Discrimination. Maybe what I experience when I'm awake comes from the same source? I don't mean my brain. That would be obvious and superfluous to say! No, what I'm referring to is the same state, if that's even the right word. The same context. The same pattern. The same distortion. Whilst everything around me may be highly confusing and seriously ambiguous, that one connection actually makes perfect sense. What it refers to, what it relates to, is mental illness.

Thursday 7th July 2016

Today's been another day fraught with nerves. We've taken my car in for its MOT. It's not the possibility that it may fail that is the real issue for me. Neither is it the likelihood that something will need doing to bring it up to shape. What worries me beyond anything else is the chance that I may have to make some kind of decision. We've tried to negate that prospect as best we can. The garage has Lesley's mobile phone number, for example, though this time, every perceptible, every conceivable, every logical position would suggest that it should be mine they have. Not only is it my car, after all, but Lesley is in meetings all day and only has access to her phone in the intervals between each one. However, when she mentioned that fact yesterday, I simply couldn't countenance the idea that I would effectively be in charge. I felt the ominous but inevitable onset of tension rising up inside me like a huge tidal wave of fraught emotion. I wouldn't be able to cope. That's the bottom line. But didn't I feel guilty! I hated myself for having to ask my wife to once again, lead from the front. I chastised myself for my weakness. I kept telling myself how pathetic I was, how unfair I'd been, how over-bearing my position, how inflexible my approach. But what else could I do? The alternative was just too terrifying. It would have led to my being able to do absolutely nothing today. I'd have had to take a tablet. Had I been in the driving seat, I would have given the easiest answer, rather than the most decisive, the most sensible or crucially, the most cost-effective. Anything to avoid being put on the spot. I must have wasted thousands of pounds in my life for the simple reason that I can't, when pressurised, react with the full force of reason and self-command on my side. How many times do you hear financial specialists advising people to shop around? To do your homework by comparing price and service. It's such an easy thing to say, and a totally sensible thing to do, but for me, it would simply entail immense indecision and confusion. I'd fall apart. It would make me ill. That's no exaggeration.

Having agreed on which one of us should be the point of contact, you may be forgiven for thinking that all my worries were over.

Well, I guess you could say that the foremost ones were, but inevitably my mind has drifted as I've tried to work this morning, thinking about the consequences of having to spend yet more money. My usual catastrophic thought connections have been 'in play'. Principally the one that says that as a result of spending too much, we won't be able to pay the bills or the mortgage, we'll lose our house, I'll lose my wife and family and so on and so forth. Even though they occur so regularly, almost mechanically and without much alteration, they always pose me the same problems and cause me the same worries. I can't just say, for example, 'I've dealt with this one before, all I need to do is go through the same thinking process again'. It doesn't work like that. No matter how hard I try to remain calm and composed, I convince myself that something, somewhere, is different. I might not even be able to say what that is. I just know that it's fresh in context and unique in character. Even the process of doing the same doesn't mean that, robotically, it just happens. This is no computer programme. There's always the same inherent difficulties and challenges, and even though I've gone through it all before, the agonies still remain.

As it happens, the car needs four new tyres and a new light bulb. There's also something wrong with one of the rear seatbelts. It hasn't passed, in other words, and the garage we've taken it too can't deal with the latter fault. It will have to go to a dealer instead. Lesley's just rung with the wonderful news! This now poses additional demands as far as arrangements go, and of course, the person that affects is Lesley. She's the one that has to adjust her timetable for today and possibly for the rest of the week. It's her inconvenience, not mine. And, once more, I can't help but feeling terribly sorry and irreparably guilty.

Friday 8th July 2016

I'm currently waiting for the results of my latest blood tests. Up until fairly recently, these never used to bother me. I knew I had to have them, primarily as a result of the medication I take, but nothing new ever used to emanate as a consequence. They were more a reassurance really, of the fact that my surgery were at least monitoring some aspect of my mental health care and were therefore taking more than a passing interest. I would go to the treatment room with a cheerful, almost care-free disposition. I'd crack the usual jokes about not finding any blood or taking too much. I'd treat it all not even as a minor inconvenience, but as a nonchalant exercise in administrative prudence. I was always told that unless I heard from them again in a week's time, there was nothing to worry about. And that was it. I never gave it another thought. The week would fly by. No phone call. My mind may be shattered and diseased, but at least my blood was Grade A! Rest assured. No problem.

How things have changed! The last few tests have come back without the positive conclusions I'd become accustomed to receiving. My liver functions have again become a cause for concern. My cholesterol levels are not so consistent and the most recent occasion revealed that I was Vitamin D deficient. If it's not one thing, it's another! I'm now no longer so self-assured. In fact, I'm now not only more wary, but I'm beginning to anticipate, to expect, bad news. What is particularly worrying is that for all of these 'afflictions', I've been taking medication. Sometimes for a long period of time. Are they no longer working? Have I become immune to their effect? Have I exhausted their use? It seems to me that, if these drugs work like my anti-depressants and anti-psychotic medication, my 'threshold' may have increased to such an extent that they are no longer any good. With the former, I tend to need increasingly larger amounts to maintain the same stability and to achieve the same level of effect and impact. Perhaps this is something similar? Or is it that these aspects of my physical health are simply getting worse?

I know what I'm expecting, if I'm honest with myself – and with you, the reader. I just know that at some point I'm going to get a call to say that I have diabetes. I've already been told that one of my current medications – I forget which – does have a tendency to increase the possibility of contracting that illness.

But if it was only that, I wouldn't be too concerned. No, my family history lets me down here. My Dad and my Grandma (his mother) developed diabetes, my Dad at a fairly late stage in his life. He was diagnosed after a particularly messy coronary and at one point, there was a chance that he may have to have a limb amputated. I remember it well. That spectre hung over his head – and ours – for many a day before, somehow, it was brought under control. Afterwards, he had to take daily blood samples, pricking his fingers until they were raw and tender. Even given this aspect of familial inheritance into account, there's still further credence to my fears and suspicions. Considering my build and size as well as my other health problems, whenever I've been brave enough to take a risk score – that obviously involves putting in height and weight dimensions – I always seem to register high on the probability measures. I'm a patient waiting to happen. It's only a matter of time. Even if I survive this occasion, there'll only be another six months to wait until the next series of tests. It's simply a stay of execution.

Saturday 9th July 2016

I had a horrible dream last night. It was the end of the summer term – and therefore of the academic year – at school. My Mum had arrived to pick me up. She was on her own. I can't recall why that was. My feeling on reflection this morning was that my Dad had already passed away, but where my brothers were I have no idea. Mum packed only my basic stuff into her car and was then preparing to drive away. My room in the boarding house was still replete with clothes, books, sports equipment, posters and the like. Why did she not want take all this with us? My initial thought was that she had forgotten which term it was and that when I pointed out her mistake, all would be well. But as soon as I tried to reason with her, she wasn't having any of it. The more I implored her, the greater the fervour of my pleas and protestations, the more entrenched her response became and the greater the degree of detachment and distance between us. She then told me the truth. She was leaving me to start a new life in New Zealand, and she was leaving now. The time for discussion and deliberation was over. Her mind was made up. She had booked her flight, made all the other necessary arrangements for herself, but as for me. I was on my own. She was taking what she wanted from my life, not to benefit me or to remind her that I was her son, but instead to hinder me in my initial need to readjust and to cope. It was an action of spite, almost of revenge. I was left in astonishment and shock. I sat there, full of tears, following the trail of her departing car until I could see it no more. As if that wasn't enough, in the meantime people had started to dump all their superfluous bits and pieces in my room. Boxes started to accumulate, to be followed by all manner of things – guitars, cricket bats, hi-fi systems, even pets (not that we were allowed them at school, of course) – until it was virtually standing room only. Once more I tried my hardest to appeal to their sense of fairness and compassion, but it was as if I was as invisible and inaudible as the air we were all breathing. The door to my room was now broken – it had been forced off its hinges – so I couldn't even try to keep the wolves at bay by barricading myself in. At any minute, my housemaster would come to ask why I was still here. I sat on the only remaining space on my bed, in anger, sorrow and trepidation, waiting anxiously for the footsteps that would seal my fate. And the thing that bothered me more than anything was the fact that at any minute now I would be forced into having to make a decision. I couldn't postpone it. I couldn't delegate responsibilities. The time was now and there was no-one left.

Not surprisingly, all this took its toll on me when I first opened my eyes and realised that I'd had another nightmare. I must have expended copious amounts of nervous energy whilst asleep. I couldn't move, never mind rouse myself from my slumber. I kept putting off the effort of getting up until finally I felt I couldn't stay there any longer. I was so tired. I could hear Lesley downstairs, already busy, but the prospect of having to do anything other than simply breathe and exist was daunting in the extreme. I finally made it, but kept what I'd gone through to myself. The strange thing was that I felt intense guilt for thinking of my Mum in the way I had whilst dreaming. It didn't matter that I couldn't help it. I felt awful. My Mum has always been there for me. She's remained steadfastly loyal, totally committed in her love and belief. Why, oh why was my depression – for I know that this lies behind these nightmares – now turning on her? Wasn't it enough that I'd already begun – on rare occasions, it has to be said – to see my Dad as some form of adversary in my nightmares? Was there no limit to its devastating impact? Was nothing sacrosanct?

Significantly – and I do believe in fate – when I looked at my emails just now, there was one from her. It was as if my real Mum had somehow foreseen my despair and wanted to reassure me that she was there, as she always is. It was gratifying and it was wonderful.

Sunday 10th July 2016
As I've said on a few occasions, the medication I'm on has a variety of different side effects, some of them predictable, others less so. One of the strangest is muscle pain. I have no idea of the physiological circumstances and connections that make this a reality. All I know is that I often get aches and pains in my limbs and across my shoulder and neck area. They're not severe as such, but they're enough to make you uncomfortable. There are also times when I feel the need to resort either to Ibuprofen gel or pills. I know I should try and resist doing this, because the pain isn't unbearable. It's what the pain leads me to contemplate in my mind that's the crucial thing. I have a tendency to ruminate, and to ruminate wildly. I make links that aren't logical. I also catastrophize. There are two ways of stopping this. The first is the long method. Of working things through cogently, of using all the experience and tactics of Cognitive Behavioural Therapy (CBT), of reaching conclusions based on common sense and reason, of making my brain work for me rather than against me. Then there is the short method. Further medication. The former I should try and use much more than I do, the latter only when the pain warrants it. That's logical! However, there are occasions – far too many of them – when I just can't countenance the hard

work and effort, the inevitable battle with anxiety and fear, that can come with using CBT. I want to rid my mind of the consequences of pain, rather than the pain itself, and I want to do it quickly rather than sensibly. I do hope that makes some sort of sense?!

However, perhaps the most bizarre side-effect is twitching. This is, of course, also muscle related, but it's still distinct in its own right. It's quite difficult to explain, but the general gist is that my legs – and, for me, it's exclusively my legs – at times feel like they are behaving totally independently of my conscious will or endeavour. As if they have, quite literally, a mind of their own. Sometimes they move themselves. On other occasions, the tension within them necessitates my having to move them to alleviate that sensation. What I have to do is stretch as much as I can. It's like waking up in the morning, but at different times in the day. Actually, it's the evening whilst I'm lying in bed watching the telly that's the worst. I will, of course, have just taken my evening medication, so logically, there's the connection. This may also explain those occasions when I'm nervous or worried, and my right leg can't keep still. It taps incessantly on the floor, as if I'm emulating morse code[28]. Again, these are occasions of annoyance rather than soreness, of discomfort rather than hurt. The fact that it happens so regularly, however, does tend to wear you down. It eats away at your confidence as well as your composure, and in public it can be upsetting. Almost inevitably, people do look your way and you can't help wondering what on earth they can be thinking. I want to reassure them that I'm not under the influence of anything, but of course, I am, aren't I? It may not be alcohol or recreational drugs, but it's something just as potent, maybe as toxic and certainly as dependent.

Monday 11th July 2016

The Euro 2016 Football Championships reached their conclusion last night. Portugal beat the host nation France 1-0 in a rather tepid affair that only came to life in the second period of extra time. In many ways, the final epitomised the rest of the competition. For large parts, the standard of football was uninspiring, teams committed to avoiding defeat rather than striving for victory, and yet there was always the potential for a surprise, or – in England's case – a seismic shock! Wales were positively uplifting – as were Iceland and, very briefly, even Albania and Hungary. The 'big guns' threatened but in the end, largely flattered to deceive. Portugal only won one game within the standard ninety minutes, but as a unit, they were strong, united, well-organised and extremely difficult to beat. The fact that they won despite their talisman, Cristiano Ronaldo, having to leave the field injured within the first twenty minutes or so, suggests that flair does not always result in a definitive and decisive advantage.

For me, the whole thing was disappointing, but, on reflection, hardly surprising.

Football is not the game it was. It might be more professional. It might have advanced in things such as fitness, sports science, tactical insight and of course, financial investment, but it is, to my mind, a poorer product now compared to the game of my youth. Modern players may be fitter, faster and stronger. They may be prepared and looked after much more meticulously and carefully. They may have a whole host of off-field advisers, trainers, managers, coaches, agents, promotional staff and the like. They are obviously much better paid. But are they better in terms of what they deliver? I'm not so sure. As I watched the game last night, I couldn't help thinking back to the first international tournament I gleefully, hungrily and avidly followed as a young boy. It was the World Cup of 1978 in Argentina. I can remember inspirational performances, games full of goals, new teams and players that were unheard of in this country. There was tension, there was controversy – I remember Clive Thomas, the Welsh referee, blowing his whistle to end a game a matter of seconds before Brazil scored what they thought was a winning goal – there was colour and there was skill in abundance. Moreover, it was a spectacle. Every game seemed refreshingly competitive, the football creative and dynamic. There was boldness and transparency. Teams wanted to win, to simply score more goals than their opponents. The idea of 'shutting up shop', of playing for extra time and penalties would have been deemed a betrayal of ethos and legacy. It was a totally different context compared to today. Football then, it should be remembered, was virtually never shown live on television. Only the FA Cup Final and international tournaments warranted live coverage. Because of this, watching a match became what can only be described as a treat. Particularly for a nine-year-old boy. I'd never seen Brazil and Argentina before. Even Peru – who famously beat Scotland – left an indelible impression, particularly their star player, Cubillas, who was able to bend the ball in ways that I hadn't even thought possible. Even now, some thirty-eight years later, I can still remember so much!

The other thing that stuck out in my mind as I watched the best of Portugal (bar the injured one!) finally hold off the best of France, was the recognition that unless you are a passionate supporter of one of the teams, football for the most part, has become quite boring. Even a little tedious. It might not always be predictable – thank God for that at least – but in other ways, it seems to be moving in the direction of performance rather than sport. You know what you are going to get. Supreme athleticism and technical accomplishment are wonderful attributes in themselves, but if they serve primarily to nullify the threat of one's opponents, games can become deadlocked, reverting to dogged battles of attrition, a contest dominated by tactical manoeuvring rather than spontaneous or even collective inspiration. The fact that these days, cameras seem to zoom in on managers and coaches and the punditry focuses as much on formations as the game-breaking player, are themselves telling illustrations of where we've gone. Interesting though it is, it's like analysing a Mozart symphony in terms of how it is put together as opposed to savouring it for what it sounds like. There's always a place for the former – and as a former Music student, I should know – but not at the expense of the latter! One has to have the thrill of completion, an end product, after all!

Tuesday 12th July 2016

I can't help thinking about all the implications from what I wrote yesterday. I'm not sure I've really got it clear in my mind as I sit and write, but there's a bit of me that suspects that I'm not ever going to anyway. All I feel capable of acknowledging for certain is that this is important for me, not just because I'm a football fan, but because it connects to my mental health on a much broader level. Anyway, please bear with me and forgive, in advance, any rambling on my part.

The first thing I need to say – in reiteration – is that watching football as a neutral, without affinity, without allegiance, but also without care and without passion, seems to me to be almost devoid of meaning. It becomes mundane. Or rather, it can become so. The alternative is to choose not just intent and all the things missing emotionally from what could be called Plan A, but also to deliberately revel in the element of chance, of unpredictability, of risk. It can elevate one to feelings akin to intoxication, to experience excitement, belonging, a sense of joy and rapture. But for me, that only happens if my team wins. In defeat, the blow is every bit as intense, though of course the feelings are diametrically contrasting. For me, football has become probably the most vivid representation of 'all or nothing'. There's no middle ground. With regards to my mental health, all my treatment and my direction of travel is towards stability. I hope for something more, but I dread anything less. When that happens – as it inevitably does – I become acutely depressed. The ravages of a depressive episode consume me from within, like the most destructive of cancers. What I'm effectively faced with in relation to football, therefore, is either to choose a path commensurate with my mental health treatment, or one that is deliberately, decidedly and – most importantly – adversely impactful. The safe, stable option of security, or its risky, potentially volatile, alternative? The former is consistent and logical. It makes sense. The latter is to side with something that may occasionally be uplifting, but is just as likely (more likely, given the teams I support!) to be appalling and catastrophic. Is this also, however, a metaphor for living one's life? Has it become that as well? Predictability, stability but monotony versus a state of trepidation and compelling, but possibly unfulfilled, expectation. I wouldn't – I can't – think of ignoring the treatment that has kept me alive. So why on earth would I put myself in the firing line? It's a gamble. There's no two ways about it. And, as usual, it being a decision, I have absolutely no idea what to do.

Wednesday 13th July 2016

If I'm struggling with life-changing decisions, I'm also agonising over far more humdrum concerns. As an example, one of my clients has stipulated that I need to have my own Public Liability Insurance in place. Not a big deal, you may think. Anyway, my enquiry to the company with whom I always deal with in relation to insurance, yielded a question as to the extent of the cover required. I didn't know, but having looked through the relevant email chains I found that the level being suggested by the company was not the level that one of my colleagues has arranged. It would have to be, wouldn't it? Immediately, I'm in a dilemma. Having concluded that I could ask for two quotes, I then thought about what may happen then. I realised that not only do I not know what to do, but I also can't decide on the process I should take to make that decision! Do I go back to my colleague? Do I ask other people? What if my original source thinks I've ignored her advice? So many questions. So many decisions. If this sounds like a rhetorical muddle to you, imagine what's going in inside my head! Whatever lead or direction I seem to follow, the only way forward seems to include taking on board more and more issues, with more and more conundrums and more and more possibilities of things going completely haywire! What a useless entity I am at times. The master of indecision. And yet, that's the last thing I really want to be. I'd love to be strong, not just appear strong. I'd welcome the opportunity to be firm and decisive. I want to be looked upon as someone who knows what to do, who is blessed not just with experience but with a moral and ethical antenna that can always find a way through the mists and fog of deliberation and confusion. The strange thing is that when it comes to big things and other people, I do have this perspective. I offer advice and guidance based on what I think is the best route for others to follow, even if this relates to monumental areas of importance and significant aspects of people's lives. But for myself. I can't decide whether to have orange squash or blackcurrant most of the time. Why this apparent inconsistency? I really don't know. I guess I should take some confidence from this. If people can't trust me or can't rely on my input in terms of its wisdom and perspicacity, they wouldn't turn to me. I should be flattered. And I am. But I should also be invigorated. And sadly, I'm not.

Thursday 14th July 2016
If there's one thing clear from the last two days' entries it's the fact that at times, I obviously think too much. Despite my best intentions, my tendency to overthink leads not to clarification and resolution but to confusion and frustration. At least more times than not! I wish I didn't do it. But try stopping my mind once it's switched out of first gear. Not only does it race at breakneck speed, but it tries to go in multiple directions all at the same time. In its desperation to solve and to connect, it becomes a hindrance, a barrier and a disability all at the same time. I become the most disjointed of beings, carried away both by my own desire to alleviate worry, panic and depression, and my inability, my incapability to do so. I once described Leeds United as being 'consistently inconsistent' – I've done it on many an occasion actually – but I am the same. I guess I'm also 'inconsistently consistent', though I won't even attempt to distinguish properly between the two!

I've spent much of the day on an Interview Panel. On the other side of the fence, so to speak. Actually, I'm not sure I like the process, irrespective of whether I'm interviewer or interviewee. It may be slightly less nerve-wracking being the former, but the interconnection is still one that can be immensely challenging in a number of ways. I find that I'm trying hard to get into the head of the person being interviewed. I'm looking not just for all the things I'm supposed to be assessing – skills, experience, competence, application and so on and so forth – but also for other things. Some of them come with the territory, I suppose. Things like character, demeanour and attitude. Others are directly connected to mental health and even more specifically, to mental illness. I do believe that if you have a long-standing relationship with the latter, you can detect its presence and its impact in others. Not just in their behaviour, but in their whole persona. The way they look, the way they sit, the way they talk, the way they make eye contact – or not as the case may be. Things such as leg movements and shifting positions can be every bit as indicative as mannerisms you may consider to be more representative. In some cases, I honestly do think you can sense depression and other illnesses just as much as more obvious traits such as anxiety, worry and stress. Of course, what you can't do is state for certain that this is the case. And, more importantly still, judge people as a result.

There is one thing though that I think is vital to consider. I may not know if any given person has a mental illness. But I also cannot say for certain that they do not. When you're dealing with people in whatever context – at work, socially, in families, making acquaintances, at interviews, in performance – if you can put the second consideration before the first, you will be behaving much more fairly and equitably. You will be addressing stigma and discrimination. You will be giving people a chance. And you'll be a better person as a result.

Friday 15th July 2016

A quiet end to the working week. I only have one engagement today and that's to go to John's Social Media Café. He wants to discuss a new initiative with me, which is always exciting as John's plans have this habit of not only coming to fruition, but also being significant in their aims and objectives. He doesn't do half measures! It's interesting that I find going to his Café a much more relaxing and comfortable experience than other social events of a similar nature. Usually, the thought of attending something so informal and geared towards discussion – networking that is – terrifies the life out of me. But not this one. There are times when it is hard. When I'm isolated, not knowing who to turn to or where to look. And I have on occasions had to resort to my coping mechanism of pretending to have conversations on my mobile phone. Just to look normal and involved. I guess these tend to be when I'm not so well. When my confidence and self-esteem are naturally lower. But most of the time, I'm actually fine. It just shows that an environment that is geared around support, that recognises disability in its many forms, that is inherently about involvement, that has human vulnerability as much as human contact very much in its DNA, can do wonders to make people feel appreciated and, dare I say it, 'normal'.

The same can be said about CLAHRC at the Leicester General Hospital. I've been doing some work with them for the last six months now and I can honestly say that there have been few occasions when I've felt like an outsider. In fact, I can't really remember any. I've been able to contribute even when I've felt low, but more importantly, I've been able to tell people – new colleagues, people only just getting to know me properly – when I'm struggling and what exactly I'm struggling with. It helps that Carol, one of Lesley's close friends, works there and is centrally involved in what I do as a consultant. But every single person I have come into contact with has made me feel valued.

To give just one example. The receptionist always greets me with a cheery hello and takes the time to talk to me. We share a laugh. We have a brief conversation. And I don't even know her name! Yesterday, as I approached the desk, she said to me 'It's not Friday is it?' She remembered – because she's obviously made it her business to remember – that I usually attend meetings on a Friday morning. How brilliant is that? I was really touched. She must have hundreds of people go through her to other meetings and events and yet somehow she'd remembered my presence and had acknowledged it. Little things like that can make a world of difference to someone with a mental illness. It's not rocket science. It's the simple things that make you feel special and give you a cause and a reason to live.

Saturday 16th July 2016

A good friend of mine is currently with the England Academy Rugby League squad on their tour of Australia. I've been thinking about him a lot because I'm aware that in the past he's had his own battles with mental illness. He's come through difficult times, but I know from personal experience how demanding a month-long sojourn away from home can be, especially for people from our community of the mentally afflicted. There are, of course, high-profile examples. Marcus Trescothick and Jonathan Trott from the world of cricket come immediately to mind. But I too tried – and failed – to cope with these challenges.

It was back in 2000 when I, an employee of the Rugby Football League, was asked to accompany the New Zealand team during the course of the World Cup tournament being held here in England and Wales. I was assigned the task of helping the touring party with practical matters whilst they were here, but in addition I also had responsibility for the Group in which they were playing which, from memory, involved Wales as hosts, but also Lebanon and the Cook Islands. Initially I was based in Gloucester, but, as the Kiwis were strong favourites to progress to the latter stages of the competition, it was highly likely that I would have to move to pastures new as they negotiated round after round. Whilst the team did indeed do what was expected on the pitch – they would eventually meet, and lose, to Australia in the final – for me, my World Cup began and ended in that hotel on the outskirts of Gloucester. I lasted no more than ten days.

Looking back with the benefit of hindsight, and of course with a diagnosis of mental illness, I should never have been there. It was clear after the first day, that I couldn't handle the prospect of being left alone to deal with a whole host of practicalities. The isolation I felt, away from my comfort zone, was crippling. I had the power to delegate, but the colleague with whom I had been assigned to work, seemed to resent the fact that I had a degree of authority that was just one step above his. I didn't blame him in this respect. The situation just wasn't managed well, and I was never sure whether the nature of the arrangements was ever properly communicated to him. As it was, the squad of players, managers, coaches, medics and officials was already a very tight-knit group of people. They had to be to succeed. Of course they knew each other well. Their sense of camaraderie was strong. They were thousands of miles from home. They knew they had to support each other off the pitch as well as on. And, young men being young men, humour and playful antics played a significant part in their gelling as a group of people on a mission. If you weren't part of this, you were immediately an outsider. I remember a coach drive back to the hotel after a night out at a restaurant in Cheltenham. I was sitting close to the front, next to the man – I can't remember his name – who compiled match facts and statistics on each individual player, when a barrage of objects started flying our way from the back of the coach. What they were, I can't recall, but I do remember being hit incessantly. It was like the very worst of school trips! I tried to play along with the situation, but inside I was hurting. I wanted to confront my tormentors, because I was convinced that I alone was the target. But how could I do that without making myself more of one? When we eventually reached the hotel, I rushed as quickly as I could without making it obvious, to the sanctuary of my room. I never wanted to come out again. When I look back, it was clear that I was in the grip of a massive depressive episode. I had been from the outset, even before I first arrived in my temporary home. I endured a birthday on the day of the first match. It was traumatic in the extreme. I couldn't talk to people properly. I couldn't do anything other than try to look occupied. I couldn't handle anyone and anything. I was living on an absolute knife edge. And there was no respite. No safe space. No outlet for my pain. How I managed not to cry or lose my composure and temper, I will never know. As the first week neared its end, I'd found one coping mechanism, and that was escape. I just got in my car and drove to Cardiff, the venue for the climactic group games and the hotel base of the other three nation's squads.

They all had liaison managers like me, so I wouldn't be called upon to do anything practically. I could invent jobs. I could make myself look useful. I could contrive to manifest myself as the supporting mechanism I should have been, yet was incapable of achieving. And I could also take my time getting there and getting back. By this time too I'd stopped eating in the hotel restaurant with the rest of the New Zealand party. I would go to McDonalds on my own, or buy sandwiches from a local supermarket. Anything to avoid having to socialise and be among a group of strangers.

I was in such a bad way. And I needed out. But how? What could I say? The truth was too pathetic in my mind. 'I'm sorry, I'm missing home and I can't cope'. I couldn't admit that to myself, never mind anyone else. Of course, I didn't know then what I know now. That I was beset with a paralysing, devastating disability. That it was called depression. That it was real. That it was consuming. That it was manifestly total and ruinous in its impact. That it was justifiable. That it was recognisable. I felt compelled to lie. I rang the person who was supposed to be my immediate contact for support and told him that the operational situation with two of us involved with the New Zealand squad hadn't worked and that I wasn't able to resurrect the type of close relationship needed to enable me to properly support them for the rest of the tournament. Or words to that effect. I tried to enforce on him that I couldn't therefore continue. That I could do something else – even though I secretly and wholeheartedly wished that not to be the case. Thankfully, he agreed with me. I also had to tell the New Zealand management something. But what? And when? I vividly remember waiting in the hotel lobby one evening whilst they had a team meeting. It went on and on. Inside I was terrified, but I couldn't show it. I'd positioned myself so that I could see down the corridor to the room where they were obviously discussing match affairs. Every time I heard any door opening or shutting, alarm bells would ring. Every time someone entered the lobby area, my heart missed a beat. When would this agony finally go away? Eventually, the players emerged from their briefing. Alone or in small groups they made their way to their rooms, obviously under the instruction that they have an early night. I waited until I could see the Team Manager and the official from the New Zealand Rugby League. I approached them and asked if they had a few minutes. I still hadn't really convinced myself that whatever I said would sound acceptable. I managed to talk despite my self-recriminations and the self-loathing that was increasing by the minute. I simply stated that for personal reasons that I didn't want to divulge, I could no longer do the job I'd been asked to do. I had to go home. A replacement would be arranged. I was sorry to let them down. They were fine about it. Disappointed – which surprised me. But it obviously wasn't that big a deal to them. The sense of relief I felt inside was overwhelming. The end was in sight. I could even count down the hours.

Those initial feelings were, however, brief. They were soon to be replaced by emotions that I've come to know only too well. I felt useless and vulnerable, afraid and anxious, incapable of logical thought and expression. I also felt embarrassed. A complete failure. A liability, even. What would the future bring? I'd never be asked to do something like this again. Whilst that felt good in the short term, it began to dawn on me that my career in sport would from now on be curtailed in various ways. I wouldn't be trusted. I'd sacrificed a future, possibly. But I'd had no choice. I had to act, even though it wasn't the way I'd wanted to. I'd been dishonest, but what other option had I had? At the time, depression wasn't on my radar as an explanatory term. I was depressed. Of that there was no doubt. But I couldn't call it depression. No-one had said I had depression. I'd used other words. Any other words. But not that one.

It's much simpler now, of course. And open as well. Looking back, it seems like another life. It's only sixteen years ago, but it's a world apart. It's not, as you will know by now, a case of a life before depression and a life during it. It's a life before it was diagnosed and a life post-diagnosis.

The one stable and continual factor, ironically but tellingly, has been the depression itself.

Sunday 17th July 2016

Time can be an alluring thing. When I'm particularly depressed – and sometimes when only slightly so – I find myself constantly looking backwards. To things I did. To things I didn't do. To things I wished I had done. To things I'd rather forget. It sometimes feels like I'm living my current life in the past. Memories seem palpably real in the sense that I can actually touch them. They're life-like. They feed on sensations, feelings and emotions as well as evidential occurrences. The one constant thing about them all is the notion that I didn't make the most of whatever it was I was doing or whatever situation I was in. If I could only have it all again? Or even a small part of it. I'd make up – quite literally – for lost time.

I've been watching the documentary series 'The World At War' over the course of the last couple of weeks. I have the full boxset. Fully twenty-six episodes. But I've never seen it in its entirety. I thought it was about time that I did! It's a compelling piece of television. Made in 1973 and 1974, it features interviews, for example, with actual participants including leading members of the political and military hierarchies of the time. I've found myself contemplating the connections that are caused by time and its peculiarities. When these people were being interviewed it was only thirty years or so on from the contexts they were being asked to describe and comment on. I myself can remember quite vividly thirty years ago. Those years seem at times to be remarkably close. In 1986, I was doing my A' Levels. I was going out with Mary, my first love. I was actively playing football and cricket. I watched football from concrete terraces, complete with overcrowding, crowd surges and the like. I was playing the Elgar 'Cello Concerto on a school Orchestra Tour. My Dad and Danny were both alive. I was slim and fashion conscious. I was politically extreme. I had hopes and desires. I had goals. I thought I knew what I wanted. But it all changed in a flash. Before I had time to enjoy it, to revel in it all, it was all over. I was also, of course, experiencing depression. I didn't know it then. I wished I had done. It would have enabled me, I think, to pace myself, to look after myself much better than I did, to reassess parameters and to be more realistic in my adventures and in the way I wanted to be active in the world. It wouldn't have stopped all the ambitions that I had, but it would definitely have made them more achievable, for the simple reason that I would have had support and I would have been able – with that support – to plan more effectively, to take things one step at a time. Moreover, I would have coped better, I suspect, with the calamities that were just around the corner. The death of my father. The break-up with Mary. The rejections from universities. The new role in my family. As it was, I persevered alone. I came close to taking my life. I turned to drink on many occasions. I didn't know where to go. I just wanted to appear strong for my family. But it was all a façade. I was tearing myself apart. I was completely lost, unable and unwilling to look at life and its opportunities with anything other than cynicism and revulsion. All for the want of a diagnosis.

Monday 18th July 2016

I've just worked out that, as a rough estimate, I've been alive for around 17,400 days. It sounds a lot, and it is a lot. I'm not sure quite what I want to read into that and what element of that longevity is the most important, but one thing that comes immediately to mind is how much of that figure was spent under the dark cloak of depression? Was I born depressed? At least in the sense that there was already something biologically malfunctioning in my brain. Or did depression descend gradually? If so, how and why did this happen? And when? I guess the latter is always going to be speculative, for the simple reason that if depression was part of my DNA even as a toddler, how on earth would I – or indeed my parents – even know that it was depression? If diagnosis didn't even occur whilst a teenager when my capability to assess and to describe was that much greater, how on earth was it ever going to happen in my formative years? Things are very different now, of course. We know a lot more about the illness, even though its causes are not quite so clear cut – the nature versus nurture debate etc. Even more crucially, we know that it can be evident in young children. And that treatment at a relatively early age can pay significant dividends. I can't help feeling that I was born at the wrong time. That I wouldn't be as ill as I am if I'd been born even twenty years later. But naturally, to ruminate over this issue is as pointless as it is intriguing. I am what I am.

On a different note, I had the pleasure of watching last night's Proms concert on BBC Four. The highlight was a performance of Faure's Requiem. What a wonderful work it is. The beauty of its construction, the sublimity of its lines, its phrasing, its depiction. It has an ethereal quality that truly encapsulates the peace and tranquillity, the serenity of passing from one life to the next. I was mesmerised. During the course of this Proms season, those other musical giants of the Requiem Mass, that of Mozart and Verdi, will be performed. They're very different, but equally as alluring. They've always seemed to draw me into their magic – as is the case with Faure's adaptation. I have to wonder why that is? It was the same with my father and indeed my grandfather. Dad, for example, dedicated his copy of Brahms' German Requiem to the memory of my Grandad. I'm not a Roman Catholic. I'm not even that religious. But somehow, the power of the music and the drama of what it conveys has a resonance that is remarkably strong. I just hope it's a good sign rather than a death wish!

Tuesday 19th July 2016

I'm expecting today to be the hottest day of the year so far. All the forecasts are predicting temperatures in excess of 30 degrees. Whilst many – undoubtedly the majority – will be savouring the moment, relishing the feeling of hot sun on skin, I am one that can only think of how I'm going to cope. To be honest, I hate hot weather. I always have done. What it is that gets me is not the propensity to burn, it's my tendency to sweat and to sweat profusely. In turn, this makes me not only uncomfortable (that much may be obvious), it gives me this feeling that I'm inherently dirty. As a result, I shy away from my fellow humans. I don't want them near me because I'm convinced I smell and that I look unclean. Yesterday was a good example. I had to attend an event at a community centre in the city. I wore a suit, not because it felt appropriate, but because the jacket would hide evidence of sweat on my shirt. As a result, I was hotter than I might have been. And of course that meant I sweated a lot more! It's a vicious circle! It really is. My bulk will always count against me when it comes to sweating, but I am aware that at least one of my medications also has this as a side effect. And given my inclination to panic, I can't help believing that all the possible circumstances are working against me. I just wish I could accept the fact that I can't really do anything about it. But I can't. I have to add that I'm not as bad as I used to be. There was a time when I would have umpteen showers a day, not necessarily to get rid of the dried sweat, but to try to install in me a contrary belief that I can't be cleaner. The problem was that as soon as I got dressed afterwards and consequently began to perspire again, I would more than not just jump back under the water. It used to take me ages before I was ready to face the world. Looking back, this was a time when my OCD was out of control. It was that aspect of my mental illness that dominated my thinking. But I've managed to address this. Well, most of the time anyway. Now it's that fear of being judged that has taken hold. I don't want anyone to have negative thoughts towards me. About anything. It really bothers me. I can't rid myself of the thought that anything, no matter how apparently slight, quickly translates into loathing and hate. It's as if people – in my mind – either like me, or positively detest me. There's no middle ground. And I can't bear contemplating the latter. So as far as sweat and cleanliness is concerned, my belief is that people will not put it into context, people will not understand that it's a matter of temperature. On the contrary, they will see, smell or detect sweat on my body, and immediately will turn against me, their feelings quickly becoming intensified as aversion, hostility and revulsion. Sweat becomes simply a reason. An excuse. It's the trigger. The catalyst. A green light to reveal their true presentiments.

Wednesday 20th July 2016

Of course one thing I need to be conscious of now is my newly-acquired Vitamin D deficiency. In addition to tablets, the one practical thing I can do – and probably need to do more of – is expose myself to the sun. It's great isn't it? To address one – just one – part of my increasingly feeble composition, I must put myself in a position where I sweat more! The rest follows like the proverbial fallen pack of cards, so that ultimately in order to deal with one – relatively insubstantial – condition, I'm furthering my chances of mental breakdown. I can't win. It's no coincidence that yesterday I felt increasingly irritated as the day went on. Physically, I was hot and sticky. My breathing was more laboured. I had little energy and if I could pant like a dog I would have done so gladly! However, it was the impact on my mental faculties that was more disturbing. Little things began to take on immense significance, out of all proportion to sound sense and reason. I was having to constantly check things with Lesley. I seemed to need extra reassurance. The mere fact that I was being forced to make decisions as a result of emails received was trying in itself. Even before I could contemplate mulling over what to do, I was already severely stressed and anxious. And then, the last straw, our television started to act as if it had a mind of our own. Every now and again, it seems to turn itself off without human input. Last night, it became an epidemic. No sooner had I switched it on again, it decided to thwart and derail me once more by hitting the 'off' button. It was doing it on purpose. At least in my mind. I sat there cursing. My language became more and more 'colourful', until eventually I was all for throwing the remote controller at the screen! I could sense Lesley becoming agitated and concerned. Thankfully, I still had an ounce of common sense and rational perception about me. I decided to go and have a shower and then lie on our bed under the fan. Removing me from the possibility of full-blown anger and frustration was the only way. It worked, but it took a while for me to calm down. Life has this habit, doesn't it, of kicking you persistently when you're already down. It leads the sufferer to believe more and more in fate. For the mentally unhealthy, all those common feelings are magnified and exacerbated in many diverse ways. You begin to think you are genuinely cursed. That there is no way out of your predicament. That resistance is futile. That you must accept your lot. Or die. There's no other way. Even though when you are lucid and when illness isn't as destructive, you do realise that you have options, that there are ways of dealing with the way your damaged mind is working – or not as the case may be – at moments of extreme vulnerability, there is no – or very little – acknowledgement of this. The secret is to recognise when you are in this position – or to have someone close recognise this for you – and to instil in yourself, if you can, a means by which you can effectively 'tread water'. You're not going to be able to reasonably and effectively think or act your way out of your predicament. Not at that moment. So you wait until you can begin that process. It's damage limitation. It works for me, but like all these things, I'm conscious that it isn't necessarily as workable or as conclusive for others. You have to find your own way of dealing with the matter. And that comes not just with experience, but with proper support. Both are crucial.

Thursday 21st July 2016

There are some wonderful organisations who do sterling work helping to address stigma as well as providing necessary support to those of us who have a mental illness. One of these is the National Survivor User Network. I get their regular Members blogs and they're always an interesting read. In the latest one my attention was drawn to a piece entitled 'Talking about night terrors'[29]. In it, a lady called Judith described clearly the type of experience that I have been having fairly regularly over the course of the last two years or so. She talked of screaming, of feeling as if she was falling and choking. She said that she would wake up and cry 'uncontrollably', that she panicked and felt shaky as a result, that the effects would endure long into the next day, that she would be reluctant to go to sleep again. She had also done some homework. She stated that for adults there would appear to be a link both to 'childhood trauma' and to an increased susceptibility to respiratory disorder. This makes perfect sense. Most of my 'terrors' relate to school. Occasionally, they revolve around my relationship with my Dad and with Danny, my sense of desperation and futility in not being able to 'cure' them of their illnesses and disabilities, of not being able to prevent their deaths. But in the main, it's been school. I can't begin to truly recognise or try to measure the impact that my school career has obviously had on my future health and prosperity. In some ways, there is a direct relationship to my father in the sense that his failing health was a continual cloud over my teenage years. The two are intertwined in so many respects. And yet it's strange that the most pleasurable and meaningful part of my time at school – my relationship with Mary – is sometimes manifest in my traumas. It's not direct memory, of course. If so, there would be no trauma. No, what tends to happen is that my mind completely distorts – indeed positively savages – the actual reality of what we had. Instead of the closeness that we shared, we become distant. Instead of the love we had, there comes anger and resentment. She moves away from me in a way that she never did in true life. All my hopes go with her. I become isolated and lonely. I become a target not just for the bullies but for everyone who should have been there to help – teachers, friends and the like. I become once more the person I was before we started going out. Insecure, vulnerable and sensitive. In one of my visions, I'm running away. I'm near the coast and there is a direct route to the cliffs overlooking the dark waters of the North Sea. In my 'terrors', I'm there on that journey to oblivion. I'm trying to avoid detection. I don't want anyone to miss me and therefore look for me. I make my way to the overhang and reflect. What do I do now? Hide for ever or take one fatal step? And yet the peace and solitude of that moment never properly materialises. No sooner am I there, trying to take it all in, than I'm surrounded by faces, by accusations, by hostility and menace. I'm caught and I'm being punished. I have to fight back. I kick out randomly and sporadically. I'm trying to push people away, but they're all around me, closing in, suffocating me, drawing every last breath out of my body. And usually, at around that point, I realise that I'm actually fighting with the bed covers, that I'm shouting and screaming, that I'm swearing profanities, that I'm in danger of attacking our Lesley, if I haven't already accidentally done so. I wake up. Or I'm woken up. I sit there, breathing hard, trying to calm myself. Trying to rid my mind of what's just happened. I can be there for what seems like hours. I have to convince myself, somehow, that it's safe to shut my eyes and go back to sleep.

What I've read in Judith's harrowing piece is simply a reflection of me. I'll reflect more on this on another occasion. I'm too upset to continue at the moment.

Friday 22<u>nd</u> July 2016

I'm not sure whether sleep apnoea counts as a 'respiratory disorder', but – following on from yesterday – if it does, then there's another potential affirmation of this latest addition to my growing list of mental afflictions. I'm still to be diagnosed with this condition, of course, and I don't want to tempt fate one way or the other, but it really does make complete sense. Ironically, I was due to be wired up by the sleep disorder people on Wednesday, but a lack of car to get to my appointment combined with my fear that I wouldn't sleep at all well given the current heat wave we're experiencing meant that I had to cancel. It's been rearranged for a fortnight's time. If I'm honest, I'm looking for an excuse to put it off. The thought of my breathing being obstructed during my sleep isn't a pleasant one. But I need to know. And I can't cancel again unless I want to be sent back to the bottom of the waiting list. So in fourteen days, I'll be assessed and then I'll know the score. From what I understand, sleep apnoea is far more common than people may imagine, so in that sense, I'll be joining an expanding club. But it's the fact that it's another thing to think about that really concerns me. I think I've got more than my fair share of health worries! I suppose there is an alternative way of looking at it, and that's the fact that it's probably better to be aware of what's going on than not. The logic isn't escaping me. If 'night terrors' tend to invoke sensations of feeling trapped and more specifically, of being choked, then it's entirely consistent to think that there is a physiological as well as a psychological explanation for what is going on. I really am being denied, albeit only fleetingly, the opportunity to breathe!

Saturday 23rd July 2016

This is hard to believe – and certainly difficult to digest – but it could just be that I appear to be the one who is mentally strong in my family at the moment. I'll come back to my deliberate choice of words shortly, but I need to begin by outlining how and why this apparent situation has arisen. To start with, Rachel – who's been back with us for this past week only – has been having some difficulties with her Sri Lankan partner, Kasal. Obviously, the geographical distance between them doesn't help the situation, but it would appear that cultural factors are at play here that elevate that sense of family loyalty and cohesion, but don't necessarily help when the relationship involves someone from outside that tradition and context. It would seem that compromises will need to be made to enable her to be truly happy, but whether they are workable is another matter. It may be a situation where head has to rule heart. Joel too has had a setback this week, but, in contrast to his sister, it's of his own making. He decided to risk playing football when his ankle obviously hadn't properly recovered, and as a consequence, he went over on it again! Luckily, he's still able to work, so his goal of accumulating enough money in the bank to enable him to ultimately get out to Australia hasn't been disrupted. However, in his mind, he'll probably be wondering about his future prospects of playing the sport he loves. If he doesn't allow proper recovery – and as a young man, patience isn't one of his virtues – a permanent weakness may develop which, of course, won't do him any good at all. Elliot, bless him, has had a real mixed bag of fortunes recently. On the academic front, his end of term report was, once more, truly magnificent. He works hard. He concentrates. He gives it his all. And he therefore deserves the successes and accolades that come his way. However, on a more personal level, he's been the subject of some incessant, but also quite random, bullying. He seems to have become a target for a reason that he can't do anything about. The school are working at addressing the situation, but it's had a depressing effect on him. At times, he doesn't want to go. He often asks me to pick him up, and at a time when he could really do with his friends rallying around, they seem to have given him very little actual support. He's pleased that school is now over for another year, so I'm hoping that the more confident and outgoing Elliot emerges once more now that the specific pressure of school is over for a while. He could do with a holiday. As indeed could Lesley. She's been struggling of late. The stress of having to cope with all the trials and tribulations of life has caught up with her a little. She's having to revise for the exams she missed as a result of the attack on her at the end of last year, and it may well be the case that memories of that time are resurfacing. She's become a little tearful and you can tell that things are occupying her mind. She's not been as confident when taking Millie out for a walk, for example.

I can't help but feel that I am of little use to Lesley – and indeed to the others – at times like this. My worries and anxieties, my daily struggles with living, all combine to make me think that instead of being there as a source of support and comfort, all I actually do is increase everyone else's burdens, because they have me to deal with as well. I can't do anything about this, other than what I'm actually doing. And that is to try and give the impression that I'm strong and that I can help. That is why I deliberately used the phrase 'appear to be' in the first sentence. I say all the right words. Or at least I think I do. I offer and give hugs. I hold people's hands. But is there any substance to my well-intentioned gestures? I just don't know. I genuinely hope so. Of course I do. I like to think I make a difference, a positive difference, to those around me. But whether I do or not, I have my doubts. Depression can be a terribly self-centred, affliction. When someone is sharing their significant concerns and worries with me and all I can actually think about is what to do to answer a routine email, when that relatively minor challenge overcomes all around it, that's depression, but it's also extremely selfish. I try to hold back the growing sense of agitation that's developing fast inside my mind, to concentrate on my role as a father and as a husband, to focus on providing that rock, that sense of security and safety that I've always tried hard to accomplish. But when your mind is playing such tricks in relation to priorities and importance, when it convinces you that unless you answer a question in a particular way, you're going to bring calamity and misfortune down upon yourself and those nearest and dearest to you, it's hard to contextualise and decipher what actually matters from what, truth be told, is really quite trivial. I do my best, but I'm my worst critic. It comes with the territory, I'm afraid. And I honestly believe I'm rubbish.

Sunday 24th July 2016

It only takes a second for a stray thought to transform into something far more disturbing. This morning I was doing the ironing – as is my wont on a Sunday – when I suddenly realised that Lesley had been a long time taking Millie for a walk. No sooner had my consciousness been aroused, I began fearing that something had happened. I couldn't rationalise it as something entirely normal – it was a nice morning, she was making the most of the weather, Millie was enjoying herself, etc. Instead, paranoia took over. My thoughts changed entirely, directed by a process that I couldn't control, a process known to depressives as 'catastrophizing'. In my new way of thinking, Lesley had been attacked again. She was lying in a ditch, where no-one could find her. Millie was gone. She'd run away in fear. As the minutes passed, Lesley was no longer injured. She was dead. And it was my fault. I should have gone with her. I should have been protective. I shouldn't have let her go. I knew she'd be accosted again. Why hadn't I acted? I began to panic. What should I do? I could get hold of her on her mobile. But what would be the result in me if she didn't answer? And if she did, would my fears somehow transmute to her. Would she suddenly become as fearful as I felt? Would I turn an innocent, leisurely walk into something entirely different? Luckily, within minutes, I saw her turn into our drive. She was back. Unharmed. Unafraid. Unaffected. Unaware.

One of the most challenging things in all this is the time-span. Within seconds I was something entirely different. Catastrophizing has that impact. Once prompted, it attaches itself like a thousand leeches. And like these blood suckers, the only way to rid oneself of their hold is to leave a thousand scars. I know I'll be consumed by these thoughts for some time to come today. Their legacy, irrespective of time, is an increased sense of doubt and insecurity. It will take some effort to regain what I had only a short time ago. However, the bigger picture is that catastrophizing not only leaves an immediate and temporary blemish on your mind, when added together with previous occasions, it becomes a more obdurate state of mind in itself. There is something horribly permanent about its manifestation. How many times have I convinced myself, for example, when Lesley goes off to work in the morning, that I'll never see her again? The feeling is more than paranoia in a sense, because you can be paranoid whilst recognising that you are being so – perhaps not at the time, but not long afterwards. This sensation becomes almost fact. I can't change it. It's out of my control. No matter what I do, it's been sanctioned by fate. More times than not, I have to resort to taking a pill, to sedate myself. It's the only thing that helps lessen the impact. It only really goes when I see her once more. She'll come through the front door. We'll greet each other. 'How's your day been?' she'll ask. 'Oh fine. No problems', I'll reply, lying through my teeth!

Monday 25th July 2016

I have a challenge to face today. For most people, this wouldn't be so, I would suspect. In fact, I'm guessing that the majority would find what I'm about to do quite exciting. On the surface, everything points to it being a positive development, something to revel in and enjoy, something fresh and yet also familiar, something that can open up new opportunities, new experiences, a new world in fact. You'll be wondering, by now, what I'm talking about! What life-changing adventure am I about to commence? What life-enriching episode am I about to undertake? The reality is, I expect, rather more mundane, for the fact is that what I am doing is changing my mobile phone. I can't help comparing how I feel at this moment with the emotions shown by my kids at various times when they've had one as a present for birthdays or at Christmas. Emotions of glee, delight, euphoria even. I can't think of a single occasion when anything but sheer unadulterated pleasure has been the reaction. And why wouldn't it be? The very fact that it is recognised as a present rather gives it away. It is a significant investment still, despite the fact that everyone seems to have one these days. And yet, for me, it's an occasion to endure. To get through.

Why is this the case? The simple explanation is that the novelty of the experience is what I dread. For a variety of reasons. I'm about to go from a situation over which I have almost total control to one in which I'm less sure of myself. My existing phone is basic to say the least –others would probably call it primitive! – but it's always done what I've wanted it to do. It rings. It allows conversation. It stores numbers. And it texts. That's it. However, about a month ago, it started to play up, so Lesley convinced me that I should move into the twenty-first century, and upgrade. Even then, I couldn't face the prospect of switching straight away. I was saved by the fact that as it was a pay-as-you-go phone, I still had substantial credit which needed to be used up otherwise I'd just lose it. I have to confess that I still felt the need to delay things by topping up on one more occasion. It was silly of me, but it was a coping mechanism. I haven't told anyone else until now! So please don't laugh or think badly of me! Anyway, Rachel kindly took charge of the transfer to another provider. She brought my new SIM for me. She also arranged a new tariff. And, prior to her going away with work, I had to take advantage of her presence by asking her also to set it up. This she did last Friday. Today, though, is the day the big change takes place. My old phone no longer works and I'm just waiting now for the new one to start functioning. As I need it for work, I can't really risk not having it alive and well, so to speak. But what if I can't work out what I need to do? What if I press the wrong button and delete something essential? What if there's something wrong with it and it actually doesn't work at all? All these possible scenarios have been running through my mind all morning. At some point today, I have to take that plunge again. That leap of faith and confidence. That focused decision to regain control – or at least to try and do so. It shouldn't be this difficult. It shouldn't even be something to worry about. But it is. On both accounts. Please wish me luck!

Tuesday 26th July 2016
Well, I managed it. Though nerves threatened to get the better of me at one point, I eventually pushed myself to turn my new mobile on. I wasn't entirely sure what I was looking at when I'd done this, mind you, but the appearance of the more obvious signs quickly began to offer a modicum of comfort. It's a sign of the times, and a testament to the fact that most people these days seem to have phones of this type, that my instruction pamphlet didn't even include some of the most basic features. I guess it just assumes that people already know! There was nothing, for example, on how to switch your phone onto silent. Or to tell you how to get to the main page from standby. Luckily, I could just ask Lesley! What is simply a matter of course for the majority, could have become a major stumbling block for dinosaurs like me.

I've decided to explore just a few things at a time, to set myself mini-targets in the overall goal of securing mastery over this new technology. That way, I don't set myself up to fail. I get quick wins. I feel competent and in control. And, most importantly of all, I don't panic. Generally speaking, I find that this methodology does work. It's what I did when first confronted with Office 365 as part of my Holocaust Memorial Day Trust induction, for example. It comes from a simple premise. That to attempt to do too much too quickly only leads to confusion and frustration. For a depressive, that can be calamitous. It can also be decisive. It could, for instance, lead you to give up altogether, to decide that you're never going to be able to understand what is required, so there is no point going any further. How many times have I been in this situation? I hate to think. Once bitten, twice shy, so the saying goes. It requires a tremendous effort to return to something that's already beaten you once. Your mindset is conditioned to defeat, to failure. You have to work tremendously hard to overturn this. It's not easy, and it often requires the input and encouragement of others. I'm fortunate in the one sense in that I don't tend to let go of a problem. It can – and often does – however, lead me into the realms of paranoia. I get so preoccupied at overcoming one hurdle at any cost that I don't always recognise what I'm doing to myself and to others as a result. I become fixated. Consumed by the recognition that unless I achieve what I've set out to do, I'm a complete failure. It's that 'all or nothing' mentality that is another key depression thinking trap. There are times when I've lost my temper, shouted at the people around me, made them angry and wary, turned them away, isolated myself, all because I want to do one simple thing that has held me up. When I realise what I've done – and it takes a while to truly register – I recoil in horror. Was it really worth it to alienate family, friends and allies? No, of course it wasn't. I never meant to, of course. But if I go too far down a solitary path which allows little deviation other than to turn around completely, I have to see it out, irrespective of the cost. I can't admit defeat. To do so would be to admit that I'm useless. It's a Catch 22 situation. Because, in the cold light of day, I feel just as bad if not worse as a result of the path I've already trodden! I lose far more than I gain.

Wednesday 27th July 2016

Sometimes I think my social skills have actually hit rock bottom. Last night was a case in question. Lesley's parents came over for tea and stayed the rest of the evening. As they have now moved to a new place not far from us, we've seen a lot more of them recently. They're lovely people and I get on well with them.

I always have done. Good company. Very easy-going. It's always good to see them. But – and there has to be a 'but' – I just find the whole dynamic, the changed dynamic that is, really challenging. I've said this before, and of course it's not them at all. Far from it. It's actually anybody, even my own kids. What it boils down to is that I find conversation not just difficult, but frightening and even irritating. Talking doesn't just weary me, it annoys me and it scares me. So many times, I almost resent anybody being near me, not because of who they are, but because of what it makes me feel about myself. I don't count Lesley and Elliot in that bracket. Or even Joel now he's been here for a while. With them, I don't have to make an effort. I can actually be silent, alone with my own thoughts, saying the odd thing now and again. But for people I'm not used to, irrespective of how close they are to me, their presence makes me realise that I'm isolated and that it's all of my own making. Or rather, it's what depression has made me become. Because the fault, the cause, lies in my own mental illness. I wish I could describe more fundamentally and accurately what goes through my head. Firstly, I must mention the physical effort. To string a sentence together becomes a task of monumental proportions. Every single word acts like a weight. Every one carries with it a consequence, a draining effect, a physical exertion. It's probably why I tend to speak more silently when in that position. I equate quietness with conserving energy. (But then I often have to repeat myself because I'm inaudible and that takes even more out of me!) I also have this doubt that anything I actually say is of relevance. It's general chit chat. That's the problem. Talking about important and weighty matters isn't so much of an issue. The mundane I see as being pointless. If I could rely on gestures and facial expressions, I will. But even they have a cost when it comes to my sapping energy levels. But it's much more than this. I can find human interaction an intimidating prospect. I think I'm in the firing line. I overthink, if I'm honest. I believe that everyone is scrutinising me. It's like my whole being is on trial. It's not that I don't know what to say, it's what it may lead others to think that's the pertinent issue. The pressure is intolerable. It becomes a physical sensation. I can actually feel it rising inside me. Like a kettle about to boil. Like compressed air about to explode. I crave protection. The release that comes with solitude. The nearest equivalent that I can think of in 'ordinary' life is the interview. For a brief period of time, you're under a microscope. Everything you say or do is being assessed. And for every second of its duration. You finish with a sigh of relief, out of shot of course, and then you realise that you're physically and mentally drained.

I only hope that people don't think badly of me. I pray also that people realise that it's not anything that they have done or are for usually there is nothing about their character or persona that leads me to think in these ways. Of course we all have mannerisms that can irritate others. But they don't necessarily constitute dislike. We may get annoyed, but at the aspect of character, not at the person. And in any case, it's precisely those mannerisms that comprise a person's individuality. It's what makes them interesting. No, the problem is me. I love my family, I love my friends. I just can't handle situations that I can't control, situations that have boundaries that are either unknown or outside my influence. This may involve time. If I know that people are around for a fixed period. An hour, for example. I can deal with that. I can pace myself. I can keep a level of self-control because I know there's a definitive end. There are other peculiarities that also constitute something certain, something unconditional. It could be the subject of the conversation, for instance. It could be the distraction provided by an activity. Even of something on the television. These things help me to shape my involvement in such a way that I can cope. But where there is nothing. When everything is free. Then the alarm bells start ringing.

Thursday 28th July 2016

Ever since I completed yesterday's entry, I've been terrified that I may somehow be misinterpreted.

I can't rid my mind of the thought that just one person may think that I was being critical of someone other than me. For a while I considered changing what I put. However, I came to the conclusion that as it was an honest appraisal of my situation and that my intention not to blame anyone else was clear, I should leave it as it is.

Of course, I'm now scared of what I decided. Rumination has set in once more. All I can do, I think, is reiterate the fact that my reaction to being around people that I love, whoever it may be, is entirely dependent on my own mental state and that, more often than not, depression plays a significant part because it serves to isolate me. No-one else does this. I could even say that I don't do this. It's depression acting. If it can talk, it can certainly act. I don't want to withdraw into myself. I don't want to tear myself away from anybody. I don't want to be lonely. I certainly don't want to feel pressurised and estranged because of who is around me. But depression is a powerful thing. It becomes overbearing, difficult if not impossible to overcome and to dominate. It's always there. It never goes away. All that changes is my own capacity to deal with it. And when I'm in a group of people – it doesn't matter who they are – it seems to come alive a bit more. It reasserts its power and its impact. Like a pervasive cancer, it slowly but surely smothers every other conscious aspect of thinking and feeling. I would go so far as to say that it feeds on human interaction. It detects the first inklings of panic and stress and then begins to devour one's inner resolve, one's composure, one's security. It's one of the most destructive elements in the entire arsenal that is depression. Because it acts at a time of need. I need people around me. I especially need the support and love of those closest to me. I'm so scared that I may turn people away. It's unbearable. It really is.

There must have been a time once, when I revelled in the company of others. When there was no automatic panic button. When I sought interaction. When I enjoyed interaction. When I came alive as a result of interaction. When I wanted to participate and contribute in that interaction. When I felt good about myself as a result of interaction.

Sadly, I can't now recall when all that was ever the case. I simply can't remember being and feeling in such ways. I must have been a different person then. Or perhaps I've always been this way. I simply don't know any more.

Friday 29th July 2016

I suspect I may be slipping into another depressive episode. I've thought this for a couple of days now and whilst I'm still uncertain as to whether this is the case – or whether It's just a minor down period – there are enough evident signs for me to be wary. Certainly, I feel increasingly pressurised without necessarily being able to pinpoint a tangible source. I also sense that element of fear that usually accompanies a significant bout. I'm less certain about what I'm doing and feel a greater need for reassurance. Most ominously though is that move towards self-withdrawal. At the moment, I'd probably describe this as 'uncomfortable' rather than anything else. It's certainly not alarming as such, but as soon as the sensation turns in that direction, I'll know I'm in trouble.

I have wondered about whether I'm experiencing some form of mid-life crisis. Indeed, I've done a little bit of digging into this on the Internet this morning. It's a much-used term, but I'm not convinced that it's actually widely understood. After reading around the subject, I'm not really any the wiser myself! Part of the problem would appear to be the fact that its symptoms, its articulations if you like, actually constitute my major mental illnesses. If depression is a common characteristic, perhaps even its most manifest, how on earth am I supposed to distinguish between its everyday expression (my normal life) and its new and accompanying by-product? If self-judgement is also evident but that is part of my routine composition, how am I able to know where the boundaries or parameters are between the norm and the exceptional? The simple answers to these questions – and there are a number of others as well – are 'I can't' or 'I'm not'. These are some of the most worrying aspects of depression or mental illness in general. If part of your everyday life, it can – and does – mask the onset of other severe illnesses. If you have a headache all the time, how are you in a position to know whether you may have a brain tumour? It's a similar analogy.

There are some apparent aspects of mid-life crises that don't seem entirely relevant. I have absolutely no desire to reassert my youthfulness by trying to be something I'm evidently not, for example. I don't crave for a younger body or to relive my past in a sexual sense. I realise my limitations and the fact that I'm not the man I once was physically. But whether a concern about my physical health, a worry about the physical consequences of my mental state, equate to the same thing, I have my doubts. What I do know is that I'm living a lot more of my life in the past. I have flashbacks. I have regrets. I don't always look forward with any degree of surety or confidence. Some of this I can't control. My dreams, or should I say my 'night terrors' are a case in point. In addition, these have also been aspects of my depression for a long time. I'm constantly wishing that I could undo the mistakes I've made. I'm always critical of what I did as well as what I am. I seem to harbour a wish to punish myself, without it being a conscious reality – if that makes sense. I don't want to, but I can't stop myself. I guess I'll see how it goes. If things become unbearable, my symptoms more severe, even critical, I'll have to seek help. I've done it before and I've come through it before. I can do it again.

Saturday 30th July 2016
Another day, and sadly, another step downwards in my descent into severe depression. Though I'm still not certain that I'm going to continue in that direction, my optimism is dwindling literally as I write. Last night was agonising. The time seemed to drag. I had little enthusiasm or motivation for doing anything other than sitting in my chair watching the cricket. The more I watched, the

less engaged I became, until at one stage it became simply a blur of activity, people in different coloured kits running around hitting or chasing a white ball in reckless but illogical abandon. I no longer had any interest but I couldn't even energise myself into changing channels. And it was Yorkshire too! That made my disinclination to enthuse even worse!

I really don't like myself at the moment. I know that's part of the depression, but it's no less palpable a feeling in itself. Not only do I consider myself useless and pathetic, it seems as if I'm deliberately making myself be these things. I know full well, if I try to be rational, that this is a fundamental element of my mental state. It's my illness that's at fault here. It's depression that is driving such feelings into a state that is actually the truth, not a belief. But I can't divorce the illness from myself. I can't accept that it's depression that lies at the heart of things. It's so difficult to explain. All I seem to do is accuse myself of neglect, of selfishness, of disinterest, of apathy. I've become these things because of me. It's my mind that I've let depression control. It's my body that I've allowed to be consumed with illness. It's all my fault because I'm weak.

Somehow, in writing this words, I've got to reassert at least a semblance of reason. I've got to force myself, tell myself and convince myself that depression is alive and kicking inside me. That I'm locked in a fight for control with something that is real. Something that is physical and substantial. Something that is not a figure of my imagination. It's about recognising the fact that my companion throughout my life, that thing inside me called depression, is actively working against all conscious and subconscious activity at the moment. That it's become large and looming, that it's spreading its tentacles into areas that often lie inert and unfeeling, that it's threatening to dominate in a way that pushes all efforts at resistance to one side.

It's strange that I can write these words without necessarily acknowledging them to be valid. But that's depression as well.

Sunday 31st July 2016

There haven't been many occasions during the course of writing this diary when I've been struggling for something to say. In fact, I can't remember any off the top of my head. But today is definitely one. Even though yesterday turned out to be OK – certainly not as bad as I was expecting when I began writing twenty-four hours ago – the overall prognosis remains the same. I tried really hard to put on a brave face – or at least a cheerful one – but inside the demons I recognise well are at work. I guess it's something to cling on to that I was able to defy myself outwardly, engage in conversation, even take a trip out for a coffee with Lesley and Elliot. That at least gives me some hope that the precipice into which I know I'm falling may not be as deep as ones I've experienced in the past. I may still be able to arrest my fall. But I have a large and growing weight on my shoulders. A weight that slowly but surely is sapping ounce by proverbial ounce of energy, confidence, determination and self-respect. I'm tired. Physically drained, but mentally expended. I'll continue to fight. That's in my nature. But as I do so, it's hard not to register the fact that I'm a David that's growing smaller and weaker whilst my Goliathan adversary is recruiting allies on all sides. What I have to keep reminding myself is that David ultimately won.

August

Monday 1st August 2016

The start of the new month brings with it both Luke's twenty-eighth birthday and Yorkshire Day. What a day to have been born! How envious am I? No doubt festivities will be forthcoming in one flat in north London as well as in a whole English county. As for me, I've tried this morning to knuckle down to work, in the hope that it offers some distraction for my feeble and troubled mind. I've got quite a bit done, if I'm honest with myself. What it hasn't resulted in though, is any sense of internalised self-fulfilment. I can't seem to recognise that tasks completed are any form of achievement. Maybe that will come through completing this diary entry? Or doing some exercise this afternoon? I have to look at gaining some small wins, in the hope that their gradual accumulation will help aid or at least trigger my recovery. I guess the very fact that I'm still able to think logically in these ways is a positive sign. I'm thinking of helping myself. I'm trying to help myself. I want to help myself. I haven't given in. I'm not at the stage where I have to admit defeat. Yet. Maybe I won't reach it. Who knows? All I do know is that if that time comes, it's not the end of the world. My resistance may be non-existent at that point. I may have to put my hands up and start the process of conserving energy for a time – which will come – when I'll be able to start pulling in the right direction. It's a bit like breaking a limb. For a while you have to accept the fact that whether it's an arm or a leg, it will be in plaster. Your body is naturally fighting the injury without your conscious effort. You can't do anything else other than rest and let nature do its work. Your mind is like that at the bottom of a depressive trough. It's hurting. It's tired. It's broken. But somewhere inside you, something is stirring. The body's powers of recovery have been called for and they are beginning to have an impact. It may be slow. But it's happening. The physical as well as mental process whereby you begin to come out of depression has started. You are not aware of this, until you begin, slowly, gradually, to recognise some signs. Then – and only then – can you consciously and deliberately begin to steer your ship forwards.

In the meantime, I'm persevering. I'm still here. I'm still standing. I'm trying hard to avoid the heavyweight blows that have already started to come my way. One thing is sufficient perhaps to illustrate my point. Appointments, whether they be work or household related, offer some sense of correlation to the idea of a punch. They have to be negotiated, but I find them much more difficult to address when I'm low. All that they entail becomes a potential problem. Even getting to where I need to be weighs worryingly on my mind. What usually is easily overcome suddenly becomes a challenge. What I would normally find hard is elevated to realms of difficulty out of all proportion to its typical state of being. What I habitually would register as difficult turns into an impossibility. And so on and so forth. Life, basically, becomes more trying. There are hurdles around every corner. I feel like Indiana Jones trying doggedly to reach his holy grail. There are arrows flying at him, swords and other weapons waiting to cut him in half. He has to step carefully to avoid falling to his doom. A giant stone ball is hurtling in his general direction. And at the end, he must make a leap of faith, to step on an invisible bridge not knowing if his eyes or his mind are deceiving him. It's not a bad analogy, now I think about it!

Tuesday 2nd August 2016

I've just returned from helping to deliver a focus group on advance planning and mental health. It went well, I think. It's difficult to gauge when you're feeling depression more acutely, as I am at the moment. People said nice things, particularly about my contribution, which focused on my own experiences and how I believed that it was important to take advantage of opportunities to plan ahead. When all is said and done, people do appreciate a personal perspective and to those who also have an intense relationship with mental illness, to hear it talked about, described and articulated by someone like themselves, can serve as an uplifting boost to morale. It means that you're not alone. That what you go through is not unique. That you can share aspects of experience that you may otherwise be reluctant to divulge. That there is no such thing as a no-go area.

It did give me a boost, but already, only two hours on, those positive feelings are beginning to wane. One thing that has been satiated though is my nervous state. I knew it would happen, but from yesterday evening onwards I began to experience real anxieties about doing the group. I foresaw problems. I anticipated issues. I predicted disaster. No matter what I did to try and forestall their onset, thinking traps galore abounded. Whether it be looming catastrophe, all or nothing thinking, expecting the negative and such like, I couldn't keep their sharp claws away from grabbing a hold of my belief systems, and conscious energies. It didn't help that I was already in a bad state of mind. Yesterday just seemed to be a day to endure, to get through as best I can. Every stage brought with it seemingly insurmountable obstacles. I couldn't even get the washing in without it becoming a drama. The final straw probably came when, as part of my new role, I was trying to draft an email to people already accustomed to Holocaust Memorial Day. It was my first one to a mass audience in this guise, and the pressure therefore seemed that bit more exacting. Already, my perfectionist tendencies were working overtime. I not only had to get the grammar and punctuation spot on, I had to ensure that there was consistency in line spacing, that writing in bold and underlined was sparingly but appropriately used, that my headings made sense and were free from any ambiguity. All in all, it became not an exercise in communication so much as a test of my mental ability to endure self-inflicted pressure. It was a test that I set myself up to fail. And I did. When I couldn't seem to get the bullet points to space properly, I ended up banging away at the keys, starting passages again and again as if that would resolve the issue. For some unaccountable reason, one – just one – of a series of points wouldn't fit into the system I had devised. I was petrified that in my efforts to put an end to this campaign against a relatively unimportant aspect of presentation, I would end up accidentally sending the message out before I'd finished work on it. That somehow, my anxiety and temper would transfer to the message itself. That recipients would, as a consequence, consider me strange, irrational, someone not to be trusted, and – calamity of calamities – imperfect. Eventually everything got on top of me and I ended up self-harming. I whacked both sides of my head with my open hands so hard that I was momentarily stunned. It did serve to shock me out of my trauma, to re-open channels of communication, to let some reason into a mind disturbed and befuddled. But at what cost? I was able to finish the email and send it off. That was the immediate task. But afterwards? I felt awful. My head was spinning, my mind was still reeling. I'd consumed so much nervous energy that all I could do was try to stay still and recuperate. Gradually, slowly but still pointedly, things began to become clearer. I calmed down. I eased off. I let things go. I became stable and functional once more. And all because of a bullet point!

Wednesday 3rd August 2016
As soon as I came downstairs this morning I was confronted by my first worry of the day. Millie, usually at her most lively when

she first sets eyes on you, was sat on the window seat not moving with a dental stick lying by her side. I tried to entice her to eat it, but she wasn't at all interested. Moments later Lesley – at the University for an exam – rang me to ask if she was OK. By that time, Millie had got to her feet and was relieving herself in the garden, so all looked well. I didn't want to worry her – she's enough to think about – so I relayed the message that all looked fine. But there's obviously something wrong. As I write, she's sitting at my feet, not wanting to move away. She's a very loyal as well as loving dog, but this isn't normal for her. Yesterday she had one of those days when she couldn't stop eating. Normally, she doesn't have the largest of appetites, but there are occasions when she just blitzes on food. I now wonder whether she's suffering from some sort of stomach ache. It's the most logical explanation. Of course, being me, logic doesn't always translate into reason and consequently relevant understanding and action. I can't focus on the most feasible solution to the conundrum. I have to look elsewhere. I have to catastrophize. I'm now worrying intensely as to whether there's something more serious at play here. But I'm powerless. I can't decide what I should do, so I'm trying to wait it out – if that's the correct terminology! Lesley will be home by lunchtime. She'll know what to do. She'll look at things reasonably and coherently. She'll come to a decision based on fact and common sense. I don't like delegating or devolving responsibility, but within my mind, I'm confused and anxious. I know I won't be able to cope if I decide to act. So I'm forcing myself to wait. And it hurts.

If only there was something that would ease my troubled mind. I really want to shut down. To rewire the connections inside my head, to give them a chance to start working again, but in a positive sense, in an alleviating fashion. Working for me rather than against me. If I was a computer, I'd rid myself of all existing data, go back to factory mode, reboot and restart. I even think I would risk ridding myself of all the knowledgeable elements to my brain, all the elements that make up past experience and present character, all the things that, in essence, comprise me. At this moment, I'd gladly sacrifice them for a chance to have a pain-free existence. However, not only is that impossible, I'm sufficiently engaged to realise that such a sacrifice would rid me of things that I can and do use in a more constructive and encouraging sense. My beliefs, my standpoints, my skills, my talents, my hobbies, my ability to help others, my inclinations, my determinations. And so on and so forth. They all come with the territory just as much as depression and mental illness. Moreover, I wouldn't be able to use my mental state, my past predicaments, my present context, my future concerns as an aid to others in similar circumstances, people who – unlike me – are not as open, people who still feel the need to hide and to deny. That, I think, would be a loss. Certainly to me. And I hope to them. It's an academic argument anyway. It's hypothetical. It's a veritable 'what if?' And I have to deal with 'what is'.

Thursday 4th August 2016

I seem, yet again, to be in the mental health equivalent of 'no man's land'. I'm really not sure where I am – and more importantly, where I'm going. On the one hand, I'm dealing quite well with everyday issues to do with communication in particular. I haven't withdrawn into my shell. I'm even able to share a joke and have a laugh on occasions. I certainly don't feel the inclination to not engage with people. I can talk. I don't feel the usual sense of talking being a real physical effort. In these respects, things are carrying on in a relatively 'normal' fashion. And yet there are times, when alone, when I either want to cry or scream in frustration. There are also occasions when I feel I can't move from the situation I'm in to the next thing. Any sense of 'looking forward' to anything has gone. I can't see any proper horizon, any ultimate goal, any future context in which I'll be able to say 'I've made it'. Endurance remains the name of the game. Sheer doggedness is the quality I need to have. An easy barometer is the fact that this time next week, we'll be on holiday in Paris. I should be excited, you may think. I should at least see an end to this mini-chapter in my life. Holidays are things to look forward to. They are what they are – a break, a treat, a change. And yet, I can't say that I see going away as anything different to what I'm currently doing to tackle life. In other words, moving from one context onto another without any respite, without any sense of alteration. Something again to endure. Hopefully, when I'm there, there will be a difference. All my powers of recovery and self-sustainment have to be focused on reaching next Wednesday without a disaster. I have to believe that I will gain something positive, mentally, from the realisation that I'll be away from the normal pressures of life. Of course, the other side of my brain, the more dominant side at the minute, keeps telling me that there will also be pressures in going away, that there will be obstacles, just different ones. As usual, the battle is within me. I can only do so much. I can influence what I do and how I go about attacking my illness, addressing my predicament, but I can't determine what will happen. Depression is too strong to be willed away, irrespective of the force of that will.

Friday 5th August 2016

This afternoon I have an appointment at the Sleep Laboratory at the General Hospital. I can't put it off, much as I'd like to, because I've already been told if I ask to rearrange again, I'll lose my place on the list and will therefore have to be re-referred. I couldn't face going to my original appointment a few weeks back. I can't remember exactly why. I think it was a combination of hot, humid nights and my thinking that my sleep patterns wouldn't be normal coupled with that old chestnut of having to face something new and unusual. Anyway, I didn't go, but now I have to. I've done all my preparations. I've worked out where I need to go, which car park I need to use, which entrance to the complex I need to go through, who I need to ask for, what information I need to take, what forms I need to complete. I know what they're going to do to me. I'll have something called an oximeter placed on one of my fingers to measure oxygen levels and my pulse. I'll have a belt around my middle which will contain another form of recording device. I'll have two bands around my waist and chest and lastly, an airflow monitor beneath my nostrils. They've given me the choice of either having them insert all this at the hospital or leaving me with the instructions necessary for me to do it myself later. I can't make up my mind what to do. I guess my inclination is towards the former. At least that way I'll know the job has been done properly. I just hope it won't be too uncomfortable. It's funny how the thought of a disrupted night's sleep seems to be alarming rather than inconvenient. Again, I know I'm making a mountain out of a mole hill, but what I detect and feel inside my head is fear rather than anything else.

But fear of what? Of diagnosis? I don't think it's that. Sleep apnoea is apparently not as unusual as you might think. And if that's what I have, in comparison to all my other ailments, it's a relatively minor thing. If resulting treatment has some impact on my night terrors then that's good of course. But I can't help thinking that what I go through so often during my sleep is nothing to do with anything physical. It all relates to my mental state and my ongoing mental illness. So if it's not potential diagnosis, what is it? Maybe it's just the prospect of having to deal with something new? Maybe it's the thought that what happens afterwards may affect some sort of change? If truth be told, as long as my dreams aren't frightening and dangerous, I don't mind that sense of vivid reality that they bring. There are times – and I know I've said this before – when what I go through in the night time hours is much more real and meaningful an experience than what I undergo during the course of a waking day. I don't want to lose that. I don't think I do anyway. But as usual, in this instance, you can't have the smooth without the rough. If this is another example of making me stable. If what comes out of this is analogous with the impact of medication, of ensuring that my graphic pattern is less extreme, more straight line, less peaks and troughs, then I'll be one more step towards becoming the robot, the zombie that is increasingly less imaginative, less potential and more conceivable, more actual. Life will become even more routinized. It may be less dramatic. It may be easier to withstand, but life is for living, isn't it? Can't I at least have some element of what other people have? Can't I hope for enjoyment and pleasure? Even some excitement? I don't want it all. Just a glimpse every now and again, to keep me going. That's not too much to ask, is it?

Saturday 6th August 2016

There were times yesterday when it truly felt like Armageddon. It was the worse day I've had for quite a while. Even as I was writing yesterday's diary entry, things had already started to go wrong. The Internet wasn't working and Microsoft Outlook refused to open. My remedy, as always, was simply to turn everything off and then on again. Whilst this seemed to rectify matters when it came to the web, Outlook stubbornly refused to budge. I left to go to John's Social Media Café and then to keep my appointment at the General Hospital, hoping beyond hope that on my return a miracle of miracles would have occurred and everything would be alright again. No such luck. The same message flashed up on my screen. The next two hours now seem a bit like a blur. Lesley, bless her, tried to resolve things by phoning a help desk and following directions. But no matter what we tried, the situation, if anything, seemed to deteriorate. I was watching my entire working life dissolve into shreds and then nothing in front of my very eyes. The software we were using seemed to change what I was expecting to see. No longer did the familiar signs, the normal pages, the usual procedures come up and take place automatically. Instead, I was constantly faced with new directions, new formats, updated programmes, all the things that serve to instantly send me into a state of panic. I started to cry. I lost all semblance of composure. I catastrophized. I could see myself having to give up work entirely simply because I had lost vital information. What I couldn't see was any way around my predicament. Outlook seemed to have vanished entirely and with it all my contacts, all my working calendar entries, all my current emails and the threads of conversations that I'd already saved for the reason that they were important. Lesley tried so hard to reassure me. She kept saying that she would deal with it, but she hadn't the time at that moment. She was having a well-deserved evening out with a friend so I couldn't detain her. There was no way I could let her go with a shadow over her head. But I couldn't calm down. Whilst all this was going on, we were having some work done on our boiler, work that, as it transpired, actually culminated in the bloody thing shutting down. What more could go wrong?

I had to take some Diazepam. It was the only way I could come close to dealing with the situation. It took some time to kick in, but as Lesley was about to leave, I felt the fuzziness begin to embrace my battered mind. I became docile, floppy and pliable. The fear and agitation went to be replaced by sensations akin to the early signs of alcohol intake. I couldn't fight anymore. I'd given in. Or rather the drug had caused my submission. I'd become weary. Everything around me was hazy. I couldn't focus. I couldn't remember what I was supposed to be doing. Probably a good thing in the cold light of day. Elliot had to help me cook the tea, or to be exact, decipher and coordinate the oven timings. At one point, I couldn't even turn the channel over on the telly. It was like trying to deal with a delicate matter requiring meticulous preparation, steady hands, deep concentration and focus whilst standing on a skateboard or the deck of a ship in stormy waters. The more you tried to put your mind to it, the greater the ferocity of the elements, the more the wind blew, the greater the speed of your journey, the more precarious your footing. I had to shut myself down. It was the only way. Even, during the course of the evening, when something came into my head that threatened to begin the descent into anxiety and fear, it quickly evaporated into memory, like a moment that was gone forever. How I managed to wire myself up with all the equipment I received from the Sleep Laboratory, I really don't know! Having taken it all back this morning, I'm half expecting to receive a call sometime soon to tell me either that nothing registered or that I technically died during the night. At the start of the day, dealing with this was at the forefront of my mind, but as it turned it, it was relegated to a relatively peripheral role in my veritable 'dies irae'[30]

I often wonder what I have done to deserve the misfortune that seems to come my way. Of course, in saying this, it has to be recognised that when I'm ill – and often when I'm not – I undoubtedly elevate all problems, all negative circumstances, all tight situations, all mistakes, all hindrances, to catastrophic status. It's a question of relativity, when it comes down to it. But in a sense, it doesn't matter how others may feel about these things. It doesn't change the fact that I see them in their worst possible light. I only see disaster. It's my health that I resent. Or rather, it's the impact of my health conditions that I see in this way. I seem to accumulate one thing after another. And whilst they may not always be draconian or life-threatening, in my mind they are. Depression actually is this, it has to be said. It's every bit as impactful as the worst possible cancer. Or it can be, at its most severe. But when you start to add up everything else that revolves around that one illness, that one disability, it just increases the burden that you feel you have to carry. Sleep apnoea – if I have it – on its own is perfectly manageable. Or so it would seem. But when it becomes another adversary for an already feeble and deteriorating body and mind, an add-on to an already long list of afflictions and symptoms, it could be the proverbial straw that breaks the camel's back.

The one thing that I have to be grateful for is that yesterday ended and today comes anew.

Sunday 7th August 2016

I don't think there's any doubt now that I'm in the grips of another depressive episode.

The last couple of days have shown me sufficient evidence to dispel any lasting hesitation or uncertainty. The one saving grace is that I know I've not reached the depths of one of its troughs. Therefore, I'm capable of fighting back using my own inbuilt resilience and determination. These attributes may be low, but they are there. And I have to use them. Of course, it's not that simple. Words do not do justice to the battle I have ahead of me. But whilst I have the capacity to realise that I face that challenge and that I have some resources with me and inside me, I remain afloat – just!

It may be interesting – and valuable for me – to outline what those ingredients for battle actually are. What are the weapons I will use? What are the tactics I need to employ?

The answer to these questions may surprise you, because they are actually everyday items, things that a non-depressive probably takes for granted as simple aspects of living. I'm referring to doing small jobs, spending brief periods of time working, using up what energy I have doing short bursts of exercise. I will read. I will watch television. I will listen to music. Not for long. Just until I start to lose concentration. Just until the time comes when I consider what I'm doing to be pointless. Just until they become – literally – a waste of time. I will make myself, and others, cups of tea. I will do my own lunch. I will put some washing on. I will hang up items on the clothes line. I will wipe the surfaces in the kitchen. I will put something back that has been left out. I will feed Millie. I will take her onto the green for ten minutes. I will venture down to the local store for some milk. I will send a couple of routine emails. I will make the beds. I'll put clothes away. I'll tidy up the cushions on the chairs. You get the picture.

Doing these things is not an automatic process, as is usually the case. They become more onerous tasks. Because they require motivation and a sense of self-will. Because they necessitate my moving from a chair. Because in my mind I'm telling myself that they don't matter. Because that part of me that is depression is urging me not to answer my own calls to action. This is the most illustrative example of actions speaking louder than words. I have, in effect, to act myself out of depression. Doing these things will make a difference. It won't be apparent straight away. Indeed, it will take all my resolve to prompt and push myself into activity. But every time I do so is to confront my demons. To stand up to their bullying nature. To say that I'm still fighting. And if I succeed, my mind will start to believe once more that I have a future that is worth living.

Monday 8th August 2016

It's a sign of my mental state at the moment that I haven't yet mentioned the fact that the new football season started this past weekend. Given the way the last one ended – with Millwall's defeat in the Play-Off Final, if you remember – and what I deliberated over in terms of my future relationship with the sport, it's probably not a bad thing that I've downplayed its launch. Indeed, I would go so far as to say that I can't remember ever feeling this disconnected from, and unenthused over, our national game. When I was a kid, especially, August was a wonderfully exciting time. Summer holidays, no school, the dying embers of the cricket season, endless days of laziness and sunshine and then, shirt-sleeved crowds full of anticipation and yearning, new kits, new signings, a new optimism would greet the beginning of yet another season-long vigil. I would eagerly count the days down. I couldn't wait for it to start. I would badger my Dad about which games we would take in. Who are Leeds playing first? Will we get off to a flyer? When does the League Cup start? Is it our year? Can I have the new shirt for my birthday? Do I prefer the home or the away one? Usually, by the third or fourth week, it began to settle down. It wouldn't take long for the realisation to dawn that the best we could hope for was mid-table mediocrity.

But this year? Millwall have started well. Leeds predictably have not. But the whole thing seems very distant. I've bought my Millwall Members Card. This was more an automatic gesture than a conscious decision. If I'd thought about it too hard, I guess there was more than a strong chance that I wouldn't have bothered. But I have, so I need now to run with it. My goal though, is not to get so worked up about what happens. I need to adopt the mantle that football fans the nation over cling to when they think about Wembley. 'Que sera sera, whatever will be, will be'. Fate combined with circumstances outside my control, will determine what happens to Millwall, Leeds and my other favourites. I can support, I can sing, I can shout, I can gesture, but I can't make any one of the many squad members who pull on the hallowed shirt either put the ball in the opponents net, or keep it out of ours. It's not my fault if we lose. It's not down to my presence if we win. I'm a relatively meaningless and powerless cog in a large wheel that turns. Where it goes, how fast it goes, whether it stops, whether it ploughs on. I can only watch and wait.

Tuesday 9th August 2016

I'm not sure how much more of this I can take at the moment. By this, I mean life. Everything I seem to touch somehow goes wrong and I can't – I just can't – believe that this is coincidence. It's me. It really is. It's as if my trepidation at dealing with life's nuances transfers itself by some form of human osmosis to anything I bring myself to touch and in particular, things that I need at a particular point in time. To bring you up to date with the saga of the boiler. It's still to be resolved. I've lost count of the number of excuses we've had to listen to. Every single person we deal with has a different story, a different explanation, a different remedy. I wouldn't mind the discrepancy between the first two as long as the last one actually worked. But it hasn't so far. We're due another visit from the company within the hour. Am I confident? Am I heck! The ironic thing is that our former boiler came with the house. It was probably over thirty years old and yet it never once showed any sign of wear and tear. And it certainly always worked.

It wasn't the boiler though that brought me to tears and cries of frustration this morning. It was something as innocuous as a battery charger. I've always used this thing to recharge the battery in my camera and though it's always been efficient, it's not the easiest or most logical piece of equipment to set up. It necessitates having to stand the battery on its end and grip it between two adjustable slots at exactly the right angle over the connection charge. When it works first time – as it did initially this morning – you think nothing of the potentially over-elaborate mechanism by which it operates. You just put it in and turn it on. Pure and simple. I left it to charge on my laptop desk, only to find within half an hour or so that Elliot had taken it off the surface and put it on the floor so that he could move and then use the desk for his own convenience. Of course, when I tried to get it to work again, it wouldn't. I began to curse Elliot. It wasn't his fault, but I just couldn't help myself. I took it downstairs to Lesley. Despite our combined efforts, we just couldn't remedy the matter. We started to adjust the settings without any real plan. It just seemed that moving them was the only logical explanation as to why it suddenly refused to work. By that time, I was in complete panic. If I couldn't get my battery to charge, I wouldn't have a camera. All of a sudden, that became the most important thing in the world. There would be no point in going on holiday without my ability to take photos. I might as well stay at home and stare at the walls. All those wildly illogical connections that lead to considered catastrophe began to work overtime. I couldn't leave it alone though. I had to keep trying, even if that meant increased desperation and irritation. Eventually I decided to take it to Curry's to ask them. Of course, no sooner had the technician had a look at it, he got it going! I'd been using the wrong points!! Despite my obvious relief, I felt such a fool. I also felt intensely deflated, worried beyond measure at the capacity of such a relatively minor thing to completely throw me sideways.

As I write this, I don't want to touch anything anymore. I'm convinced that I carry a curse, that the more I engage with life, the greater the chance that it will let me down. That I need protection, some form of temporary respite, a refuge perhaps. Anything that will channel my energies into something that doesn't have the potential to hit me back.

Perhaps what I actually need is a holiday? I hope so, because this time tomorrow we'll be on a plane at Luton Airport about to take off for Paris. A break will, I am sure, help in some way to restore at least some degree of confidence and assuredness.

But what I really need is a break from life. Or alternatively, a break from me. And neither of them are possible.

Wednesday 10th August 2016

Our summer holiday begins in a couple of hours time. I am looking forward to it. I think. But I have to negotiate all the travel arrangements before I can properly relax, and at the moment they are at the forefront of my mind. As is my custom, I've tried to be as thorough as possible by way of preparation. I know what we need to do when we land. Where to go for tickets. Where the trains depart for central Paris. How frequently they go. Where we need to get off. Which Metro line we then need to take. It's all down on paper. But, of course, the practice may be different from the planning. There are things that I'm not sure about. What the best method – and most cost effective – is in relation to getting around Paris during our stay. What to ask for as a result. And these things are weighing heavy inside my head. I can't do any more. I had to keep telling myself that yesterday. I've planned as much as I can. The rest is down to experience.

In a way I wish we were going either at the end or the beginning of the day rather than the middle. My reasoning – and it may well be suspect – is that negotiating all the stages that involve getting from airport to hotel would be a lot easier if there were fewer people about. Sometimes it's the pressure of people around me that conspire to elevate the challenge I face. If, for example, I'm at a ticket booth with a long queue behind me, I can sense people's eyes focused on me and what I'm doing. There's nowhere else to go. They want me out of the way so that they, themselves, can be served. Their impatience and their scrutiny are hard to handle. In the past I've sometimes deliberately waited until the flow of people slows down before even approaching someone for help. And then when you get on the bus or train and it's full, your whole demeanour as well as your actions seem to become the preserve of every single person in the compartment. I'm terrified that I'll do something to make people laugh or stare harder. Putting your luggage away on a rack or in a holding space. Getting to your seat without tripping over something or losing your balance. It all adds up.

One thing that did help me was a website that not only explained where to go at Charles de Gaulle Airport to catch your transfer train into the city, but actually showed you in up-to-date photographs what you need to negotiate. This was brilliant. I can't tell you how useful such a thing is. It put you at the scene. It explained the signs that you will see. It even highlighted what you need to look for on the photo. For someone with a mental illness, someone prone to panic – irrespective of the extent of preparation – a website such as this is a real godsend. Indeed, I would hazard a guess that whoever came up with the idea and whoever chose what to show had mental illness in mind. It's things like this that can make a real difference to people. I just wish that more organisations thought so clearly and comprehensively about the perils that people like me have to negotiate and then did something about it. It wouldn't take away completely the nerves and the anxiety. But it would certainly alleviate their harshest effects.

Thursday 11th August 2016

My worst fears came true. As soon as we landed, I went into panic mode. No matter how much I tried to control what was whirring around in my mind, nothing seemed to help. Charles de Gaulle Airport is huge. Irrespective of the fact that I knew what to look for, the simple reality of a plethora of signs, directions, information points, service areas and the like only served to bewilder me and hamper my attempts to negotiate a safe and easy path to our train. It was literally a case of too much information. Eventually we had to ask where to go to buy our tickets. I'd been told not to use the machines because a particular card was needed that wasn't dispensed from them. However, they all seemed to sell what we were after. So what to do? We were directed to a ticket hall, but rather than it proving to be the resolution to our quandary, it only increased my confusion and consternation, because what we were offered was a type of ticket/card that I hadn't even considered a possibility. It was cheaper. It was simpler. It included everything. But it wasn't on my radar and as a consequence, I couldn't deal with the decision we had to make. Lesley had to do it. She took charge whilst I dissolved into merciless self-recrimination and nervous paranoia. The issue was compounded by the fact that a photograph was needed to fully validate the card and the only machine we could find – after a walk to another terminal – worked for Lesley and me, but not for Elliot! After spending 15 Euros without an end result, we realised that we could simply ask the hotel to photocopy his passport photo and stick that on instead! For free! Oh the joys of a clear and logical mind.

The whole experience was intensely disturbing. It proved to me that no matter how much preparation I do, no matter how deep I delve into foreseeing problems, no matter how determined I am to forge my own path, there are times when circumstances combine to elevate depression to a level that it is hard even to realise. It dominates. It oversees everything. It is able to fight off all attempts to make it unsteady and less imperious. It can be controlled. But it takes time to do that, and if the situation dictates that you have no or little of that one precious commodity, you are relatively powerless and need the composure and practical assistance of people around you. Such was the case yesterday.

Friday 12th August 2016

I was able to put the anxieties of travelling behind me and enjoy yesterday, our first day in Paris. We did a lot, starting at the Place de la Concorde, and ending up in Le Marais, an evocative area of the capital, formerly the Jewish quarter, but one still resplendent with kosher shops, restaurants and the living presence of my religion.

Sadly, it also included many plaques that told the story of former residents, deported from their homes by the Nazis to end their lives across the continent. One – that commemorating the life of

Paulette Wajncwaig – was particularly hard to take. She was only one month old at the time of her detention and deportation.

Today we began at Sacre Coeur. Whilst I relied on the Funicular railway to negotiate the steep climb from the Metro station, Lesley and Elliot decided on the more physical option and walked. When we met up again at the top shortly after, it was clear that there was something wrong. On their way up the steps, both had been accosted by one of many young men trying to force tourists to buy their cheap wares. They had been grabbed by the arm and only after a strong rebuke was the grasp relinquished. For Lesley, all the painful memories of her ordeal last December – when she was attacked whilst taking Millie for a walk – came flooding back, as did the tears. Despite my informing the police, the same thing threatened to happen on the way back down. This time Elliot alone was their target. I flipped, angrily confronting the people in question, who, unbelievably, couldn't understand why I was so incensed. Nothing gives anyone the right to lay their hands on someone else in such a way as to intimidate and frighten them. Being able to at least make this point and to stand up to them made me feel a little better, because, truth be told, I felt that I had let Lesley and Elliot down by not being at their side previously. Why, oh why, had I decided to be lazy and use the railway? To me, those feelings of regret, remorse and inadequacy were my punishment for a dereliction of duty. I felt I had to suffer. To feel the consequences. I hadn't lived up to my responsibilities. I was probably being harsh on myself, but, to my mind, I deserved it.

Saturday 13th August 2016

I haven't started too many entries with these words, but what a wonderful day today has been! We made it to the top of the Eiffel Tower and were afforded the most marvellous views of Paris. Blue, cloudless, skies ensured that we had unhampered vision, and I took many a panoramic photo which, when I get home and put them onto my PC, should leave us with many enduring memories. It's funny though, but it wasn't what I could see looking out that left the most lasting impression. The genius that was the engineer and architect, Gustave Eiffel, not only had the power and presence of a superlative tower in mind when he was drawing up his plans. On a much more modest level, he incorporated for himself a small office, where not only could he meet business contacts, other clients and distinguished visitors, he could also be free from distraction and conduct further experiments. Not a surprise, you would think. But it was where it was that was the endearing factor. Right at the top. Eiffel obviously needed his own space and seclusion for work, but it is tempting to think that there may have been another factor. That he needed those same things for his peace of mind. I can't think of a better location for a bolt hole. I'd be tempted to live more than just a working day in such a place. Away from everything and everyone. Master of my own creation. Commander of my own space. Liberator from my own pressures, tensions and the strains of life.

We ended our day in a similar vein, this time by climbing the three hundred or so steps to the top of the Arc de Triomphe. Elliot was keen to go as dusk gave way to night and boy, was he right in his insistence. The magic of twilight and the serenity of darkness combined with artificial lights across the city to produce not only a visual sensation of some magnificence but also a sense of peaceful tranquillity. The Eiffel Tower was already light up, but on the hour, it transforms into a sparkling light show akin to the world's largest Christmas tree. However, for me it was the sense of proportion and power that emanated from the position of the arch, as a centrepiece for many avenues leading away in long straight lines – including of course, the Champs-Élysées – that caught my imagination. It reminded me of my childhood fascination with Napoleon and his military victories, the reason, of course, for its construction in the first place. The other thing that I found much more poignant and a cause for reflection was the tomb of the unknown soldier of the Great War and its memorial flame, a reminder that militarism has its consequences, many of them fatal.

Sunday 14th August 2016

Today was another day for the most thoughtful of contemplation. We visited Paris' excellent Holocaust Museum in the morning before I left the other two to make my way alone to Drancy, the sight of a large transit camp for Jewish prisoners during the Nazi genocide. There's definitely a limit to the extent to which most people can endure tales of prejudice, persecution and mass murder. However, for me, with my long-standing interest in the Holocaust, my toleration levels are set at a much different measure. When I'm away on my own in November – as I intend to be again this year – my whole trip is focused around visiting places of significance to former Jewish communities as well as sites at which their subjugation, deportation and death became fact. I can deal with that. I do deal with that. I'm not always sure how I do, but I do. I'm on my own wavelength. I'm beset with my own ambitions. I'm ready to deal with the challenges that come my way. I'm in a phase of mind that is quite particular. In a word, I'm prepared. Such was my state of mind as I negotiated the suburban Paris bus system to eventually find myself at a memorial site in front of what is, truth be told, a fairly typical housing development. Drancy was always this. It had been built as a vast horseshoe-shaped complex for people to live in relatively cheap apartments and it resorted to the same once the Holocaust was over. For a short period of time though, it became the last fixed abode in their country of birth for fully 65,000 French Jews, living in cramped, dirty and inhumane conditions prior to their deportation eastwards across Europe. It seems disturbing to think that people now live where all this horror once was an aspect of life. But the fact remains that people don't really choose to live here. Their poverty dictates where they live and how they live. Somehow, they have to force the past from their minds and focus only on the demands of the present. When you are, socio-economically, near the bottom of the ladder, this isn't as difficult to do as one may think. It is simple necessity. (And I have been there myself.) The past merges into the present. As to the future? Well, that's another story.

Monday 15th August 2016

Elliot, obviously tired from the exertions of previous days, wanted a relaxing day today. So we took a boat trip on the Seine.

I don't think it was quite what he had in mind for relaxation, but I think it did the trick even if we were out for longer than we had originally intended.

Seeing Paris by boat is an absolute must. You don't just see the tourist sites. You witness ordinary Parisians doing what ordinary Parisians do. Walking by the river. Sitting in the sun. Having a drink and a chat. Taking a leisurely lunch by the water. Making phone calls away from the hustle and bustle of the city's offices and streets. Even – and I think this is a relatively recent craze – writing your name and that of your partner on a padlock and including it along with thousands of others on a metal fence specifically designed for that purpose. The effect is quite stunning, particularly when the metal of different shapes and colours, shines in the sun. It glows in a peculiarly mesmeric fashion. You find yourself transfixed by the beauty of the sight, its visual impact as well as the intensity of the emotions that obviously radiate from each single contribution.

Such an experience was such a contrast from the horrible sensation I had on Saturday night. For some unaccountable reason, the thought entered my head that Lesley was going to die. What began as a totally irrational fear quickly became a tsunami of horrific contemplation. I couldn't do anything about it. As much as I willed my brain to change tack, to rid itself of the magnitude of what it had enforced, the more the vision became stubbornly entrenched. Lesley was asleep at the time, and I had to keep looking over to check that she was still breathing. Such was the immediate reality of the situation. What disturbed me most was the fact that the emotional consequences that death would bring didn't seem to enter my consciousness. I actually wanted them to, but my brain wouldn't relent. It was as if it was saying to me clearly and unequivocally, that there was a detachment between emotion and practicality. That of course you're going to be upset, but that's the least of your troubles. What was terrifying was the solitude, the fact that I would be left alone to cope not just with me, but with the kids as well. What was being reinforced was my inability to cope without Lesley. That is an aspect of the reality that such a situation would bring. Of course it is. But of greater magnitude would be my sense of loss, not my practical adjustment to life without my soul mate. The distinction is important, but at the time, what mattered most was how I needed to react. I could go through life fearing the possibility of death, or I could re-orientate my mind into recognising that such thinking serves no purpose other than to scare and maim.

I can't go through life worrying about what may happen. I have to deal with the reality of what I can influence and control. Realising and discerning the boundaries of what these are not always so apparently straightforward, however.

Tuesday 16th August 2016

I'm glad to say that Lesley was very much with me, alive and well, when I awoke this morning. I'd told her about Saturday's thoughts and she reassured me that she had no intention of dying! It's funny – but telling – how such a response, one of humour and candour – actually had a massively reassuring impact. It was as if the fact that Lesley had dispelled the thought from her own mind, automatically precipitated a correlating effect, transferring that logic and surety to my own. I believed her. So it isn't going to happen. This is every bit as illogical as the initial thought itself, but I don't want to dwell on it because if I do, I'll just go round in circles. I need peace of mind more than anything else. If only I could switch my brain off when it serves to punish me or to reflect on traumatic possibilities. If only I could just stop thinking at times.

Our last full day in Paris wasn't actually spent there. We took the RER C train line to its terminus, Versailles, the chateau and the gardens of the 'Sun King', Louis XIV. Nothing illustrates the grandeur of regal France and its history more than here. It truly is a stunning location. Everything is on a different level, a more superlative and grandiose stage. Even the fountains work in synchronisation with music of the period. The hot weather and the clear blue sky once more served to highlight a vision. However, this wasn't a view as such, more the elevation of opulence and privilege. And nothing epitomised that more than gold. It was everywhere, from the external gates, to embellishments on the doors and windows, to candelabras, to the rims of portraits, to enduring images of the sun. Beautiful though these images were, the republican and the socialist in me couldn't help reflecting on the diversity of circumstances, of the legacy of advantage and its opposing state, of the hypocrisy behind the notion of 'serving one's people'. It's no wonder the French populace at the time of one of Louis' familial successors – a people accustomed to poverty, deprivation and starvation – decided ultimately that enough was enough. That unfairness had reached its limit and that they had the power to do something about it. Their methods in the Revolution may have been brutal and certainly unedifying in the extreme, but their cause was surely just and true. But that's enough of politics for one day!

Wednesday 17th August 2016

Luckily, the journey home didn't bring with it any of the trials and tribulations of last Wednesday. I coped. Actually, I coped quite well. It helped that we now had more confidence and experience of the Paris transport system. I knew what I was doing this time, and was even able to negotiate a shortened and far more manageable route via two Metro lines which prevented not only an unnecessarily long sojourn down Line 7, but also the hike that always seemed to prevail at the larger stops when changing lines or systems. I was quite proud of myself!

If this holiday has reinforced anything, it's the fact that I must do something about my physical health. I have to tackle head on the fact that there is a relationship between physical and mental states, that aspects of my mental illness – not least some of the medication – has a significant impact on how my body works and copes, but that – crucially – I still can do something that mediates some of the physical consequences. The only alternative is to accept that the relationship works without my conscious interference. It is perhaps to resign myself to accepting a certain body shape and image. To acknowledging that I will always be what I am because of mental illness. I can't afford to do that any longer. For the simple fact is that I struggled to cope with much of the physical demands such a holiday placed on me. We walked on average around five miles a day. We walked up steps at Metro stations, and even up the entirety of the Arc de Triomphe. I did it all, but I was constantly tired. And I was also very slow. Of course the hot weather didn't help, but when I looked at myself in shop windows and other reflective sources, I didn't like what I saw. I looked old and laboured. I looked strained and short of breath. And I looked fat.

Losing some weight isn't just an exercise in body image. It's become vital for my ongoing health. It will help with my blood pressure as well as my cholesterol levels. It will probably have an effect on any potential sleep disorder. And, just as importantly, it will make me feel more positive about myself. I have to give it a real go this time. Even if that means addressing all those old feelings about food being the enemy. Even if it involves or results in some unhealthy obsessions. Even if I simply inculcate a new challenge to my mental faculties. I really do think I have no choice. Because to continue as I am means risking much more. I can't help believing that all this is relatively simple. I have to change. Or I'll die.

Thursday 18th August 2016

As we left Paris yesterday, my thoughts were very much with my Dad. One of my many cherished memories of yesteryear was not only going as a very young boy with him on one of his school trips to France and to the capital, but in hearing him speak French and enthuse about the possibilities for human interaction that lie from a greater ability to communicate. He was, of course, a French teacher, someone fluent in that language, but his mission if you like had a much more humanitarian value at its core. He believed in the concept of Europe. He maintained that its people needed to learn lessons from the past and that greater understanding, acceptance and respect were not only attainable but vital. Whilst I share this vision, linguistic practicalities are things that sadly have never really been within my immediate grasp. It's funny that Lesley believes that I have a flair, a natural inclination, for language. I like to think that this is so to some extent with regard to English. I've had two books published, so I can't be that bad! However, with regard to foreign languages, I've never been able to go further than the most basic, elementary level. In comparison with my Dad, I'm a complete novice. I wish I wasn't. Indeed, it's one of my lifetime regrets that I've never had the aptitude of my father, the skills necessarily to master one or more unfamiliar tongue. The nearest I've come, ironically, is with Czech. I say 'ironically' because Czech has never been – and probably never will be – a language that permeates the formal state education system in this country. It was my determination not to be excluded when visiting Prague, as well as my desire to be respectful to its people, that led to me teaching myself the basics. I did quite well for a long time. I used it when I was there – even if the locals seemed much keener to try out their English than to listen to my attempts to speak like them – and I'm convinced it had an impact. People smiled when I tried. They congratulated me on my attempts. They corrected me when I went wrong. And I even got free drinks and, I'm pretty sure, larger portions in restaurants. It also enabled me to do things like use the local transport system, to talk to people in the suburban areas, to make enquiries at Holocaust and other relevant sites. It helped me to feel a connection.

One thing my Dad always said was important in relation to learning French was to 'speak it like a Frenchman or Frenchwoman'. To imitate the intonation, the accent even. This isn't always easy, but it's certainly easier in relation to French than it is to Czech. The latter has sounds that don't exist in the

English tongue or vocabulary! It's right to try though, and with a trip to Berlin on the horizon at the end of the year, I'm going to work with Elliot to see if we can't help each other become much more confident as well as competent, in German. I'm also planning on visiting Vilnius in November, so a few words of basic Lithuanian would certainly come in handy.

Perhaps it's not too late for me to meet my own expectations as far as languages are concerned? Not being fluent in anything other than English has been – as I mentioned just now – one of my life's regrets. But surely there's still time? I think I need to set myself some goals, to address this gap in my life in the same way as my desire for better physical health. Challenging aims and ambitions are, by their very nature, difficult to attain. And for a depressive, the mental strength and stamina required can be onerous and problematic to achieve, never mind instil as a basic requirement for progress. It's that much harder when you see your 'natural' inclination or propensity to be one related to failure. But I have to try. And try I will.

Friday 19th August 2016

One thing that I've become more conscious than normal about recently is the fact that I seem to be living constantly on the edge of a very steep precipice. I know this is hardly new news, so to speak, but it seems to have become much more focused – if that's the right word – and certainly more perceptible. Every single thing has the potential to knock me completely off my stride. Not just the big things in life – relationships, jobs, security and such like – but the most mundane, run-of-the-mill occurrences. Like a battery charger not working, for example. I actually feel like a mountain climber walking along the narrowest of paths at the top of a ridge, with huge voids opening up on either side of me. One slip, one loss of balance, one heavy wind, one bout of snow. They all threaten to derail me and send me tumbling to a terminal fate. But they have also become metaphors for life's challenges. I'm living my life in a way that is not conducive to short term stability, never mind mid-term safety or long term prosperity. I'm evidentially nervous, continually fraught with worry and concern, expecting the worse to happen, anticipating disaster around every corner.

Maybe this is why I also feel increasingly volatile, ready to lose my cool and my temper at the slightest provocation. It doesn't take much to set me off. In France, the inability of some people to queue properly and appropriately – in other words, fairly – threatened to hijack the sense of relaxation one tends naturally to feel when on holiday. It really got to me at times. No matter how hard I tried to put things in perspective, to tell myself that it really wasn't worth bothering about, nothing seemed to douse the fire that was burning within me. And at other times too, the behaviour of people around me, their mannerisms, their antics, their demeanour, all seemed at times to grate like a long nail on a blackboard. They weren't doing anything other than being human. But that wasn't any form of consolation, alleviation of, or suppression for, my mental agitation. I must sound like the very worst side of Victor Meldrew![31] It bothers me. It really does. I don't want to be at war with humankind. And yet I feel there are occasions when the best place for me is an uninhabited island, a place where I can escape and – probably more importantly – a place where I can be confined by others tired of my habits and deportment.

I suspect this is something that I'll come back to quite a lot in the forthcoming weeks.

Saturday 20th August 2016

Of course one of the drawbacks of any holiday is the return to normality. The difference between vacation and routine life though is never quite as marked for depressives or indeed for anyone experiencing long-term mental ill health. The reason is quite obvious. Your illness simply doesn't disappear as you work on your tan, sit in a bar, see the sights or whatever else you choose to do to occupy your time. It may take a back seat. It may become less burdensome. But on the other hand, it may actually accentuate other areas of depression that lie more dormant when you are at home going through the motions of living. The change in context, for example, can bring with it huge challenges. I've talked a lot over the course of the last couple of weeks about the perils of travelling, but that's not the only thing that has to be addressed. New adventures, new experiences, a change in climate, negotiating unfamiliar languages, different sleeping routines. All these are directly relevant. What you may not be expecting to hear though is the pressure that can come to bear simply to be happy! After all, holidays are supposed to be enjoyed aren't they? I deliberately used the word 'simply' two sentences ago, to make the point that for depressives this is certainly no simple, straightforward task or transformation in character. There is deep irony in that word. If it was so 'simple' to become more cheery, to enjoy oneself, then depression wouldn't be the constricting, acute illness that it is. In fact, it probably wouldn't exist as a medical condition. You would just tell yourself to put a smile on your face, turn your 'happy mode' on, laugh and be merry!

As if it was that 'simple'!

This pressure that I referred to just now can be really intense. Though it wasn't so much the case with regard to Paris, I remember so many occasions when I've felt that I should try to achieve the impossible and put depression to one side, if not for me, then for my family. I really have tried to do this, putting aside all logic and common sense. But on many an occasion, the harder I've tried, the greater I've fallen. I can turn my mouth into a smile. That's a physical sensation. But I can't hope to replicate any emotional conversion. I can make a joke, even make people laugh. But that involves simply saying words. Again, a physical task. Emotionally, I'm usually crying inside. I end up putting on a mask for my family. They need a break as well, but one of the breaks they probably need the most is from my mental state. In other words, from me! I've often encouraged Lesley and the others to go away on their own or together, without my presence.

That way, I know they won't have to suffer my company and that of my illness.

In a nutshell, holidays for me are like any other occasion when happiness is expected.

If I'm unwell, if my depression is particularly bad, they become trials of endurance and exercises in deception. They involve hiding away as much as showing my face. They require patience and enormous willpower. They necessitate having to confront yourself, to go to war with your own mentality. They are exhausting. They can be shattering.

When things are not so bad, the problems diminish. They never go away completely, but they become much more manageable. And sometimes – heaven forbid – you do genuinely have a good time. It is possible. Though usually in small doses. As always, with holidays it's a question of balance and of relativity.

And Paris was one of my better ones.

Sunday 21st August 2016

The issue of 'control' can at times be a double-edged sword. At this moment in my life, this is a real issue with respect to what I guess could be described as 'routine' or 'normal' medication. By this, I mean the sort of stuff you can buy over the counter rather than via prescription. I've come to realise that I'm taking more and more. In fact, I've probably become over-reliant, such has been the extent of my use and for quite some time as well. What sort of drugs am I talking about? Well, ordinary Paracetamol and Ibuprofen for a start. But also Sudafed for sinus pain and IBS Relief for…well, IBS[32]. I am also not averse to taking pills for tension headaches and, very occasionally, migraine tablets and hayfever remedies. The reason why 'control' lies at the heart of this is firstly that I take them to try and reassert it at the earliest possible opportunity. I can't seem to let things see how they pan out for a while. I can't, for example, lie in bed with the first inklings of a sinus-induced headache and try to massage my nose and temple area. I can't go to sleep with the confidence that the pain will go away naturally. I have to act immediately, because – in my mind – if I don't, things will only go one way. The symptoms will become worse and I'll become significantly unwell. The same is the case with stomach aches and a rumbling tummy. Unless I resort to taking the IBS stuff that I know works, I'm convinced that what starts as a minor, unsettling feeling will translate, very quickly, into a full-blown irritable bowel. My mind only works in this direction. I therefore feel that I have no choice in what I've been doing.

What this means, in effect, is that I'm taking such medication with my mental state foremost in mind. The physical discomfort and any pain are a secondary matter. They're simply not as important. Unless I act immediately, my mind will make things worse. When I've tried to resist the temptation simply to pop a pill, more often than not – in fact, virtually every time – I ruminate and ruminate until I'm utterly convinced the pain is worse. What I guess is happening is that my anxiety is ruling the roost, telling me – reinforcing it in my head – that my physical symptoms are deteriorating. When in actual fact, they're probably not.

I do hope that makes sense.

The second reason for the centrality of control is, in a sense, the diametric opposite. The more I take medication to alleviate the first signs of pain in an effort to regain mastery of my situation, the less controlled my substance use actually is. I just take pills automatically, sometimes without conscious awareness. It has become at times an automated process, the medication becoming the master over my own feeble attempts to cope. Rather than see dealing with the situation logically, without immediate recourse to tablets, as a sign of strength and 'control', what I do has shifted that mastery to what I'm putting in my mouth, putting all my eggs, if you like, in that alternative basket. Recently, there have been times when something has obviously been triggered in my brain, something that has caused alarm and consternation, as soon as I've taken a pill – for whatever affliction. I've started to tell myself that I'm overdosing. That I'm damaging my insides. That all pills are inherently evil and destructive. I've gone from one extreme to the other. It is classic 'black and white', 'all or nothing' thinking. My conclusion, therefore, is that I need to try and resist that massive pull towards immediate remedy. I have to try and give nature a chance. In that way, at some point, I may once more regain a sense of perspective that I've lost, a perspective that I haven't had for a long while.

Monday 22nd August 2016

I started work again today after my summer break. Actually, if I'm honest, I'd already delved into emails and work programmes over the course of the weekend, but today was officially my first day back. When I was at the Council, I'd return to hundreds upon hundreds of messages. Things are a little more sedate now, and certainly more manageable, but even so, I've felt a pressure this morning that was a little disturbing, a pressure that focused on hitting the ground running, being able to pick up literally as I left off. I know this is unrealistic. I am well aware that I'm creating a rod for my own back, but I just couldn't help myself. Once again, it boils down to that word 'control', a word that is increasingly haunting me and my attempts to cope with all that life throws my way. I persuaded myself that unless I gained a perspective on my work straight away, unless I could field enquiries and know what I'm supposed to be doing virtually instantaneously, I wouldn't be able to 'reel it in', to be in charge, to assert myself, to keep a check on everything of relevance, to anticipate problems and challenges and deal with them. I have felt this many times before, but the timescale is different this time. Previously, I would make allowances for the fact that I'd been away from things, give myself a little licence, be realistic in my plans and ambitions. All that seems not to matter anymore. I have to know and act now. There have been times this morning when having to look something up or find the relevant information on a website has been a duel between realism and my push for instant knowledge. I've been very conscious of a rising sense of tension and anxiety within me, but I can't seem to quell it in any way. This can't be good for me. I hate to think what my blood pressure is like!

Tuesday 23rd August 2016

The issue of control is obviously closely related to that of 'perfectionism', a trait that I know is common to many people with depression, myself included. How I wish that I could at least sometimes settle for second best? But I can't. I've never been able to. It is, of course, ironic that much of what we do in our lives is based around the notion that you should always strive for perfection, even if it is an unrealistic proposition. At school, this is particularly the case, and having found myself glued to the television watching the recent Olympics, the thought that any one of our elite competitors was aiming for anything other than top marks or victory is virtually unthinkable. However, perfectionism is also an element in so many everyday things that we all take part in. We try and cook the perfect dish. We look to take the perfect photo. We search for the best deal possible when buying insurance or a new car. And so on and so forth. In so many things, therefore, perfectionism is considered a prized asset. But for depressives? That's potentially a different story.

Whenever something comes together that embraces that element of being the best, it can be a real confidence booster. Passing an exam. Planning an activity. Writing a blog. Creating a new piece of art. Even things like doing the gardening, decorating a room or building a piece of furniture are part of this process. But what happens if something goes wrong? What happens if you don't succeed? What if you can't succeed? The impact can be devastating. To someone accustomed to black or white thinking, anything that is not superlative runs the risk of being crap. There's nothing in between. Accordingly, what I try to do sometimes is not aim for 100%, but tell myself that 70% is perfectly fine. That there's nothing wrong with a minor imperfection. That even if things go disastrously haywire, even if what you're trying to do breaks down completely, you can always try again. It doesn't matter. Failure is a part of life. You can learn from it etc. You get the picture I hope! This is so easily said rather than done. It takes a complete reorientation of the mind to even begin to think in these ways. But it's worth persevering with. It may necessitate help from others. In fact, it probably will. Because if this was a simple, straightforward, task, you'd already be doing it. You wouldn't be conditioned to do otherwise. You probably wouldn't even be mentally unhealthy or ill. When I first set myself this target – and I can't remember the context – I remember feeling so bad for so long afterwards. I knew what I'd done was not perfect. The desire, the temptation, to intervene, to remedy, was overwhelming. I was in agony. In real anguish. I couldn't believe that I could feel so incomplete and so inadequate. But eventually the feelings do subside and the more you practice – no matter how difficult it is – the better you become.

It's worth dwelling on this as a conclusion. In University education, you don't need 100% to get a First Class degree. 70% is just as valid.

Wednesday 24th August 2016

I am always concerned about how other people feel and think about me. In truth, I look at people who profess that they don't care about this with a mixture of envy and incredulity! For me, it is vitally important. But in all honesty, it's probably too important. By this I mean that I not only try to create a positive impression, I worry about every potential eventuality that may prevent that and sometimes, in anticipation, even try to remedy things before they've actually happened! This of course relates to what I've been saying about control and also about perfectionism. Not only is anything I do either flawless or terrible. I, as a person, am the same as well. I'm liked or disliked. I'm admired or detested. I'm brilliant or disastrous. I'm knowledgeable or stupid. I'm great or shit!

If I detect the slightest sense of reservation that someone may have towards me, I can literally go to pieces. I either do my utmost to change a mind (a mind that may not actually need changing), doing my best to ingratiate myself with somebody, to do everything I can to make them like me. Or I resign myself to the fact that I'm hated and disappear from the scene, with the resolve that I will avoid that person in the future, to the best of my ability. It becomes a real mission. It takes enormous amounts of will-power and determination, attributes that when I'm ill I really don't have. It is also really tiring. Going through life with such a focus is certainly not a recipe for positive mental health.

One thing I did this morning may serve as an example. I realised yesterday that I would have to draft an email to some work contacts in which what I needed to say may not be well received. It wasn't that I had categorically bad news to relate. It was the possibility that they may not take things in the way I hoped they would. It hung over my head like the darkest of clouds as I thought about it last night, even to the extent of constant rumination at one point. I was searching for the right words. It became an obsession, but the more I focused on it, the less clear things became. So, this morning arrives and I start fiddling around with word combinations. I needed to be clear, but also to at least sound conciliatory and positive. The words just wouldn't come. Whatever I put, I discarded. Something was always wrong, at least in my mind. Eventually, I decided to send a copy of what I'd done to a colleague to get their perspective. Within the hour, a reply was received, suggesting some modifications, but reinforcing to me the reality that this wasn't the big deal that I'd made it become. What mattered more than anything was that the recipients of my email thought positively about me. I couldn't conceive of the possibility that the opposite may actually come to bear.

The logical extension of all this is that you try your utmost to ensure that everything you do that relates to someone else – which I guess is most things when you come to think about it – is done faultlessly and leads to a favourable response. You work at ensuring that every single person thinks well of you. That no one, no single person – whether close or distant – has any cause to consider you in a bad light. The only way to do this is to be the impossible – perfect, without blemish. It's an unattainable task. You are bound to fail, and with failure comes self-recrimination. And so the cycle begins again!

Thursday 25th August 2016

A slight deviation from the theme of the week. This morning was yet another round of blood tests at the Doctor's. This actually constituted my annual check-up which begs the question of what I had only a month or so ago! As nothing came of giving that sample in terms of a follow-up, I'm going on the presumption that I'm OK. But what exactly I'm OK with, I haven't a clue! Looking at the letter I had from the surgery, what they're testing this time are kidneys, liver, thyroid, sugar and cholesterol, with the added bonus of a blood pressure and pulse check. I'm expecting conflicting results, but as long as I don't add another component to my already sizeable list of ailments, I'll be happy. I already know my blood pressure outcome, and, for me, it was sensational. 130 over 90 constitutes progress, and progress of a substantial nature. Even the fact that the nurse considered it only 'acceptable' didn't dampen my spirits unduly. If I could I would have danced out of the treatment room! As it is, I'm going to be referred once more to the hypertension clinic. Nothing surprising there though. I was expecting it.

I'm sure nobody likes doctor's surgeries, and I'm certainly no different. But I also find them interesting places in which to 'people watch'. One thing always amuses me. The number of times old acquaintances meet up and can't help asking each other how they are. Nine times out of ten, the answer is the same. 'I'm very well, thanks. Can't complain. What about you?' So what on earth are they doing in a surgery waiting to see a doctor? In addition, there are occasions when people's demeanour changes significantly within the course of a few minutes. They can be sitting there, engrossed in conversation, sharing a joke and a funny story, all smiles and laughter. And then they get called to go in. It's their turn, you see. All of a sudden, a solemn visage takes over. I swear that some begin to breathe heavily or develop a limp. Pain and discomfort suddenly descend. They have to put on their 'ill' face to justify their being there. And they say that only kids are selective in their behaviour?!

As for me, I just sit quietly, resigned and bored. My foot inevitably starts tapping, which shows I must be slightly nervous. I really can't wait to get in and get out. As quickly as I can. I try to make it pleasurable for whoever's seeing me. If it's a nurse – as it was this morning – I go on the reckoning that it must be intensely tedious taking blood sample after blood sample. (I guess they get sufficient practice, though, which is reassuring). So I try to enliven proceedings with some variation on the old Tony Hancock sketch about giving too much blood. If it's a doctor and I'm there regarding depression, it's a bit more challenging. Even though some of the world's most notable depressives have been comic geniuses – or is it genii? – it is difficult to find anything remotely comical about your predicament. I try with the occasional smart comment, but my heart isn't in it. It's usually tired and almost inevitably soulful. What can you say when you're feeling so desperate? What is there to say? I just wish sometimes there was some kind of quick barometer that can measure your mental state, in the same fashion as a thermometer or blood pressure machine. That would be a wonderful invention. It would save a lot of time and certainly a lot of anguish. And it would stop me feeling the need to try and make some light of proceedings. The doctor rarely laughs, by the way. So I fail even in that small feat.

Friday 26th August 2016

I was supposed to be meeting a friend for coffee yesterday afternoon but in the morning the prospect of having to go out and socialise again – I was already committed to a meeting earlier in the day – was just too much so I sent her a message and a text to give my apologies and to ask if we could postpone until next week. I've now discovered that somehow she can't have got either message and I feel absolutely mortified.

I do this too often. I commit myself to something weeks in advance and then, when it comes to the day itself, my mental state isn't strong enough to withstand the barrage of obstacles that come my way from within, so I plead forgiveness. I should know better. At the time it seemed perfectly logical to arrange a number of appointments on the one day. In effect, to concentrate them. But this imposes real demands on my mental stamina and yesterday, I just couldn't take it. I had things I needed to do as well so that was the message I sent her, but I couldn't bring myself to admit that whilst I could do one meeting, I couldn't do two and it was hers that I'd have to sacrifice – it being the second in the day.

I now feel desolate, devoid of any sense of dignity and integrity.

What must she think of me? Why couldn't I just open up? She knows me well enough. She is well aware of my mental illness. I didn't lie to her, but I still feel that I've let her down and I now fear for the consequences. It's not just the possibility that she may feel differently towards me, that she may no longer see me in the same light, that she may not wish even to be my friend. It's the fact that all these things will transpire to cause me excruciating pain with regards to confidence and self-esteem.

It's hitting me already. I feel false as I write these words. I'm beating myself up inside. I can barely face looking myself in the mirror.

I guess all this just shows that no matter how open you are about your mental illness – and I always have been that way – it's a stance that you can't always maintain. Sometimes it is easier, and less painful, to focus on other reasons for whatever it is you're doing – or not doing in this case. Being continually transparent is not easy. It puts you on a sort of pedestal. But there's another factor. When your whole life is affected by mental illness. When everything you do has an impact on your mental state. When – to varying degrees of course – there isn't any situation in which your mental faculties and their deficiencies are at play. It's hard to keep relaying that information, that reality, to others. I'm scared that people only see me because of my depression. That I have nothing else to offer. That mental illness becomes my 'lingua franca' almost. That I have to continually talk about it if I'm being totally honest about the way I live my life. I can't do that. I don't want to do that. Deep down, it only reinforces what I fear I've become. A walking epitome of mental self-destruction.

Saturday 27th August 2016

I was watching an old episode of 'Porridge' the other day. I love 'Porridge'. The character of Fletch is surely one of the most memorable creations in the entire history of British comedy. Of course it is the genius that was Ronnie Barker that brought him to life, endearing him to viewers across the generations, giving him – and Fletch – a sense of immortality. I could watch these old classics time and time again. And I do. Even though you know what's coming, it doesn't seem to matter. The delivery of the lines. The mannerisms of the characters. The facial expressions. You do have to deal with the dated, inherent, discrimination of the times. The derogatory references to identities. The use of words that are as unacceptable as they are offensive. They do make you wince and wonder. But that aside – recognising that the series was a product of its era – there is a certain reverence that descends when you realise that the combination of actors and plot produced something that has lasted.

And lasted well.

'Porridge' is, first and foremost, funny. But it also has its serious side and there are moments and situations that are poignant and telling, occasions which should make us as viewers think and reflect.

The episode in question is one such an example. It focuses almost exclusively on a nocturnal conversation between Fletch and Lennie Godber. For those that need reminding, Lennie is a prison first-timer, young, inexperienced and frightened. He has been 'billeted' with Fletch, who is, of course, a dab hand. The latter recognises – though he's probably loath to admit it – that he has a certain responsibility for ensuring that his latest cellmate does his time and gets through the experience with at least a modicum of respect still intact.

This particular conversation is all about survival, and in it, Fletch talks about the concept of 'little victories', doing and achieving small tasks and feats that collectively build up powers of resilience and tolerance, attributes that can serve as coping mechanisms. It struck me that such a concept also applies to dealing with the sentence that can be mental illness. Being able to dissect what you do in life into small, individual elements, each one of which is attainable in the sense that you realise and do them, and do them well and without consequence. In essence, things that make you realise that you can win and achieve. These might be everyday things that others take for granted. Making a cup of tea. Cleaning a window. Sending an email. Putting some washing on the line. Hoovering the front room. Reading a work document. They key is that they have to be unique in their own right. Each one has its importance in isolation and independence from any other. Take my last example for instance. If you see reading something relevant to work as part of a larger, more complex and challenging assignment, then it may be that you are pushing yourself too much. You don't see its value in and of itself. You only see it as a reflection of something that you may be struggling to cope with. The danger here is that whatever you do within that overall perspective you only see the big picture and that picture is too daunting and oppressive within your own mind. Only by dividing things up into small portions can you actually succeed. Otherwise, you are setting yourself up to fail.

This isn't as easy to do as it may seem.

What you are essentially doing is adjusting, re-orientating your behaviour and thinking in tandem. It doesn't just happen. It takes practice. You have to persevere. You'll have doubts. You'll have worries. You'll believe fervently that you'll never be able to change. You'll find it hard. You'll look for short cuts, easier routes. But in most cases, there aren't any. This is it. If you can gain some element of mastery then you're on the right road.

It doesn't take depression away, but it does help to make it manageable, for at least some of the time.

Think of it this way. You have to win each battle before you can win a war.

Sunday 28th August 2016
Of course the approach that I outlined yesterday – that of 'little victories' – does have some consequences, one of which is probably an inability to multi-task, or at least to do so successfully.

I don't necessarily buy-in to the gender stereotype that is often cited here, but I do concede that I myself find multi-tasking challenging. Not because I'm a man though, but because of my mental illness. If I'm focused on one thing at a time as a means of coping and of achieving, it is rare that I can adequately switch that focus between my main concentration and that of anything else. If I do so, or even if I think of doing so, I risk not only failing in the original mission I have set myself, my sense of self-control is also threatened. One thing can then lead very quickly onto another. If I don't succeed to the level I have set myself, that perfectionist element within me quickly tells me off. I become intensely self-critical. I doubt my own abilities to adapt. I see only failure and despair. In effect, I'm right back to where I started!

There is another danger though. Whereas it is entirely true that the more you practice breaking down larger tasks into constituent parts, dividing up your day into small individual components, over each of which you can gain both satisfaction and a mastery, the more it becomes engrained as a coping mechanism, the less able you are to do things any other way. If, all of a sudden, you are faced with multiple obstacles, with having to make decisions and choices across a spectrum of contexts, there is a likelihood that you will quickly go into panic mode. Your brain, you see, is not able to adapt or even to register what is required in the time fate has allocated to you. It's not sufficiently flexible, neither is it orientated towards action across a number of fields at the same time. Therein lies the contradiction. The more you practice your method of coping – the more it becomes second nature – the less effective you become when confronted with any other thinking mechanism, particularly those that demand adjustability and versatility. Life rarely allows you to be one-dimensional, sadly. It's just not like that.

I have to say that I only require this method of coping when my illness is particularly pronounced. The 'little victories' concept is not one that comes into play when I am as I usually am. It varies, of course. It's a question of balance and relativity. I can, for example, employ the practice to suit a particular situation and quickly change out of its thinking essentials when I no longer need it. But only when I'm relatively well. When it comes down to it therefore, it's probably true to say that I can multi-task most of the time, but I can't when I'm really depressed. It poses too many challenges. It holds too many risks.

For those people not affected or conditioned by mental illness, this is probably something that is alien to their experience of life. They do not have to make concessions or even think about what techniques to employ. They just do what comes naturally. They cope. And if they don't, it's not a calamity. That's just life. The stakes though are so much higher for people like me. If we get it wrong, our descent into darkness and confusion can become alarmingly sudden. You're spiralling out of control before you even realise what's happening and it's not easy to wrestle it back.

Monday 29th August 2016

Today is a Bank Holiday. It's also the last day of Elliot's summer break. Tomorrow he's back at school. I know he's not looking forward to it, but he won't be the only one. His consolation – and mine – is that at least he can return home once his lessons are over. At his age, I had boarding school to deal with. When I look at him now – and he is quite mature for his age – I wonder how on earth, at thirteen, I ever survived that experience. Not only did I have the challenge of being away from parents and family respite, I also had the social class stigma to face. It wasn't easy at all. The people around me – most of them at any rate – were so different to me in so many respects. They had things I didn't have – materially I mean – but they also talked and behaved in ways that I had not come across before. Moreover, there was something about them, a sense of privilege and of self-assumed 'superiority' that is hard to describe, but was nevertheless something essentially 'real' and tangible. I don't even know that there is a word that can actually encapsulate or define this. They had a way of life that was completely alien to my upbringing, but what that word was, I still can't accurately say. I should state that that doesn't mean that they were all necessarily hostile or ambivalent to my situation. There were some lovely people. Teachers as well as students. I also had many friends, people to whom I warmed to, people that would help and soothe the passage. But I still seem to come back to that word 'alien'. I was alien to most of them. And some of them made me feel intensely 'other worldly'.

As I write, Elliot is still to surface from his room. In contrast, Lesley and Rachel were up at five o'clock. They're doing a car boot sale, their 'stock' consisting mainly of Elliot's old toys and books. It's raining so I hope they also took some umbrellas! Joel is in London with Luke. They're both going to the Notting Hill Carnival. They're regular attendees actually, two of the faces, experienced carnival goers.

So at the moment, it's very quiet here at home.

I like it. Noise can grate inside my mind at times. It's one of the barometers of my mental state. When I'm on my way down, sounds seem not only to magnify but to increase in intensity and discomfort. What passes for ordinary background noise or even things that wouldn't even normally register suddenly transform in a way that is disturbing. It's like developing some form of periodic tinnitus. I guess it may be because you're more on edge. Your senses are heightened. You're expecting conflict. You're anticipating turmoil. Every little thing has the capacity to turn into something which you have to deal with, something you can't ignore. I'm beginning to feel like that again, which isn't a good sign.

Tuesday 30th August 2016

It really feels like the end of summer today. The house is quiet as I sit here at my desk. Elliot's back at school and everyone else is at work. I just have Millie for company. Whilst quietness is what I crave at the moment, I can't help feeling a little sad as one more summer leaves me behind and our home reverts back to normality. It's not necessarily the season that I'll miss. In many ways, I loathe the summer period, the heat and the humidity in particular. No, it's the fact that time moves resolutely on, ticking constantly like some world-weary sentence, a reminder that for me I feel compelled to make the most of what I have and yet, with my disability, I am at times incapable of doing so. I have been fixated by one element of this recently. I've thought about the number of books that I haven't read, the amount of music I haven't listened to, the experiences in other spheres that in some cases I haven't even begun, the places I've never visited, the languages I haven't spoken. It's as if I've set myself one of those impossible missions. To learn as much as possible about the world around me. Sadly, the flip side to the proverbial coin, is that unless I do so, I'll have missed out. My life will have been incomplete. I will have wasted the time and opportunities made available to me. I will have failed.

It's remarkable how persistent this particularly belief has become. I can't even recognise the fact that some things are already beyond me. I'll never play professional sport, for example. Unless I take up darts! I'll never climb the highest mountains. I'll never sail across an ocean. I'll never travel in space and look down upon the earth. My age and disability count against me here. I also seem incapable of accepting the blatant truth that it is impossible for one single person to do everything that is on my insurmountable list. There can't be a person who speaks every language known to humankind. To listen to every piece of music is an impossibility. As is to read every book. There is too much that lies unknown. And too little time. It is pure folly to think that any one person has or can achieve proficiency in every given field. Or that a single human being has the inclination and interest to immerse themselves in everything. And yet I still scold myself. I still beat myself up. My mind still berates me and accuses me of laziness and disinterest.

I have to tell myself and make myself believe that every person is limited, myself included. That I can only do so much. That I have to pick and choose. That I'm not a robot, a machine that devours without sensation. That to be so is to ignore that human component that does make life interesting and worthwhile. Those elements of feeling, of response, of reflection. The ability to dwell on what you know and what you learn and savour.

Wednesday 31st August 2016
I booked my flights and hotel for Vilnius yesterday afternoon. Every year I spend a few days by myself visiting Jewish and Holocaust-related sites somewhere in Central or Eastern

Europe. This year, I'm venturing further east than I've ever been so far. Despite the nature of the trip, I always look forward to these short breaks. Not only are they a time when I can be by myself, they are also an occasion for me to do entirely what I want to do, to immerse myself in my interests, to be focused, to become absorbed in the topic of my choice, to indulge myself in learning and knowledge, to appreciate the emotions that inevitably come. The subject matter is challenging but I go well prepared. Vilnius promises to be a real trip into the unknown. A new country for a start. But also a place that I know little about in terms of its Holocaust history. I'll do my homework beforehand. I'll know what to look for and where to go. I'll prepare a travel plan so that I do things in a logical order geographically. I'll assess whether I need to use public transport and if so, what tram or bus to catch. I'll gauge how much time to spend in various places, how long it will take me to get there, what I can expect to see and if there are any logistical arrangements I need to make before I venture out. It's all quite meticulously done. Why I do this, you can probably guess. It's not just a case of having to make these preparations to make the best use of my time. It's also a necessity, part of my need to maintain control. It enables me to take the immediate decision-making out of the equation, for example. I'll already have done it at home. It gives me a structure within which to operate, a framework within which I can feel comfortable, a timetable that is comprehensive as well as easy to navigate. It serves to ease my mind, basically.

There will inevitably be challenging moments, but from experience, I can anticipate what they may be. I won't know the specific context, of course. As I said, I've never been to Vilnius before. But the more you travel around the eastern half of our continent, the more you become aware of how things generally work, what you'll have to negotiate and where you'll need to go should problems arise. Every country I've been to is different, of course, but there are also many commonalities. One thing I will need to do this time is learn some basic Lithuanian. Not because there will be an impregnable language barrier. English is widely spoken. But because it is courteous to do so and it reaps its rewards when you see people appreciating your attempts to converse. Even if you fail miserably!

At times depression is so inconsistent in the way it works. I seem to accept that I won't be able to master the language before I go. Even the fact that I'll probably get things horrendously wrong in terms of pronunciation. Why can I do this, but give myself such a hard time over other aspects of my life? Why does perfectionism not come into play here? It never has done. I do my best. I try my hardest to blend in, to do what the locals do. But I know I'll come up short. However, it doesn't seem to matter in this context. Why this is I just don't know. I'm also able to use public transport when I'm abroad on these visits, but when I'm here, in my own city, the prospect of using a bus freaks me out. And you've heard about my experience negotiating trains on a number of occasions. It's totally illogical. It's more than that actually. It's inexplicable. Maybe it's down to my preparation? Maybe it's because my linguistic inabilities 'shelter' or 'isolate' me from my fellow passengers and their curiosities? I'd love to know the secret.

September

Thursday 1st September 2016

At the start of a new month and indeed a new season, I think this is probably an opportune time to take stock of where I am and how I am. Perhaps I ought to make this a more regular occurrence? I can't, if truth be told, ever remember deliberately motivating myself to do this before. I do it incidentally – if that's the right word. I'm always assessing where I am in some respects, but never completely. What I think I need is a complete health check. A systematic health MOT. And it probably needs to happen more than once a year.

Anyway, enough preamble. Mentally, I'm OK. I think. Though at times it seems as such, I haven't had a sustained period of low mood for quite some time. I've had moments, days even, but not anything like the prolonged intensity that I've become accustomed to. What I gain in one respect, however, I lose in another. What has definitely become more acute – particularly recently – are all the other manifestations of mental illness, the other symptoms of depression. Here I'm talking about anxiety, panic and stress. I'm talking about the inability to make decisions, the need for reassurance, the nervous discomfort in the presence of others. I'm referring to common thinking traps. Catastrophizing. Black and white, all or nothing cogitation. The ability to make mountains out of molehills. To fall apart at the first sign of trouble. To worry unnecessarily. To ruminate over dark feelings. All these things seem to have become elevated as my ability to cope with low mood has increased. If I'm honest and had a choice, I'd go for low mood every time. These are the things I'll need to mention when I next see my consultant.

Physically, I'm in limbo. Ever since I returned from Paris, I've been determined to do something about my physical state. I'm exercising more regularly. I'm watching what I eat and how much I eat. I'm resisting everything, including temptation – to coin Oscar Wilde. I suspect it's starting to have an impact. I feel like I've lost a little weight and even some flab. It could just be an illusion though. I haven't checked my weight yet. I've been too scared to do so just in case my perceptions aren't matched by reality. I'm scared of the psychological consequences. What I can't escape from, of course, is what I already know. My liver functions are suspect. I'm on medication for high blood pressure and cholesterol. My BMI (Body Mass Index) tells me I'm obese. I've just been checked for sleep apnoea and am currently awaiting the results. I experience regular 'night terrors'. More than anything though, I feel knackered and lethargic. I know it's almost certainly associated with all the medication I take – medication that I need to keep my mental state in check – but there is that fear within me that I will go the way of my father. That I will succumb to heart disease and diabetes. Whether that fear has any tangible substance is another matter. I hope it's just a reflection of my mental illness, my tendency to worry and to think the worst. But I can't allow for that indefinitely. I have to take measures that I hope will work. And I have, to be fair to myself.

Family wise, things are normal. I'm so blessed with my nearest and dearest. Lesley continues to be my saviour, my confidant and treasure. Elliot is developing into the most beautiful of human beings, someone with real compassion, awareness and understanding. I've been lucky to have Rachel and Joel around me too. They are uniquely talented, but there's so much more to them than their intellectual capacities. The same could be said of Luke, even though I don't see him as much as I would like. When I inherited my ready-made family eighteen and a half years ago, I couldn't have dreamed that I would be so fortunate in my choice of children as much as my choice of wife.

With regard to work, I've managed to make some kind of living for myself as a consultant. This time last year, I was approaching the end of my time at the Council. The future looked decidedly shaky. I had no idea what was to come. I worried – as is my wont. A large part of me thought it was the end. That I'd never recover. That I'd lose what stature I thought I'd accumulated over the years. That things would be downhill from now on. But they haven't been. I've been able to choose what I do and I think I've chosen wisely. I'm still working in equality and diversity, but in a different area, and I've been able to use my passion and knowledge of the Holocaust and other genocides to undertake some work encouraging more people to commemorate Holocaust Memorial Day and to share its important legacies.

And I've written a published book! I'm still to absorb what that actually means, if truth be told. But there is within me a heightened sense of achievement – at least in this field.

In summary, my challenge is to utilise the good things that have happened to me, the positive elements in my life, so that they start to impact in areas that are still immersed in dark clouds. Of course, that is the task that every depressive – indeed every person with a mental illness – has to try and take on, if they are to really challenge their inner turmoil. I'm fighting. I always have done. Sometimes I'm fighting without direction or purpose. Those sleeping habits that come with 'night terrors' – the kicking the punching, the screaming, the crying, the thrashing about in bed – are really a metaphor for my life more generally. I hurt myself. I endanger the person closest to me. (Quite innocently and imperceptibly, I should add.) I lose control. I don't know what I'm doing. It's all automatic. It feeds on insecurities. Or rather it allows depression to take over completely. In its most destructive manner. I can't tackle it this way. I have to choose my fights. When I have them. What weapons I use. What tactics to employ. What experiences I bring to bear. This is the real task. The only one that will see me live with depression effectively. The only one that can arrest the potential slide to oblivion. The only one that will keep me one step ahead. The only one that will make life worth living.

Friday 2nd September 2016

I may have been tempting fate in some of what I wrote yesterday, for my mood has taken a turn for the worse. I don't know at this stage, of course, whether this is a temporary aberration or something more prolonged. It just had to happen though didn't it? I state that my mood has steadied and, as if by some perverted magic and twisted logic, within hours the dark clouds begin to descend. I've tried to reason this out. The catalyst seemed to be some minor problems with the car. However, rather than deal with the matter – which I did – and see it in perspective as something to be expected in a vehicle that age – which I also did – for some reason my mood took a blow from which it is yet to recover. I tried to rally. I attempted to make conversation with Lesley, to show some interest in what she was doing, to raise a smile and even a laugh, but inside I was crying out in frustration and despair. Why? WHY? If only I had an answer. There's little I can do when this happens other than to keep going and try not to wallow, overthink and overcomplicate things. I need to try and let my behaviour, my actions, impact on my emotions and thoughts. In a positive sense. To that end, I've kept my appointments today even though I found them both a strain and an effort. In the first meeting – at the General Hospital – I tried to make a contribution, to input into proceedings, but I didn't seem to be able to say anything constructive or particularly insightful. I found myself struggling to keep pace and focus. The more I persevered, the less effective I felt I became. I began to think that people would be wondering what on earth I was doing there, and what I was being paid for. That old chestnut about justifying my presence. I can't really remember what I said, if I'm honest. It was obviously that memorable! In the second, a good friend opened up and confided in me that he had fears about his mental health. I again tried my best to give the advice and guidance he needed but I can't believe I lived up to anywhere near his expectations and my own. He's made an appointment to see his doctor tomorrow morning which is the right action, but I feel I've let him down. A rambling, incoherent, inconsistent me is not what he requires at the moment. Just when I needed to be firm, thorough, decisive and reassuring, my competence and ability to communicate effectively went AWOL. I just hope he could see through the mist and fog of my own efforts.

I must give out some signals when I feel so futile and ineffective. It's ironic that another person I usually see on Friday mornings also turned to me to ask for help and all I could do was reinforce the need for him to have confidence and self-belief! Those very qualities that I seem to lack at the moment. He seems to think that I am some walking authority on current job vacancies because every time we meet he asks if I have anything for him. If I don't – and realistically, how can I have? – I see the disappointment in his eyes. Disappointment in me just as much as the outcome. Looking into his face this morning, all I seemed to see was accusation and recrimination. But do people see behind my façade? Am I just as useless at putting on an act? When I try to be positive, to give what people expect me to give, despite my own tears and frustrations, are people able to penetrate my disguise? I guess some will and some do. Those that know me well will be able to note when things are wrong. Some people also have that innate ability not just to see, but to contextualise and understand.

I sometimes think that rather than try to battle through I should just hold my hands up every time and just say 'look, please don't expect anything from me, because I'm hurting at the moment and anything I say or do will be crap'. Or words to that effect. Instead of persevering and trying to give the impression that everything is normal, just be honest and say it isn't. I'm scared though as to how people would react. It's not that I don't want to admit when I'm struggling. That isn't me either. It's just that you don't always know how people will take being confronted with the truth. And I don't always have the ability to be tactful as well as open-ended. It's 'control' again, I'm afraid. Even when I'm feeling low – perhaps especially when I'm feeling low – I still feel the need to keep myself in check. I don't want to break down in tears. I certainly don't want to raise my voice in temper or, heaven forbid, hit myself and self-harm. I don't want to shout and scream. I don't want to let myself go. I actually want to be measured and calm. Even though I don't feel that way at all. The rambling, agitated, volatile me isn't nice. It can be scary. It can disturb. It may be honest, but perhaps honesty isn't always the best policy?

Saturday 3rd September 2016

No change in my mood. At times like this it's virtually impossible to find any form of respite or satisfaction. That activity or moment in which I genuinely feel anything like happiness. Everything becomes mundane, even activities that I customarily enjoy. It really is like going through the motions. I live by biological means in the sense that I breathe, eat, sleep etc. Anything else seems to be beyond me, certainly beyond my ability to attach and associate positive feelings or emotions to whatever it is I think or do. I'm never content with the moment. I'm constantly trying to catch up with whatever's next. I tell myself and try to put into practice a sense of looking forward to something, that notion that whatever looms on the horizon has to be, and is, better than my present state. But I fail every time. When I reach that destiny, what greets me is simply more of the same. As I know I've said before, it's a bit like trying to catch a bus that is always, tantalisingly, out of reach. Irrespective of my efforts to get on board. I drive myself, imploring my legs to one last effort, but just as I think I'm there, it pulls away again.

Actually, I'm still able to get something from reading though, so all is not lost. Maybe that's the thing I need to concentrate on at the moment, whilst I still retain the tiniest of positive connections? I'll have to choose my books wisely though in the sense that I don't want to set myself up to fail by tasking myself with reading something challenging or of considerable length. This is what life has become, when deciding what to read becomes an issue, a challenge to negotiate.

I've also tried to do two simple things at a time, to give myself an alternative focus when concentration and desire begin to dwindle. This works to an extent. It's not like multi-tasking. There's no goal as such, no end product. It's not a challenge in the sense that I have to make decisions or to grapple with the realities of my activity. It can literally come down to a different visual perspective. Last night I went on my lap-top whilst watching the telly and I've also got into the habit of reading outside whilst using my phone for sports updates and looking at the changing nature of the sky. It works for me. I can read a couple of pages, put the book down, look around me, listen to the environment, read some more, check the cricket scores and so on and so forth. Time seems to pass more quickly this way. Which is one good thing in my predicament. And at least I'm still using my senses and giving myself some options.

The one positive thing I should try and internalise is that with all that I've said, I've shown to myself that I'm not taking this lying down. I am still battling. I'm not resigned to defeat. I'm doing what I can. That's all I can do, after all is said and done.

Sunday 4th September 2016
My mood stays the same, but at least I got through another day in melancholia. That's something to hold onto. There was a point yesterday when I thought that time had stood still. When I

reckoned that I had another ten hours or so to survive until bed, and I seriously wondered how I was going to do it. However, Lesley had made an appointment for a test drive, so that gave me an item in my day, an appointment, to focus around, to be busy, to give me a change of scenery, to take up some time. It worked to an extent, especially as I persuaded her to stop in town on the way home for a coffee and a brief wander around the shops. The truth was that I just didn't want to go home. I couldn't face the monotony of depression and the same four walls, the low mood and my usual routines. At least not that early in the day.

We're going to have to make a decision shortly with regard to a new car. Hence the test drive. I say 'we', but of course I really mean Lesley. Our trusty Peugeot is becoming a little...well, untrustworthy. We're now spending more on repairs and servicing than the actual value of the car itself. Every time I venture out now, I can sense the tension and nerves within me. I expect something to go wrong. Driving has become a test of application and mental strength. And I'm sadly lacking in both at the moment. Having a car for most people is a necessity. To get them from A to B and back again on a daily basis, whether that be for work, domestic duties, seeing friends, visiting places and so on. For me, it's all of these things, but it's also a means of escape and effectively of recuperation. I may not actually choose to use it. And when I'm really ill, I barely do. It's more the fact that it's available to me as an option. I can get out if I want to. I can use it to take me to places that do have a positive impact on my mental health. I can devote some time to the journey and for a visit. I can realise an achievement, by perhaps going to a shop or even something as basic as filling it up with petrol. However, if I've lost confidence in the basic function of a vehicle, that option becomes less viable. I'm trapped, in other words.

We visited a dealer yesterday. I had to ask Lesley not to ask my opinion if she could help it. It's not that I don't have one, it's just that I can't decide what it is! That's difficult to do though. What I was asking was quite strange, when you think about it. To go as a couple to look at the feasibility of buying something important, but to allow only one person to talk and to make decisions. What on earth would people think of me? I hadn't thought it through, so for appearances sake I tried to contribute when I felt I could, even if it was just to reinforce what Lesley was saying. I didn't take my driving licence so only Lesley was able to take the car out. To be honest, I hadn't realised the need to bring it, but even when I did, I couldn't face that sense of scrutiny that would inevitably arise if I was in the hot seat. Plus the fact that it would have been a new environment, a car that I wasn't used to. I would need to do a test drive for myself and my ability to cope with a test drive, before I did the actual test drive itself! Try getting your head around that one!

We do need to think about what we're doing, of course. It's a major investment after all. But at some point, a decision has to be made. We can't go on for too long deliberating and researching possibilities. When that time comes I will again ruminate long and hard. Even if it's not me that ultimately decides, that won't stop that process of self-examination and critical reflection. Inevitably though that process won't just be in relation to the car, it will be about my involvement in the process itself. Did I do all that I could? Was I at least of some use to Lesley? Did I have some value? Am I still valuable?

Monday 5th September 2016

I know I'm not well. All the usual signs are there, but more than anything there is a great emptiness, a void that is working hard to prevent me from climbing the ladder to recovery once more. What the void really represents is life, all its facets and characteristics, all that gives living a purpose and a motivation, all that produces within us the necessary tools and attributes that are necessary for us not just to function but to do so with some positive association. I can't effectively do anything until that void begins to fill itself once more. I can continue to do what I'm doing. Little things, small tasks, routine habits. But they themselves do not constitute what is missing inside me. It's only when that feature that gives life its meaning begins to connect these elements together and moreover, gives each specific feature an injection of feeling, a boost of emotional adrenalin if you like, that I'll begin my ascent. I just hope it comes sooner rather than later.

I do have to be thankful though this morning. For some inexplicable reason, yesterday afternoon my PC threatened to do what it did a number of weeks ago and lose all my Outlook data. In trying to renew our Office subscription, some rogue element within the machine I'm looking at as I write told us that Outlook wouldn't open. It was doing all the same things again. I've spent so much time in the intervening period trying to restore my system, painstakingly entering data on people, groups and organisations, that to have it all consigned to the dustbin by a click of a mouse would have been hard to take. All I could see was catastrophe in front of my very eyes. Luckily within minutes, Joel had figured out what was happening and had rectified matters. I could have kissed him! I really don't know what I'd have done had the worst come to the worst. I felt physically sick as well as drained. All the lights were going out inside me, one by one. The last vestige of hope and ambition was being driven away. It's no wonder my head felt heavy for the rest of the evening. I survived though. Just.

Tuesday 6th September 2016

One of the problems in writing a diary is the fact that you are almost bound at times to repeat yourself. It may even be the case that I've used the same analogies and examples more than once during the course of the eight months I've been doing this. When writing my book on the Holocaust, I was meticulous in planning what I was going to say and when I was going to say it. Indeed, the planning stage, the outlining of the text, took a long time to put together. But when it was done, I knew I only had to follow what I'd decided upon. That didn't mean it was easy to write, of course. Just that it was prepared and logical. With this diary, it is different. I don't really know what I'm going to write about from one day to the next. I've identified themes and issues that I know I need to cover at some point, things that are a necessary component of any depressive's journey. But it wouldn't be an authentic diary if too much planning was involved. And more than anything, I do want this journal to be true, a faithful and genuine representation of all that I go through.

I'm also conscious of the certainty that at times I will totally contradict myself! That I will –perhaps even during the course of one single entry – confuse you the reader by saying things that not only do not make complete sense, but also seem to refute or question what I've said previously. I make no apologies for this. It is, after all, simply a reflection of the way the mind of someone battling with mental illness works. Though the search for consistency and logic is inherently linked to the issue of control, the reality is that I am fully aware that there are occasions – and sometimes long periods – when, despite my best efforts, I fail when it comes to these particular attributes. When your mind is racing. When it is confused and unclear. When it is struggling to combat the most severe consequences and symptoms of depression, it does the very basics, but nothing more. It operates. That is all. It doesn't close down – much as sometimes I would wish it did. But it can't deal with complexity and ambiguity. It can't penetrate and decipher the challenges that come with daily life. It isn't in any position to achieve what you ordinarily rely upon as a requirement of everyday thinking. It's ill. That's the bottom line.

It's important therefore to see the brain in the same way as any other part of one's body. When you've injured your leg, your ability to run or even walk is compromised. When you have a stomach ache, your normal capacity to eat is affected. You get the idea. The same is true of the brain. Why wouldn't it be?

At the moment, I'm struggling to stay afloat. My mental illness is presently overwhelming. My mind isn't well. It needs attention. It requires rest and recuperation. It shouldn't be expected to behave as it normally does – even if that normality is still suffused with depression. It's a question really of relativity. I'm moving more and more towards one end, the dangerous, scary extreme. I'm usually in the middle somewhere. Very occasionally I venture towards the positive side, but ordinarily I can't hope to stay there for any considerable amount of time. I've become accustomed to my position. That doesn't mean I don't fight. It doesn't equate to resignation. It's just reality. And the reality here and now is that I'm once more in a battle for my life. I don't think that's a melodramatic statement. I don't mean to suggest that I'm doing so all the time. What I mean is that when depression becomes more severe, there is an inherent danger that your mind loosens and becomes dominated to the extent that ominous, menacing and unpredictable thoughts enter into the equation. They sometimes become overbearing. They can take over your conscious and subconscious being. Add that to the fact that combatting depression is wearisome – it takes it out of you – and you have a serious and disturbing combination of elements. I'm fully prepared for the possibility that I will question my desire to live at some point. That's what normally happens and there is nothing in my present circumstances to suggest that this is an exception to the rule. As best I can, I have to be prepared for such an eventuality. And more than ever, I'll need the help of others.

Wednesday 7th September 2016

I had a horrible dream last night. For some reason, I'd returned to school to join two old teachers in making music. However, aside from my first chord, my ability to play my 'cello seemed to evaporate into thin air. The more desperate my attempts to keep up and retain some modicum of musicality, the less efficient and accomplished I became. It was as if I'd gone backwards, my proficiency and authority gradually diminishing before my very eyes. Before long, I was only capable of playing long notes in first position[33]. Quickly that became open strings. I was a novice once more. All vestiges of the reputation I had gained at school as a decent, competent musician had gone. But that wasn't the end of it. Fate then decreed that my 'cello itself become the target of decay and unrealised dreams. It began to fall apart at the seams. The bridge fell off, the strings could no longer withstand the pressure required to function, the sound post came away, the veneer became coarse. What was once a beautiful instrument with a wonderful, rich and resonating sound, had transformed itself into its most basic element – a lump of wood.

I tried once this was done to hide the disaster from my father. To convince him that all was well. That I wasn't neglecting his request, his instruction for me to devote hours to practice. To fulfil his wish that I succeed in becoming a professional musician. But what could I do? The evidence was too damning. It's probably not a coincidence – given how the subconscious mind works – that only the other day I was listening to a CD of Rostropovich[34] playing the Chopin Sonata, a piece I performed in public as part of my undergraduate finals exams in Durham some twenty-five years ago. As my ears marvelled at the sound, it was hard to believe that I was ever capable of playing something so technically difficult. But I was. And I did. Once. What a waste. Why did I not discipline myself when I had the skills and talent to propel myself to a successful professional career? Why did I give up when I did? Why couldn't I energise and motivate myself? Why did I need my Dad so badly to give me that purpose? Why did he have to die when he did?

Disconcertedly, last night's saga wasn't over. In the small hours, I once again succumbed to the trauma of nightmare. I was still at school, but this time all those boys in my boarding house that were younger than me when I was in the sixth form had become adversaries. They were all bigger than me and every single one of them was intent on causing me physical as well as emotional upset. They pushed me about. They punched me. They wouldn't let me get away. It was as if they were addressing the call of some long-established vendetta. I had become, once more, the victim of bullying behaviour. Only there was no respite whatsoever. Wherever I turned, they were there. I soiled myself (in my dream, that is!) in my desperation to escape. Only there was no sanctuary or refuge and certainly no peace. I had to force my eyes to open to put an end to it all. On three separate occasions I went back to sleep, but there was no rest. Fearful of a return to where I'd been, my mind – for once – worked for me. Every time I found myself once more by that precipice, I made myself wake up and put it behind me. I have no idea how that worked, of what strange force or magnetism I was able to draw upon, but I was grateful at last for an end to my suffering.

Thursday 8th September 2016

I've spent this morning over at Leicester Racecourse at the AGM of my local NHS mental health trust. Although I am a member, and, of course, a service-user, I did have an ulterior motive in attending as I hoped to recruit more people to some work I'm helping with in relation to advance planning. As it was, I only managed to generate interest once, but that didn't mean my time was necessarily wasted. It was interesting to see and hear what the Trust itself sees as its current situation. Its review of the year and assessment of activity is naturally of interest given my disability, but it's always fascinating to see how organisations manage to convey positive messages irrespective of the climate of the times and the factual setbacks that can occur through things such as formal inspections. I fully accept that there is a positive element to bad news and sure enough, we heard many references to 'areas that we need to improve' and 'lessons we need to learn'. However, we were told, courtesy of the Chief Executive, that there have been 'significant areas of progress'. I have no reason to doubt him or indeed any other of the presenters. The facts are available should one wish to see them. It's how you interpret and utilise them to paint optimistic pictures of the way forward that is key to how bodies such as these take people like me along with them. They have my support. It's inherent in my membership. However, I have to say that I myself do not see any signs of change in the type, level and frequency of service. More significantly perhaps, every time I talk to other service-users, they say the same. Politicians tell us all the time that there needs to be greater financial investment and are quick to parade themselves when there is. But the rhetoric – and more tellingly, the money – doesn't always translate into a changed service. Change for the better that is. The waiting lists and times seem to be just as long. There are obviously issues over funding of some treatments. There appear to be shortages of staff and working conditions within the NHS, by all accounts, are at an all-time low. I do admire staff for the way they work given this climate, and we are fortunate that the NHS still retains both credibility and that purpose for which many readily give of their time and service. I do wish the Trust well, but I know they are in for another uneasy ride in the next financial year.

Given my current low mood, I couldn't do some things whilst I was there. What hits me the most is the increased sensitivity of my emotions and of my senses when I'm ill. I was genuinely scared to enter the building. I passed a door leading into the main room and all I could see was a succession of faces all involved in intense conversations. The hum from the room was disturbing. Of course it wasn't anything unusual. This is how these things are. What changes is me and my ability to cope. I steadied myself, took the plunge and entered but I felt essentially like a fish out of water. It was as if all heads turned to look at me. Factually, they didn't. Not one. But the feeling was the complete opposite. I was being scrutinised once more, my every move and action subject to critical examination, my intent and whole appearance questioned. It's a horrible feeling and what makes it worse is the fact that it doesn't go away. I tried to look inconspicuous. I got myself a coffee. I pretended to play around on my phone. There were stands all around me, services that I would almost certainly have found interesting, maybe even useful, but to move in their direction would signal a movement of intent. And I just couldn't do it. The prospect of having to talk to people I didn't know. To even be in the presence of strangers was just too much. I looked for an outlet and found a couple of familiar faces, but when they moved on, I was left alone in trepidation once more. I sat myself down and awaited the formal proceedings. I can deal with that, because there's a set pattern, a tried and trusted formula. I can hide, if you like, amongst the audience. I become anonymous. But once it was over and lunch was announced, I decided to make my exit. I just couldn't face the informality of socialising and networking. It would have destroyed me today. Organisations really need to find innovative ways of addressing this issue because I am pretty certain I was not the only one to feel as I did. Particularly given that mental health is pre-eminent in the remit of the Trust. But I've yet to find anyone that ever manages successfully to broker this novelty. It's all the same usual methods. They work for most people, but not for all and that simply isn't good enough. Yes, I can look on a website. Yes I can read the reports. But how do you replicate both face-to-face engagement and interaction and be attune to people's mental health needs and requirements at the same time? It's not easy. But there must be a way.

Friday 9th September 2016

I feel unbelievably tired today. I didn't sleep well (another school-based nightmare), but that's not the foremost reason for my lethargy. No, it's simply a reflection of my state of mind and of mood. The physiological machinations that connect mental wellbeing and mood levels in particular with tiredness are unknown to me – and would probably be beyond my capacity to appreciate. All I know is that connection there is. And a direct one at that. I had dropped Lesley in the city centre and had a bit of time to spare before my own meeting, so I decided to have a wander. Almost immediately, I was aware that my feet were almost being dragged along by the rest of me. I was breathing heavily. Every single step was an effort. The weight that I've talked about in the past seemed that bit more cumbersome and protracted. That sense of heaviness was pronounced. There was nothing I could do to dispel these sensations. They stay with me for as long as my mood is at a certain level. When I start to feel brighter, I also begin to feel lighter. It is that causal in effect and impact.

A deep sense of irony – almost of a comical nature – is also strong at the moment. At every meeting I've been to since my mood started to dip, I've been greeted by the statement 'you look really well'. My immediate response would be 'how' if I didn't wish to dismiss the notion by simply accepting it and carrying on. I do wonder whether it is the case that people are just being nice, and that they wish to be positive and encouraging. Or do I genuinely appear to be well even if I feel lousy? If the latter, I must be a fabulous actor. The other possibility is that the last time I saw these individuals I must have looked absolutely terrible. Everything in relative terms!

The fatigue that I mentioned earlier also plays a part here. If walking is draining, if breathing is laboured, if other bodily movements are more challenging, then the same must be the case with regard to talking. It becomes much more of an effort. In fact it is essentially energy-sapping. For many people this is probably hard to conceptualise. But there is a real focus within me on trying my best to limit what I propel through my mouth using my vocal chords. I'm conserving energy. I try to express things as succinctly as possible without coming across as rude or abrupt. If that happens, it leads to much more damaging thought processes – thinking traps in essence. If I can get away with one word answers, I do. I also try to turn questions around or to ask whoever it is I'm speaking with to do all the work. 'How are you?' when addressed to me, tends to precipitate the response 'I'm fine, what about you?' The other factor is that I really don't want to talk about me. I find myself decidedly uninspiring. I can't see anything I'm doing as being of interest to anyone else. How, when you come to think of it, do you describe the sense of nothingness and mundaneness that you consider as being your existence? I'd rather everyone else talked about themselves. I can nod my head and smile. I can look interested and engaged. That's all much easier to do than talk.

That being said, conversations generally are much more demanding in themselves, whether I'm talking or listening. I guess it comes down to things like concentration, an attribute that is also called into question when mood is low. I was very conscious of that today. I found myself working really hard to stay with the discussion, to retain the thread that connected me with what was going on. It's so hard mentally, but also physically. It's no wonder that I seek the solace of my own company. Even if I don't like myself, it's just easier to cope with.

Saturday 10th September 2016

I know that when I'm low I spend a lot of the time sitting in my chair, staring into the distance. I'm aware of the stillness around me, but it's as if I feel incapable or unworthy of upsetting the calm. You see that 'calm' represents both nothingness and the status quo. The theory is that the longer I stay in that moment, the longer the moment becomes and the less chance there is of anything infiltrating both me and the situation I'm in. And that's a good thing. Because in my present state, interference always equates to the negativity of anxiety, stress and worry. It's as if I can cope with time standing still. I become accustomed to it. I equate to it. It loses its fear eventually. Interference means change and change in ways I can't always anticipate or foresee. Change, in my distorted thinking, brings uncertainty, and uncertainty means having to adapt. Adaptation requires action, and action means decision making. The spiral effectively continues until I'm once more in that state of nervous tension. When I'm like this, I don't see this as likely, I see it as inevitable.

My best option, therefore, is to stay still, let time go on without my active participation. The consequences may be less stressful, but they don't come without their challenges. The inertia you are trying your hardest to create and maintain isn't possible indefinitely. Try sitting in one position without movement. Eventually – and it comes quicker than you think – you feel a yearning to shift yourself, even if it's only to move your legs. Your mind tells you that you are uncomfortable, that you have to do something about it. And that's only your own physical movement. Inevitably, change also happens in the environment around you. Life outside your own body doesn't somehow sympathise with your predicament. It's not a televisual trick. You can't literally halt time. Something will disturb the tranquillity you've done your best to achieve. And the thing is that this happens continually. You can't live in a vacuum. It's impossible. It's probably only a matter of seconds before change hits you, even if you don't want it to.

Sunday 11th September 2016

I've been on my own this weekend. My own choice. As Rachel is shortly to fly back to Sri Lanka, she had arranged a family weekend retreat to celebrate her birthday a little early. I'd love to have gone, been with everyone, and joined in the revelry, but I just couldn't. Initially, I'd planned just to go for the day yesterday – they've been there since Friday night and are due back this afternoon – but even that shortened prospect began to fill me with real anxiety as last week progressed. I knew I wouldn't be able to do it.

I can't accurately and completely describe how horrible this is. When my mental illness comes between me and my family I resent it enormously. It's not that I don't love them. Of course that's not the case. It's simply the interaction, the social dynamics, the conversations and the expectation of happiness that I can't face. Those of you who enjoy simply being in a room and talking, enjoying the company of others, chipping in now and again, making others laugh, swapping anecdotes and stories, I envy you. It may be difficult to understand how all these factors – every one of which is deemed positive and natural – can suffocate and stifle, can set someone apart, imprison them within themselves. That's my reality when I'm low in mood. The tension and anxiety with me becomes impossible to withstand. I want to join in, but every movement I make seems to magnify my predicament. I desperately want to be like everyone else. But I'm not. I'm like a kettle waiting to boil, full of pent up frustration, wanting a release. But I can't control how that release will come and what it will look and sound like. What I'm scared of is that my mental state will express itself in whatever I say or do. That it will be inappropriate or scary in response. My depression literally talking and behaving. Staying silent isn't a remedy. It singles you out if you don't do as others do. You become terribly self-conscious. You feel that what you say and what you do is going to lead to everyone looking in your direction, whereas it's anonymity and invisibility that you crave. That's not a recipe for successful interaction.

But I am faced with an impossible quandary. Do I do my best to fit in, put on a brave face and endure? Or do I face facts, recognise my limitations and withdraw? I can handle the first option for a short while. Sometimes it even leads to brief glimpses of normality, when I genuinely do enjoy the situation – however temporary it may be. But it's always time-limited. I habitually need an escape route or outlet. I have to take myself away, to re-energise, to reflect, to do what I need to do to go again. I'm very conscious though that this puts demands not just on me, but on other people too, particularly Lesley. I don't want her to be worrying about how I am when she should be enjoying people's company, particularly that of her own family. I don't want her having to negotiate my mental state at times of togetherness. I just want her to do what everyone else is doing. Withdrawal becomes therefore the better option. I suffer as a consequence. Though I can cope with myself, I don't enjoy my own company when I'm like this. But coping is the limit of my horizons. It's what I have to try and achieve. Nothing else is remotely possible. And faced with the choice between solitude and group, I tend to cope best when I isolate myself from others, and perhaps also from life itself.

Monday 12th September 2016

I made the mistake yesterday afternoon of calling my Mum. Obviously a statement like that needs quantifying. It wasn't, needless to say, that I didn't want to hear her voice or catch up on her news. It wasn't even that I didn't want to talk to her and tell her how I am. No, it was because I was incapable of engaging in conversation. And it showed. Almost as soon as I'd dialled the number and heard her answering, I knew that I was in trouble. The words wouldn't come. There was no incentive or desire inside me to speak and the more it went on, the greater became my wish to just put the phone down with a quick apology. Even acknowledging what she was saying became an onerous task. What must she think of me? I think at the end I could hear the worry in her voice. It seemed like she was hanging on, wanting the reassurance that I was OK. But what could I tell her? The fact is I'm not OK. I'm ill. No matter what I try to do to hide that fact from my nearest and dearest, I know I'm not convincing. You can't mask it completely. There are too many symptoms and signs of distress. Even if you manage to disguise one, you will be betrayed by another.

What was also apparent mid-conversation was the fact that I couldn't remember certain words. My mind went blank on more than one occasion. This is becoming a much more frequent occurrence. It's strange to say this – in fact it's probably quite bizarre – but I only hope this new phenomenon is related to my current mental illness. I don't want to add early dementia to my ever-increasing curriculum vitae! I've tried to rationalise this. And I may have succeeded. If, because of my mental state, I'm more tired. If, as a consequence, it becomes increasingly difficult to get the machine that is my body to work. If the limit of my expectation is that everything inside of me operates only to the level entitled 'coping'. Then it makes complete sense that my brain is as affected as any other bit of me. That element within my brain that powers things such as recollection and memory will, quite naturally, be reduced in its efficiency. It makes sense. When I'm not well, I need longer to digest things, to register what's happening, what's being said, what others are doing. And so on and so forth. By natural correlation, what comes out of me as a response will need a little longer as well. I can usually find the words eventually. They just don't always come when I need them. I'm existing in classic slow-motion!

Tuesday 13th September 2016

All of a sudden, life has become scary. I guess what I'm really saying is that I feel intimidated by everything around me that involves people. Nothing's happened in the big wide world to make me feel this way. It's entirely internal. It's me. Everyday interaction – of whatever kind – has suddenly taken on a new dimension. Whatever I do and wherever I am, I'm not sure of myself. I don't know how I'm coming across. I feel tense and wary. I desperately want to be normal, but I've forgotten what that actually constitutes. Even the most routine of occurrences sees me in some sort of spotlight – self-imposed but no less draconian in its impact – in which I'm being assessed, scrutinised, examined. But for what? I've thought about that question a lot and the only answer I can realistically propose is 'for my sanity'. As an example, when I was sitting with Lesley last night watching Panorama deal with the issue of gambling addiction, we started to debate the very nature of addiction itself and how organisations tasked to deal with its consequences should go about doing so. I must have come across as heated and even aggressive. I thought I was just being forthright. Now I know it can be a fine balance, but it made me realise that what I think I am and how I think I am is no longer necessarily reality. I'm something different. I didn't feel angry. Only frustrated at not being able to say precisely what I felt. The words, the reasoning, just wouldn't come. But I had no idea as to my persona. The same was also true when I was telling Elliot to come off his laptop and go for a shower. When he didn't go immediately – because he was finishing off something – I immediately felt a tension within me and I had to keep on at him until eventually he did raise himself from his seat and make his way upstairs. I didn't think I was doing anything other than offering a strong reminder, but now I'm not so sure.

All this has made me feel that the only safe situation for me is to withdraw from everyone. I can then be as opinionated and forceful as I want to be – only with myself. I can deal with things in my own way without impacting on anyone else. If I don't like my own company – as I said on Sunday – at least in doing this I'm not imposing it on those around me. Refuge. Isolation. Sanctuary. Whatever the word is, that's my goal, my preservation, my means of survival. Of course, this just isn't realistic. To go outside my own house at the minute is a real challenge. We went to test drive a new car yesterday evening. But could I willingly and happily engage with the process? No, I couldn't. Lesley had to do it all – drive, ask questions, negotiate, decide. Everything. I sat there like a proverbial spare part, trying to fit in, but feeling out of my depth, scared to say or do anything. Afterwards, I ruminated long and hard as to what the people at the dealers showroom must have thought. What I realised was that I can't keep life at bay. I'm not Robinson Crusoe. I'm not locked away, forgotten, in a padded cell. I'm alive and that means I have no choice in terms of dealing with what life throws at me. It isn't going to protect me. It isn't going to leave me alone. I have to stick with it, not matter how hard that is. I can do some things to help ease my turmoil. But telling everything and everyone to go away, isn't one of them.

I will get better. I have to keep reminding myself of this until eventually it starts to happen.

Oh and by the way, we bought a Kia Sportage. Just in case you were wondering!

Wednesday 14th September 2016

After work today, Lesley is travelling up to Lincolnshire to see her Mum who is currently in hospital after a knee operation. She won't be back until tomorrow night. Whilst of course this is a necessary trip, for me it means increased anxiety and a heightened awareness of my OCD. When Lesley isn't around, the wariness returns, as do the checking procedures that are my only means of coping with it. I am miles better than I used to be. In fact, it's virtually unrecognisable compared to the situation some fifteen odd years ago when my whole life was hampered by my inability to leave rooms and buildings without constant vigilance and the security of routine. I remember a time, for example, when I was renting an office on behalf of my employers at the home of a community organisation here in Leicester. It used to take me some 45 minutes at the end of the day to get out and start my journey home. I can still recollect the pattern of behaviour that I would have to repeat each day. Firstly, I had to go to the toilet and ensure that all the windows were closed and the taps fully turned off. Any drip would stifle and upset me. I'd immediately believe that as a result there would be a flood, the building would be unusable, I would lose my office facility and therefore my job. I'd then return to my office, turn all the switches off and unplug every machine. Each plug would have to be laid down in a particular fashion and left in the same place every night. I would then ensure that all windows were closed and fully locked, that the curtains were drawn across so that no light whatsoever could get in, before carrying what I believed I needed to take home to my car. There were certain items that I felt I couldn't leave in the building overnight. I'd worry that if there was a burglary such material would be stolen. I'd then be sued for negligence. I'd lose my job and then my home. Full catastrophization (if that's a word?). Finally, I'd return to the office once more and do a final check. Or rather I'd have to go through a routine cycle of checking. Seven times! That was my number. If I couldn't do this, or if there was some slight alteration to my habits. If the phone went, for example, or someone else entered to say goodbye. If I saw something that wasn't correctly in position, or I'd forgotten to put something away, I'd have to start all over again. Oh, I forgot to mention the phone. I'd have to pick up and put down the receiver seven times. If I didn't do this, I would convince myself that someone was still on the line, that as a consequence, I'd run up a huge bill, lose my job etc. You know the rest. Finally, the worst bit. Locking my door. This one activity would frighten me more than anything, because almost inevitably there would be other people still around the building. Everything else I could do in secret. No-one could see me. But here I was potentially in the full glare of human scrutiny. I had to lock the door and check it was locked…seven times. I can't begin to describe the tension within me as I forced myself through this predicament whilst trying not to let on and let others see what I could only believe was pure madness. And this was every day. Every single day.

Every now and again there is a return to OCD of this magnitude. But only rarely. For most of the time, I'm not conscious of this need to check. If I do over elaborate, I don't realise it. I still check things, but not in a specific manner or pattern. And I don't have to repeat myself seven times over. Only when Lesley isn't around do the behaviours of my past threaten to disturb my present. So tonight I will check the oven, make sure the doors are locked, the lights are switched off etc. I will do so much more vigilantly than is normal. I will take longer to do so. I will feel the need to temper my anxiety. But it won't dictate my mood or my behaviour as it used to. I'm winning this particular battle. And have been for a while. That's something to be proud of, I guess.

Thursday 15th September 2016

I managed. That's about the limit to what I can say. My brain adapted to the situation by applying some form of logic. That everything was fine in the house when Lesley left yesterday morning, so if I don't disturb anything, there will be nothing to fear. It kind of makes sense, if you think about it, but of course what it does do is restrict just about every single action that you wish to take. Unavoidably as well, there are things that inevitably you have to do. You can't not switch a light on when it's dark, for example. You can't avoid locking up the house. You can't resist opening windows when the temperature is unbearably hot and sticky. You can't get a glass of water without turning on a tap.

So whilst I did my level best to disturb the status quo as little as possible, I had to put myself in positions where my OCD would raise its ugly head. And it did.

Being conscious about everything that you do, everything that you touch, every movement you make is wearisome. You find yourself trying to remember exactly what you did, so that the exact reverse is possible. This may appear strange to you, but it again is logical. The only problem is that when I use the term 'exact', I mean precisely that. If I feel that there was any difference at all, I'm back to square one again. And I risk having to repeat things seven times until I feel reasonably confident that I've 'remedied' the situation. The difference I'm talking about may be the length of time it took, or the sequence of actions involved.

I ought to make one thing abundantly clear. If I do have to do things seven times, that doesn't necessarily equate to resolution or satisfaction in my mind. It's not as if as soon as I hit the number seven I automatically relax and can therefore leave things alone. It's just not that simple. It is more than likely that I'll still ruminate, and do so with an intensity and fear that is still hard to stomach and even harder to rectify. Many's the time I've been unable to resist the temptation to look and check once more. And then the cycle begins again. What 'seven' allows me to do is to take stock. To use everything I've learned through techniques such as Cognitive Behavioural Therapy, to apply that learning to my predicament, to reason things out using common notions such as likelihood and predictability. Where I've changed is that I've become more able to do this at the first sign of trouble. When the number is one, in other words, not seven. The ability to do this doesn't come naturally to someone with OCD. In fact, it's the exact opposite. But if you are able to apply systematically the awareness and skills involved in therapeutic instruction, it can make a massive difference. Enough to make you believe that you have mastered things, even if occasionally there is a return to the insanity of the past.

Friday 16th September 2016

A matter of minutes after I'd finished yesterday's diary entry, my Mum called to tell me that she'd been to the doctors, had some tests done and had been told that she had skin cancer. Though it took a while for this news to truly sink in, now that it has, I am truly devastated. She sounded so frail and fragile on the phone, so unsure of herself, it genuinely felt that my heart was breaking. I've had some challenging times in my life, some horrible moments, some shattering obstacles to face, but this is up there with the worst of them. It's not only that this is happening to someone I love to bits, it's the fact that I feel so ill-equipped to offer the kind of solid, dependable support she needs. I am barely able to look after myself. I just wish that it was happening to me. I could probably cope more readily with that, the pain, the worry, the uncertainty. It wouldn't see it as adding much to the way I'm facing my current crisis with depression. In fact, it may well deflect attention away from my mental state. But I'm aware that I'm thinking out loud, rather than thinking things through. In fact, I'm not really sure what I'm saying.

Words just don't feel adequate at the moment. I can't express myself in the way I would wish. I need you the reader to sense my anguish, rather than read about it. To imagine. To envisage. To conceptualise. To try and put yourself in my shoes. To feel and to internalise. I don't have anything left in the tank other than my emotion. That isn't enough. But it's all I have.

Saturday 17th September 2016
I journeyed over to Whitchurch today to see my Mum.

I feared the start of the day. In fact, I'd wished so fervently beforehand that it was all over. I didn't want to face what I knew I wouldn't be able to avoid. Every single feeling was negative. I couldn't see beyond my own fears and I worried about my ability to cope. I knew I had to be strong, decisive, firm, but equally as assured, relaxed and comforting. How would my Mum be? What would be her reaction when she saw me?

I determined on the drive over that what was required was to put on a face. Even if I felt wretched and fragile myself, I couldn't let my Mum see that side of me. It was thirty years ago all over again. My own mental state had to be secondary, to be put firmly to one side. What mattered wasn't me inside, but what I said and how I looked. I remembered my Dad's letter. His request for me to look after her after he'd gone. That's what had to come first. And for that to happen I had to quell every sinew of anxiety, every tiny morsel of depression. I knew that that was, in so many ways, an impossible task. It couldn't be sustained indefinitely. But I might be able to do so for a few hours, at least as long as I was with her. And I did.

She wasn't nearly as vulnerable as I thought she might be. Of course, I knew full well that she too was wearing a mask. How ironic that both of us were trying so hard to quell our mutual worries and fears. But we did. And as a consequence, I was able – I think – to offer some pearls of wisdom gleaned from many years of having to face my own mental trials and tribulations. I talked of the benefits of CBT, of trying to rationalise one's worries, one's initial, fear-driven conclusions. I tried to make her see that she had always been a fighter. That she had overcome so many obstacles in the past. That this was simply another one. I tried to make reason her goal. To instil in her the strength that I knew was there, lying dormant and pushed aside maybe, but still within her. To make her realise that she wasn't alone. That there were practical answers and solutions to every single possible predicament.

Did it work? I think so. There were no tears. Visible ones anyway. It was still, however, with a heavy heart that I drove quietly and slowly away from my childhood home. I remembered a photograph that I have on my PC. Taken some time in the seventies, I guess. Of us all standing proudly in front of the house. A family intact. Optimistic and cheerful. And then, only then, did the tears come.

Sunday 18th September 2016

I was shattered when I got home yesterday evening. But at least I felt that I'd done something positive. Who knows, I may even be able to use my stance from yesterday in a constructive way to combat my current depression?

It comes down again to Fletch's 'little victories', doesn't it?

I just hope my Mum is feeling something similar. But I can't do any more than what I did during the course of my time with her. Only keep up that persona. Reinforce those messages. Keep saying the right things. Keep encouraging her. Keep telling her that I'm here.

She sees the specialist within the customary two-week period for cancer patients. That will be her next ordeal. She'll worry, of course. But she'll get through it. She knows hospitals and medical appointments so well. It's precisely her familiarity, her past experiences that she as to draw upon. It may well be the case that she's in a much better position to cope as a result of the fact that she's always been ill herself with her heart condition. At least compared with someone facing illness of this kind for the first time. The many occasions we had to face the medical profession head on with Dad and Danny will also be something to utilise in a positive way. It's again ironic that all the horrors we've had to undergo during the course of our lives may well stand us in a better, stronger and more durable stead.

Monday 19th September 2016

The start of yet another working week. I was more conscious than ever today that I'm currently working at limited capacity. I seem to be slower at the uptake. Things take longer to register and to deal with. I can't focus as quickly and as completely as I can when I'm well. I have to expect this. It's nothing new, after all. Usually, I adjust simply by allowing myself the luxury of added time, or limiting what I have to do during any given period. But today was one of those days when both these coping mechanisms were impossible to activate for the simple reason that impatience got the better of me. I wanted to get things done, to put them to bed quickly, irrespective of their complexity, without consciously realising the inherent need for thought and reflection. It seems such a paradox. Total inconsistency. Rather than recognise the need to ease my mind into whatever it set its task to be, I wanted to rush through things to eradicate that recognition, to avoid the thinking process entirely. To run on automatic pilot. It was as if thinking itself was painful, too trying, too exacting, too cumbersome. I just wanted to exist. Not to consciously do so, not to burden my mind with complications or problems. Not even to do the basics. Not to register, not to reason, not to deliberate. Just to be.

How I got through the two meetings I'd scheduled for myself I really don't know. Both focused on my Holocaust Memorial Day work and both seemed to go well. What I said seemed pertinent and worthwhile. I took on what was said to me. I made note of what actions I need to do as follow-ups. But if you asked me to say whether I was fully conscious of my contribution. If you pressed me on the mental processes that were at play, that I brought to the fore, that I used as tools, I would have to resort to my metaphorical 'hard drive'. It was there within me. The rock, the pedestal that I can fall back on when times are tough. But it was nothing more than that.

I'm probably being inherently self-critical. Perhaps I'm not doing myself justice or allowing myself the laxity that one needs when times are tough? I just don't know. All I can say for certain is that I'm not totally conscious of what words I'm using now as I write this entry. I don't know whether I'm making sense, or whether I'm once more having to draw upon my inner reserves. My intellectual, decipherable DNA, so to speak. It feels akin to driving a car and getting to a destination without active or involved aforethought, without realising the mechanical and sensory journey that is also involved. Suddenly I'm there. How, why and by what means is secondary and actually, quite irrelevant.

Tuesday 20th September 2016

I had to take Elliot to his first CAMHS CBT session this morning. He did remarkably well. Very composed. Lucid in his responses. Thorough and comprehensive in his self-assessments. I was really proud of him, especially as I know from my own experiences what challenges and difficulties are involved. It's no easy matter to have to talk succinctly and in some detail about very personal affairs and concerns, particularly when you are meeting someone for the first time. And for one so young, it really is quite astonishing. He has started on a path that will almost certainly be troubling and painful, even occasionally devastating, but one paved with remedial intentions, one that can be liberating and, if all goes well, life-enhancing. Our task as parents is to continually remind him of this, that he can progress, that change is possible, that he has within him the same capabilities that can inspire recovery. That he has qualities that will improve his life, freeing him from the restrictions that he currently endures.

For me, to witness my little boy go through similar experiences to my own is nothing less than shattering. I can't help blaming myself. I've tried my best to rationalise things, to use what I know to come to conclusions that are logical and trustworthy, but I can't. Everywhere I look, every turn I take, every thought process I go through, they all lead to the same incriminating judgment. I should have seen this coming. I should have forestalled it. I should have intervened earlier. I should have been firmer, more decisive, more insightful. I should have spent longer with him when it first began to materialise. I should have been able to see the dangers ahead. I should. I should. I should. Is there ever a more punitive beginning to a sentence than these two small words?

It's not too late though. He can turn things around. He's clever. He's aware. He knows what he's facing. He's not a reluctant speaker. He's very forward in his observations. He is not embarrassed to admit or to divulge. He knows he has support. He knows what we as parents can do and what we can't. And – to come back to those words again – what we should do and what we shouldn't.

It's ironic – but certainly not strange – that when I woke this morning, I anticipated my bigger challenge to be what came after his appointment. Today is the last day that we can use our

Peugeot. Its insurance cover runs out at midnight tonight. As we intend to sell it on the open market, I was tasked with taking it to a car wash for a thorough clean, inside and out. This prospect, I have to admit, filled my mind last night with all sorts of horrific thoughts. I knew where I had to go, but I hadn't done this on my own before. I wasn't sure what to ask for, where actually to park, where to wait. It was all new to me. And it's novelty that I find difficult to come to terms with. Where most people just go with the flow, I over think. I see problems. I expect challenges. I get so fearful. It just consumes me. What is worse, I'm obsessed with how I look to others. It's not just that I get scared, it's that I look scared as well. How do I deceive those around me? How do I convince people that I'm fine and in control? How do I deal with this potential 'double whammy'? It comes down to damage limitation. Or at least it did this morning. I was helped by the fact that I had Elliot with me. It was a distraction and a diversion. And a welcome one. The irony – if it needs spelling out – is that I can adjust to my role as a compassionate parent, I can be that safety net that Elliot needs, I can say and do what is right in this context. But what I can't seem to do as readily and as comfortably, is deal with the practicalities of something as routine as washing the car. Life can be very weird.

Wednesday 21st September 2016

At the minute the world seems a very scary place. I'm not referring to prominent news items such as terrorist attacks or various criminal activities. Or even natural disasters. What I mean is the world around me, in all its manifestations. The world immediately outside my front door. The world inhabited by ordinary people doing everyday things. Just to illustrate the point. I decided to put £10 worth of petrol in the Peugeot late yesterday afternoon (I was conscious that it needed something in the tank for anyone interested in buying to have a quick drive), and accordingly journeyed down to our local garage. As soon as I pulled out of the drive, my radar switched automatically to 'threat status'. The driver of every car that came close became immediately menacing, as if a sudden outburst of road rage was imminent. Every person that looked like crossing the road in front of me became adversarial. In my mind, I mean. The prospect of contact. That's what it was. Of having to engage with someone else. Of having to cope with situations that loomed, accompanied by a dark cloud, rather than actual physical, tangible experiences. Even when I was paying for the petrol – a simple process, one hardly necessitating communication other than the transference of money – I was aware that my heart was beating a little faster. I was anticipating problems. I was expecting confrontation. This happens continually when I'm not well. It's part of the illness that is depression.

What I need to return to is refuge, a sanctuary, a haven where nobody can get to me. A place where my madness can venture without it affecting anyone else. A place where it can just be what it is. A place where judgments, perspectives, responses do not hold me to account. A place where people cannot enter, where they can't intervene, where they no longer have the ability to impact upon my fragile mind.

Luckily for me, Lesley and my family provide this necessary and supportive environment. But even so there are times when only solitude – complete solitude – can keep the world at arm's length. In my home, there are places I can go to when this feeling is acute. Outside on the patio. Our bedroom. However, there are occasions when the temptation to go somewhere else, somewhere remote, is really strong. When I'm on a train, I often look out at the countryside as we speed through it, and imagine myself hiding away in a thick wood or in a lone shed. I wonder what it would be like to camp out under the stars with nothing and no-one around me. With no resources to draw upon other than my own. It becomes a yearning. The only complications of life are those immediate to my situation. Where can I get food and drink? Where can I be so that nobody can find me? How will I pass the time? Everything else is irrelevant. It just doesn't matter.

I just want to be in a world of my own. A world without pain or anger. A world without responsibilities and obligations. A world without complexity. A world without worry, without danger.

A world without people.

Thursday 22<u>nd</u> September 2016

What I wrote yesterday certainly set me thinking. It would be dishonest of me not to say that there are times when I do contemplate getting in my car and driving off somewhere – anywhere – where I can't easily be found. Sometimes the temptation to do so is almost irresistible. Two things always hold me back. Firstly, and most crucially, I know that Lesley and my family would be fraught with worry. I'd have to let her know I was OK. She'd ask me where I was. It's inevitable. What would I say? I'd have to lie or at least be diplomatic with the truth. 'I'm fine. I can't tell you where I am, but don't worry'. It wouldn't work, and the last thing I'd want to do is inflict more anxiety on her and anyone else. The second reason is more practical. Where, realistically, would I go that is that secluded and isolated? I'd always thought the north of Scotland, but of course I'd leave a trail that would easily be picked up. I'd have an evening of sanctuary at most, before someone, somewhere would decipher my whereabouts. My car would be the giveaway. That only leaves abroad. That would be easier in terms of hiding the evidence of my getaway. It's what Stephen Fry did, if you remember, on one occasion when the depressive side of his illness got the better of him. He got on a ferry and made for France. Sooner or later, though, I'd have to come back. That's the bottom line. And what would I have achieved?

What I do have though is my trip away in November, my annual visit to a Holocaust-related city or area of Eastern Europe. Primarily this is for research, for my own interest, to widen the scope of my experiences. But it also acts – partly at least – as an escape from normality. I can do what I want, when I want. I am free of the routines of regular life. I don't have to be conscious of the impact of my illness on those around me. It's a break for them too. It's difficult not to feel the solitude, those same sensations I've just talked about, the sensations of my dreams, when you're in the middle of nowhere, by yourself, at some remote spot in the Polish countryside. However, the silence of these places is deafening. They resound to the sounds, the appalling sounds, of what once happened in your midst. The cries of the persecuted victims, the murdered millions, do much more than simply touch your imagination. They are real in every sense but actuality. They are also sounds that have a resonance, not just in the fact that I have a connection with them through my faith, but in the very personal impact on my own battle with fate. Their cries become my cries. It's strange, but I often find companionship when I'm there, a companionship not confined to historical interdependence, but one that is every bit as real and as valid as I am today, a companionship of kindred hearts and souls, of anguish and devastation. The important thing for me, is that, unlike them, I can walk away and return to the land of the living.

Friday 23rd September 2016

We collected our new car this morning – a Kia Sportage. Nevertheless, even this momentous occasion – and serious delving into our financial pockets – had to take secondary status to the news I gleaned from my Mum last night. It appears that she doesn't have skin cancer after all. She had seen the specialist earlier in the day and he had firmly discounted that possibility. Obviously my first and primary reaction was one of immense relief. Having seen her reaction to the initial prognosis, I just couldn't see how she was going to deal with illness of this kind – particularly its possible longevity – without it severely impacting on her own mental health. It was that that formed the centre of my advice – for what it was worth – when I saw her last Saturday. It would, it doesn't need to be said, have taken its toll on my own mental reserves – what's left of them – as well. Sometimes it's much harder to cope with someone else's adversity and all that that entails, and if it's your Mum, well that only exacerbates and heightens the emotional intensity. Perversely – very perversely – I think I would have been better placed to do so than most. I seem to 'thrive' (and I'm aware of the connotations of this word) at times of distress for people around me. I can cope with that. It makes me feel like I have a purpose again. I can make a difference to someone else. I can do the right things. Say the right things. Without having to address the issue of self-reflection or internal analysis. It really is a case of 'do as I say, not as I do'. I can turn the spotlight onto someone else. The focus is on them. Not me. Please don't get me wrong. I don't mean to imply that I somehow look forward to other people's misfortune. That would be dangerous as well as inaccurate. It's just that as I am so accustomed to sadness, to affliction, to hardship, to despair, I seem capable – and curiously willing – to help others come to terms with their adverse situations, even if I can't deal with my own.

That was highlighted magnificently – and uncannily opportunely – when we got back from the dealers this morning and I attempted to boot up my PC. As soon as I opened Outlook I was hit with a message telling me that Office couldn't be verified and I had to address the problem through the Control Panel. Brilliant! It didn't tell me why there was a problem or even what to do when I got the Panel open in front of me. As Lesley was incapacitated – she had a severe migraine – I had to try and deal with the problem myself. Nightmare. Though the process was entirely logical – involving an online conversation with a Microsoft technician, allowing her remote access to my system – it couldn't prevent me from scaling the heights of anxiety and wanton despair. I was banging my head. I was screaming at the machine. I was scared to press any button, even the ones to which I'd been directed. My whole demeanour changed in a matter of seconds. I became a wild beast. Totally out of control. Eventually, what she was doing in front of my very eyes became accessible – not just visually but logically with respect to my ability to follow – and the fire inside me began to cool. But it took a long while for it to dampen completely.

If, for argument's sake, I had been working on someone else's machine. If I was helping them to deal with their problem. I know I would have been calmness personified. I just know. As a consequence, one answer to my problems appears pretty obvious. Somehow, I have to distance myself from the situation in which I find myself. Become objective. Treat it as an external matter. Try looking at it from a different perspective – a less involved one, more dispassionate, more focused, more controlled. Like a lot of things within the realm of mental health, the remedy may appear entirely succinct and clear. Straightforward even. But doing it is another matter entirely. If your mind always did what you willed it to do, there wouldn't be a problem. There wouldn't be such a thing as mental illness, I guess. Sadly, it really isn't that simple.

Saturday 24th September 2016

So to the car. At the moment it stands proudly in our drive. Its novelty is stunning. It gleams. Every bit of it. Its interior is blessed with every conceivable element of modern technology. It helps you reverse. It tells you when you're changing lane. You can specifically adjust the temperature of your seat. In so many ways it just drives itself. You start it up. Tell it where you want to go. Point it in the right direction. And the rest just comes with the minimum of human effort.

I would even go so far as to say that it's beautiful. It's only done 15 miles on the clock. It's the first new car I've ever had. And therein lies one heck of a problem for a depressive like me. You see, the very fact that it is virtually unblemished – the wheels have accumulated a bit of dirt, but that's about all – makes it harder for me to use it. It is perfection. And I have to yield to what is perfect. I have to strive to achieve it. I have it in my DNA. I have to constantly have that essence in my outlook. Anything I do now, is to lessen that perfection. Moreover, driving it, doing with it what it's constructed to do, increases the possibility that I may damage it. As I write, the very thought of dirt, let alone a scratch, on its bodywork is horrific. It disturbs me more than words can say. We specifically bought a car with a big boot so that we can put Millie there rather than on the back seat. Thus preventing hairs, mud, dirty water and the rest from 'contaminating' the seated area. But all that does is transfer the issue to the back of the car. The only thing that could possibly work in limiting my sensitivities, reducing my anxiety, is for her to be thoroughly washed every time we have to drive her anywhere. And that's just not realistic. The same actually goes for us. The possibility of drinks being spilled. Despite the fact that we have built-in drink trays. The prospect of dirty hands and soiled clothes. The thought of shopping items leaking or spilling. It all adds up. And that's just the inside. It is simply impossible for a car not to show signs of usage from the very first time you turn the key in the ignition. I don't want it to rain, because that may blemish the windows. I don't want to drive in the country because mud on the roads will transfer. I don't want to drive in the city because it increases the accident risk. I don't want to leave it in a car park because someone may scrape its side.

All told, all I really want to do is to leave it where it is and admire it from our front window!

Sunday 25th September 2016

I was so proud of our Elliot today. At lunchtime we both took part in a monthly event that focuses on mental health and our responses to it. Each one has a theme and on this occasion, that theme was young people and bullying. Though Elliot volunteered enthusiastically at the time the theme was announced, he had begun to have second thoughts as the date of the event drew near. I tried to reassure him that this was entirely natural and that his contribution would be both unique and valuable. Even though the wobbles did set in, he composed himself, set about finalising what he wanted to say, practised his delivery, thereby preparing himself meticulously and with a steely resolve. I was slightly surprised when he told me he wanted to deliver his material last (there were two other speakers, myself included), as I'd anticipated some element of 'getting it out of the way'. But that was what he wanted to do.

When the time came, he was absolutely fantastic. People warmed to him. They respected his words but also importantly his honesty and his determination to get his own story and set of circumstances across. Perhaps most significantly of all, his personality endeared itself to his audience, the majority of whom were adults from different communities. I'm not sure that I could have done what he did today at his slender age. He has a gift of communication that I'm quite sure he doesn't yet appreciate or even realise, but is actually readily apparent if not yet fully developed. When that time comes, people will relish the opportunity to listen to him because he has important things to say and equally important feelings to share.

I'm so glad I'm part of initiatives such as the one we've both experienced today. There are so many now that recognise the necessity of breaking down barriers with regard to mental health that for too long have remained entrenched and unyielding. This one – entitled 'Jamila's Legacy' – is particularly pertinent because its inspiration is a very good friend of mine who has, over the years, been able to share her health issues and her vulnerability with me whilst being a support to me at the same time. It's not just loyalty and friendship that draws me to her projects, it's the fact that she commands respect and devotion simply by being who she is. She's the type of person that people feel comfortable with, that people can relate to, someone that gives much more than she will ever take, a person that devotes her time to being a source of reassurance and support. I'm truly blessed to have her as a friend. At the same time, I know that exposing Elliot to her ways, her demeanour, her character and her industry, will benefit him. Being able to speak in public is not easy. But when you're divulging inner fears, when you're relaying very personal experiences, things that can be embarrassing, things that are upsetting. When you're allowing access into your heart as well as your head, it is much more challenging. However, if you're helped by the environment, an environment framed by good people with sound convictions and intentions, the process becomes easier, more logical and more natural. It also becomes – or can do – more therapeutic. You gain from it. It may be cathartic, a release of pent-up feelings and emotions. It may also be necessary in terms of addressing long-held personal issues. The experience can therefore be invigorating, perhaps even life-changing. The more Elliot realises this for himself, the more he will warm to the task. I'm sure of it.

Monday 26th September 2016

I've spent today at a training event at the Leicester Diabetes Centre. The subject was...not surprisingly...diabetes. How to recognise it. How to diagnose it. How to treat it. Its symptoms. Long term effects. Causes etc. It was actually really, really good. What worries I had at the start with regard to interaction and the extent of personal involvement were quickly dispelled. If you remember, it's never a straightforward process when it comes to how trainers expect participation from their audience – what they task people to do, how much they put people in the 'firing line', what 'ice-breakers' they consider appropriate and so on and so forth. It can become a real test of nerve and mental aptitude if tasks are set that somehow ask you to gauge your own personal level of expertise, knowledge and confidence. If, quite naturally – for a depressive anyway – you automatically consider yourself deficient at best, and downright inept at worst, you will never get a true assessment of the qualities you're trying to judge. Even though I've written a book on the Holocaust and journeyed around the continent visiting numerous sites, I would still look upon my own levels of competence and command in a very negative way. Today though was a good experience. Quickly put at ease, the people there were welcoming and engaging. I didn't feel constrained in divulging my own health circumstances and the very real fears I have about developing diabetes. I had supportive colleagues around me. I knew where I was going. I'd been in the room before. I even had Lisa, a good friend of mine for many years, greet me at Reception.

As to what I learned, it really was quite a revelation in so many ways. The complexities of the disease I had some knowledge about, particularly from my Dad's experience, even though it was a very long time ago. He was diagnosed with diabetes after one of his many coronaries and came very close to losing his leg as a result. He had to inject himself and monitor his glucose levels by pricking a finger and testing the blood every day. I knew about untreated diabetes, but hadn't quite appreciated the links to other afflictions – eyesight, blood pressure, cholesterol levels, kidney functions, cardio vascular disease, even boils. I hadn't much idea about what to look for in terms of a healthy, balanced diet either. Again, I knew the basics, but things such as different types of fat, weighing up calories, fats and sugar contents, recognising what foods are actually not as good for you as you may first imagine, were all relatively new to me in terms of detail anyway. As someone with a family history of diabetes – my grandmother was also a diabetic – and with a high risk score, it is naturally of direct personal relevance as well as interest. I do have regular blood sugar tests as part of my routine checks, but the fact that on occasion I do have periods when all of a sudden I feel very faint, weary, dizzy and lethargic and that my remedy is to sit down and eat or drink something very sweet very quickly, has made me very conscious of the fact that my levels obviously do fluctuate and that it's something I need to be very wary of and continue to monitor.

One thing I did learn today though made me quite cross.

I didn't know that if you were a diabetic as soon as you require medication, your prescriptions are free. That is also the case for medication relating to any side effects or correlating conditions such as high blood pressure or even depression. Now, I don't have a problem with this in itself, but it can't be reasonable or in any way fair to make distinctions between illnesses as to what constitutes or qualifies for free medication. For the simple fact is that I have to pay for all my drugs. My mental illness and all its associated factors are every bit as debilitating and as long term as diabetes and indeed other conditions which also qualify for free medication. So why should someone with a long-term mental illness have to pay and someone with diabetes not? It goes against every single morsel of fairness and equity. It also serves, yet again, to elevate physical illness when compared to mental equivalents. Parity, once more, would appear to be completely lacking.

Tuesday 27th September 2016
Listening to the radio this morning, I was disturbed to hear a well-known presenter refer to someone in fun as "a total nut job".

This tells us many things, not one of which is remotely funny or even acceptable.

First and foremost, it reveals the ignorance of the person in question, and perhaps also something about his values and standards. And yet, I found myself asking the question 'is ignorance really an adequate defence'? Surely it is not beyond reason to accept the fact that, in this day and age in particular, using such terminology is likely to offend? This was an educated man, after all. Is it really stretching credulity to believe that he didn't even think of the consequences of using such a word? Really? Children younger than Elliot are aware of terminological boundaries, parameters that should not be crossed. Not all of them of course. But certainly some. If not many. So how can someone given the privilege of communicating to a vast audience not realise what these are?

It is high time that everybody – not just people who are known to the public and have their ears – starts to recognise that terms such as 'nut job' are every bit as offensive and degrading as others which have, thankfully, become less common in their usage but which can still be heard – and immediately condemned – in reference to other minority identities. I'm not even going to give examples, not only because you will know what I'm referring to, but also because even to illustrate my point by specific reference runs the high risk of offending someone. Mental health still lags a long way behind other identity areas, but it shouldn't do. It simply shouldn't. All we need to do as a community is recognise that words can offend. We should all internalise why that is the case, what the connotations are, what feelings are aroused, what anguish can be caused and so on and so forth. This doesn't need a complex educational programme. It just needs to be recognised. And actioned. We're not talking about a serious intellectual challenge here. We're talking about basic decency. Honest courtesy. And utmost respect.

The presenter in question then went on to use the terms 'idiosyncrasies' and 'mad' very shortly afterwards, in reference to the same person.

Now let's examine those words. To use the first in the context of mental illness is nonsensical. I don't know a single human being who doesn't have idiosyncrasies. It's what makes every one of us unique and individual. It's what captivates and attracts. It's what provides interest and makes us special.

So if we accept that that's a given and applies to everyone, let's turn to the word 'mad'.

What actually is madness? Irrational behaviour? Inconceivable logic? Disturbing thoughts? It's certainly all of these and more. Now again, which one of us isn't 'guilty' (and I use that word advisedly) of one and all of these human mannerisms? Madness can still, nevertheless, be a stigmatising term. That much is true. I've used it often to describe elements of my own behaviour and thinking. I use it, not because I'm mentally ill, but because I am human and not everything I do is logical, rational and predictable. For some – and I guess this applies to our presenter – it serves to separate those that are 'sane', those that are normal, non-threatening, routinely orientated, from those that are not. Or at least are considered as such. It thereby isolates the mentally ill. It makes them 'different', not in the sense that I stated before – that we are all different – but in a way that is damaging and potentially demonising. It suggests that we pose a danger. That we actually need to be set apart. It does everything that we in the mental health community of service-users, activists, professionals and supporters, are trying to counter. It makes our challenge that bit harder.

As if living with a mental illness is not challenging enough?

Wednesday 28th September 2016

I've spent the bulk of today in Birmingham at a workshop organised by the Holocaust Memorial Day Trust (HMDT) – for whom, of course, I now work as a freelance Support Worker. Its focus was Holocaust Memorial Day 2017 and it was one of a series of workshops taking place across the country in a bid to promote awareness of the commemoration and to encourage activity around its annual theme. I am part of the workshop taking place in Derby on 18th October. However, I was more than happy to support my colleague and equivalent in the west of the Midlands. She has been a real source of support to me as she's been in situ for a year longer, and so to reciprocate was not only logical and convenient but also a real pleasure. It was an exceptional performance from all concerned today. Many issues were covered and it certainly provided a very sound basis for the attentive audience to go away and construct events and activities of their own. The theme for 2017 is 'How Can Life Go On?' This has been deliberately devised to extend the range of opportunities, simply because it's a far more complex issue to consider. There are so many facets that are both relevant and significant, so many areas to ponder, so many questions to consider and it offers everybody a real opportunity to stamp their own individual mark on what is an extensive and varied terrain. I'm really looking forward to my opportunity to share the stage with colleagues three weeks today.

My main challenge of the day was – surprise, surprise – the train getting to Birmingham in the first place. To begin with, it was already packed when it drew up at Leicester Station. There simply weren't enough carriages to cope with the number of people wanting to travel. Luckily – or so I thought – I'd reserved a seat. However, as soon as I got on, I found someone sitting where I should have been. Worse still, there was no sign of a reservation in that seat, or indeed any other. A seat was free just over the aisle so I quickly took it and breathed a huge and long sigh of relief. I'd be OK now, I told myself. No such luck. No sooner had we pulled out of Leicester, when an announcement was made apologising for the absence of 'reserved seat' signs, but also asking that passengers still honour their designated reservation. I now began to panic, for although someone was sitting in my seat (and I was reluctant to draw attention to that fact), I now had to consider the fact that I might well be sitting in someone else's!

At every stop, I waited in trepidation to be challenged. One by one they came and went, and I remained on tenterhooks. You can imagine my relief when, two stops short of Birmingham New Street, the train was so full that people were standing in every conceivable place at the ends of carriages and right down their middle. Even if somebody wanted to claim their reservation, they simply weren't able to get to their seat!

Since I've been home, I've considered whether or not to contact the train company and point out to them the anxiety that their arrangements – or lack of them – had caused me. On balance, I don't think I've actually got a choice. They need to know how highly charged and disconcerted someone with a mental illness can become when confronted by the obstacles and challenges I've faced today. If I don't say something, how can I expect things to change?

Thursday 29th September 2016

I really want a quiet day today. It's curious just how much a busy one like yesterday leaves its mark. Of course when I say this I don't just mean 'busy' in the sense of actively doing lots of things, I mean 'busy' in relation to the impact on the brain and its mental aftermath. These days, simply travelling by train uses up so many reserves of mental fortitude and stamina, there is bound to be a consequence. And I feel it every time. Last night my head was still reeling from the vigour of what I'd been through, I felt I had to take a tension headache tablet to soothe it. I wasn't stressed or uptight, so there wasn't anything there that would lead me to consider Diazepam. I was just tense. Pure and simple. The other thing that needs to be borne in mind is the anticipation that always comes with a day out. This isn't necessarily positive anticipation. More than likely it's its reverse. I worry and fret about the logistics of the day. When I realise that I can't do any more in terms of preparation. When my efforts at control have reached their natural conclusion, but there is still more beyond which I can't influence. I know there will be a reaction and a variety of repercussions. I guess when it comes down to it, I have to accept that at times like these, I live my life on the very edge. Nervous tension becomes the norm rather than the exception.

So what am I planning to do today?

I have a number of phone calls in relation to Holocaust Memorial Day activities. I have to pick up my monthly prescription from Boots. I have to address the emails that amass when you miss a day of scrutiny. I have to prepare for my fortnightly meeting at the General Hospital. I want to do some exercise. I'll take Millie out on the green for a runabout. I'll peg the washing out. Make myself something to eat. These promise to be much more routine affairs. Things I can handle. The only anomaly is talking on the phone. I know I'll be nervous beforehand. It's not my natural domain. It's something that I try to avoid if I can. Even though these will be positive calls, even potentially exciting, I'll not be able to rid my mind of the immediacy of the discussion, of the fact that it is a verbal tennis match, one point leading to a response and so on. I'll not be able to quell completely the anxiety that this induces. I'll put pressure on myself. I'll feel the pressure of the context. To perform. To be correct. To be helpful. To be 'normal'.

Friday 30th September 2016

In the early hours of this morning I had another really horrific night terror. In the cold of light of day, I can't remember the context or even the details. I wonder why that is? Why does the mind not always retrieve the contents of our dreams and our nightmares? How can something so traumatic be wiped from memory as a result of a couple of hours sleep? There must be sound psychological, neurological and probably a few other 'something logical' reasons for this. I should take the time to find out really.

All I do remember is waking myself up after kicking out, and waking up with a severe tension headache. Though I took some more tension-focused pills, I wondered afterwards whether I really needed to do so, as just sitting up and trying to calm myself did alleviate the harshness of the pain. I don't want to get into the habit of resorting to this medication as I believe it can be addictive. It's just so hard to wrestle control of my mind when my immediate, automatic, inclination is to search for a tablet.

I feel OK now. I've been to a meeting and was able to contribute, even though I still feel really tired. It does take a while to get out of my system – both the trauma and the resulting drug.

There's a programme I really want to watch on the television tonight. It's a celebration of Terry Wogan and his fifty years working for the BBC. I had a lot of time for Terry. Over and above his obvious talent, he always came across as a nice guy, full of charm, respect for other people and genuinely interested in the world around him. His ability to communicate is the stuff of legend. Indeed, it's hard to think of a more effective and insightful communicator. Someone who took the time to get to know people and to reflect that in what he himself said and did. Our Danny loved him. He always watched his programmes. He never missed one if he could help it. My Dad always used to measure the character and quality of a person by how they related and interacted with Danny. Terry, had he known him, would immediately have become his friend. I just know that to be the case.

Anyway, reflecting on the type of programme I'm expecting to see, it made me think that we very rarely in society take the time to celebrate someone's life whilst they are actually alive. Most of the tribute type shows that relate to personalities are produced after they've passed away. The only exception that comes to mind as I write is the old 'This is Your Life' series, and I'm not even sure if that's still going. Upon the death of any person of stature, there are tributes, interviews with former friends, colleagues and family, specifically produced shows, re-runs of past hits and the like. The same is true of us mere mortals. Obituaries appear in papers, people gather at funerals and wakes to remember and to honour. Social media comes alive with people saying nice things and remembering amusing anecdotes or stories that personified the character and nature of the person in question. Now, how's this for an idea? What about doing all this whilst the person is around to appreciate it and savour the sentiment? How about making this a regular course of action for everybody? What an impact that could have on people struggling with their mental health. At the immediate sign of distress or even as part of recovery, this would make a massive difference. My self-esteem and sense of self-worth plummet to virtually nothing when I'm grappling with a depressive episode/nervous breakdown. Whilst I rely on a 'metaphorical' injection of medication (tablets rather than a needle), what I could really do with as well is a real injection of confidence and motivation. And what better way than to have positive images of oneself projected and reinforced by people you value and even just by people who know of you?

I'll leave you this month with that thought.

October

Saturday 1st October 2016
I'm starting October and the last quarter of the year with a trip to Walsall to watch Millwall. Though I've passed their ground many times – it's right by a busy stretch of the M6 – and have even stayed at the hotel that's on its complex, I've never actually been to a game there, so this is another tick to add to the list of venues still to experience.

It's also, of course, a test of my new approach to football, particularly as it's also my first live game of the season. (I can't remember the last time it's taken until October to achieve that monumental feat!). So what do I need to look out for, to heed, and what can I allow myself to indulge in? If that's the right word.

Basically, it comes down not to my actions as such, but in the meaning I attach to them. I can sing and shout. I can berate the referee (within acceptable norms, of course). I can celebrate if we score. I can be pissed off if we concede. In fact, I can do anything that I've traditionally done in the past – within reason. It's how all this makes me feel that actually counts. Or rather, it's more about how I react within my mind to anything negative. If we lose, I need to keep a perspective that says that it's not the end of the world. If we let one in in the last minute that means we draw rather than win, I have to tell myself – somehow – that that's life, that there are worse things happening in the world, or even to me and my family, that there's always next week. You get the drift. It's a matter of logic, of rationality, of that word 'perspective', of keeping one's feet firmly on the ground. It's a test of how I apply CBT techniques, of using what I've learned and what I know to work – to some extent – in a context in which I've never felt able or inclined to use them before. I can do it. I have to do it.

I can allow myself, some five hours before the game kicks off, to say this. It's a measure of how entrenched depression is within me that I've come to this stage. That I have to treat doing something that I used to enjoy without consequence as a serious test of my mental aptitude. That I have to recognise an experience that the vast majority of people around me will consider to be meaningful entertainment, a diversion from normal, routine, everyday life, as an evaluation of my psychological strength and make-up. That I have to say to myself – and insist that I internalise – the fact that this isn't a distraction, it isn't something that can be put to one side and treated as a cathartic release. On the contrary, it's fundamental to my existence. Football is therefore not a peripheral activity. It's real and it has the ability to harm me if I can't control that word 'perspective'. I wonder how many of my fellow fans, people that I'll be sitting alongside, singing with, shouting in unison, can say the same? How many of them will be wrestling with their inner demons as they watch what is, when it comes down to it, a form of pleasure?

Sunday 2nd October 2016

On reflection, a 2-1 defeat may well have been the best thing to happen to me yesterday. If that sounds absurd, just hear me out. Losing the game tested straight away all those things I mentioned in my previous entry. It immediately confronted me with the question of whether I could keep things in perspective. And, I'm glad to say, I think I succeeded. I was helped by the fact that all my other teams managed a win, but all in all, I was content with the fact that I didn't go away thinking it was the calamity of all calamities. I even countered the thought that did keep returning to my besieged mind. That of Millwall being so bad they could get relegated. I kept saying that I could do little to impact on that possibility. That I couldn't influence in any meaningful or real sense the way our supposed superstars did their jobs. That I was doing all I could. Supporting, singing, cheering, trying to put off the opposition, abusing (kindly) the referee. I even made myself think that if they went down, I could go to grounds I'd never been to before. In other words, that there was a positive amidst apparent disaster! It wasn't easy, because like the four hundred or so other hardy souls who were standing in the away end, defeat was a disappointment and a real setback. I tried to think logically. That the vast majority, angry and dejected as they were at ten to five, would soon be having a drink on the way home, would get back to London or from whence they came and then have a night out or a take away tea in front of the telly. That they would, in effect, quickly get on with the normal things that people do on a Saturday evening.

As to the game itself, it was typical Millwall. We had the better players and the better chances. We won the corner count nine to none. We hit the bar with an audacious free kick from inside our own half. We had all the pressure in the last twenty minutes or so. We looked threatening all the time. But we didn't get any breaks at all. And defensively, at times we're a shambles. We conceded goals early in each half. Sloppy goals. Easily preventable. But at the minute we always seem to be playing catch-up. What we need is a bit of luck. And probably a new centre-half. Sadly, we're not Chelsea, Manchester City or any other of the so-called big guns. We can't go out and spend money, because we haven't got any. We have a choice between a seasoned veteran or a young novice to partner Byron Webster at the back. At the moment, Tony Craig (the former) has the nod, but I'm not sure for how long. Tony is Millwall through and through, but sadly he seems to have lost the faith of the fans. Everything he did yesterday was criticised. Fairly in some cases, but often not. If he ever scored, it would be considered a fluke! Personally, I think we need to blood the youngsters. Give Tony a coaching role. Get him involved in back-room affairs. Let him influence off the pitch rather than on.

Anyway, on to today. I am shortly to have my baptism in the new car. The initial seven-day insurance from the dealer only covered Lesley, so I haven't been able to whet my ever-growing appetite to give it a go. I have though to address the nerves, the anxiety and the worry that are accompanying my more positive inclinations. I'm scared. That's the bottom line. I'm trying really hard to rid my mind of the thought that I'm the one who is going to hit another car or scrape its side in parking. That it's inevitable. I'm also having to deal with the fact that in using the car, I'm soiling it. I mentioned this before. But now, as I wait in anticipation for my debut, that thought is really banging away inside my head. Alongside that, there is the multitude of buttons, the electronic technology that comes with a new vehicle these days. All the gadgets, all the opportunities. It's as if I need to know exactly what they do and how they work before I even sit in the front seat. I need to know. Not want to know. I need to know. It's as simple as that. And I need to know now. It's as if the prospect of driving without total familiarisation cannot be countenanced. I'll let you know how I get on tomorrow.

Monday 3rd October 2016

My car debut was almost over before it had even started. Having got in and adjusted my seat and the mirrors, I turned the key in the ignition…and nothing happened. It just seemed totally dead. We couldn't work out what was going on. Lesley started perusing all the manuals, I started to panic and Elliot, sitting in the back and oblivious to all that was going on, carried on listening to his music! Eventually, clueless as we were, we resorted to ringing the Kia showroom in Leicester. 'Did you have your foot on the clutch?' They responded. 'No, I replied', immediately doing as I'd been instructed. And sure enough, the engine roared into life. I'd always been taught to keep things in neutral and had never started a car by engaging the clutch. Lesley, by contrast, must do this naturally. Hence there'd never been a problem when she'd had to start the car. Feeling just a tad foolish and certainly embarrassed, we thanked them profusely and finally, after ten minutes of confused frustration, we were off.

It was such a smooth, almost serene, drive. The car doesn't just go, it glides. As if skating on ice. Almost noiseless, utterly responsive and effortless in its manoeuvring, it aroused those practically dormant feelings of joy when doing something that is, in effect, beautiful. I just wonder how long that sensation will last? Because it won't. At some point, what I experienced for the first time yesterday will become less an event and more of a routine. It will become the norm. I guess what I have to do is try and retain as much of the former for as long as possible. To treat driving as just that…a treat. That means tangible things such as using it sparingly but also engaging all my senses whenever I'm in the driving seat. How does it sound? What does it feel like? The smell of new material. The view from my elevated position in the front. Even the belief that I'm not driving a car, but rather a work of art. It reminded me of an exercise I was once asked to do in a CBT group therapy session. Forgive me if I've already recounted this story, but even if I have, it's worth repeating. We were all given a Starburst sweet (an Opal Fruit to those of us of an older generation), and told just to put it in our mouth. 'Do not, under any circumstance, begin chewing', was the accompanying instruction. We were then asked to assess not just its taste, but its texture, its shape, its irregularities. 'What's beginning to happen in your mouth?' Increased saliva for one. 'What's beginning to happen in your mind?' We're getting not just a sense of flavour, but a desire to bite. Then, we were told to just lick it. Again, do not chew. What was being tested, you see, was not our resolve to give in to temptation, but our elevated use of sensations. When you ordinarily chew a sweet, you don't necessarily give in to that feeling alone. Even though it's pleasant, you're experiencing it as one of a number of different actions, most of them totally unrelated. You're watching television. You're walking to the shops. You're doing the ironing. You're making a drink. Moreover, you're not focusing. You're not conditioning your brain to be restrictive and totally absorbed in the one thing. You're negating some of life's pleasantries. You just take them for granted, without immersing yourself, indulging your cravings. What the sweet exercise teaches you is to live in the moment. And to live totally in the moment. To revel and luxuriate. To use everything you have to indulge yourself in something positive. To shut out competing tendencies, conflicting thoughts and emotions. To concentrate. To adjust your mind. To exert control. It does work. I can vouch for it.

Tuesday 4th October 2016

Elliot had the third of his CAMHS CBT sessions this morning. I know he's finding it challenging and still probably a little daunting, but at least he has now recognised what I already knew from the beginning, that he has to put the work in himself outside of the appointments for it to have any chance of success. It's like most things, the more you put in, the more you get out. And Elliot is fortunate in having a positive work ethos that encompasses and embraces challenges such as this one. This will be his hardest test to date. There's no doubt about that. But he's already shown a willingness to knuckle down and put himself in situations that he would ordinarily avoid, situations that are the key to unlocking the door to a life without OCD. I've been with him for every session and, even though I know what's coming from my own experiences, it's a different but equally challenging assignment for me, because the most I can do is encourage. I can't do it for him. I can't even reassure him. I have to engage with him and be with him as he faces each particular trial, each individual context, each building block. Your natural inclination as a parent is to reassure, to protect, to get in the way of each potential obstacle, to block each one, to push them away, to take the full force, the inevitable blow, yourself. But in this case, that wouldn't be helping him. It would, in fact, be doing the opposite. I would, in essence, be protecting him from his own capacity to heal himself.

One thing his therapist did today surprised even me though. Right at the end, he got a mint sweet out of a container and proceeded to let it deliberately touch the soles of both his and Elliot's shoes, then his skin and then the door handles. He wasn't stopping there though. We ventured outside the room where he thrust it at every door in view. Still not finished, he then took us into the staff toilets. There the sweet touched the toilet floor, the toilet seat, the taps and then the inside of the door. I could sense Elliot's anxiety rising at every new surface. I suspect he thought he would be asked to eat the sweet himself. I have to admit, I wasn't sure where exactly we were going with this until we returned to the room. There, his therapist proceeded to put the sweet in his mouth and chew it. It was a lesson of sorts, and a very strong one. He told Elliot that he'd never had to take a day off sick as a result of this, that he'd done it hundreds upon hundreds of times, that he'd become immune 'mentally' to the risks, that he was firmly in control of the situation, that he'd chosen his actions wisely and methodically, that he'd kept the emotional side of his brain in check, that reason rather than sentiment was in the driving seat. I'm not sure I could have done what he did. And sure enough, we both felt a little reluctant to shake his hand at the end of the session, knowing where it had been. But we did. Elliot even resisted the temptation – and it must have been a strong one – to wash his hands in the toilet before we left for school. I guess it was the equivalent of demonstrating that one can overcome one's fears and natural inclinations by putting a spider in the hands of an arachnophobe, by treating vertigo through abseiling, by jumping into the deep end as a novice swimmer. I just hope it opened Elliot's eyes to what is possible. If so, it could be the most important lesson he's ever learned in his young life so far.

Wednesday 5th October 2016

It's my turn to see a consultant today, though if I'm honest with myself – and you – I'm not sure it's going to be that profitable. You see, my regular consultant has found himself a new job elsewhere in the Trust and so today I'm seeing a locum until they find a permanent replacement. I'm really disappointed that my bloke has left. We started off on the right foot and were really beginning to gel. He had an insight and an approach that made me feel valued as well as comfortable. He'd begun to get to the real essence of my long-term condition. Moreover, he was straight as a die. He told me how it is. He made no bones of the fact that this was something that I'd have to live with for the rest of my life, but that that didn't mean there weren't things that could be done to alleviate my pain, to address my symptoms, to make my life worth living. And we were just starting to get to grips with possibilities as well as actualities, long term ideas as well as short-term remedies. And now he's gone. I can't blame him, of course. He's had a better offer. It's obviously a step up on the ladder. It's a new, added, challenge. He would have been foolish to refuse. Even the way he personally wrote me a letter to let me know showed the quality of the man. I believe him when he said that it was a hard decision to make and that he was sorry we couldn't continue. But there it is. I now have to start afresh, and that always makes me worried.

I've seen locums before and I have to say – only from my experience – that they were wasted appointments. I suspect they're tasked with ensuring that there is nothing glaringly wrong rather than actually moving things forward. What can they realistically do? They won't be seeing me again. All they need to ensure is that I haven't dramatically deteriorated – which I haven't – and that I have no plans to take my own life – which at the moment I don't. We'll go through my past history. He or she will look at my last set of notes. Determine what medication I'm on. Assess how I currently am. And that will be that.

I have to go though. Not because I'm convinced I'll get anything out of it, but because for my own peace of mind I have to show willing. I have to go through the motions. If I don't, it's akin to admitting defeat – even though that may be a temporary state. I also have to go for Lesley. I have to demonstrate to her that I'm still fighting, that I'm still believing, that I'm still intent on doing what is best for me – and, of course, for her.

Thursday 6th October 2016

I'm quite emotional as I write this. I've just watched a documentary film on BBC iPlayer called 'A World Without Down's Syndrome'. It was beautifully put together. Presented by the actress Sally Phillips, it focused not just on her own journey as the mother of a boy with Down's but as someone tackling directly, as an informed activist and concerned citizen, the issues that surround pre-natal screening and all the resultant ramifications. I have to say that I'm hurting right now. I'm really hurting. I feel like I'm one entire open wound, savage and raw, susceptible to everything that increases pain, infection and fever. There are so many things I'd like to say but somehow I can't find the words. I don't even know where to begin. My only consolation is that I've already committed myself to writing a book on Danny, my brother, a book that will focus on everything that was raised in the programme, and lots more besides, a book that looks at the issues from a perspective that is seldom heard, that of a sibling. Only an assignment of that magnitude can truly do justice to what needs to be said. I owe that to Danny, the single greatest influence on my life.

What I will say for now is this. One of the central questions raised by the film is whether one considers Down's Syndrome to be a disease or a person? A condition or a human being? For Sally, and I surmise for everyone who is related to or has strong experience of people such as her Olly and my Danny, the latter will always hold sway. How can it not? We know the joys and the sorrows of living with or socialising alongside people who are every bit as human as anyone else. I would go further actually. Danny enriched our lives in such an all-consuming fashion that his presence was almost 'superhuman'. He had the ability to bring us together in a way that was totally unique. I don't know a single person who has Down's Syndrome that has not had the same absorbing impact. Down's is therefore an identifiable human being. First and last. Danny was Down's in the same way as I am depression. It doesn't define me. But it does characterise me. And it does so positively in so many ways. Both conditions are at times debilitating. Both are causes for health concern. Both are limiting in some ways. But both serve to identify us as who we are and both deserve respect for what they bring not just to themselves but to people around them. I wouldn't be me without depression. Danny without Down's Syndrome would be someone else entirely.

What makes me angry is when that ability to connect is questioned. When someone, distant and deliberately objective – I think I prefer the word 'obtuse' – questions whether one person's life is worth as much as somebody else's. When somebody sees someone in the Down's Syndrome community as inherently deficient or lacking in some undefined and pseudo-scientific way. When someone sees a person as being less deserving of the opportunity of life itself. There are also people who, couched in the world and terminology of science and medicine, do not impose such opinions, but move so-called scientific development to such an extent as to lead others to make judgements and decisions based on that 'information'. They proclaim that science isn't about morality. It just states the facts and leads others to decide. To me, that is a dereliction of duty if the other side of the equation isn't brought just as forcefully and comprehensively into play.

A world without Down's Syndrome? To me, that's unthinkable. It's also disturbing.

And where does it end? Will there be a stage sometime in the future when pre-natal tests can be undertaken to determine whether a new person will have depression, schizophrenia, bipolar disorder, OCD and any other mental – or indeed physical – condition? There's nothing to suggest that won't be the case. It's where we seem to be going. What does that tell us about the world now though? That everyone who has one or more of these – or indeed any other long-term ailment or disease – is somehow a second-class citizen? That we are not as deserving as those who are without? That our lives are worth less in fact? That we should be ashamed or embarrassed? That we should hide ourselves away? I don't think I'm being melodramatic in what I'm saying here. I'm genuinely frightened as to what may materialise in the future.

I've realised one thing as I draw this challenging entry to an end. That I've always been an open wound. Not just because of what I have. But because of what societal thought and action has done to me and to my brother.

Friday 7th October 2016

I should have gone on to John's event at the West End Centre after my meeting ended this morning, but I had what I described as a 'real mental health moment' and decided to go home instead. What it was sounds decidedly insubstantial now, perhaps even a bit pathetic, but it was so strong within me that I succumbed to its power, though admittedly with a bit of a whimper. Effectively I'd convinced myself that I was going to crash the car. My reasoning went as follows. The car park at the Centre is small and on Fridays crammed with vehicles parked in every conceivable space – official and otherwise. My car is now bigger and as a result more difficult to negotiate and to fit. I couldn't get it out of my mind that not only would it be hit by somebody trying either to get in or out, but as a result, my whole composure would desert me and I would go on some rampant vehicle damage spree. I would deliberately charge into everything I could find. I would say to myself that my own car was damaged goods anyway, so to inflict more destruction was both logical and reasonable. It also didn't matter. The feeling inside me was peculiar in its intensity. This wasn't something that I seemed to imagine or rationalise, it was something that I was actually foreseeing. In other words, it was bound to happen.

I can remember many years ago taking my Mum's car on a particularly windy night to a party in Wallasey on the Wirral. My friend's house was on the water front and whilst we were inside, a stone had obviously been whipped up by the frenzied weather and had shattered the rear windscreen. I drove home scared out of my wits, with a force ten gale blowing through the car. Anyway, the next morning when I told Mum what I'd done, she was, quite naturally, more than a little irate. It wasn't the response that I was looking or hoping for and I immediately lost it, threatening with intent to kick the living daylights out of the vehicle. I was consumed with a rage that I didn't know I had within me. It was forcing me to act against all my natural inclinations. I was out of control as much as out of order. I've never forgotten it. It was that scary.

Well this morning, that particularly episode seemed to penetrate every thinking angle and every visual frame. I couldn't get rid of it. The more I tried, the more obdurate it became. It was threatening me directly. It was telling me that this is what I could expect. That I couldn't prevent it. If I went in one direction. If I put myself in a position in which there could be not just a repetition but savage repetition, it would consume me once more like an eternal fire, full of rage and volatile intent. I didn't want to confront it. I didn't want to put myself in a position of challenge. I didn't want to face the battle. So I walked – or in this case, drove – away.

I'm embarrassed now. I feel not only that I've let John down, but I've given in to myself, to my demons. I've told myself not to use what I know, what I've learned, to bring myself down from confrontation, but instead to flee. As always appears to be the case when you let your fears dominate, the consequence can be devastating in a different way. I know that for the rest of the day, I'll ruminate. I'll be harsh on myself. I'll be prone to severe self-recrimination. I'll let the hidden voices have their say. They'll judge me. They'll scold me. They won't let me go. Eventually, they'll subside, but it will take a while.

Saturday 8th October 2016

I did something really stupid last night. I went to the cinema with Elliot and Lesley to celebrate Elliot's fourteenth birthday, but before we left I took my night-time tablets, all six of them. I still can't explain what made me take them then rather than before bed, but I did and I suffered as a result. As soon as we'd sat down, my legs started to twitch. Before long I just couldn't keep still for more than a matter of seconds. I seemed to be constantly restless. I was moving about in my seat, trying desperately not to make it obvious or disturb the people sitting behind us. But I just couldn't help it. All the time, there was this powerful urge to shift position. I tried crossing my legs, holding my legs, stretching my legs out as far as I could. But nothing worked. At the same time as this was going on, I realised that I was gradually becoming more and more heavy in my head, increasingly dozy, lethargic and under the influence. The medication was kicking in. Whilst this, of course, happens every day, usually it will happen whilst I'm in bed watching the telly, or even during my sleep. I therefore don't notice it. I began to panic as to whether I'd be able to get up at the end of the film and even make it back to the car. I kept looking at my watch, imploring the film to end. Whilst I had to keep my head in one position, my legs were moving around like a frenzied Irish dancer! Finally, finally my predicament was over. I staggered, literally staggered to the car. How I stopped myself from falling over, I really don't know.

I'll know not to do that again. It made me realise how strong the medication is that I'm on. The twitching is, of course, related. It's there as one of the potential side effects in the extensive leaflet that accompanies what I take. However, whilst I do get these muscle spasms and urges to move whenever I'm in bed, it's usually tolerable and often virtually imperceptible. And to think that there was a time when my doctor changed the strongest of the tablets from modified to immediate release – because it's cheaper. I remember on more than one occasion to all intents and purposes passing out. How on earth did my body tolerate that? I guess after years of intake, my system has got used to it. It's adjusted itself accordingly, slowly but surely. God help me if I ever have to come off them. I know that's not going to happen, but I can't stop myself wondering what would be the consequence if, for some inexplicable reason, the drugs I take were to become suddenly unavailable. It would be a physical as well as mental catastrophe.

Elliot had a decent birthday, I hope. It's never great when you have to go to school, but a trip to the cinema plus a party tonight where he's hosting eight of his friends, can't be bad. He's also had an expensive laptop as a present. He's had to forego any other present now and at Christmas, but he happily accepted those conditions. He deserves it. He really does. He's had a lot to put up with over the course of the last year. A descent into mental illness, bullying at school, increased demands educationally as he's a high achiever, family illnesses and a bit more besides. He's retained both his dignity and his ambition, and that's something really to be proud of. I am so in awe of him. He is often the catalyst to my efforts to keep going. He gives me determination and a reason to persevere. And he's absolutely beautiful.

Sunday 9th October 2016

Elliot's party passed off without incident or catastrophe. The worst that happened was the inevitable mess caused by confetti cannons. Oh, and Millie, in the excitement, urinated on the floor! He seemed to have a thoroughly enjoyable time. I'm not quite sure what they all did as Lesley and I were banished to our room upstairs. We ventured downstairs every now and again, but they were all so pre-occupied I'm not sure they even registered our presence!

One of the outcomes was that I was forbidden from watching the Super League Grand Final. I followed it through my phone, but that hardly compensated. I missed a cracker by all accounts. But there again, it's a fixture – and a sport – that never fails to thrill and amaze. I know I'm biased, but it still has to be said.

Luke has been with us this weekend. We're adjusting to the news that Lesley's Dad has stomach cancer. He's in a bad way at the minute, thoroughly exhausted most of the time, his appetite severely curtailed. A hospital trip looms this week, an appointment that will give us the full news and consequences. It's going to be hard, particularly for Lesley, of course. I think Luke being here has given her a lift. I know the main purpose of his visit was to see his Grandad, but it's been comforting to see her feel a little less restrictive in the way she's been handling it. She's trying her best to maintain a cheerful, positive face and a strong character, but there always has to be a time for letting one's true feelings and natural disposition come out. And it did yesterday. I held on to her whilst the tears flowed. It's not nice to see such honest distress and fear, but, for want of a better phrase, such things are better out than in. She needs a release. And that's my purpose. She copes with me every day of the year. She deals with my constant ruminations and anxieties. She picks up the pieces of my despair and my low moods. In a perverse way, it's good to be able to respond and to reciprocate. I just wish the circumstances were different.

Monday 10th October 2016

Today is World Mental Health Day. That being the case, I spent most of it at an event organised by a good friend of mine at Leicester's African Caribbean Centre. The focus wasn't specifically on mental health – though that was a recurrent theme – but on health more generally. There were stalls there covering a whole range of issues and illnesses and the speeches and presentations were likewise very wide-ranging. What was interesting – though when you think about it not surprising – was how much depression was almost a common thread irrespective of health condition. The links are very strong in some cases – diabetes being a good example – but in others it still rears its invasive head. I suspect in a lot of cases, when people are diagnosed with things like cancer and coronary heart disease, the depression that accompanies it isn't treated with the same level of severity as it would be in a stand-alone situation. It's simply seen as a by-product, when in actual fact it can be as devastating as the physical illness itself. If not more so. I know an old friend from my Council days who was told to expect depression when she was diagnosed with Multiple Sclerosis. As far as I know, she gets all that she is entitled to in the way of assistance with the latter, but nothing with respect to the former. And yet, a positive frame of mind is often mentioned as a necessity when you are confronted with the devastation of a terminal physical illness. There's something obviously missing there, isn't there?

As I sat through various talks on the likes of heart disease, diabetes, prostrate cancer, eye conditions and hearing loss, I was very conscious that the antennae that is fear and worry had been triggered inside me. I convinced myself that I had everything that was being talked about. I analysed every specific symptom. I asked myself question after question. Do I do that? Have I seen a change in this? Am I experiencing that? And so on and so forth. It was yet another test of mental stamina. Yet another battle with spiralling internal anxieties. When all was said and done, my immediate conclusion was that there was no hope for me. I had – or would develop – every major illness known to humankind. I tried to laugh it off by mentioning my train of thought to colleagues. They laughed. So I tried to reciprocate. And did. It worked, but only until the next thing came up to focus my weary and trying mind. It plays such tricks on me. Such appalling tricks as well. Just attempting to keep up with it saps my energies, and that's before I do what I can to re-exert control.

I have to work so hard, it's no wonder I'm shattered most of the time. Oh for hibernation. Or just a switch off every now and again!

Tuesday 11th October 2016

It's strange, but encouraging, how quickly I seem to have adapted to life away from the Council. I was there last night at an Inter Faith Forum event. I've only been back once I think since I left at the end of September last year and so I was still extremely nervous as I parked the car and made my way around to Main Reception. But this time – as opposed to the previous occurrence – what was whirring through my mind was not recognition, but estrangement. I knew now that this was an alien environment to me. I no longer belonged. And, to be honest, it felt good. When I saw previous colleagues, it was as if they were from another life. When I ventured into rooms that I once knew so well, there was no longer a sense of familiarity. The connection that was once there had truly been severed. I was firmly a member of the public. Not a former Local Government worker.

No longer do I automatically describe myself when meeting someone for the first time in terms of what I used to do. That doesn't mean, of course, that I've forgotten what I went through or negated the knowledge and experience that I gained working in the same fields that I've now made my specialism as a consultant. It's just that there's been a definite role reversal. I'm looking forward now, not backwards. Last night, I was very conscious of what I can only describe as beguiling and often confusing 'council talk', of the way they do things in a public sector organisation, of the ethos and atmosphere, of the culture of the place. I heard of intentions and planning, of policies and strategies, of authorisation, of consultation, of engagement and involvement. Words that used to mean a lot, but which now I find myself questioning more and more in terms of actuality and reality.

All that been said, I'm not sure I'm ever going to lose my inhibitions and the prevailing sense of dread whenever I'm faced with the prospect of going through the front door of that building. The scars are too deep, too lasting. It's such a pity. I gave a lot of my life to the work I did there. And, sadly, it nearly took my life as well. I can't forget that.

Wednesday 12th October 2016
Something really out of the ordinary happened to me yesterday afternoon. I was asked to appear on the Ben Jackson show on BBC Radio Leicester, ostensibly to talk about Holocaust Memorial Day, though what they were keen to do was to put that work in context and look at me and what I've done more broadly. That meant conversations about music, rugby league, school, equality and mental health alongside reflections on my journeys around Central and Eastern Europe.

I think it went well. It's always difficult to judge when you're in the middle of it all, but Ben was keen to have me back, so that must count for something. It always amazes me how comfortable I feel talking on the radio. It also makes me ask the question why it is that I can talk with such ease into a microphone but I often can't handle the day-to-day conversations that are far more routine and unexceptional. Is it something to do with the anonymity that comes with radio studios? I'm a name, but not a face. I can't see my audience. I don't know if nobody is listening, or – in this case – half of Leicestershire.

Of course it's not just the ability to talk per se that's of significance here. It's the fact that I can talk about such meaty matters as well. Yesterday, amongst other things, I talked about suicide, about mass graves in Sobibór[35], about alienation at school. Not trivial affairs, by any stretch of the imagination. And I can do this relatively easily. So why does the prospect of arranging an appointment with someone, or asking for a particular service, cause me such anguish? I guess I'm a contradiction. That's the only thing I can say with anything like certainty.

Our conversation about mental health was useful, I thought. The focus was on language and how mental health issues and conditions have become 'normalised' in everyday speech. People refer to 'OCD moments', for example. It's common to hear the phrase 'I lost the will to live' in reference not to suicidal ideation, but to things such as challenging meetings or discussions. What I said was that people need to think a little more deeply about using such analogies and respect the fact that OCD, depression and suicide are serious conditions and states of being. They're not, to those who experience them in this way, in any way a trivial matter. I've often felt genuinely cut to the core by people casually using words in this way. It hurts to think that people can be so loose about something that has come so close to taking my life, and which continues to affect me so significantly every single day. This isn't in any way 'political correctness'. It's about respect and consideration. I know that in the past, my negative feelings and emotions have been exacerbated because of simple things such as language and casual reference. It's made me analyse myself much more intensely, and much less positively. On some occasions, it's been the final straw, the one that broke the camel's back. My reactions have been extreme. I've become more volatile, more morose, more depressed. I've become less focused, less controlled, less bothered about life and less inclined to want to continue. The links are that direct.

If, as a result of what I said on air yesterday, someone out there – just one person – reviews his or her behaviour and thinks a little more profoundly and cautiously, then it will all have been worthwhile.

Thursday 13th October 2016

I had a day at home yesterday. No work commitments. No meetings arranged. No targets fulfilled. I'd deliberately done this because it was Yom Kippur. Even though I'm not at all religious in the sense that I feel I should be part of a community (formalised religion just isn't me), I still wanted to observe and honour the day in my own individual way. I also had a conversation with God. That's all. I asked for a good year to come. What that means, of course, depends on the person and his or her circumstances. I can't, for example, expect twelve months without depression, OCD or the ever-developing affliction that is anxiety. But what I can hope for is a period during which I can cope with what I have. A little bit of joy, fulfilment and achievement would also be very welcome.

I took advantage of the day and the circumstances to produce an itinerary for my forthcoming trip to Vilnius. I have to plan ahead to make the most of my visit, to ensure that I'm aware of what I wish to see so that, even if I don't manage to do everything, at least I'm conscious of that fact and can be selective if need be. I also go into intense detail. There is an order to follow, meticulously prepared, with travel arrangements to boot. I know where I want to go, when I want to go and how to get to where I need to be. I've studied the public transport system in Vilnius, analysed which bus or trolleybus to use, where it drops off, its ultimate destination and the timings involved. I've even looked into what the respective vehicles look like! There are still some uncertainties, however. Do I, for example, take the easy option at the Airport and take a taxi to my hotel? Or do I immediately test my abilities and use the express bus? Which of course is a lot cheaper. Is it possible to buy three-day travel passes at the Tourist Information Centre at the Airport itself? Or will I have to use a kiosk or make a specific trip to the Railway Station? To visit the forests of Paneriai, the site of despicable murder during the Holocaust, I need to take a train from Vilnius. I know the ultimate destination of the train I need to take, but I'm not sure of the frequency, the cost, or even what I need to look out for when buying tickets. And I'm assuming that people speak English!

So there are still things that will bother me until I confront them. Nothing I've considered is without concern or worry. That's the reality. But again, I am comforted by the confidence I felt yesterday. It wasn't complete by any stretch of the imagination. I'm far from being complacent – if I ever can be given my mental state. But what I do have is some sort of strength that enables me to negotiate the trams, buses and trains of a country that I've never visited, whilst the prospect of doing the same thing at home completely terrifies me. How is that logical? Or possible? I really do not know. It's been the same wherever I've gone in the past. In Poland, Germany, the Czech Republic, the Netherlands. Somehow I can do it in these places, but not in Wigston or in the city of Leicester! It may be because in Central or Eastern Europe the transport systems are not just more straightforward/less complex, they're also completely integrated. Indeed, in every Polish city I've ever been to, there is a consistency, a simplicity, an expectation, that makes travelling around less burdensome and far easier to circumvent. It may also, of course, be down to preparation. What I did yesterday, for instance. If I spent the same amount of time focusing on what happens in my own city, it probably becomes entirely logical and less daunting as well. All I know for certain is that as soon as I've got over the hurdle of purchasing my ticket, I'll be free to roam as I want to. One little step to open up the logistics of travel as well as the confidence required to do so.

Friday 14th October 2016

I felt really low last night. For some reason, despair and despondency hit me all of a sudden and once there in my consciousness, nothing I could do could dispel them. They're still with me this morning as I write this entry. The overwhelming thought is that I can't do anything right. Like an inverted Midas, everything I touch, everything on which I focus, every single test or task that comes my way, turns to ashes. There for a second, they dissolve in front of my very eyes and disappear in a gust, never to return. Once more, this situation is largely inexplicable. I've had a couple of disagreements with people, but those in themselves are not weighty enough to provide the context for my state of mind. They may have been the catalysts, but not the cause. Again, I have to accept that it's that bedrock we call depression that is behind all this. Of course it is. I know that. You know that. At least you should do by now! My mind is full of troubling, disturbing thoughts. I now doubt every single thing that I do. I'm expecting catastrophe, but I don't know how or with what I can circumvent disaster. I'm like a balloon in the sky – fragile, vulnerable, susceptible totally to the weather, blown this way and that by the wind.

Saturday 15th October 2016

If I hoped – remote though that hope may have been – that yesterday could only get better after what I'd written early in the morning, those hopes were soon to be shattered. Around midday I had a text from Lesley, accompanying her Dad at his cancer appointment, to say that there was nothing they could do other than palliative care, and that it was now simply a matter of time. Even though we'd all feared – and half suspected – that this would be the case, to have it confirmed was still a mortal blow. Lesley stayed with her parents for the rest of the day before coming home and beginning the process of letting the kids know the situation. Tears flowed in abundance. It was so difficult to see her in obvious pain, but still going through the process of being a mother and a protector. She was fantastic. I told Elliot when he came back from school. I'm not sure he's totally accepted or taken in the repercussions. But that will come in time and when it does, I'll be there for him.

The one thing we don't know at the moment is how long we can expect life to continue. He didn't want to know when confronted with that predicament at the hospital, and Lesley had to respect his choice, but realistically, I think we have to know what we're dealing with and for how long even if he wants to remain deliberately unaware. There are things – plans – that need to be considered and made, most pertinently perhaps whether and at what stage Rachel comes home from Sri Lanka. It's such a difficult thing to grapple with. Almost impossible, in fact. Because there is no obvious right or wrong way. As individuals we have choice and accordingly, we will differ in what we choose. All the considerations we had to weigh up when faced with the news that Danny was going to die some twenty years ago came flooding back and it was hard to have to tackle once more the doubts I've always retained as to whether we did the right thing or not back then. We chose not to tell Danny, but as time has gone on, I've often wondered whether that was the correct course, or whether we should have respected his human right to choose for himself. Of course, when dealing with a learning disability, things are not as straight forward. The very fact that it was Mum and I that faced the consultant in her office, rather than Danny himself, is symptomatic and crucial when it comes to thinking of the interface between people and the decision-making process that inevitably kicks in. Would telling Danny have brutally scared him? Would it have been beyond his capability to take in? Would it only have devolved our responsibilities? Was it kind? I just don't know. I didn't know then, and I don't know now. All I do know is that it's haunted me ever since.

As if Lesley's news from the hospital wasn't bad enough, I then had to take a phone call from my Mum in the evening, telling me that my Auntie Mayla is in hospital in Northallerton. She has a chest infection apparently, but there are concerns about the impact of this on her heart. Mum recounted the news she'd heard from my cousin Jane, that if she did make it home there would need to be some drastic changes to her living situation, that her independence, her proud independence, may have to be compromised to reflect how she now is. I think this news hit me as hard as the more immediate concern about Lesley and her parents. As my Dad's sister, I've always seen my role with regard to Mayla as more than just one of a loving nephew. Ever since 1988, when my Dad passed away, I reasoned that I should now take his place and that meant a change in the relationship with my Aunt. It's funny, but I've always imagined her continuing, year after year, defying age and disability. I've always thought of her as virtually omnipresent, impregnable, the continual living connection to my late father. It now seems that that final connecting thread, the living lifeline, is to be severed in the not too distant future. And I'll be heartbroken.

Sunday 16th October 2016
After writing what I did yesterday, I have been wondering just how much having to make decisions about Danny has played a part in my own mental illness?

My conclusion is damning and inevitable. It has to have. The only consolation – and it is a consolation – is that I know I already had depression prior to the last defining decision we had to make, that relating to whether or not to tell him of his final prognosis. The thought of everything being conditional on one decision alone is somehow too awful to contemplate. And as I write these words, I'm struggling to make it clear within myself – as well as to you – that depression was simply a part of my DNA and not conditional on any one person or situation. I can't face having to address the possibility that if Danny hadn't been who he was, or if my Dad hadn't been as ill as he was, or if I hadn't had to become a substitute father to both my brothers, that somehow I would have been free from the demons that pulled me into the depths of mental illness. It's a question to which I'll never know the answer. I can deliberate and reflect all I want, but I won't reach finality in terms of closure. As much as the logical side of me is saying that there's no point even thinking about this, the mental illness within me is telling me to ruminate and to speculate.

I do think there is a definitive connection though between my ability – I should probably say 'inability' – to make decisions per se and that one choice we had to make following the consultant's news surrounding Danny's future. Of this, I'm far more certain. I can't quantify it. I can't evidence it. But deep down I know. I didn't at the time though, in the sense that the full gravity of what we were doing hadn't hit me then. But the hours – probably days –

I've spent since deliberating, reflecting, wondering, have confirmed things within my own mind.

I guess as well that what I went through with respect to Danny and my Dad has brought me much closer to the prospect of death. Indeed, I can safely and honestly say that my relationship with the ultimate state of every human being is curiously but comfortably an immediate one. It doesn't scare me in itself. I've been so close to it in the past – both in my own brushes with suicide as well as the actuality of the fate of my brother and father. What does frighten me is its novelty. If it was possible, I'd like to have a dummy run, so that what I eventually have to face is not something new. It's instead something entirely familiar. This shouldn't surprise you as it's entirely consistent with the way I feel and have to deal with any new situation. It's not what happens from then on when you die that is the formidable obstacle to any sense of solace or surety, it's having to breach the challenge that is its initial manifestation. The former is probably what frightens most people. Is there a state of being after life? Is there life after death? Whereas for me, my belief and faith is consistent and positive here. It's my mental state in dealing with novelty that is far more threatening and ominous.

On to lighter affairs. I went to Northampton yesterday to see the home team take on my Millwall. With pessimism flowing through my veins, I made the relatively short journey down the M1 to sit amongst the travelling cohorts from South London. And we won! We should have won more comfortably than we did, but then that's the Millwall way. A 3-1 victory was more than welcome and for once, a small degree of confidence for the season ahead has been permitted to enter my system. How long it will stay there remains to be seen!

Monday 17th October 2016

In the middle of the night, I woke up with really bad sinus pain, so I took a couple of tablets. As soon as I felt them taking effect, I was conscious that I also felt a little queasy. That feeling has stayed with me this morning. I remembered that whenever I buy them I'm asked whether I take anything for high blood pressure. Not wanting to get drawn into a conversation about my regular medication – and also, of course, conscious that I probably shouldn't be having them – I always lie. I say no. How I feel this morning, I suspect, is the reason for the probing. Effectively, I've overdosed. Not dramatically. Not dangerously. But certainly noticeably. This is another one of those perennial dilemmas. Do I put up with a bit of pain above my eyes just so that I can stay within the parameters set by what I have to take daily? Or do I sacrifice safety and compromise by seeking immediate gratification? And suffer the after effects? There's no easy answer. There wouldn't be, would there? I reason that I should use tablets like this very sparingly, so that the odd one here and there is less likely to do any noticeable damage. But is that wise? The medics will obviously say no. But then they don't have to put up with pain that others – those not on the medication I have to take – simply eradicate by popping a pill.

Tuesday 18th October 2016

Elliot has had one blinder of a day. To begin with, he had his CAMHS appointment, which went really well, even if he probably didn't realise or appreciate it at the time. He has made positive and significant strides forward. He's now able to do things that he wouldn't have imagined possible only a short time ago. And, as importantly, he's able to contemplate tackling obstacles and challenges that he once considered insurmountable and impregnable. I can see the progress. His counsellor can see the progress. Elliot probably doesn't realise the full enormity of what he's doing at the moment, but that time will come, and when it does, I can see only bright times ahead with respect to combatting his OCD. He's naturally quite taciturn and soft in his responses, and I know he has problems with the style of the guy he's seeing and obviously with what he's being asked to do, but when he reflects – as he will do – he will see all that he's going through as necessary and unavoidable if he is to beat the illness.

I have more confidence in him than I do in myself. Which probably says as much about me as it does about him.

I then asked him to accompany me to an event I was helping to present in Derby. It was the regional workshop for Holocaust Memorial Day (HMD), put on by HMD Trust staff and myself to help those interested in organising activities with their planning, preparation and promotion. Again, Elliot took it in his stride. He didn't want to actively engage in the process – it was geared towards an adult audience after all – but he sat there quietly taking it all in, offered me some interesting thoughts and insights and, tellingly, helped me cope with my own nerves when I had to take the lead. He is so polite and enthusiastic, never judgemental, always encouraging, and I hope he thinks seriously about volunteering as a Youth Champion in this important field of work and life. He has already declared his interest and he would be a real asset. I think the first-hand experience he has gained from travelling to sites in France and Germany has had a telling impact and, of course, he has seen discrimination in its various forms and is unswerving in his position on how we as a society need to address built-in and accumulated hate and prejudice. He has a lot to say and so much to offer.

My pride in him more than made up for my disappointment at the fact that of thirty-one people who signed up for the workshop, not even half turned up. I know I've been guilty of this in the past – something that I will return to tomorrow – and of course, people have very good reasons for giving apologies as often things do crop up at very short notice. But in the heat of things this afternoon, I couldn't help but take it personally. I know I shouldn't. I fully accept that it's my depression talking and acting. But it felt resounding, deeply upsetting and strangely condemning. It was catastrophization at its most punishingly severe. You see, I felt it was my presence that was the turn-off. That if I hadn't been there, people would have come. I have no evidence for this. There is nothing to substantiate this draconian line of thought. But it still infected the way I perceived things and even now, as I reflect, I find it hard to distance myself from what I know to be falsehoods and untruths. Sometime tonight, as I watch the telly or follow the football scores on my phone, my mind will finally dispel the negative associations and predilections, but it won't let go without a battle. That much I know for certain.

Wednesday 19th October 2016
Yesterday I mentioned the issue of not being able to fulfil appointments. I think this deserves a little unpicking because for me – and I'm guessing for a lot of people with a mental illness – it's not necessarily as straightforward as it may seem. Sometimes things do occur that make it impossible for me to attend, but that's the same with anyone, irrespective of disability or any other identity characteristic. Far more often, however, what prevents me from honouring the commitment I've made, is the state of my mental health at the time. You see, when booking your place on a workshop, or a course; when responding to an invitation to attend a seminar or a ceremony, you do so ahead of the event. Sometimes that can be a matter of weeks or even months. At the time you say 'yes', you're feeling fine. There's no problem. There are no inhibitions. However, often as a result of what you're having to put yourself through to go to whatever it is you've booked, you wake up on the morning and you simply can't go through with it. Your nerves and anxiety get the better of you. Sometimes, it's worse. You're in the midst of a depressive episode. Simply getting past your front door is an achievement. You just can't motivate yourself to do anything about your predicament. You don't want to let anyone down of course, but you can't put yourself through something that you know is going to have a devastating impact on your health. You could well be setting yourself up to fail. When this happens, there have been times when I've been able to apologise and tell the truth, the whole truth. To say that I'm too ill mentally to cope. Nevertheless, especially if you don't know the individuals concerned, it's often far easier to tell a white lie. You don't want to elicit sympathy. You don't want them to go out of their way to

make you feel comfortable because you feel that you're being intrusive, too demanding, too particular even. Perhaps it's also because you don't want to draw attention to yourself or make a fuss. Often, it's just because you don't want to have a conversation. If you're me, you feel horribly guilty afterwards. You punish yourself not only for what you perceive as 'cowardice', impudence, rudeness or disrespect. You also slate yourself for not being honest. But even these punitive repercussions are better than the prospect of physically getting yourself to and inside a venue.

Today, I'm happy to say, I managed it. I attended a consultation event that focussed on the NHS Workforce Disability Equality Standard (or WDES for short). It was very interesting and hugely important. Enabling disabled workers to feel confident and valued within an organisation is vital to the long-term success of that organisation, as well, of course, as all the benefits that should come to a worker by right. Far too often, though, this just doesn't happen. People are discriminated against. People are subject to extra scrutiny. People feel they have to justify their existence. People don't feel appreciated. There are also other factors to consider. The higher up an organisation you go in terms of hierarchy, the less chance you are of seeing someone with a disability. I also suspect that far more disabled workers are leaving public sector bodies because they can't cope with the demands and stresses that are brought to bear, especially if these are augmented by their medical condition. I'm one of them, after all. So for the NHS to recognise that their work in the fields of race and ethnicity needs to be replicated – and adapted in some respects – to embrace disability as well, is a positive development. The discussions were valuable, I felt. I did sense though a definite tension between my experiences and my identity as a disabled man and activist and that of those present from NHS Human Resources and Management. The latter, to me, seemed far too entrenched and inflexible. 'There are rules, and they must be applied. There has to be consistency'. Well no, that isn't necessarily the case. You need to be adaptable and so often it's not the rules that need bending as such – that might not always be possible let alone desirable – it's the way that they're implemented. You can still ensure that people feel valued, useful and welcome, even when you're giving them bad news or having to enact something that is applicable across the boards. Perhaps, ultimately, it comes down to this. Equality is often defined as being 'treating everyone the same'. Actually, that is incorrect. To enable equal access and opportunity, you need to be flexible and you need to show consideration to people's particular needs. That's why we have things such as British Sign Language. It's why there are flexible working arrangements. It's why hearing loops were invented. It's why there are disabled toilets and lifts in buildings. It's why you need to consider using community languages. It's why using verbal imagery is vital for those with learning impairments or literacy issues. I could go on ad infinitum.

I was happy, as the event drew to a close, to accept an invitation to become some form of Disability Ambassador for this work. It must have meant I'd made some sort of positive impression and that someone there valued what I had to say and what I can bring to the table.

Thursday 20th October 2016

The subject of jobs follows on nicely from what I wrote yesterday. It's a sensitive area for those of us with a mental illness, and it's sensitive for a variety of reasons. To begin with, employment is something that we aspire to in the same way as any other person. We know that given the right environment, having a rewarding job gives an immense boost to one's self-esteem. It provides aspiration and a purpose. It enables commitment and helps with social skills. And, of course, there is a financial benefit, a regular income, a means of paying the bills, even of treating oneself every now and again. However, the issue of employment brings with it a number of intense challenges. Will I be able to cope? What if the pressure becomes too much? Will my employer make reasonable adjustments to help me do what I need to do? What if I have to take disability-related sick leave?

What about my other work colleagues? Do I tell them about my mental illness, or do I keep quiet? Do I actually self-declare my disability? What if I'm asked to do something that I'm simply not capable of? How do I respond to social invitations when I know that I'm really afraid of those informal occasions when people get together over a meal or a drink?

It's difficult. As you can see. And I haven't even touched on the issue of stigma and discrimination. If I tell my boss or my manager. If I open up to those around me. How will they respond? Will they shy away from me? Will they be positive and supportive? Will they fear or doubt me? Am I opening up a whole can of worms?

Whole books could be written on this. It really is that important and significant. As it is, I'll confine myself to a number of points.

Firstly, I think it's both realistic and crucial to say that nothing is beyond us. The history of mental illness tells us that people with a wide variety of conditions and degrees of severity have not only been able to cope with a job, they've actually flourished. This shouldn't really be a surprise because it's the same as anyone with a disability. In fact it's the same as anyone, full stop. Just look at those individuals who have been able to prosper in what they do. Winston Churchill, Abraham Lincoln, Ludwig van Beethoven, Howard Hughes, Stephen Fry, Robbie Williams, Sigmund Freud. I could go on. Every one of these people has been or is mentally ill. Has it stopped them? No. They've had to overcome the challenges that inevitably come with their mental illness. But they've succeeded. In fact, in lots of cases, their mental condition has provided a stimulus, an inspiration, to elevate them to unprecedented heights of achievement.

The key – and this is my second point – for anyone in the world of work, is the context. The right environment, a supportive workplace, encouraging colleagues, the ability and opportunity to ask for assistance. To make adjustments and to allow people to be as they are. Individuals with specific needs. If this is in place, and particularly if one is motivated and inspired to request the little things that make such a difference, then there is nothing we cannot do.

People with mental illnesses, in my experience, actually go beyond the call of duty when it comes to work. Because we're sensitive to the issue of having at some stage to take time off to help us overcome depressive episodes or similar crises, we spend the time when we are at work focusing more intensely, making every minute count. We even overwork. We build up hours in advance as some sort of compensation. This isn't necessarily a good thing, but it demonstrates commitment and a positive work ethic. Things that, stereotypically, people seem to doubt us as having. In all my time at the Council, I was never in deficit with regard to working hours. I never had to make up time. It was always the reverse. I had to be told to take time off in lieu.

On the surface, some positions, high profile ones, seem to involve pressure that would be hard to deal with on a consistent basis. That comes with the territory when it involves people with massive responsibilities. However, given the individuals I mentioned earlier, and the thousands of others who succeed irrespective of the status and pressure involved in what they do, such positions, though inevitably more challenging, are not insurmountable. We can do it. And we do. Where I would have a problem, ironically, is with my physical acumen. The lethargy that comes with my mental illness and the resultant medication, would severely curtail what I would be able to cope with physically. I wouldn't be able to do normal, everyday, things, because I don't have the energy. Even the most mundane or monotonous of physical tasks would be difficult to endure on a consistent basis. It's one of the paradoxes of my disability. What would bring me down is more likely to be a physical dimension than a mental one.

In conclusion therefore, I think it really comes down to this.

Don't judge us. Don't be scared of us. Don't doubt us. Just give us an opportunity. Just let us be what we can be. A valued asset.

Friday 21st October 2016

As is often the case, after I'd finished yesterday's entry I then thought of something else I needed to add! It may be that I've mentioned this previously, but after nine and half months I just can't remember!

What I felt needed adding is this. Whatever job I've ever done, I've always felt that I can do it competently and diligently. However, I have to acknowledge that there have been times when I haven't been able to do it comprehensively because when my disability is acute, there are limitations. This doesn't just relate to periods off work, but sometimes to spells when I've had to focus on things that don't place demands on my mental state and put aside for the time being tasks that I just can't face or complete. This has often put me in the position where I've had to fight my corner. I've had to respond to the accusation – that may be too strong a word, but it's the first that came to mind – that I'm not able to do my job per se. Every time, for example, I've had to undergo an Occupational Health Assessment, this issue has cropped up, and every time I answer it in the same way. What I say is significant I think for anyone with a mental illness that faces the challenge of this situation. What I do is point out the obvious. That I'm no different from anyone else who has a normal, everyday, illness. Think about it. Can someone in the midst of a severe migraine work at a desk staring at a computer screen? Can someone with a bad back actually sit at that desk in the first place? Can someone with an ear infection or a perforated ear drum working in a call centre be expected to answer or make phone call after phone call? Can a footballer recovering from a broken leg sprint around the pitch and even kick a ball properly? Can someone with a fever or high temperature realistically negotiate a backlog of meeting engagements? Can someone who has lost his or her voice be expected to deliver a key-note speech? I could go on and on here. The answer to all these questions is 'no'. And yet, their competence and capability to do their job in itself isn't questioned at all! Wayne Rooney, recovering from a hamstring injury that prevents him from playing, suddenly doesn't change into someone incapable of being a footballer! The Prime Minister, laid up with flu or a viral infection, isn't then considered as being unfit to perform that role in perpetuity! You get my drift, I hope.

On so many occasions I've felt that I've had to justify my ability to do my job. I've had to implore people to understand that when I'm well I can do anything. I've had to plead. I've had to beg for understanding and appreciation. Every time this has happened, I've felt degraded and powerless. I've had to control my irritation and my anger. I've had to focus intently on maintaining a calm and composed demeanour, despite the provocation of the situation. I've had to prove that I'm mentally alert and astute, that I'm not insane or delusional. I've had to prove that I'm me.

To say that's unfair is, I would argue, an understatement. And yet, that has been the reality.

Saturday 22nd October 2016

The end of another week. It's been relatively busy, especially in the first half, but it's also given me time to think about things and, I hope, to be a proper and effective support to Lesley. She's doing really well. Having to cope with the impending passing of a loved one is one of life's most awful tasks. What to do and what to say are not necessarily straightforward or obvious. And it's difficult not to stop yourself becoming subsumed by absolutely everything, the psychological baggage as well as the practicalities of support. Of course, I have experience of what she's going through. I've lost both a Dad and a brother. I've known the trauma of negotiating the finality of death. I've had to cope with knowing about imminent passing. I've had to make decisions not just about what to do, but the way to do it. I've also had to cope with my own mental demise, with mental illness compounded by the sensation of loss. So, for once, I feel that I have an advantage, a knowledge, that I can use to help my wife. I have, for the time being, become her equal with respect to caring responsibilities. She's now more dependent on me. I feel strong, if I'm honest with myself. I can deal with this. It's not just the fact that I've had personal experience within my own family. It's the fact that I've confronted the prospect of my own death on many occasions. In the most perverse way imaginable, it's a time when I'm actually feeling grateful for having a past association with suicide. Death has been close, and it has become close as a result.

Sunday 23rd October 2016

I had a familiar dream last night. Well, in reality, another night terror. Again, it was school and once more it involved Mary. As has been the custom in previous occurrences, the context was one of forced separation. We were there on our last day at school, intent on spending as much of it as we could together. However, circumstances – every single one of them – was just as determined to prevent us from doing so. This time, it wasn't any individual person. It was what I can only describe as fate. What I remember quite vividly is arranging to meet her at 2.00 pm. I set out from my boarding house on a bike, a new bike, in good time not only to be there as planned, but in advance – as is my wont. No sooner had I left than I kept meeting other people who wanted to talk to me and whom I couldn't refuse. Teachers, past work colleagues (completely out of context), family members come immediately to mind. I was also drawn back to my room where I hadn't finished packing. To be honest, I'd hardly started. Once more, I'd been distracted, but I now faced a race against time because I needed to be out and on my way home. Somehow, what should have been a straightforward task, was becoming more complex and onerous by the minute. As soon as I'd packed one thing in my trunk or suitcase, more items appeared that needed to be dealt with. Things that I didn't even recognise as my own. I was being punished. I knew that. But even so, I felt I had enough determination and inner strength to withstand whatever it was that was intent on destroying my lasting legacy of my school-time love. To cut a longer story short, that inner compulsion simply wasn't enough. I missed the appointment and no matter where I searched, I couldn't find Mary.

What should I glean from all this? Firstly, I've been telling myself this morning that it wasn't true. My last day at school was spent almost entirely with Mary. It was a day of intense joy mixed with true sadness and worry. Our youthful idyll was at an end. We didn't know what the future would bring. I know this was the reality, but, as has been the case in the past, the truth has been distorted by demons and circumstances thrown at me from within my own mind. I also know that what I previously called fate could – and should – be seen and labelled as depression. It's my mental illness that prevents calm and surety. It's precisely that which tortures and confuses me, that tries to impose on me a recollection that was the complete opposite of the truth. One that just wants to hurt me and cause me intense pain and sorrow.

Finally, I have to face the uncomfortable fact that dreams such as these tend to overwhelm me either when I'm in the middle of a battle with a depressive episode, or when I'm on my way there.

As I know I'm not in the former, that only leaves me with one explanation.

Monday 24th October 2016

Yesterday, I undertook a quick review of what I've written over the course of the year and one thing that struck me almost immediately was the fact that I'm consistently writing less and less. I saw this as almost inevitable. You start a new venture full of enthusiasm, particularly as you're conscious of the fact that you have a lot to say. I remember making a deliberate decision to pace myself, not to fire the passion within me by allowing myself the luxury of getting into all the major issues straight away. It's why I quickly created a list of everything that I could think of that needed to be addressed, a list that has accompanied my writing as the year has progressed. I should state straight away – just in case I may have subconsciously misled you – that I'm still enthusiastic about this project. That's never really wavered, despite the equally inevitable consideration that it's sometimes difficult to motivate yourself to write when you can't think or conjure up anything remotely interesting or relevant to mention. It may, in fact, be the case that you, the reader, have a different perspective that enables or leads you to see as significant and fascinating, things that I barely touch upon during the course of a daily entry. Actually, come to think of it, that's also pretty inevitable! We're all different and unique, after all!

It has been a difficult balance to maintain what I hope is the interest of anyone reading this diary whilst focusing on what has been happening to me, physically, tangibly and psychologically. To ensure that this is a readable and engaging piece of work just as much as it is accurate in getting across the reality of my situation. In the hope that I get what I'm doing published at some point, I'm fully conscious of the need to make my diary an attractive proposition to any potential publisher. That necessitates the balance I've just mentioned being evident throughout. With this in mind, I have become increasingly concerned as to whether the quality of my written word is consistent just as much as it meets the standards expected and required for publication. At the end of the day, I want this to be read. Because it has to be before it can be of any practical use.

I guess this is one occasion when my perfectionist streak is positively an asset. I do critically review each entry and when everything is completed at the end of the year, I will spend a considerable amount of time reviewing everything once more. I do question every example of punctuation, every grammatical usage, whether each and every word is the most suitable and whether, when joined together as a phrase, they flow as well as make sense. I am meticulous as much as I am pedantic. I know

I overdo it. That my main challenge is to be putting an end to a process that, for me, could last forever. I have to say to myself that there is a percentage of satisfaction that I need to obtain, and that that does not equate to the maximum. Seventy, rather than a hundred per cent.

Tuesday 25th October 2016
It hasn't been the greatest start to a day. To begin with I had the most horrendous of nightmares. It was so bad that it physically woke me up. Indeed, it took me a few minutes in the middle of the night to gather my thoughts, compose myself and to recognise that it was just the product of an overactive and depressed imagination.

Even now though, I find it hard to stomach what it was that was being inflicted on my tortured mind by my tortured mind.

For some reason, I'd left my boarding school and had returned to my previous comprehensive to complete my academic studies. It was my second day and as I left the building I became conscious of the fact that my return had now become headline news. Everybody seemed to be staring at me, but not in a curious or comforting manner. It seemed that I'd aroused feelings of real anger and resentment. My one ally, my old mate Jason, tried his best to ease the path for me, but it was useless. As I walked through the crowds, the comments and accusations began. These were quickly followed by threats and physical intimidation. I had no recourse left within me, no inner resolve or genuine defence. Though I could guess, I didn't know why so many people seemed intent not only on punishing me but on inflicting real pain. Was it because they felt I'd deserted them? That, in going to a public school, I considered myself above them? That I was different to them? Had I become an alien on my home turf? As I finally left the immediate surroundings of the school, it quickly became clear that it wasn't just my fellow pupils that had been antagonised, it was the whole town. A rage of abuse greeted and followed my steps. Some had even conspired to let weapons do their talking. I was poked by metal rods. I was dodging knives and avoiding missiles. There was no respite, not even when I finally reached home. A crowd of angry people besieged our tiny house. Every one of them was known to me. Every one had a specific grief, a particular cause with which to admonish and brutalise me. I tried to placate them. To appeal for mercy. I said I would help people with their troubles. I would give my time and my energy only for them. I would answer their grievances by committing the rest of my life to their service, even though to do so – given the numbers involved – was unfeasible and unimaginable. It was just as I was pleading my case that my mind finally gave way and, in its agony, stimulated my body to come back to life. My eyes opened and the path to clarity and recovery had begun once more.

As if all that wasn't enough, as I drove Elliot to his CAMHS appointment, I'm convinced that I went through a red light. To be fair to my conscience, I'd already committed myself, so it wasn't as if there was actual intent, but as soon as I'd done the deed, I began to feel the recriminations. Immediate catastrophization set in. The train of thought was predictable, but no less real or impacting. From one split-second decision I finally concluded that I'd lose both what work I've managed to accrue as a consultant and then, much more disastrously, my wife and family. There was no doubt in my mind. That was going to happen. One thing would lead to another, an inevitable pathway to ultimate destruction. I've calmed down a bit, but it's still there in the back of my mind as I write. I've told myself that there's nothing I can now do. I can't turn back the clock. I can't undo what has been done. I'll just have to wait and see. Of course, to someone suffering from mental illness, to someone who needs both certainty and security, to someone that constantly strives to reach and maintain definitive control, that is much easier said than achieved. But that's what I'm left with.

Please God, let me be OK. And let the rest of the day pass without incident or concern.

Wednesday 26th October 2016

It did. Indeed I had rather a good day after my morning escapades. However, once more, what I went through only served to emphasise how terribly close I am at times to complete mental collapse.

I'm so often on that ledge above the precipice, it's becoming familiar territory. That may not be a bad thing in a perverse sort of way. The more a climber puts him or herself in those positions of danger and overcomes the inherent physical and mental obstacles, the more secure and sure-footed they become. I suspect it's no different from learning how to ride a bike or drive a car. At the start of the learning process, you're consumed by fears and anxieties. Once you gain familiarity, it becomes second nature. You also become more attuned to the dangers involved. You see them before they actually materialise. You prepare for them.

However, I don't want to appear resigned to fate, or complacent in the face of risk and peril. I'd much rather not be on that ledge at all. That's the safest way of looking at it. But I'm there more often than I'm not. That's the reality. The majority of the time, I'm there attached to a guiding rope, steady on my feet, well-equipped and with favourable weather conditions. But sometimes, all those assets, all those securities, simply disappear. I may as well be attempting the task in trainers, shorts, with nothing to hold on to, with a mist quickly enveloping my being. It's one precarious step at a time. During the course of that simple physical movement, I'm expecting to fall. I know every conceivable circumstance is against me. So what do I do? I tell you, I just stay there. I freeze. I subject myself to all the worries and fears imaginable. I can't move forwards or backwards. The only way to survive is to cling on for as long as it takes. Fate will determine when the weather breaks, when someone comes to help me, when they bring with them the necessary equipment I need to negotiate my predicament, when I gain confidence and overcome the fear, when I'm able to make the decision as to which direction to go. Only then do I make progress once more.

Thursday 27<u>th</u> October 2016

On my way to Loughborough this morning, I was listening to Radio Five Live. For those of you who aren't regular listeners, there is a daily phone-in for an hour or so, either on a burning topical issue or one less time-specific but equally significant. Today there was a discussion on bullying and the breakdown of relationships in the workplace. Obviously, given my background and experiences, this was one that was particularly close to home. I was astonished to hear a so-called expert opine that it was as much the responsibility of a person being mistreated to 'clear the air' by instigating and stimulating discussion, even on a one-to-one basis with each relevant and respective colleague. His argument was that somebody needed to begin proceedings otherwise the tension would continue. It actually made me quite angry. But in some respects, I too have put myself into that position, voluntarily, in the past, by feeling that I should talk to people about my mental illness and how it impacts upon me in the hope that that will increase people's awareness, or at least their propensity to want to learn. However, it just can't be right that someone subject to mistreatment – whether you call it bullying or not is largely incidental I feel – should feel that unless they do something themselves, the behaviour to which they have been subjected isn't consequently and as thoroughly addressed as it should be. And if mental illness is the influential or deciding factor, a situation that will undoubtedly impact upon a person's ability or capability to take the lead when it comes to communication, then the injustice is all the more apparent. Surely that can't be fair?

It made me that cross that I ended up turning the radio off!

The event to which I was going focused on various aspects of health. I was there with a colleague to promote the need for people to find out if they are at risk of contracting Type 2

Diabetes. It's part of the health service work that I'm now involved with over at the General Hospital. It's also a hot issue at the moment given the current prevalence of the disease and the impact it is having and will continue to have on NHS budgets. What I found really interesting today was that so many of the people that came to our stall to talk about diabetes ended up discussing their own mental health or that of a loved one. Depression often accompanies diabetes, as is also true of many other physical illnesses and disabilities. And yet, as I've said before, it is often marginalised in comparison with its physical co-manifestation. It can't be a coincidence that people wanted to focus on the need for specific treatment in relation to their mental health to help them – and others – cope with the challenge of their physical affliction. The two are intrinsically related, of course. They are interdependent facets of one large health issue. It struck me that it may be the case – particularly with men I suspect – that the way to open Pandora's box in relation to mental health is through tackling and focusing on physical factors. On other health challenges. It may be admission or awareness via the back door. But anything has to be better than silence, tacit recognition or – worst of all – ignorance.

Friday 28th October 2016

I made my routine call on Boots the Chemist yesterday to pick up my monthly bag of prescriptions. The fact that it does come in a bag now is, naturally, a telling fact. I looked down at the drawer full of other medication waiting to be claimed and as I did so, I could immediately pick out what would be mine. It wasn't difficult. It was the biggest. We went through the regularity of checking that all was there. I signed the forms, including the request for 'same again' in November, and then, once more, I left with the tablets that would keep me alive and relatively sane for another thirty days. Just for once though, rather than simply go through the motions, I started thinking about the enormity of what has become with regard to my medication. I wondered, for example, just how many anti-depressants and anti-psychotic drugs I've ever taken. I tried to do the maths, but quickly gave up. Not because it was a complex process, but because it revealed to me something quite frightening. I'm not talking about my dependence on tablets – though that is revealing and unnerving in itself. No, it was the sensation that, if taken in the wrong manner, I could have killed myself by overdose many times over. Substituting that rather draconian summation for something more mundane, I've probably overdone the medication in other ways by using regular over the counter stuff in addition to what I ordinarily have to take. And I've done this remarkably often. I've not shied away from taking stuff to deal with an irritable bowel or sinus pain. I've not hesitated to take ibuprofen or something stronger to help soothe the pain of a headache or an aching muscle. And, with the medication I have to take to address high blood pressure and cholesterol, it's a veritable cocktail of toxic drugs that regularly enter and consume my system. It's quite scary really. But I have no real choice. I'm dependent. Not in a physiological sense, but psychologically. I've channelled my mind to accept that these are necessary and effective items that help to keep me relatively stable. To reverse that thinking process would, I now feel, be to court disaster.

Saturday 29th October 2016

One of the visitors to our stall at the Health Event on Thursday told a familiar story. Her husband has diabetes. His condition is manageable most of the time. However, there are occasions – fleeting though they may be – when things become more serious, less controlled and obviously more ominous. What he wants when this occurs, is to retain as much control as he possibly can so that he feels that he's dealing with the situation to the best of his ability. He also wants something more than he's currently getting to feel that he's actually improving. What he doesn't want is that notion of 'treading water'. He wants progress. That's the long and short of it.

I knew exactly what she was describing, because I believe I'm in the same boat to some extent. When I go through the routine of appointments and assessments. When what transpires is continuation without deviation. When I'm told that I'm stable and the best I can be, despite feeling low and anxious, irrespective of the fluctuations in mood and the symptoms that take me close to self-harm and perhaps worse. Then I get frustrated and feel powerless. What is more, a sense of futility takes over. Is this what life has become? Is this the most I can expect? I become resigned to my fate, without motivation and the ability to get myself out of this most devastating of thinking traps. Effectively, I believe that I'm caught in a much broader cage. In what can only be described as a mental health 'no man's land'. I'm too ill to relax my treatment, but I'm not ill enough to warrant immediate specialist attention and care. I'm stuck, confined by the parameters of my disability and my condition.

As a consequence, I often wish that my illness was more severe. That may seem an odd thing to say and is perhaps difficult to comprehend and appreciate. But it's true. If I threatened my own health, or that of others, my freedom would be removed. Though I don't think I could ever do the latter, the former at times becomes a much more dominant and appealing prospect in a mind struggling to come to terms with deterioration. If I self-harmed more. If I had a visible breakdown. If I took further steps towards suicide. Then someone, somewhere, would have to take notice. My agony would be more apparent. Rather than try and keep it inside – which is what I do most of the time – I would instead be physically as well as metaphorically, calling for help. If I could relinquish that compulsion within me to retain control. If I wasn't concerned about the impact of my health status on others. If I felt that crying or shouting was more effective. The situation I'm leading into may be different. For one, I would be sectioned, hospitalised, institutionalised. Other treatments, commensurate with that position, would be considered. They may work. They may not. But I'd be in with a chance of improvement.

What stops this situation is not always the fact that I'm not sufficiently ill. Ironically, it could actually be the complete reverse. That I'm too ill to believe that anything would work or that there is any future for me outside the maintenance of stability. It's that trap again. A veritable but inadequate status quo rather than the risk of improvement or decline. I'm an immovable object on a steep ledge rather than an energetic climber able to choose what to do and not afraid of the ramifications. I have to be satisfied. But at times, the recognition that the forces of nature as well as that of my own inner-self are constraining rather than compelling, stifling rather than emancipating, is hard to bear.

Sunday 30th October 2016
My forty-eighth birthday! It started well. I got an extra hour in bed with the clocks going back. And I woke to some lovely birthday greetings from my family and through social media. I'm a lucky man. We haven't planned much for the day, but that's been my choice. I don't really want a fuss and I'm relaxed when I can just spend some time at home without the pressure of having to conform to happiness, if that makes sense. Of course it is a happy occasion – or it should be – but sometimes there is an inherent compulsion to look and be happy when that isn't necessarily how you feel inside. It's like Christmas or, more routinely, weekends. There is an expectation, a dictate imposed from without, from circumstances, from the supposed nature of the day. And if your supply of cheer can't meet that required demand, it only reinforces your alienation and can lead you to greater despair.

As it is, we're going to a café for a snack at lunchtime. Something short and simple. We may go on to do a little shopping afterwards, and I've put in a request for stew and dumplings for my birthday dinner!

I have a tendency – which comes directly from my mental illness – to read into other things going on around me as to whether my birthday celebration has had an impact, or conversely, whether situations elsewhere will determine the forthcoming year I am to face. It goes back to somehow seeing a direct connection between my circumstances and the world around me. That my fate is the fate of the world. Or – to flip the coin over – that the nature of the world at this given moment will indicate what I can expect to experience myself. It's no different to thinking that if Millwall or Leeds lose, it's my fault. That's exactly the correlation I mean. It is ludicrous. I know it is. But, despite my best attempts, I can never rid myself of this tendency for intense self-analysis. I won't dwell on this because my mind has already been overworked in this fashion today and there's hardly ever a definitive conclusion. I'll leave you with this, as an illustration. All my football teams won yesterday and yet, within twenty minutes of switching the test match on this morning, England went from 100 for none, to 127 for five! What can you read into that?

Monday 31st October 2016

Thinking more about what I wrote on Saturday leads me to contemplate what sort of treatments for mental illness may be available in the future. Elliot's counsellor said an interesting thing the other week, for example. Speculating, he stated that there will probably come a time when all you would need to do to address someone's OCD is attach some contraption to the side of one's head and turn a switch. Effectively, something magical is employed to cut all sorts of corners – and time – to address something that has taken a long while to come to fruition. It could be that simple, he said. You just turn OCD off. Given human development when it comes to technological knowhow, I can't say that I disagree with him. But is it 'magical'? Or something quite different? As we were leaving the appointment, I couldn't help draw analogies with ECT – or to give it its full moniker, Electroconvulsive Therapy. ECT is one of those elements of mental health care that 'helps' – if that's the word – to trigger all sorts of stereotypical and unwanted associations. We've all seen the black and white films of people being 'wired up', having electric currents passed through their brain, their bodies jumping and twisting in response. It looks draconian, and it is – surely – just that. However – and there always seems to be one of those

– it would seem that ECT is not solely a thing of the past. Not that long ago, one of my previous consultants asked me if I would be averse to having this treatment. In my initial surprise, it took me a while to respond. Truth be told, it wasn't surprise as such. I was decidedly shocked. He explained that there would appear to be a new wave of enthusiasm to reinstate something that I thought was a relic of a previous, bygone, era. I don't think he put it in quite that manner. But that was the gist of it. My answer was unequivocal, when it came. 'Yes', I said. 'I'm up for anything, if you think it has a chance of bettering my life'. So there may well come a time, particularly if my situation either deteriorates or stays static for too long, when I might well be faced with this option. Of course, the key to this is a belief that it may work. There's no point, in my view, in instigating any sort of treatment unless you feel that it has a chance of making a difference. You have to believe. Have some confidence. Some hope. And, when it comes down to it, if you ask me today if I thought ECT could make a positive impact, I would say 'yes'.

The only problem is, if you asked me the same question tomorrow, I might well give a different answer!

November

Tuesday 1st November 2016
Elliot's CAMHS appointment was a little different today. Principally because Elliot wasn't involved! His consultant wanted one of the weekly sessions to be with us, his parents, ostensibly I think to explain his course of action and the principles that lie behind it, as well as to guide us in our efforts to support our son. Much of what he had to say was familiar to me, but there again, I'm a bit of a seasoned campaigner where OCD is concerned. It was interesting to see how he described psychological concepts, mannerisms and developments that have become largely second nature. You do these things without question, sometimes without thought, and it's good on occasions to take stock and re-examine the whys and wherefores. It puts things into a perspective that you can allow to be taken for granted. For Lesley, of course, it's different. She doesn't have the condition. All her experience comes from observation. And from dealing with the consequences. It may be, as a result, that she is far more attune to what happens, because of the inherent greater detachment that she brings to bear. Whether she is able to put

her finger on why things happen, to explain as well as to describe, is another matter. It may be a more challenging task. Or am I deluding myself into believing, without question, that you have to have something to genuinely appreciate and understand it fully? I just don't know.

One issue I did raise this morning was the predicament I sometimes find myself in with regard to Elliot and his OCD, a predicament that results directly from my own experience of the condition. I said that there are occasions when I don't know whether it is better to talk to him about what I find challenging and how I deal with things, or, alternatively, try to hide my own symptoms and manifestations. At least from him. The former has the benefit of being the more open and honest approach. It sets the parameters and boundaries. It shows that he's not alone. It potentially encourages a certain response and reciprocal approach. If that worked for me, it can work for him etc. On the flip side, such an outlook may actually be counterproductive, simply because it demonstrates that after all these years, I'm still not free of my own obsessive and compulsive traits. It may serve to deflate and to depress. To give the impression that it can't actually be beaten in its totality.

I'm not sure I've ever really thought this through. I've always gone with the flow, convinced that transparency is always the best option. But is it?

When it comes down to it, there's no easy or straightforward answer to this question. Much depends on circumstance and sometimes on occasion. One way may seem right in one context or on one day, whereas it doesn't on another and the next. It also depends on the individual. People do get better – completely better. They conquer their demons, their afflictions, their fears. These things vanish, never to return. At least in terms of severity. Elliot can be such a person. He's young enough. He's intelligent. He's adaptable. And, what has become really apparent within the last week or so, he's really motivated. I had years of the unknown. Where nothing was diagnosed. Where my illnesses were allowed to nurture and to progress, to become entrenched, to become solid, to permeate all elements of my character, my behaviour and my life.

At the end of the day, I'm convinced my approach is the best one. I need to be me. The vulnerable as well as the strong me. The honest, clear and open me. The me that is both mental illness and a coping mechanism. A disability as well as a response. The afflicted as well as the purveyor of experience and recovery.

Wednesday 2nd November 2016

Yesterday's appointment has made me reflect on the current state of my own OCD. Probably the starting point is to say that it's always worse when I'm on my own, or even just when Lesley isn't around. I still check things, irrespective of whether I have company or not, but I'll only – normally – do so once. What happens is what I call a 'delegation of responsibility'. It doesn't matter if someone else actually does go and shadow what I do to address my obsessive and compulsive concerns, it's enough for me to believe that they're in the house as well and therefore the onus that I think rests solely with me when I'm on my own, is somehow shared. I should add that there is a difference between my reliance on Lesley on the one hand, and my belief that anyone else will act as she does. In other words, my OCD lessens or completely disappears when Lesley is here, but still remains obstinately and tantalisingly present when I'm with someone else.

Having dealt with the issue of other people, let me now tell you what bothers me. It may be just as quick to say what doesn't, because the one thing I have mastered over the years is contamination. This is probably the most enduring and obdurate element of most people's OCD. It's certainly Elliot's. For me, however, I can deal with things such as poo, dirt or germs. I no longer feel the need to wash my hands over and over again, or readily refrain from situations in which I may have to handle things that I believe are dirty or infected. As I mentioned in an earlier post, my biggest test years ago was actually blood. I fervently believed that my blood was tainted. I would panic if I cut something or if I had a nose bleed. My belief that I was now destined to spread some fatal disease was absolute. One hundred per cent. I would immediately seek a plaster or bandage. It didn't matter if it was only a paper cut, a wound that would heal within minutes. I had to patch myself up straight away before I did anything else. I then was engulfed by the procedure of washing, which if you think about your average plaster, usually means that all the stickiness evaporates virtually instantaneously. Time and time again, I would use plaster after plaster until I eventually found satisfaction. The tension would ease and my breathing would return to normal. Life could go on.

That's all over now. What remains are locks, gas and electricity. I still go through the same elaborate procedures every time I have to lock something, use the cooker or the central heating system, or turn something on or off. I'm certainly not as bad as I once was, but it's still there, a reminder perhaps of days gone by when I would be imprisoned in a situation by my own fears, but certainly an ever-present demonstration of my inability to completely let go. If anything, dealing with electrical things is the worst. I simply find electricity scary. If I could, I would turn everything off at the socket and unplug every plug. Every day. But I can't do that. We wouldn't have much use for a freezer if I did give in to my fears, and it's simply impracticable to turn off things such as washing machines or dishwashers after every single use. It would also mean that the electric currents that spark our heating and hot water would be turned on and off more times than is necessarily healthy. I've tried to convince myself over the years that the more I fiddle with things, the greater the chance of something going wrong. The greater the danger, in other words. This process of frightening myself into submission has worked to some extent. However, the temptation – and it's an agonising one – to give in and to continually turn switches one way, then the other, can be so acute at times. It's positively destructive. I know it's playing with me. It's trying to tempt me into relenting, to persuade me to listen to my obsessions and compulsions. And yet it's precisely those moments that are the key to recovery. The more you put yourself into positions when you have to make one choice or the other and the more you turn away from OCD, the greater your chance of beating it. You need to physically as well as psychologically reject the condition and what it's making you become, the way it's making you act, the train of thought that is fuelling what is essentially an addiction.

Practice. That's the solution. It's not easy, but it can be done.

Thursday 3rd November 2016

I attended a consultation event at City Hall yesterday. It concerned proposals to create what were termed 'resilience and recovery hubs' throughout Leicester, Leicestershire and Rutland. I try to attend as many events that I can that relate to mental health and this one, considering that it focused on significant transformations in service delivery, I felt was particularly important. The concept is sound. It involves Clinical Commissioning Groups and local authorities joining forces, amalgamating budgets, working more closely together, creating a new point and method of delivery, making it easier and more simple for people to understand and to use. The problem, as always, is money. In many ways, the pretext, the reason for the development, I believe, is fundamentally flawed. You see, first and foremost, it's not about improving the way things are done. Even though that may well transpire. No, it's about saving costs. The budget is limited. More limited than we initially thought. And therein, sadly, is the predicament we're in. As far as I can see, the tenders that they will at some stage be inviting organisations to bid for, are so constrained as to make them unworkable. The ideal candidate – in fact the only candidate that will truthfully be able to do the work – will need to be local, familiar with the geography and demography of the area in question, well versed in mental health service delivery, have the confidence of local communities, be a trusted vehicle for engagement, be able to link statutory and third sector bodies. All good so far! But then, it will also have to use its own resources to fully implement the administration and the methods of delivery because what money it gains will quickly go on staffing and general, but necessary, costs such as petrol and office rental. What organisation, realistically, is going to bid for something that may well, ultimately, cost them money? Voluntary sector groups won't be able to afford to do that, and those in the private sector – heaven forbid – won't find anything attractive in the proposition to begin with!

Sadly, therefore, it's another example of the poor relation that mental health has become, is, and continues to be. The representatives of the proposal did a sterling job trying to answer and address all these – and other – issues that came their way during the event. But their hands are tied. They know the score. They can't hide the cracks. But they can't admit defeat or potential failure. In the absence of a greater budget, ultimately from central government, things such as this – great ideas admittedly – are destined to be virtually infeasible. I say 'virtually', because I try to live in hope. Perhaps the budget can be increased? Perhaps there can be some form of sponsorship? Perhaps someone will come forward – altruistic to the core – that will save the day and be willing to take a chance as well as a loss?

Time will tell.

Friday 4th November 2016

I completed my preparations for Vilnius yesterday. To be honest, I don't think I could be more thorough. As usual, I've been over everything from start to finish. I've studied guide books and maps. I've made my own notes. I've checked my cameras work. I've looked through all the instructions in relation to parking, flying, travelling the other end and my accommodation. I've printed out all the relevant documents. I've checked-in both ways online. I know what clothes I'm going to take and where to pack them. I've been quite meticulous. It's not necessarily that I want to be, of course. It's because I need to be. I have no choice if I'm going to take that plunge into a domain that is unfamiliar as well as daunting. You see, the biggest hurdle with trips such as this is conquering my own fears. To do so, to be in with a fighting chance, I have to exert as much control beforehand over what is actually to come. I have to go to the limits, all that is physically and psychologically possible. Short of doing a dummy run, I think I've done that.

As the week has gone on, that curious mixture of excitement and trepidation has begun to merge. Sometimes one achieves precedence over the other, but there is never a time when I'm completely immersed unilaterally, if you follow my meaning. There will be some amongst you that finds the whole essence of planning and scheduling uncomfortable when it comes to taking a holiday. I do myself to a certain degree. I'd love to be able to go with the flow, to do what comes naturally at the time, to be free and easy, relaxed and spontaneous. But I can't. Not only do I need to be able to envisage what is to come, to know beforehand what I will have to face in terms of arrangements, the perfectionist streak in me comes rising to the fore and tells me, implores me, dictates to me, that I have to take full advantage of where I'm going and what I'm thinking of doing. If I don't, I've failed. Yes, even a holiday isn't free of the need for perfection! I can cope far better when I'm with other people. Indeed, when with Lesley, I'm able to relinquish that need for control to such an extent that we can and do decide what to do on the spur of the moment and are as opportunistic in our planning as anyone else. When I'm on my own, however, I'm not able to be this way. Perhaps it's simply down to my travelling companion? The physical companion that is my wife, or its psychological counterpart that is depression.

Saturday 5th November 2016
With Lesley spending more time with her parents helping them with practicalities as well as emotional support, much of the onus on domestic duties has now fallen to me. In one way, I'm glad,

as it makes me feel useful – as well as taking some of the obvious pressure off Lesley's broad shoulders. The problem comes not with my inclination to clean, tidy up, do the washing, shopping etc. Instead it revolves around that one word that is my perennial nemesis – perfection. If my goal in dealing with the perfectionist streak that is part of my depression is to aim not for one hundred percent, but for thirty percent less, that will translate – when it comes to cleaning – with overlooking things that are obviously dirty or dusty. It has to. Somehow, I have to force myself not to be meticulous and comprehensive. But, more critically, not to assess myself in terms of whether I've succeeded or not. A blemish, a stain, a piece of engrained dirt. All these things can be missed. Indeed, in a way, they have to be. The alternative is for me to search methodically, time consumingly, obsessively for every single thing that is not clean. It's telling, for example, that the room I usually start with – the kitchen – I spend the most time addressing. Yesterday afternoon, I spent ages on my knees cleaning every millimetre of cupboard and appliance. Once I'd started in that manner, I couldn't then relent. I had to continue. It was only when I'd finished that room, that I forced myself to re-think my strategy. To compel myself not to persevere in that fashion. To continually tell myself that seventy per cent was perfectly acceptable.

Sunday 6th November 2016

In less than twenty-four hours' time, I'll begin my big Lithuanian adventure. I have to be honest and say, right now, that I wish it had already begun and that I was already ensconced in my hotel room, prepared and ready to hit the streets. It's not just the travelling that scares me, it's the logistical hurdles I know I'll have to negotiate and master in order for me to take those first steps – map, guide and camera in hand. More than anything it's being able to source and then obtain the necessary public transport card that will see me through the week. Every guide book I've consulted has described slightly different arrangements. In one, I can buy it at a Tourist Information Centre. In another, it can only be bought at a specific Tourist Information Centre. In one more, they can be obtained through kiosks at stops. And in one more still, only at specific kiosks. You see my dilemma. Until I get one in my hand, I'll be worrying. It could be that, as there is a Centre at the airport, I can get one virtually as soon as I land. That's obviously the best case scenario. But since when has a depressive believed – to any sense of satisfaction and purpose – that the preferred option will actually come to fruition? I'm expecting a saga.

Dealing with the flight though remains my first task to address. I actually love flying. I've never really had a problem with fear in relation to the flight itself. It's getting onto the plane in the first place that is my most difficult obstacle. Every time I go, I buy the most comprehensive package. Priority boarding, dedicated seating, excess baggage. Whatever it constitutes and what is available, short of extra leg room, I'll choose it every time. My nightmare is getting onto a crowded plane, with hand luggage and a large coat. Finding my choice of seats severely limited and with no cabin space to put my stuff, I'm walking up and down, everyone looking at me. I trip. I bump into people. I begin to panic. People see my torture, my rapidly escalating concern and anxiety. They know I'm suffering, that I'm starting to lose it, but still they sit there and stare, rather than offer to help. It is, of course, the identical situation to the one I face getting onto trains. It's such a tangible ordeal. I can feel it now, even as I write. It's therefore essential to maintaining my composure and controlling my fears, that I get on to the plane as soon as possible, whilst everyone else is still concerning themselves with their own affairs. I don't mind spending the extra money. To be honest, I don't really have a choice. That's the only way I can exert the necessary control that I need.

My preparations, of course, can only go so far. There are things outside my power to influence. One of which is the weather. It's going to be cold in Vilnius. I've studied the local weather forecast meticulously over the course of the last few days and it seems that temperatures are going to struggle to get over freezing. Again, I don't mind the cold. Indeed, I often relish it. It stops me from sweating, for one! It's the impact of the conditions on things such as flying that will stay with me until the moment I leave Vilnius on Friday evening on my return to Luton. I've kept reminding myself that planes can and do fly from places accustomed to harsh weather conditions. Airports in Eastern Europe – unlike here – do not come to an abrupt halt at the first sign of snow. No, what is staying with me this time, is the fact that on my last sojourn to Poland, last December, I was stuck at Łódź for three hours whilst they replaced some light bulbs, without which we were marooned. I know that wasn't down to the weather, but the reminder of a problem remains slightly unsettling.

All this again emphasises the significance of that word 'control'. I've done as much as I can. I'm now susceptible and condemned to fate. If everything goes without a hitch – and there's no logical, rational reason why it shouldn't – I'll be fine and I'll have a productive and enjoyable week.

If something goes wrong, however.....

Wish me good fortune!

Monday 7th November 2016

Well I made it! A car journey down the M1 to Luton, a bus from the car park to the airport, a flight across the northern reaches of the European mainland, a local bus to the nearest stop and finally, some eight hours after leaving home, I'm here in the hotel, my base for the next four days. Despite constantly being on edge, there were no real problems. The only time when my anxiety levels were raised was waiting for the bus to take me to the airport terminal in Luton. As I glanced over the Departures board, I couldn't see my designated flight to Vilnius at all. There were flights highlighted both before and afterwards, but no Wizzair flight W68004! What could this mean? Had it been cancelled? No, that couldn't be the case as one of the other entries was for a cancelled flight. Had the times been changed?

No. I'd had constant emails from the airline over the previous two or three weeks, the last one only a day or so beforehand, warning me of roadworks on the M1 approach to Luton. Surely, they'd have told me of something far more important – an altered timetable? All I could realistically do was to try to hold my fears in check and wait until I got to the airport when all would be revealed. As we left the car park, I was willing the bus onwards to its destination. Every stop, every traffic light, every bit of congestion, only served to increase my anxieties, to punish me for my doubts. Eventually, after virtually running into the Departures hall, I had the chance to check the situation and there, in glowing electric lights, on the main information board, was my flight. I breathed a massive sigh of relief. I suspect it was as audible as it was tangible! There was a plane to take me to Vilnius and shortly I'd be on it!

Tuesday 8th November 2016
Disaster struck as soon as I switched my mobile on.

For some reason, I couldn't send texts or make phone calls. I cursed my decision, made some months previously, to upgrade my phone. Its predecessor, for all its basic features, always did the job. There was never a problem. Every time I went abroad, it switched automatically to the local provider. The only thing I ever had to adjust was the time, to reflect its new, temporary, locality. Why, oh why, was this happening? I sat on my bed and tried to think it through. I came to the conclusion that it must be something to do with the tariff I'm on. Admittedly, it is the cheapest. Though it serves me well at home, I suspected that it was inadequate when it came to foreign travel. Though there was an option to upgrade, I was too scared of having to input things like my bank details without the reassuring presence of Lesley and the four walls of my home. I got it into my head that somehow, I would miss some safeguarding detail, oversee some measure of security. My financial affairs and any forthcoming transaction would be available for all and sundry to see and to take advantage of. I'd be opening myself up to all sorts of perils, saying to every prospective, opportunistic thief, 'come and grab what I can't hide', 'take advantage of my naivety', 'rob me to your heart's and wallet's content'.

The rapidity as well as the strength of this process of catastrophization was too much to contemplate.

Then, another thought struck me. How could I let Lesley know that I was alright if I couldn't text or phone her? She would almost certainly be worried and that prospect really scared me. I tried to use the hotel's phone, but was informed by Reception that that only covered internal and local calls. I couldn't ring out. The receptionist suggested the Internet. Facebook seemed to be my salvation. Straight away, I sent messages to Lesley and to my three boys. Then the thought struck me. What if they didn't access them? It would be so out of character. What are the chances of all four of them deciding not to look at their respective Facebook pages for the duration of the next twenty-four hours or even longer? It was a possibility though, and where there was uncertainty, there was a persistent nagging pressure on me to try to reduce it, to temper it, to eradicate it and so therefore save my increasingly fragile mental state.

I had to allow for the probability – as it seemed – that someone out there would heed and act upon my message, and so I set out to fulfil the object of my journey, to see the sights related to Jewish history and the specificity of the Holocaust, to meet the requirements I'd set myself in my detailed timetable.

No matter how much I tried though, I couldn't stop myself worrying. I kept thinking of the repercussions of no contact. Not only would Lesley be frantic, but how on earth was I to cope without having the option of speaking to her, or sending her a text, whenever I wanted to or felt the need? When I got back to my hotel base, I hastily checked Facebook. To my dismay, there was no message for me. Not one. I decided to send a message to Sammy, who I could see had been on Facebook only minutes before. If that didn't work by morning, I'd have to do something more drastic.

And all for the want of a working mobile phone!

Wednesday 9th November 2016

Sammy came to the rescue! He'd seen my SOS and had contacted Lesley. Once more, I breathed a huge sigh of relief, cathartic and tension-consuming in its process and effect. It didn't negate the feelings of isolation that still peppered my besieged mind, but at least I could feel content in the fact that Lesley knew what was going on and the reasons why I hadn't been in touch. I could, at least, do what I needed to do, go to where I'd targeted as sights, safe in the knowledge that one pressure had eased, even though the larger, more significant one still remained.

After traipsing the streets of the former Jewish ghettos yesterday, today was a day for museums. The Vilna Gaon Jewish State Museum operates out of three sites, two of whom I would visit during the course of the day. The latter, dealing specifically with the story of the Holocaust in Vilnius and Lithuania, was the most taxing as well as interesting. It wasn't an easy place to find. The address belied the fact that it was set back from the main road. I knew that I was looking for something quite particular, a green painted wooden structure, with a number of memorials in the small square outside its front door. Snow had begun to fall as I made my way to the entrance, having to ring a bell to elicit the attention of the museum staff. Some two hours later, having devoured every bit of detail, every element of the tragedy, every nuance of the local context, I made my own contribution to the visitor's book, thanked the staff profusely and made my way out into what remained of the day's light. Despite the enormity of what I'd just put myself through, I was satisfied. Gaps in knowledge that I needed to fill, had been. Stories that I'd not encountered previously, had registered. The satisfaction was academic and intellectual, based on learning, awareness and understanding. Nevertheless, how could one ever be satisfied, as a human being – on a more mortal, fundamental level – knowing what had happened, what could still happen, indeed what was happening again? Once that measure of personal interest had been absorbed, I could only reflect, sadly, on a world that has never really learned its lessons. Antisemitism is still rife. Xenophobic, nationalistic sentiments are frequent. Attitudes that should have been put to bed, are still prevalent. Indeed, the more I reflected, the more I deduced that this world is still a dangerous place if you are a minority, if you share some vulnerabilities, if you are specific in intent and approach, if your identity somehow 'doesn't fit'. As a Jewish man with a mental illness. As a political activist and commentator. As someone who chooses to work with 'targeted' communities, who identifies with those who are vulnerable and in need of support and advocacy, I'm not safe in such a world.

It shouldn't be, but that's just the way it is.

Thursday 10th November 2016

That same sense of desolation and concern prevailed as I negotiated the local rail network to visit the third site of the Jewish State Museum, the one that I knew would prove to be the most challenging. The forests of Paneriai lie some eight kilometres outside the city. As the Holocaust intensified in its severity and destruction, between seventy and a hundred thousand people, the majority of whom were Jews, were taken into the woods and murdered, their bodies being dumped in mass graves. It must have been an appalling sight. Could humanity ever steep as low as this? As I made my way on foot from the local railway station, I was conscious that I was on my own, literally in the middle of nowhere. Though a small mini-bus had passed me, obviously on its way to the memorial, nobody else seemed to be going my way. The world was oblivious to my feelings as I adjusted to what I knew I would shortly have to face. It was difficult. Words are simply inadequate to accurately and fully describe what was going through my mind and what then as a consequence impacted on the rest of me. I felt angry as well as disconsolate. Wretched, disturbed, anguished, crushed. But also intensely cold and frightened. It wasn't quite the same as seeing the excavations of similar graves at Sobibór in Poland – that was truly Dante-esque in pain and savagery. But it was close. The settled snow, of course, concealed the ground, but it couldn't obscure the true revelation of what had happened in this cold, dark place so many years ago. It was a shattering experience for me. Particularly as I was alone, away from any other living human contact. The focus of the place consumed me and indeed was me. It was as if I was some form of ambassador for the living, someone charged at that moment and time, with reflecting the memory of the past in the context of a live present and an uncertain future. It was a responsibility that I couldn't avoid, even if I had wished to. It is indeed something that I do feel is intrinsic to my role in life in so many ways. I only hope I live up to the expectations and hopes of those taken from this world in such a demeaning, brutal and tragic fashion, left to lie in places such as this.

Friday 11th November 2016

Today I had to face the fears that had been growing inside me for the previous two days. Even as early as Wednesday night, I began to have thoughts, strange premonitions even, that things would go wrong when it came to my journey home. Indeed, I had to really fight to reinsert a degree of calmness on a number of occasions, such was the ferocity of the attack upon my nerves, the intensity of the feelings and their 'realistic' nature and impact. I ended up physically, audibly, telling myself off. Telling myself not to think the worst. That there was no evidence that things would be as I feared.

But what was it that was making me so worked up?

Simply this. That on Friday evening, my flight would be cancelled. That I'd then have to make some decisions as to what to do. That I'd have to act upon them. That I'd have to take a degree of control that I was unaccustomed to having to face on my own. That I wouldn't have the luxury and comfort of a wife to confide in and consult. What had been resolved in my mind was something draconian and devastating. That I'd have to make my way to the British Embassy and ask for their help, saying, honestly and truthfully, that I was incapable of sorting out the logistical mess of cancellation on my own, that I was in the midst of a panic attack or breakdown that I knew was inevitable, that I wasn't well enough to face the consequences of changed plans and altered arrangements. That was my only option in the face of calamity.

As the day went on, I knew I was struggling to keep myself calm and focused. Nothing seemed to be wrong. The weather conditions were fine. Planes were landing and taking off from Vilnius Airport. I'd had no direct communication to warn or to heed. Even as I went through the process of checking-in, of going through security, of waiting at the gate, I was expecting trouble around every corner, at any time, from all directions. Even when I'd taken my seat inside the plane by the window, when the cabin doors were locked and we were ready to go, I still expected an announcement to come, telling us all to disembark and make our way back into the terminal. I willed us to move. The more I implored movement, the more obdurate our position seemed to be. Someone, somewhere, aware of my agitation, was playing a cruel game, lengthening each second, halting time for everyone but myself. Every change in circumstance was a change to be endured and overcome. They became personal challenges, tests of my mental strength and dexterity. I thought I'd be fine when we took to the air. I usually am. But this time, the thought quickly came to me that we would either crash or have to land elsewhere. At any second, I was expecting turbulence to rock us either to oblivion or to necessitate a change in our circumstances, one that once more I would not be able to adjust myself to. Indeed, at one point, the prospect of crashing was the more attractive proposition. In that scenario, I didn't have to do anything but die. There was no other choice or decision to be made. I could leave things to fate. I could prevail upon that to decide my outcome and my way forward, limited though that would have been.

Nothing happened. We landed at Luton twenty minutes early. I wondered – as I once more reflected on what I've become mentally – if anyone else around me was aware of what depression had just put myself through? Was my disturbed state evident to anyone else? Did anyone else appreciate or care? To people going through the boredom and monotony of one more journey, of dealing without thought or worry with every logistical arrangement. To people who are able to get on a plane when nearly full. Of people who see transport as easy and as natural a process as walking through a door, of switching on a television set, of making themselves a meal. To these people, can they really envisage or understand what it is to endure a challenge as demanding to me as it is simple to them? Can they truly imagine?

I suspect not. But there again, that's one of the reasons why I'm writing this diary. To make people more aware, so that they can – if they choose – offer themselves as a way of negotiating the hardships of others, of simply holding out a helping hand in friendship, empathy and compassion.

Saturday 12th November 2016

Back on 'terra firma', in the comfort of my own bedroom, in the security and safety of her embrace, I told Lesley everything that I'd been through over the course of the last few days. She was right, I think, when she said that it all hinged on my inability to speak to her. Had I been able to do so, I could have talked through my fears and received the necessary strength from her to withstand the assault on my mental state. She also, would have been able to act for me. To take away the pressures that always come with making arrangements.

To be honest, I've been thinking as to whether I'll be able to negotiate trips such as this into the future. Have I indeed reached my limit with respect to my ability to cope? I sincerely hope not. Because when I'm there – wherever 'there' is – if I didn't have the end journey to contemplate, like a looming, darkening presence on the horizon, I think I'd be fine. I do enjoy what I do. I do things at my own pace. And I can cope. I can deal with getting myself food. Even with local transport arrangements. Whilst in Vilnius, I brought myself a three-day bus pass from a local kiosk. I was able to ask for the right train ticket to Paneriai, as well as checking timetables and types of train. I could communicate and make myself understood in the museums. I was never lost. I always knew what was around the corner – metaphorically as well as geographically. It's because I prepare, of course. That's the secret. Doing your homework beforehand. I had a handle on the local bus and trolley-bus service whilst at my desk at home. I'd gone over it so many times. I knew when things opened. What food to expect. The price of everyday items.

What I can't cope with is any sense of uncertainty. That's when I really need help.

Perhaps there's a way of getting some assistance from airlines and at airports? After all, people with physical disabilities ask for and receive appropriate aid and support. I saw this on numerous occasions both in Luton and Vilnius. Why should those of us with a mental disability be any different? The answer to this, sadly, is still two-fold. Firstly, there shouldn't be any disparity. But secondly – unfortunately – there is. It's exactly the same as asking a member of staff at a railway station in England to get you to your seat on a pending train. You're counting on them being aware of mental illness and how it affects people. You're hoping that they're knowledgeable and understanding, but also that they're not discriminatory. That they don't see you as somebody strange and peculiar, someone that expects personal service for some other reason other than disability. You don't want to see reluctance in their approach or a bemused face. You don't want them to feel that you're asking for anything out of the ordinary. You also don't want them to feel sorry for you. But I suspect that, for all those reasons, that is still the case more times than not.

I think I've given myself something else to do. The only way to deal effectively and conclusively with the perception of ignorance is to inform. To tell people how it is. To ask the right questions of the right people. And to insist on answers. On practical, remedial actions. It's part of the fight for parity for mental health. And it's a fight in which I have to participate if I'm not to become victim to my growing fears and inhibitions and never go abroad by myself again.

Sunday 13th November 2016
I'm having a quiet day today. I need to recuperate, mentally as well as physically, before facing the demands of work and everyday life once more. Luckily, I don't have much in the diary to do this week. And if I wanted, I could actual cancel some of the things that are in there. But let's take things a day at a time. The process of readjustment is not always straightforward. It is more challenging for someone with a mental illness. You won't be surprised at that fact. It's not that there's necessarily anything different in terms of what you need to do. It's your capability of doing those universal tasks that is the question at hand. Your mind exerts its own pressure. It reinstates dormant associations, some of which are perplexing and have become strange and remote. It reinvigorates the process of practical exertion by elevating, to arduous and formidable status, feats and measures that others simply take for granted.

But that's a task for tomorrow, not today.

Monday 14th November 2016
It has been a gentle start to the working week. I've spent most of the morning at the Leicester Diabetes Centre, manning a stall devoted to the work of the Centre for BME Health of which I am a part. The event was organised to commemorate World

Diabetes Day, an increasingly important occasion in the health observation calendar given the prevalence of diabetes in modern societies. It was good to get back into the swing of things in such a hospitable and friendly environment and with people I know and respect. One thing I did notice was how tired I got simply talking. I probably spoke more in two hours than I did in the whole of the time I was away in Lithuania and it really took its toll. Put succinctly, I just wasn't used to it. I did a lot of talking to myself in my own head last week. It helps to keep some semblance of normality when I'm on my own, even though I suspect that on occasions words came out of my mouth and were audible enough to provoke a reaction of mild curiosity amongst those close enough to actually hear me. I'm not always conscious that I do this, so it must look strange and perhaps even a degree threatening, given the often cited saying that equates talking to yourself with madness. But we do all do this. This isn't something strictly and specifically confined to people with a mental illness. It's much more common. Look around you next time you're in a public place. You'll see what I mean.

I do find talking a struggle at times. I know I've said this before but it's worth reiterating. It's not only a physical sensation. One of tiredness, exertion and muscle strain. It's also mentally demanding. I sometimes feel that unless I actually say something, people will feel that I'm remote and inaccessible. This often means that I talk simply to try to mask what's actually going on inside my head. That it becomes a coping mechanism, a means of avoiding discussing or allowing to register what is much more challenging and frightening – my mental illness. And yet I don't really enjoy it at all. I struggle to find interesting things to say. I can't always keep up with changes in topic. I'm always conscious of saying something stupid or offensive. I worry about the impact and repercussion of a spoken word or phrase. And once it's over, I'm drained. I can't describe to you the full enormity of what I mean here. I guess it's a combination of a variety of things – relief, concern, anxiety, dread, disappointment. There are too many to mention. But it doesn't end there. I will mercilessly and obsessively review and reflect.

I will brutally take to pieces what I believed I said and if I can't remember, I will urge my already tired brain to recollect and to confirm. It's important to remember that this isn't some natural process of reaffirming some consequential contribution to a meeting, an interview or an event. It's about everyday, commonplace conversations. Routine, rather than exceptional. My mind doesn't always distinguish between the two. To me, everything becomes significant and far-reaching. Nothing can be left to chance. It's agonisingly punishing. Yet I can't help but do it. I don't know any other way.

Tuesday 15th November 2016
Thinking back to what I wrote yesterday, two things come immediately to mind.

Firstly, what I described towards the end, that process of reviewing and reflecting, is related directly to that strive for perfection. It is so engrained within my psyche that even mundane conversations, the sort that happen without much conscious deliberation, are not immune from that desire to be without fault or flaw. It's as if every single word matters, even a monosyllabic 'yes' or 'no'. Most of the time I don't realise I'm doing this. The process starts automatically and before I know it, I'm in the middle of intense terminological scrutiny, analysing and judging, contemplating and ruminating, rarely satisfied, always looking, searching for excellence. It becomes a real psychological effort to revert to what I guess most people would see as 'normality'. To tell myself that it doesn't matter. That I shouldn't beat myself up about it. That any process of 'normal' communication includes elements of spontaneity as well as deliberation. That I have to admit the likelihood and the desirability of the former.

My 'normal' here, you see, is different from those who don't think and act as I do, those of you without the perfectionist tendency that comes from the type of mental illness that I've had for so long.

The second observation perhaps involves an element of contradiction. I talked about the need to talk, of speech as a disguise for vulnerability and illness. However, I am very much aware that when I'm really ill, or during those moments of intense anxiety, I'm hardly able to talk at all. When I no longer feel the need to try and make an effort, to hide my situation, I become an open, transparent mute, incapable of conscious will, devoid of motivation and aspiration. I need my own silence and isolation. During these times, I'm probably at my lowest ebb. Life is barely worth it, so why bother to function in ways that characterise life at its most basic level? Why put yourself through the agony and exertion of talking when you have nothing to say? Why make the effort to be something you don't want to be? I've had so many times like this and no doubt will do again in the future. The irony is that in doing and saying nothing, life actually becomes more demanding. There have been times when I've had months upon months of this – seven months being my maximum. This is depression at its most severe. It's the bottom rung of life. You're edging towards the abyss. You feel its allure. It constantly tempts you with its power and permanence. And yet, somehow, I've always managed to hang on.

One of the signs of recovery, interestingly, is when I start to want to say a few words, to exercise my vocal cords, to begin that process of communicating more willingly and freely. When that happens, life starts again.

Wednesday 16th November 2016
Elliot had his latest CAMHS OCD appointment yesterday.

He's doing astonishingly well. Indeed, there is little we have to do now to motivate him to do thoroughly the tasks he has been set. He just gets on with them. That transformation in his approach has been as obvious as it's been necessary. He has realised that unless he himself has the determination to crack it, he'll be left in some form of OCD wilderness, unable to move, uncertain as to direction, unwilling to take chances. And the challenges that he's been set are not easy ones. They all involve pre-meditated, deliberate contamination. Making himself 'dirty' as it were, so that he can address the issues 'head-on'. It goes against every single, miniscule morsel of OCD substance, all the things – the coping mechanisms – that he's devised and used for so long. He's now realised that, rather than combat the condition, what he's been doing – innocently and naively – is fuel the fire that then serves to obliterate any chance of recovery.

Elliot now has a great chance of beating OCD once and for all. The reason is not only this new, developed and refreshed psyche. It's also his age. Put succinctly, his OCD has been active only for a relatively short period of time. Given the right guidance and the adaptability of youth, there is nothing that stands in his way other than an obstinate determination not to change. For me, however, it's not quite that straightforward. His counsellor said as much in one of his earlier sessions. For adults, many of whom – like me – have had decades of immersion in OCD, the prognosis isn't quite as positive. It's years of unchecked practice, of engrained behaviour, that have to be undone. The manifestations of the condition have a permanence and a resonance that can prove too much when it comes to defeating one's fears and changing one's behaviour. I know I'm a lot better than I was some twenty years ago. But it's still there. I can always sense its presence. And at times it rears up its ugly head to become the shattering experience I can still remember as normal.

Things could have been different for me if, when I was a younger man, I had known the very words 'Obsessive Compulsive Disorder'. If there had been awareness of the condition. If it had a degree of 'validity'. If there wasn't such a stigma towards mental illness. If I hadn't felt that what I had was genuine madness.

If, as a result, I hadn't been so reluctant to seek help, terrified of the consequences.

But 'if' can be a dangerous and destructive word.

Thursday 17th November 2016

I'm very conscious of the fact that I need to keep my life manageable. By this, I don't just mean controllable, but within parameters relating to things such as pressure and overload. This doesn't just apply to obvious contexts such as work, but actually to everything I do – or at least try to do. Yesterday was a good example. I'd spent much of it at an event focusing on the crucial relationship between religion, belief and sexuality. It was scheduled to end at 3.00 pm, but when it overran, the rest of my timetable threatened to fall apart like a house of cards. With a little bit of luck, I managed to retrieve the situation and be home within the hour, but then, rather than immediately begin the next thing on my list, I had to deal with a school issue which took a little more time than I actually had. Once I'd begun my next phase of work, what I'd intended to do was occasionally interrupted by the vagaries of emails and phone calls. So much so that I felt compelled to do more than I'd anticipated and planned for as some sort of recompense. Amidst all of this, I hoovered up, changed the washing, emptied the dishwasher, sorted out clean clothes, fed Millie and a few more things that I now can't remember!

The point of this recollection is not to demonstrate what I did or even, necessarily, how busy I am, but to emphasise the fact that I find it difficult to adjust to things that I hadn't anticipated and that if I don't allow for such eventualities, I'm actually setting myself up to fail. It's not that I'm giving myself too much to do, therefore – my diary is probably much less demanding than most working people – it's that I have to give it some slack and allow for slippage. Ordinarily, I'm quite good at this, but sometimes, in my efforts to keep up with things that I think need doing, I rely on good fortune and fate rather than make the necessary allowances. And that can be fatal for a depressive who believes that such things always conspire against you.

What I need at times is that type of rest when you actually put yourself consciously into oblivion. When you shut your brain off and think of nothing, or at least of something warm and comforting. It can emanate from a bit of meaningless telly, for example. The problem is, though, that the more you try to instil relevant images and thoughts into your brain, to will and impose them on your psyche, the more your brain works against you. It tends to do everything you don't want it to do. You can test this yourself. Think of something entirely random – an elephant, for example – and then try to go a whole minute without conjuring up the image you selected. I'll bet you can't do it. It's actually virtually impossible.

Increasingly, therefore, in the absence of the mental fortitude to knowingly and deliberately relax, I have to resort to the only thing that I know can work, and that is sleep. Sometimes, I even have to aid that process through medication. I'm not sleeping because I'm physically exhausted. I'm sleeping because my mental state is at threat and I know I have to close. I'm no different from a PC wishing to install necessary updates. You have to shut down and restart to gain the benefit.

Friday 18th November 2016

Every now and again I get a really disturbing thought or image that both penetrates and stays in my mind. With it comes a fervent and total belief that whatever it is I'm seeing or thinking will inevitably come true. I had just such an experience last night. For some illogical and unexpected reason, what fixated my mind was the conviction that Elliot was about to die. Even for a second such a contemplation is hard to stomach, such is the punitive and horrific nature of the belief. But this went on for some thirty odd minutes. I couldn't dispel the thought. In fact, the more I tried, the more obstinate and fixed it became. (This, of course, harks back to what I mentioned in yesterday's entry). Irrespective of the fact that I was at my wit's end. That I was suffering intensely. That I was indeed breaking up inside. That this was pure torture. At some point my brain turned to the question of what I should do. My immediate inclination was to rush to him to plead with him to stay safe, to remain living. But, realistically, how could I do that? There was nothing in what he was doing, or in what he ordinarily does, to suggest that he's in any particular danger. He doesn't have a terminal disease either. To say anything would only serve to disturb and worry him, and that's before you address the issue of what words to use. I watched him laughing away in conversation with one of his friends. He was fine. How could I break that particular moment to divulge the paranoia that was consuming me from within? There was no-one else to turn to? Lesley was still to come home. Joel was at the gym. I had to ride it out. That was my only option. I knew eventually it would subside. The only question was when.

At times like this, it makes me more conscious than ever of my vulnerability and the precarious nature of my existence. It also leads me to scrutinise, to truly assess whether my life is worth living. I would have done anything during those torturous thirty minutes to ensure that the only death in question was my own. Only that way would I be free from the unpredictability of my psychological state, to put an end to the way my brain malfunctions, to cease, once and for all, the barrage that life inflicts on my fragile being.

When, at last, the feelings began to disappear, the images becoming more and more remote, I started to breathe more easily. Things reverted back to normality, even if that normality involves mental illness in its more restrained state. I was no longer panicking. I'd ceased to be paranoid. I was thoroughly shattered. Physically exhausted. But at least I was still alive.

And more importantly, so was Elliot.

Saturday 19th November 2016
If I have a favourite time of year, it is the lead up to Christmas. Christmas Day itself is often too much for me. The expected, sometimes enforced, high spirits. The need to be happy, or at

least to appear so. The challenges that come with extra communication, of talking and listening for long periods of time. Of being around people that you don't see on an everyday basis, even though they are, of course, family. It all adds up to extra pressure, self-enforced though some of that may be. I manage by doing things in small doses, and by tactical retreats when the need arises. The month or so beforehand, though, is an entirely different matter. I allow myself to get swept away in the emotion and excitement of this special time of year. Or at least I try to.

As has been the case in previous years, I deliberately start early. I try to stretch the duration of time. This doesn't translate into putting up our Christmas tree in October, or even beginning the Christmas shopping at the start of November. What I do is gradual, but meaningful. I watch DVDs that I only view at this time of year. Indeed, I have a schedule of programmes – Christmas films, shows that I associate with Christmas – that I will make my way through. Not in any particularly order, and not confined to certain dates. Often I'll watch them more than once. I allow myself, for once, the luxury of flexibility and spontaneity. I'll listen to Christmas music – songs, carols, larger compositions. Music that not only is directly influenced by Christmas, but which in my mind, always invokes particularly fond and welcome images. I will search for depictions of snow on my PC. Of winter settings festooned with lights, old-fashioned, traditional houses, trees glittering with ice, people insulating themselves from the cold in woollen hats and scarves.

All this is, of course, connected to my mental health. My desire to draw out this period of time is not just one that relates to the specificities of the season, it's an attempt to instil some wonderful sense of enjoyment and expectation in my life. It's a deliberate venture to give myself some happiness, to keep the wolves of depression at bay. It doesn't always work. But as it's engineered, developed and undertaken by me and me alone, I am, to a certain extent, in control. Whether you'd call this a coping mechanism, I'm not sure. What I reason is actually quite simple. That I deserve to have some degree of cheer and hope in this world. When this doesn't come naturally – because of my mental illness – I have to try and manufacture it, to create the seeds from which some remote but fleeting ember of joyous flame can shine, even temporarily. I have to give myself a chance.

Sunday 20th November 2016

One thing I'm struggling to get a handle on at the moment is the propensity for things to go wrong with and in our house. We have a television that, from time to time, switches itself over. We have a shower door that has come off its hinges. We have electric sockets that have somehow been smashed. We have a brand new boiler that, for some unaccountable reason, is not on the same wavelength with the electrical circuits that translate into heat and hot water. As a result, once on, it stays on. And it takes no notice of the thermostat. We also have temperamental electricity full stop, meaning that a short circuit or a move on a trip switch is always likely. I could go on. There have always been problems with the house. Nothing major. Usually. But I can't recall a time when there hasn't been at least one outstanding issue that has required our attention. This may actually be the norm, of course. But I doubt it. We really seem to be 'blessed' with more than our fair share of bad luck.

What this does, of course, is place constant demands on my mental strength. Particularly at times when Lesley is away. I worry. Unnecessarily most of the time. But I can't seem to use reason and logic when it comes to the likelihood not only of things going wrong, but of my ability to put them right. Put simply, I expect it every day. I even find myself on many occasion deliberating as to what I should do given a crisis – and to me these things are always just that – and coming up with anticipatory plans of action. Before anything actually happens. You see, I feel I have to have an immediate solution. The more I try to think in response to an incident, at the time of the situation, the more I am likely to get so worked up that I can't effectively do anything constructive or remedial. I tend to do the first thing that comes into my mind, such is my desperation to deal with the matter at hand. And sometimes, of course, that can be fatal, making whatever the situation is, worse. It's as if I need my own manual. A guide to my own house. Something to instruct me what to do given any eventuality. Something akin to what you find in a hotel as a guide and information for residents. Actually, when I come to think of it, putting something like that together is not a bad idea. It could help not just me, but anyone faced with similar problems, dilemmas that need resolving, issues that need addressing. Anyone who, like me, cannot think properly when stressed and anxious. Anyone with a mental illness, in fact.

Monday 21st November 2016

Of course Christmas on the horizon means a further and sustained attack on our finances! I know that this applies to everybody, not just us, but somehow that doesn't really negate the worries I feel about the issue.

At the outset, I have to say that I do my fair share of spending. (Or should that be overspending?) If ever there was a time during the year when the contradictions that often accompany mental illness are at play, it's now. There's a large bit of me, you see, that sees spending money on presents for my loved ones as part of the festive spirit, as a necessary element in my attempt to embrace the lead up to Christmas, to create some enjoyment and revelry for myself. However, at the very same time that I'm visiting more shops or – as is more the custom these days – buying things online, I'm scared of the consequences. Every single item that I purchase leads to critical self-examination. I ask myself 'am I doing the right thing?' 'Can we afford it?' Every pound spent is a pound analysed. Very soon, that process of catastrophisation comes into play. You'll know the score by now. I spend money on a CD for someone. I then get it into my head that that one item is the straw that broke the camel's back. That, as a consequence, we tip the financial scales heavily in favour of debt. That we can't afford to pay our bills, and then our mortgage. That we lose the house, and ultimately the sanctuary of my marriage and family togetherness. It's a vicious circle, without respite or resolution.

Last year, whilst I wasn't working, I did have the luxury of my voluntary redundancy package to fall back on. Twelve months on, I'm not bringing in nearly as much money as I was. I'm working. And I'm very busy at times. I'm actually contributing more than I thought I would – financially, that is – and I can't really see what more I can do, such is my need to balance work and stress. However, there are occasions when I feel profound guilt. I chose to leave my job at the Council. Irrespective of the fact that I didn't really have much choice if I wanted to stay remotely sane, it was still my decision to do what I did. I knew what the consequences were likely to be. I suspected that I would have problems coming to terms with the fact that I'd be earning less and that we'd have to rely much more on Lesley's regular – and much more substantial – income. What I didn't know was how much that scenario would play on my pride as well as the practicalities of our shared finances. What I couldn't anticipate was the extent to which guilt has remained, almost a permanent feature of my life. Guilt and pride are a toxic combination. When added to the practicalities of dealing with mental illness, they are difficult to withstand and to accommodate.

I'm punishing myself. I know that. I keep telling myself to acknowledge the inevitability of the choice I made to leave full-time employment. To realise that I'm better off in so many other ways, even if that isn't in the pocket. That money isn't everything. That we're in a much more advantageous position, financially, than many. That I'm contributing as much as I can. Sometimes that thought process works and stems the tide of irrepressible guilt. Often it doesn't, and I'm left to stew, to ruminate and dwell, to reflect and to wonder. To ask myself that question: 'What have I done?'

Tuesday 22nd November 2016

On our way to school after his weekly CAMHS appointment this morning, Elliot – who'd been very quiet in the car – confided in me that he sometimes feels that life isn't worth living. Though he wasn't telling me that he'd had more definitive suicidal thoughts or even that he'd self-harmed in any way, this was still a colossal acknowledgement. (I've deliberately avoided the words 'revelation' – because I've suspected this to be the case in the past – or 'confession' – because it's not something to be ashamed of) No sooner had we made the last turn towards the school gates, then the floodgates opened and he, freely, willingly, overwhelmingly and unashamedly, burst into tears. I decided to reverse tracks and took him home. I couldn't let him go into school in that state. When in the confines of our own kitchen, we hugged each other and chatted things through. In many ways, the pressure of becoming an adult at an early age is taking its toll. However, there are other things – additional challenges if you like – that are at play here. Things that are, and will remain, private, confined to the comfort of our family. I will say that some do relate to my own mental state. I never underestimate the impact my illness must have on Elliot – and indeed the others. I can see the same tensions and uncertainties in him that I faced in relation to my own father. Wondering, constantly ruminating, on whether what he had in terms of physical as well as mental, afflictions and torment will somehow transfer down the genealogical path. That I would become like him. And that Elliot will become like me.

I think our talk had the desired impact. He seems much more relaxed and comfortable now. I thank God that we have an openness, a clarity, in our relationship. That as a result we are good friends as well as father and son. That we can talk about heavy stuff without fear of embarrassment, without suspicion that there is something missing in our communication and in our confidence. Being open about mental illness is a key component to this. Indeed, if we were anything other than totally transparent, I don't think we'd really be able to handle effectively the normalities of our lives, complex and demanding that they are. It was the same with Dad and myself.

I've had a good role model. I just hope I can live up to his expectations and those of Elliot and the rest of my family.

Wednesday 23rd November 2016

I've thought long and hard about what I wrote at the end of yesterday's entry because in many ways it does encapsulate a significant element of my mental illness. The word around which everything seems to pivot in this context is 'pressure'. The pressure to be as my Dad would wish. The pressure to be as my son requires. The pressure to be a moral and ethical fulcrum. The pressure to do the right thing. The pressure to always be accommodating and generous with my time and in my manner. Harking back to the sustained period of psychotherapy I underwent many years ago now – it lasted for some forty weeks – I know that we focused enormously on the issue of expectation when it came to my Dad, the onus that I felt always stayed with me to be a living him after he'd died. We did come to the conclusion that this was an unfair pressure in many ways, that it was impossible to sustain to the level I felt justified its existence. We talked for hours about the ramifications of this for the way I saw my father. About how it had impacted on me in the past, first and foremost, and about what I should perhaps be doing to make the adjustments necessary for me to move on.

Ever since that time I've tried my best to put things in a better, more stable, more realistic, perspective. To realise that my Dad wasn't some Nietzschean Übermensch' (Superman). That he was – and always was – mortal flesh and bone, prone to error and miscalculation, sometimes wrong and unfair, occasionally despicable and horrid. (It's funny – but telling – how hard it was to write those words). Being able to see things properly, as they were, has enabled me to see my own promises to him in a more reasonable light. It's also helped me in my relationship with Elliot and, it has to be said, with Rachel, Luke and Joel as well. It has made me recognise my own being, my own humanity, its failures and weaknesses just as much as its successes and strengths.

The only pressure that I exert now is one that comes from within my mind. It stems entirely from my depression and my OCD and has managed to put my Dad – and indeed anyone else – to one side. I deliberately used the word 'only' to reinforce the irony of the statement. The pressure has in no way been negated. If anything it has increased over the years. What has changed – along with its intensity – has been its source. I can't blame anyone else, or point to them or a specific context as the source of my problems – though, to be fair to me, I've never knowingly done that. I can only say, with a fervent belief, that all the things that impact on me and lead me into negative thinking and destructive behaviour, emanate from the living mechanism that is depression. Life outside provides the catalysts, the final straws if you like, but life within is where the beating drum of continual affliction reverberates and resonates, throbbing like the most intense of pains.

Thursday 24th November 2016

John put on an excellent event at the Centre for Integrated Living yesterday afternoon. Entitled a Disability Policy Day, he'd invited a small, selective group of people to outline what they considered to be important pieces of work for the organisation to focus on in the coming year or more. For me that meant a deliberate effort – a campaign even – to 'mainstream' mental health awareness and to make organisations in particular accountable for the extent and nature of their work in this regard. For public sector organisations, this should be happening anyway. Mental illness is one component of the vast disability spectrum, and disability is one of the nine protected characteristics defined by the Equality Act 2010. Nevertheless, it being the law, doesn't always translate – as it should – into good practice and effective procedures. However, I want things to go much further. I want private businesses to address all the issues pertinent to this 'policy', to make themselves viable and attractive propositions in which people with mental ill health can work without compromise, worry or fear. I also want the public at large to be more knowledgeable. To recognise the impact of mental illness and to become much more empathetic and compassionate. To campaign for equality alongside those of us with a direct, vested interest. It can happen. It will take time. But where there's a will, there's a way.

Towards the end of the session, I made the point that, unlike other areas of equality, we in the disability domain rarely focus on the achievements of our forefathers and foremothers. To recognise the sacrifices made by disabled people in the past. To acknowledge the historical fight for disability-related social justice and equality. And we should do. I had my brother in mind here. Our Danny, denied a heart-lung transplant that would have saved his life because he had Down's Syndrome, was a direct victim of a system that should have been there to help him when he needed it. Instead, he was condemned to die. The words uttered by the consultant when he gave the shattering news to my parents will forever resonate inside my head. 'You will be hard pressed to find any surgeon who would operate on a child like this'. Yesterday, I sat alongside the mother of a young man with Down's Syndrome who had been operated on when he was a child. She said very clearly and without hesitation, that Danny's sacrifice – and those of thousands of others in a similar situation – had paved the way for a change of mind – and, irrespective of the pun, of heart – in the medical profession. People are now living because of the injustices of the past. I could have cried.

I now want to tell my brother's story. The Centre will help provide outlets for me to do that in public. However, it is an immense tale, one of struggle, full of joy and sadness, heartache and pain, achievement and irony. One that needs a much larger platform, a bigger arena, a more sustained outlet. Accordingly, once I've finished this diary, I will be turning my attention to writing about my brother. It's something that I can no longer put off. It will be agony in many respects, but it has to be done. It will be the hardest task of my life. It will reduce me to tears. It will lead me to ruminate wildly. But our Danny deserves lasting recognition of what he was and what he did. I only hope I'm capable of giving him that.

Friday 25th November 2016

Pressure. That's what I'm feeling at the moment. It's not a particular kind of pressure. It doesn't stem from a specific situation, context or issue. It's something far broader in scope. The broadest it can be, because it's the pressure appropriate to, and originating from, life itself. Though it's easy to imagine what that involves – we all feel different forms and levels of pressure at times – it may be less easy to consider that ordinary, mundane, routine things, things that most people tend to take for granted, can elicit a sensation that the majority only feel in relation to something considered 'pressurised'. A work interview, a presentation, an awkward meeting, a difficult journey etc. For me just now, everything seems to involve that peculiar tightening in the chest and anxiety in the mind.

Take this morning for example. When I opened the bag containing my recent batch of medicine yesterday, I found that the pharmacist hadn't included one item. OK. No problem. Just return, point that out, and you'll receive what you're missing. Simple. Not a bit of it. I deliberated long and hard before I went to bed. What if they didn't believe me? What if they refused to give me something they thought I'd already had? Even though this has happened before, and there had been no problem then, that didn't quell the worry that was rapidly consuming body and mind. Conscious of the fact that my medication focuses on my mental illness and its associated afflictions, I've had to deal with the deciphering look that is trying to enter my thought process, to ascertain whether my intentions are to overdose. Whether that is true or not – the look that is – that's how I've interpreted it. Irrespective of the fact that if I wanted to at any time, I could kill myself by swallowing a whole cocktail of drugs, it's that moment of communication, of contact, between deliverer and receiver that tests my durability, my honesty and, of course, my state of mind. I thought it was there again this morning. However, I passed the test, and now have my full monthly entitlement of medication of differing strengths, sizes, colours and ingredients.

Now, there are countless lessons that can be deduced and learned from this. Among them is perhaps the most obvious. That you worry unnecessarily. That you put yourself through stress needlessly. Of course that's the case. I know I do it. But stopping it. Now that's another matter. There can be a tendency to see mental illness and the 'irrational', 'illogical' behaviour that emanates from it, in very simple, dichotomised ways. That you recognise that what you're feeling and thinking and how your acting and behaving is 'strange', 'inappropriate', 'melodramatic' and any other suitable adjective that comes to mind. And if you do so, all you need to do is change. Stop and think and do something else. But think about it for a minute. If it was really that simple, there wouldn't be such as a thing as mental illness. Human beings are not robots. They're not programmed to behave in specific, 'approved' ways. We all have choice, and we all have different levels and natures with regard to a whole host of things, whether they be termed 'standards' or 'morals' in a very broad, all-consuming sense, or in relation to something very specific. Some people can look over the edge of high cliffs. Others won't come anywhere near that position. Some people see nothing wrong in eating dead animals. For others, that's something that they – very literally – cannot stomach. I could go on. The fact is that for me, and for many millions across this planet, worrying, feeling anxious, being depressed or obsessive, seeing problems around every corner – all these things are entirely 'normal'. They've become so over the years, as engrained as any other characteristic of me. What I have to do when they threaten to overwhelm me, is to try and become exceptional. To think and act out of character. And to keep doing so until at least some component of that different train of thought and of its resultant behaviour, begins to change in a direction that doesn't bother me or threaten to harm or kill me. That's as challenging to me as climbing Everest single-handed without ropes would be to someone suffering from vertigo. It's remotely possible, but it's bloody difficult!

I want to conclude by mentioning my Dad. He would have been eighty-four years old today. I can't really imagine him at such an age. I lost him to heart disease when he was only fifty-five. I wish he was here. That I could talk to him and listen to the sound of his voice. Sadly, after all this time, I've forgotten what that was like.

Saturday 26th November 2016

I had to resort to taking Diazepam last night. Our temperamental heating system had warranted yet another service call — it's never worked properly since the new boiler was installed in the summer — and I'd firmly believed as a consequence that, at last, we'd cracked the issue at hand. All seemed to be well as the serviceman left the house. He'd programmed the timings we wanted. He'd demonstrated how things worked and what I needed to do to change what had been set. All systems go. For two and a bit hours everything was fine. The system moved seamlessly from one programme to the next. The changes I'd expected to see on our wireless thermostat were visible. The heating was on, the amendments apparent by the temperature of the room. And then, it gradually started to get colder rather than warmer. At first, I just thought it was my imagination. My catastrophizing mind at work once more. But soon, it was impossible to ignore. No longer could I pretend that it wasn't happening. The heating had, for some reason, turned itself off. I tried everything I could think of within the parameters that the serviceman had set. I adjusted the thermostat. I checked its connection. Nothing. In desperation I decided to resort to using our old system, the one I'd been assured was no longer needed and had become obsolete. And, sure enough, as soon as I turned it back on, the familiar humming was audible within seconds. It shouldn't have worked. But it did.

By this time, I was in a state. This was something that I'd overseen on my own. It was supposed to be good news to give to Lesley when she came home. But, yet again, it had all fallen apart. I had to call Lesley. I don't know why really. She couldn't practically do anything. She was at the hairdressers. It was another cry for help, I guess. I must have sounded distressed because she was home within the quarter hour, abandoning her plans to go food shopping. By then, though, I'd taken a tablet. It didn't kick in for a while, but when it did, the tension began to go as the wooziness increased. From then on, I was in a world largely of my own. Every time I got up from my seat, I felt a little dizzy and unsteady. I couldn't always focus and concentrate on what was being said around me. Even making coffee became a real effort. I craved sleep and oblivion. Only with that would I finally relax and let nature do its course.

If only people knew the potential consequences of something going wrong, something routine and commonplace. But that's one of the reasons for writing this diary. So that people do know and appreciate the type of life I lead, one in which mental illness oversees and influences absolutely everything.

Sunday 27th November 2016

I'd been planning to take Lesley's Dad to see Leicester City yesterday. The club had responded magnificently to a request I made to help us secure tickets so that he could see the club he's supported all his life one last time. They couldn't have been more helpful. Not only did they provide tickets free of charge, they arranged for car parking and wheelchair access and were always available to address every single detail we asked for. Right up to the last minute, they were making adjustments to the arrangements so that Ray could literally turn up and enter the ground without any hassle or delay. Sadly, despite his fervent hopes and determination to go, he felt he would be in too much discomfort and pain, so we had to inform the club we wouldn't be able to attend. When I spoke to him, he was in tears, devastated and inconsolable. There is still hope that he may be able to go to another fixture – the club have kindly left that option open – so it's not a case of 'last chance scenario'.

When I relayed that news to him, he did perk up, so we'll just have to see how things pan out.

For me, I was so disappointed for him. This was the one thing I wanted to do before he passed away, to show him how much his love and support has meant to me over the years. Of course, this being me, the fact of negotiating all the arrangements and overseeing his welfare on my own, even for just a short time, was playing with my sensitivities and the complexity of my mental illness. The plan meant, for example, that I'd have to get to the ground much later than I would normally do if I was on my own. I know that would increase my anxiety in terms of feeling visible, particularly as we needed a wheelchair for Ray. I also had to deal with the issue of what to do should things not go to plan. Would I be able to think on my feet? Would I be able to make adjustments on my own? And what if Ray suddenly deteriorated and needed medical assistance? Would I be able to act calmly and swiftly? Would I be able to stall the fears and anxieties that I know would be threatening to engulf me?

It brought back memories of taking my own Dad to a match at Everton at a time when the coronary disease that would eventually kill him was already severe and life-threatening. On the way back to Kirkdale station after the game, he stopped and clutched his chest. I found a wall for him to sit on and thankfully the moment – and the pain – passed. But I was faced with the predicament of what to do in the middle of a Liverpool street, isolated and vulnerable, away from the safety and security of home. And this was a time before mobile phones! That feeling has never really left me. Looking back now, it was probably one more nail in the coffin that was and is depression, one more element in the life sentence that I've had to endure since childhood.

Monday 28th November 2016

We're living in challenging times. This is particularly the case for Lesley, of course, as she watches her Dad's health gradually deteriorate. The same goes for our kids. Watching a much-loved relative, especially a granddad who has always put them and others first, succumb to something as devastating as cancer, is as devastating as it is cruel. Yet, dying is a part of life. I've known that from an early age. For me, though, much as I'm saddened by the predicament that we're in, I also have to face the uncertainty that comes with caring for someone nearing the end. Though those responsibilities don't directly lie with me, I have to step up to the plate and deal with the home front, if you like. What I find testing to the extreme is the fact that plans can change at any moment. I've geared myself up to one course of action, one scenario, one situation, and then, all of a sudden, I have to make adjustments. That doesn't necessarily mean having to do something. More often than not, it's an adjustment of the mind that is forced upon me by circumstances beyond anyone's control. If, for example, I'm expecting Lesley home at a certain time, and I'm waiting for that time in order to check something with her, something that's been bothering me, and then she's delayed for one reason or another, I rapidly lose the control that I've spent considerable time and effort trying to achieve and accommodate. I thereby panic. I overestimate the severity and immediacy of the issue. I'm craving resolution, satisfaction in my head. More often than not, I'll have to resort to phoning her. Just at a time when she doesn't need my distraction. The only alternative, when things get really rough, is to pop a pill.

For a couple of hours or so yesterday, we were united as a complete family. Rachel has come home from Sri Lanka for a month – ostensibly to be with her granddad – and Luke and Megan, his partner, were up for the weekend from London. It's wonderful to see them. Of course it is. And I know that Lesley in particular cherishes that special type of togetherness that only families bring. I do as well, even though I'm very much aware that a new configuration of people – however temporary that may be – brings with it new demands on my mental state. What it is that I find challenging is the novelty. New conversations, new arrangements and plans, changes in the normality which has served to keep me sane and within parameters that I've learned to manage. It adds up to pressure. And also guilt. Because the last thing that I want or actually intend is to feel aggrieved that changes have had to be made. It's very, very difficult to explain. I hate the sensation of adaptation but I'm equally hateful towards the fact that I can't deal with it. And when that comes to people, particularly loved ones, it's a very bitter feeling. I want to be around those that I love the most, even though I realise that with that, comes a need to be more flexible and more accommodating. Things I'm no good at any more.

The pressure that I mean doesn't come from people either. It comes from within. My family are wonderful in allowing me to do what I need to cope. I don't have to make excuses or beg forgiveness. They know and they understand. When it comes down to it, I guess the pressure that I'm talking about relates to the frustration I feel at the way life has become for me and the way I am when changes have to be made. I resent it. My foibles. My circumstances. My peculiarities. My entrenched positions. But most of all. I resent my illness. My depression.

Tuesday 29th November 2016

I watched the second of a two-part documentary on the closure of the last deep coal mine in the UK last night. I found it really moving. It's hard to believe after the legacy of so many years that that is now it. We as a country have abandoned the mining industry and with it the communities that served it so well for so long. My thoughts kept returning to my Uncle Harold – my great-Uncle Harold in fact – a man who spent some fifty years of his life working in various pits in West Yorkshire. I remember well the certificate he received from the National Coal Board to commemorate and honour his service. It was given pride of place in the living room of his small flat in Beeston, South Leeds. Coming to think of it, aside from a mirror, it was the only thing that adorned the wall. He always talked with fondness of his time as a miner, particularly of the community of people he knew as colleagues and friends. Considering that he probably spent some fifteen actual years of his life underground, it's hard not just to admire the sacrifice he made as a result of the work he did, but to reflect on the pride that emanated from his status as a miner. Last night's documentary certainly reinforced that. Indeed, the last scene showed a man moving on in work terms, being offered a new job as an engineer on the railways. When asked about that change in direction, in terms of what that now made him, he replied, without hesitation and with obvious pride and dedication, 'I'll always be a coal miner'.

As we witnessed one pitman after another deliberating on what to do, trying to adjust to life after the colliery, it made me realise that my life, in so many ways, is also about a struggle to deal with adjustment. For me, that battle is an everyday occurrence and it doesn't simply focus on one major component of my life, such as a job. It actually relates to everything, at least everything that I consider as being my norm. Following on from what I said yesterday, I know I have a tendency to make what you may call a routine some kind of fixed entity. Doing so helps me to establish and to maintain some modicum of control. But life doesn't – and can't –revolve around something that never changes. That's just not life. It's not realistic. The reality is that in order to stay alive and to feel alive, we continually make adjustments, most of them small, some of them even indiscernible, almost unnoticeable, subconsciously activated. Though my thought processes and the behaviour to which they relate attempts to counter what is both natural and inevitable, to make myself almost robotic as a way of coping, I have to recognise that in trying to do that I'm actually stifling life itself. In so many ways, my life focuses on that continual battle not just for control but for change. To adjust to adjustments, if you like. I guess what would be best for me is a more recognisable and decipherable balance. And one in which I can live in a way that others simply take for granted. At times that will inevitably mean taking a chance, sacrificing the strictness and inflexibility of control for something that may make life more meaningful and enjoyable.

Of course, it may not. But that's the chance I probably have to take.

Wednesday 30th November 2016

The last day of the penultimate month of the year. As I enter the final lap of the gruelling race that has been this diary, I can't help but wonder where I actually am in the finishing stakes. Am I ahead? Still competing? Or lagging behind? I guess, when it comes down to it, it depends on which criteria you want to use as an assessment. I've never been short of something to say. A positive thing. But has what I have said truly revealed or at least given an indication of the full reality of my mental state and thereby, of my life? That, I'm not so sure.

All I can say, with – for once – a heavy degree of certainty, is that I've been truthful and honest. It may be, therefore, that if I haven't passed the test relating to the burning question I've just posed, that words may actually not be adequate when it comes to full revelation. I strongly suspect that may be the case. I'll leave that with you as I draw November to a close.

December

Thursday 1st December 2016

Over the course of just sixteen hours, last night and this morning, I had two major instances of blind panic. Though neither was enough to constitute a full-blown panic attack, both threatened to derail me just the same. Both also involved a journey in a car and the prospect of being late for an appointment. Irrespective of the mitigating circumstances of heavy traffic and aside from the fact that I could and did call ahead to warn that I may be delayed, it's disturbing just how much the very thought of keeping others waiting whilst contemplating walking in to a context where people are already there really shook me to my core. I found it so hard to deal with – remember this is the prospect rather than actuality – that on both occasions I contemplated simply giving up and going home. The fact that I didn't is not down to any conscious decision on my part. I just let fate decide, trying literally to cope with every single second of what had by now become a real ordeal. I could even have parked up, walked to where I needed to be, and then decided not to go ahead. I've done it before. It is a viable option for me.

I've made all the effort, gone through intense anxieties and then, at the last minute, with resolution in sight, I've bottled it and turned away. The thought of opening that door, entering that space, simply too much.

I wonder how much of my life is given to worrying about something that may never happen? (I don't mean having a fleeting thought here, by the way, I mean considerable rumination) I actually hate to think. It happens every day. Often more than once. I can't seem to stop myself. I can challenge my thinking. I can deploy the techniques I've learned over the years to get myself out of the thinking trap, but I can't seem to stop the process by which I'm hit, mentally – with an impact every bit as shuddering as the most powerful of rugby tackles – with the agonising dilemma and uncertainty of deliberation. My mind races ahead of me. It starts to make connections almost before I can grasp the need for remedial action. I would say that it has a mind of its own, if it wasn't such a poor metaphor. It's as if I have no way of satisfying its insatiable demand, its mission to cause psychological chaos. I have no means of reigning it in, nothing to use to still its destructive path. I literally have to wait until it sets its own scene, steadying itself to establish a challenge that I really don't need. My brain is then forced to try to adapt and to reason, to provide the evidence and justification for whatever action comes as a result. Often, I just can't do that. And I resent having to. Remember, this isn't about what you may consider to be a 'genuine' or 'normal' conundrum or challenge. This is about something that most people wouldn't even recognise as anything other than automatic behaviour. And it keeps coming at me. It doesn't leave me alone.

What never really helps is seeing how other people placed in a similar situation simply get on with it. You can see that it hasn't bothered them one bit. They don't even have to consider using or thinking of that word 'cope'. Their mental state hasn't been tested at all. I'm so jealous of them. I sometimes want to cry out, shake them out of their 'normality' and implore them to realise and understand that what they have just done as a matter of course, has cost me a bucket load of nervous energy. Physically, it's made me sick. The anxiety within me has turned me to jelly, to someone on the verge of collapse.

I've only just made it through, I want to tell them.

I've survived. But look at the cost. Look at what I've become.

Friday 2nd December 2016

I've mentioned before that a while ago now, a good friend of mine told me that in her place of work hot-desking was to be initiated with no apparent exceptions to the new rule.

As she herself has a disability that necessitates her working close to the exit to the room, she was understandably concerned. Firstly, that she would have to be flexible with regard to desks, and secondly – and just as crucially – that if she did voice her concern and was thereby allowed to remain where she was, that somehow she may well feel pressure to divulge to her colleagues why that was the case. She's a very private person. Though she's informed her manager of her disability, she hasn't made it public knowledge. She simply doesn't want to. She's therefore in a 'no-win' situation and not one of her own making. All I could say to her was that as her condition constitutes a disability – even if she doesn't see it as that or acknowledge it as such – she is protected under the Equality Act. That effectively means that her employer is legally as well as morally bound to make reasonable adjustments to allow her to work effectively and comfortably as well as she can. The issue of her colleagues is one that her manager has to, well…manage.

It, of course, made me think as to what I would do in her situation.

OCD doesn't really allow for the flexibility inherent in hot-desking arrangements. In fact, it actively and directly works against it. There is no way that I could enter a workplace not knowing where I would be sitting. In addition, when I did work in an open-plan office, my positioning was as crucial as my friend's. In the same way that the prospect of walking down a train carriage to my seat leads to increased palpitations and considerable fear, the same applies to an office situation. Moreover, I have to have things organised and placed where I work. I could always tell when someone had been sitting at my seat in my absence. Subtle changes and movement of items would always serve to throw me. I'd spend considerable time afterwards trying to reconcile things in my head, worrying ostensibly as to what else may have been altered. When my OCD is severe, the simplest of changes, of a pen not in its place, of a ruler moved elsewhere, of a book or report opened and left. All would lead me to worry and to ruminate. I wouldn't be able to get on with my work until I'd reassured myself that all was well, that there was nothing to worry about, that any alterations were accidental, that they didn't constitute doom. This may seem melodramatic. But OCD plays havoc with your mind if allowed to roam freely and without impediment. It restricts you. It castigates you. It accuses you, berates and betrays you.

The one thing in my favour to a certain extent was the fact that I was open about my mental illness. That didn't, of course, equate to total awareness in those around me, but there was little – I considered – that I could do about that. It wasn't my fault that some people didn't wish to engage with the challenge of understanding. I couldn't help it if others who did know the score chose to hold it against me by being fearful, mistrusting or suspicious. I did what I could to help them as well as myself. I couldn't do any more. For my friend, transparency is not something that she wishes for herself with regard to her own disability. And why should she? She has her reasons. And they are sound ones. We've had a many a conversation about the pros and cons of being open. It's not something she feels comfortable with. She has enough on her plate dealing with the ravages of her illness, without worrying about how others may see her.

Sadly, it's a predicament that many disabled workers have to face. And it's not fair on them.

Saturday 3rd December 2016

For some reason, I was physically shattered yesterday. So much so that, in my efforts to put up and dress our Christmas Tree, I had to keep stopping for a breather and a drink. As I'm fitter than I have been for quite a while, I'm attributing that temporary state of exhaustion to the demands on my mental health. It has to be that. The relationship between mental exertion – whatever it is – and physical lethargy is a close one. Those of you that work in offices will know full well that you can have a demanding day and be absolutely knackered as a consequence, whilst all you've done is sit in a seat focusing on a computer screen. Whilst you may think that the muscles that you've used most are in your fingers, that's not actually true. Because literally, they're in your head.

Being anxious and fearful is just as exacting as the mental agility, dexterity and knowledge you need for work. In fact, I can probably say – without the evidence to actually demonstrate – that the things you experience as a result of mental illness are much more taxing and onerous. Simply because the emotions are both stronger and have negative meaning and connotations. If what you need to cope psychologically could be seen as battery strength – quite a suitable analogy I would suggest – then being afraid of something, powerfully afraid that is, will consume a much greater percentage of what you have in your locker. Indeed, on occasions, it can completely obliterate anything that you need to keep yourself going. It's no surprise therefore, that you simply have to rest and let your battery/brain recharge.

If, therefore – and I hope you're following my train of thinking! – you consider the relationship between brain and body as one of interdependence, if one is depleted, devoid of energy and strength, that will immediately impact on the other.

Anyway, enough of the pseudo-science!

Today, we're journeying over to Shrewsbury to see my family, have a meal and exchange Christmas gifts. We're taking a full contingent for the first time in a long while. Luke and Megan are meeting us there having come up from London, whilst Rachel will, of course, be with the three of us travelling from Leicester. As much as I can do, I'm looking forward to it. Social occasions are no longer the effortless, undemanding, joyful experiences they used to be for me. But I'll cope. And maybe even have minutes when that past returns? Who knows.

Sunday 4th December 2016

For much of yesterday afternoon, I was absolutely fine. It was so good to see my Mum, indeed all my family. Sammy's kids are wonderful. Really boisterous, good-humoured, characters both. I love the interaction I have with them. I find it really easy, natural even. It's always been the case, ever since depression became so deeply embedded some fifteen years ago now. When I'm in conversation or in the company of children, I seem to reach them at a level that doesn't place so many demands on the conformity I often feel necessary to accommodate my mental illness. It's as if what I am doesn't matter anymore. Perhaps it's because I'm acting, pretending that things are fine? Perhaps it's because I'm less conscious of what lies within me? That I don't have to explain or apologise for aspects of my behaviour? Of course, Elliot and I have a relationship that is both the same and more as well. With him, I can talk with confidence and with an openness that occasionally, I suspect, belies his age, whilst still being fully aware of his youth and the need to be – first and foremost – his Dad. I guess when it comes down to it, I remember what my own father told me was his aspiration for the relationships he had with his own children – that he wanted to be their friend as well as their parent. It's a good policy.

Anyway, back to yesterday. Everything was going so well. The food and company were wonderful. There was lots of laughter.

The conversation was easy. The interaction between everyone was without constraint – full, instinctive, uninhibited and genuine. And then, I hit the wall. I knew it would come at some point. I don't know why it does and I can never accurately predict when it will, but as soon as I became aware of the change within me, that transformation became complete almost instantaneously. I've tried to explain it to Lesley this morning, but I'm not sure I can ever truly and accurately do it justice. Simply because I don't understand it myself. When it happens, I become someone else. All of a sudden, I'm consumed with fear and anxiety. It's as if I've become exposed in some way. My mental frailty becomes obvious, visually apparent, naked in the spotlight of normality that surrounds it. I can't talk. I can't look at anyone. I need to be somewhere else, somewhere on my own. Everything I say or do is an effort and feels strange, almost other worldly. I become so tense, it's positively scary. I look around for an exit, but there isn't one – at least one that doesn't draw attention to what I've become. Yesterday, I had to ask Lesley to instigate a move. It had become too dominant a sensation to try and see it out without intervention. Sometimes, when I know that there will be a change soon in the context in which I'm in, I can do that. I can tell myself not to worry, that in ten minutes time the situation will be over naturally, without force or unnatural break. But often, there isn't such an outlet. So I have to create one.

Though I punish myself incessantly afterwards – out of guilt mainly – I know that I can't avoid what has just happened. It's part of my illness, as 'natural' if you like as having a headache when you're stressed, or sweating when you're hot. It comes. It goes. Life carries on. If only I could always look at it in that way.

Monday 5th December 2016

I finished my latest book yesterday. It was heavy stuff, focusing on the legacy of the Holocaust, the same topic as my own only much more theoretical and academic in its manner and outlook. I've always been a keen reader. My library is testament to that. I can't resist adding to it, even though there are a significant number of books on the shelves upstairs that I'm still to get round to reading. I guess that the subjects of what you read tell you a lot about the reader. In my case, history and non-fiction rule. I have books on the Holocaust, naturally, but also about the two World Wars, Jack the Ripper, Ireland, the Kennedy Assassination, the Titanic, Mallory and Irvine, Germany, Prague, Judaism, the Russian Revolution, rugby league, Leeds United and Millwall, amongst others. I also have a few books on depression. Mainly personal stories and reflections. What I don't have is a sizeable collection of fiction. This is one area of life in which I differ considerably from my father. He loved literature. He was always espousing the need to read widely, but to delve into the classics, to experience for yourself just why they are so. I tried. But without success. I remember when I first went to University, in the autumn term at Durham in 1988, I thought that I should use the opportunity of Higher Education, to broaden my mind and to, at last, begin the journey that my Dad had always talked about – from experience. I read 'Great Expectations'. Sadly, that was the extent of my immersion. In recent years, I've tried again, though my choice is reflective of my wider interests. I've read fiction that relates to the Holocaust, to antisemitism, to the Nazi period in Germany. I've enjoyed it. I have to say that. I just wish, though, that I'd had my Dad's love of literature from an early age. There are now – and this is a direct consequence of my depression – too many books that I want to get through before I die. The perfectionism within me has set its own target. There are even times when what it's telling me is that I have to read every single book that has ever been written on particular topics. That I can't call myself an 'expert', even on something that I've immersed myself in for years such as the Holocaust, unless I've actually done that. It's pressure of a kind that, of course, I don't need. But rid myself of it? Easier said than done. The other thing that it tells me is that I have to read every word of a book, even the acknowledgements, the reviews, sometimes even the Index. If I don't do so, I can't claim to have read it in its entirety and therefore I haven't managed to squeeze every literal ounce of information from its pages. I have to try so hard to dispel these calls for the absolute. I do succeed, eventually, but it's not easy. Once more, I remind myself of my target of 70%. That doesn't mean that I only read seven tenths of the book, of course. That would be stupid. No, what it does is say that certain things within the cover don't matter. That I can let them be. That I haven't let down the author. That I've still succeeded and gained the benefit.

If only this one thing, this simple process, the joy that should be reading, could be natural?

As it is, I'm now wondering whether the perfectionism within my depression can account for my reluctance to read literature when I was younger? That it wasn't laziness, or disinterest, but mental illness. There may be some substance to this. But there's no point in looking back. What's done is done.

Tuesday 6th December 2016

I'm really tired again this morning. I would say that that was due to the hours I spent yesterday putting together a new Ikea bed in our spare room, but I actually think there's something more fundamental at play here. My inclination is to think that I've actually been overstretching myself for some time. And I don't mean physically. Like I said on Saturday, mental exertion can be just as taxing and energy-consuming as the most physical of labours. At the moment, every single task that I set myself to do feels like a marathon, and yet I can't seem to settle myself to rest either. I feel guilty when I'm sitting down. As if something somewhere within me is scolding me for even attempting to recuperate. I know what it is I'm doing. I'm putting myself under a pressure that is too much to bear. And I can't seem to help it.

The only thing that I know will work without me having to ruminate constantly is to take Diazepam. But I'm also aware that that really isn't the answer. It will bring me relief – not instantly, but within a short space of time – but I also know that I'll look back at some point and deliberate once more over my lack of faith in my mental ability to find a way out of my unease. I don't want to resort to medication if I can help it. But sometimes the temptation is too strong. I simply can't face the hours of soul-searching.

When it comes down to it, the only way I can describe what's going on in my head at the moment is to say that I'm not happy – or maybe satisfied is a more appropriate word – whatever it is I'm doing. Unless I'm doing something astronomically significant, something of such proportion that it will serve to change the world – or at least the world around me – I feel I'm a waste of time. And when have I ever made such an impact? I can't face the mediocrity that I feel I am. I punish myself for my lack of energy, bravery and industry. Only by saving the world will I actually feel some degree of satisfaction.

And even then, I suspect, I'll still find some fault in what I've done or haven't done.

Wednesday 7th December 2016

I had more vivid dreams last night. Once more, one of them revolved around school and yet again, I was there out of context, a forty-eight year old man as a pupil, older than many of the staff. The ability to interpret dreams, or at least to attempt to do so, I would suggest is an absolute necessity for anyone with a mental illness. So much of my life is spent energised in my mind whilst asleep for it not to be an important source of meaning. Particularly when the same dream keeps coming back, time and time again. In saying this, I've almost forced myself to declare what I think emanates out of that one repetitive dream about school. I guess, firstly, it says that it was a crucial environment in my life, that it had a resonance that was much more than a basic account of formal education. As such, it relates directly to the issue of feeling out of place, of being a stranger, an outsider. It also demonstrates a fundamental clash, perhaps even a contradiction. That the longer I spend there, the more familiar I am about the place and how it works, and yet, as I've said, that doesn't translate into acceptance. I'm destined always to be the person who can't move on, but is trapped in a world that is an alien environment, uncomfortable in so many ways.

Everyone I know that has a mental illness acknowledges that interpretation of thoughts – as well as dreams – is an important part of dealing with their condition. If you think about it, that's probably as obvious as saying that it gets colder in the winter, or even that night follows day. We're constantly embraced in a process of learning from what goes on in our head, whether that be conscious thought or subconscious fantasies. We have to do this to a certain extent if we want to at least partially understand why we are as we are. If we want to tackle head-on our conditions, to try to address the origin, perpetuation and vitality of what makes us think and act as we do. It is that vital.

One of the consequences of all this is that we become experts. In some respects, we become our own therapists. We know what things mean. We recognise traits and mannerisms. We are conscious of their significance.

That doesn't mean that we can do without external help, whether that be from doctors, consultants or other specialists in psychology or psychotherapy. It also doesn't mean that we can deal with what we know, perceive or admit. But it does give us a little bit of a head start.

Thursday 8th December 2016

Yesterday I received a message on Facebook from an old friend asking me to give him a ring. I haven't seen or heard from him in years. I knew him, first and foremost, as a rugby player. Hard as nails and as dedicated and as reliable as they come, he was one of those players that never really shone in a match simply because what he did enabled others to do so. He laid the platform, if you like. Rugby league can be gruelling, but he was someone who epitomised what is always needed in a team game, someone who sacrificed the glory to ensure that his teammates had a greater chance of a success. Probably the best thing I can say about him was that his name was always one of the first on a team-sheet.

Call it intuition, but I seemed to know beforehand what it was that he wanted to talk to me about. It wasn't a suspicion. It was far more definite than that. In fact, I had already rehearsed the conversation. Sure enough, after the opening pleasantries, he got straight to the point. He was struggling with mental illness. He told me that he'd been diagnosed with bipolar disorder, but that recently, things had got on top of him, so much so that he was living – temporarily – away from his wife and kids. He was coping – just – but what he needed, I guess, was a sounding board. It was hard to take in. It wasn't the fact that he'd opened up to me. It was the pain in his voice. I managed to have a decent conversation with him. I urged him to stick with it. I told him that he was doing all the right things, that building up the relationships he has with his family in the manner he is – he's seeing his kids for short spells and has daily conversations with his wife – is likely to strengthen their interdependence, their connection as a unit. That being honest and open is the way to go. And, more importantly than anything, I left him my number with the instruction that he was to call me any time he felt he needed an outlet.

For people without a true understanding of mental illness, people who tend towards the stereotypical, it could be said that he was 'the last person they'd suspect of being mentally ill'. I've heard that phrase so many times – often in relation to me. Whenever I hear it now, I respond with a question of my own. 'Why?' Is it because I crack a joke every now and again? Is it because I try to give solid advice and guidance to others? Is it because I'm working? And perhaps, most fundamentally of all – is it because I'm a man?

Men's mental health is such an important challenge for society as a whole. It needs sustained as well as immediate attention. It requires necessary interventions. But most of all, it needs a basis from which to grow. And that basis has to involve addressing at their core all the gender assumptions and misconceptions that abound in the world in which we live. It's no coincidence that men seem to turn to me – a fellow man – for help. I've lost count of the number over the years. I urge them to think in terms of what is right and what is strong, what is helpful and what provides solace and support. Strength is perhaps the key ingredient here. Simply because there is still an inclination to see opening up emotionally and psychologically as something that is inherently weak. Whereas, in fact, it is exactly the opposite. It takes a strong person to 'confess' and to 'admit', even though these are terms I actually detest. For many men, that's probably the biggest hurdle there is. Just acknowledging that they have a problem, an illness of the mind. 'If men could cry more too', I hear myself saying. But that's easier said than done. For many of us – men that is – anger is a more realistic and 'acceptable' response to our worries and anxieties. 'Acceptable' in terms of gender stereotype, I mean. The problem, of course, comes when anger is inflicted on someone else. Not necessarily physically – which of course is totally unacceptable – but visually and audibly. I hate the thought that raising my voice in frustration at my limitations causes other people concern – particularly my own family. But I know – and it's a consolation of sorts – that I would never hit another person. I just thump myself around the head if things became too much. That has been – to date – the limit of my self-destruction, the extent of my pain. It has to be said – and to be believed – that we are far more likely to hurt ourselves than to inflict pain on anyone else.

I could go on and on here. There are so many facets to the issue of men's mental health that need urgent review and attention. As long as I'm breathing, I'll do what I can. But it needs a much more general response, one that is sympathetic as well as empathetic. One that is comforting and assuring. One that does not stigmatise or blame. One that recognises the pressures and the social forces at play. One that is fundamentally compassionate.

Friday 9th December 2016
Lesley flew off to Budapest yesterday for a three-day break with two of her friends. There's no doubt at all that she needs this short holiday more than anything, such has been the strain on her mentally as well as physically recently. Almost as soon as she went though, the doubts and anxieties began to descend on me. At various times during the course of the day, horrible, savage visions and thoughts entered my mind. Images of myself alone, destitute and grieving came and went with a regularity that was hard to cope with. I knew this would happen, of course. It always does when she's not with me, even for a short period of time. Nevertheless, it's something I'd gladly sacrifice for the knowledge that she's enjoying herself in a carefree environment. She deserves it so much.

As for me, my method of coping is to set myself little challenges, and to think of every one of them as an achievement when completed. Some of them are physical. Some mental. Some even relate to time. If I can get to five o'clock, for example, with the house intact, everything working, jobs done etc. It's hard to sustain at times, but the reality is that I need it as a system. I wish I didn't. But I do. It's as simple as that.

Saturday 10th December 2016
Elliot and I are shortly to join the throngs of people doing their Christmas shopping in Leicester city centre. We're going to make a day of it by having lunch and going to the cinema as well. I'm really looking forward to spending some quality time with my boy. He's had it rough of late and I just hope that having a day devoted to him will boost the confidence as well as energy levels that I know have been sagging lately.

As is always the case, I'll have to negotiate at least two significant obstacles.

Firstly, parking the car. The earlier we go, of course, the less I'll fret about this, but even so, the thought of having to negotiate a packed car park and the even more worrying contemplation that there may not be a space available, will loom like the proverbial dark cloud over me until I've safely turned the key in the ignition and locked the doors. Then, and only then, will I be able to put that particular hurdle to bed, knowing that it's behind me and that I don't have to contemplate thinking on my feet and making alternative arrangements. It's a similar scenario with regard to my second potential nemesis. Finding a table in a packed fast-food restaurant. The only thing that compounds my anxieties here is the thought that I might be searching for a seat whilst also carrying a tray full of food. It takes all my powers of concentration to ensure that I don't tip it over, thereby drawing everyone's attention to my predicament and the mess I've created. The thought of that is simply too horrific to imagine.

As you can see, my mental reserves will be tested to the extreme in dealing with two situations that, for most people, are everyday occurrences, free of anxiety and threat. I often think of how many other people are, at that same moment, going through something similar. Is the person behind me in the queue to enter the car park someone exactly like myself? Is he or she cursing me for having the temerity to be ahead, to have first pick of available spaces? Looking around the restaurant, can I see the same portrait of uncertainty and worry in the faces of any of my fellow diners? Or are they, like me, doing their level best, to mask what's going on in their heads?

There's one saving grace in a busy day in the shops. I'm far less likely to stand out when I'm looking through their wares. And consequently, the likelihood of being approached by a shop assistant to ask if I want any help is significantly reduced. Both scenarios are ones that I positively hate. At times, I just can't deal with them. At my worst, if I see a completely empty shop, I will avoid it like the plague, at least until I see other people entering the premises. Equally, I will have one eye on the assistant who is there ready to pounce, and, almost like an old Benny Hill sketch, I'll move around the shop floor in a macabre game of avoiding any form of verbal contact, hoping beyond hope that my 'antagonist' will give up and focus on some other duty.

So, wish me luck as I psych myself up for what is to come!

Sunday 11th December 2016

Two weeks today is not only Christmas Day, but the beginning of Hanukkah. I have to say that, despite my best efforts, I feel distinctly disengaged from the festivities and the increasing anticipation of what is to come. As I've said before, I've made a conscious attempt to extend the season so that I have a better chance of revelling and enjoying what is usually my most favourite time of the year. But up till now, it hasn't worked. What I feel inside is, to be honest, a sense of nothingness. At least nothing that is positive in nature. It hasn't escaped my attention that that sense of nullity, the void that is there, hasn't extended to include all the elements that accompany mental illness. I don't appear ever to be immune from them. The anxiety, the fear, the low mood, the anger, the frustration. They just carry on as normal. But things that I hoped would be inspired by listening to Christmas music, watching Christmas TV programmes, putting up Christmas trees and seeing the lights around our streets, just haven't registered on my 'Richter scale' of emotional sensitivity. There is still time, of course. And we're going to Berlin on Friday. Maybe the beauty, the noise, the rich aroma of a German Christmas will do the trick? I sincerely hope so.

Everything went really well in town yesterday. Indeed, if we'd set out a plan, some idea of our ideal scenario, we couldn't have wished for any deviation. It was that good. We had a drink and did our shopping within a couple of hours maximum. That left us the luxury of an hour and a half to have lunch before going to the cinema. Elliot was wonderful company. We get on so well. I cherish the time I have with him that is ours, and ours alone. And I know he does too.

I guess, looking back at what I said initially today, I may be doing the festive period and my response to it, a disservice. Because being with Elliot yesterday, doing what we had to do, was, of course, Christmas. And I did feel something inside.

Maybe – and not for the first time – my son is my true saviour?

Monday 12th December 2016

I spent much of yesterday in London, attending a focus group organised by Mind and British Gas. The purpose of the event was to gather the views and experiences of a selection of people with mental illnesses, all in relation to the services provided by the latter. With specific adjustments and a tailored service in mind, it was good to see a major energy supplier and of course a British company of such stature, looking to increase their understanding and awareness of customers who are mentally ill. I attended a similar event last year and one of the first things the British Gas representative did was to update us on what had happened as a result. It would be foolish to think that radical and significant changes happen overnight. That's not the British way! But at least he was able to give us some indication – through practical examples – that what we fed back had been listened to and taken seriously. It's always difficult to gauge the sincerity and integrity of any service provider in such a situation. Are they content simply to be seen to make an effort at community engagement? Is the process more important than the results? Are they simply ticking boxes? Their representatives always appear to be genuine in their intent – and yesterday was no exception. But nodding heads and continual agreement do not necessarily translate into an improved service. I get the feeling though, that British Gas really do mean what they say. Why would they instigate a follow-up process if that wasn't the case? Why would they invest the time and effort of additional engagement if they had no intention of translating feedback into action? The answers to both these questions, of course, do not necessarily validate their stated motive. But their approach, I guess, does. And, though it may be only intuition, I was much more confident about the whole process and outcome than I was twelve months ago. Time will tell.

Much of my own contribution to proceedings related to things that I've already talked about during the course of this diary, namely the specifics of interaction and communication between phone operators and service engineers.

However, the one thing I really wanted to get across yesterday was that an organisation such as British Gas needs to have a much broader concept as to what constitutes 'vulnerability'. I get the impression that sometimes people – and I'm thinking of service providers here – see only elderly people in this way. Of course, age is a defining factor in relation to this, but firstly, not all old people are actually 'vulnerable' simply as a result of their age, and secondly, there are other groups in society who are also vulnerable, and vulnerable in similar and in different ways. If you think about consumer affairs programmes such as 'Watchdog', you regularly get features that focus on companies exploiting elderly people, playing on their anxieties and worries, the confusion of new products and so-called emergency situations. When was the last time you saw someone with a mental illness depicted in the same light? I can't recall this ever happening, if I'm honest.

In order for this to be rectified, there needs to be a strong focus on relevant, comprehensive and thorough training in relation to mental health and mental illness. All employees need to receive this not only once, but regularly as part of their employment. The outcomes of training need to be monitored, and monitored systematically and properly. And training needs to involve people like me, people with lived experiences. We all said this yesterday. It was universally emphasised, strongly advocated, purposefully driven.

Let's hope the response from the company is equally so.

Tuesday 13th December 2016

Every time you put people united by mental illness in the same room, you seem to get immediate telepathy. And it's so comforting. For lots of people with a variety of mental illnesses, life can be very alienating. Your experiences and the way you interpret them are not the same as others. You feel strange, peculiar, at odds with the world. You're very conscious of your illness and the separation that comes with it. How can you truly get someone who doesn't have the relevant experience, to understand the negative and detrimental impact of everyday situations? And yet, when you're together with others of a similar background and ilk, it's all natural. Normality changes from society's as a whole, to yours and yours alone. When you start describing something as apparently mundane as answering a telephone – in terms of the anxiety that that process induces – you are confronted not by bewildered, confused and curious faces, but by ones that are nodding in agreement, ones that are empathetic and knowing. Because your difficulties are their difficulties. They feel the same. They react the same. The consequences and the impact are the same.

It was so good to be with people like me yesterday.

I felt such a genuine sense of community. It was empowering, if I'm honest. Liberating even. We finished each other's sentences. We could reach out and validate each other's views and experiences. We 'revelled' in our own world outlooks. We shared so much. It was difficult, really difficult, to leave that behind and to walk out into London's grey and suddenly menacing streets when the event finished. To leave behind the security of 'madness' (and I hope you appreciate my deliberate use of that word) for a world in which I don't readily fit, a world that in so many ways treats me as an alien, an outsider, someone to be suspicious about or even feared.

The normality of insanity. Now there's a phrase to think about.

Wednesday 14th December 2016
I went to a Time to Change meeting yesterday afternoon.

Time to Change is a charity that focuses directly on the stigma and discrimination associated with mental health. It encourages people to have conversations and instigates processes that make such opportunities feasible and comfortable. It actually does a great job and I have a lot of time for it.

Back to the meeting though. To be honest, all the usual issues were raised. People talked about their experiences at work, experiences that I know so well from my own past. The need for action was discussed, as you would expect. But somehow, for me at any rate, one subject dominated, and that related to the pledges, statements and platitudes expressed by organisations and their leaders. You may be aware of the sort of thing I mean. When you hear of somebody's avowed intention to make their place of work discrimination free, 'mental health friendly' or such like. When you listen to people espousing equality, decrying prejudice, stating that they understand, that they want to listen, that they're putting in place appropriate policies. The issue for me – and I got quite agitated when I expressed it – is whether such words or actions actually mean anything? When you hear of people still having to face the same challenges. When you listen to cases of blatant prejudice within organisations where you know there are statements and policies that should – should – not only deal with such eventualities but prevent them from arising in the first place, you have to wonder. You also begin to question things such as sincerity, honesty and transparency. I have no doubt that some people at least genuinely believe what they're saying. But if that's the case, they have to be responsible for addressing matters when things go wrong. I'm no utopian. I know how the world works. I know how big organisations work. But sometimes the disconnect between word and practice is too marked, too overt, too obvious. Organisations need to be made accountable. They have to answer for what happens within them. Because for so many people, for far too long, the battle is isolating as well as punishing. Stigma and discrimination is too much for them to cope with, particularly when they are having to fight the harsh reality of mental illness. That's enough of a fight for anyone.

Thursday 15th December 2016

I met up with a good friend of mine yesterday lunchtime. I haven't seen her for a while and it was great to catch up, particularly as whilst we were together she received the news that she'd been successful in a job interview.

We were work colleagues many years ago, but it was really after her partner took his own life that I got to know her properly. I guess I became a bit of a sounding board for her, a means by which she could try to understand more completely the pressures and the illness that had infiltrated and dominated his mind and which led him to take the steps he did. I was more than happy to do what I could to help her adjust to life afterwards. I remember long conversations with her as she tried to deal not just with her own tragedy, but that of his immediate family. People are different. That's what makes us human in many respects. And accordingly, people's reactions to something as savage and desperate as suicide can and do differ, and sometimes even clash and conflict.

The family in this case seemed to withdraw within themselves. An understandable reaction, of course, but one at odds with my friend's inclinations and needs.

What she wanted to do was to reach out. To draw attention to suicide and its impact.

She devoted her life at that time to awareness and fundraising. She even climbed Kilimanjaro as part of her new mission. She's been a real inspiration to me. Someone who has been there to help me in my many times of trouble and crisis. She's also become an activist as a result of her experiences. Someone to listen to and learn from. Someone purposeful and determined.

Someone not content to accept the status quo. Someone who wants real change. Someone to fight our corner. And boy, do we need people like that.

Friday 16th December 2016

Berlin. The start of our six-day break in the German capital, a favourite destination for us at this time of year. Everything was going relatively smoothly. I'd negotiated the psychological hurdles of travel, helped this time out by having Lesley and Elliot by my side. As we left the S-Bahn at Zoologischer Garten and made our way towards our final destination, I allowed myself to revel in the combined luxury of relief, contentment and success. I'd made it. Even as we entered the hotel lobby, I felt totally reassured. In ten minutes time we'd be appreciating the warmth and comfort of a temporary home from home.

But then it all went wrong. The first sign of disquiet was the bemused look on the receptionist's face. She couldn't find our booking. A manager was called. Delving into the recent mists of administrative time and complexity, he finally declared to us that our booking had been cancelled in July. By this time, I was sinking. I knew it had been too good to be true. There just had to be a spanner in the works, and here it was. What transpired was that the company we had made the reservation with in May had subsequently gone bankrupt without informing us and without, crucially, paying the hotel. They tried to find a solution, but it meant us having to pay again and at a less generous rate. Even then, we'd have to switch rooms mid-stay as the hotel was effectively full and they were trying their utmost to squeeze us in to a situation with few real options. Eventually, they were kind enough to arrange for us to stay at a local competitor at a rate commensurate with our original booking, so once more we traipsed out into the Berlin night, suitcases trailing behind us, rattling on the city's cobbled walkways. Three weary and perplexed additions to the city's nocturnal domesticity.

At least we didn't have far to go. It was, quite literally, around the corner. An inauspicious start, but at least we had a roof over our heads and beds to sleep in. I couldn't help but wonder what we had done to deserve this succession of problems, inconveniences and simple bad luck. Would we ever get a break?

Saturday 17th December 2016

Of course, this being me, I couldn't switch off from the situation we'd had to deal with last night. Financial worries now blighted my battered mind. I had to focus on worse-case scenario. I couldn't go anywhere else. Would we get our money back? Yes. Lesley seemed confident that as she'd made the booking on her credit card, it wouldn't be a problem. The crux of the matter for me though was that at this moment in time, she couldn't guarantee that. It wasn't confirmed, signed, sealed or delivered. My catastrophizing brain was working overtime, making connections and deductions that only served to intensify my already heightened fears and concerns. I had to work overtime to try and bring myself around. All I could do was to focus on what I had the ability to influence and control, and that was the here and now. So, determined but far from confident, I joined my wife and son as we made our way as tourists into the heart of Berlin.

We covered a lot today. Starting at Nollendorfplatz, the next stop down on the U2 Unter-Bahn line, I was able to give Lesley and Elliot a tour of what was and still is, the beating heart of Berlin's LGBT community. We then made our way to the architectural masterpiece that is Potsdamer Platz, venturing into the Film and Television Museum, before paying a brief visit to the Nikolaiviertel quarter. One of Berlin's attractions is that it never stands still. There is always something being built or altered and the city authorities never seem to do anything by half. Perhaps the most pertinent example of this is the development on the site of the old Schloss and East Germany's Palast der Republik. This being Berlin, what is now being built was subject not just to planning and architectural concerns and strictures, but to ideological insight and argument. Should the new building be a reflection of Berlin's imperial past or it's more recent, communistic essence? Which part of history should hold sway? Which was more defining? More persuasive? More appreciative? More memorable? Though the old won the day – a new incantation of the Kaiser's old home is slowly emerging from the temporal and physical void that had been allowed to exist – it's probably significant that no-one really seems to have thought about option three. Doing something completely different. History rules in the German capital.

Sunday 18th December 2016

We spent the morning and the early afternoon in Wannsee, one of the city's affluent and picturesque suburbs, home to its most prosperous but also to a building that encapsulates the contradiction that is – and perhaps always will be – Berlin. For on the shore of the lake, amidst the peace and tranquillity of woods and water, stands a villa that is every bit as beautiful and resplendent as its neighbours – more so probably – but one which will forever be tainted by evil. On 20th January 1942, leading Nazis and state bureaucrats met here, under the stewardship of Reinhard Heydrich, head of the Reich Main Security Office and Reichsprotektor of Bohemia and Moravia. What they discussed, deliberated on and concluded – all in the span of an hour – was to shape the course of history. Their mission was to provide the administrative and operational structure to the Final Solution, the murder of European Jews. What we now know as the Shoah, or the Holocaust. The contrast between geographical surrounding and human intent is never more acute than here. If one could only rid one's mind of what happened within the walls of the building, one could appreciate the beauty of the location. But of course, one can't. How is that even remotely possible? As a Jewish man, it's hard to come to somewhere like this. But I'm well versed in that challenge. I've spent over ten years travelling to a succession of places connected to murder, violence, prejudice and inhumanity. To the sites of concentration and extermination camps, to what is left of the ghettos, to burial sites and old police buildings. Irrespective of its physical nature and surroundings, the House of the Wannsee Conference – as it has become known – will forever be condemned in the minds of well-intentioned people. It will never lose the darkness that engulfs it. As generation gives way to generation, we need to pass the baton on. Remember, reflect and make sure that 'never again' really does mean what it states.

Monday 19th December 2016

What on earth can I realistically say about today? No sooner had we returned to our hotel this evening than a breaking news story appeared on the television. Just around the corner from where we were, at the site of a Christmas market we knew so well, there had been a terrorist attack. A hijacked lorry had veered, deliberately, off the main road into the heart of the market, targeting people and stalls alike. Even as we approached our hotel, we'd seen that the police had cordoned off the street ahead of us. A crime had obviously occurred, but we had no inclination to believe or even consider what had actually happened. We didn't give it much of a thought. However, as we sat there, stunned, watching the television, all three of us were shocked beyond measure. It was a surreal experience. We could hear the wail of emergency sirens in the distance even as we watched, engrossed and consumed by shock and despair, the reality of events on TV.

I need to put this into context.

The Christmas market on Breitscheidplatz is a venue we have been to many times. We always stay close by. We even know where individual stalls are located. We've eaten there. We've drank there. We've bought souvenirs there. We've joined fellow tourists and locals in revelling in the festive atmosphere of a place we associate with joy, laughter and community. It's a place where you can just wallow in the time of the year. You can people watch. You can enjoy people's wonder and excitement.

There is a tangible sense of anticipation and wonder. People go there simply to be.

We'd been there on both Saturday and Sunday nights, our last stop before adjourning to our hotel. Last night, we'd even bought Elliot a waffle at a stall that we now know would have been directly in the path of the weapon that was the vehicle. And at the same time of night. We could put ourselves directly in the shoes of those that were less fortunate than ourselves, those that had simply been there on a different night to us.

As we continued to watch, the realisation dawned that we had been unbelievably lucky. Our decision to eat in the centre of the city and to visit a large book store that we know on Friedrichstrasse, rather than stay local, may even have saved our lives. If we had been half an hour earlier, we may well have been tempted to go, once more, to the market for a final something to eat or drink. If we had approached the area from the other side, as had been our want in years past, we would have walked down the side of the market that was tragically hit. So many 'ifs.

The strange thing was that I'd had an uneasy feeling all day. For some reason, I'd got it into my head that something was going to happen to Lesley. As a result, I kept her close. I watched where she was walking, where she stopped, where she even looked like going. I tried to be a protective shield. Without telling her – because I knew that would worry her – I'd allowed my anxieties to permeate into something more than just psychological concern. I felt I had to act. To give in to my fears, if you like. To try, once more, to re-establish and reassert control. To prevent something that I had no way of knowing would actually happen.

I would gladly have given my life to protect her. Luckily for me on this most awful of days, I didn't have to.

Tuesday 20th December 2016

It was a very different Berlin today. You felt you could almost touch the shock, the numbness, the confusion and uncertainty. People were in a daze. No longer sure of themselves and of their environment. As if another potential calamity was around every single corner. What had been normality had changed decisively and excruciatingly. It was hard to negotiate. We tried our best to do what we would have done in the manner in which we would have done it. To see places, to visit sites, to use public transport, to be where other people were. My idea to go to Spandau, some way out of the city, was probably a good one, given the circumstances. Even here though, there was a noticeable difference in context and outlook. None of the Christmas markets were open. People almost seemed to avoid each other. You could sense the apprehension.

We felt that we needed to go to the site of the tragedy, to share the grief and anguish of those around us. To remember those that died – now twelve in number. To honour their memory and to show solidarity with a city that has known trying times in the past and must once more, turn to its reserves of strength and courage to enable life to continue.

In the evening we made our way to the Brandenburg Gate, illuminated in the colours of the German national flag and that of the city of Berlin. TV crews were everywhere, but the crowds that normally dominate the streets were conspicuous by their absence. People were staying indoors. They'd withdrawn to safety and sanctuary. The darkness of the night seemed metaphorically disturbing. Shadows were no longer enough. Light could no longer protect. Doubt had replaced it in the consciousness of the city's people.

The world, I guess, needs to recognise the needs of a city gradually coming to terms with one more awful cataclysm. One more discernible setback.

We all need to be Berliners now, to paraphrase the immortal words of Jack Kennedy.

Wednesday 21st December 2016

For us, the real consequence of what we'd been through in Berlin these last twenty-four hours can be gleamed by the fact that we weren't entirely sorry to be leaving. I never thought I'd ever leave the city feeling this way. I love Berlin so much. If I had my life again, I could see myself living here permanently. It feels welcoming and it's a city in which elements of my past coincide with important features that reflect my interests and passions. It's always got something to attract people. It changes, of course, but it does so in a fashion that is almost deliberately intoxicating. Nowhere on Earth, I believe, does so more purposefully and more completely. It poses challenges. It requires a connection, one that is adaptable, one that is deliberate, and one that if you can internalise and realise what it constitutes, enhances your sense of belonging and your appreciation of history. Indeed, history comes alive here. And if you're historically minded, there's nowhere better.

Of course it's one thing to be leaving a place, it's another to negotiate the practicalities of that departure. Even though I had Lesley and Elliot with me, I was still consumed by the same fears and worries. If only time travel were possible. I'd only need it to help me deal with the vagaries of actual travel. I'm not greedy. I don't want to see into the future. I don't want to go back into the past. I just want the present to disappear in an instant. As it happened, I was fine. I managed to keep my fears from showing. Or at least I think I did. I did try to explain to Lesley, someone who is sceptical about the advantages of Priority or Speedy Boarding, just why something that like that is a positive godsend to a depressive or someone with another mental illness. I talked not just about the need to get things over with as quickly as possible, but of the reassurance of knowing that you had control over the situation. I tried to explain the worries that accompany getting on to a public means of transport. Of worrying about the possibility of being seen to be flustered. Of being able to negotiate a physical space without having to think about other people at the same time. Of being as anonymous and as invisible as you possibly can be.

There are so many things to consider. So many individual concerns to think of, each one of which has the potential to be the straw that broke the camel's back. It can be a lesson in endurance as much as fear. Once you've got over one thing, another quickly emerges from the shadows to dominate your thinking, to focus your mind in a negative way, to occupy it completely and destructively. There never seems to be an end. Once you think you're on the final lap, you realise that something else is blocking your way, something that can actually prevent the culmination of your mission, the end of your suffering. You still have work to do. It can still derail you.

Like the proverbial item on the Monopoly Board, you can be sent backwards – spiralling backwards – by an element of chance.

<u>Thursday 22nd December 2016</u>
It is good to be home. Even though you are immediately confronted by the vicissitudes of everyday life, there are, of course, those elements of safety and familiarity that only really come from the auspices of your own home. Nevertheless, when I do return – even from a brief break – I do find it difficult to keep my obsessional traits in check. I know that my OCD is heightened. Why it is so, I'm not always too sure. And to be honest, it probably doesn't matter that much when you are faced with the practical realisation of what it involves. Within minutes of coming through the door last night, for instance, I knew that someone had been sitting in my usual seat in the living room. It wasn't at the right angle and it had a box of handkerchiefs by its side. When I went upstairs, I knew that someone had been on our bed. The cushions weren't where I usually put them, and the duvet was back to front. At my desk, someone had put extra documents and pieces of paper to the side of my working area.

Now. The issue at hand isn't that someone has had the temerity to invade my space. If that was the case, I would never be able to adjust to the fact that other people live within the confines of that boundary. It's the prospect that, in doing something entirely normal and routine, they have broken the protective shield that I've placed around that context. This may actually be something that animals feel more intensely than humans. A dog seems to register a fellow canine coming close to what he or she considers is theirs. It's not just territorial in spatial terms, it's what that territory actually represents that is crucial. Normality. Control. Ownership. These are traits – concepts, emotions, practicalities – that somehow become magnified in importance for someone with OCD. And changes within them are hard to come to terms with.

Friday 23rd December 2016

With two days left before Christmas, I'm still struggling to feel remotely festive in mood. I think I've now concluded that it just isn't going to happen this year. Despite my intentions and the planning behind them, I've now reached a stage where the only thing I can realistically do is force myself. And that simply doesn't work. I know from my battles with mental illness that you can only do so much to influence your thinking and behaviour. You can't simply wish something to be or not to be and expect it simply to happen. At least for anything like a meaningful period of time. I know from my experience of Cognitive Behavioural Therapy that there is a lot you can do to help yourself, but to change utterly, completely and sincerely just like that isn't realistic or possible. I wish it was. It would mean I could cancel my mental illness with the click of my fingers. But it isn't. At least for a depressive. At least for me.

So I will try my best to indulge and to join in. I'll revert to operational measures that have worked in the past. Short spells. Small doses. Escape when necessary. Rebooting and reenergising. Perhaps even silent reflection. A period in actual darkness maybe. I'll do what I need to do even if that means isolating myself from everybody else. To carry on once that feeling descends – that feeling that quickly consumes me and becomes intense panic, anxiety, frustration and irritation – is a recipe for disaster. I'll do or say something that may hurt. And I don't want to inflict that on anyone.

Saturday 24th December 2016

I think I'm in some form of shock as an aftermath of Monday's incident in Berlin. I can't seem to get certain thoughts and images out of my head. They all revolve around what would have happened had Elliot and/or Lesley been in the direct path of disaster. The prospect of what could have been and how I would react are just so disturbing, I can't properly describe the power and intensity behind the feeling. I keep seeing bodies trapped under wheels, sides of Christmas stalls bearing down on those underneath them, a lorry that isn't stopping, a vehicle dragging people, trees, wood and much more. And through it all, I see Lesley and Elliot. I'm dealing in 'what if's'. I know I shouldn't be. That doing so is courting adversity. Lesley told me yesterday that this was a central component of what she'd learned from the counselling she underwent following the attack on her last year. That somehow, one has to rid oneself of that particular line of thinking. That it's inherently self-destructive. But at the moment, I can't stop it.

It's significant that I can't see myself in the visions of catastrophe. I'm not lying on the pavement, injured or dead. Indeed, there's a part of me – and a strong one at that – that almost wishes that I could have stood there and absorbed some of the impact, to prevent others being maimed or worse. I wouldn't mind injury, even fatality. It's not something I dread. I haven't for some while. What I can't stomach or contemplate is how I'd be if the worse happened to any of my loved ones. I said to Lesley yesterday that had she and Elliot been killed on Monday night, I would immediately have taken my own life. I'm not sure how I would have done it. My warped thinking hasn't taken me there yet. I hope it stops before I get remotely near. But I would have done it. Somehow. Somewhere.

Sunday 25th December 2016

Christmas Day. A day of wonder and joy. A day for family and harmony. A day for giving and for receiving. I could go on. Christmas Day should be the culmination of a full year of living, of coping with whatever life throws at you, of normality, routine and, for lots of people, monotony and sheer grind. But what if the expectation of the occasion can never be realised? What if the pressure to conform and to 'let go' is simply too much? What if you simply can't be merry and jolly? For just about every depressed person I know, this day, more than any other, is one to endure rather than enjoy. Much as we all try, I'm sure, you can't simply switch from one state of mind to another, particularly when the 'other' is virtually alien to your existence.

I thought I'd share with you something that I wrote on Facebook four years ago:

"It's Christmas morning. I know for a lot of people with depression how hard today could be. From personal experience, I find it difficult if not impossible to cope with all the things that I used to enjoy and which people without this mental illness find natural and wonderful about Christmas Day – the change from normality, the gathering of people, the excitement, the social aspect of playing games and simply chatting. It also, for many people with depression, serves to intensify and demonstrate the difference between their mood and that of the people around them. So, to all of you suffering with depression today, I wish you love, solidarity and solace. I hope you get the most out of the day that you can. For those of you who have someone in their surroundings who has depression, I thank you for your understanding and patience. To all of you, Merry Christmas."

What I wrote is as true today as it was in 2012. Indeed, it never changes. Short of a miraculous cure that so far has avoided humankind, it never will either.

Monday 26th December

I have my ways of coping with Christmas Day, and yesterday, I did cope. My family were wonderful, as they always are. They let me be as I need to be. They understand. They don't pressurise me or raise their expectations. Of course, that doesn't stop the habitual feeling of personal guilt from descending once more. As soon as I put into effect something that helps me to deal with one aspect of the day, I feel guilty for having to do so. It comes with the territory, I'm afraid. You'd think it would mitigate itself given time, but it doesn't. Not really. It's simply something else you have to address. To, in effect, cope with your coping strategy.

I guess this is one more example of the complexity of depression. It has many layers and they don't always complement each other. Indeed, if anything, logic, harmony and the ability to 'fit' are rare. It's more the case that you get glaring contradictions. It's difficult to explain. For those of you who appreciate the fact that in fashion – and in other areas – some colours inevitably clash, it would be like trying to enforce cohesion on a situation that goes completely against common sense and rationality, a fashionable 'no-no'. Perhaps it's better to use the metaphor of trying to force a square object into a round hole?

The other thing that does need to be said, however, is that occasionally – perhaps more than we think, actually – what others may, without question, consider random and unsuitable, obtuse and ill-fitting, makes perfect sense for us. As depressives, we don't think as others do in this respect. Even the contradictions appear logical!

We also have a tendency to choose the most difficult, perhaps even the most onerous, method of adjusting. I've used the word 'choose' here, but most of the time, there isn't actually a choice. If we've done it a certain way in the past. If we've followed a well-trodden path. We'll do so again. Even if there is a better, easier, more troublesome way given to us. Familiarity rules, you see.

Instead of simply finding the 'correct' space, we'll 'choose' to fit that square into the same hole, by shaving it's edges to make it round!

Tuesday 27th December 2016
At various times yesterday I felt decidedly depressed. Though it lifted a little in the evening, it's still with me this morning as I write. I'm not sure yet whether this is simply a reaction to the end of Christmas and all the hopes I invested in it, or whether it's something more fundamental, yet another bout of illness to which I can't ascribe a cause or reason other than what it is. It is, of course, too early to tell. Even though the symptoms are exactly the same, it would be better for me if it was the former. That would, at least, allow me some element of reason and perhaps even some sense of how long it will take for me to emerge at the other end. The latter is much more frightening. If it is solely depression as a result of depression, I'm entering that world in which there are simply no rules. I know what I'll need to do to try and cope, but I can't predict or remotely guess how low my mood will fall, how deep the chasm, how much it will take out of me and how long it will last. I'll be in living hell once more.

Wednesday 28th December 2016
I don't know what's going on inside my head at the moment. I seem to spend half my time looking backwards, trying almost to recreate situations of yesteryear, whilst the other half conjures up images of pending doom, disasters that may happen. Virtually nowhere in this existence is today, the here and now. I can no longer seem to live for the present. What worries me is

that I suspect that the reason behind all this is the fact that my current predicament is less palatable than the extremes of past and future. That's my deduction. And, if I'm honest, I know that it's true.

The desire to reflect and to remember is powerful as well as understandable. What I'm trying to muster in my befuddled mind is not just a visual image, but all the sensations that went along with it. I'm being selective, of course. What predominates is the most memorable for all the right reasons, times when I must have been happy, even if it's difficult to recall what that actually feels like now. I guess the rationale is to sensationalise things that were as a result of my inability to do the same with things that are. That makes total common sense. The problem that results, however, is actually three-fold. Firstly, it highlights the gulf between what I must have been and what I am now, today, on 28th December 2016. Secondly, my brain has the ability to distort, to change in subtle and alarming ways things that happened so that they cease to be memories of fondness and become instead something that serves only to alarm and to accuse. My Dad, for instance, suddenly becomes someone who had no time for me whatsoever. He's an adversary rather than a friend. The same could be said of Mary in this respect. Lastly, there is a part of me that worries intensely about what I'm trying to do. I know it isn't good for me, but there's something else, something far more terrifying. It is said that a dying person sees his or her whole life flashing before their eyes towards their end. Is this what's actually happening to me? Only in apparent slow motion? Is it a prophecy? Is there something on the horizon that is too dreadful to contemplate, something that I can't do anything to prevent?

I need to see my consultant, whoever that is at the moment. You'll remember that my previous one has left for pastures new. I'm supposed to see someone next month, but so far I've had no news, either of whom or when. I think that, in addition to depression and OCD, I'm actually suffering from some form of Post-Traumatic Stress Disorder as a result of what happened in

Berlin. I keep getting horrific thoughts. I can't get certain images out of my mind. Images of what might have been. Even my dreams have turned in this direction. I see Elliot in particular in positions of absolute danger and yet my power to intervene seems to be thwarted, prevented even. I literally can't do anything about it.

I can't go on like this. Something has to give.

Thursday 29th December 2016

I started doing my tax return the other day. It's a job I've been putting off, but I don't want to leave it until the last minute – the deadline is the end of January – so I thought I'd be brave and take the plunge. It's some years now since I last had to do one. Then, it was a solely a paper job. Now, of course, the online option exists. All the assistance and guidance you need is available at the touch of a button. Or at least, that's what the system proclaimed. And, yes, it's true. By hovering over a question mark at the end of virtually every question, you can get the sort of help that most people would probably find invaluable. However, what it can't do, what it's not designed to do, is to help someone with a mental illness. Because there is a fundamental problem that all the technical words and specific assistance cannot address and that relates to the impact of doing something so important and official within the mind of someone like me. I knew it would happen. I could cope with telling the form what my name is, when I was born, even my National Insurance number. But as soon as we got into questions that had a potential consequence, panic and anxiety soon threatened to consume me once more. I began to worry intensely about whether I'd said the right thing. Every single question led me to ruminate negatively and destructively. What if I – however innocent in intent – answered incorrectly? I'd be fined. I'd be imprisoned. I'd be separated from my family. I'd lose my house, my work, everything I owned. I began to skip over questions, so fraught with tension had I become. I wanted it to end. Luckily, of course, I have a safety valve. She's called Lesley. She instructed me not to submit it until she'd been through what I'd put. As a result, I have the reassurance that I crave and that I desperately need. I know that she'll be thorough. She'll take time over every single question, every issue, every statement. She'll deliberate and she'll be decisive. Basically, she'll do it properly.

But what if you haven't got someone to do that for you? What happens then?

Processes like this one need something more. Yes, there is the option for anyone with a mental illness to seek the help of a local or national mental health organisation. But, to my mind, there is an onus, a duty, on officialdom – in this case the Inland Revenue – to recognise vulnerability and to offer specific help and actual reassurance. They themselves must take deliberate steps in this direction. They will need help. And I guess that's where the larger mental health organisations can really make a difference. By giving specific advice and guidance, by helping to raise understanding and to demonstrate awareness, they can guide the official body to take steps that, to some extent at least, can help the user. We're probably talking about mitigation here, rather than comprehensive removal. Mental illness is too strong, too stubborn, too penetrative to disappear completely in mind and practice. I'm never going to endure any process like this without there being an impact on my mental health. But if some of the harshness, the severity of worry, can be taken away. That would really be something.

Friday 30th December 2016
As we near the end of 2016, it's traditional not just to look ahead to the New Year, but to think about resolutions, things we want to change about ourselves and our environment.

I have to admit, I've never really been strong on this. I guess that too can be attributed to my mental illness. To not wanting to put even more pressure upon myself. To avoid any element of perfectionism if I can. To not really wishing to look too far ahead.

To taking each day as it comes. However, this year, I don't think I've got much of a choice. I have to do something about my physical health. It's ironic that, for someone with a mental illness, someone whose mind is ill to all intents and purposes, it's not that that becomes the focus. It's as if I can accept that that part of me is sick, beyond definitive repair, destroyed even. But physically, unless I do something radical to change me, the doom that infects my brain, the destructive thinking, the fatalistic trait within me, distorting and twisting my thinking one way and then the other, will – inevitably – become reality.

Let's look at the facts.

I have a fatty liver. I have to take medication to control my blood pressure and my cholesterol levels. I am technically obese. My risk of diabetes is high. And I have a family history of heart disease. I'm not exactly sitting pretty!

At various stages of this year, I have worked to do something about this. And, I think, with some degree of success. I do gentle exercise most days of the week, for example. I've been able to walk greater distances and for a longer duration. But what I need to do is sustain this over a longer time period and – perhaps most importantly of all – look towards a healthier diet. I've reached a stage in my life when this has become a necessity, rather than something I would like to happen. To change my past attempts into a more prosperous future, what I really need to do is to 'mainstream' these steps, to make them become as routine a part of life as brushing my teeth and taking a shower.

Of course, if I succeed, not only will I feel better physically, it will impact – positively – on my mental health. It's win-win! It sounds so simple. I can almost taste its outcome. But at the moment, it's all so tantalisingly out of reach. Please God, give me the strength of mind and body to help myself to survive, to give me some sort of life free from pain, stress and worry.

Saturday 31st December 2016

Well, I made it! There were times – many times – during the year when I wasn't sure that I had the motivation to carry on writing. There were lots of occasions when I thought I didn't have anything to say. But I obviously did, on both counts. I'll leave any concluding pearls of wisdom – if indeed I have any – to the Afterthoughts. That leaves me free to draw the calendar to an end, logically, systematically and, of course, chronologically.

A sort of peace has descended on our house as we approach the end of 2016. Rachel has returned to Sri Lanka. Luke is on holiday in New York. Joel is spending the New Year in London. So it's just the three of us, plus Millie, once more.

It's funny that peace is what I crave most of the time. As my mental illness continues to devour me, so I seem to be more sensitive than ever to noise, of any kind. However, the irony is that peace seems almost to stimulate and prompt the type of rumination that I know is self-destructive. Before I even know it, I find myself reflecting on what might have been, what I should have done, what opportunities I missed and so on and so forth. Living my life in the past, once more.

The mind is a complex system of connections and, in my case, misconnections. It's simply bewildering as well as fascinating. It's almost miraculous in how it works. And yet, if fuelled in the wrong way, if broken in particular pieces, that small lump of muscle, matter and whatever else – biologically – it constitutes, can serve to isolate, accuse, befuddle and confuse. It creates, allows and stimulates low mood. It instils paranoia and a fervent drive to absolute perfection. It enforces pressure. It allows one to wallow, negatively, in the past. It generates a fear of what is to come. It fashions restlessness and unease. It acts as much against you as in your favour.

What I'm describing, once more and for the last time in this diary, is mental illness.

But much more than that. It's me.

Afterthoughts

Perhaps the first thing I need to say relates to style. I'm fully aware, having looked through the final product, that there is repetition in my text. However, I've resisted the temptation – significant though it's been – to go back and revise, on the pretext that to do so would have altered the day-by-day nature that characterises both my writing and indeed my life.

Moving on to the substance of my words. I'm very conscious of the fact that this has been my story, my experience of depression and OCD, my viewpoint on issues that are essentially relevant to me. There will be things I've not talked about at all or only done so fleetingly –perhaps even casually, you may feel. Alcohol is one thing that comes immediately to mind. As I don't drink, it's not something that affects me. Certain treatments, certain medication, certain procedures, certain perspectives on mental illness may also be missing from your expectations. But what I have done – or at least I hope I've done – is relayed things as I see them and as I've experienced them.

One very positive development in 2016 has been my involvement in new work and with new colleagues. I have been so fortunate to find people who are not only professional in their jobs and in their outlooks, but people who have taken it upon themselves to look after me and to make me feel welcome and valued. Their understanding of mental illness has helped here, of course, but what they have done goes far beyond showing how knowledge can translate into practical, pro-active and remedial activity. I'm so grateful to staff at CLAHRC and at the Holocaust Memorial Day Trust for their care, compassion and empathy, as well as their commitment to change. It's great to belong.

Whilst I'm in that deliberating mood, it has dawned on me that it's actually quite difficult to offer many definitive concluding thoughts or statements, firstly because there is no natural conclusion to what I've offered other than that determined by a calendar. This has been nothing more than a snapshot of my life. It actually amounts to approximately 2.1% of what I've lived so far. My diary didn't begin at a particular stage of my mental illness and it hasn't ended as such either.

What I can say, on reflection, is that in comparison to many other years, 2016 wasn't a bad one. Though I had periods of severe depression, none of the episodes I had stayed with me for long. When I think back to the time when I had to endure seven months of intense pain and mental anguish, when I reflect upon periods off work, time spent gazing at the four walls of my living room, no motivation, no incentive to do anything other than sit and ruminate, I can't help but think that I've been fortunate during the past twelve months. I've managed to cope – for most of the time at least. I've kept active. I successfully secured and negotiated things for me to do that will bring in some money. I've been able to write and to speak in public. I've tried to be supportive to my family, to friends and to people around me. I've even been able to handle some social occasions.

On the flip side – and, for a depressive, there always is one – what I seem to have added to my mental health portfolio is a form of intense paranoia. More and more frequently, I find myself wresting with truly horrific thoughts. They aren't fleeting either. They last, and some have now become firmly entrenched. I've tried my hardest to deal with them using techniques that I've learned over the years, but I get the feeling that they've become much too powerful for me to cope with using my existing arsenal. What I have within me and at my disposal is simply inadequate. Sometimes the demons thrashing around within my head have led me to resort to medication. To literally dull my senses and put me to sleep. I haven't been able to logically dismiss them. To drive them away by myself. They've tortured me to the extent that I've questioned my ability to cope. Even to whether I want to cope.

At the time of writing, I still haven't got a date for my next consultant's appointment. When I do see whoever it is, I'll need to be thorough and honest in what I say. To be fair to me, that's always been my way – or at least my intention. I do know though that in times gone by I have tried to put a positive slant on things that perhaps has distorted the reality of my situation. I've never missed anything out. Not knowingly anyway. But I've perhaps focused on what I've been able to do rather than what I haven't. On what I've achieved, rather than what I've struggled with.

I guess that leads nicely on to one firm recommendation for anyone experiencing mental ill health. You need to talk. I would be trite to say that it's as simple as that, because it's far from being so. However, if you can open up to someone, anyone, it's a step in the right direction. Whom you choose is really up to you. It doesn't have to be family. Or a friend, necessarily. But it has to be someone that you can trust, someone that can help you and guide you to begin or continue a journey that is challenging, gruelling, sometimes soul-destroying, but essentially meaningful and potentially life-saving.

There are many people within our community of the mentally ill that are perfectly willing to listen and to give you their time and the benefit of their experience. There would be more if the stigma and discrimination that still surrounds mental ill health could lift even further. It still seems odd to me that, given the prevalence of mental illness within our society, there remains an obdurate, at times unyielding, taboo surrounding the subject. Misconceptions abound. As do stereotypes. Yet, as adults at least, we all know what it feels like to be low in mood. We all know the challenges of life. Every person over a certain age has had to deal with death. We've all had setbacks that have had a psychological consequence. Why, on earth, do we still persist with this essentially Victorian attitude towards something that potentially impacts on every single one of us? It stifles us as a society. And, more crucially, it condemns those that are in real need to an extra challenge – one of our own making, one focused on ignorance and sheer spite, one that punishes and sets people apart, one that can be too much to bear.

We all need, therefore, to talk about mental illness. We need to encourage and stimulate conversations, ordinary conversations, informal conversations, everyday conversations. Mental health – as opposed to illness – is a potential way in. Specific projects, specific initiatives, specific areas of life – such as advance planning, for instance – can serve a much broader purpose. There are wonderful techniques that can be used. Mind Apples is one that comes to mind. Based on the precept that we have to focus as much on our mental as well as physical health and using the concept that there are certain givens that we need to fuel positive health outcomes, Mind Apples simply involves people saying what they do to help themselves become stronger mentally, particularly when their reserves of energy are depleted and vulnerability strikes. Every time I've organised such a session, there has always been at least one person that has started to open up about more penetrative matters. Even though it's not the intention to 'out' the mentally ill, the environment of calmness, of mutual support, of refreshing self-revelation, does help to at least begin to unlock whatever Pandora's box has been created. Essentially, it's because people feel valued. Their vulnerability is addressed. They see the potential for talk, even if at that moment in time, they don't choose to do so.

To seek help for some form of distress is a very natural inclination. If you think about it, we do it all the time. Usually for everyday, mundane things. Seeking help and support for mental discomfort, pain or torment, really shouldn't be anything different. It's a very logical extension. But often, that doesn't equate or translate. For all the reasons I've posited in this section and indeed at various times throughout the year, people are stopped in their tracks. What they've now entered is seen as being something remote from things that have happened in their past. It's a new stage. A new environment. A new world. And yes, it is, to a certain extent. But it's also fundamentally connected to things that have already happened in people's lives, things that people go through every single day. It employs emotions and feelings that have always been there. Perhaps not to the same extent, maybe. But the basics have always been within us. As babies, did we not cry? As toddlers, were we not frustrated? Did we never feel sadness or loss as a child? We've always had our mental health. From the very first breath we took. Mental illness is, in essence, simply an addendum to that. Yes it's frightening. Yes it's daunting. Yes it can be horrific. Yes it's alienating. Yes it has the ability to maim and tragically, to kill. But it's not unnatural. That's the point.

So, as a very direct form of advice to anyone in pain or need, please seek help. Take someone you trust with you if you're afraid of what a doctor may tell you. Of if you're not sure what to say. Have the courage of your convictions. You are stronger than you may feel. And you're certainly not alone. Mental health charities, groups and organisations are wonderful sources of support and practical assistance. There are phonelines and there are websites. There's an abundance of information, all geared towards providing you with what you need in terms of material and, just as importantly, reassurance. And when you're within the system, do as you're instructed. Follow the guidance given. Question it, if you need to. But don't unilaterally abandon instruction or advice. Medication may not be for everyone. Some may choose, for sound reasons, not to go down that path. But if you have, and you're comfortable with it, follow the process that's been outlined for you. Report any side effects. Talk about fears and worries. Raise and ask questions. But give it time to work. And if it doesn't, tell your doctor or consultant. If you've been given an appointment, please honour it. You may feel that you have nothing to say or report, but building a relationship, a meaningful one, with someone who is tasked to help you, will always be a positive step. No change is no change. But it's the process that counts. In all these things, the more you immerse yourself into the 'culture' – if you like – of support and awareness, the greater your ability to make choices of your own that are based on sound reasoning and practical knowhow. The more involved you are, the more you'll feel. Your own awareness of what's going on inside your mind will develop. You'll become your own expert. You'll be able to enter into conversations with clinical and non-clinical mental health staff at a level commensurate with genuine personal attention and treatment. You'll be able to seek and secure specific advice. You'll be able to talk with more confidence and more openness. You'll be able to help yourself much more readily, constructively and thoroughly. You'll also be an in a position to offer real support and assistance to those in need, those that are not quite where you are within that process, those that are still on the bottom rung of the ladder.

I've had a lifetime's immersion in these issues and more. And, as a result, I can tell you this. Depression is many things, the vast majority of which have the potential to hurt, destabilise and distort. Depression is powerful and it can be destructive. It has the ability to alienate and to confuse. It leads you to question what you're doing, where you are, and even if you want to be. Let's be brutally honest. It can and does, in many cases, kill. But there is another side to it, perhaps one that is only truly realised if you openly and candidly absorb yourself in its complexities. If you choose to get to know it as much as you are able. This is a side that can, at its best, be genuinely, life-enriching. I am firmly of the belief that being a depressive makes you much more sensitive to how other people tick. It makes you more attune to issues of vulnerability. It enables you to reach out to people in need, people in despair, people who may feel their lives are crumbling in the wake of mental anguish. And it gives you, when you do so, a degree of empathy as well as sympathy that I think would be hard to realise if you weren't akin to that mind and to what mental illness can do.

In short, it makes you a better person. It releases that side of humanity that truly makes us more human. It makes a difference, and in doing so, it enriches life at its core.

My thoughts and prayers are with you all.

Endnotes

[1] Entitled 'More Fool Me'.
[2] Lesley has been a law student at the University for a number of years, receiving a first class undergraduate degree and now following a postgraduate course.
[3] Diazepam must only be taken under the exact direction of a GP or consultant. It's addictive as well as powerful. See
http://www.netdoctor.co.uk/medicines/depression/a6560/diazepam/

[1] See http://www.oxforddictionaries.com/definition/english/depression
[2] Not at this Authority, I should add
[3] See http://www.theguardian.com/society/2016/feb/04/female-suicide-rate-in-england-highest-for-a-decade-in-2014-figures-reveal
[4] See http://www.theguardian.com/society/2016/feb/15/nhs-vows-to-transform-mental-health-services-with-extra-1bn-a-year
[5] Translated as 'The Abduction from the Seraglio'.
[6] See http://www.equalityhumanrights.com/private-and-public-sector-guidance/guidance-all/protected-characteristics
[10] Child and Adolescent Mental Health Services.
[11] 'Suspended Disbelief: Reflections on the Holocaust' by Julian Harrison. Published by GG Books UK
[12] The BBC's current affairs programme.
[13] As Liverpool was fairly close to my home, I used to take the train in and watch matches – usually at Everton it must be said, but also at Anfield.
[14] From the BBC comedy series 'The Office'.
[15] Tottenham needed to win the game to keep the Premiership race alive. Despite being 2-0 up at half-time, Chelsea came back to grab a draw, ensuring that Leicester City could no longer be caught at the top of the table.
[16] See https://rethinkyourmind.co.uk/
[17] Irritable Bowel Syndrome.
[18] For those of you interested in finding out more, I wrote a book about the competition's early years and my part in the story, entitled 'Beyond the Heartlands: The History of the Rugby League Conference'. See https://www.amazon.co.uk/Beyond-Heartlands-History-League-Conference/dp/1903659175
[19] As we lived in North Shropshire, Wrexham was one of the closest clubs to my home. They had also just been promoted to the old Second Division and were entering probably the most successful period in the club's history.
[20] Wrexham's home ground.
[21] Presuming we use our three substitutes.
[22] See Wednesday 10th February 2016.
[23] British Exit from the European Union.
[24] I should point out that the words I've used here are a reflection of my warped and ill state of mind at the time. They are what I thought inside. In no way, shape or form do I consider them appropriate as terms to be used for anyone suffering with this illness, and would never think of doing so.
[25] The same could be said with this word.
[26] This sounds grandiose, but it's only Elliot's (and Joel's before him) old bedroom!

[27] Though what exactly constitutes 'normal' is, of course, another totally absorbing topic!
[28] I've talked previously about this in relation to waiting for my consultant appointment.
[29] See https://judithhaire.wordpress.com/2016/07/16/talking-about-night-terrors/
[30] 'Day of wrath' in the Roman Catholic Requiem Mass.
[31] From the BBC hit comedy 'One Foot in the Grave'
[32] Irritable Bowel Syndrome.
[33] The most basic left hand position.
[34] Mstislav Rostropovich, the celebrated Russian 'cellist.
[35] Sobibór was a Nazi extermination camp in eastern Poland.

Bibliography

All photographs used in 'A Year in Melancholia' are my own and copyright © Julian Harrison

Biography

After working in academia and then in rugby league development and promotion, Julian Harrison has spent the last seventeen years of his life working in community engagement, development and in the specific areas of equality, diversity, community cohesion and human rights. Indeed, he is recognised and respected for this work both in his adopted home city of Leicester and wider afield.

Originally trained as a musician – he gained a music scholarship to Gordonstoun and then studied music at the University of Durham – he went on to pursue other interests gaining further qualifications from the Universities of Leicester and Leeds. However, his ongoing passion for social justice and history resulted in an immersion in exploring themes related to the Holocaust. During the course of the last decade he has spent many weeks visiting Holocaust related sites in Germany, the Czech Republic, France, the Netherlands, Lithuania, Austria and Poland, undertaking research and taking photographs. His experiences formed the backdrop for his book 'Suspended Disbelief: Reflections on the Holocaust', published in June 2016.

His identity as a passionate campaigner for human rights also stems from his own mental illness (he has clinical depression and Obsessive Compulsive Disorder). He devotes a lot of his time to encouraging a greater awareness and understanding of mental ill health, offering advice and guidance to those directly affected and addressing the stigma and discrimination that still seems to accompany mental illness. He has spoken in the media, to organisations and in public on these matters and has recently completed a record in diary form of living with depression.

Julian Harrison lives in Leicestershire. He is married (to Lesley) and has four children and a dog.